A Tale of Flowering Fortunes

A Tale of Flowering Fortunes

ANNALS OF JAPANESE ARISTOCRATIC LIFE IN THE HEIAN PERIOD

Translated, with an Introduction and Notes, by

William H. and Helen Craig McCullough

VOLUME ONE

Stanford University Press, Stanford, California

1980

Stanford University Press
Stanford, California

© 1980 by the Board of Trustees of the
Leland Stanford Junior University

Printed in the United States of America
ISBN 0-8047-1039-2
LC 78-66183

Published with the assistance of
the Japan Foundation and
the National Endowment for the Humanities

In memoriam

PETER A. BOODBERG

(*1903–1972*)

PREFACE

Eiga monogatari ("A Tale of Flowering Fortunes") is a chronicle of the great aristocratic family of Fujiwara at the peak of its power and affluence during the tenth and eleventh centuries. Written probably by one or more female contemporaries, or near contemporaries, of most of the events described, the work in its present form falls into two sharply distinct parts. The first, consisting of thirty chapters and covering the years from about 946 to 1028, deals primarily with the life and times of Michinaga (966–1028), the greatest of the Fujiwara Regents. The second, in ten chapters, treats Michinaga's heirs and successors down to 1092, in the time of Morozane (1042–1101). The thirty-chapter "Main Section" (*seihen*), as it is sometimes called, is the heart of the work, both because of its bulk and because of its superior historical and literary interest. The "Continuation" (*zokuhen*), a dry, imitative chronicle, contains little to interest the modern reader, except for an occasional bit of factual information. Our translation includes only the Main Section, and the introductory remarks below apply almost exclusively to it. (A short description of the Continuation will be found in the Introduction, n. 78.)

In preparing this study and translation, we have received support from the United States Office of Education (Fulbright–Hays Center Faculty Fellowship, 1967–68) and the Center for Japanese and Korean Studies at Berkeley, and we wish to express our gratitude to both. We should also like to thank Dorothy Birch and Sasaki Shinzaburō for reading and criticizing the textile notes, Raymond Tang, Director of the East Asiatic Library, University of California, Berkeley, for permission to illustrate the text with xylographic prints from a seventeenth-century *Eiga* text in the library's collection, John Weatherhill, Inc. for permission to quote from *The Threefold Lotus Sutra*, and Barbara Mnookin of Stanford University Press for a superb editorial performance. It is a special pleasure to acknowledge the unstinting help and advice we have received from Professor Matsumura Hiroji, whose profound knowledge of *Eiga*, and of Heian literature in general, has guided us throughout. Our indebtedness cannot be expressed adequately in a few words, but some measure of its extent will be found in the ubiquity of his name in our notes.

We are keenly aware that the philological and literary weaknesses of the Translation are an unfitting memorial to the great scholar and teacher to whom this book is dedicated. We wished, nevertheless, to make some public acknowledgment of the pervasive influence his example and instruction have exercised upon our notion of the nature of literary scholarship, and he generously agreed, a few months before his death in June 1972, that we might do so.

W.H.M.

H.C.M.

CONTENTS

VOLUME ONE

CONTENTS

TRANSLATORS' NOTE

THE TEXT

The Translation is based chiefly on the text edited by Matsumura Hiroji and Yamanaka Yutaka in Iwanami Shoten, *Nihon koten bungaku taikei* (NKBT), a modern printing, with certain orthographic revisions, of the oldest known complete *Eiga* manuscript, which is now usually called the Umezawa manuscript, after the name of its present owner. When the sense has seemed to require it, we have occasionally followed other texts or made emendations suggested by commentators.

The Umezawa manuscript is a composite work in which the calligraphy and paper size of the first twenty chapters differ from those of the last twenty. Although both halves belong to a single textual line and are dated, on the basis of calligraphic style and format, to no later than the middle of the Kamakura period (1185–1333)—i.e. to within approximately 150 years of the last datable event in the work (1092)—it is not known when they were combined into their present form. Despite some deficiencies, the Umezawa manuscript is considered by the chief authorities to be the best available text, closer to the original than any other known version. Also sometimes called the Sanjōnishi manuscript, after its former owners, it is an officially designated National Treasure.

Matsumura, the leading expert on *Eiga* texts, has established three main lines of filiation: (1) the Old Texts (*kohon*), represented by the Umezawa manuscript; (2) the Variant Texts (*ihon*), the oldest complete manuscript of which is dated to the Muromachi period (1392–1573) or earlier; and (3) the Vulgate Texts (*rufubon*), the oldest complete manuscript of which is dated to the late fifteenth century. The Variant Texts differ substantially from the Old Texts, most notably in the absence of the second part, or "Continuation" (Chapters 31–40). In the Vulgate Texts, which appear to represent some kind of process of textual amalgamation or revision, over half of the chapters are very close to, or identical with, the Old Texts, and the rest closely resemble the Variant Texts.

In addition to the three main textual lines, there is a miscellaneous group of unfiliated fragmentary texts. These include what is perhaps the oldest known *Eiga* manuscript fragment, the Kobayashi manuscript, which is thought to date from no later than the early Kamakura period. The Kobayashi manuscript, consisting of Chapters 27 and 28, was stolen from an exhibition at the Ueno Museum in 1940; so far as is known, it survives now only in two photographs, in the collation notes to the *Kokushi taikei* edition of *Eiga*, and in a handwritten copy of the first two-thirds of Chapter 27 (the last third was destroyed in an American air raid in May 1945). Although the text cannot be filiated with any of the main groups, it is closer to the Variant Texts than to either of the other two lines.*

We are particularly indebted to the annotations of Matsumura and Yamanaka in the NKBT edition (EM, in our notes), and to Matsumura's *Eiga monogatari zenchūshaku* (EMZ), which provides abundant exegesis of textual problems and a complete rendering into modern Japanese. Three other works have been helpful: (1) Wada Hidematsu and Satō Kyū, *Eiga monogatari shōkai*, the first full-scale commentary and still a work of impressive scholarship; (2) Yosano Akiko, tr., *Eiga monogatari*, a reissue of a well-known poet's free adaptation into modern Japanese (first published 1914); and (3) Yokoyama Seiga, *Gendaigoban Eiga monogatari*.

DATES

The Heian Court usually designated years by "year titles" or "era names" (*nengō*), which changed with some frequency. During the period of our concern, no year title remained operative for much longer than twenty years, and most were superseded within less than a decade. The titles had meaning—they were usually auspicious two-character phrases chosen from Chinese sources, such as Tengyō, "Heavenly Felicitation," a phrase drawn from *Han-shu*—but we have left them untranslated, since they function as proper nouns, useful for purposes of identification and reference, and are most easily recognized in transliterated form. They served as bases from which years were counted—e.g. first year of Tengyō, second year of Tengyō—but were themselves connected only by accidents

---

* Matsumura's *Eiga monogatari no kenkyū* is the principal reference on the texts. For a brief, up-to-date statement of his views, see his *Eiga monogatari zenchūshaku*, 1: 10–16. The *Eiga* text printed in the Wada and Satō work cited in the next paragraph is based on the two chief versions of the Vulgate Texts line: the old typographical edition and the xylograph edition of 1656. *Eiga monogatari ihon* in the Koten Bunko series contains one of the chief Variant Texts, the Tomioka B (*otsu*). The surviving copy of the Kobayashi manuscript is printed in Matsumura, *Eiga monogatari no kenkyū*, 2: 253–300.

of history. Enchō follows Engi as a historical fact, rather than through a systematic ordering of titles.

The years designated by the use of titles corresponded in general, but not exactly, to Western years. Although the basic orientation of the calendar was solar, the year was usually divided into twelve periods approximately equivalent to the lunations, with the result that a calendar year was about eleven days shorter than a solar year. Periodic adjustments were therefore necessary to keep the two in general correspondence. Since the Japanese year also began slightly later than the Western, its first day might fall at any time between January 15 and February 15; and it always corresponded to parts of two Western years. For example, the fourth year of Manju (the year of Michinaga's death) began on February 10, 1027, and ended on January 29, 1028. Consequently, in order to convert the date of a Japanese event into its Western equivalent, it is necessary to know the month, and frequently the precise day, of the event's occurrence. In the case of Michinaga's death, for instance, if we had known only that it took place in the Twelfth Month, we would have been unable to say whether he died in 1027 or 1028, since the First Day of the Twelfth Month corresponded to December 31, 1027. We can say he died in 1028 only because we have the exact day of his death, the Fourth Day of the Twelfth Month.

In the many cases where events mentioned in the text are dated only by year, it would therefore be proper to give the corresponding Western date as two years—e.g. 1027/1028 for the fourth year of Manju. In the Translation and notes, however, we have listed only the Western year to which the Japanese year generally corresponds—in the above example, 1027—leaving it to the reader to understand that the Japanese date excluded the first part of the Western year and included as much as a month and a half of the following year.

Months in the Japanese calendar were numbered from one to twelve, but it is important to remember that they did not correspond to their numerical equivalents in the Western calendar. The Seventh Month, for example, always included part of August, and in a given year might fall as late as the latter half of August and the first half of September.

In order to bring the calendrical year back into general correspondence with the solar, an intercalary month was inserted every third year or so. The term "intercalary Fourth Month" designates an extra month inserted after the regular Fourth Month, and so forth.

In the notes to the Translation, Japanese dates are sometimes cited in the form 4 xii 1027, which is to be understood to mean Fourth Day of the

Twelfth Month in the Japanese year generally corresponding to 1027. In the case of an intercalary month, the Roman numeral is preceded by a hyphen: 4 –xii 1027.

The Japanese calendar was also divided into four seasons, which corresponded only roughly to those of the Western calendar. Each was defined in two ways: (1) according to the months of the year, and (2) according to the "twenty-four fortnights" (*nijūshi sekki*), which were calculated on the basis of the solar year. The system was as follows:

Season	Months	Twenty-four fortnights
Spring	1–3	Feb. 5–May 5
Summer	4–6	May 6–Aug. 7
Fall	7–9	Aug. 8–Nov. 7
Winter	10–12	Nov. 8–Feb. 4

PERSONAL NAMES, AGES, AND GENEALOGIES

Throughout, we have usually omitted the particle *no*, inserted in the Heian period between a clan name and a given name: thus Fujiwara Michinaga, not Fujiwara no Michinaga. The particle has been retained following one- and two-syllable clan names: Ki no Tsurayuki, Ono no Komachi.

As in most Heian texts, people are seldom referred to in *Eiga* by their proper names. Instead, official and toponymic titles, sobriquets, and other less specific terms of personal reference ("eldest Prince," "wife of His Lordship") are used; and when a person's circumstances change, so too does the method of referring to him. Since the result for the modern reader is apt to be bafflement, we have routinely employed a single name for each person throughout the Translation, often suppressing titles and other identifying tags. Our frequent use of given names (Michinaga, Shōshi) is, we recognize, a particular betrayal of the original text, in which they very rarely appear.

As a general rule, we have adopted Sino-Japanese (*on*) readings for female personal names, since Japanese (*kun*) readings are usually impossible to establish.

Ages recorded in the Translation are calculated in the Japanese manner, according to the number of calendar years during which the person had lived. Unless otherwise indicated (by the use of the notation *sai*), ages mentioned in the notes are calculated in the Western manner.

With occasional minor modifications, genealogical tables follow *Sonpi bunmyaku*, which ordinarily lists lay sons (including monks who had lay careers, however short), clerical sons, and daughters, in that order. Listings within the three categories are by approximate order of birth when known.

SCOPE AND NATURE OF ANNOTATIONS

The primary purpose of the annotations is to facilitate understanding of the text. We have sometimes commented on inaccuracies and distortions, but have not thought it appropriate to call attention to all of the author's minor misstatements. (The interested reader should consult EM and EMZ.) Whenever possible, we have used foot-of-page notes. When information has seemed too lengthy or complex to carry in that manner, it has been cast in the form of supplementary notes, which will be found at the backs of the appropriate volumes. The supplementary notes are keyed to the foot-of-page notes, where they are referred to as s.n. 1, s.n. 2, and so forth.

In both sets of notes, citations of works employ short forms. For complete authors' names, titles, and publication data, see the Works Cited section, pp. 855–64. The following abbreviations are used in the notes:

EM   *Eiga monogatari*, ed. Matsumura Hiroji and Yamanaka Yutaka, Vols. 75–76 of NKBT.

EMZ   Matsumura Hiroji, *Eiga monogatari zenchūshaku*, in *Nihon koten hyōshaku zenchūshaku sōsho*. In progress. Tōkyō, 1969–.

Genji   Murasaki Shikibu, *Genji monogatari*, ed. Yamagishi Tokuhei, Vols. 14–18 of NKBT.

GR   Hanawa Hokiichi, comp., *Shinkō Gunsho ruijū*, ed. Sakamoto Kōtarō et al. 24 vols. Tōkyō, 1938–39.

KT   Kuroita Katsumi, ed., *Kokushi taikei*. Rev. ed. 66 vols. Tōkyō, 1929–64.

Mak.   Sei Shōnagon, *Makura no sōshi*, ed. Ikeda Kikan and Kishigami Shinji, Vol. 19 of NKBT.

NKBT   Takagi Ichinosuke et al., eds., *Nihon koten bungaku taikei*. 102 vols. Tōkyō, 1957–68.

Shōkai Wada Hidematsu and Satō Kyū, *Eiga monogatari shōkai*. 17 vols. Tōkyō, 1907.

ZGR   Hanawa Hokiichi and Hanawa Tadatomi, *Zoku Gunsho ruijū*. 71 vols. Tōkyō, 1923–30.

Introduction

No waning
In the glory
Of the full moon—
This world
Is indeed my world!

MICHINAGA
(*Shōyūki,* 16 x Kannin 2)

INTRODUCTION

By 946, the year with which the *Eiga* chronicle begins in earnest, the courtier class at Kyōto had emerged from its long apprenticeship to Chinese masters, and was developing styles, attitudes, interests, and values that later generations of Japanese were to look back on as among the truest and best expressions of the native genius. A burst of cultural activity, affecting almost every aspect of life during the tenth and eleventh centuries, was approaching its climax in the realm of literature, where the perfection of a simple, efficient writing system had liberated Japanese authors from the cumbersome Chinese character and was resulting in an outpouring of some of the most remarkable writing the world has seen. In Imperially commissioned anthologies, in private collections, in contests, and in the day-to-day social intercourse of the aristocracy, poetry flourished as never before. New kinds of prose emerged—the poem tale, the travel account, the literary diary, the miscellany of random notes—and at the beginning of the eleventh century Murasaki Shikibu's celebrated novel, *The Tale of Genji*, established fiction as a major art. It was in that milieu, and as part of the same impulse toward native interests and modes of expression, that *Eiga monogatari* came to be written.

The notion of a chronological history was not alien to eleventh-century Japanese minds. For members of Court society "history" was in fact virtually synonymous with "chronicle," since the histories with which they were likely to be in any way familiar were either pure chronicles or chronicles plus various appended materials, notably official biographies. Such were the classics of Chinese historiography—*Tso-chuan, Shih-chi, Han-shu,* and *Hou Han-shu*—which had long figured in the education of the Kyōto aristocracy, and such also were the Chinese-style Six National Histories, compiled by order of the Court between 720 and 901. Quite naturally, when the author of *Eiga monogatari* took up her brush to write a history of contemporary times, she cast her work in the form of a chronicle. But if *Eiga* is traditional in form, it is decidedly untraditional in almost every other respect.

From around the first half of the sixth century on, the ruling family in Japan appears to have made a more or less continuous effort at record-keeping. As far as is known, however, none of the products of that labor survived into the Heian period (794–1185); and for the Kyōto courtier, as for us, native history-writing began only with the first of the Six National Histories, *Nihon shoki* (completed in 720).[1] The earlier parts of *Nihon shoki* consist chiefly of myths and legends about the origins of the country and the ruling house, but as the chronicle approaches the time of its compilation it becomes an increasingly straightforward factual record of political events centering on the Court of the reigning Emperor. The succeeding National Histories continue the pattern, becoming ever more voluminous and detailed, and concentrating increasingly on the internal workings of the Court itself.

The content of the Six National Histories, and especially of the last five, is almost entirely public and official, as one might expect of official compilations initiated by government order and put together by committees of appointed bureaucrats. Month by month and day by day, they record in Chinese, with little descriptive embellishment, the march of what were deemed significant events: the accession and subsequent activities of Emperors, the appointment of Crown Princes and Ministers of State, the issuance of Imperial edicts and government orders, the promulgation of regulations concerning dress, the construction or destruction of Palace buildings, the appearance of omens, the changing of year titles, the great Court ceremonies and rituals, the deaths of prominent men, Imperial marriages and births, the reception of foreign embassies, and miscellaneous events calculated to illustrate or promote public morality. The treatment is usually laconic in the extreme, with little or no attempt to re-create a scene or to offer more than the most cursory critical comment and interpretation. The chronicles are, of course, immensely important sources for Court history during the centuries they cover, and they also contain material on broader social and political issues, but the long lists of official appointments, the mechanical notation of the round of official activities, and the many similar instances of an uninspired bureaucratic mentality at work make them virtual paradigms of aridity.

The failure of the National Histories to establish a historiographical

1. On Japanese historical writing before *Nihon shoki*, see Robinson 1961, pp. 215–16; and Sakamoto 1958, pp. 1–7.

tradition comparable in quality and length to their Chinese models may no doubt be interpreted as simply a specific instance of the general failure of Chinese civilization to transplant itself unchanged to Japanese shores, despite the willing assistance of many hands. Chinese historiography was probably even less suited to the needs and interests of Japanese society than to those of a modern state. It was sponsored by, and served the interests of, a government that ruled over a great and diverse empire, dependent for its security and well-being on an efficient, centrally directed administration. It was underlain by a conviction that history was a veritable textbook of government, and by a system of thought that placed primary emphasis on moral worth, defined mainly in social or political terms.

Thus the Chinese historian's chronicle dealt with events whose impact was felt far beyond the narrow confines of the Court: dramatic events such as wars against barbarians, internal revolts, the rise and fall of dynasties, and great engineering feats, but also bureaucratic and governmental events that were of intrinsic interest and importance because the fortunes of the central administration were at least in part the fortunes of the entire empire. A basic chronicle of such events, supplemented by biographies of leading officials, literati, and other key figures, produced for the Chinese a kind of history that was uniquely suited to their society and to their conception of what determined its development.

But Chinese-style history made little sense for the Japanese. Once the political and social reforms begun in the seventh century were completed, a chronicle of the activities of the central government resulted in a monotonous record of repetitive events with little obvious bearing on the direction in which Japanese society was moving. The Imperial dynasty was stable—eternal both in theory and in practice—and in so far as political authority changed hands at all, it did so not by revolution, but by an evolutionary process of decay and growth. No great armed revolts wracked the society until the end of the twelfth century; no foreign invasions seriously threatened the stability of native institutions until the end of the thirteenth. The forces that were changing and moving Japanese society from the eighth century on were less and less related to the actions of the central government, and thus increasingly beyond the purview of official history. Subtle, almost imperceptible shifts in rural landholding and personal relationships were virtually impossible to treat in a Court chronicle or in biographies of Court figures, even though their cumulative effect produced revolutionary change, both at Court and in society at large.

Moreover, as Fujiwara leaders asserted control over the Court in the ninth century, much—in the end perhaps most—of the significant political action at Kyōto was determined and carried out in the private chambers of Fujiwara mansions, whither official history did not usually penetrate. The material with which the Court's historiographical office had to work was consequently of limited scope and interest, resulting in histories that served not the grand purpose of Chinese historiography—the moral and political guidance of rulers and ministers—but simply the need of a Court bureaucracy for administrative, ceremonial, and ritualistic precedents.[2] Even the Chinese interest in biography received little more than perfunctory recognition in the pages of the National Histories, perhaps because the Japanese of those centuries were never convinced that individual moral worth, as revealed in political rectitude and sagacity, was a primary political force.

As experimentation with the various facets of Chinese civilization proceeded, and as the institutional basis for much of the experimentation withered or changed, there was growing dissatisfaction with the sterility of Chinese-style histories. An attempt to continue the National History series, undertaken in the mid-tenth century, resulted in the draft of a large work called *Shinkokushi* (New National History), but the text was never completed; and after 969, when the office in charge of the project was abolished, no more was heard of official historiography at the Imperial Court.[3]

The cessation of the National History series coincided approximately with the final subordination of the Emperor and his governmental apparatus to the control of the Fujiwara Regents, and one can scarcely doubt that the two developments were related. The National Histories, as records of the Court government, lost much of their meaning when the government ceased in large part to function, and for the remainder was controlled, as it were, from outside the Imperial Palace. Even the function of the histories as repositories of precedents and standards for ceremonial and ritual action was being steadily usurped by courtiers' diaries, which had begun to be kept in the ninth century, and which were becoming increasingly numerous and detailed by the end of the tenth. The transfer of public, formally instituted power to private hands inevitably meant, no doubt, that historiography would follow the same route. At any rate, it was not long after 969 that the need for a new, private kind of history began to be recognized.

2. A point made by Bitō 1962–64, p. 22.
3. On *Shinkokushi*, see Sakamoto 1958, p. 53. The work has not survived.

Perhaps the first person to articulate dissatisfaction with the National Histories and to advocate the claims of a different kind of history was Murasaki Shikibu, whose great work of fiction rather curiously earned her a sobriquet incorporating the title of the first of the Six National Histories —Nihongi no Mitsubone, Lady "Chronicle of Japan."[4] In the famous discussion of "tales" (*monogatari*) in the "Hotaru" chapter of *Genji*, Murasaki has Prince Genji state the view that it is "tales" that "record all that has happened in the world since the age of the gods," whereas *Nihon shoki* and the other National Histories show "only one aspect of events."[5] She goes on through Genji to develop the point that tales spring from the direct observation of life, that they are not fantasies, and that despite their fictional elements, their contrived construction, and their idiosyncrasies of style and tone, they are the medium through which the truth about human existence is revealed. She seems to be saying, in other words, that although official chronicles may have their uses in government, we must turn to tales if we want to know how people have actually lived, and what they have felt and thought.

Although the true meaning of this much-studied passage is obscured by the difficulty of its language and by the fact that Genji may have been speaking at least half in jest, it can be and usually is interpreted as in some sense a defense of the art of fiction.[6] The context of the discussion makes it clear that Genji is talking about written tales, and in his day such tales seem always to have been at least partly fictional. But it is important for our purposes to note that Murasaki's contemporaries did not usually regard "fiction" as a separate prose category. Rather, they spoke of monogatari, "tales" or "colloquial narratives," which might be fictional, semifictional, or nonfictional. In Heian usage the word monogatari referred most commonly to the kind of more or less factual stories told by one person to another in ordinary conversation—anecdotes, gossip, simple accounts of everyday happenings. The derivative use to refer to written fiction was of decidedly less frequent occurrence.[7]

4. *Murasaki Shikibu nikki*, p. 500.

5. *Genji*, 2: 432. The translation is from Cranston 1971, p. 209.

6. Studies by Japanese scholars are legion. For comment by Western scholars, see Cranston 1971, pp. 207–13, and the works mentioned in his n. 1. See also Harper 1973, 2: 56–61.

7. In the "Miyuki" chapter of *Genji* (3: 82), Murasaki speaks of *amayo no monogatari*, "rainy night tales," in reference to the rainy night conversation about women in the "Hahakigi" chapter. For another example of the conversational monogatari, see *Mak.*, pp. 123–24, the passage beginning *saemon no jō Norimitsu ga kite, monogatari nado suru ni*; in Morris 1967, 1: 78, "In the course of our conversation . . ." For a brief discussion of the use and meaning of monogatari in the Heian period, see Oka 1972, pp. 179–82.

Whether written or spoken and whether fiction or nonfiction, the mono-gatari was differentiated from other types of expression chiefly by the fact that it told a connected story in the colloquial language. In addition to that specific denotation, the word must have connoted the particular type of subject matter that seems to have been the almost invariable staple of col-loquial narratives: births, love affairs, marriages, deaths, amusements, re-ligious observances, and similar events in the daily private lives of the aristocracy.

For a Japanese of the eleventh century, therefore, the thrust of Genji's remarks may not have been the paradoxical claim that fiction is truth, as Abe Akio has put it,[8] but the rather more straightforward notion that the realities of aristocratic existence were to be found in colloquial narratives. It may be true, as Abe maintains, that Murasaki's point in the monogatari discussion was not that monogatari were superior as history to the National Histories, or that the monogatari form was appropriate to the writing of history, but that the tales should be judged on the basis of their own methods and aims, rather than being dismissed, as was commonly done, because they failed to meet the standards of factual accuracy observed in official historiography.[9] Nevertheless, the discussion, by its unfavorable comparison of the National Histories with the tales and by its stress on the realism of the latter, clearly implied the notion of monogatari as his-tory. And with the almost sensational example of *Genji* itself at hand, it could have required little effort of the imagination to conceive of employ-ing the monogatari form as a vehicle for true history. At any rate, once *Genji* began to circulate at Court, only a short time elapsed—perhaps less than a decade—before one of Murasaki's readers began to write *Eiga monogatari*, a work that can be thought of as the historical side of the monogatari coin whose obverse was the fictional *Genji*.

The ambiguity of the word monogatari may have obscured the signif-icance of *Eiga*'s historiographical achievement even to its original author, who perhaps saw herself as inventing no more than a variation on Mura-saki's richly developed narrative theme. The sharp conceptual distinction that the modern mind tends to draw between *Genji*, a work of fiction, and *Eiga*, a work of history, is only partially valid, and to Heian readers it might have seemed considerably exaggerated. If we today can see that some parts of *Genji* are rather thinly disguised descriptions of actual per-sons and events, Murasaki's contemporaries must have been even more

8. Abe 1960, p. 34.   9. Abe 1963, pp. 1–13.

conscious of the work's underlying historical base.[10] For them and for the *Eiga* author, the haziness of the distinction between fiction and nonfiction was not simply a semantic problem: fiction actually was history in a very real sense. And as we shall try to show, history was also to some extent fiction.

'EIGA' AS A WORK OF HISTORY

Despite such confusions, *Eiga*'s original author could not have been completely unaware of the new historiographical ground she was breaking as she conceived and wrote her work. The historicity of her materials, the chronicle form into which she put them, and the chronological link between her narrative and the last of the Six National Histories show unmistakably that she intended to write history, and she could scarcely have failed to recognize that the result of her labors was unlike any other history that had been written in Japan.[11]

In the first place, she wrote in Japanese, which in itself must have struck both her and her contemporaries as a daring innovation. Japanese prose had been restricted chiefly to what were considered frivolous writings suitable for women and children—fairy tales, fantasies, romances, and the like—and the use of the language for such a scholarly subject as history was entirely unprecedented. Earlier historians had always preferred to write in literary Chinese, which was a reasonable enough choice, given contemporary intellectual experience and the prevalent Sinitic conception of what constituted history. After all, what better language to use in writing about the affairs of a Sinified state than Chinese?

But Chinese in the hands of early Japanese historians was an awkward, recalcitrant instrument, seldom, if ever, genuinely expressive of native feeling or thought. The flat, banal sentences of the Six National Histories are convincing evidence that the Japanese historian who remained wedded to Chinese was unlikely ever to come to grips with the realities of Japanese life, especially in so far as they depended on the subtleties of human character, motivation, emotion, attitudes, and values.

The *Eiga* author's choice of Japanese for her history made it possible to

10. For some possible historical sources for *Genji*, see Yamanaka 1962, pp. 48–98.
11. We accept the usual view that the first thirty *Eiga* chapters were written before *Ōkagami*, a work of similar subject matter and language, but it should be noted that the relative dates of the two histories are still a matter of some controversy. If *Ōkagami* preceded *Eiga*, *Eiga* would have to be regarded not as innovative, but as historiographically regressive. See below, "*Eiga* and the Historical Tale."

escape the constraints imposed by an alien tongue, and to deal effectively with realms of experience and feeling that had been largely beyond the reach of previous generations of historians. Thanks to the fluency and freedom of expression afforded by her native language, she was able to present a picture of Japanese history that, if it was still distorted and idealized, was nevertheless a much more convincing representation of human life than anything in the works of her historiographical predecessors.

Yet important and innovative as the author's use of Japanese was, her choice was undoubtedly dictated at least as much by her times and her sex as by conscious purpose. In eleventh-century Japan, women were not usually trained in the art of Chinese reading and composition, and both social convention and practical necessity required them to use Japanese when they wished to write. So close, in fact, was the association between women and written Japanese that the orthography of the language was sometimes called the "female hand." As far as we know, no Heian woman ever wrote a single piece of prose in Chinese, and one can assume, on the basis of unflattering references in tales to Sinitically learned ladies, that our author's contemporaries would have been shocked and scornful if she had written her work in that language.

The effective use of Japanese for historical narrative was a practical possibility for the author only because the language had already been molded into a sensitive tool of expression through a century or more of use and experimentation by female authors. The language of those women naturally reflected their own interests and preoccupations, which were focused not on the mundane side of everyday existence—politics, military revolts, landholding, and the like—but on the emotional and sensuous aspects of aristocratic life. It was not particularly well suited to the clear explication of the more traditional subjects of history, since it lacked suitable conventions and techniques of exposition, but for descriptions of personal relationships, human feelings, natural beauty, and the immediate surroundings and private concerns of the aristocracy, it was a richly expressive medium, capable of great beauty and precision. For the Heian historian who wished to write about such subjects, it constituted an ideal vehicle; for the historian to whom no other language was available, the subjects on which it had been honed were an almost inescapable choice.

Inspired in all likelihood by the example of *The Tale of Genji*, and possibly also by Murasaki's discussion of monogatari, our author employed the language of the Heian monogatari to shift the emphasis of history away from the impersonal, official world of the earlier Emperor-centered chronicles and toward a more realistic, personal, almost domestic view of aristocratic life—a view that emphasized the quality of events at least as much as the simple fact of their occurrence. The tedious chronicling of Court affairs characteristic of the Six National Histories was not completely suppressed, but it was usually submerged in a mass of material that found its closest affinities with the Heian monogatari and especially with *The Tale of Genji*.

Although the new material was various in type, the greater part of it can be described as having to do with the aspects of Heian life that most directly engaged the personal interests of the aristocracy: marriages, pregnancies, births, deaths, and rivalries in the Imperial harem, because those were the things that determined aristocratic status and fortune; festivals, entertainments, pilgrimages to shrines and temples, religious events, literary occasions, Court ceremonies, and individual triumphs and tragedies, because those appear to have been the significant experiences of life for most members of the Court circle. The almost complete absence of broader political, military, diplomatic, religious, and economic events leaves the reader with the impression that he has only skimmed the surface of history, and from a modern analytical point of view that is no doubt true, even if we accept the Heian aristocrat's position that the history of the Court and the aristocracy was History. But it must be remembered that history in the mid-Heian period moved slowly and undramatically, and that life at the capital was mainly a round of small, personal events.

Other available sources for the period reflect essentially the same state of affairs, as a glance at any standard chronology will reveal. Occasional provincial revolts scarcely impinged on the consciousness of Court society, and even those disappeared at the height of Fujiwara supremacy. Court politics, revolving around the Fujiwara and Imperial families, consisted for the most part in a relatively genteel quest for personal advantage, with little attention to such abstract notions as state policy or the public welfare. Relations with the continent were reduced to the odd traveling monk or Chinese merchantman visiting Kyūshū. It was, in other words, a period when the capital at Heian knew little in the way of earthshaking events. If *Eiga* seems superficial or narrow to us today, that is at least in part because it is a faithful product of its time and place. For a stable aristocratic society in which heredity and family relationships determined personal power and fortune, births and marriages loomed as large, and were of as consuming interest to members of the society, as wars were to feudal knights, or as stock mergers are to modern tycoons.[12]

In addition to introducing a new language and new kinds of subject matter to the writing of Japanese history, *Eiga* made a major contribution to the emergence of topic as a historiographical concept. In the sense that the Six National Histories had recorded only major governmental events (rather than everything that had happened or a random scattering of miscellaneous incidents), they had led the way in the employment of topical principles, but only at the most diffuse and least useful level; and although there had been tentative gestures toward sharper definition in several short biographical and historical accounts written before the eleventh century,[13] those works had not represented a radical departure from the Histories' brief biographies or from some of their more integrated series of entries— e.g. the *Nihon shoki* passages describing the succession dispute before the accession of Emperor Tenmu (r. 673–86).[14] The *Eiga* author was the first to take the critical step of using a narrowly defined topic in large-scale historical writing. And if she did not quite manage by herself to arrive at a complete understanding of the meaning and potentialities of the tool, her progress toward that goal meant that the appearance of genuinely topical Japanese histories was merely a matter of time.

In order to account for all the material in *Eiga*, it would be necessary to define its area of concern as the generality of Court affairs and aristocratic life at the capital. Its overall topic, in other words, is scarcely more sharply focused than that of the National Histories. But a closer look reveals a kind of layering of topics, consisting of a thin outer shell concerned with Court and aristocratic life, a somewhat thicker middle layer devoted to the fortunes of the main Fujiwara line, and a central core given over to the spectacularly glorious life of Michinaga and his immediate family. The three layers are not completely unrelated, since the first two function to

12. A point made by Oka 1968a, p. 445. For a highly perceptive discussion of the inward-looking, stagnant nature of early and mid-Heian society, see Nagahara 1973, pp. 3–21.

13. Biographical writings include such Nara and early Heian works as *Kaden* (the biographies of Fujiwara Kamatari [614–69] and Fujiwara Muchimaro [680–737]; GR, 3: 689–96), *Jōgū Shōtoku hōō teisetsu* (Prince Shōtoku [574–622]; GR, 3: 679–84); and *Fujiwara no Yasunori den* (ZGR, 8-ge: 65–71). Topical history writing in the period is represented by a single example, *Shōmonki* (GR, 16: 1–14), a mid-tenth-century account of the revolt of Taira Masakado (d. 940). None of the above works amounts to more than a few pages in a modern printing.

14. Aston 1956, pp. 301ff; *Nihon shoki*, 2: 307. Possibly Sugawara Michizane's *Ruijū kokushi* (892) should also be counted among the precursors of topical histories in Japan. In it, the material contained in the Six National Histories is rearranged into various subject categories and quoted verbatim.

some extent as the context within which the core subject is treated, but the relationship between layers is frequently tenuous or totally absent, and even where obvious connections could have been drawn between them, the author usually fails to do so. Her work as a whole, therefore, lacks unity of topic, except in the broad sense mentioned. Nevertheless, its core, which accounts for by far the bulk of the content, is focused on a single, well-defined subject, and there is some use of subtopics, as in Chapter 15, which includes a general summation of Michinaga's religious works.

The author's decision to concentrate on Michinaga's career was in part a natural result of the kind of history she was interested in recording, for Michinaga was, after all, not only the dominant Court figure of his age, but the Fujiwara Regent *par excellence*, the very archetype of the Heian noble. But she must also have been strongly influenced by the tradition of the monogatari, which typically centered on personal histories rather than on events, and she probably owed a particular debt in that respect to *The Tale of Genji*. The major part of Murasaki's work is a chronologically arranged account of the life of a brilliant Court hero, a man who was very likely modeled to some extent on Michinaga himself. For a historian writing about Michinaga's times in the monogatari tradition, and especially for one who seems to have owed so much otherwise to the already famous *Tale of Genji*, the choice of a similarly biographical approach was perhaps inevitable.

The author made another contribution to the development of Japanese historical writing by treating her topic thematically. Whereas the official Histories had been essentially themeless chronicles of government activity, in which disparate facts were catalogued without regard for their cumulative narrative effect, the bulk of the material in *Eiga* has clearly been selected and presented under the guiding principle of a single, overriding theme: the splendor of aristocratic life, as seen especially in Michinaga's career. The primacy of the theme is revealed in the very title of the work; as far as we know, it is the first one in the Japanese literary and historical tradition to incorporate an abstract, thematically derived nominal construction: *eiga*, "flowering fortunes."[15] The titles of earlier histories and monogatari seem to have been uniformly derived from the subjects of the works they identified—i.e. to have been based either on personal or place names (e.g. *The Tale of Genji*, *Chronicle of Japan*) or on straightforward

15. Possible exceptions are works with titles whose meanings are obscure today, such as *Tales of Ise* (*Ise monogatari*).

descriptions of content (*The National Histories Classified*, *Record of Ancient Matters*). *Eiga*'s innovativeness in the use of theme was thus directly reflected in the uniqueness of its title.

It should be noted that early sources use two different sets of titles for the work: *Yotsugi* or *Yotsugi monogatari* and *Eiga* or *Eiga monogatari*. The first set followed the established mode of title-making, since *yotsugi* meant something like "generational succession" (or "successor"), an obvious description of the work's subject or materials, rather than of its theme.[16] But though the earliest independent sources use the *Yotsugi* titles in references to the work, internal evidence indicates they probably came later.[17] The fascicules (*satsu*) of the oldest complete manuscript, dating from the mid-Kamakura period or before, bear the name *Eiga monogatari*, both as an inner-page title and as a cover title,[18] and in Chapter 36 (i.e. in the "Continuation") there is an explicit reference to "an earlier chapter of *Eiga*" (*eiga no kami no maki*),[19] which the context identifies as Chapter 24. If the text has not suffered interpolation or emendation, the occurrence of the *Eiga* title in Chapter 36 proves the work to have been known under that name at least by the time the last ten chapters were written—i.e. by about 1100, which is perhaps a decade earlier than the oldest known *Yotsugi* reference.[20]

16. Yotsugi is commonly believed to have been a generic name for any privately compiled chronicle spanning a number of generations or reigns. *Ōkagami* was also called *Yotsugi monogatari* and *Yotsugi Ōkagami*; its chronological continuation, *Imakagami*, was sometimes alternatively referred to as *Shoku yotsugi* (Yotsugi Continued) or *Shin yotsugi monogatari* (The New Yotsugi Tale); and *Imakagami*'s successor was known as *Iyayotsugi* (Still More Yotsugi). Moreover, a late-thirteenth- or early-fourteenth-century work, *Godai teiō monogatari*, p. 325, uses yotsugi in a clearly generic sense, speaking of "National Histories, yotsugi, and family records" (*kokushi, yotsugi, ieie no ki*). On the other hand, late Heian and early Kamakura citations of *Eiga* as *Yotsugi* or *Yotsugi monogatari* certainly suggest an established title, rather than a generic term; and an entry in a somewhat later book catalogue, *Honchō shojaku mokuroku*, leaves no doubt that *Yotsugi* was being used as a specific title for *Eiga* in the medieval era. See Matsumura 1956–67, 1: 515–16; Iwahashi 1956–58, 2: 329; and Bitō 1962–64, p. 26.

17. *Eiga* is called *Yotsugi* or *Yotsugi monogatari* in Fujiwara Kiyosuke (1104–77), *Fukuro sōshi*, p. 16, and in three works by Kiyosuke's adoptive brother, Kenshō (c. 1130–1210): *Kokinshūjo chū*, pp. 141–42; *Kakinomoto no ason Hitomaro kanmon*, p. 45; and *Shūchūshō*, p. 53. The references are all specific enough to provide positive identification with material in extant *Eiga* texts. For discussion of the references, see Matsumura 1956–67, 1: 194–96; and Iwahashi 1956–58, 2: 329. For another probable early use of the *Yotsugi* title in reference to *Eiga*, see n. 66. References to *Eiga* or *Eiga monogatari* occur in Ken'a (1261–1338), *Nihongi shishō*, quoted in Matsumura 1956–67, 1: 240; *Eiga monogatari mokuroku*, the Kanazawa Bunko text of which is in the hand of Ken'a (Matsumura 1956–67, 2: 54; text printed in *ibid.*, 1: 172–78); and other Kamakura-period texts.

18. Matsumura 1956–67, 3: 176.   19. EM, 2: 458.

20. The apparent reference to *Eiga* in *Sanuki no suke nikki* (n. 66, below) is thought to be the earliest mention of the work in an independent source.

Further support for the conclusion that *Eiga* was the original title is found in the use of the word in the text, where it occurs three times, always in reference to Michinaga's prosperity.[21] A combination of circumstances suggests that the occurrences were the result of a carefully considered, thematically motivated decision.

"Eiga" was, to begin with, an uncommon item in the vocabulary of mid-Heian writers of Japanese. It was Chinese in origin, and as such belonged to a small, rather special group of recognizably foreign loan words and derivatives that had found their way into the Japanese lexicon by the middle of the eleventh century. Most such words were Buddhist terms, names of imported articles (e.g. incenses, plants, implements), or terms having to do with the Court bureaucracy, such as official titles; but there were also a few general-vocabulary items, adopted, it may be conjectured, because they conveyed certain meanings more easily, more effectively, or more impressively than any possible Japanese equivalent. Such, for example, were *rei* ("precedent"), *ko* ("the late"), *daiji* ("important matter"), *yō* ("manner"), *aigyō* ("endearing charm"), and *en* ("ethereal charm," "rich beauty"). Some of the group (e.g. rei, yō, and en) appear so often in Heian texts that they must have conveyed little or no suggestion of foreignness, but others were more sparingly employed—aigyō, for instance—and they undoubtedly gave a special flavor to the passages in which they figured.

In the Heian period eiga was one of the rarest of the general-vocabulary loan words, occurring, as far as is known, only three times in extant Japanese texts dating from before the compilation of *Eiga monogatari*. The word presumably did not spring spontaneously to the mind of a mid-Heian writer of Japanese, and one may plausibly suppose that our author chose it for rather particular reasons.

Most fundamental to the choice, no doubt, were the meaning and connotations of the word, which perfectly suited the author's thematic purpose. According to early dictionaries and commentaries, the original meaning of the Chinese binomial term *jung-hua*, of which eiga is the Japanese reflex, was "flowers and blossoms," with *jung (ei)* referring to the flowers of plants, and *hua (ga)* to tree blossoms. The word seems to have been most often employed, however, in its derived sense of "flowering fortunes," "worldly success," "glory"[22]—the sense always attached to it in Japan.

---

21. The word yotsugi, it may be noted, does not appear.
22. The derived meaning occurs early in Chinese literature, e.g. in *Chuang-tzu*, 3: ch. 7, 28b, and in *Shih-chi*, p. 692 (the occurrence here is in an addendum to the text made by the Han scholar Ch'u Shao-sun). The works of Six Dynasties and T'ang poets, however, are more likely to have been the conduits through which eiga entered the Heian vocabulary. It appears

The "flowers and blossoms" were not, it is important to note, imagistic symbols of all types of glory, spiritual as well as profane. In both Chinese and Japanese usage, they referred specifically to a thoroughly material and secular prosperity, the chief ingredients of which were high public office, power, and wealth.[23] Semantically speaking, the word described precisely the kind of glory that Michinaga exemplified, and that the author sought to portray.

The connotative appropriateness of eiga to the author's theme was perhaps enhanced by an allusive potential derived from *Ise monogatari* (Tales of Ise), a classic tenth-century collection of "poem tales" that served subsequent generations of Heian writers as a stock source of allusions. One of the stories in the collection describes Ariwara Narihira's composition of a poem at a party in honor of a certain Fujiwara Masachika. The decorations for the event included a large cluster of wisteria blossoms—a happy choice, because the name of the plant (*fuji*) formed part of Masachika's family name. The guests had been composing poems about the wisteria when Narihira arrived and was persuaded to join them. He recited:

Saku hana no	Longer than ever before
Shita ni kakururu	Is the wisteria's shadow—
Hito o ōmi	So many are those
Arishi ni masaru	Who find shelter
Fuji no kage kamo.	Beneath its blossoms!

The tale concludes with the following exchange: "'What is the point of your poem?' someone asked. 'I was thinking about the full-blown state of the Chancellor's flowering fortunes [eiga], and about the especially flourishing condition of the Fujiwara family,' he replied. The critics were satisfied."[24]

One may find the point of the tale unclear, but the poem itself appears to be a congratulatory piece, celebrating the great worldly success of Masachika's family, the Fujiwara, which had recently attained unprecedented heights of power and prestige with the appointment of its head, Chancellor Yoshifusa (804–72), as the first Regent of non-Imperial blood. In other words, Narihira uses the wisteria as a metaphor for the Fujiwara, com-

---

with some frequency in the Six Dynasties anthology *Wen-hsüan* and in the poetry of Li Po and Po Chü-i, probably the Chinese writings best known in Court circles during the Heian period; and its adoption from those acknowledged models of stylistic excellence would have been a natural development.

23. See the *Shih-chi* passage cited in the previous note for a typical equation of eiga with wealth and honors (*fu-kuei*).

24. After McCullough 1968, pp. 138–39.

paring the long cluster to the mighty family's ever-increasing prosperity. And the word eiga is central to his explanation of the poem's meaning. *Saku hana* ("blossoms," "blooming flowers"), which is to be taken in the sense of "flowering fortunes"/"worldly success," is almost a direct Japanese equivalent of the basic meaning of eiga; and *sakayuru*, "flourishing" (an etymological echo of saku, "bloom"), which appears in "the especially flourishing condition of the Fujiwara family," is a possible rendering of the initial *ei*. Thus the tale not only associates eiga closely with the Fujiwara, but also seems to endow it with a congratulatory element, connoting specific praise of the family's period of outstanding success and power, which began with Yoshifusa and culminated under the leadership of *Eiga*'s hero, Michinaga.[25]

It seems possible that our author was consciously alluding to the *Ise* tale when she used eiga to describe Michinaga's career. Since the word is the key to the meaning of the tale, explaining the poem and tying together the story's elements, anyone who remembered the tale itself could scarcely forget it. And *Ise*'s near-canonical status guaranteed that it would be familiar to most, if not all, contemporary readers. Furthermore, the tale may well have served as the word's *locus classicus* for writers of Japanese, since its use there marks the first known occurrence in a Japanese text.

The allusion in *Eiga*, if such it was, not only expanded the word's connotations in an appropriate manner, but also made an explicit semantic connection between the family name Fujiwara ("Wisteria Plain") and the "flowers and blossoms" of the title, preparing the reader for the floral imagery that runs throughout the work in descriptions of Michinaga's family and career. The birth of his first Imperial grandson, for example, is called "the first blossom in the flowering of Michinaga's fortunes"; an infant Imperial granddaughter is compared to a flower in bud; two of his sons, Norimichi and Yorimune, participating in a parade, seem to the spectators to fit the occasion "as perfectly as a flower its season"; and he himself is likened to an eternal flower of incomparable scent and color.

The selection of Michinaga's glory as a theme naturally led the author to stress the years of her protagonist's greatest power and influence. The density of treatment increases in almost direct proportion to his prosperity, starting at its lowest point, in Chapters 1 through 4, with a relatively sketchy account of the fifty years between 946 and 996, a period during which Michinaga was either unborn or still in the early stages of his career; and rising progressively to a level at which seventeen chapters, representing

25. There is some doubt about the true meaning of the tale. See n. 35, below.

50 percent of the work's total length, are required to describe the final eleven years of his life, when, as he said, all the world seemed to belong to him.[26] In terms of descriptive intensity, the climax comes in Chapters 17 through 26, which deal with the period during which the fortunes of Michinaga and his immediate family were at their zenith. The reigning Emperor was his grandson, the Empress was his daughter, two of the three other living Imperial ladies were also his daughters, another daughter was married to a former Crown Prince who had received the title of Retired Emperor, still another daughter was married to the current Crown Prince (who was also his grandson), a son directed the Court government as Regent, and another son held one of the chief ministerial titles.

Buddhist activities, mentioned frequently throughout the narrative, come to dominate other concerns as the description intensifies in the latter half of the work. The development is in part a natural one, since Michinaga ended his formal involvement in Court and secular affairs by entering holy orders in 1019 (Chapter 15), and since he was thereafter much involved in religious enterprises, especially the construction and dedication of the great Hōjōji, which might legitimately have been regarded as the crowning achievement of his long career, and a fitting monument to Fujiwara dominion. The religious orientation can also be taken to reflect the author's personal interests, and, perhaps more particularly, the nature of the sources available to her.

The pronounced Buddhist tone of the work, especially in the second half, is reinforced by a seemingly purposeful structural resemblance to the *Lotus Sutra*, a scripture that figures prominently in *Eiga* as a principal object of Michinaga's worship. Chapter 15, "Doubts," which separates the author's account of Michinaga's secular career from that of his life as a Buddhist Novice, constitutes a clear numerical and functional analogue to the crucial fifteenth chapter in the *Lotus*, "Gushing Forth," which stands between an initial section concerned with the historical Buddha, Śākyamuni, and a final section revealing the eternal buddha;[27] and the parallelism is

26. The average distribution of *Eiga* material is as follows: Chapters 1–2 (946–85), two pages per year; Chapters 3–4 (986–96), five pages per year (in 986 Emperor Ichijō accedes and Kaneie, Michinaga's father, becomes Regent); Chapters 5–12 (996–1017), ten pages per year (Michinaga becomes chief minister in 996 and Regent in 1016); Chapters 13–30 (1017–28), twenty-nine pages per year.

27. The pivotal nature of the "Gushing Forth" chapter was recognized as early as the fifth century A.D. In the sixth century, Chih-i (531–97) formulated the standard interpretation of the division, identifying the first part of the sutra as the "realm of trace" (*chi-men*) and the second part as the "realm of origin" (*pen-men*). See Katō et al. 1975, p. 238; and Ui 1949, 2: 82–88.

underlined by references and allusions in "Doubts" to "Gushing Forth."[28]
This correspondence, which can scarcely be accidental, strongly suggests
that the division of the "Main Section" (*seihen*) into thirty chapters was
inspired by the structure of the *Threefold Lotus Sutra* (*hokke sanbukyō*).[29]
The *Lotus Sutra* itself has only twenty-eight chapters (*hon*), but it was
often bracketed, in Buddhist discussions and rituals, with two one-*kan*
sutras, *Muryōgikyō* (Sutra of Innumerable Meanings) and *Kanfugengyō*
(Sutra of Meditation on the Bodhisattva Fugen). *Muryōgikyō* was regarded as the "opening sutra" of the *Lotus*, and *Kanfugengyō* as the "closing sutra"; and the three together were called the *Threefold Lotus Sutra*,
of which there were thus thirty parts.

The *Lotus* trilogy was worshiped and explicated in the "Thirty Expositions of the *Lotus Sutra*" (*hokke sanjikkō*), a type of Buddhist service
closely associated with Michinaga. In the normal fifteen- or thirty-day
schedule of the service, the "opening sutra" was expounded in the first session, the individual chapters of the *Lotus* followed seriatim in each of the
next twenty-eight sessions, and the service concluded with the exposition
of the "closing sutra" in the thirtieth session.[30] *Eiga* depicts Michinaga as
a regular and frequent sponsor of Thirty Expositions services after his rise
to power, and it is quite possible that he was their originator, since he
commissioned the first one of which we have knowledge.[31] At any rate,
they remained so closely associated with him and his descendants as to lead
one scholar to suggest that they were "special Fujiwara ceremon[ies], intended to promote the felicity of the House";[32] and their thirty-part structure would have been an obviously appropriate model for a chronicle of his
life.

The heavily Buddhistic content of the narrative, taken in conjunction
with its structure, might suggest a reading as a kind of latter-day sutra,
in which Michinaga is celebrated as a Flowering Fortunes Buddha—an
interpretation the author encourages by likening her protagonist to a
buddha on several occasions, and by reporting evidence that he was a re-
incarnation of either Kōbō Daishi or Shōtoku Taishi.[33] But it would be

28. See the Translation, p. 515, where an allusion to the "Gushing Forth" chapter provides
the title "Doubts."
29. The correspondence between the *Eiga* chapter divisions and the thirty parts of the
Threefold Lotus Sutra was first noted by Haga 1928.
30. Chōken (d. 1203), *Hokke sanjikkō honshaku*.
31. In 1004. *Midō kanpakuki*, 1: 94 (10 vi Kankō 1).
32. De Visser 1935, 2: 696.
33. Translation, pp. 501–2. Note also that Chapter 30 ("Crane Grove"), which describes
Michinaga's death, is named for the place where Śākyamuni is said to have entered nirvana.

a mistake, we believe, to go so far. The author herself hints that Michinaga was, after all, something less than a buddha,[34] and she seems in reality to have seen his religious works as merely another aspect of the "flowering fortunes" that constitute her main theme. Just as her interest in secular history is not so much in cause and effect as in spectacle and drama, so her treatment of Michinaga's pious works concerns itself less with the meaning of his acts than with their visual impact. The famous description of the Hōjōji and its dedication (Chapters 17 and 18) is more detailed than that of any other single subject in the book, but in kind it follows a familiar pattern—the admiring, exclamatory account of aristocratic splendor and opulence. Clearly, it is not because of the temple's religious significance that the author allows it so much space, but because it is, in her eyes, the wonder of the age and the ultimate expression of Michinaga's glory.

It is curious, certainly, that a work with such a pronounced Buddhistic coloration should bear the title "Flowering Fortunes," the connotations of which are all secular. In early Chinese and Japanese usage, the word eiga often functioned as a kind of antonymous correlate of eternal moral or spiritual riches, appearing in contexts that implied the ephemerality, inconsequentiality, and final meaninglessness of worldly prosperity. Particularly in a Buddhist context, negative connotations seem always to have been present, since a cardinal tenet of Buddhist teaching was the transience of worldly success, as well as of all other mundane concerns.[35]

34. After his death, she reports a dream revealing his rebirth in the *lowest* realm of Amitābha's paradise. Translation, p. 770.

35. A poem by Po Chü-i contains the lines "Flowering fortunes last but an instant; / Of what use to seek and obtain them?" *Po-shih ch'ang-ch'ing-chi*, 24: ch. 51, 12b. Li Po likens "flowering fortunes" to the impermanence of "water in the eastward-flowing streams." "Teng kao wang ssu hsi," *Li T'ai-po wen chi*, ch. 2, 7b. In *Wen-hsüan* the word occurs six times, always in association with notions of transience: 11: ch. 21, 7b–8a; 23: ch. 25, 16b–26a (two occurrences); 9: ch. 16, 26a; 17: ch. 32, 15b; and 22: ch. 43, 8b–9a. Of the three pre-*Eiga* Japanese occurrences, two clearly have similar associations, and one is ambiguous. The unequivocal examples both appear in *Genji*. In one, Yūgiri earns praise because, although "he was born into so eminent a house and might have been expected to amuse himself solely with worldly 'flowers and blossoms' [*sekai no eiga*]," he has studied with the devotion and ardor of the ambitious poor (2: 280); in the other, a monk remarks that people seem to find it impossible to face the austerity of a religious life "as long as they remain involved in the pursuit of secular 'flowers and blossoms' [*seken no eiga*]" (5: 398). In the first instance, Waley (1935, p. 404), translates eiga as "brilliant gaieties," which misses the more exact sense of the word but conveys well, in the Confucian context, its connotation of frivolity; in the second, Seidensticker (1976, p. 1072), accurately renders the connotation with "illusory triumphs and glories." There is a similar association with frivolous pursuits in *Hamamatsu chūnagon monogatari*, p. 334. The third pre-*Eiga* use occurs in the *Ise* tale discussed above, where the context seems to lack the contrast needed to elicit negative connotations. The diary of Fujiwara Morosuke (908–60), which refers to the "flowering fortunes" of his family when five of his sons receive promotions in rank on the same day, shows that eiga had a positive sense when there was no such context. *Kyūreki*, p. 28 (7 i Tentoku 4). But the bad relations

Troubled, perhaps, by the potential associations of the word, the author seems to have found it necessary to deny that they applied to Michinaga. At the end of a long paean to his Buddhist endeavors, she says, in the pivotal Chapter 15 (Translation, p. 515):

There is a difference between fact and aspiration for people in this world, regardless of their statuses. Though a tree may wish to remain motionless, winds never cease to blow; though a son may intend to be filial, parents do not live forever. Whatever lives dies. A life span may be immeasurably long, but there is always a limit. Those who prosper must decline; where there is meeting, parting will follow. All is cause and effect; nothing is eternal. Fortunes that prospered yesterday may decline today. Even spring blossoms and autumn leaves are spoiled and lose their beauty when they are enshrouded by spring haze and autumn mist. And after a gust of wind scatters them, they are nothing but debris in a garden or froth on the water. *It is only the flowering fortunes of this lord [Michinaga] that, now having begun to bloom, will not be hidden from sight during a thousand years of spring hazes and autumn mists.* No wind disturbs their branches, which grow ever more redolent with scent—rare and splendid as *udumbara* blossoms, peerlessly fragrant as the blue lotus, fairest of water-flowers.

Although Michinaga's "flowering fortunes" are linked through sense and imagery with the symbols of change and ephemerality in the earlier part of the passage, they are, the author seems to be saying, exempt from natural law and beyond the purview of Buddhist doctrine.

The contradiction in this apparent piece of blasphemy is so jarring and unexpected that one may at first be tempted to suspect the author of some grandly ironical design—to believe that she intended, by her juxtaposition of Buddhist piety and secular grandeur, to move her readers to reflections on the inevitable end of her protagonist's glory. But this was almost certainly not the case, for the work as a whole is too ingenuously exuberant in its praise and admiration of Michinaga's career, secular and religious alike, to lend credence to an ironical interpretation. At any rate, if irony was intended, the too-complete success of the author's dissimulation elsewhere defeats her purpose.

In our view, the passage is a further demonstration that the author saw

---

between Narihira and Fujiwara Yoshifusa, coupled with the pervasive *Wen-hsüan* influence on contemporary poets, raises doubts about the meaning of the *Ise* use. It is even possible that Narihira had in mind two specific *Wen-hsüan* uses (ch. 21, 7b–8a, "Ta pin hsi," and ch. 25, 16b–26a, "Yung shih pa-shou"), where the reference is to the fortunes of tyrants, who might reasonably have reminded him of the Fujiwara "tyrant," Yoshifusa. On Narihira and his relationship with the Fujiwara, see McCullough 1968, pp. 41–49. Eiga occurs several times in Buddhist contexts in the late Heian *Konjaku monogatari*, always as an antonym of the eternal values of the true religious life (3: 199, 202, 274, 384, 404, 531).

Michinaga's religious works as a principal manifestation of his "flowering fortunes," and that (like most Heian aristocrats) she was little bothered by contradictions of thought or doctrine, which she overcame by ignoring them. The structural and verbal allusions to the *Lotus Sutra* are literary flourishes, surely, rather than ironic religious comment. Similarly, the likening of Michinaga to a buddha and the assertion of the immortality of his secular glory are merely specimens of the hyperbole in which the work abounds, signifying no more than the predictions of unending life that had for centuries been de rigueur in congratulatory poems addressed to exalted personages. The author's identification of religious works with secular splendor coincided with a general tendency among Heian aristocrats to convert Buddhism to worldly ends. For most members of the nobility, Buddhism was at least as much an instrument for material benefit in the present life as a path to spiritual enlightenment, and the author was no doubt justified in regarding Michinaga's temple buildings, images, pilgrimages, and religious services in the same thematic light as the mansions, costly furnishings, regal journeys, and extravagant ceremonies that had glorified his lay years. All were expressions of his wealth and power; all were equally petals of his "flowering fortunes."

The author's understanding of the concept of theme may have been influenced by Murasaki Shikibu's remarks on the monogatari writer's attitude toward her subject. When an author "wants to write favorably about something," Murasaki remarks, "she will select only good things to tell about, but when she wants to appeal to readers, she will give them a collection of strange and wicked things. But in neither case does she ever write about matters outside the ordinary world of men."[36]

Murasaki is apparently saying that an author writes from a particular point of view, or with a particular aim, which will lead to emphasis on one or another aspect of a subject, but that the material will always remain realistic in spite of such artificial shaping. The idealized portrait of Prince Genji in her novel seems to be an application of that principle. It is unlikely that such a paragon ever existed, but each of Genji's component parts was probably realized more or less perfectly in an individual living courtier, or at least was held to be an ideal that men were capable of attaining. The Shining Prince was the sum of all that was good in the eyes of the Heian aristocrat—an artificial creation, but representative nevertheless of prized traits actually to be found, or potentially realizable, in Murasaki's social world.

36. *Genji*, 2: 432.

In the sense that the *Eiga* author wanted to "write favorably about something"—in the sense that she selected everything good she could think of to record concerning that "something"—her treatment of the capital aristocracy, and especially of the Fujiwara family and Michinaga, seems to be a direct application of Murasaki's remarks to historical materials. Although she occasionally allows herself a mild word or two of criticism, as in Chapter 16, where she comments unfavorably on the competitive attitude of Grand Empress Kenshi's ladies in copying out chapters of the *Lotus Sutra*, her account is for the most part eulogistic in content and tone. Whether writing about the sumptuousness of a Fujiwara mansion, the disestablishment of a Crown Prince, the entrance of a noble youth into holy orders, the marriage of an aristocratic girl, or the death of an Emperor, she always manages to find the "good"—to strike a positive, approving note. The atmosphere of the work as a whole is therefore affirmative, with emphasis on the happier moments and aspects of life—fine houses, magnificent furnishings, beautiful clothes, elaborate gardens, elegant pastimes, great temples and religious services—and even when death, tragedy, or some lesser misfortune intrudes, it serves merely to reveal another highly regarded side of aristocratic character: refinement of feeling and emotional sensitivity.

It is true that the author makes passing references to the Buddhistic concept of *mappō* ("latter dharma"), and to the Chinese-derived political notion of *masse* ("latter ages"), both of which imply a marked deterioration in the quality of human beings and their society, but there is little evidence in her account to suggest that she actually saw the contemporary world in a pessimistic light. On the contrary, she writes as if Michinaga's times were the very apex of civilization, imperfect only in the sense that all human affairs are transitory, and even this conventional piece of wisdom receives little stress in her pages.[37]

Michinaga in particular becomes a model of aristocratic virtue. The author saw him as the grandest, most "glorious" courtier Japan had ever known, and it was clearly her intention to include in her chronicle nothing that would contradict that view. When he is introduced in Chapter 3, his character is described as "extraordinary and ideal in every respect," and we are treated thereafter to a constant parade of evidence in support of the encomium: dazzling events and spectacles testifying to the great man's glory, elegant scenes of domestic beauty and harmony demonstrating the

---

37. Some writers attach greater importance to the notions of mappō, masse, and the transitoriness of human affairs as they appear in *Eiga*. See, for example, Nishio 1961, pp. 83–84.

blissfulness of his life, and saintly acts of piety, compassion, and generosity revealing the incomparable fineness of his nature. Seldom is there a suggestion that he was less than perfect; nowhere is there more than a faint reflection of the political infighting, economic exploitation of inferiors, merciless treatment of rivals, callous use of people, jealousies, enmities, and spite that marked his career in real life. But if the author's treatment seems more hagiography than biography, it is nevertheless important to bear in mind that the idealization was achieved not primarily by falsification of the record—although, as we shall see, there may have been some of that too—but by selection and emphasis, by describing "all the good things" and suppressing or brushing over the rest.

Although the author made Michinaga's career the core of her work, she did not attempt either a complete account of his life and times or a searching examination of his character. He is already twenty years old when he enters her pages (Chapter 3), and details concerning his official and private activities do not become voluminous until Chapter 6, when he is nearing the peak of his power and affluence. Important pieces of information about his career are omitted—his appointment as Chancellor, for instance—and concentration on external magnificence substitutes for exploration of the deeper recesses of mind and character. The author's preoccupation with glory and splendor reduces her hero, in the end, to a one-dimensional cut-out. He may indeed have been uninteresting—there are enough dull despots in history to permit the conjecture—but we are not told enough to let us judge even that much.[38] We see little of his real qualities as a human being: none of his warts and wrinkles, none of his passions, none of his human foibles, nothing of the drive and ambition that made him the most powerful figure of his age.

Nor are his better qualities convincingly presented. His acts of compassion and piety, for example, are described in such superficial, conventional terms that little sense of the living man emerges. The failure of the author to portray Michinaga as a recognizable human being gives her account a curiously unreal, detached quality, dilutes the image of aristocratic glory she sought to convey, and partially, at least, defeats her thematic purpose.

The author's inability to handle her core topic and theme with complete success was probably due to a variety of reasons, but one principal cause was her attempt to combine two antithetical forms, the monogatari and the chronicle. On the one hand, her basic orientation in language, materials,

38. The case for dullness receives some support, however, from his own diary, *Midō kanpakuki*, and from other contemporary sources. See also Kitayama 1970.

and treatment was toward the monogatari; on the other, conceiving her work to be in some sense a successor to the National Histories, she adopted the chronicle form as her fundamental organizing principle. In order to provide continuity with the Six National Histories, she began with the reign of Emperor Uda, the successor to the last Emperor treated in the Histories, even though the period that interested her started considerably later, with the accession of Emperor Murakami.[39] Moreover, we find conspicuous remnants of the official chronicler's interests and style alongside her monogatari-like materials. Throughout the work there are brief notations of miscellaneous public events—deaths of prominent men, appointments to office and rank, the occurrence or nonoccurrence of ceremonies and religious rites, genealogical events in the Imperial Family and the nobility, and so forth. Emphasis on chronology and the traditional materials of history is most pronounced in the earlier chapters, where the largest spans of time are condensed into the least space, but it persists even where the monogatari element is strongest.

Despite her recognition of the possibility of a new kind of history, the author thus failed to escape completely from the influence of traditional historiography. Although she was often vague about dating or allowed the pace of her narrative to supersede strict insistence on chronological development, the basic chronicle format and the introduction of numerous unrelated facts produced a disjointed, episodic work in which the full potentialities of the monogatari approach remain unrealized. *Eiga monogatari* is not a well-constructed, sharply focused account of Michinaga and his times, but rather a series of sketches, vignettes, and anecdotes, hung on a chronological framework beginning well before Michinaga's day, and embracing much material that is only tangentially pertinent to his life and career or to the general history of the period.

But if the author's use of topic and theme was far from ideal, her work nevertheless established a major new field of historiography in Japan. The official-chronicle tradition, revived at the beginning of the Kamakura period, continued vigorous and productive into the Edo period, spawning such monuments of scholarship as *Azumakagami, Dainihonshi,* and *Tokugawa jikki.* The liveliest and most provocative reading, however, came from thematically and topically oriented histories of the kind pioneered by the anonymous author of *Eiga monogatari.* The "mirror" series of histories

39. Abe 1963, p. 11, suggests that *Eiga* was originally intended as a continuation of the never-completed *Shinkokushi,* which covered the three reigns between the last of the Six National Histories and Murakami—i.e. Uda, Daigo, and Suzaku.

inaugurated with *Ōkagami* in the late eleventh or early twelfth century; the two chief theoretical works of medieval historiography, *Gukanshō* and *Jinnō shōtōki*; the military tales of the thirteenth and later centuries; and the many miscellaneous biographies of the medieval and modern eras may all be seen as having flowed in one sense or another from the *Eiga* topical tradition.

By adopting a descriptive approach to the treatment of her materials, the author made still another major contribution to Japanese historiography. In the chronicle style of the Six National Histories, the emphasis had been on a concise recording of facts, with little or no descriptive elaboration. More often than not, an entry in a National History simply notes a fact: there has been an eclipse, so-and-so has been appointed to such-and-such a rank, relief supplies have been granted to such-and-such provinces because of such-and-such natural calamities. Even in the case of the most spectacular events, such as the burning of Ōtenmon Gate at the Imperial Palace in 866, the details tend to be purely factual: the main incidents involved, the identities of the participants, what happened to them, official orders or decrees issued in connection with the crime, and so on.[40]

Dissatisfied with this bare-bones approach to history, our author seeks instead to re-create a scene as a physical and emotional experience. When one of Michinaga's daughters marries, we are not simply told the name of the bridegroom and the date of the nuptials. We receive descriptions of the bride's appearance, of the costumes of her ladies-in-waiting, of the decorations of the bridal chamber, and of the marriage ceremony itself, as well as some sense of the joys and anguish of the occasion. When a birth occurs, the author may describe the special fittings of the lying-in room, the preparations for the delivery, the expectant mother's mixed feelings of anticipation and foreboding, the anxious concern of her parents and husband, and the overwhelming confusion of noise and incense smoke created by the monks as they perform their protective rites. When Michinaga erects a Buddhist temple, the reader occupies a grandstand seat at the dedication ceremonies, and later accompanies some nuns as they tour the establishment, noting with awe the wonders of its furnishings. When a Court figure is sent into exile, the author's concern is not so much with the circumstances of his disgrace, his past career, or pertinent official documents—the sort of thing found in the *Sandai jitsuroku* record of Tomo no Yoshio's exile after the burning of Ōtenmon Gate—as with the human drama of the event, the grief of the banished minister as he takes leave of

40. The Ōtenmon Gate affair is recorded in *Sandai jitsuroku*, pp. 195ff (8 ix Jōgan 8).

his sister and widowed mother, his emotional visit to his father's grave, and later his secret reunion with his dying mother. Such subjects and such treatment are a far cry indeed from the lean, hard-fact, highly political world of the National Histories.

Clearly, the author's descriptive method owed much to the monogatari tradition. The fact that *Eiga monogatari* is sometimes viewed as primarily a work of literature, rather than a history, shows the extent of the book's indebtedness to monogatari techniques and conventions. Dialogue and direct quotations of thought and poetry, which appear only sporadically in the National Histories after *Nihon shoki*, here occur on almost every page, serving, as in a monogatari, to add immediacy and realism to the narrative, and especially to convey the emotional quality of an occasion.

The author also follows her monogatari predecessors in interjecting herself directly into her material. She describes functions as if they were happening before her eyes, endowing them with a sensuous, pictorial quality typical of the monogatari style; she responds repeatedly to the emotive value of events with exclamations of "How sad!" "How moving!" "How splendid!" and "How lovely!"; and she sometimes places herself squarely in the middle of a scene, commenting, for example, that she could not be sure who was present because it was dark, or that she stopped recording the poems composed because the hour grew late. Like many poets and monogatari authors before her, she makes nature a symbol of human emotions and moods, although she employs the technique far more sparingly than, say, Murasaki Shikibu does in *The Tale of Genji*. A description of a brilliantly fine day frames an account of a great festival or ceremony, harmonizing with and emphasizing the splendor and joy of the occasion; the gloom of a heavy snow reflects the mood of mourners at a funeral.

Finally, the author may also have been inspired by the monogatari tradition to divide her narrative into gracefully titled chapters, and, more significantly, to arrange her material in such a way as to achieve tonal and dramatic contrasts. Matsumura Hiroji and Kawakita Noboru have pointed out that there is a contrast between "light" and "dark" chapters in the first part of *Eiga*, i.e. that chapters centering on gloomy, sad events (5, 7, 9, 10) are juxtaposed with others devoted to bright, joyful occasions (6, 8, 11).[41] Kawakita has further noted the possibly intentional distortion of historical fact to achieve dramatic intensity, as in Chapter 5, where a pregnant Empress's grandfather (Takashina Naritada) is depicted as praying

41. Matsumura 1956–67, 1: 445; Kawakita 1968, pp. 217–19. Kawakita (1969, pp. 10–14) finds similar intentional contrasts within individual chapters as well.

for the safe delivery of the child, although he had in fact died before its conception.[42]

The author's innovations in subject matter, treatment, and language, although frequently marred by imperfections of concept and execution, marked an important milestone in the evolution of Japanese historical writing, making it no longer an insipid reflection of Chinese practice but a live and genuinely felt response to perceived reality. She was no better than her predecessors at recognizing and describing the fundamental forces that guided the nation's history—she would perhaps have felt little interest in them had they been pointed out to her—but she was intimately familiar with the concerns and values of the hothouse social world inhabited by the Kyōto aristocracy, and she succeeded to a remarkable degree in capturing the essence of that world as it seemed to some, at least, of its denizens. Her success may have been due in part to her innocence of historical theory. Unconstrained by the heavy-handed didacticism of Chinese historiography or by any other complex interpretative framework, she was free to pursue the simple principle of human interest that Murasaki Shikibu had laid down as the basic motivation of the monogatari.

Monogatari were written, Murasaki said, when an author was so moved by events in people's lives that she could no longer keep them to herself.[43] For Murasaki, as for our author, monogatari were written neither to interpret nor to guide human behavior, but to record some of life's most impressive and moving moments, regardless of their moral value or intrinsic importance.

In the case of *Eiga*, this view led to something approaching what a modern logician of historical writing has called the "prodigious fallacy"—the fallacy that "mistakes sensation for significance . . . the erroneous idea that a historian's task is to describe portents and prodigies, and events marvelous, stupendous, fantastic, extraordinary, wonderful, superlative, astonishing, and monstrous—and further, that the more marvelous, stupendous, etc., an event is, the more historic and eventful it becomes."[44]

Such a principle of selection is obviously "dysfunctional to the historicity" of a historian's interpretation, resulting in a kind of journalistic approach that in itself tells little or nothing about the underlying dynamics of a society. Yet it is precisely this that makes *Eiga* an important historical work: because, like a modern newspaper, it is a record of society rather than an

---

42. Kawakita 1968, pp. 143–47. We shall return to this case and look at another possible example of distortion for dramatic effect in our later discussion of the historicity of the work.

43. *Genji*, 2: 432.   44. Fischer 1970, pp. 70–71.

interpretation of it; because it mirrors tastes, attitudes, values, and beliefs in an unanalytical fashion, making little or no attempt to tailor its accounts to fit the historical importance of the events treated. One can in fact be grateful for the author's interpretative restraint, since the intellectual climate of her day was not conducive to rigorous thinking. Even if she had attempted a deeper analysis of her materials, it is unlikely that she could have produced anything more substantial than the primitive theorizing of medieval Japan's best-known analytical history, *Gukanshō*, which today serves mainly to illuminate the confusion of its author's mind.

Interpretation is not, to be sure, wholly lacking in *Eiga*. The choice and treatment of materials inevitably entailed at least a minimal degree of analysis, evaluation, and synthesis. But there is nothing in the design of the account that could have taxed the author's intellectual capacities. Her work was shaped by a simple judgment concerning the intrinsic value and importance of aristocratic society, and by the recognition of a few facts, which were probably considered self-evident, about that society: the commanding role played by the Fujiwara family; the central importance of blood and marital ties (especially with the Emperor) in determining status and power; and, conversely, the critical role played by powerful non-Imperial relatives in deciding the fortunes of Empresses, Crown Princes, and Emperors. Within that modest framework, which is never explicitly formulated by the author herself, a selection of materials was made—primarily from Murasaki's lyrical point of view, it seems—resulting first in concentration on the dramatic figure of Michinaga, and then on the impressive and moving events of his life and times, regardless of whether or not they served to explain historical developments.[45]

'EIGA' AND THE HISTORICAL TALE

Not only in the broad sense described above, but in a narrower sense as well, the appearance of *Eiga monogatari* meant the beginning of a new kind of historical writing in Japan. *Eiga* became the first of six similarly oriented, closely interconnected works, known collectively to modern historiographers and literary historians as *rekishi monogatari*, "historical tales,"

45. Inoue (1957, p. 107) maintains that *Eiga monogatari*, like *Genji monogatari, Ōkagami*, and *Gukanshō*, represents an attempt to understand the reasons for the instability of life in the mid- and late Heian periods. In the sense that the author saw family and marriage as determining factors in individual fortunes, that is perhaps true, but the emphasis of the narrative is clearly not on explaining events, even in those simple terms, but in recording and describing them.

which together cover the history of the Imperial Court from its putative origins in 660 B.C. to the overthrow of the Kamakura Shogunate in 1333.[46] The "historical tale" group is reasonably homogeneous in language, type of subject matter, and emphasis on the theme of aristocratic glory;[47] and particular relationships between individual *rekishi monogatari* further knit it into a clearly recognizable series that includes some of the most significant historical and literary writing of the Heian and medieval periods.

Eiga played a dual role in the evolution of the historical tale. First, and no doubt most significantly, it appears to have been the direct source and inspiration of *Ōkagami* (Great Mirror), the acknowledged masterpiece of the group. Second, it established the characteristic features of the *rekishi monogatari*, and as progenitor and molder of the series, contributed ultimately to further important refinements of historical understanding in Japan.

Although *Ōkagami*'s date has not been firmly established, the weight of expert opinion today favors the view that it was written not long after the composition of the first thirty chapters of *Eiga*—probably late in the eleventh century or early in the twelfth.[48] The author seems to have been familiar with *Eiga*, and to have drawn from it not only the linguistic style of the monogatari and the general subject of the Court aristocracy, but also his central topic—the history of the Fujiwara line culminating in Michinaga—and much of his material.

Despite his apparently heavy reliance on *Eiga* for language, subject, topic, and materials, the *Ōkagami* author was in many respects the most inventive writer in the historical-tale line. To begin with, he replaced *Eiga*'s annalistic approach by an organization somewhat reminiscent of the official Chinese histories. A brief initial section (corresponding vaguely to

46. The other major extant tales are *Ōkagami* (Great Mirror), by an author thought to have been male, writing probably in the last half of the eleventh century or the early twelfth century, covering the period 850–1025; *Imakagami* (Mirror of the Present), by Fujiwara Tametsune, in 1170 (?), covering the period 1025–1170; *Mizukagami* (Water Mirror), by Nakayama Tadachika (?), in the twelfth century, covering the period 660 B.C.–A.D. 850; and *Masukagami* (Clear Mirror), by an unknown author (1338–76), covering the period 1180–1333. The sixth work, *Iyoyotsugi* (Still More Yotsugi), covering the years 1170–80, has not survived.

47. The historical tale's emphasis on glory was noted long ago by Jien (1155–1225) in *Gukanshō*, p. 129. Referring to the tales as yotsugi monogatari, he says that "they all seek to record only good things (*yoki koto*)." See also Matsumura 1956–67, 1: 518–19.

48. Some scholars have argued that *Ōkagami* was written shortly after 1025, the year of its narrative present, but most authorities postulate a later date. *Eiga*'s date is discussed below. For a survey of scholarly opinion on the date of *Ōkagami* and a discussion thereof, see Matsumura 1961, pp. 111–22.

the Chinese *pen-chi*, "Imperial annals") provided vital statistics and a few general remarks or anecdotes about the fourteen Emperors who reigned in Japan between 850 and 1025 (the narrative present of *Ōkagami*); a second, main section (corresponding to the Chinese *lieh-chuan*, "biographies") was given over to "biographies" of the Fujiwara leaders from Tokihira (871–909) to Michinaga; and a third, final section (considered by some scholars to correspond to the Chinese *chih*, "monographs") contained miscellaneous information and stories about various members of the Imperial, Fujiwara, and Minamoto families.

The *Ōkagami* author also introduced the useful fiction that his narrative was drawn from a lengthy discourse and conversation—the result of a chance meeting in 1025 at the Urin'in—in which the main participants were two immensely aged men, both of whom had lived during most of the period he proposed to describe. The device afforded him a convenient means of inserting occasional alternative versions or interpretations of incidents, usually with the apparent aim of offering a slightly more critical look behind the scenes of Fujiwara power. It also served, of course, to enliven the account and to give the materials a degree of narrative unity, based on the personal viewpoint of a single direct observer. Through the alternative accounts, as well as in the main body of his work, the author made substantial additions to the *Eiga* materials, both in the kinds of events treated and in the details provided.

Ōkagami is no better history than *Eiga*, but the sharper focus on the Fujiwara leaders achieved through its new, Sinitically inspired organization, the greater compactness of its account (it is not much more than one-third as long as the first thirty chapters of *Eiga*), the liveliness and provocativeness of its narrative, the author's ear for a good story and his ability to tell it, and the vigor of the writing all conspire to make the work a better piece of literature than its pioneering predecessor. In immediately succeeding generations, it probably enjoyed by far the wider readership of the two,[49] and it seems to have become the chief model for the subsequent historical tales.

Although the later tales were less successful as literature, two of them made further noteworthy contributions to the evolution of the concept of history in Japan. *Mizukagami* (Water Mirror), which is generally thought to date from the late twelfth century, pointed the way to a nonbiographical notion of topic in its emphasis on revolts against Imperial authority, and

49. See the discussion of *Eiga*'s readership below.

it also made what appears to have been the first Japanese attempt to interpret history according to an explicitly stated theory—i.e. the belief that the
world evolves through a continuous cycle of four periods (*kalpas*), characterized by greater or lesser human capacity to understand the Buddhist
dharma. The work was thus a conceptual predecessor of *Gukanshō* and
may have been an important influence on that famous work of medieval
historiography.

The use of topic was further refined and extended in *Masukagami* (Clear
Mirror), a fourteenth-century historical tale that focused on Court-Bakufu
relations, and particularly on the attempts of Emperors Go-Toba and Go-
Daigo to recapture from the Bakufu the substance of political authority.
In the conception of his topic, the author may have been influenced by the
example of the thirteenth-century "military tales" (*gunki*, or *senki*, *monogatari*), which were similarly concerned with describing a narrowly defined
series of related historical events. If so, the evolution of the historical tale
apparent in *Masukagami* was inspired by a group of works that probably
owed their own existence, in part at least, to the example of the earlier
historical tales, especially *Eiga* and *Ōkagami*. In a sense, therefore, the succession of influences stemming from *Eiga* came full circle and stopped
with *Masukagami*, the last of the major historical tales. By the time of its
composition, the courtly life that had been the subject of the historical tale
was fast disappearing beneath the weight of military rule and an emerging
feudal society, and subsequent historiographers inevitably turned their attention to other subjects and other forms.[50]

Whether indirectly through *Ōkagami* or directly in its own right, *Eiga*
exercised a continuing and central influence on the historical tale, for it
was *Eiga*'s language, *Eiga*'s type of subject and materials, and *Eiga*'s notion
of topic and theme that defined the salient features of the group. The literary and historiographical importance of the work is therefore not confined to its own unique achievements. Individual offspring substantially
enriched the medieval literary world, especially in the case of *Ōkagami* and
Masukagami, and the historical-tale line as a whole demonstrated for the
medieval historian significant new ways of organizing and looking at history.

50. The contributions of *Mizukagami* and *Masukagami* to the evolution of historical
consciousness in Japan, and the relationship between the historical tale and the gunki monogatari, are discussed in Matsumoto 1959, pp. 5–47; Nishio 1961, pp. 91–93; and Ishida
1963, p. 66. On the historical tale in general, see Matsumura 1961, *passim*; Sakamoto 1958,
pp. 73–85; and Robinson and Beasley 1961, pp. 229–38.

HISTORICITY OF 'EIGA'

Given the author's point of view, her adulatory attitude toward Michinaga and his family, and the influence of the monogatari tradition on her work, it is not surprising to find that her text is marred by various types of historical error and distortion. Simple, apparently inadvertent misstatements of fact, which seem to be of little or no significance, are the most common. The majority are inaccurate datings of events, usually involving mistakes of a few days or at most a month, but sometimes amounting to several years. A fairly rough calculation suggests that perhaps 15–20 percent of the dates given in the text or implied by its chronological scheme disagree with other sources, and in nearly all cases it is clear that it is the *Eiga* author who is at fault.[51]

Mistakes in the attribution of official titles and ranks are fairly common, resulting most often from anachronistic usage: an individual will actually have held a particular title or rank, but not at the time indicated. Other types of minor errors occur sporadically throughout the text—the mislocation of persons and events, misinformation about the number or order of offspring, the erroneous recording of natural disasters, and so forth—making it necessary to exercise caution in accepting any particular item that cannot be corroborated from another source. These miscellaneous mistakes are, nevertheless, relatively infrequent, and if the chronological errors and anachronistic use of titles and ranks are excepted, it is legitimate to say that on the whole the basic facts concerning events are accurately stated. The author did not invent incidents, nor did she often err in presenting factual information.[52]

The text is, however, compromised in another respect—one with more serious implications for its historicity than these petty factual slips and bobbles. This has to do with the author's apparent willingness to use her imagination in fleshing out the details of events, perhaps especially when she wished to depict their scenic aspects and the emotional states of the people

51. A glance at the notes accompanying the Translation will yield numerous examples of chronological errors, and of the sources by which they can be established. The chief sources for the purpose are diaries of contemporary courtiers and early chronicles in the National Histories tradition (e.g. *Nihon kiryaku, Honchō seiki*). For a nearly complete listing, see Yamanaka 1962, pp. 200–215.

52. Kanō (1971, pp. 1–3) has counted 385 factual errors in the first thirty chapters, of which 210 are chronological, 101 have to do with offices and ranks, and 74 are miscellaneous.

involved. Much or most of such material quite possibly came from written sources or from her own recollection. Heian aristocratic women filled diaries and notebooks with descriptions of scenes, feelings, moods, states of mind, and emotional responses, frequently buttressed by the quotation of conversation and poetry; and it is clear that the author made extensive use of those generally authentic materials.[53] But in several instances, at least, her description is demonstrably imaginary, a fact that naturally casts doubt on similar uncorroborated materials elsewhere in the chronicle. In Chapter 8, for example, Michinaga's son Yorimichi is represented as having been appointed Imperial Messenger to the Kamo Festival in 1005, and considerable attention is given to the details of the preparations for his participation in the procession to the shrine, to the procession itself, and to Michinaga's happiness as he observes "the childish grace of the plump little envoy" passing before his viewing-stand. But we know from unimpeachable sources that Yorimichi was not the Kamo Messenger in 1005, and indeed there is no evidence that he ever served in that capacity. It is possible, of course, that the author has merely confused people and places, but whatever the reason, the account remains fictional.[54]

In one sense, the author's occasional indulgence in fiction does relatively little harm to the historical worth of her work, provided that the invention functions as a kind of contextual supplement to the narrative, without betraying the basic atmosphere and movement of historical developments. Michinaga was in the midst of his years of greatest splendor at the time of the 1005 Kamo Festival, and had his son been the Festival Messenger in that year, as he might have been, the brilliance of the procession would probably have been just as *Eiga* describes it. Although the account does not represent historical fact, it is nevertheless history in the sense that fiction often is history—i.e. it is a faithful representation of real circumstances.

But the author sometimes distorted historical events to such an extent and in such a way as to significantly alter their meaning, and those instances raise grave questions about the historical worth of the work as a whole. The best-documented case occurs in Chapter 5, where the circumstances surrounding the exile and subsequent pardon of Michinaga's cousins, Korechika and Takaie, are recounted.[55] The chief facts of that famous

53. See the discussion of sources below.

54. Other cases of imaginative description occur in Chapter 1, where the author mentions the grief of the Junior Consort Hōshi after the death of her father, Morotada, whom she actually predeceased by more than two years; and in the passage in Chapter 5 mentioned earlier.

55. The case is discussed in Kawakita 1968, pp. 63, 146; Matsumura 1971, pp. 6–9; and Yamanaka 1967, p. 50.

incident are well established: in the Fourth Month of the second year of Chōtoku (996), Korechika was exiled to Kyūshū and his brother Takaie to Izumo, charged with involvement in an arrow attack on ex-Emperor Kazan, and with other acts hostile to the Court; in the Fourth Month of the third year of Chōtoku (997), the brothers were pardoned in an amnesty declared because of an illness of the Imperial Lady Senshi.[56]

The *Eiga* account dates the pardon a full year later, in the Fourth Month of the fourth year of Chōtoku (998), and attributes it not to an attempt to cure Senshi, but to Emperor Ichijō's solicitude for the welfare of a son who had been borne to him in the previous month by Empress Teishi, sister to Korechika and Takaie. (One of *Eiga*'s constant themes is the dependence of Princely fortunes on the support of maternal relatives.) This interpretation of events is possible only because *Eiga* also misdates the birth of Teishi's child, assigning it to the Third Month of the fourth year of Chōtoku (998), instead of to its correct date in the Eleventh Month of the first year of Chōhō (999).[57]

Although it is clear that the author has seriously misrepresented the circumstances surrounding the exile, her reasons for doing so are less obvious. The chief focus of Chapter 5, the chapter in which the exile and pardon are described, is on the decline in the fortunes of Korechika and his sister Teishi after the death of their father, Michitaka. It is possible, therefore, that the chronology was rearranged in order to enhance the unity and emotional impact of that theme. By placing the Prince's birth before the pardon, the author was able to describe, first, Teishi's pathetic state as she faced childbirth without the support of her immediate family, and second, the joy of Korechika and Takaie when they learned in exile that they had become uncles to an Imperial son, an event auguring well for the restoration of the family fortunes. Furthermore, by tying the birth to the pardon, the author not only succeeded in giving more weight to the principal theme, but also managed to introduce an affecting picture of Imperial compassion.

But was the distortion deliberately introduced for those purposes? Possibly so, although the circumstances of the exile and pardon were dramatic enough in themselves to require no embellishment; and whatever the increment in emotional impact and unity resulting from the misdatings, it could have been achieved equally well, one would think, by other means

---

56. The two principal sources for the event are the diary of Fujiwara Sanesuke (d. 1046), *Shōyūki*, 2: 7–9 (24 iv Chōtoku 2), 32 (5 iv Chōtoku 3); and *Nihon kiryaku,*, 2: 185, 187–88.

57. *Shōyūki*, 2: 70 (7 xi Chōhō 1); *Gonki*, 1: 84.

that would not have flown in the face of well-known history. It is difficult
to understand, in fact, why the author should have intentionally falsified
so celebrated an incident, when some readers, at least, were almost certain
to recognize her errors. Further speculation along such lines is no doubt
pointless, but one cannot dismiss the possibility that the explanation lies
simply in a faulty memory, aided, perhaps, by a romantic imagination.[58]

Aside from the Korechika-Takaie case, there appear to be only a few
relatively minor instances in which the distortion of historical truth for
the sake of dramatic or literary effect may be suspected.[59] Probably somewhat more common is another type of misrepresentation, designed to protect and enhance the good name of Michinaga and his branch of the
Fujiwara family. A prime example occurs in Chapter 13, where the central topic is the resignation of the heir apparent, Crown Prince Atsuakira
(Koichijōin), and his marriage to Michinaga's daughter Kanshi.

Prince Atsuakira was the eldest son of Emperor Sanjō by his senior consort, Seishi, a daughter of a relatively uninfluential line of the Fujiwara
family. Within the context of Heian politics, his appointment as Crown
Prince in 1016, the year of his father's abdication, represented a potential
threat to the continued ascendency of Michinaga and his line at Court;
and one need not be unduly cynical to suspect Michinaga of somehow engineering the Prince's resignation, which followed the death of ex-Emperor
Sanjō in 1017 by less than three months. Although contemporary sources
other than *Eiga* are silent concerning Michinaga's role, *Ōkagami* offers a
convincing version of the resignation in which Michinaga is rather clearly
the moving force. According to a young man present at the Urin'in "conversation," Atsuakira, abandoned by everyone after his father's death and
alarmed by rumors of Michinaga's displeasure, decided that he would have
to resign his title before he was forcibly divested of it—a decision that was
immediately accepted by the exultant Michinaga.[60]

In *Eiga*, however, the resignation is depicted as springing from Atsuakira's own longing for a return to his former carefree existence, and Michinaga is not only innocent of self-seeking manipulation, but actually tries

58. Yamanaka (1962, pp. 129–36) sees the influence of *Genji monogatari* on the *Eiga* version of Korechika's exile, suggesting that the model for the episode was Genji's exile to
Suma. This does not, however, adequately account for the specific historical mistakes in *Eiga*.
The relationship of *Eiga* to *Genji* is undoubtedly very close in materials relating to Korechika,
who seems to have served as one of the chief models for Prince Genji.

59. Another case involves the Coming-of-Age ceremony for Prince Tamehira described in
Chapter 1. See the Translation, p. 81. For others, see Matsumura 1974, pp. 349–50, 352–55.

60. Yamagiwa 1967, pp. 83–91; *Ōkagami*, pp. 102–10.

to persuade Atsuakira to reconsider. He agrees at last to withdraw his opposition only because the Prince threatens to become a monk.

There are other instances in which historical circumstances suggest that bias in favor of Michinaga may have resulted in falsification or distortion. Michinaga's kindly concern for Prince Atsuyasu in Chapter 6, his magnanimous attitude toward the Imperial consort Seishi in Chapter 10, his solicitude for the health of Emperor Sanjō in Chapter 12, the rather dark picture drawn of his brother and rival, Michikane, in Chapter 3—all of these seem improbable for one reason or another. And there is, in fact, independent evidence to support the reader's suspicions in the cases of Seishi and Emperor Sanjō.[61] The author's desire to present a uniformly glowing picture of Michinaga's career may also explain her failure to record such inauspicious events as her protagonist's long, serious illness in 998.[62]

DATE AND AUTHORSHIP

The ultimate significance of *Eiga*'s factual errors, omissions, fictional embroidery, distortions, and bias depends to some extent on the date and authorship of the work. It may be well, therefore, to introduce at this point a brief résumé of what is known or inferred about those two very vexed questions.

If we restrict ourselves to indisputable fact, we can say only (1) that *Eiga monogatari* achieved its present forty-chapter form at some time between 1092, the year of the latest datable event it describes, and the Kan'ei era (1624–44), when the oldest known dated manuscript was transcribed;[63] and (2) that the identity of the author or authors is unknown. As with all other Heian monogatari, the older manuscripts bear no explicit indication of date or authorship. But other evidence sheds a certain amount of ad-

---

61. According to *Shōyūki*, 3: 4 (9 iv Chōwa 1), 11–16 (27 iv Chōwa 1), Michinaga, far from taking an avuncular interest in Seishi, actively discouraged the attendance of nobles at the ceremony investing her with the rank of Empress—an event he had already managed to overshadow by scheduling his daughter Kenshi's reentry into the Palace for the same date. The author's description of Michinaga's concern for Emperor Sanjō is also belied by Sanesuke (*Shōyūki*, 4: 65 [4 viii Chōwa 4]), who depicts him as badgering the ailing sovereign into retirement in order to prepare the way for the accession of his own grandson, Emperor Go-Ichijō. It must be remembered, however, that Sanesuke disliked Michinaga, and that his diary, though contemporary, may have been no less biased than *Eiga*. For a fuller discussion of these cases of distortion, see Yamanaka, 1962, pp. 283–89.

62. EMZ, 2: 115–16.

63. Tōkyō University manuscript formerly owned by Kume Motobumi. It was destroyed in the 1923 earthquake. Matsumura 1956–67, 1: 12.

ditional light. Calligraphic experts push the date of the oldest surviving forty-chapter manuscript back to around the middle of the thirteenth century or before,[64] and references in twelfth-century writings demonstrate the existence, within some eighty years of its last datable event, of at least a relative of the present text.[65] One early reference suggests, in fact, that an *Eiga* text was circulating by the first decade or so of the twelfth century, i.e. within twenty or thirty years of the final event the work records.[66] Beyond this the evidence is neither so certain nor so undisputed, but most scholarly opinion today would probably support two additional conclusions: (1) the first thirty chapters and the last ten were composed at different times and by different authors; and (2) the first thirty chapters were written, or achieved their present form, not long after 1028, the latest date they contain.[67]

There are several pieces of relevant evidence. In the first place, *Eiga* itself draws a clear line of demarcation between Chapter 30, which recounts the death of Michinaga, and Chapter 31. After describing the death rites and touching on one or two related matters, the author ends Chapter 30 with a brief passage in which she calls on "someone who witnesses or hears about" subsequent developments to record them—an injunction that certainly sounds as though she had intended to leave the history of Michinaga's successors to other hands.

The ascription to different authors is further supported by a gap of nearly three years between the events with which Chapter 30 ends and those with with Chapter 31 begins; by marked differences of quality and content between the two parts; and by the opening passage of Chapter 31, which can be read as a kind of scene-setting recapitulation preliminary to a new author's continuation of the original: "Although Michinaga was dead, Yorimichi, Norimichi, Shōshi, Ishi, and many of His Lordship's other children were still alive, and thus the family's situation remained splendid indeed. It was unfortunate that Kishi and Kenshi were gone, but the world is never entirely as one would wish it. Things must have

---

64. Two manuscripts are actually involved. See p. xi.

65. See n. 17, above.

66. *Sanuki no suke nikki*, pp. 415–16, refers to *Yotsugi* as a work in which one finds mention of the *ōgashira*, a kind of emblematic banner used at the Guards headquarters in the Imperial Palace on ceremonial occasions. *Yotsugi*, as we know, was a title used for *Eiga*, which mentions the *ōgashira* in Chapter 33 (not included in the Translation). *Sanuki no suke nikki* is thought to date from about 1110.

67. These conclusions are based on evidence first marshaled into a comprehensive argument in *Shōkai*, pp. 8–25. The argument has been accepted and elaborated by such leading *Eiga* scholars as Matsumura Hiroji, Yamanaka Yutaka, and Kawakita Noboru.

been very much the same after the death of Genji, the Shining Prince. All was splendor, and yet there was also a feeling of sadness for those who remained. It was as it had been [in *Genji*] when only the Akashi Empress, Yūgiri, and Kaoru were left."

Furthermore, the author of the first thirty chapters writes as if her narrative present were somewhere between 1026 and 1045, a span of years centering on the period just after the final events in Chapter 30, and preceding or coinciding with the beginning of the period covered in Chapters 31 to 40. The first sentence of Chapter 1 shows the narrative present to have been no later than 1045. "There have been more than sixty Emperors in this country since its beginnings," says the opening clause, thus establishing the present in or before the reign of the sixty-ninth Emperor, Go-Suzaku (r. 1036–45), and at the same time excluding most of the period covered in the last ten chapters, which extend the chronicle to the time of the seventy-third Emperor, Horikawa (r. 1087–1107).

In Chapter 15 the author remarks that a lamp lit at the dedication of a temple building in 1019 "has never gone out to this day, more than twenty years later," a statement that would place the narrative present somewhere between 1040 and 1048. However, there is firm evidence to show that the building was actually dedicated in 1005,[68] and it is possible that the author's calculations were based on the earlier year, in which case the narrative present would fall between 1026 and 1034.[69]

The evidence concerning the time of the narrative present in the first thirty chapters, coupled with the sharp line of demarcation between those chapters and the other ten, points rather clearly to the conclusion that the thirty were written or edited into their present form during the fifteen or so years following the date of the last entry in Chapter 30 (1028)—i.e. between about 1030 and 1045. There is, however, a certain amount of contradictory evidence, which can be construed to mean that they were completed a good deal later, and that their author was identical with the author of the last ten chapters.

In Chapter 11, for example, *Eiga* compares the infancy of Princess Teishi (later Yōmeimon'in), Michinaga's first Imperial granddaughter, to a flow-

68. The event is recorded under that date in Michinaga's diary, *Midō kanpakuki*, 1: 162 (19 x Kankō 2), and a document of supplication (*ganmon*) composed for the occasion is similarly dated. The document is preserved in *Honchō monzui*, pp. 324–26. *Shōyūki*, 2: 132, also mentions the event under the same date.

69. Matsumura (1956–67, 2: 139–54) discusses the problem of the dating in Chapter 15, and also points out that the final section of Chapter 30 seems to suggest a narrative present in the reign of Go-Ichijō (r. 1016–36). See the Translation, p. 774.

er in bud (*tsubomihana*), "for although the present might be a time of uncertainty and impatient waiting, the petals of a brilliant destiny would one day unfold." If that hint of future good fortune refers, as some believe, to the fact that Princess Teishi eventually became the mother of Emperor Go-Sanjō (r. 1068–73), one could then conclude that the passage was written no earlier than Go-Sanjō's reign.[70] Supporting evidence has been found in Chapter 6, which mentions a tale called *Hatsuyuki no monogatari* (The Tale of the First Snow). The story, no longer extant, has been dated by one scholar to the 1060's or 1070's—i.e. to about the reign of Go-Sanjō—on the basis of a reference in *Mumyō zōshi*, the well-known late-twelfth- or early-thirteenth-century critique of literature and women.[71] Kawasaki Hiroko has demonstrated, moreover, that a triplex respect language formation peculiar to *Eiga* occurs in all forty chapters—a stylistic feature that could be taken to indicate a single author or editor for the whole, and thus, obviously, a much later date for the first part.[72]

In support of the single-author argument, it has also been pointed out that the break after Michinaga's death may not be evidence of a new brush, but may rather represent a conscious echo of *Genji monogatari*, in which there is a similar chronological gap at the time of Prince Genji's death.[73] *The Tale of Genji* was already a famous piece of literature in Murasaki's own day, and it is quite conceivable that a later writer would have elected to use one of its conspicuous structural features in order to suggest to her readers a similarity between Michinaga and the Shining Prince.

The various bits of evidence in favor of a later date are a good deal less than unambiguous, however, and as a whole they do not seem sufficient to warrant the rejection of the text's more explicit indications. It is unnecessary, for instance, to assume that the prognosticatory remark concerning Princess Teishi must have been written after her son's accession. As Wada Hidematsu and Satō Kyū have pointed out, Teishi, who was Michinaga's special favorite, had become a consort of the Crown Prince (Go-Suzaku) in 1027, and had given birth to the future Emperor Go-Sanjō in 1034.[74] By 1028, the date of Michinaga's death, it would have required no special prescience to guess that the Princess was destined for great things, and the

---

70. This inference was first drawn by Haga (1928, p. 51). His view has been accepted by, among others, Oka (1968b, p. 123) and Inoue (1970, p. 24).

71. Matsuo 1963, pp. 510–17.

72. Kawasaki 1971, pp. 75–84. Iwano (1962, pp. 114–27) appears to have been the first to notice the author's peculiar use of triplex respect language (*oboshi* + *sase* + *tamau*).

73. Oka 1968a, p. 432.   74. *Shōkai*, Shukan no jō, pp. 14–15.

birth of Go-Sanjō a few years later would have made her "brilliant destiny" even more obvious.

The argument based on *Hatsuyuki no monogatari* is also shaky. Since
the work has not survived, there is no way of determining whether or not
the brief mentions of it in *Eiga* and *Mumyō zōshi* refer to the same text,
and the histories of other old monogatari provide little ground for assuming that they do. Furthermore, the dating of the *Mumyō zōshi* work to
the latter half of the eleventh century is speculative, resting on the inferred
dating of a group of tales, and on the assumption that *Hatsuyuki* discussed
other tales from the same period. The text of *Mumyō zōshi* in fact requires
us at most to understand that *Hatsuyuki* dealt with post-*Genji* tales, which
means that the work might date from almost any decade of the eleventh
century except the first.[75]

As Kawasaki herself notes, the linguistic evidence for single authorship
turns out to be similarly ambiguous. Although the use of triplex respect
language throughout the forty chapters seems to suggest a single author,
or at least closely related authors, other evidence of the same sort points
in the opposite direction. For instance, Kawasaki has discovered that the
respect language form *oboshi* + verb is used more than twice as often as
the triplex form in the first thirty chapters (443 occurrences against 197),
but that the triplex form is nearly a third more frequent than *oboshi* + verb
in the last ten (64 against 50); and she has found nothing in the nature of
the content that would seem to account for the differences.[76]

Moreover, Nomura Kazumi, in a study of more than 100 "important"
Eiga vocabulary items, has found striking differences in usage between
the first thirty and the last ten chapters.[77] For example, common words
such as *medetashi*, *okashi*, and *monosu* are used two to six times more
frequently in Chapters 31–40 than in Chapters 1–30; and there are twelve

---

75. The *Mumyō zōshi* reference to *Hatsuyuki* occurs in a discussion of monogatari that
occupies most of the work. The first and lengthiest section is devoted to *Genji*. A second part
deals with what are probably all post-*Genji* tales, and a third with contemporary works. The
woman who is the chief speaker remarks, at the end of the discussion of *Genji* and the post-
Genji tales, that there are many other notable monogatari worthy of attention, but
that she does not have time to discuss them. She says in conclusion, "Consult the tale called
Hatsuyuki. Things about tales appear there." Then she turns to works by two contemporary
authors, Fujiwara Takanobu (1142–1205) and Fujiwara Teika (1162–1241). There is nothing to indicate conclusively what the dates of the tales discussed in *Hatsuyuki* were, although
the position of the reference in *Mumyō zōshi* and the speaker's expressed contempt for pre-
Genji tales make it reasonable to suppose that most, at least, were post-*Genji*. For the *Mumyō*
zōshi reference, see Tomikura 1973, p. 247.

76. Kawasaki 1971, pp. 79, 83–84.   77. Nomura 1963, pp. 12–18.

words or phrases that occur between nineteen and 118 times in Chapters 1–30, but not at all in the last ten chapters. (The item that occurs 118 times is *kakaru hodo*, "meanwhile.") Nomura has found thirteen other words —e.g. *haberi* (288 occurrences in Chapters 1–30) and *sate* (185 occurrences) —that appear between thirty-seven and 288 times in Chapters 1–30, but only once or twice in Chapters 31–40. The differences he identifies are not traceable to any particular chapter or chapters, which might indicate the influence of undigested source material, but are characteristic of the two parts in their entirety.

Finally, the structural similarity between *Eiga* and *Genji* does not in itself warrant the conclusion that *Eiga* was written by a single author. Quite conceivably, a second author simply made use of the *Genji* model in effecting a transition to her own narrative. It is, after all, the author of Chapter 31 who draws attention to the *Genji* parallel by comparing the post-Michinaga era to the period after Genji's death.

In our view, the single-author theory is greatly weakened by the marked differences in theme, treatment, and tone that distinguish the first thirty chapters from the last ten. Unable to find a protagonist comparable to Michinaga—or indeed any central subject at all—the author of the last section has presented her material as a heterogeneous assortment of facts and incidents. In place of the chatty anecdotes and enthusiastic descriptions that enliven the earlier pages, she offers a perfunctory, abbreviated, imitative record of the cycle of aristocratic life, negative and pessimistic in tone. There is, in brief, a pronounced falling off in both quality and quantity, together with a shift in atmosphere and tone, which can best be accounted for by the assumption of a change in authors.[78]

78. The last ten chapters have been consigned to deserved oblivion. Covering the period from late 1030 or early 1031 to 1092, they offer only flat, repetitive accounts of Imperial excursions, banquets, competitions, and other familiar events, which in many cases consist almost entirely of quoted poems or descriptions of feminine attire. Influenced no doubt by the currently fashionable idea of mappō, the author frequently suggests that the world is in decline, that old practices are being corrupted, and that even the mighty suffer. Mild criticism is sometimes leveled against the Fujiwara themselves or against such august figures as Emperor Go-Suzaku; and it is perhaps the same disenchanted spirit that leads in Chapter 38 to an unfavorable comparison between the reign of Emperor Go-Reizei, who was dominated by his uncle, Fujiwara Yorimichi, and that of the more independent-minded Go-Sanjō—the most extended piece of criticism and interpretation in all of *Eiga* (EM, 2: 489–90). As indicated earlier, there is external evidence to show that the zokuhen (or at least one of its chapters) was in existence by the first decade of the twelfth century. Since the account ends with a year of no particular significance in Court history (1092), it is generally assumed that the concluding chapter was written in that year or shortly thereafter. It is possible that the ten chapters were the work of more than one author, but none has been convincingly identified, despite much speculation and theorizing. Perhaps all that can usefully be said on the subject

In the absence of convincing evidence to the contrary, perhaps a majority of leading *Eiga* scholars tend to accept the text's more obvious testimony concerning its date and the process of its composition, and to place the completion of the first thirty chapters at some time between about 1030 and 1045. Those particular dates are of considerable interest because they provide powerful support for what may be the oldest surviving statement concerning the author's identity.

The attribution appears in a brief miscellany of historical notes and extracts called *Nihongi shishō*, compiled by the Buddhist monk Ken'a (1261–1338), who was the second head of the Shōmyōji at Kanazawa in Musashi. According to Ken'a, the author of *Eiga monogatari* was the celebrated poet Akazome Emon, whose poetry shows her to have been alive between 976 and 1041.[79] Although Akazome could not have been the author of all forty chapters, since she would have been over 120 years old by 1092 (the date of the latest event recorded in Chapter 40), her dates would agree very well with authorship of the first thirty chapters—the section of the work to which Ken'a may in fact have been referring. An extant thirty-chapter *Eiga* manuscript, lacking the final ten chapters, has been dated to about the year 1400, and the text it reproduces is thought to be even older—to derive, possibly, from a revision of the original in the late Heian period.[80] It is therefore entirely possible that Ken'a's attribution referred only to the initial thirty chapters. Nevertheless, his testimony needs to be treated with caution. His book was written two centuries after *Eiga*'s completion, and his period was one in which attributions of authorship were notoriously cavalier. But Akazome is so plausible a candidate as to make the identification more persuasive than any of the alternative theories that have been proposed.

To begin with, *Eiga* was almost certainly written by someone of Akazome's sex. A few modern scholars have argued for male authorship of at least part of the work, and a late Kamakura or Muromachi catalogue attributes a forty-chapter version to a specific man, Fujiwara Tamenari (fl. 1160–78), but the overwhelming weight of modern informed opinion favors

---

of authorship is that the writer or writers probably served among the ladies-in-waiting at the Imperial Court. For discussions of the zokuhen's date and authorship, see Matsumura 1956–67, 1: 563–618, 3: 249–60; Nomura 1963, pp. 11–27; and Sakamoto 1958, p. 74.

79. *Nihongi shishō* has not been printed, but its note on *Eiga* is quoted by Matsumura 1956–67, 1: 240. A manuscript in Ken'a's hand is owned by the Tōkyō University Library. For descriptions, see Matsumura 1956–67, 1: 246; Yamaguchi 1952, p. 34; and Nishioka 1963, pp. 152–53.

80. The extant manuscript is the so-called Tomioka kōhon of the Variant Text line.

female authorship.[81] Even a cursory reading of one or two chapters will
show why. The materials, the treatment, and the point of view are so
emphatically feminine that it is difficult to believe that any man of the
Heian period could have been responsible for them. Although Michinaga
is the protagonist, the reader sees him most often in relation to the women
of his family, and women and their affairs dominate the account to an extent that would scarcely be conceivable if the author were an eleventh-
century male historian. The special attention given to births and marriages,
the frequent and detailed descriptions of female attire and apartments,
and the countless intimate scenes of exclusively female life are almost certainly the reflection of feminine interests and opportunities for observation, as is also the nearly total absence of such male pursuits as football,
archery, drinking parties, and the conduct of Court and family business.
Moreover, in so far as events are described and not merely chronicled, they
are usually seen as a woman might have seen them. When an Empress gives
birth, the reader may find himself in the delivery room, where only women
were normally permitted; when a Court ceremony takes place, the view
is likely to be from behind the blinds of a chamber occupied by attendant ladies-in-waiting; when a temple is dedicated, the spectacle may be
seen through the eyes of visiting nuns. Nowhere is there evidence of an
unequivocally masculine spirit. And finally, the force of tradition also favors female authorship, since prose writing in Japanese during the eleventh
century was preeminently the preserve of aristocratic ladies.

Akazome's close relationship to Michinaga's family also lends credibility
to Ken'a's attribution. It is clear that our author knew a great deal about
the family's affairs, and that she viewed its chief members—especially
Michinaga, his wife Rinshi, and their daughter Shōshi, Empress to Emperor Ichijō—with uncritical, ingenuously admiring eyes. Akazome seems
to fit the description exactly. An early Kamakura source tells us that she
was one of Rinshi's ladies-in-waiting,[82] a statement confirmed by her own
poetry collection. Some of the poems indicate that she was in Rinshi's
service before the latter's marriage to Michinaga, and numerous compositions written for or about Michinaga and Rinshi or in connection with
events at their mansion show that she remained on intimate terms with

---

81. Two prominent modern scholars who have attributed some or all of *Eiga* to male
authorship are Origuchi (1950, p. 294) and Yamanaka (1962, pp. 158–94). Yamanaka's
attribution applies only to the first fourteen chapters. The attribution to Tamenari appears
in *Honchō shojaku mokuroku*, p. 533, where *Eiga* is referred to under its alternative title
Yotsugi.

82. *Waka iroha* (1198?), p. 132.

her mistress after the wedding.[83] Other poems reflect a warm relationship with Shōshi, whom she appears to have visited with some frequency after the death of Emperor Ichijō.[84] There is much similar evidence elsewhere in the collection—including, significantly, a final note in which Akazome states that she has compiled the work for presentation to Yorimichi, Michinaga's son.

Akazome's marriage to Ōe Masahira (952–1012) constitutes another possible link with *Eiga*. The Ōe, a noted family of savants, had been involved in a number of scholarly and literary enterprises, including the compilation of *Montoku jitsuroku*, one of the Six National Histories, and the preparation of *Shinkokushi*, the abortive continuation of the series.[85] After her marriage into such a family, Akazome may well have been stimulated to try her own hand at history writing, especially if, as seems probable, there were family archives of historical materials to draw on. The point is an important one, because the *Eiga* author, who seems to have made use of a considerable range of sources, must have had some kind of library at her disposal. One scholar, impressed by the significance of the Ōe connection, has even suggested that the *Eiga* project was initiated by the Ōe and inherited by Akazome after her husband's death.[86]

Akazome's claim is further buttressed by her Buddhistic interests and connections. Her poetry reveals a deeply religious nature, especially during her later years; and one composition makes it reasonably certain that she entered holy orders after Masahira's death in 1012,[87] so that she would presumably have been in a position to acquire and use the kinds of materials on which *Eiga* seems to draw heavily. It is generally believed, for example, that much of the Hōjōji material was based on descriptions provided by nuns who had visited the temple at the time of its founding—sources most easily accessible, one may conjecture, to an author who was herself a nun. On the other hand, pronounced Buddhist interests and even entry into Buddhist orders were commonplace among the Heian aristocracy. To be a nun was probably little more distinctive than to be a widow.

Akazome's sex, her close ties to Michinaga's family, her marriage into the historically-minded house of Ōe, and her religious bent all argue the case for her authorship. Resting as it does on the speculative dating of *Eiga* itself, on a late source, and on a group of author's characteristics that were

---

83. The poems are cited and discussed in Matsumura 1956–67, 1: 247–50.
84. *Ibid.*, pp. 250, 254–55.   85. Iwahashi 1956–58, 1: 314, 328.
86. Yamanaka 1962, p. 194.
87. *Akazome Emon shū*, p. 419. The preface to the poem says that it was composed when Akazome's daughter sent some seaweed "for the *ama.*" Ama puns on "nun" and "sea worker."

undoubtedly shared by a number of Akazome's contemporaries, the case is obviously not watertight. Nevertheless, if the inferred date of *Eiga* is correct, we can say, at least, that most available evidence tends to point toward Akazome, and that if she was not the author, the work must have been written by some person or persons very much like her.

Even if Akazome's authorship were to be established beyond question, the contribution to our understanding of her book would be limited, because she herself is a shadowy figure. Her father is usually identified as Akazome Tokimochi, an obscure officer in the Right Gate Guards (Uemon, whence her sobriquet, Emon), but a brief twelfth-century biography states that her true father was Taira Kanemori (d. 990), one of the "Thirty-Six Immortals of Poetry"—i.e. one of the thirty-six Japanese poets to whom the celebrated critic Fujiwara Kintō (996–1041) gave his accolade by including their work in an anthology he compiled.[88] Her birth date can be placed in the early 960's or late 950's, since she must have been at least in her teens by around 975, when she is known to have written a poem for her younger sister's use in addressing a suitor. Her poems reflect a rather serious love affair with Ōe Tamemoto, but it was Tamemoto's cousin Masahira whom she finally married. She bore Masahira two children: a son, Takachika (d. 1046), who achieved some prominence as a Court scholar and stylist in Chinese, and a daughter, Gō Jijū, a poet in her own right, who seems to have served Michinaga's second daughter, Empress Kenshi (994–1027), and later Kenshi's daughter Yōmeimon'in (1013–94). As noted earlier, Akazome appears to have been in the service of Michinaga's wife, Rinshi, and to have remained with or close to her after her marriage to Michinaga in 987. Her own husband, Masahira, held a series of provincial posts, including the governorship of Owari, whither Akazome accompanied him on two occasions, once for a stay of several years between 1001 and 1004, and again, probably in 1009, for a shorter stay.

At some point after Masahira's death in 1012, Akazome apparently became a Buddhist nun, but she seems not to have cut herself off from secular concerns. Her poetry, in any case, demonstrates continued involvement with the world of the Court; as late as 1041, she was still composing contest entries. Since her last datable work comes from 1041, after which her name disappears from contemporary sources, it is probably safe to assume that she died during the 1040's, at the age of eighty or more.[89]

88. *Fukuro sōshi*, p. 68.
89. Akazome's biography is discussed by Matsumura 1956–67, 1: 246–67, 3: 345–66; Yamanaka 1962, pp. 181–83; and Oka 1957, pp. 356–66.

Apart from these miscellaneous scraps of information, gleaned mostly from the poetry collection, little else is known about Akazome, except that she was acquainted with the leading literary women of her day—notably Izumi Shikibu, Sei Shōnagon, Ise no Tayū, and Sagami—and that her poetry earned the qualified admiration of Murasaki Shikibu, who said of it in her diary, "Although [Akazome's work] is not particularly distinguished, it shows true refinement. She does not scatter around poems on any and every topic just because she is a poet, but all of her work that I have heard, including poems composed on the most trivial occasions, is done in a style that puts one to shame."[90]

Scanty though the details of Akazome's biography are, her identification as the author of *Eiga monogatari* would shed a certain amount of light on the work's virtues and shortcomings. It would mean, in the first place, that the bulk of the material was written by a contemporary of the events described, since even Chapter 1, for well over half its length, falls within Akazome's lifetime. By the beginning of Chapter 2 (972), *Eiga* is treating a period of which she must have had at least childhood memories, and by the date of the events recorded in the last half of the chapter, she was an adult. Akazome also unquestionably witnessed many or most of the events described. As a talented poet in Rinshi's service, she enjoyed innumerable opportunities to observe aristocratic society during the mid-Heian period —opportunities that must have been nearly unsurpassed, at least by any other woman. She was probably with Rinshi by about 985; and thereafter, except for her two sojourns in Owari, she was more or less continuously at or near the center of life in the capital, and thus in a position to write a narrative in which, from Chapter 3 on, the author frequently had personal knowledge of the events described.

In view of the errors and distortions discussed earlier, it may be thought that the author could not possibly have been a firsthand observer of most of the events recorded, and that the attribution to Akazome must consequently be dismissed. The memoirs of generals and statesmen remind us, however, that fidelity to historical fact is not always a virtue of participants in events. In Akazome's case, her personal circumstances might almost have guaranteed precisely the kinds of historical lapses we find.

At the time when *Eiga* was probably set down, Akazome was at least in her seventies, an active but aged poet looking back over forty or fifty years of service in, and dependency on, Rinshi's family. Writing in the

90. *Murasaki Shikibu nikki*, p. 495.

monogatari tradition about the house and society she had known for four
or five decades, such a woman could have produced an accurate chronicle
only if she had been a historian dedicated to absolute truth, with a complete set of reliable, detailed documents at her disposal. Needless to say,
that is unlikely to have been the case.

If Akazome was indeed our author, she must have relied heavily on her
own memory, filling in gaps and providing details from such documents
as were available. The documents, we may suppose, would have consisted
mostly of poems, letters, diaries, and descriptive accounts of events, often
poorly dated and of dubious reliability. When both memory and documents
failed her, it is difficult to believe that she would have scrupled to use her
imagination in reconstructing missing facts and episodes. Everything in
the literary tradition she knew—the poem tales, the literary diaries, the
fictional tales that had probably provided at least some of the inspiration
for her work—would have suggested a fairly loose interpretation of the
demands of historical truth, which in any case presumably would have
weighed no more heavily on her than on the aged everywhere when they
describe the great events of their past.

If *Eiga* was written under such circumstances, its errors, biases, and
distortions come to seem the natural products of its authorship. The minor
factual errors in which the work abounds are the sort of thing one would
expect of an old woman trying to piece together a chronicle from memory
and from a limited number of heterogenous sources, which must often
have been undated or dated only by month or year. The distribution of
factual errors is similarly explicable. Nearly 90 percent are concentrated in
the first 60 percent of the text (through Chapter 16), indicating a fairly
high degree of reliability for the period that would have been freshest in
the author's mind, and for which documentation would probably have
been most easily available.[91] Even the mistakes involving people whom
Akazome knew intimately—their official titles at particular times, the precise order of their children's births, and so forth—are consistent with the
kind and degree of accuracy we ordinarily expect in personal reminiscences.[92]

91. The figures on distribution are based on Kanō 1971, p. 3. Kanō thinks that the author's
faulty memory was responsible for as many as half of the factual errors in the text (p. 6).

92. In a series of articles dating from 1967, Inoue Chie has attempted to show that Akazome could not have been the author of *Eiga* because the book makes critical mistakes about
people she was very close to, e.g. Fujiwara Michitsuna. Inoue's arguments seem to be based
on the fallacious assumption that a writer would not be in error about people intimately
involved with his own past. Moreover, her strongest evidence is sometimes seriously flawed.
For instance, she contends that *Eiga*'s reference to Michitsuna as the oldest of Kaneie's sons,

Nor should we be surprised by an occasional blunder of greater mag-
nitude. In the case of the exile of Korechika and Takaie, for instance, it is
entirely plausible that Akazome had forgotten the exact sequence of events
after more than thirty years, and that she either lacked suitable documents
with which to refresh her memory or simply did not bother to consult
them. Her interest was in the pathos of the exile, not in its particular facts;
and even if she had been sure of the facts, it is possible—although to our
minds unlikely—that she would have ignored them in order to achieve the
kind of picture she wanted to present. Certainly, the monogatari tradition
would have supported her, as it would have in the instances of fanciful
embroidery that can sometimes be detected. The work's biases, too, are
what one might expect of a woman who had been heavily dependent on
Rinshi and Michinaga during most of her lifetime, and whose children
were similarly indebted to them and their descendants. It is even possible
to interpret *Eiga*'s faintly critical attitude toward Empress Kenshi, Michinaga's second daughter, as a reflection of Akazome's partiality for Kenshi's
older sister, Empress Shōshi.

The author of *Eiga* (whether Akazome, as the burden of the evidence
suggests, or some other woman) was a sensitive observer living at or near
the center of Japanese civilization during one of its most creative phases.
Her work possesses lasting value, not only as a simple repository of historical fact and incident, but also as an authentic reflection of the rhythm
and tone of the life she witnessed. Despite her limited perspective and obvious failures as a historian, she left what is unquestionably one of our
truest contemporary pictures of Heian aristocratic society. She was neither
as successful as Murasaki Shikibu in evoking the atmosphere of a specific
time and place nor as accurate and detailed as a diarist like Fujiwara
Sanesuke, but her chronicle is a direct, if somewhat distorted, representation

---

yorozu no ani, betrays an ignorance of which neither Akazome nor any other contemporary
could have been guilty. But one finds in fact that two contemporary diaries also refer to him in
almost precisely the same terms—*ikkakei,* "elder brother of the entire house," and *kakei,*
"elder brother of the house." *Gonki,* 1: 120–21 (7 iv Chōhō 2); *Shōyūki,* 2: 257 (15 vi
Kannin 3). The explanation for this apparent anomaly is that after the death of Kaneie's eldest
son, Michitaka, in 995, Michitsuna, the second son, was generally referred to by contemporaries as the family's oldest brother, and *Eiga*'s reference to him as such, far from proving
a later date for the work, may actually indicate that the author was relying on her memory or
contemporary documents, rather than on records, which would have shown immediately what
the genealogical facts were. Inoue notes the *Gonki* reference to Michitsuna, but forces an unnatural interpretation on it, and she ignores the *Shōyūki* reference, where Michitsuna himself
is quoted as saying to Michinaga, "I am the elder brother of the entire house." Her conclusions
seem to have been accepted only by scholars already committed to the view that the first thirty
chapters were written during or after the 1070's.

of actual persons and events, as Murasaki's *Genji* was not; and she often managed to invest it with a physical and psychological realism that Sane-suke seldom, if ever, achieved in his tedious recording of Court and family activities. Although a faulty memory and scanty or unreliable sources may have led her into frequent factual errors, we can assume that her selection and treatment of materials provide a generally accurate measure of the values, attitudes, and tastes of her contemporaries, and that the tempo of events suggested by her chronological arrangement of materials reflects life as she had found it in the great households of the Heian aristocracy.

This is not to say, of course, that *Eiga monogatari* can be accepted at face value. It puts forward what is often an idealized or romanticized view of people and events; and the reader must be particularly wary when such things as values, tastes, and attitudes become the subject of explicit discussion. But the work is nevertheless the single most important overview of Michinaga's age to have survived from the hand of a contemporary, and as such it is of prime historical importance.

SOURCES AND THEIR USE

Although *Eiga* may have been based in considerable part on the personal recollections of its author, it is undoubtedly indebted to other sources for much material. Its time span of 141 years (887–1028), its bulk, and the detail of its facts and descriptions guarantee *a priori* that no single author's memory could have furnished all of its contents; and positive evidence of the use of sources in particular instances is also fairly plentiful throughout the text. The author herself does not usually reveal that she has made use of any sources, let alone identify them, but distinguishing characteristics of language, style, format, or content often point with more or less clarity to materials that were probably drawn from elsewhere. For example, the detailed and circumstantial accounts of the Putting On of the Train ceremony for Princess Teishi in Chapter 19 and of the illness and death of Grand Empress Kenshi in Chapter 29 were very likely based on records kept by ladies who had been present during the events described.[93]

Much or most of the verse quoted apparently came from other sources. The nature and arrangement of the poems composed after the death of Emperor Ichijō in Chapter 9, for example, strongly suggest the "Laments" section of a poetry collection; and the long lists of poems included in the descriptions of ceremonies, poetry contests, and banquets (e.g. the Thanks-

93. Matsumura 1956–67, 3: 123–25.

giving services of 1012 in Chapter 10) were almost certainly taken from records of a type known to have been commonly made of such events.[94]

In other instances the nature of the text implies the use of records or original documents, as in the case of the Buddhist monk's sermon for the dedication of Kenshi's *Lotus Sutra* in Chapter 16, or the supplication for the services after Empress Seishi's death in Chapter 25.[95] If the author did not construct those rather involved passages out of whole cloth, she must have obtained them from some source other than her own memory.

Such inferences, drawn from the characteristics of the *Eiga* text and from our knowledge of the contemporary literature, make it possible to suggest a few of the general types of sources on which the author seems to have based her account: individual poetry collections, diaries kept by Court ladies, accounts of ceremonies and rites, records of competitions, sightseeing journals, original documents, and perhaps well-known tales in general circulation among the aristocracy.[96] A positive attribution of specific material to specific sources is possible, however, in only two instances. In one, the author uncharacteristically reveals the source as she questions its reliability; in the other, the source has survived for comparison.

The first case occurs in Chapter 17, one of the seven so-called Hōjōji chapters, which deal with the construction and dedication of the Hōjōji buildings and statues. In many respects, those chapters, especially Chapters 15, 17, and 18, constitute the climax of *Eiga monogatari*. The intensity and detail of the narrative technique, the brilliance of the events described, the high incidence of allusion to and quotation from Buddhist texts, and the shift toward a more ornate, Sinified style set off the Hōjōji material rather distinctly from the rest of the book, making it more effective, both as history and as literature, than any other section.

The author's revelation of what was at least one of her sources for Chapter 17 is therefore of more than ordinary interest, because it casts light on the composition of the core of her work. The identification comes at the end of a well-known passage, a long, circumstantial account of the dedication of the Hōjōji's main hall. After remarking that "those fortunate enough to have seen and heard everything close at hand" would be in a position to provide especially accurate information, the author—or possibly the author of her source—expresses misgivings about her own version, which is based, she says, on oral information from "ignorant nuns" who

94. *Ibid.*, 1: 279–80, 3: 184–90.   95. *Ibid.*, 1: 280.
96. The most detailed discussion of these possible sources is in *ibid.*, 1: 277–408, 3: 181–230.

had been among the spectators (Translation, p. 559). The "ignorant nuns" were presumably also the source of much, if not most, of the remainder of the Hōjōji materials. In all probability, they can be identified with the nuns whose tour of the precincts makes up the bulk of Chapter 18. If so, the obviously free access to the temple that they are shown to have had in Chapter 18, together with specific attribution of crucial material to them in Chapter 17, makes it reasonable to suppose that their diaries, reports, and reminiscences directly or indirectly supplied the basic content of the Hōjōji chapters.

Although the author reveals her source for the dedication, and although some inferences can be drawn concerning the origins of related material, the Hōjōji chapters do not show how sources were employed. For information concerning the author's methodology, we must turn to the single section for which an original source survives—a lengthy one in Chapter 8, dealing with the birth of Empress Shōshi's first son, Prince Atsuhira (later Emperor Go-Ichijō). The source was the diary of Murasaki Shikibu (*Murasaki Shikibu nikki*). The author does not acknowledge her indebtedness, but textual comparison reveals a close relationship, amounting to near identity in relatively extended passages.

As a lady-in-waiting to Empress Shōshi, Murasaki was in a position to have firsthand knowledge of events surrounding the Prince's birth. Since the content of *Murasaki Shikibu nikki* appears to be authentically hers— dating, it is conjectured, from around the year 1010—there can be little doubt that it was at least ultimately the source of the *Eiga* account. In other words, *Eiga* was not the source of the diary description, nor did the relationship result from the use of a common source or sources.[97]

It is conceivable that our author's reliance on the diary was indirect, i.e. that she drew on it via another, temporally intermediate, account of the birth. But the probable near contemporaneity of *Eiga* with the diary and the absence of any evidence pointing to the existence of a third account support the simpler hypothesis.

The use of material from *Murasaki Shikibu nikki* begins with the diary's opening passage in the early fall of 1008 and continues to the end of the year. For the entire period, the author seems to have relied almost exclusively on Murasaki, adding little in the way of substantive comment or descriptive detail. Third sources record other events that might have been considered appropriate for inclusion, but except in two minor instances the coverage never leaves the world of the diary. Buddhist services, Shintō

97. On the relationship between *Eiga* and Murasaki's diary, see Oka 1957, pp. 310–13.

observances, pilgrimages, official appointments, ceremonies, deaths, and various other happenings at Court and among the nobility—incidents that would ordinarily have been grist for *Eiga*'s mill—do not appear unless they are also to be found in the diary, even when they directly involve Michinaga.[98]

There is nothing particularly noteworthy about the cases in which the author has introduced new material, or at least material absent from extant versions of the diary. The two together occupy less than two-thirds of a page in a modern printing, as opposed to seventeen pages for the entire diary-based section. The first case consists of bare mentions of two annual events, followed by a short description of Michinaga's prayers for an early delivery (Translation, p. 270). In the second the author quotes, with some embellishment, a poem composed by the Kamo Virgin for an event discussed by the diary (Translation, p. 292). The mention of Michinaga's prayers adds an interesting, if puzzling, detail to the description of the Prince's birth, but there seems no obvious reason for the inclusion of the Kamo Virgin's poem—unless, of course, it was present in the *Murasaki Shikibu nikki* text used by the author.

If the author's narrative for the latter part of 1008 was based almost entirely on *Murasaki Shikibu nikki*, her employment of the diary was nevertheless highly selective. Of the portion on which she drew—the first two-thirds, devoted to the months before and after the birth of Prince Atsuhira in the fifth year of Kankō—she made direct use of only about 50 percent. As a rule, she omitted entries concerning Murasaki's personal affairs, private thoughts, and feelings, or dealing with the gossip and incidental life of Empress Shōshi's household, and chose to concentrate instead on the more formal and public activities having to do with the birth: religious services to ensure a safe delivery, postnatal celebrations, the Imperial visit to Michinaga's mansion (where the birth had occurred), the Empress's return to the Palace, and so forth. Traces of the diary's more personal and anecdotal side remain—notably in the description of the circumstances leading up to Murasaki's poem on the night of the Fiftieth Day (Translation, p. 287), and in the Gosechi story about Sakyō (p. 291)—but even those minor aberrations are closely connected with the chief events

---

98. For a record of significant events during the period for which the diary served as the author's source, see *Dainihon shiryō*, pt. 2, 6: 153–524. Our discussion here relies heavily on a detailed analysis of the relationship between the diary and Chapter 8 of *Eiga* made by Imakōji 1970, pp. 56–213. Imakōji's exhaustive chart comparing the content of the two works is especially helpful (pp. 64–165). See also Matsumura's commentary in EMZ, 2: 408–513.

and figures of the *Eiga* account, and they scarcely disturb the sharp focus on the joyous pomp and display with which Michinaga welcomed his first Imperial grandson.

Diary materials were used in a variety of ways. In some cases, they were reproduced verbatim, except for a few minor verbal variations—the result, perhaps (at least in some cases), not of the author's desire to improve on Murasaki's language, but of differences between her manuscript of *Murasaki Shikibu nikki* and present texts. More commonly, the diary was subjected to varying degrees of editing and rewriting, with greater brevity the typical outcome. Long and often repetitious descriptions of costumes, lists of the names of participants in events, and similar minutiae were the usual objects of condensation, which was achieved by cutting unwanted material from a quoted passage, or by more or less extensive rewriting, or by some combination of the two. A desire to avoid redundancy and needless detail may also have led the author to ignore the final third of Murasaki's work, which includes, among other events appropriate to the chronicle, material relating to the birth of Empress Shōshi's second son. Or it may be, as Shirai Tatsuko has suggested,[99] that the author's text of the diary did not include the final part. In any case, material from the last third of the diary, which covers the sixth year of Kankō (1009) and the First Month of the following year, is conspicuously absent.

Generally speaking, the author's revisions were faithful to her source's basic sense, even when she transferred the description of one event to another,[100] but in a number of instances they produced minor betrayals of chronology, some of which led to obfuscation of meaning. Fairly often (nearly twenty times all together), the sequence of events recorded on a single day is at least slightly confused in the *Eiga* account, or events are related out of order under the wrong date, as in one case where the result is a thoroughly garbled text.[101] Such chronological blunders may occasionally have come from careless editing or copying, but most of them can probably be regarded as reflections of the author's demonstrated willingness

99. Shirai 1971, pp. 124–32.
100. *Eiga*'s description of the seating of the senior nobles and courtiers at the Fifth Night banquet appears to be drawn from Murasaki's account of the Third Night banquet (*Murasaki Shikibu nikki*, p. 455), but since *Shōyūki*, 2: 147 (15 ix Kankō 5), shows that the seating arrangements on the Fifth and Third Nights were identical, the *Eiga* version remains valid. The relationship between the *Eiga* Fifth Night passage and the diary is discussed by Hagitani 1971–73, 1: 282–83.
101. The more important chronological confusions are indicated in the notes to the Translation. For a complete listing, see Imakōji 1970, pp. 186–88. For the garbled text, see the Translation, p. 280, n. 93.

to engage in minor chronological deception when it suited her convenience.

In one particularly egregious case of editing, injudicious cuts have emasculated a revealing story told by Murasaki about life in Empress Shōshi's menage. The story concerns the aging Lady Sakyō, who had once been in the service of Empress Shōshi's rival, the Imperial consort Gishi, but had descended, on the occasion being described in the diary, to a menial role in one of the annual Court ceremonies. Sakyō tried to avoid the notice of people at the Palace who had known her in her better days, but she was recognized, and Empress Shōshi's ladies purposely humiliated her by sending her a poem and a small collection of gifts to make her aware that she had been seen and her fallen estate noted.

In *Eiga* the basic outline remains the same, but the key fact—that the object of the exercise was to embarrass and humiliate the unfortunate lady—is wholly expunged, except in so far as it can be dimly inferred from the lady's circumstances. The author may have felt, with justice, that the cruelty of Shōshi's attendants did not harmonize with her idealized portrait of Michinaga and his family, but whatever her motive, she presents a bowdlerized version so pointless as to be almost unintelligible.

These instances of confusion and obfuscation notwithstanding, significant misstatement and misrepresentation are rare in the *Eiga* account, and the author shows herself, on the whole, a reliable interpreter of sources. She engages in no serious falsification of events, except in the case of the incident involving Lady Sakyō, and she does not treat diary material in such a way as to change the reader's sense of the events recorded.

Apart from selection, revision, and rewriting, the author's contributions to Murasaki's account are relatively slight, consisting mostly of a few transitional words or sentences between diary passages, or of incidental comment or descriptive embellishment. The additions have no significant effect on the general course of the account, which remains very much as it was in the diary, not only in content but also to a considerable extent in language.

To provide a more concrete illustration of the manner in which the diary was employed, we quote below, in parallel columns, the opening passage of *Murasaki Shikibu nikki* and the corresponding *Eiga* section.[102] Although the author's use of material here is slightly atypical, in that her account contains an unusual number of items and observations absent from the diary, the section is otherwise representative. In the first few lines, the

102. The column on the left is from the Translation, p. 270, and the column on the right from *Murasaki Shikibu nikki*, p. 443.

identity of the language is less complete than the translations make it appear, but the suppressed differences are all minor—e.g. *keshiki* for *kewai*, *onoono* for *onogajishi*, the insertion of an intensifier (*ito*), the omission of a pluralizing suffix (*-domo*)—and they do not materially alter the sense of the text.

Eiga monogatari	*Murasaki Shikibu nikki*
With the coming of autumn, the beauty of the Tsuchimikado Mansion surpassed description. The trees bordering the lake and the massed shrubs beside the stream blazed in a myriad shades of red and yellow, and the beauty of the atmosphere	With the coming of autumn, the beauty of the Tsuchimikado Mansion surpassed description. The trees bordering the lake and the massed shrubs beside the stream blazed in a myriad shades of red and yellow, and the ethereal charm of the atmosphere
lent a special poignance to the voices that constantly chanted the sacred writings, their accents drifting on the cool breeze, and mingling all through the night with the perpetual murmur of the brook.	lent a special poignance to the voices that constantly chanted the sacred writings, their accents drifting on the cool breeze, and blending all through the night with the perpetual murmur of the brook.
Everyone was busy with the Hokoin Eight Expositions until the First, and then the Weaver Maid Festival came and went. One could not help reflecting that the people who occupied themselves with such events were like so many sheep bound for the slaughterhouse.	
Empress Shōshi's child was due in the Ninth Month. Michinaga had been praying that it would arrive in the Eighth, but he abandoned his supplications when others persuaded him that there was a fixed term in such matters, and that what he sought was wrong.	
	Although Her Majesty must have been suffering as she listened to the trivial chatter of her attendants, she betrayed no outward sign of distress. Her qualities require no praise from me, of course, but I continue to marvel that my usual

Eiga monogatari   *Murasaki Shikibu nikki*

state of mind undergoes a complete change whenever I am in her presence. All else is forgotten, and I feel that I should [long ago] have found service with someone like her to make my life easier to bear.

It was still well before dawn, and the tree shadows loomed dark beneath a cloud-veiled moon.

"I wish someone would attend to the shutters," a voice said.

"The maids aren't here yet, I imagine."

"Let the Lady Chamberlains do it."

As the time drew near, every conceivable prayer was recited for the Empress's safety. Among the religious ceremonies, there was a Five Great Mystic Kings service, conducted throughout in a manner beyond criticism.

While that exchange was taking place, the predawn bell rang out, heralding the beginning of the five-altar rites. The assistant monks raised their voices, each determined not to be outdone by the others, and the sound of their imposing and holy chanting echoed far and near through the mansion. It was all quite unlike the ordinary run of religious events—even to the thunder of footsteps on the gallery bridge as the Kannon'in Archbishop and his entourage of twenty assistants left the east wing to perform their mystic incantations.

Shōsan, the Kannon'in Archbishop, brought along an entourage of twenty assistants, each of whom took a turn at performing the sacred invocations. Apartments in every corner of the grounds had been equipped as retiring rooms, even such places as the horse-racing pavilion and the library. Watching the monks stream back and forth between the outlying buildings and the scene of the services, one could not help noticing that some of the older men were exceedingly ugly—and yet their faces commanded deep respect. It was a moving experience to follow one of those venerable figures in one's mind's eye

The Hōjūji abbot was staying in the horse-racing pavilion, the Henchiji Bishop was in the library, and others were similarly disposed.

It was a moving experience to mentally follow one of those monks attired in full ritual dress as he

Eiga monogatari	*Murasaki Shikibu nikki*
as he proceeded back across the elegant Chinese bridges and through the trees to his quarters. The Holy Teacher Shin'yo, I believe, officiated in vestments of red at the altar dedicated to Kuṇḍalī, and the Holy Teacher Shōzen bowed before Daiitoku.	proceeded back across the elegant Chinese bridges and through the trees to his quarters. The Holy Teacher Saisa bowed before Daiitoku.
Immediately after the Five Great Mystic Kings service, the Ninnaji Archbishop Gakyō performed the *Peacock Sutra* ritual. Thus rite followed rite in rapid succession, until a new day at last dawned. It had been an ear-shattering, weird night, and those who were inclined to nervousness came away with giddy heads and racing hearts.	The day dawned as the others arrived.

Our author has made generally effective use of the diary, selecting key entries relevant to her immediate purpose, condensing, where possible, to eliminate material not directly related to that purpose, stitching discrete passages into a reasonably faithful and well-integrated account, and, with miscellaneous garnishings of detail and opinion, shaping the whole to serve her overall aim: a eulogistic recording of Michinaga's glorious career. The result is marred, however, by her failure to shift the first-person perspective of Murasaki's sentences to an appropriately neutral or third-person view. The diary was written as a first-person narrative, and although the frequent ambiguity of Heian Japanese with respect to grammatical subject often permitted the adoption of Murasaki's language without specific commitment to a subject perspective, a natural reading of the *Eiga* account clearly implies a first-person point of view—i.e. the section reads as though the author were reporting, in her own words, things she had personally witnessed.

If the diary no longer existed, the *Eiga* description of the Tsuchimikado Mansion at the time of Empress Shōshi's lying-in (Translation, p. 270) would unquestionably be understood as the product of the author's own observation, as would the account of the Jōdoji Bishop's bewilderment at the time of the bathing ceremony for the newborn Prince (Translation, p. 275), the description of the ladies' costumes on the same occasion, and similar mentions of what appear to be personal reactions to scenes described. Such disregard of grammatical niceties might be interpreted as derivative applications of the monogatari convention, which permits authors to insert themselves directly into their materials, were it not for other cases in which the retention of Murasaki's first-person view leads not merely to the appropriation of her responses, but to the actual misrepresentation of circumstances, suggesting either careless editing or plagiaristic intent.

For example, in describing a ceremony celebrating the birth of Prince Atsuhira, Murasaki says, "The Third Night banquet was presented by the Master and other officials of the Empress's Household. The Commander of the Left Gate Guards provided the banquet services for the Empress, which consisted, as well as I could see, of aloeswood standing trays, silver plates, and things of that sort" (*Murasaki Shikibu nikki*, p. 454). Our author incorporates the passage verbatim (Translation, p. 275), including the phrase, "as well as I could see" (*kuwashiku wa mizu*), without any warning to her readers that it is not her own firsthand report.

In another case, Murasaki describes in first-person style an occasion on which she has been forced to compose a poem for Michinaga (*Murasaki Shikibu nikki*, p. 471):

Anticipating a trying evening of drunkenness, Sanuki no Saishō and I had agreed to steal away at the conclusion of the ceremonies. Just as we were about to leave, the east room was invaded by a boisterous party of gentlemen—Michinaga's sons, Middle Captain Tsunefusa, and some others—and we were obliged to take refuge behind a curtain-stand. Sweeping aside the curtains, Michinaga caught us and made us stay, saying that he would let us go if we gave him a poem. The situation was so distressing and embarrassing that I could not refuse.

> How to count them
> On this Fiftieth Day?
> So many
> The thousands of years
> Of the young lord's life.

The author has again adopted Murasaki's account almost without change, making it appear that she herself was involved in the incident and composed the poem (p. 287).

Such cases might be thought to result from the mechanical copying of source material or simple inattention to implied grammatical subjects (the first-person pronoun does not appear either in the diary or in *Eiga*), but another passage suggests more strongly that the author intended to put forward Murasaki's account as her own.

That passage occurs in a description of the Fifth Night banquet for

Prince Atsuhira, which is clearly a much revised and condensed borrowing from the diary (Translation, p. 278). Toward the end, the author, following her source, observes that poems were composed that night. She then adds the following clause, which does not appear in present texts of the diary: "I was too distracted by the noise to hear them [i.e. the poems] properly, and when I made inquiries, they proved to be so disorganized, and so complicated by allusions to particular circumstances, that it was hopeless to try to record them." There follows at once an almost direct quotation from the diary, describing the concern of the ladies about the poems they would be called on to recite when the winebowl was passed and recording a poem prepared by Murasaki for the occasion.

In the diary, Murasaki's poem is quoted in isolation without mention of its author, treatment that identifies it as the work of Murasaki herself; in *Eiga* the first-person stance is abandoned, and a line is added explicitly attributing it to Murasaki. On the one hand, therefore, the author inserts a first-person statement absent from present texts of the diary—a statement that in effect appropriates the diary account as her own—while on the other, she makes a point of identifying Murasaki as the third-person composer of the poem. Her handling of the poem here stands in direct contrast to the technique she employs in describing the later occasion of the Fiftieth Day ceremonies (noted above), when the result of her verbatim use of the diary is the plagiarism of Murasaki's composition.

Perhaps the simplest way of reconciling these apparently contradictory approaches would be to assume that the author wanted her account to be read as a record of her own observations—i.e. that she was engaged in plagiarism—but that for some reason she wished, or felt compelled, to identify Murasaki as the author of the Fifth Night poem. It is possible, for instance, that unlike the Fifth Night poem, which was too well known to permit appropriation, the later poem had remained obscure, thus eliminating the need for scruples about its attribution. The Fiftieth Day poem did not in fact appear in an Imperial anthology until the latter half of the thirteenth century, whereas the Fifth Night poem was included in *Goshūishū* (completed 1086), the first Imperial anthology to be compiled after the poem's composition—a circumstance indicative, perhaps, of a certain amount of early fame and recognition.[103]

103. The *Goshūishū* poem is No. 433 in *Kokka taikan*. (Poems in Imperial anthologies are cited hereafter by *Kokka taikan* numbers.) The Fiftieth Day poem, *Shokukokinshū* 1895, also appears in Fujiwara Kiyosuke's *Shokushikashū* (1165 or after), p. 683, where it is attributed to Michinaga. Both compositions are included in Murasaki's poetry collection, *Murasaki Shikibu shū*, pp. 809–10.

Such reasoning is at best highly speculative, and since other equally plausible, if slightly more complex, interpretations could be adduced, the question of the author's intentions is better laid aside. For present purposes, the matter of primary importance is not the author's intentions themselves, but their effect on her use of sources, and here it is clear that she leads her readers badly astray, whether through inadvertence or not, by retaining Murasaki's first-person perspective.

Despite her heavy reliance on Murasaki's diary, the author appears to have made some use of supplementary materials in preparing her description of Prince Atsuhira's birth, thus demonstrating at least a rudimentary skill in the historian's art of drawing on multiple sources to construct a single account. Cases in point are the two events mentioned earlier—Michinaga's prayers for a premature delivery and the episode of the Kamo Virgin's poem—and three minor facts inserted in passages that otherwise derive entirely from the diary.[104] None of the additions can be authenticated from contemporary sources,[105] but their very insignificance may serve as a kind of guarantee of reliability, since it is difficult to see why the author would have bothered to invent them. Unless they were present in a lost version of the diary,[106] she presumably inserted them from other sources, either because of what seemed to her their intrinsic interest or for other, more particular reasons.

In several cases, facts provided by the author differ from those in the diary, but most or all of the discrepancies are probably the result of copyist errors, rather than of changes or corrections introduced from alternative sources.[107] In only one or two instances does there seem to be any real in-

104. Two of the insertions occur in the account of the Five Great Mystic Kings service, where the author adds the information that Shin'yo was the officiant at the Kundali altar, and that the Ninnaji Archbishop performed the *Peacock Sutra* ritual. The third consists of a brief note about presents received by Fifth Rank courtiers in connection with the Fifth Night ceremonies. Translation, p. 279; *Murasaki Shikibu nikki*, p. 458.

105. There is some support for the statement about Shin'yo (n. 104) in *Osan buruiki* (or *Gosan buruiki*), *Dainihon shiryō*, pt. 2, 6: 173, which contains a headnote to a quotation from an anonymous work (*Juchiki*), saying that Shin'yo was in charge of the Kundali altar at a Five Great Mystic Kings service on the day of Atsuhira's birth in the Ninth Month. But the service mentioned in *Eiga* and the diary seems to have taken place a month or two before the birth of the Prince, and the *Osan buruiki* reference may not be relevant. Even if it is, the work is of unknown date, and the headnote, the source of which is not clear in the *Dainihon shiryō* version, may have been drawn either directly or indirectly from *Eiga* itself. On the other hand, Michinaga's diary, *Midō kanpakuki*, 1: 263 (24 vii Kankō 5), shows that Shin'yo did participate in prayers for Empress Shōshi during her pregnancy.

106. A distinct possibility in the case of the Fifth Night presents (n. 104). See Hagitani 1971–73, 1: 310.

107. For example, *Eiga* lists Tō no Sanmi, and the diary Tachibana no Sanmi, as the name of the lady who offered refreshments to Emperor Ichijō when he visited the Tsuchimika-

dication of the use of sources to revise *Murasaki Shikibu nikki*, and even then the possibility of miscopying remains strong. One such case occurs when the diary names the Henchiji Bishop (p. 453), and *Eiga* the Jōdoji Bishop (Translation, p. 275), as the monk who performed the "rites of bodily protection" (*goshin*) during Prince Atsuhira's bathing ceremony. Since no temple by the name of Henchiji is known to have existed in the eleventh century, whereas the Jōdoji was an established Kyōto institution, and since a Jōdoji Bishop named Myōku unquestionably participated in prayers for Empress Shōshi during her pregnancy,[108] the discrepancy may represent a genuine correction made by the author on the basis of better information. If so, it is an interesting comment on her concern for historical accuracy, but we cannot be sure that we are not again dealing with an inattentive copyist. As was pointed out long ago by Ikeda Kikan and others, the Henchiji in extant *Murasaki Shikibu nikki* texts may have resulted from a misreading of the cursive forms of the Chinese characters for Jōdoji, leading either to an intermediate rendering of Henchiji in characters, or directly to the present *kana* version.[109] In other words, *Eiga* may be a faithful version of Murasaki's original wording. The issue is further clouded, it may be noted, by a reference in an anonymous work quoted in *Osan buruiki*, which names the Provisional Archbishop Shōsan as the monk who performed the "mystic invocations at the Imperial bath" (*oyu no kaji*).[110] If "mystic invocations at the Imperial bath" and "rites of bodily protection" are two names for the same thing, and if the *Osan buruiki* source is reliable, both the diary and *Eiga* are apparently mistaken.[111]

---

do Mansion. *Murasaki Shikibu nikki*, p. 465; Translation, p. 282, where the original Tō no Sanmi is rendered Fujiwara Sanmi. Reliable sources show that the diary is correct; and since no obvious purpose was served by the change, the simplest and most plausible explanation seems to be that either the author or a copyist confused the characters for Tō (the "fuji" of Fujiwara) and Tachibana, as might easily have happened with a document written in cursive script. In a related passage, *Eiga* lists the Hour of the Tiger (3:00–5:00 A.M.), and the diary the Hour of the Dragon (7:00–9:00 A.M.), as the time at which the Emperor was expected to reach the Tsuchimikado Mansion. Translation, p. 281; *Murasaki Shikibu nikki*, p. 462. No other contemporary source notes the scheduled arrival time, but it is known that the Imperial party did not leave the Palace until around 9:30 or later (*Midō kanpakuki*, 1: 271 [16 x Kankō 5]), and *Eiga*'s improbably early hour again appears to be the result of orthographic error, rather than of deliberate revision. Other sources indicate an even later hour for the trip. See Chapter 8, n. 98).

108. *Midō kanpakuki*, 1: 263 (24 vii Kankō 5).

109. Hagitani 1971–73, 1: 53.

110. Quoted in *Dainihon shiryō*, pt. 2, 6: 174. See also Hagitani 1971–73, 1: 56.

111. Another possible case of correction occurs in the description of the Emperor's visit to the Tsuchimikado Mansion. The diary (p. 467) identifies Fujiwara Sanenari as the Assistant Master of the Empress's Household (Miya no Suke), but *Eiga* (Translation, p. 284) correctly calls him the Provisional Assistant Master (Gon no Suke).

It is unlikely that texts comparable to *Murasaki Shikibu nikki,* a source ideally suited to the author's needs, were available in sufficient quantity to have enabled her to construct her entire book in the manner described above. But if her use of the diary can be considered representative, it seems clear that she was sometimes, at least, more editor than author. Given a full account of an event—as she may have possessed, for example, when she composed the Hōjōji chapters—she may have shortened, rewritten, revised, and even occasionally corrected, but her own contributions to basic content probably remained negligible: an odd fact here and there, an interesting episode or two, and very little else. Her treatment of the diary suggests that she impressed her style, purposes, and interests on source materials chiefly through selection, rewriting, the introduction of transitional passages, and occasional independent comment, making no consistent effort either to supplement her main source or to collate it with other works.

Since she was little concerned with sustained interpretation, criticism, or evaluation, her ultimate product, when she worked from a congenial text, must always have been highly derivative, even when it was not an outright duplicate of the original. In the sense that she seems seldom to have betrayed literal meaning or intent, she was, for her time and place, a surprisingly faithful editor. Nevertheless, too-exact reproduction of language sometimes resulted in plagiarism and deception, whether deliberate or not. That is the most serious criticism we can level against her use of sources, because it calls into question the integrity of any material written from a first-person point of view, and virtually precludes confident conclusions about the authorship of the work as a whole.

READERSHIP

Very little is known about the audience reached by *Eiga* during the two or three centuries immediately following its composition, but the paucity of references to it in contemporary writings indicates that it was not widely read, and Kawakita may be right in supposing that it remained rather exclusively the property of the Fujiwara for some time.[112] Even if the family did not actively seek to preserve it as a "secret" treasure, the great size of the manuscript and the formidable cost of having it copied would have imposed severe limitations on its circulation, and interest was no doubt further diminished by the existence of *Ōkagami,* which treated roughly

112. Kawakita 1968, p. 39.

the same period and subjects in a fraction of the space, and with markedly superior literary effect. But whatever Fujiwara intentions may have been, and despite *Eiga*'s bulk and its competition, the chronicle did not remain unknown. The sources cited in the discussion of date and titles and the existence of several partial manuscripts attributed to the thirteenth and fourteenth centuries[113] suggest a modest but constant circulation in aristocratic quarters throughout most of its earlier history.

It was probably not until the fifteenth and sixteenth centuries that the work began to attract any considerable amount of serious attention and study. Those were times of almost continuous warfare, during which the activities of contending military lords increasingly threatened the Kyōto aristocracy, its institutions, and its civilization. Moved at first, perhaps, chiefly by nostalgia for the great days of the Imperial past, and then, as war laid the city waste and poverty gripped the Court, by an urgently felt need to preserve and restore Court traditions, a number of bookish courtiers took up the study of the major literary and historical documents of the Heian period, an age that seemed to medieval eyes the very embodiment of aristocratic ideals. There followed an unprecedented flourishing of native classical studies, which produced several learned works on Court ceremonies, rites, and usages, as well as numerous commentaries on masterpieces of the Court's literary past—principally *Man'yōshū*, *Kokinshū*, *Ise monogatari*, and especially *Genji monogatari*.[114]

Although only one minor *Eiga* study survives from those centuries, the chronicle was a mine of information for scholars bent on imbibing and restoring classical glories, and it is evident that it was included in the contemporary enthusiasm for Heian writings. As early as the first half of the fifteenth century, it was apparently highly enough prized for a manuscript to be sold at a price sufficient to defray a substantial share of the construction costs of a temple,[115] and the Court's interest had resulted in the

113. One complete manuscript and at least six fragments are attributable to the thirteenth and fourteenth centuries. One of the fragments (which has not survived) was in the hand of Yoshida Kenkō (1283?–1350?), the author of *Tsurezuregusa*; another is attributed to the poet Fujiwara Tameie (1198–1275). See Matsumura 1956–67, 1: 7–10, 155–58, 162, 197–98, 2: 23–38, 49–50, 3: 22, 25.

114. For a brief survey of the studies and of the intellectual climate that generated them, see Haga Kōshirō's remarks in Kodama et al. 1956–58, 7: 204–11.

115. Under a date in 1432, the diary of Go-Sukōin (1372–1456) mentions an earlier sale of an *Eiga* manuscript for temple-building purposes; and the ex-Emperor adds later that straitened circumstances are forcing him to sell the same manuscript to his own son, the reigning Emperor, Go-Hanazono (1419–70, r. 1428–64). The manuscript in question had probably belonged to the scholarly Emperor Hanazono (1297–1348, r. 1308–18). For Go-

acquisition of at least two manuscripts by the end of the century.[116] Diary entries dating from that time to the late sixteenth century suggest a continuing effort to correct errors (probably both textual and factual) in the Court manuscripts,[117] and they also reveal that on one occasion a section of the text was read aloud at the Palace in the Imperial presence.[118]

Sanjōnishi Sanetaka, the celebrated Court official, poet, scholar, and diarist, acquired a complete *Eiga* manuscript at great cost in 1509. He spent the following year or more in reading it; and it was perhaps then that he made the extracts and brief notes that are now partially preserved in the library of Matsuda Takeo.[119] During his long life of more than eighty years, Sanetaka became a leading figure in aristocratic studies of the classical past, devoting particular attention to the recovery of the Court ceremonies, rites, and usages lost during the cataclysmic Ōnin Wars (1467–77).[120] As his extracts and notes show, his historical studies were chiefly responsible for his interest in *Eiga*, which can be traced as far back as

Sukōin's remarks, see *Kanmon gyoki*, 2: 41–42 (27 vi and 4 viii Eikyō 4). References to *Eiga* in early sources are conveniently summarized in a chronological chart in Matsumura 1956–67, 3: 373–416.

116. I.e. the one acquired by Go-Hanazono (see the preceding note) and another presented to Emperor Go-Tsuchimikado (1442–1500, r. 1464–1500) by Konoe Masaie (1444–1505) and several other courtiers in 1483. On the latter, see Matsumura 1961, p. 309; and *Gohōkōinki*, 1: 383 (30 iii Bunmei 15).

117. For example, Nakamikado Nobutane (1442–1525), *Nobutanekyōki*, 1: 147 (22 iv Bunmei 12); Sanjōnishi Sanetaka (1455–1537), *Sanetakakōki*, 1: 450 (21 viii Bunmei 15); and *Oyudono no ue no nikki*, 9: 11 (3 and 7 ii Keichō 3). See also Haga 1945, pp. 139–40.

118. *Sanetakakōki*, 2: 468 (17 -viii Entoku 2). The reading was actually of *Kayanoin gyōkō komakurabe ekotoba*, a scroll painting of scenes in Chapter 23 ("An Imperial Visit to the Horse Races"), with accompanying descriptive texts quoted from the chapter. The work is thought to date from the late thirteenth or early fourteenth century. Four fragments are known to survive, one in the Seikadō Library in Tōkyō, another in the collection of Kubo Sōtarō (Ōsaka), and two formerly owned by Kanō Seisen (1796–1846). A copy of various fragments made by Seisen is owned by the Tōkyō National Musem. See Matsumura 1956–67, 2: 95–114; Akiyama 1968, plate 63 (from the Kubo fragment) and p. 109; *Nihon emakimono zenshū*, vol. 17, color plate 2 (from the Kubo fragment), gravure plate 6 (from the Seikadō fragment); and Tanaka 1951, pp. 431–33, and Mizunoo 1957, p. 293 (the two Seisen fragments).

119. The purchase of the manuscript is noted in *Sanetakakōki*, 5:279–80 (4 and 8 xi Eishō 6); the reading of it in *ibid.*, 5: 476 (7 iii Eishō 8). The entries describing the purchase contain lacunae, making it difficult to be certain about the cost, but the sum involved was at least 100 rolls of cloth, i.e. well over 1,000 yards of material about fourteen inches wide. The text acquired by Sanetaka was apparently the one now known as the Umezawa (or Sanjōnishi) manuscript. Six years earlier, in 1503, Sanetaka had expressed great interest in the sale of an *Eiga* manuscript that had once been owned by Ashikaga Yoshimasa (1436–90), but the 1509 purchase came from Kitabatake Zaishin (1468–1511), and there is no traceable connection between it and Yoshimasa's text. On the sale of the latter, see *Sanetakakōki*, 4: 175 (5 ix Bunki 3). For Sanetaka's *Eiga* extracts and his notes thereon, see Matsumura 1956–67, 1: 619–28.

120. See Haga Kōshirō, in Kodama et al. 1956–58, 7: 204–11.

1483, when he took part in the collation or correction of a manuscript at the Imperial Palace.[121]

Sanetaka's clearly expressed enthusiasm for *Eiga*[122] was doubtless shared to some extent by a number of his fellow courtiers, but the work probably did not become generally available, even to the aristocracy, until the seventeenth century, when it was printed in both typographical and xylograph editions.[123] Although the size of the printings was presumably small,[124] they must have resulted in a greatly expanded audience from the seventeenth century on, and it is probably to them that we owe a number of ground-breaking studies, produced by such nativist scholars as Nomura Naofusa (d. 1729), Andō Tameakira (1659–1716), and Dohi Tsunehira (1707–82).[125] An abridged and illustrated xylograph version published in Kyōto, perhaps around the middle of the seventeenth century,[126] made the work considerably more accessible to the general reader, and may have prompted the appearance in 1680 of a *jōruri* (puppet) play called *Akazome Emon Eiga monogatari,* which tells how Akazome happened to write her book and describes a love triangle in which she became involved while working on it at Yorimichi's Uji villa.[127]

Even under the most generous assumptions, however, it seems unlikely that *Eiga* reached more than a narrow circle of readers during the Tokugawa period. It is a work written by Heian Court aristocrats for their contemporary peers, and throughout its history it has remained very much what it appears to have been almost from the beginning: the nearly exclusive property of learned students of the native classical tradition.

121. *Sanetakakōki,* 1: 450 (21 viii Bunmei 15).

122. *Ibid.,* 5: 476 (7 iii Eishō 8).

123. The typographical edition, which is undated, is thought to have been printed around the Kan'ei era (1624–43). See Matsumura 1956–67, 1: 28; and Kawase 1967, 1: 529, 2: 894. The xylograph is dated 1656. Matsumura 1956–67, 1: 28–29.

124. Kawase 1967, 1: 529, 2: 894, lists only twenty-two partial or complete extant copies of the typographical edition.

125. See the chart in Matsumura 1956–67, 3: 373–416, for a brief listing of studies made by those and many other Tokugawa-period scholars.

126. Matsumura (1956–67, 1: 34) refers to this as the "illustrated nine-volume extract text" (*eiri kyūkan shōshutsubon*), and says that it may have been first printed at some time between about 1650 and 1670. It was reprinted in 1806. A copy in the possession of the East Asiatic Library at Berkeley, Calif., is from the first printing.

127. The play, attributed to Chikamatsu Monzaemon (1653–1725), is printed in Fujii 1925–28, 1: 349–83.

A Tale of Flowering Fortunes

I

THE
MOON-VIEWING
BANQUET

THERE have been more than sixty[1] Emperors in this country since its beginnings, but I cannot describe all of their reigns in detail. I shall merely attempt to speak of the most recent.

Once there was a sovereign called Uda.[2] Of that Emperor's many sons, the successor to the throne was the eldest, Prince Atsuhito, who has become known as the Virtuous Emperor Daigo and whose reign is still held up as a glorious example.[3] Emperor Daigo took several consorts during his thirty-three years on the throne, and became the father of sixteen Princes and numerous Princesses.[4]

Minister of State Mototsune, the Chancellor in those days, died during the reign of Emperor Uda.[5] Mototsune was the third son of Middle Counselor Nagara (Chancellor Fuyutsugu's eldest son, who was posthumously

1. Emperor Go-Ichijō (r. 1016–36), whose reign was the last to be described in the *Eiga seihen*, was the sixty-eighth.

2. Uda (867–931; r. 887–97), the Teiji Imperial Personage (Teiji no In), was the fifty-ninth Emperor.

3. According to a generally reliable source, Emperor Uda had ten sons. *Honchō kōin shōunroku*, p. 424. Emperor Daigo (885–930; r. 897–930), the Engi Emperor, was admired both as a statesman and as a patron of learning and the arts. *Engishiki*, the great tenth-century compendium of administrative regulations; *Sandai jitsuroku*, the last of the Six National Histories; and *Kokinshū*, the first Imperial anthology of Japanese poetry, were all compiled at his direction.

4. The Princes included two future Emperors, Suzaku (923–52; r. 930–46) and Murakami (926–67; r. 946–67). There were also four sons on whom the Minamoto surname was bestowed, including Takaakira (914–82), whose exile to Kyūshū is described toward the end of this chapter. For details on Daigo's consorts and offspring, see EM, 1: 474.

5. Mototsune died in 891 at the age of fifty-five. For information concerning Court ranks and offices, see Appendix A.

granted the title of Chancellor).[6] After his death he was honored with the posthumous name Shōsenkō.[7] He had four sons, of whom the eldest, Tokihira, rose to the office of Minister of the Left and died at the age of thirty-nine; the second, Nakahira, became Minister of the Left and died at seventy-one; the third, Kanehira, held Third Rank; and the fourth, Minister of State Tadahira, served as Chancellor for many years.[8]

Mototsune had a daughter who was one of Emperor Daigo's Junior Consorts.[9] She bore several children, among them the sovereign's eleventh son, Prince Hiroakira, who ascended the throne, reigned for sixteen years, and then abdicated. That Emperor is known as Emperor Suzaku.[10] Emperor Suzaku was succeeded on the Thirteenth of the Fourth Month in the ninth year of Tengyō [946] by Prince Nariakira,[11] his full brother and Emperor Daigo's fourteenth son.

Ex-Emperor Suzaku had no sons, but his consort, the Princess,[12] gave birth to a delightful little daughter, and after the death of the mother, which occurred when the child was three,[13] he cared for her with great tenderness and compassion. His one desire was to see her installed as Empress, and he fretted constantly because there was no precedent for such a thing.[14] The daughter's name was Princess Shōshi.[15]

The new ruler, Emperor Murakami, was all that anyone could have wished. Emperor Daigo's reign had been a brilliant one, and now with this virile, majestic, wise, and learned sovereign, Yao's son seemed Yao

6. See supplementary note (hereafter s.n.) 1.

7. A posthumous name (*imina*) was usually conferred by the Court on a Chancellor who died as a layman. This kind of imina consisted of the Chinese character *kō*, a title of respect, preceded by two characters indicative of the Confucian virtues exemplified by the late Minister. Shōsenkō seems to have meant Eloquent Lord, or perhaps Lord Who Refused to Mince Words.

8. See s.n. 2.

9. Fujiwara Onshi (885–954), Mototsune's fourth daughter, became a Junior Consort (Nyōgo) in 901 and Empress (Kōgō) in 923. Her two Imperial sons, Suzaku and Murakami, named her Grand Empress (931) and Senior Grand Empress (946), respectively.

10. So called from his place of residence as an ex-Emperor, near the intersection of Sanjō and Suzaku avenues. He later became a monk and moved to the Ninnaji (950).

11. Emperor Murakami.

12. Princess Kishi (d. 950), daughter of one of Emperor Daigo's sons by Empress Onshi, Prince Yasuakira (903–23), who died while Crown Prince. Princess Kishi's mother was a daughter of Fujiwara Tokihira (871–909).

13. A mistake. The princess died in the year of the child's birth. EM, 1: 474, s.n. 15.

14. Many earlier Princesses had in fact become Empresses, and Suzaku's daughter herself married the future Emperor Reizei (950–1011; r. 967–69) a number of years later (963), becoming Empress after his accession in 967. The difficulty seems to have been that there was no precedent for making a baby an Empress. EM, 1: 474, s.n. 16.

15. Princess Shōshi (950–1000) reappears in *Eiga* from time to time as a wealthy childless woman, estranged from her mentally ill husband and deeply involved in Buddhist activities. She received the titles of Grand Empress and Senior Grand Empress in 973 and 986, respectively.

himself.[16] Emperor Murakami was also a gifted poet, and a man who combined great compassion with a robust enjoyment of gaiety and splendor. Of his many consorts, some pleased him more than others, but he always refrained from exposing anyone to humiliation or pity. Controlling his inclinations with admirable self-restraint, he treated each of the ladies with a solicitude so unfailing that no disagreeable incidents, awkwardness, suspicions, or jealousies marred their relations with one another. Those who produced offspring were recognized in a fitting manner, and the childless ones were summoned to help him dispel the tedium of ritual seclusion by playing *go*, backgammon, character parts, or jackstones while he watched.[17] It is small wonder that the ladies lived together in harmony and amicability! The very wind, it seemed, was moved by the Emperor's generous spirit to leave the boughs in peace—to spare the blossoms that scented the tranquil air of spring and the crimson and yellow leaves that lingered quietly on autumnal branches.

The Chancellor who governed the realm during that reign was Mototsune's fourth son, Tadahira, an uncle of Emperor Murakami.[18] Tadahira had five sons. The eldest, Saneyori, was Minister of the Left and lived at the Ononomiya; the second, Morosuke, was Minister of the Right and lived at Kujō. Little is known of the third. The fourth, Morouji, was a Major Counselor, and the Fifth, Morotada, also served as Minister of the Left. Morotada lived at Koichijō.[19] Thus Tadahira's sons became exalted personages. They had many children of their own, especially Morosuke, a man of amorous inclinations, whose numerous wives gave birth to eleven sons and six daughters.[20] Saneyori had only three sons,[21] although there were also some daughters. One daughter married the son of a Princess, the second was a Junior Consort, and the others were variously situated.[22]

16. The reigns of Daigo and Murakami have traditionally been bracketed together as "the glorious reigns of Engi and Tenryaku," periods during which the arts flourished, Court life was brilliant, and the Emperor played a relatively prominent political role. (Engi [901–23] and Tenryaku [947–57] are era names.) Unlike the legendary Chinese ruler Yao, who was obliged to select Shun as his heir because his own son was unworthy, Emperor Daigo, says the author, had a son who was his father's equal.

17. See s.n. 3.

18. See s.n. 2. Mototsune had served as Chancellor from 880 to his death in 891, after which there had been a hiatus until Tadahira's appointment in 936. Tadahira (880–949) held the office only during the first four years of Murakami's twenty-two-year reign. It was as Regent, rather than as Chancellor, that he "governed the realm."

19. For details on Tadahira's sons, see s.n. 4.

20. For a list of Morosuke's children, see s.n. 5.

21. Atsutoshi (912–47), who died at thirty-six (sai); Yoritada (924–89), a Regent (977–86) and Chancellor (978–89); and Tadatoshi (928–73), a Consultant.

22. The "son of a Princess" may be Takaakira, whose mother, a Minamoto, could conceivably have been born a Princess. Saneyori (900–970) is known to have had one daughter,

Emperor Murakami's consorts at play. "Those who produced offspring were recognized in a fitting manner, and the childless ones were summoned to help [the Emperor] dispel the tedium of ritual seclusion by playing *go*, backgammon, character parts, or jackstones while he watched." The Emperor sits behind a partially raised bamboo blind in the upper part of the lefthand panel. Curtain-stands appear

just to the right of the sliding-door partitions on the extreme left, and a veranda runs outside the raised blinds on the right. The absence of a roof, enabling the viewer to look down into the room, and the cloudlike formations at top and bottom are artistic conventions.

Morotada had two sons and a daughter, but one of the sons died young.[23]

Of Emperor Murakami's many Junior Consorts, Morosuke's daughter Anshi occupied the foremost position.[24] Among the others were Kishi, the daughter of the Emperor's brother, Prince Shigeakira, the Minister of Ceremonial;[25] Sōshi, the daughter of another Imperial brother, Prince Yoakira, the Minister of Central Affairs (Sōshi was called the Reikeiden Consort);[26] Masahime, the Azechi Concubine, a daughter of the Azechi Major Counselor Arihira;[27] Hōshi, Morotada's beautiful daughter (called the Sen'yōden Consort);[28] and Keishi, the Hirohata Lady of the Bedchamber, who was a daughter of the Hirohata Middle Counselor Moroaki.[29] Those were all ladies who bore children—there were many childless ones as well. I almost forgot to say that a daughter of Motokata, the Minister of Popular Affairs, also entered the Palace as a bride.[30]

Two Crown Princes had died in succession not many years earlier.[31] The

---

Keishi (d. 942), who acted briefly as a Junior Consort of Emperor Suzaku before returning home for unknown reasons. Another daughter, Jusshi (933–47), Emperor Murakami's Kokiden Junior Consort, died of smallpox at the age of fourteen; a third was one of Takaakira's wives. See EM, 1: 475, s.n. 21; and *Honchō kōin shōunroku*, p. 428.

23. See s.n. 6.

24. For details on Anshi (927–64), see s.n. 7.

25. Prince Shigeakira (906–54), Murakami's half-brother, was known for his learning, polite accomplishments, and luxurious tastes. In 948, after the death of Kishi's mother, he married Anshi's sister Tōshi (d. 975), with whom Emperor Murakami later fell in love. His daughter Kishi (929–85), who entered the Palace as a bride in 949, was called Saigū no Nyōgo because she had served in her childhood as Ise Virgin (Saigū). Unable to compete with strong consorts like Anshi and Hōshi, Kishi spent most of her time at home, where she held poetry contests and created a salon frequented by some of the leading literary lights of the day. She was herself a superior poet.

26. Prince Yoakira (904–37), another half-brother of Murakami, fathered three sons, Shigemitsu (923–98), Yasumitsu (924–95), and Nobumitsu (927–76), who all figure in *Eiga* as Minamoto *kugyō* (senior nobles). His daughter Sōshi (930–1008) took Buddhist vows after Murakami's death.

27. Masahime (d. 967) was also called the Azechi Lady of the Bedchamber. She appears to have entered the Palace around 948. Her father, Fujiwara Arihira (892–970), served briefly as a figurehead Minister of the Left before his death in 970 at the age of 78. Azechi (Inspector), originally a title used of an official sent to the provinces to review the work of local officials, had by this time become a nominal additional post for a Middle or Major Counselor.

28. See s.n. 6.

29. Little is known of Keishi, other than that she had a reputation for wit and intelligence. Her father, Minamoto Moroaki (903–55), died a Middle Counselor. Hirohata, the locality in which Moroaki lived, is thought to have been an area east of Kyōgoku Avenue and south of Konoe Avenue, in the vicinity of the present Ritsumeikan University, but the identification is uncertain. See Kakimoto 1966, 2: 128; and *Kagerō nikki*, p. 349, s.n. 97.

30. Fujiwara Motokata (888–953) was a Middle Counselor from 941 until 951, when he advanced to the position of Major Counselor, his highest office. (The text below is mistaken in making him a Major Counselor in 950.) He was named Minister of Popular Affairs in 947. His daughter, Sukehime, who held the title of Concubine (Kōi), took Buddhist vows when Murakami died.

31. They were Prince Yasuakira and his son Yoshiyori (921–25), predecessors of Prince

office was now vacant again, and the Imperial consorts were annoyed and depressed by their seeming inability to produce a son. To the joy of her family, Anshi became pregnant, but the baby disappointed everyone by turning out to be a girl,[32] and furthermore it lived only a short time. Then Motokata's daughter left the Palace, announcing that she too was with child;[33] and while people were predicting a glorious future for her if it should be a boy, she gave birth to His Majesty's first son, Prince Hirohira.[34] The event caused a tremendous stir. The Emperor sent the baby a sword and provided everything needed for the customary ceremonies.[35] Major Counselor Motokata, overcome with joy, never doubted for a moment that his grandson would be nominated to fill the vacant post of Crown Prince.

Meanwhile people began to say that Anshi was pregnant again. Moto-kata told himself that even if the stories were true, she would probably only produce another daughter, but Tadahira and Morosuke were elated.[36] Quite naturally, the Emperor's own predominant feelings were happiness and relief. Whatever the future might bring, he reflected, he had a son.

After an illness of several months, Chancellor Tadahira died on the Fourteenth of the Eighth Month in the third year of Tenryaku [949]. He was seventy and had served as a Minister of State for thirty-six years. His sons held the distinguished offices of Minister of the Left and Minister of the Right, the Emperor himself was a close relative, and the consorts from his family were enviably situated. Anshi and Hōshi both left the Palace to go into mourning.[37]

The loss of Tadahira, a clement and humane ruler, was much regretted. He was granted the posthumous name Teishinkō, Upright and Faithful Lord, and the sad days slipped by in a series of impressive Buddhist services.[38] Saneyori, the Minister of the Left, became head of the government.[39]

Hiroakira (Emperor Suzaku) as Emperor Daigo's heir apparent. No Crown Prince had been appointed after the accession of Murakami.

32. Princess Shōshi (948–51).

33. In the Heian period, it was customary for an Imperial consort to leave the Palace when she was about three months pregnant. The principal reason was to prevent the defilement of the Palace by the emission of blood, either at the normal term of the pregnancy or because of a miscarriage or premature delivery. It seems also to have been felt that Buddhist prayers and other important prenatal care could best be provided in the woman's own home. On Shintō precautions against female bleeding in general, see Nakamura 1962, p. 22.

34. During his short lifetime, Prince Hirohira (950–71) held the titles of Minister of War and Governor-General of the Dazaifu (Kyūshū Government Office).

35. See s.n. 8.

36. Tadahira had died in 949, before the birth of Prince Hirohira.

37. See s.n. 9.   38. See s.n. 10.

39. Although the text could be construed to mean that Saneyori replaced his father as Regent, the regency remained vacant until the accession of Murakami's successor, Reizei.

Morosuke took second place, but everyone agreed that he was his brother's equal.

So the year ended. On the Twenty-fourth of the Fifth Month in the fourth year of Tenryaku [950], Anshi was delivered of a son, Prince Norihira.[40] A sword was dispatched posthaste from the Palace, and the peculiarly auspicious nature of the occasion created great excitement. After Major Counselor Motokata heard the news, his chest felt so tight that his food stuck in his throat. "What a terrible blow!" he thought. "Our hopes will never be realized now." Tormented by anxiety, he began to suspect that his health was collapsing, and morbid notions ran through his head. "If I am to die, let it be as soon as possible, now that things have come to this pass."[41]

I could not possibly do justice to the splendor of the ceremonies that took place while the mother and child were in the lying-in chamber at the Kujō Mansion.[42] Morosuke must have felt that such a stroke of luck would never come his way again, and it would be natural to suppose that Saneyori also found the event more agreeable than the birth of Prince Hirohira. Not a care troubled the serenity of the Emperor's mind. It was, he thought happily, exactly what he would have wished.

Soon the Fiftieth Day ceremonies[43] came and went, and on the Twenty-third of the Seventh Month, just as he was beginning his third month of life, Prince Norihira became the heir apparent. If only Tadahira had not died, thought Morosuke, weeping in spite of himself.[44] Meanwhile Prince Hirohira's mother had taken to her bed, where, in a display of grief that others considered excessive, she refused to swallow even a sip of water.

Since each of the Imperial consorts was determined not to be outdone by the others, they conceived and gave birth to an impressive array of children as the swift years passed. Masahime bore the sovereign's third

40. The future Emperor Reizei.

41. He prefers not to live to see the appointment of Anshi's son as Crown Prince.

42. The reference is probably to the bath ceremonies and other early rituals, such as the first suckling and the severance of the umbilical cord. Since other sources indicate that Prince Norihira was born in a house belonging to Fujiwara Tōnori, the ceremonies presumably took place there, rather than at Morosuke's Kujō Mansion. Tōnori (d. 953), a provincial governor, is to be distinguished from Anshi's brother of the same name (d. 989). He later received an appointment in the Crown Prince's Household. See *Dainihonshi*, 2: 212; and *Sonpi bunmyaku*, 2: 441.

43. *Ika*, held on or about the fiftieth day after a birth. Using chopsticks, the father or maternal grandfather fed the baby from an assortment of fifty special rice cakes (*ika no mochii*), probably as a formal indication that the infant's diet would thenceforth include solid food. The event, which took place at night, was accompanied by an elaborate banquet at which the guests composed poems predicting long life for the child. See Chapter 8, below; Nakamura 1962, pp. 83–91; and Watanabe 1964, pp. 90–92.

44. Tears on joyous occasions were considered inauspicious.

son, Prince Munehira, and his third daughter, Princess Hōshi; Anshi his fourth and fifth sons, Princes Tamehira and Morihira; Hōshi his sixth and eighth sons, Princes Masahira and Nagahira (Prince Masahira died young, but Prince Nagahira's childhood was uneventful); Sōshi the seventh son, Prince Tomohira, and the sixth daughter, Rakushi; Kishi the fourth daughter, Kishi; Keishi the fifth daughter, Seishi; Masahime the ninth son, Prince Akihira; and Anshi the seventh, ninth, and tenth daughters, Princesses Hoshi, Shishi, and Senshi. Such a succession of births was splendid indeed—there were nine Princes and ten Princesses.[45]

It seemed to the Emperor that one of his consorts, Keishi, possessed a remarkably subtle mind. Once he sent each of the ladies the same poem:

Ōsaka mo	Since no barrier remains
Hate wa yukiki no	At Ōsaka
Seki mo izu	Where people come and go,
Tazunete toiko	Pray visit me—
Kinaba kaesaji.	If you come, you will not be sent back.[46]

Though they responded in various ways, only Keishi sent him incense—proof, he thought, of her superior sensibility. Such discernment was not to have been expected of all, but he could not help wishing for the Nakoso Barrier[47] when a certain lady went so far as to present herself at his apartments in gorgeous attire. People say his regard for her cooled after that.

Hōshi was a great beauty. The Emperor, to whom she was very dear, taught her to play in a charming manner on his own favorite instrument, the thirteen-stringed zither.[48] With no formal instruction, but merely from being present during the lessons, her brother, Lesser Captain Naritoki,[49]

45. The author fails to mention Princesses Rishi (the second daughter) and Shūshi (the eighth). See s.n. 11 for a list of Murakami's children.

46. The poem seems to say, "Although I have been longing to see you, others have stood in the way. Now, however, the coast is clear." The real message is concealed in the initial and final syllables of its five lines, which may be read: *Awasetakimono sukoshi*, "Please send me a little incense." (*Ha* and *wa*, *su* and *zu*, and *shi* and *ji* were orthographically identical in the Heian period.) Incense, used for perfuming the air and scenting garments, was compounded from basic materials such as sandalwood, musk, and clovewood, which were pulverized, bound together with honey or some other sweet agent, and kneaded into hard balls. See Ikeda 1967, pp. 276–81. The Ōsaka Barrier, often mentioned in poetry because of the orthographic identity of its initial syllable with *au* ("meet"), had originally been established to protect the capital in case of emergency, but by the mid-Heian period it had lost its military effectiveness. It was situated in the mountains on the road between the Ōmi and Yamashiro basins, within the area of the present city of Ōtsu.

47. On the Hitachi-Mutsu provincial boundary in northern Japan. Its name can be interpreted to mean "Don't come."

48. *Sō no koto*, a predecessor of the modern koto. See Kishibe 1969, pp. 20, 39.

49. See s.n. 6. Naritoki (941–95) was a Lesser Captain from 961 to 967.

also developed an excellent technique, and the Emperor, intrigued by his proficiency, gave him some personal instruction. Afterward, Naritoki was the first person summoned whenever there was to be music, and he always performed with great skill.

Although Tadahira's sons were brothers, they were not at all alike. Saneyori's taste was faultless, and he composed excellent poetry, but there was a quality of inscrutability about him that people found disconcerting. Morosuke was quiet, generous to acquaintances as well as to close friends. When someone called on him after staying away a long time, he showed no displeasure, but behaved with as much cordiality as though meeting the person for the first time. (That may be why most of Tadahira's old dependents found their way to the Kujō Mansion.) Morotada was pleasant to his intimates and cool to outsiders, and his very positive likes and dislikes were plainly reflected in his actions.

As the Crown Prince grew older, he developed into a handsome lad. The Emperor relied in a gratifying manner on Morosuke, whose position had been made even more secure by the births of the Fourth and Fifth Princes.

Meanwhile, on the Twenty-seventh of the Seventh Month in the second year of Tentoku [958], Morosuke's daughter was granted Imperial rank.[50] That lady, Fujiwara Anshi, was thenceforth to be called Empress. One of the Emperor's brothers, Prince Takaakira, who had become a commoner bearing the Minamoto surname, was selected to serve as Master of the Empress's Household,[51] and all the other Household officials were chosen with equal care. Everything worthwhile in life seemed to have come Morosuke's way! Saneyori could only lament the death of his own daughter.

In a certain year, Saneyori lost his beloved eldest son, Lesser Captain Atsutoshi. During the mourning period, while he was still dazed with grief, someone sent him a horse from the east, saying that it was for Atsutoshi. When Saneyori saw the animal, he composed a poem:

Mada shiranu	Someone, it seems,
Hito mo arikeri	Had not yet heard.
Azumaji ni	Better for me had I too
Ware mo yukite zo	Journeyed to an eastern province
Sumu bekarikeru.	And made it my home.

50. The date was actually the Twenty-seventh of the Tenth Month.
51. Probably because his wife was Anshi's younger sister. In 958 Takaakira was a Major Counselor, an office he held until his promotion to Minister of the Left in 967. His period of exile as nominal head of the Dazaifu, which lasted from 969 to 972, ended his official career.

Poetry was an interest close to Saneyori's heart. Emperor Murakami, who was also skilled in the art, exchanged verses with him from time to time.

Long ago, in the fifth year of Tenpyō Shōhō [758], during the reign of the Takano Empress, a sovereign had instructed the Tachibana Minister of the Left and a group of other senior nobles and courtiers to compile the *Collection for Ten Thousand Generations*.[52] A more recent ruler, Emperor Daigo, had commissioned the brilliant *Collection of Early and Modern Times* in twenty sections, an anthology that was now more than twenty years old.[53] As the contribution of his reign, Emperor Murakami ordered a third collection, to consist of old and new poems that had not found a place in the *Collection of Early and Modern Times*. Since the new book was in the nature of a sequel, the Emperor gave it the name *Later Collection*,[54] and by his order it also contained twenty sections. It included, I believe, a rather large number of Saneyori's compositions.[55] The Emperor had wanted it to contain something comparable to Ki no Tsurayuki's splendid Preface to the *Collection of Early and Modern Times*, but he had reluctantly concluded that the great Tsurayuki had evoked the past, mused on the present, and predicted the future with such skill that nobody at his Court could equal the performance.

Of Saneyori's two remaining sons, the third, Tadatoshi, no sooner achieved the office of Commander of the Right Gate Guards than he died, leaving only Yoritada, the second. Yoritada was still a minor figure at Court, but Saneyori was afraid to promote him too rapidly, because Tadatoshi had got no further than the Gate Guards in spite of having been made a senior noble while only a boy.[56]

Saneyori adopted the third of Tadatoshi's numerous sons, naming him

52. This may be the earliest extant mention of the old theory that *Man'yōshū*, the great eighth-century collection of verse, is, in part at least, an Imperially commissioned anthology compiled by Tachibana Moroe (684–757). See EM, 1: 477, s.n. 31. The Takano Empress was Kōken (718–70; r. 749–58 and, as Shōtoku, 764–70).

53. "Twenty years" is thought to be a copyist's error for "forty years." *Kokinshū*, the first Imperial anthology of Japanese poetry, was probably presented to the throne in 905.

54. *Gosenshū*, commissioned in 951 and put into its present form some time between 955 and 966.

55. *Gosenshū* contains 1,426 poems by some 200 authors, of whom Ki no Tsurayuki (884–946), with seventy-seven, is the best represented. Saneyori, with ten, is in a three-way tie for eighth place. For Tsurayuki's significance as a poet, and as author of the Preface mentioned below, see Brower and Miner 1961, Chapter 5.

56. This paragraph, which is out of chronological order, makes it appear that Tadatoshi, who died in 973, predeceased Saneyori, although he outlived him by three years. Tadatoshi was not a boy when he became a kugyō (he was thirty-nine), nor was Yoritada kept in minor offices (he was a Middle Counselor of Third Rank at the time of Saneyori's death).

Sanesuke.[57] He also reared the many sons and daughters of Atsutoshi.[58]

Anshi's sister Tōshi[59] was the wife of Prince Shigeakira, the Minister of Ceremonial. She bore and reared two daughters.[60]

Major Counselor Motokata died in the Third Month of the year in which the Crown Prince turned four [953], and both the First Prince and the Prince's mother, Sukehime, followed him in death, one after another.[61] That, I am sure, is why the Crown Prince suddenly began to indulge in the lunatic antics of someone possessed by malignant spirits. At times his behavior was heart-rending. In outward appearance he was a fine, handsome child—a precious gem, one might say, marred by a single flaw. Most alarming of all was the seeming immunity of the spirits to the esoteric rites that were continually performed on the Prince's behalf in front of many altars.[62] His mental processes and facial expressions remained abnormal, and his demeanor and voice were pathetically unchildlike and repulsive. The Emperor and Empress were frantic with worry.

The approach of the Crown Prince's Coming-of-Age ceremony[63] nevertheless excited lively interest among Princes and noblemen with marriageable daughters. Under the circumstances, the Imperial couple had little heart for the selection of a consort, but they knew of the loving care that had been lavished on Princess Shōshi by the late ex-Emperor Suzaku, who had hoped to make her an Imperial bride, and so they decided to bring the Princess into the Palace. The other aspirants were obliged to forget their dreams.

Prince Shigeakira's wife Tōshi, though not in service at the Palace, had formed the habit of visiting Anshi to watch some of the more interesting Court events. One day the Emperor caught a glimpse of her. Somehow or other he must get to know her, he thought to himself; and he broached the

---

57. Sanesuke (957–1046), one of the major figures of the mid-Heian period, was admired by his contemporaries both for his mastery of scholarship and the arts and for a courage and probity that were rare at the Imperial Court. Promoted slowly by members of Kaneie's branch of the family, he became a Provisional Major Counselor in 1001, a Major Counselor in 1009, and Minister of the Right in 1021. He received Junior First Rank in 1037. His voluminous diary, *Shōyūki*, is a valuable resource for the historian.

58. Atsutoshi seems to have had only two daughters and a son. The latter was the famous calligrapher Sukemasa (944–98), a kugyō who never progressed beyond the office of Consultant. One of the daughters is said to have been a wife of Morosuke's son Tamemitsu (942–92). *Sonpi bunmyaku*, 2: 1.

59. As described below, Tōshi entered Emperor Murakami's Palace after the deaths of Anshi and Prince Shigeakira. She became a Handmaid (Naishi) during the reign of Emperor En'yū (959–91; r. 969–84).

60. The daughters cannot be identified with any known offspring of Prince Shigeakira.

61. Although Motokata died in 953, Prince Hirohira lived until 971, and Sukehime until at least 967.

62. See s.n. 12.   63. *Genpuku*. See s.n. 13.

matter to Anshi with great earnestness. The indulgent Empress allowed him two or three meetings, which she pretended not to notice, but such favors seemed meager to a man burning with desire. She must let them meet again, he insisted. Presently Anshi sent off a formal invitation asking Tōshi to come to Court, but then it was her sister who hung back, fearful that it would not be the part of prudence to appear too often in the Imperial presence. And while matters were at that stage the Emperor communicated with Tōshi himself, employing trusted ladies-in-waiting as emissaries, and persuaded her to come to the Palace in strict secrecy. He also instructed the Office of Palace Works to make elegant articles suitable for feminine use. As was natural enough under the circumstances, the repetition of such commands made it inevitable that gossip should reach Empress Anshi's ears. The Empress flew into a rage, the Emperor lost his nerve, Tōshi quaked with fear, and the affair ended. Tōshi was pretty, sweet, and fashionable—and probably also something of a flirt, for otherwise such a thing would have been unlikely to happen. The Emperor bore his loss in gloomy silence.

Meanwhile all the courtiers and senior nobles were making a great fuss over the Fourth Prince, Tamehira, who was his parents' special favorite. When the Prince was twelve or thirteen, the Emperor began to prepare for his Coming-of-Age ceremony. Every senior noble with an eligible daughter was excited by the prospect. Minamoto Takaakira, the Master of the Empress's Household and Major Captain of the Bodyguards of the Left, hinted that he would like to have the Prince marry his only daughter, whom he had reared with every possible care; and both the Emperor and Anshi were pleased with the proposal.[64] Takaakira set happily about the arrangements, and on the very night of the Coming-of-Age ceremony he sent his daughter off to the Palace.[65]

It was usual to celebrate a Prince's nuptial rites in the home of the bride. The decision that Takaakira's daughter should go as a bride to the Palace would have occasioned no comment if she had been a new Imperial consort, but it was considered remarkably novel and modern under the circumstances. Their Majesties' welcome was as warm as anyone could have desired.

64. The genpuku of Prince Tamehira (952-1010) took place in 965, more than a year after Anshi's death. Takaakira appears to have had at least two daughters in addition to the one in question here. One, the wife of Minamoto Shigenobu (922-95), is said to have been adopted by Morosuke; the other, Meishi, later a consort of Michinaga (966-1028), was "very young" at the time of her father's exile (969), and may not have been born until after 965.
65. The marriage was celebrated late in 966. EM, 1: 478, s.n. 39.

To Morosuke's concern, it was rumored that Prince Shigeakira, the Minister of Ceremonial, had been suffering for several days from a grave malady. Presently the Prince died.[66] The Emperor rejoiced in secret at the removal of one of the barriers between him and Tōshi, but there was still Anshi's displeasure to consider. When the mourning period ended, Prince Tamehira was promoted to First Rank, with the title Minister of Ceremonial.[67]

Around the same time Morosuke began to feel out of sorts. A disorder of the nervous system was diagnosed,[68] and hot baths and medicines were prescribed, but before long he sank so low that Anshi went home.

None of Morosuke's numerous sons had attained a position of much influence (the one with the highest office was only a Middle Captain),[69] and the Emperor was distressed by the prospective loss of a man who was the sole trustworthy support of the heir apparent, to say nothing of the Fourth and Fifth Princes. So great was his anxiety that he ordered the performance of Buddhist rituals on the minister's behalf, a mark of favor that excited general envy. On the Second of the Fifth Month in the fourth year of Tentoku [960], Morosuke took religious vows, and on the Fourth, at the age of fifty-three, he breathed his last. Never was an untimely death more universally lamented. "He would have been an ideal Regent for my son," the unhappy Emperor thought again and again. Still, things were certain to go well as long as Empress Anshi remained at Court, because no one would presume to disregard her wishes.

The melancholy last rites took place, culminating in Buddhist services commissioned by Empress Anshi shortly after the Tenth of the Sixth Month.[70] "It is time to reconcile yourself; come back to the Palace," the

66. This event took place in 954, eleven years before Prince Tamehira's genpuku.

67. If *Eiga* is correct, the Prince took office at the age of two. Independent sources indicate only that he held the position by 978. EM, 1: 39, n. 26.

68. *Kaze.* Since the victims frequently succumbed, the ailment, mentioned thirteen times in *Eiga* but never described in detail, is unlikely to have been the common cold, now called kaze. Most scholars explain it as a general term for a wide range of disorders, both chronic and acute, that were predominantly ailments of the nervous system (lung, liver, and stomach trouble, paralysis, epilepsy, etc.), and that were believed to be caused by vapors entering the body. Treatments included religious rites, medicines (such as steamed garlic or magnolia-bark tea), hot baths, and the dousing of part or all of the patient's body with water. EM, 1: 478, s.n. 40; Ishimura 1964, p. 561; Hattori 1955, pp. 188–91.

69. In 960 Morosuke's three oldest sons, Koretada (924–72), Kanemichi (925–77), and Kaneie (929–90), held the offices of Provisional Middle Captain, Assistant Commander of the Military Guards, and Gentleman-in-waiting.

70. "Tenth" is a mistake for "Twentieth." The reference is to the Forty-ninth Day services, which took place on the Twenty-second.

Emperor said then, but Anshi replied that she would stay away during the summer heat.[71]

Akitada, one of Tokihira's sons, was made Minister of the Right.[72] Saneyori's influence as Minister of the Left increased as a result of his brother's death.

Through fear of the spirits possessing the Crown Prince, his consort spent most of her time away from the Palace.

Time passed swiftly. I should like to write of each of the many interesting and delightful events that took place at Court, but that would be impossible. Emperor Murakami was devoted to all of his fine, handsome children, especially Anshi's. The Imperial couple never ceased to lament Morosuke's premature death.

The uncertainty of life preyed on the Emperor's mind. He often considered abdicating so that he might end his days in peace, but when he thought of the magnificent ceremonies that had followed the deaths of earlier reigning sovereigns, it seemed a pity to give all that up.

Prince Tamehira, who was getting to be quite grown up, would have liked to leave the Palace for a residence of his own. His parents still felt the same about him, but a queer turn of events made it seem best to pass him by and let the succession go to the Fifth Prince, in spite of the latter's youth.[73] Emperor Murakami must often have wished that Morosuke had lived awhile longer.

The Emperor's seventh son, Prince Tomohira, was remarkably quick for one so young.[74] His mother, Princess Sōshi, must have been an intelligent woman. The Azechi Concubine Masahime, though not an Imperial favorite, enjoyed a secure position because of her many children.[75] Prince Shigeakira's daughter Kishi, who had not been blessed with issue,[76] found it difficult to visit the Emperor, even though he still sent her letters

71. The text implies that she was still at the Kujō Mansion, where she had stayed during Morosuke's illness, but she seems actually to have returned to the Palace before her father's death and then, after his death, to have gone to the Ichijō Mansion of her brother, Koretada. EM, 1: 40, n. 3.

72. Of Tokihira's three sons, the first and third, Yasutada (890–936) and Atsutada (906–43), had already died, leaving Akitada (898–965) the sole male representative of the family. Minister of the Right (Udaijin) was his highest post.

73. The "queer turn of events," which did not come until after Anshi's death, was the general climate of Fujiwara hostility toward Prince Tamehira created by his marriage in 966 to the daughter of an outsider, Minamoto Takaakira.

74. Prince Tomohira was born after Anshi's death, described below.

75. Three.

76. She was in fact the mother of a daughter, as the author herself has noted. See s.n. 11.

whenever he happened to recall that she was really very elegant and beautiful.

Meanwhile Empress Anshi had started another pregnancy. It was an anxious time for Emperor Murakami. Strangely persistent and acute in comparison with earlier occasions, the Empress's sufferings aroused premonitions of disaster even in her own mind. Both at Court and at her home, seven-altar rites and continuous prayers were recited on her behalf.[77] The constant repetition of sutras had some little effect, and from time to time she seemed improved, but she invariably suffered a relapse whenever the Emperor's spirits lightened a bit. After several months had dragged on in the same manner, she prepared to withdraw from the Palace. "Stay just a while longer," the Emperor begged, but she went off anyway, unwilling to run the risk of remaining.[78] The prayers for her safety were redoubled. That such danger should threaten this lady, the mother of so many of his children, naturally distressed the Emperor almost beyond endurance.

The strain of Anshi's illness made the Emperor lose interest in all his customary diversions, even his beloved concerts, and that in turn alarmed Saneyori. After all, Saneyori reflected, His Majesty had always been accustomed to entertainment, and his constant moping was a painful contrast to his ordinary behavior. The minister took the precaution of ordering prayers to safeguard the Imperial health.

"It is solely because of the Empress that we have had order and consideration in the Imperial harem. There would be many unpleasant developments if she were to die," people said. The consorts were nervous and unhappy.

The Empress's condition worsened steadily. Anxiety ran high within the Court and outside, and the Emperor sent off one message of inquiry after another. Prince Tamehira had taken the opportunity to move away, leaving his father more lonesome and depressed than ever. Anshi sent word that her daughters were to remain in the Palace for the present. She also forbade Prince Morihira to join her, for the possessing spirits, she

77. See s.n. 12. Seven-altar rites, which included safe deliveries among their presumed benefits, employed the Seven Healing Buddhas as their main objects of worship and featured recitations of the *Yakushi Sutra*. Their celebration at the Kokiden on this occasion (ii 964) followed a precedent established by Morosuke prior to the birth of Princess Shishi. "Continuous prayers" (*chōnichi no mizuhō*) was a general term for all magical rituals of indeterminate duration performed by members of esoteric sects to secure specific worldly benefits. EM, 1: 479, s.n. 45.

78. It was thought that the continued presence of a pregnant woman in the Palace might provoke the wrath of the gods. See n. 33. No other source reports that Anshi left the Palace. She appears to have died in one of the buildings assigned to the Bureau of Grounds. EM, 1: 42, n. 2.

said, might take a notion to attack him. Emperor Murakami, confronted with that evidence of her frame of mind, felt his own misgivings double.

In spite of his worries, the Emperor took care to visit the Imperial children, convinced that they must be disconsolate without their mother. He tried in every way to make them happy, but tears filled his eyes as he reflected again and again that they might soon be orphaned. Though he concealed his agitation as best he could, his feelings were beyond control. That Anshi should have been attacked by evil spirits just when she was expecting a child—that, he thought, was what made her situation so dangerous. She had grown alarmingly weak in the course of her long illness, and it seemed that each breath might be her last.

Emperor Murakami's most trusted ladies went by turns to observe the Empress's condition. Alarmed by their reports, the Emperor ordered more and more prayers, until at length the clamor was quite deafening, but nothing seemed to help. He was frantic with worry.

Of the many spirits that tormented the Empress, the most frightening was Major Counselor Motokata's, which seemed determined to claim her life. The spirit also revealed an intense hatred of Crown Prince Norihira. Gloomy thoughts filled the Crown Prince's mind, and messengers shuttled in and out of the Imperial Palace day and night. The Empress's brothers were in despair.

Finally the pains of approaching childbirth added to Empress Anshi's misery. The necessary preparations took place, and the assembled monks set up a tremendous chanting of sutras.[79] Anshi seemed alarmingly close to death. It was not even certain that she was still breathing. The throng of people in the chamber and its environs all joined in frantic supplications to the gods and buddhas, and presently, to their great delight, a baby's cry was heard. Then there was a commotion about the afterbirth, but in the midst of it all Anshi's spirit fled. It was the Twenty-ninth of the Fourth Month in the fourth year of Ōwa [964].[80] Words cannot describe such an event. I must leave it to the reader's imagination.

79. When a birth was imminent, the woman and her attendants put on white clothing; the lying-in chamber was equipped with white curtains and screens, white-edged mats, etc.; and Buddhist esoteric rites were performed to ensure a safe delivery. For the confinement of an Empress, it was usual for a number of "large rituals" (daihō) to be performed simultaneously by the head monks of the main Shingon and Tendai temples, each with his own entourage. "Goma smoke filled the building," says Heike monogatari, 1: 218, in its description of one such event. "The sound of bells echoed to the clouds, and the chanting voices made the listeners' hair stand on end."

80. The Twenty-ninth, the date of Anshi's death, was the fifth day after the baby's birth. EM, 1: 479, s.n. 48.

That night all the Empress's children left the Palace.[81] The new baby was a girl.[82] The infant's small brothers and sisters were still too young to understand what had happened, but the example of the surrounding adults made them cry.[83] It was most understandable that Prince Tamehira should have flung himself weeping onto the floor. Half-crazed by the news, the Emperor wept aloud with a frightening lack of restraint, and the Crown Prince grieved in a manner so pathetic that all who saw him were moved to tears. (The Prince was in full possession of his faculties while Motokata's spirit was busy with Anshi.) It would be idle merely to call such an occasion sad.

Jijū no Myōbu, whom Anshi had intended to choose as the baby's nurse, set straight about her duties in spite of what had happened. "Alas! If only Her Majesty had come through safely again, how happy we should all be now," Anshi's brothers and ladies-in-waiting kept saying through their tears. Their grief was but natural.

Since the lifeless body could not remain as it was, plans for the cremation were made after an interval of two days. Never were funeral ceremonies more heart-rending.[84] Anshi's body, borne in her own string-decorated carriage,[85] was escorted by the courtiers and senior nobles with whom she had had close ties, a company so numerous that few officials of any consequence could, it seemed, be missing. Most poignant of all was the spectacle of Prince Tamehira as he walked behind the carriage in his somber mourning garb. There were the customary incense and lamp litters, and people of both sexes wore coarse mourning garments over their formal costumes. Every aspect of the ceremonies was indescribably awe-inspiring. Since mourning was prescribed for both the Emperor and the Crown Prince, it was quite as though the parent of a reigning monarch had died, except that the courtiers were attired in garments of bluish-gray.[86]

81. Presumably because they were defiled. EM, 1: 43, n. 44.

82. Princess Senshi (964–1035).

83. In 964 the oldest of Anshi's children, Crown Prince Norihira, was fourteen, and the second oldest, Prince Tamehira, was twelve. Princess Hoshi (953–92) was eleven; Princess Shishi (955–1015) was nine; Prince Morihira (959–91) was five.

84. See s.n. 14.

85. *Itoge no kuruma.* The term, no longer understood, is thought by some scholars to indicate a variety of *birōge no kuruma*, one of the more opulent types of Heian carriage, thatched with bleached, chopped palm leaves (*birō*) from Kyūshū. Scattered literary references indicate the existence of three kinds of *itoge no kuruma*: (1) red, used only by ladies serving as official messengers at the Kamo Festival; (2) purple, used by Junior Consorts, Concubines, and members of the Handmaids' Office, and probably by other ladies of good family; and (3) green (*ao*), used by Empresses, Crown Princes, Regents, and Princes of the Blood. Anshi's was presumably green.

86. *Usunibi. Nibiiro* (dark gray) was the prescribed color after the death of an Emperor.

At the close of the short summer night, all of Anshi's brothers, both lay and clerical, set out together on the pious journey to Kohata.[87]

"Everyone must die sooner or later," the Emperor thought. "But I had not expected to lose her 'yesterday or today.'"[88] Those who witnessed the depth of his feeling could not help marveling at the good fortune of Morosuke's family. Indeed, many who approached the affair from a subject's viewpoint said, "Sad as it is, Anshi was lucky to die while His Majesty was still on the throne."[89]

Prince Morihira was then in his fifth or sixth year, not even old enough to wear mourning.[90] It was pitiful to see him.

The various Buddhist rituals followed the regular pattern, except that everything was more impressive and elaborate than usual. The Emperor kept to a strict regimen of ritual purity, refusing to receive any of the consorts in his bedchamber, even for a few moments of harmless amusement, and abandoning all his customary pursuits so that he might engage in pious works on Anshi's behalf.

The services[91] were celebrated on the Seventeenth of the Sixth Month. Not even the rains of the Fifth Month could have been more abundant than the tears of the grief-stricken mourners, whose sleeves were as drenched as the garments of peasants toiling in the rice fields. Officials from the government bureaus saw to the details of the rites, patterning them after the most imposing Court ceremonies.

All the monks returned to their temples after the Forty-ninth Day services, leaving the Kujō Mansion silent and lonely. But the chief courtiers and senior nobles called as in the past to inquire after the Princes and Princesses, who were still living in the house. It was touching to see Anshi's brothers in attendance there, and the deep mourning worn by the older

87. Anshi was cremated at Kaguraoka, a hill east of Yoshida Shrine in the present Sakyō-ku, Kyōto. The ceremony had been scheduled for the night of the Seventh of the Fifth Month, but high water on the Kamo River forced a postponement until the following morning, and the bones were gathered at the unorthodox hour of 2:00 P.M. or thereabouts. *Nihon kiryaku*, 2: 92 (8 v Kōhō 1). *Eiga* is probably wrong, therefore, in saying that the brothers set out "at the close of the short summer night." Kohata, in the northernmost part of the present Uji-shi, Kyōto-fu, was a Fujiwara burial ground, the final resting place of many family heads and Imperial consorts. The visit of Morosuke's sons was to transport their sister's ashes.

88. An allusion to *Kokinshū* 861, the death poem of Ariwara Narihira (825–80): Tsui ni yuku / michi to wa kanete / kikishikado / kinō kyō to wa / omowazarishi o. ("This road, I have long been told, man travels in the end—yet I had not thought to go yesterday or today.")

89. Because her funeral and the associated rituals would otherwise have been less impressive.

90. Mourning was not prescribed for children under the age of seven (sai). EM, 1: 479, s.n. 51.

91. The Forty-ninth Day services, held at the Hosshōji. *Nihon kiryaku*, 2: 93 (17 vi Kōhō 1).

children was also most pathetic. There were two or three Palace women about—the nurse Jijū, Shōni, and Suke, members of Anshi's entourage who had also been in the Emperor's service.[92]

All those things were sad indeed, and they affected Emperor Murakami deeply. But men are a wretched lot. Toward the end of the Sixth Month the Emperor sent off a letter to Prince Shigeakira's widow Tōshi, who was, he felt sure, also suffering from a sense of loneliness and bereavement. The news was a shock to Anshi's younger brothers[93]—and indeed to the older ones as well—for Morosuke's sons had relied on their sister as on a father or master, and her death had been like the extinction of a torch for them all.

When Anshi's children visited the Palace, a discreet entrance was also arranged for the new Princess.[94] The sight of her made the Emperor's heart ache with pity and grief. She was a sweet, appealing infant. For her Fiftieth Day ceremonies, which took place in the city,[95] everyone wore garments of unrelieved black.

Although Tōshi had been happy to receive the Emperor's letter after so long a silence, she felt nervous and timid whenever she thought of the spirits of the dead.[96] A succession of other messengers arrived with notes urging her to come to the Palace, but she felt that she was not in a position to consult her inclinations. While she was still trying to make up her mind, the Emperor had a confidential talk with some of her brothers. It was up to them, he said, to see that she came. It grieved the brothers to recall that Anshi had always pretended ignorance of this liaison, even though she must have known about it for years, but they assented respectfully and went straight to Tōshi's house. "You had better waste no time in presenting yourself at the Palace," they said.

To Tōshi the proposal seemed a bit improper. "This would not be the first time . . . ," she murmured in confusion. But they insisted that it was all perfectly natural.

92. Nothing is known of Jijū. Shōni and Suke are perhaps to be identified with two obscure women whose names appear in connection with Court poetry contests, and, in Shōni's case, in several anthologies of verse. EM, 1: 479, s.n. 53; 1: 480, s.n. 54.

93. With the exception of Koretada and Kanemichi, all the brothers were younger than Anshi.

94. Offspring of the Heian nobility ordinarily lived in their mothers' homes. As the author mentions elsewhere, it had once been thought necessary to wait as long as six or seven years before taking an Imperial child to meet his or her father. The custom was no longer rigidly observed in Murakami's day, but it was still considered improper for an infant to be brought into the Palace.

95. Probably at the Kujō Mansion.

96. Anshi and Prince Shigeakira. The spirits, if displeased, might attack her.

The Emperor probably instructed the Palace Storehouse Bureau to send over everything that was needed for a formal entry.[97]

Presently Tōshi decided to go ahead. In spite of her brothers' earlier advice, they were uncooperative when it came to the actual preparations. Their behavior must have cost her many misgivings, but she made her entrance and took up residence in the Tōkaden. From then on, it was always Tōshi who shared the Emperor's bed. The other consorts had no chance to visit the Imperial Apartments.

"His Majesty might have been less hasty," grumbled Anshi's attendants and the children's nurses. "This is hardly the time for such conduct." Some of them even put about the scandalous story that a curse uttered by Tōshi had been the cause of Anshi's death.

Outraged that such a thing should have happened while they were still mourning the friendly and considerate Empress, the Imperial consorts vented their jealousy and dissatisfaction in cruel slanders and criticisms. Emperor Murakami's neglect of state affairs also led to caustic comment, for after Tōshi's arrival he was closeted with her day and night. Now that she was living in the Palace, he loved her even better than in the hopeless days when resignation had seemed his only course, and he would gladly have given her the title of Empress if she had not borne another man's children. He made her a Principal Handmaid instead.[98]

The brothers sulked awhile, but the Emperor's devotion to Tōshi was beyond question, and in the end they seem to have consoled themselves with the reflection that she was, after all, their sister, however frail such a tie might prove.

To Saneyori the affair seemed lamentable. "What a pity that an indiscretion in his later years should have brought censure on a sovereign so universally admired," he said. Seldom indeed did the Emperor invite another consort to share his bed, and whenever Tōshi was with him he slept until all hours in the morning, showing a shocking lack of concern

97. As an Imperial bride. Preparations for the presentation of an Imperial bride, an event known as *judai*, were extremely expensive and time-consuming for the girl's family. They included arrangements necessary in connection with the bride's acquisition of Court rank, the selection and outfitting of ladies-in-waiting, the accumulation of a gorgeous trousseau, the borrowing or manufacture of carriages and other things required for the bridal procession, the assembling of elegant furnishings for the bride's Palace apartments, arrangements for elaborate entertainments, the provision of many kinds of presents, and a wide variety of religious activities. In Tōshi's case, the scale of the event was probably considerably reduced. (It is known, for example, that she did not receive Court rank.) See Chapter 8, below; and Joüon des Longrais 1965, *passim*.

98. According to *Nihon kiryaku*, 2: 114 (10 x Anna 2), it was not until after the death of Emperor Murakami that Tōshi became a Principal Handmaid.

for his responsibilities. "Why doesn't His Majesty sleep at night?" the scandalized gentlemen and ladies-in-waiting could not help thinking.

Having heard that his third daughter, Princess Hōshi, played the zither[99] with exceptional skill, Emperor Murakami had suggested several times to the girl's mother, Masahime, that she let her perform for him; and Masahime, greatly pleased, had made her preparations[100] and brought the Princess to the Palace. One day when the Emperor had nothing better to do, he crossed over to Masahime's apartments.

"Where is Princess Hōshi?" he asked.

"Come here," said Masahime to the Princess.

The Princess, a sweet-faced, elegant child of twelve or thirteen, advanced on her knees. It was a pity she could not have been a shade less formal. The Emperor, who felt the same warm affection for all his children, gazed at her with loving eyes, but perhaps he noticed a certain resemblance to her mother, who, despite her beauty, was somewhat stiff, conservative, and old-fashioned—not quite the sort of person one longs to meet. The Princess, however, was still young, and she made an agreeable impression of grace and charm. As she began to perform with admirable skill, the Emperor said to her mother, "Are you listening? What's that she's playing?"

Masahime inched forward on her knees, three-foot curtains[101] and all—at which the Emperor looked annoyed—and answered, "She is playing a song that goes like this":

> Journeying on a road with others,
> I came upon a sutra-roll.
> I took it up;
> I opened it and chanted.
> Of all the teachings
> Of the Enlightened One,
> It was the *Heart Sutra*
> Of the great *Prajñā*![102]

99. Koto. The character used in the text suggests that the Princess played the *kin no koto*, a seven-stringed instrument.

100. This probably means that she assembled new costumes for herself, her ladies, and the Princess.

101. "Curtains" translates *kichō*, a portable curtain-stand set up inside a room to ensure privacy and keep out drafts. Usually about three or four feet tall and six or eight feet long, a kichō consisted of black lacquered supporting members (a foot, two vertical supports, and a top horizontal bar) to which trailing silk curtains (*katabira*) decorated with streamers were attached. It appears to have been an invention of the early tenth century.

102. Probably unfamiliar to the Emperor because it was an *imayō* ("modern song"). The vocal genre known as imayō, still a relative novelty at Court during Murakami's reign, reached

Her reply was really too obtuse, the Emperor thought.[103] To her em-barrassment, he made no attempt to respond, and his rather evident exas-peration probably caused a good deal of gossip afterward. That kind of thing happened too.

"When Her Majesty the Empress presented the Ninth Princess,[104] every-thing was quite perfect," said the Emperor's ladies-in-waiting, who mourned the late Empress with touching devotion. Indeed Anshi had been so gen-erous, so truly the mother of the nation, so kind and considerate in her relations with other consorts, that even her rivals remembered her with affection.

Those were happy days for Tōshi, except for a sad event involving her brother Takamitsu, the Lesser Captain. Takamitsu was one of Morosuke's favorite sons, known in his childhood as Machiosa no Kimi.[105] He had been in wretched spirits since Anshi's death. One night, as a brilliant full moon rose in the sky, he composed a poem:

> Kaku bakari   In this world
> Hegataku miyuru   Where life is so hard,
> Yo no naka ni   How enviable the moon,
> Urayamashiku mo   Clear and untroubled![106]
> Sumeru tsuki kana.

He became a Buddhist monk at dawn on the following morning.[107] The Emperor was deeply affected, and everyone felt a poignant sense of loss.

Takamitsu lived with exemplary piety in a hermitage at a place called Tōnomine, but he could not forget his daughter, a sweet child of three or four, whose beloved memory had pursued him up the mountainside, and

---

the peak of its popularity in the late Heian period. Numerous sets of lyrics were sung, with musical accompaniment, to the melodies of a few favorite *gagaku* (Court music) compositions, notably the well-known "Etenraku." The lyrics were often adapted from simple Buddhist hymns, but there were many secular and Shintō pieces as well. The form was irregular, al-though there was a tendency to shape it into four or eight lines of alternating five-syllable and seven- or eight-syllable length. For the *Heart Sutra*, a one-page summary of the great *Wisdom Sutras* (Hannyagyō; Skt. *Prajñāpāramitā-sūtra*), see Ch'en 1964, p. 58.

103. Because she had launched into a long-winded explanation instead of giving the name of the song.

104. Princess Shishi. The text implies that the preceding episode was Emperor Murakami's first encounter with Masahime's daughter. *Shōkai*, 1: 78.

105. Or Machiosagimi. For a son of a Regent family the pre-genpuku name (*warawana*) ended in *kimi* (or *gimi*); for others of the nobility, in *maro*. EM, 1: 49, n. 40.

106. The poem, in which the moon symbolizes the peace of mind that comes from Buddhist enlightenment, hints at Takamitsu's desire to become a monk.

107. Takamitsu (b. ca. 940) is remembered as a poet and as the protagonist of the tale mentioned below. He took Buddhist vows in the Twelfth Month of 961, i.e. before the death of Empress Anshi.

so he kept in touch with the mother.[108] The little girl cried "Papa" whenever she saw a man's picture on a folding screen. If I remember correctly,
a story has been written about it all.[109] Someone is sure to mention Takamitsu whenever people speak of sad things.

Time passed swiftly, and soon it was the twentieth year of Emperor
Murakami's reign. His Majesty would have liked to abdicate in order to
be able to do as he pleased for a change, but the senior nobles refused to
hear of it.

The Emperor planned a moon-viewing banquet for the night of the
Fifteenth of the Eighth Month in the third year of Kōhō [966].[110] Two opposing teams were to produce artificial gardens in front of the Seiryōden.[111]
The leader of the Left was Chamberlain Lesser Captain Naritoki, the
Superintendent of the Office of Painting,[112] who was the son of Morotada
and the elder brother of the Sen'yōden Consort Hōshi. The leader of the
Right was Morosuke's ninth son, Tamemitsu, the Lesser Captain who
supervised the Office of Palace Works. Both sides worked furiously, determined not to be outdone. The contestants from the Office of Painting
submitted a painted landscape tray depicting flowering plants of heavenly
beauty, a garden stream, and massive rocks. Various kinds of insects were
lodged in a rustic fence made of silver foil. The artists had also painted a
view of the Ōi River, showing figures strolling nearby and cormorant boats
with basket fires. Near the insects there was a poem.[113]

The Office of Palace Works presented an interesting tray, carved with
great ingenuity to resemble a beach at high tide, which they had planted

108. Takamitsu's wife was a daughter of Morosuke's full brother Morouji (913?–70).
Their daughter later married one of Emperor Murakami's sons, Prince Akihira (954?–1013),
and became the mother of a daughter who married Fujiwara Kintō (966–1041). Shōkai, 5:
131. Tōnomine, a hill inside the boundaries of the present Sakurai-shi, Shiki-gun, Nara-ken,
was the site of a Buddhist temple and the burial place of Kamatari, founder of the house of
Fujiwara. Takamitsu moved there after a preliminary sojourn at Mount Hiei.

109. Tōnomine shōshō monogatari, also known as Takamitsu nikki. (One kan; thought
to have been compiled by someone in Takamitsu's service.) The work, an account of Takamitsu's renunciation of the world, consists primarily of melancholy poems exchanged between
the new monk and his wife and sisters, including Anshi, during his stay at Mount Hiei.

110. See s.n. 15.

111. Other sources specify the location as the twin courtyards on the west side of the
Seiryōden. EM, 1: 480, s.n. 57. The judging presumably took place on one of the adjacent
verandas. See the illustration opposite.

112. Edokoro, of which little is known aside from the fact that it occupied a small building
near Kenshunmon Gate and employed numerous skilled artists, who produced not only
paintings but also pictorial designs for ladies' trains and formal jackets. Wada 1953, p. 181.

113. Landscape trays (suhama) were low trays, irregularly shaped to suggest the indenta-
tions of a shoreline, on which real or artificial plants, birds, rocks, etc. were arranged. See
s.n. 16.

Emperor Murakami's moon-viewing banquet at the Seiryōden. "The contestants from the Office of Painting submitted a painted landscape tray depicting flowering plants of heavenly beauty, a garden stream, and massive rocks. Various kinds of insects were lodged in a rustic fence made of silver foil. The artists had also painted a view of the Ōi River, showing figures strolling nearby and cormorant boats with basket-fires. . . . The Office of Palace Works presented an interesting tray, carved with great ingenuity to resemble a beach at high tide, which they had planted with artificial flowers and carved bamboo and pines."

with artificial flowers and carved bamboo and pines. Their poem was attached to a spray of fresh *ominaeshi*.[114]

The poem of the Left:

Kimi ga tame	We did not tell the crickets
Hana uesomu to	That the flowers were planted
Tsugenedomo	For His Majesty's sake,
Chiyo matsumushi no	Yet their song echoes our hope
Ne ni zo nakinuru.	For a reign of a thousand years.[115]

The poem of the Right:

Kokoro shite	Though to some you may appear
Kotoshi wa nioe	Man-made flowers—
Ominaeshi	This year,
Sakanu hana zo to	*Ominaeshi*,
Hito wa miru tomo.	Bloom with all your might.

There was music, and gifts were distributed among the many senior nobles in attendance.[116] Once again memories of Anshi moved the Emperor and others to tears. "When the Empress was alive, occasions like this were wonderfully gay and amusing," they lamented.[117] However diverting the entertainment, the desire to abdicate was never absent from Emperor Murakami's mind.

Thus the seasons alternated, the months and days passed, and the fourth year of Kōhō [967] began. The Emperor, who had been ailing for some months, was observing one period of ritual seclusion after another. Fearing the worst, he was also sponsoring sutra-readings and multiple-altar rites, but nothing seemed to help.[118] Motokata's ranting ghost had appeared—a sure sign, the Emperor thought in despair, that his days were numbered.

114. *Patrinia scabiosaefolia*, sometimes called maidenflower. The ominaeshi, one of the "seven plants of autumn," is a long-stemmed perennial bearing clusters of small yellow flowers.

115. *Chiyo*, the sound made by the crickets, can mean "a thousand years." There is also a play on *chiyo matsu*, "await a thousand years," and *matsumushi*, "cricket."

116. The gifts probably consisted of garments and/or cloth. Hagitani 1957–69, 2: 461.

117. Probably a reference to the famous poetry contest held in the Third Month of the fourth year of Tentoku (960), which also took place on the Seiryōden and Kōrōden verandas overlooking the two patio gardens. Staged on a lavish scale by Emperor Murakami at the request of the ladies of the Court, the event ended at 5:00 A.M. with the withdrawal of the Emperor and the subsequent exit, dancing, of the inebriated guests. See *ibid.*, 2: 339–416.

118. According to *Nihon kiryaku*, 2: 100 (14 v Kōhō 4), the Emperor fell ill only twelve days before his death. The pious works included the expounding of the *Benevolent King Sutra* at a number of temples, and the erection in twenty-six provinces of sixty pillars bearing sacred texts. EM, 1: 480, s.n. 58.

He had previously been eager to abdicate, but now he must have thought, "If death is inevitable, let me meet it as a reigning monarch."[119]

When the Emperor had sunk very low, Saneyori ventured a private inquiry. "If the worst happens, who is to be the next Crown Prince?" he asked. "It was always my wish to nominate Prince Tamehira," the Emperor replied, "but that has become impossible, so I suppose it must be Prince Morihira."[120] Saneyori assented respectfully.

It would be idle merely to say that the Emperor's desperate state reduced the Imperial Family and consorts to tears. Terrified of becoming a laughingstock, Tōshi was pitifully distraught.

In spite of all that could be done, Emperor Murakami breathed his last on the Twenty-fifth of the Fifth Month. Crown Prince Norihira succeeded to the throne.[121]

Alas! To what can one possibly compare Emperor Murakami's tragic death? It was as though banks of clouds had come from nowhere to enshroud a celestial orb shining in all its glory, or as though every light in the Imperial Palace had been snuffed out. How meaningless it is to call such an event "inexpressibly sad"! The courtiers and senior nobles stamped the floor in an agony of grief, sobbing, "We shall never see such a ruler again! If only we might perish too!"

Since there had been no public announcement about the identity of the new Crown Prince, people were free to speculate as they pleased. It was really rather amusing. "Saneyori must know," everyone said. "Why is he so closemouthed?"

All the last rites were celebrated with the utmost magnificence. On the night of the funeral, special duties were assigned at an appointments ceremony, during which the tears of the participants and the pervading atmosphere of gloom and sorrow were in mournful contrast to the joyous excitement that ordinarily accompanied the announcement of new appointments. Scarcely a courtier or senior noble was left without a function; and indeed, with so many accompanying the body, the Courtiers' Hall was all but deserted.

Amid ceremonies splendid beyond description, the Emperor was laid to rest at Murakami,[122] and at the close of the short summer night the

---

119. It appears, however, that he actually took religious vows on the first day of his illness. *Ichidai yōki*, p. 137.

120. Prince Tamehira lacked influential support. Morosuke and Anshi, his only Fujiwara backers after his marriage to Minamoto Takaakira's daughter, were both dead.

121. Emperor Reizei.

122. Thus the name by which he is now known. The site of his tomb is in Sakyō-ku, Kyōto, behind the Myōkōji.

mourners went back to the city. The last rites for an abdicated Emperor, though dignified and impressive, do not differ notably from those for a subject, but all agreed that this funeral for a reigning sovereign had been a rare and marvelous spectacle.

The days slipped by in a series of Buddhist services,[123] each celebrated with great pomp and solemnity, but all very much the same. It was touching to see the Imperial children and consorts in their garments of black. In a sense, the period of national mourning was no different from any other, but so widespread were the observances that the people of the nation seemed transformed into a congregation of crows. Surely, one felt, there could be no mountain left in Japan where beech trees still survived![124]

When things had more or less returned to normal after the final Buddhist rituals, it was generally supposed that the name of the new Crown Prince would be announced soon. At Prince Tamehira's, where word from Saneyori had been awaited in an atmosphere of discreet expectancy, the minister's prolonged silence created painful misgivings. Takaakira was also greatly worried by the possibility that his son-in-law might be passed over.

On the First of the Ninth Month, Prince Morihira became the Crown Prince. He was nine years old, and Emperor Reizei was eighteen. The new Emperor's consort, Princess Shōshi, received the title of Empress on the day of his accession,[125] thus happily fulfilling the cherished ambition of her father, ex-Emperor Suzaku. Consultant Tomohira became Master of the Empress's Household, Middle Counselor Morouji, Master of the Crown Prince's Household, and Morotada, Mentor to the Crown Prince.[126] Morouji and Morotada were Morosuke's brothers. Morosuke's sons were probably still too junior for such appointments.[127]

When Emperor Reizei was in possession of his faculties, his manner much resembled that of Emperor Murakami. He was, if anything, hand-

123. The Forty-ninth Day services, held in the Seiryōden, are said by Heian chroniclers to have been especially impressive. EM, 1: 53, n. 26.

124. Shades of gray and black in textiles were produced from the nuts and bark of beech trees (*shii*, a term that referred to genera of the beech family [Fagaceae], usually to varieties of the *Catanopsis cuspidata*, a relative of the California and Oregon chinquapin, but sometimes also to *Lithocarpus edulis* and *L. glabra*, close relatives of the oak).

125. Actually on 4 ix 967.

126. On Morouji and Morotada, see s.n. 4. Morotada was a Major Counselor (Dainagon) at the time. Fujiwara Tomohira (917–74; sometimes called Tomonari), the "repulsively fat" but able and ambitious son of a former Minister of the Right, made an enemy of the future Regent Koretada when the two were competing for a Consultancy, and therefore never advanced beyond the office of Middle Counselor.

127. See s.n. 17.

somer than his father. What a pity that the malignant spirits persecuted him so mercilessly!

The Imperial Purification and Thanksgiving did not take place that year.[128]

Saneyori became Chancellor on the Thirteenth of the Twelfth Month.[129] Takaakira replaced him as Minister of the Left, and Morotada became Minister of the Right. But Takaakira's promotion failed to console him for his son-in-law's cruel and unexpected disappointment.

The year ended, and in the following year [968] the era name was changed to Anna. The New Year appointments brought happiness to many of the nobility, among them Morosuke's eldest son, Koretada, who took his place among the more exalted of the senior nobles by assuming the office of Major Counselor.[130] Koretada at once set about making a Junior Consort of Kaishi, the eldest of his numerous daughters, whom he intended to present in the Second Month.[131] Empress Shōshi withdrew from the Palace when she heard the news. In any case, the Empress frequently lived elsewhere out of fear of the spirits that possessed the Emperor.

The reader may imagine the splendor of the new consort's entry on the First of the Second Month. Emperor Reizei took to her at once, and she became pregnant very soon. Indeed, it all happened so quickly that Koretada, in some trepidation, took all possible pains with the prayers.[132] The Emperor was delighted. Everything went off beautifully when Kaishi made her announcement and left the Palace during her third month. Morosuke's luck was as good as ever, the gossips said. Even after her departure, the Emperor thought about her with great solicitude.

Meanwhile Empress Shōshi had returned. She was a lady of the utmost nobility, dignity, and elegance.

Now that the mourning robes of the preceding year had been laid aside,

128. See s.n. 18.

129. He already held the office of Regent (Kanpaku), to which he had been appointed in the Sixth Month.

130. Koretada had been named a Provisional Major Counselor in the Twelfth Month of 967. He did not become a Major Counselor proper until 969.

131. Kaishi (945–75), who probably was Koretada's second daughter, had actually married Reizei while he was still Crown Prince, had become an Imperial Concubine at the time of his accession, and had received the title of Junior Consort in the Ninth Month of 967. The following account of her presentation is therefore not to be taken seriously. She later had two daughters, as well as a son, the future Emperor Kazan (968–1008; r. 984–86), whose birth is described below. During her son's reign she was given the posthumous title of Grand Empress.

132. For a safe delivery.

there was a great fuss about the Purification and Thanksgiving ceremonies. Those were times in which many auspicious and entertaining events took place—and many moving and sad ones too.

Since Major Counselor Koretada lived at Ichijō, he was known as the Ichijō Lord.[133] His daughter, the Junior Consort, gave birth to her child just as things had quieted down a bit after the rush of preparations for the great ceremonies.[134] Most fortunately, as everyone remarked, it was a boy. It would be idle to attempt a description of all the events that took place while the child was in the lying-in chamber. A procession of callers, including Chancellor Saneyori, kept the premises crowded and noisy. On the Seventh Night, the mansion was visited by the entire student contingent from the Kangakuin,[135] as well as by the staffs of the ministries of Ceremonial and Popular Affairs, all of whom performed respectful obeisances in honor of the infant who would, they were confident, one day reign over the empire. What a shame, thought the happy grandfather, that Morosuke could not have lived to witness the sight. He would still have been only a little past sixty.

The Fiftieth Day ceremonies, following in due course those of the Seventh, were celebrated with indescribable splendor.

It may be supposed that Takaakira, the Genji Minister of State, was much affected by Prince Tamehira's disappointment. Emperor Murakami's remarkable partiality for the Prince had been common gossip, but that had not been enough to secure him the succession. Perhaps misfortune was the Prince's lot in life. To ascend the Imperial throne is not easy, however it may appear.

During Prince Tamehira's boyhood, the Emperor and Empress had once arranged an outing for him on a Day of the Rat.[136] The Emperor had had the Prince's mount brought in so that he might superintend the saddling, and had sent the youth off along the path beside the Kokiden[137] after an in-

133. See s.n. 19.
134. The child was born on the Twenty-sixth of the Tenth Month of 968, the date of the Imperial Purification. *Nihon kiryaku*, 1: 109 (26 x Anna 1).
135. The Kangakuin, founded by Fuyutsugu (775–826) in 811 and supervised by successive heads of the house, contributed to the education of Fijuwara youths, and to their official advancement, by providing them with financial assistance and lodgings during their period of study at the adjacent state university (Daigaku), and by supporting them in their efforts to gain office after graduation. On auspicious family occasions, such as the installation of an Empress, the birth of an Imperial child, or the appointment of a Minister of State, the students came with their Superintendents to convey congratulations, present songs (*rōei*), and receive gifts.
136. In 964. Prince Tamehira was twelve at the time. See s.n. 20.
137. The path ran alongside the western veranda of the Kokiden, Anshi's residence. The

spection of the entire company, including the falconers and dog handlers. The enormous retinue included Shigemitsu no Ason, the Middle Captain of the Left; Nobumitsu no Ason, the Head Chamberlain Middle Captain of the Right; Yasumitsu no Ason, the Senior Assistant Minister of Ceremonial; Kanemichi no Ason, the Provisional Master of the Empress's Household; and Kaneie no Ason, the Senior Assistant Minister of War—all brothers of the Empress or sons of Prince Yoakira, the Minister of Central Affairs, who was a son of Emperor Daigo.[138] (By this time they were all grown men.[139]) They were a splendid sight as they scattered over Funaoka Hill in their elegant hunting robes, accompanied by three or four carriage-loads of the Empress's ladies, whose white silk trains, decorated with seashore patterns, trailed below the blinds of their conveyances. It was odd afterward to hear tales of the comments of those ladies, who had kept repeating that Prince Tamehira's prospects were as flourishing as the luxuriant green pine trees on Funaoka Hill. The Prince's misfortune provoked much sympathetic comment, even from outsiders. "Prince Tamehira seemed certain to be the next Emperor," people said. "What happened to him? He lost the throne when he married Takaakira's daughter."

Because of the severity of Emperor Reizei's possession, he was kept under constant surveillance by the senior nobles and members of his mother's family; and rumors of impending abdication, inspired by his melancholy condition, recurred with disagreeable frequency. It was widely held that a short reign always succeeded a long one, and everyone expected the Emperor to step down once he had begun his third year (in the second year of Anna [969]). But then some disturbing stories began to circulate, and a most unpleasant charge was directed against Minamoto Takaakira, the Minister of the Left, who had, it seemed, formulated plans for a revolt because of what had happened to Prince Tamehira. Most people considered the accusation shameful, but whether the gods and buddhas had been negligent[140] or whether Takaakira's intentions had indeed been questionable, the Imperial Police surrounded the minister's mansion on the Twenty-sixth of the Third Month, and an emissary read out an Imperial Decree: "For the crime of having attempted to overthrow the Emperor, you are

---

party headed north toward Funaoka, a small hill outside the city that was a favorite destination for such outings.

138. See s.n. 21.

139. "By this time" (*ima*) appears to mean "around the beginning of Emperor Reizei's reign," the period with which the author has most recently been dealing. As indicated in s.n. 21, however, all five men were already adults at the time of the outing in 964.

140. I.e. had failed to protect him.

to be sent into exile as Provisional Governor-General of the Dazaifu."

The police bundled Takaakira off in a wickerwork carriage, which they held to be quite good enough for a man with no rank.[141] Prince Tamehira begged desperately to share his fate, certain that he was to blame for a misfortune which would have been unspeakably dreadful in any case. I shall not waste time by trying to describe the feelings of the accused man's wife, daughters, and sons inside the mansion; the reader can perhaps imagine them.[142] Long familiar with tales of the exile of another great minister, Sugawara Michizane, [143] and now dazed by the same cruel blow, they wept and lamented in pathetic fashion.

The police had restrained Takaakira's older sons when they tried to follow the carriage; but when the Court learned of the frenzied grief of the minister's youngest and favorite son, it was decreed that he alone might accompany the exile, although he was obliged to ride on horseback instead of sharing the carriage. He was a lad of not more than eleven or twelve.[144]

Takaakira's banishment was the most distressing event of the era—far worse than anyone's death, for death is, after all, a natural occurrence. Everyone was shocked and indignant that such a tragedy should have struck down a man who bore the Minamoto surname and was the first son of the wise and saintly Emperor Daigo.[145]

Had Prince Tamehira been free to consult his inclinations, he would have become a monk, but it was impossible for him to abandon his frail young children,[146] to say nothing of the mother-in-law who now looked

141. The kind of carriage used, called *ajiroguruma*, was made of bamboo or cypress-bark wickerwork. The body was usually green with yellow figures. As a Minister of State, Takaakira would have been entitled to the more highly regarded *birōge no kuruma* (palm-leaf carriage), but the wickerwork carriage was a respectable conveyance, used frequently on ordinary occasions by even the highest officials, and forbidden to persons of Sixth or lower rank.

142. Takaakira's principal wife was Morosuke's third daughter, San no Kimi (?–?). His sons by her were (1) Tadataka (?–?), who became a monk in 969; (2) Korekata (b. before 960), never a kugyō; (3) Toshikata (960–1027), later a friend of the Regent Michitaka (953–95), a Provisional Major Counselor and for many years an official in Empress Shōshi's successive Households; and (4) Tsunefusa (969–1023), eventually a Middle Counselor. He is known to have had at least two daughters (later married to Fujiwara Michinaga and Minamoto Shigenobu) in addition to the one who married Prince Tamehira, but it is not certain that San no Kimi was their mother. EM, 1: 58, n. 2; *Sonpi bunmyaku*, 3: 462ff.

143. Michizane (845–903), probably the most famous exile in Japanese history, was a Minister of the Right whose career was destroyed by the Fujiwara.

144. The reference is presumably to Takaakira's third son, Toshikata, who was ten (sai) in 969. The youngest son, Tsunefusa, was born in 969.

145. Takaakira was Emperor Daigo's tenth son. It is possible that a copyist's error has changed the meaning of the text, which may have read (correctly), "the first son . . . to assume the Minamoto surname."

146. In the course of his life, the Prince fathered six known Minamoto sons, none of whom

to him as her sole support. I need not say that his spirits were miserably depressed. At Takaakira's mansion where he lived,[147] the stagnant, inert waters of the weed-choked pond and stream seemed to symbolize the heavy hearts of the grief-stricken household, and the once meticulously tended plants rioted and tangled in an indescribably dismal manner. His brain numbed by despair, the Prince gave himself up to mournful recollections of earlier days, weeping so constantly that his sleeves were never dry, and living completely in the past. It was a tragic and shocking affair.

Takaakira's youngest daughter, a little girl of five or six, was taken in to be tenderly reared as a Princess by the minister's brother, Emperor Daigo's fifteenth son, who had no daughter of his own.[148] Everyone considered the adoption touching.

It was reported that Takaakira had become a monk.[149]

Time passed, and presently the announcement of the Emperor's abdication created a stir. (No doubt heaven had ordained that it was time for his reign to end.) The event took place on the Thirteenth of the Eighth Month in the second year of Anna [969]. After the abdication, the eleven-year-old Crown Prince assumed the Imperial dignity.[150] To the delight of the grandfather, Koretada, the heir apparency passed to the retired sovereign's infant son, Prince Morosada.

Since the ex-Emperor had gone to live at the Reizeiin,[151] he came to be known as Reizeiin.

The Crown Prince was two years old.

---

rose beyond the office of Consultant (Sangi); and at least three daughters, including Princess Enshi (972–98; Nyōgo of Emperor Kazan; later wife of Fujiwara Sanesuke) and Princess Kyōshi (b. 984; Ise Virgin, 986–1011). Since Yorisada (977–1020), who is believed to have been the second son, was not born until 977; since Enshi and Kyōshi, the only other offspring for whom birth dates are available, were also born well after 969; and since Tamehira himself was only seventeen in 969, it is unlikely that his responsibilities embraced more than one or two children at the time of Takaakira's exile.

147. The Nishinomiya Mansion, said to have occupied a site north of Shijō and west of Suzaku. EM, 1: 59, n. 18.

148. The child was Meishi, who married Michinaga in 988. If *Eiga* is correct, she was a year or two older than Michinaga, who was four (sai) in 969. After the death of her uncle, Prince Moriakira (928–86), she became the protégée of Michinaga's sister Senshi (962–1002), the consort of Emperor En'yū. *Ōkagami*, p. 208.

149. According to other sources, Takaakira took Buddhist vows an hour or two before the order for his demotion was issued. EMZ, 1: 160.

150. Emperor En'yū, third son of Murakami and Anshi. His successor was the son of Reizei and Kaishi, Emperor Kazan, whose birth has just been described.

151. The Reizeiin was bounded by four avenues: Ōimikado, Nijō, Horikawa, and Ōmiya. A palatial establishment built by Emperor Saga in the ninth century, it served for 200 or more years as an interim residence for reigning and retired Emperors, and as a repository for books and other Imperial possessions. It was destroyed by fire in 949, was rebuilt in 960, and burned again in 970, after which it was not rebuilt until 1008.

Saneyori was named Regent; Morotada, Minister of the Left.[152] Then
on the Fifteenth of the Tenth Month, just as everyone was busy with preparations for the forthcoming Purification and Thanksgiving, it was announced that Morotada had died at the age of fifty. He had been ailing
for some time. His daughter Hōshi (the Sen'yōden Consort), his sons, and
all his other relatives were dazed with grief.[153] In view of the imminence of
the Thanksgiving, it was considered a great pity that his brother, the Regent Saneyori, would have to go into mourning, but the Court limited
Saneyori's mourning period to a month, pointing out that Morotada had
been only a younger half-brother.[154] The old customs are sadly disregarded.

The rest of the year passed swiftly in the usual round of ceremonies for
the dead. At the exorcism rites[155] on the last day of the old year, it was
amusing to watch the little Emperor's glee as he brandished the rattle
drums presented by one of the courtiers.

New Year's Day ushered in the first year of Tenroku [970]. Brilliant skies
added to the splendor of the traditional ceremonies.[156]

Arihira, the nobleman who had replaced Morotada as Minister of the
Left, fell ill and died on the Twenty-seventh of the First Month at the age
of seventy-eight—an ominous event at the beginning of a new year.[157]
Everyone close to him went into mourning. Koretada was the new Minister
of the Right.[158]

To Saneyori's alarm, he was finding it difficult to visit the Imperial Palace
because of a disorder of the nervous system; and Koretada was being
discreetly cultivated by gentlemen who assumed that he would succeed
to the regency if anything happened. (Saneyori's second son, Yoritada, was
then a mere Major Captain in the Bodyguards of the Left.[159]) Saneyori

152. Morotada's promotion (25 iii 969) had preceded the accession of En'yū.
153. Hōshi had died in 967. It is not clear whether Sadatoki was still alive, or whether
Naritoki was in fact Morotada's only surviving child.
154. The mourning period for a half-brother with a different father was one month, but
in this case it was the mothers who were different. (Morotada's mother was a daughter of
Fujiwara Yoshiari; Saneyori's, a daughter of Emperor Uda.) *Eiga* is wrong, however, in
saying that the Thanksgiving ceremonies took place in 969. As was usual when an Emperor ascended the throne after the Seventh Month, they were held in the following year.
See s.n. 9; s.n. 18; and EM, 1: 481, s.n. 68.
155. *Tsuina*. See s.n. 22.   156. See s.n. 23.
157. Since inauspicious events were considered capable of establishing a precedent for the
coming months, they were especially unwelcome at the beginning of the year. The date given
here, however, is that of Arihira's appointment as Minister of the Left. He died in the Tenth
Month.
158. He had replaced Arihira in the First Month.
159. Yoritada, then thirty-six, was a Middle Counselor and Major Captain of the Right.

was soon critically ill, and his evident misery, coupled with his advanced years, excited the gravest fears for this minister who had clung with such tenacity to life, surviving two of his younger brothers.[160] He took all possible precautions, but a man's existence cannot be prolonged at will, and in spite of every effort he died on the Eighteenth of the Fifth Month. He received the posthumous name Seishinkō, Honorable and Prudent Lord. It was admirable that he should have died without transferring the regency to Yoritada. His age was seventy-one. We live, alas, in a world of sorrows.

Major Counselor Morouji, the last of Tadahira's four sons, died on the Fourteenth of the Seventh Month. He was fifty-five.

On the Twentieth of the Fifth Month, the regency was conferred on Koretada, who thenceforth governed as he pleased, enjoying a favored position as grandfather of the Crown Prince and uncle of the Emperor.[161] There seemed no end to the good fortune of Morosuke's house.

The new Minister of the Left was Minamoto Kaneakira, another of Emperor Daigo's sons who had acquired a commoner's surname.[162] The beauty of Kaneakira's writing was beyond description. One hears frequent praise of calligraphers like Michikaze,[163] but Kaneakira's writing was a marvel of elegance and grace. Yoritada, Saneyori's son, became Minister of the Right.[164]

The second year of Tenroku arrived [971], bringing with it the Coming-of-Age ceremony for the thirteen-year-old Emperor.[165] Imperial Household Minister Kanemichi, Morosuke's second son, who was next in age to the Regent, presented his daughter Kōshi as an Imperial bride.[166] (The Re-

160. Morosuke (d. 960) and Morotada (d. 969).

161. Crown Prince Morosada was the son of Koretada's daughter Kaishi, and Emperor En'yū was the son of Koretada's sister Anshi.

162. Prince Kaneakira (914–87), who had become a Minamoto in 921, was named Minister of the Left in the Eleventh Month of 971, rather than in 970 as the author implies. He lost the post in 977, when, at the instigation of the then Regent, Kanemichi, who wanted to promote Yoritada, the Emperor restored his Princely status and gave him the nominal office of Central Affairs Minister. Considered the best calligrapher of his day, he was also a literatus of some distinction.

163. Ono no Michikaze (894–966), often called Tōfū, a calligrapher who moved away from Chinese models and laid the foundation for the more graceful Japanese style. Michikaze, Fujiwara Sukemasa, and Fujiwara Yukinari (972–1028) have traditionally been called the Three Masters of Japanese-Style Calligraphy (sanseki).

164. In xi 971.

165. Emperor En'yū's genpuku took place in 972, when he was fourteen (sai). Nihon kiryaku, 2: 120 (3 i Tenroku 3).

166. Kōshi (947–79) was not presented until the Second Month of 973, after the appointment of her father as Regent in the Eleventh Month of the preceding year. She became a Junior Consort in the Fourth Month and Empress in the Seventh, but died six years later.

gent's own remaining daughters were still too young for marriage, a circumstance that must have caused their father great chagrin.[167]) Kanemichi lived in the Horikawa Mansion, to which he had made extensive alterations.[168] His daughter was very pretty, and the Emperor took to her in spite of his youth.[169]

Emperor En'yū conferred First Rank on Princess Shishi, the sister to whom he was closest. The presence of the charming Princess, who had also been a favorite of their father, Emperor Murakami, lent a touch of gaiety to the lonely Palace.[170]

It was during Emperor En'yū's reign that the Tenth Princess became Kamo Virgin.[171]

Morosuke's third son, Middle Counselor Kaneie, had two daughters, whom he had reared with great care.[172] Since the Crown Prince was still an infant, Kaneie presented Chōshi, the elder, to ex-Emperor Reizei, thus avoiding the appearance of direct competition with Kanemichi, whose daughter was already married to Emperor En'yū.[173] Most people considered the match a mistake.[174]

The Regent's daughter Kaishi, who as Emperor Reizei's consort had given birth to the new Crown Prince, had also become the mother of two daughters. One of them had soon died, but the other, Princess Sonshi, had survived. She was a child of radiant beauty, born after her father's abdica-

167. Partly because Koretada died at the age of forty-eight in the third year of his regency, and partly because Takakata (b. 953) and Yoshitaka (b. 954), his two sons by his principal wife, Keishi (b. 925), died in the epidemic of 974, none of his children except the Imperial consort Kaishi enjoyed noteworthy careers. Little is known of the other daughters, aside from the fact that they eventually married members of the Court circle, such as Fujiwara Tamemitsu (942–92) and Prince Tametaka (977–1002). Of his eight sons, only one, Middle Counselor Yoshichika (957–1008), became a kugyō.

168. See s.n. 24.   169. Kōshi was twelve years his senior.

170. First Rank (ippon) was conferred on Princess Shishi in the Third Month of 972. The text implies that the orphaned Emperor, thirteen years old in 972, had no intimates aside from his full siblings, Anshi's other children. Both of his brothers, ex-Emperor Reizei and Prince Tamehira, had left the Palace; and of his four sisters, the oldest, Shōshi, had died in 951; the second, Hoshi, had gone off in 968 to serve as Ise Virgin; and the fourth, Senshi, was only nine years old. Princess Shishi, an attractive girl of seventeen, was thus a natural object of affection for her younger brother. Shishi received First Rank when she held a wisteria-viewing party, attended by the Emperor, in the Nashitsubo. Nihon kiryaku, 2: 121 (25 iii Tenroku 3).

171. This was Anshi's last daughter, Princess Senshi, who established an enduring record by serving as Kamo Virgin from 975 to 1031. See s.n. 25.

172. Chōshi (d. 982) and Senshi (962–1002). On their careers, see s.n. 26.

173. The actual sequence of events was as follows: Tenth Month of 968, Chōshi marries Reizei; Eighth Month of 969, Emperor En'yū succeeds Reizei, and Reizei's fourteen-month-old son by Kaishi (the future Emperor Kazan) becomes Crown Prince; Second Month of 973, En'yū takes Kōshi as a consort.

174. Perhaps because of Reizei's insanity.

tion; and since the Crown Prince's position made it impossible for his
mother to see him, except on her infrequent visits to the Palace, Kaishi
consoled herself with this little Princess.[175]

Prince Nagahira, Emperor Murakami's son by Hōshi, was a handsome
lad, but as he matured it became evident that his mind was distressingly
slow.[176] His uncle Naritoki, who was a Consultant at the time, attended
to all the boy's needs and gave him a home in the main building of his
own Koichijō Mansion.[177] Naritoki was married to the daughter of Minamoto Nobumitsu, the Biwa Major Counselor (the lady's mother had been
a daughter of Middle Counselor Atsutada), and the couple had become the
parents of a beautiful daughter, Seishi, who was their great pride.[178] In
spite of his youth, Prince Nagahira took it into his head that he was in love
with Seishi.[179] He made a nuisance of himself about it to Naritoki, who
was solely responsible for him because the boy's mother had died in the
meantime, but Naritoki refused to humor him, and finally kept him away
from Seishi altogether. The Prince had always been an unpleasant child,
perverse in addition to his stupidity; and his present infatuation, although
it did him credit in a sense, was not likely to meet with Naritoki's approval.

Naritoki had another foster son, his nephew Sanekata, as well as a son
of his own, Seishi's older brother, Chōmeigimi, both of whom were being
reared by Nobumitsu's wife at the Biwa Mansion.[180] Sanekata and Chōmeigimi were always teasing Prince Nagahira, cackling in derision when they
succeeded in making him screw up his face and burst into tears; but the
Prince insisted on loitering about the premises because of his romantic

175. Both of Kaishi's daughters were born while Reizei was still Crown Prince. The
first, Princess Sōshi (964–86), was actually the longer-lived of the two, and presumably the
one with whom Kaishi "consoled herself," since Princess Sonshi (966–85) was sent at the age
of two to serve as Kamo Virgin. (Sonshi retired as Virgin after Kaishi's death in 975, entered
the Palace as one of En'yū's consorts in 980, and became a nun soon afterward.) The Crown
Prince was living in the Imperial Palace, which Kaishi had left at the time of her husband's
abdication.

176. On the mental retardation of Prince Nagahira (965–88), see also Ōkagami, pp.97–99.
He died at the age of twenty-three after having held the nominal title of War Minister.

177. The Prince had been orphaned in 967 by the successive deaths of his parents. Since
his grandfather, Morotada, was also dead, Naritoki was probably his closest remaining maternal
relative.

178. See s.n. 27.

179. He would have been about seven years old in 972, but the author must have had a
later period in mind, since 972 was the year of Seishi's birth. He is referred to as a twelve-
year-old in the following paragraph.

180. Sanekata (d. 998) later had an official career that ended in 995, when he was relieved
of his post as Middle Captain and sent off to serve as governor of Mutsu Province in northeastern Japan—a punishment, according to one of the many legends associated with his name,
for having quarreled publicly with the calligrapher Yukinari in the Courtiers' Hall. He is best
remembered as a poet.

devotion to Seishi. To Naritoki the situation was exceedingly irritating. What a shame, he thought, that a child of twelve should be so intractable.

One day Naritoki happened to be present when Sanekata and Chōmei-gimi persuaded the Prince to mount a horse from the mansion's stables. "You must practice your horsemanship," they told him; "otherwise you won't know how to ride. Princes always ride on important occasions." The Prince stretched himself flat on the horse's back, his face scarlet, while his tormenters howled with glee.

"Lift him down," said Naritoki, pained by the spectacle. "He seems to be afraid." Still chortling, the Prince's cousins lowered him to the ground, where his mouth was discovered to be crammed with horsehair. Naritoki was furious, but the ladies-in-waiting went off into gales of laughter.

Around that time, someone told Naritoki that ex-Emperor Reizei's Empress, Princess Shōshi, who was bored with her childless existence, wanted to adopt Prince Nagahira so that he might visit her.

"What a stroke of luck!" Naritoki said. "The Empress is a woman of immense wealth; people say she has inherited all of ex-Emperor Suzaku's property.[181] This will make the Prince's fortune."

After having selected an auspicious day, Naritoki took the Prince for his first visit. Empress Shōshi was waiting for them, confident that any child educated by Naritoki would be exceptional, even though this one had lost his mother at an early age; and she was enchanted when the Consultant arrived with his charge, whom he had dressed in impeccable taste. The Prince's lustrous hair hung to his knees in back, and he wore the informal costume of a nobleman with a pleasing air of elegance. The Empress summoned him into the sitting room of her main hall, gave presents to his attendants, and sent him home with suitable remembrances. Though he had made no response to her attempts at conversation, other than to turn red, she interpreted his reticence as the mark of a refined and gentle nature.

Prince Nagahira's silence remained unbroken on subsequent visits; but just as the Empress was beginning to wonder about him, it happened that she fell ill. Naritoki instructed the Prince to call and pay his respects.

"What shall I say when I get there?" the Prince asked.

"Say, 'I've heard you are not feeling well,' and so forth."

When the boy reached Empress Shōshi's palace, she allowed him to come inside as usual, and he recited his speech so prettily that she forgot her aches and pains.

"Please come to see me again whenever you like," she replied.

181. Shōshi was Suzaku's only child.

Prince Nagahira riding a horse. "One day . . . Sanekata and Chōmeigimi persuaded the Prince to mount a horse from the mansion's stables. 'You must practice your horsemanship,' they told him; 'otherwise you won't know how to ride. Princes always ride on important occasions.' The Prince stretched himself flat on the horse's back, his face scarlet, while his tormenters howled with glee."

Back at Naritoki's house the Prince reported, "I said what you told me to, and I got it exactly right."

"Why must you use such language? The Empress is a very important lady," Naritoki scolded, annoyed by his stupidity.[182]

"Oh yes, oh yes, that's right," the Prince mumbled. Naritoki felt that he was beyond hope.

Meanwhile the third year of Tenroku arrived [972]. On New Year's Day, Naritoki dressed the Prince in magnificent robes and sent him off to Empress Shōshi's palace[183]—forgetting, however, to coach him in an appropriate salutation. When the Prince made his bow in front of the hall, the Empress was delighted by his grace and beauty. Sending out a splendid cushion for his use, she dispatched a number of important, elegantly costumed ladies to fetch him inside. He entered with a dignified tread and seated himself punctiliously on the cushion, looking so distinguished that the ladies were lost in admiration. Eager to hear him speak, they seated themselves in rows, screening their faces with fans and trying to get as close to the front as possible. "It's dreadfully embarrassing to have to appear before a gentleman who is used to seeing Naritoki's beautiful daughter," they murmured. But the Prince's words, uttered after a preliminary throat-clearing, were startling indeed. "I have heard you are not feeling well, so I have come to see you," he said. On the occasion of this ceremonious New Year call, he had repeated the speech taught him by Naritoki during the Empress's illness the year before.

The Empress was too astonished to respond, but her ladies burst into peals of laughter. "We must tell everyone what the Prince said!" they whispered to one another.

The Prince turned an angry red. "What's the matter?" he demanded. "I said just what my uncle told me to say last year when the Empress was sick. What's so funny? You have a lot of ladies who like to make fun of people. I hate it here; I'm never coming back." He stormed out of the palace with shocking rudeness.

At Koichijō the Prince said to Naritoki, "Something awful happened." "What do you mean?" Naritoki asked.

"I'm not going back to the Empress's any more. I'll let you kill me first." "Tell me what's the matter, can't you?" said Naritoki.

"When I said, 'I have heard you are not feeling well, so I have come to

---

182. The Prince had used the neutral verb *iu* ("say") instead of the humble form necessitated by the Empress's exalted status.

183. To pay his New Year respects.

see you'—well, there must have been ten or twenty ladies in the room, and they all began to laugh out loud. It made me so furious that I left right away and came home."

Naritoki was speechless with vexation.

"Why don't you say something? Was anything wrong with my speech? You told me what to say last year when I visited the Empress, and I didn't forget a word. What did I do wrong?" the Prince demanded.

There seemed to be nothing for Naritoki to say.

2

THE MIDDLE COUNSELOR'S QUEST AT KAZAN

THE Ichijō Regent Koretada had fallen prey to a stubborn ailment that gave him an insatiable craving for water. He was confident of recovery, for he was still young and had occupied the regency for only three years,[1] but the months brought no improvement. His visits to the Palace ceased,[2] and the situation began to excite general uneasiness. During the Ninth Month a visitor called on his son, Lesser Captain Yoshitaka,[3] to inquire after his health. Yoshitaka replied with a poem:

> Yū magure   As I gaze at the garden
> Ko shigeki niwa o   Dense with trees
> Nagametsutsu   In the gathering dusk,
> Ko no ha to tomo ni   My tears
> Otsuru namida ka.   Fall with the leaves.[4]

On the First of the Eleventh Month in the third year of Tenroku [972], with his family in the state of anxiety revealed by Yoshitaka's poem, Koretada's life came to an end. It would be idle to speak of the grief and bewilderment of his children—the Junior Consort Kaishi, the other daughters, First Lesser Captain Takakata, and Later Lesser Captain Yoshitaka.[5]

Yoshitaka had always been uncommonly pious, even as a child. He was

1. Koretada was forty-eight in 972. He had become Regent in 970.
2. He resigned the regency in the Tenth Month of 972. *Nihon kiryaku,* 2: 121 (10 and 23 x Tenroku 3).
3. Yoshitaka (954–74) never rose beyond the office of Lesser Captain but was a poet of some repute. Ten of his poems are preserved in Imperial anthologies.
4. A slightly different version of the poem appears as no. 393 in the sixth Imperial anthology, *Shikashū* (ca. 1151–54).
5. See Chapter 1, n. 167.

forever reading the *Lotus Sutra* and daydreaming about taking Buddhist vows, but had resigned himself to secular life because of his reluctance to part with his little son, the offspring of an alliance of some years' standing with a daughter of Yasumitsu, the Momozono Middle Counselor. (Yasumitsu was a son of the late Minister of Central Affairs, Prince Yoakira.[6]) He composed this poem as the guests were taking their leave at the end of the melancholy mourning period, after the performance of every conceivable Buddhist ritual:

Ima wa tote	I must watch alone
Tobiwakarenuru	In the old nest
Muratori no	Whence all the birds
Furusu ni hitori	Have flown,
Nagamubeki kana.	"Since it is over . . ."[7]

Koremasa, the Master of the Palace Repairs Office,[8] responded:

Hane narabu	Unless you forget us
Tori to narite wa	We shall not desert you—
Chigiri tomo	We who have become birds
Hito wasurezuba	With wings abreast
Kareji to zo omou.	And vowed eternal love.

Koretada had turned forty-nine that year. Since he had been Chancellor at the time of his death,[9] he received the posthumous name Kentokukō, Modest and Virtuous Lord. He was succeeded as Regent by the eldest of his brothers, Palace Minister Kanemichi, who was Morosuke's second son.[10]

Presently the name of the era was changed and the first year of Ten'en [973] began. All went well. Kanemichi set about elevating Kōshi to Imperial rank at the earliest moment. It was considered a pity that Koretada had not lived to see the Crown Prince ascend the throne.

Kōshi was granted Imperial status on the First of the Seventh Month in that year. She became known as Chūgū.[11] The former Empress, ex-

---

6. See s.n. 28.

7. The "old nest" was Koretada's Ichijō Mansion, where the mourners had stayed for forty-nine days. A slightly different version of the poem appears as no. 567 in *Goshūishū*, the fourth Imperial anthology (1086).

8. Minamoto Koremasa (906?–80), a minor kugyō who held the office of Consultant.

9. Appointed in 971.

10. Kanemichi, a Provisional Middle Counselor at the time of Koretada's death, skipped the office of Major Counselor and became Palace Minister on the day of his appointment as Kanpaku (27 xi 972).

11. The title granted was Kōgō, but she was called Chūgū because her household office, as was most often the case when there was only one Empress, was called Chūgūshiki rather than Kōgōshiki. See Appendix A, n. 35. She had been made a Junior Consort two months earlier.

Emperor Reizei's consort Shōshi, was named Grand Empress. Kōshi was enviably situated indeed; others could only long for equal good fortune. The Emperor divided his time between her apartments and those of his sister, Princess Shishi of First Rank, and life at the Palace was gay and modish.

The new Regent, the Horikawa Lord Kanemichi, now bore the title of Kanpaku.[12] His four or five sons[13] became leaders of fashion, preening themselves on their sudden prominence.

In those days Morosuke's third son, Kaneie, was usually called the Higashisanjō Major Captain of the Right or the Major Counselor.[14] Ex-Emperor Reizei had shown a gratifying partiality for Kaneie's daughter Chōshi, and the Major Captain was anxious to present his second daughter, Senshi, to Emperor En'yū, who had personally mentioned the matter to him. But Kaneie and Kanemichi had been on bad terms for some time, and Kaneie hesitated to introduce Senshi into the Palace as a rival to his brother's daughter, who had already been named Empress.

As the second year of Ten'en [974] began, Kanemichi became Chancellor.[15] Seeing him in a position of unparalleled influence, people talked of little but the good fortune of Morosuke's line. All affairs of state were administered by Kanemichi in consultation with his intimate friend Minister of State Yoritada, who was Saneyori's second son.[16]

That year a smallpox epidemic raged among all classes of the populace, striking terror into every heart and killing gently born men and women in appalling numbers. Among the victims were Takakata and Yoshitaka, the sons of the former Regent, Koretada. They died one after another on the same day, leaving their mother prostrate with grief.[17] It would be impossible to do justice to the feelings of that lady, whose bereavement came to be cited as an example of the suffering caused by the epidemic.

The animosity between Kaneie and Kanemichi was considered extremely odd. Kanemichi stayed on the alert for a way of bringing his brother down,

12. His predecessor had been styled Sesshō.
13. See s.n. 29.
14. Kaneie had become Major Captain of the Right in 970 and Major Counselor in 972. On Higashisanjō, see s.n. 30.
15. He was thus promoted over the heads of the Minister of the Right (Yoritada) and the Minister of the Left (Minamoto Kaneakira). The office of Chancellor had been vacant since the death of Koretada in the Eleventh Month of 972.
16. Yoritada had become Minister of the Right in 971.
17. The brothers died on the Sixteenth of the Ninth Month, 974. Their mother, Princess Keishi (b. 925), was a daughter of Prince Yoakira. After the death of Reizei's consort Kaishi in 975, it was Keishi who cared for Kaishi's son, the future Emperor Kazan.

a goal more easily envisioned than realized. Meanwhile Kaneie, having returned to the idea of presenting Senshi, was busy with unobtrusive preparations—for after all, he thought, what was there to fear?

Only the Kan'in separated the Horikawa and Higashisanjō mansions.[18] Whenever a horse or carriage arrived at Higashisanjō, Kanemichi's people would report the caller's identity to their master, who would sneer, "Yes, I've heard that So-and-so is one of Kaneie's toadies." Some of Kaneie's friends, frightened by the Regent's hostility, took to paying their calls under cover of darkness.

Perhaps through divine intervention, Kanemichi learned of Kaneie's plan to present Senshi at Court. "This is intolerable!" he said. "How dare he try such a scheme when His Majesty has already selected my daughter as Empress? He wants to ruin me." When that remark and others like it were repeated to Kaneie, he canceled his plans in disgust. Sooner or later, he told himself, a more favorable opportunity would arise.

Time passed swiftly, and soon the Jōgen era began [976–78].[19] Ex-Emperor Reizei's consort Chōshi had been pregnant since the preceding summer. Hearing that prayers of many kinds were being commissioned in anticipation of the birth, which was expected in the Second or Third Month, Kanemichi commented, "People tell me Kaneie is praying for a boy so he can run the country." Kaneie was disturbed and annoyed by such unpleasant remarks, but he did not consider them grounds for leaving his daughter's fate to chance. He redoubled his pious exertions.

Chōshi gave birth to a fine baby boy in the Third Month.[20] In his lucid moments, the mad ex-Emperor showed every appearance of delight, showering his consort with thoughtful attentions.

"Kaneie must be pleased with himself now that his daughter has produced the ex-Emperor's second son. It delights me to think of it," said the

18. The two establishments were only a few hundred feet apart. The Kan'in, south of Nijō and west of Nishinotōin, had been the principal residence of Fuyutsugu, but had apparently passed into obscure hands after his death, no doubt because all of his children were sons who built houses of their own. The owner in 974 may have been Fujiwara Munetada, the Master of the Right Capital Office, from whom Kanemichi is believed to have acquired the property in 976. Kanemichi moved there in order to place the whole Horikawa Mansion at the disposal of Emperor En'yū, who had gone to Horikawa after the Dairi fire earlier in the year. Kanemichi's son Asateru (951–95) moved with his father and later inherited the Kan'in property. *Sonpi bunmyaku*, 1: 9; Tsunoda 1963, p. 26; Takamure 1966, 1: 373.

19. The era name was changed in the Seventh Month of 976 after two major catastrophes, the Palace fire in the Fifth Month and a devastating earthquake in the Sixth.

20. Prince Okisada (976–1017), the future Emperor Sanjō (r. 1011–16). He was actually born in the First Month, before the adoption of the new era name. *Shōkai*, 1: 148; *Honchō kōin shōunroku*, p. 429.

Chancellor. Kaneie could find no explanation for his brother's ill nature.

Presently a fire at the Palace required Emperor En'yū to occupy apartments that Kanemichi pronounced unsuitable,[21] and the Regent set hastily to work on extensive construction projects and improvements that were calculated to make a second Dairi of his own Horikawa Mansion, where he intended to establish the sovereign until the Imperial residence could be rebuilt. Since the move to Horikawa was to take place on the Twenty-sixth of the Third Month in the second year of Jōgen [977], there was much urgent work for all. His Majesty arrived on the appointed day, followed at night by the Empress.[22] The Horikawa Mansion was thenceforth referred to as the Town Palace,[23] and everyone marveled at its splendor.

Reflecting one day on the uncertainty of human existence, Kanemichi determined to secure a promotion for Yoritada, the Minister of the Right, in order to place him next in line for the regency. At the time, the Minister of the Left was Minamoto Kaneakira, Emperor Daigo's sixteenth son. Kanemichi used Kaneakira's indifferent health as a pretext for restoring him to Princely status, and named Yoritada Minister of the Left in his place. Major Counselor Masanobu became Minister of the Right.[24]

Meanwhile, Kanemichi's own health was failing. "Who knows when I might die?" he thought. "I'll have to get rid of Kaneie so Yoritada can be the next Regent." He broached the subject to the Emperor whenever he had a chance. "Now that our precious Captain Kaneie has his hands on a son of ex-Emperor Reizei, there's only one thing on his mind. He even

21. The Apartments of the Empress's Household (Shiki no Sōshi).

22. According to *Nihon kiryaku*, 2: 131 (26 vii Jōgen 1), En'yū moved to the Horikawa Mansion about ten weeks after the fire, i.e. in the Seventh Month of 976. Kōshi joined him there about two weeks later. See EM, 1: 75, nn. 27, 28.

23. *Sato dairi*; also *ima dairi*. Compare Morris 1967, 2: 285 and *passim*: the Palace of Today. Although En'yū was not the first Heian Emperor to reside elsewhere during repair or reconstruction work at the Dairi, his predecessors had stayed at the Reizeiin, an Imperial estate in the city, rather than in a subject's house. En'yū's departure from precedent, presumably occasioned by the fact that ex-Emperor Reizei was living in the Reizeiin, marked the beginning of a practice that grew increasingly common as multiplying fires and dwindling financial resources made the Dairi uninhabitable for months or years at a time. For a list of the Emperors' principal interim residences, see the table in Appendix B.

24. These events occurred in the Fourth Month of 977. Minamoto Masanobu (920–93), whose daughter Rinshi (964–1053) later became Michinaga's principal consort, was a prominent figure in his own right. His father was Prince Atsumi (893–967), a full brother of Emperor Daigo; his mother was a daughter of Fujiwara Tokihira; and his full brother was Shigenobu (922–95), who himself became Minister of the Left in 994. In addition to his social prominence, Masanobu was a musician of outstanding ability, a leader in the musical renaissance that took place during the reign of Emperor Ichijō (r. 986–1011). Kaneko 1939, 1: 339; Satō 1929, p. 637.

offers prayers about it."[25] And after announcing that his illness would compel him to stay elsewhere while the Emperor resided in the Horikawa Palace,[26] he dragged himself into the Imperial presence to complain about his brother's shortcomings as an official. "The Court is in danger as long as men like Kaneie hold high positions. We ought to make an example of him," he kept insisting.

On the Eleventh of the Tenth Month in the second year of Jōgen [977], Kanemichi finally stripped Kaneie of the office of Major Captain, appointing him Minister of Civil Affairs instead. He would have liked to deprive him of all official status, but nothing more than a demotion seemed practicable, since there was no real evidence of wrongdoing. Exile to Kyūshū or some other remote place would have been just the thing, he thought, if only a decent pretext could have been devised. Middle Counselor Naritoki, Morotada's son, replaced Kaneie as Major Captain.

Kaneie shut himself up behind locked gates, embittered and outraged by the world's cruelty. His indignant sons also retired from society.

Meanwhile Kanemichi had sunk so low that little hope was held for his recovery. After his earlier visit to the Palace[27]—the one that had cost Kaneie his Captain's title—he made a second and final appearance to dispose of pending matters. There was great curiosity about the substance of the audience, but no announcement was made. On the Fourth of the Eleventh Month the Regent was granted equality with the three Empresses,[28] and on the Eighth he breathed his last at the age of fifty-three. He received the posthumous name Chūgikō, Loyal and Excellent Lord. It was a pity that he had chosen to inflict such a harsh blow on his brother when so little time on earth was left him.

In order to honor Kanemichi's last request, which had been that the Ononomiya Minister Yoritada should succeed him, the Emperor named Yoritada to the regency on the Eleventh,[29] thus placing all governmental authority in his hands. Everyone considered it a surprising appointment.

---

25. The Crown Prince, Morosada, was Kaneie's nephew, Reizei's son by Kaishi. According to Kanemichi, Kaneie's prayers were designed to get both En'yū and Morosada out of the way so that his grandson, Reizei's first son by Chōshi, could succeed to the throne.

26. I.e. the Horikawa Mansion. A building inhabited by a member of the Imperial Family automatically became a palace.

27. The Emperor had returned to the rebuilt Dairi in the Seventh Month of 977. *Nihon kiryaku*, 2: 134 (29 vii Jōgen 2).

28. See s.n. 31.

29. Yoritada was appointed on the Eleventh of the Tenth Month; i.e. before Kanemichi's death. *Nihon kiryaku*, 2: 135 (11 x Jōgen 2).

Empress Kōshi was inconsolable, and Provisional Major Counselor Asateru and Middle Counselor Akimitsu grieved in a pathetic manner.

After having given birth to a Prince in the preceding year, Kaneie's daughter Chōshi bore a son in this year as well.[30] Her father's future seemed promising indeed.

The last rites for Kanemichi followed the usual pattern.

As the new year began, Minister of the Left Yoritada enjoyed an enviable position. He began to give serious consideration to the possibility of presenting his eldest daughter at Court.[31]

Winter came swiftly, and with it a change in the era name; it was now the first year of Tengen [978].[32] At an appointments ceremony on the Second of the Tenth Month, Yoritada had become Chancellor. Masanobu was the new Minister of the Left, and Kaneie the Minister of the Right. Kaneie owed his promotion to Yoritada, who had kept insisting to the Emperor that it was unthinkable for an innocent man to be deprived of his title and forced into seclusion. No doubt Kaneie attributed his deliverance to the gods and buddhas.

Still angered by Kanemichi's behavior, Kaneie presented his second daughter, Senshi, as an Imperial bride, paying no attention to the feelings of Empress Kōshi, whose presence had restrained others. Gratitude to Kanemichi had deterred Yoritada, even though he would have liked his own daughter, Junshi, to enter the Palace first.[33] But it was not surprising that Kaneie should have acted while the Regent hesitated. The match was a success, and the Emperor grew fond of Senshi. Empress Kōshi could not help blaming her father's heartlessness for the rude and contemptuous treatment to which she was now being subjected.

With a sweet, friendly, pretty sister installed in the Umetsubo, Senshi's brothers overcame some of their feelings of constraint. Meanwhile Kaneie's prospects became even brighter when Chōshi gave birth to a third son.[34]

As the second year of Tengen began [979], Senshi was still the Imperial

30. Prince Tametaka (977–1002), who as an adult held the titles of President of the Board of Censors and Governor-General of the Dazaifu. He is perhaps best remembered as one of the lovers of Izumi Shikibu. See Cranston 1969, pp. 8–9.

31. Junshi (957–1017). See s.n. 32.

32. The era name was changed on the Twenty-ninth of the Eleventh Month, shortly after the events described next.

33. Senshi was presented on the Seventeenth of the Eighth Month, 978, which according to other sources was three months after Junshi became a Junior Consort.

34. Prince Atsumichi (981–1007), born not in 978, as the text implies, but three years later. He succeeded his brother, Tametaka, both as Governor-General of the Dazaifu and as Izumi Shikibu's lover.

favorite. At the direction of the Empress's Household and the Court, prayers of all kinds were being recited for Empress Kōshi, who had been ailing for some months, but she died on the Second[35] of the Sixth Month, leaving the Emperor depressed and full of vain regrets. "Kaneie's luck is improving; Senshi is certain to be named Empress," predicted the gossips.

The Empress's death had caused the cancelation of the wrestling matches,[36] and the Court was quiet and lonely. Yoritada took charge of the last rites, apparently regarding the task as an obligation imposed both by his office and by his personal debt to Kanemichi. Asateru and Akimitsu were inconsolable.

That winter Yoritada presented his daughter Junshi at Court. The brilliance of the occasion, though in a sense a reflection of the Regent's exalted position, nevertheless owed much to his refined and elegant tastes. Emperor En'yū seemed less attracted to Junshi than to the sociable, amusing Senshi, but not even an Emperor could disregard Yoritada's wishes, and Junshi was in no danger of neglect.

Meanwhile Senshi had begun to suffer from a mysterious indisposition. Kaneie was greatly alarmed until it became clear that she was going to bear a child. To avoid gossip, her condition was kept quiet for the first two months, but such things cannot be concealed for long, and the Emperor was informed in the third month. He was delighted, and Princess Shishi also rejoiced in the happiness of her friend.

The Emperor made no secret of his reluctance and disappointment as Senshi prepared to retire to the Higashisanjō Mansion, but there was no question of her staying, and she took a ceremonious leave, attended by all the senior nobles. Everyone agreed that Kaneie would some day become the most powerful man in Japan.

Having by that time enjoyed a considerable reign, Emperor En'yū was looking forward to his abdication, and he was thus much concerned by his lack of a son.[37] There was no way of ascertaining the sex of Senshi's unborn child, but he took an optimistic view of her pregnancy and commissioned innumerable prayers. With continuous prayers and sutra-recitations in progress both at the Imperial Palace and at Kaneie's house, there seemed no reason for anxiety about the birth. Meanwhile one may imagine Yoritada's unhappiness. "There's nothing to worry about," he probably told

35. The Third, according to *Nihon kiryaku*, 2: 140 (3 vi Tengen 2).
36. Held annually in the Seventh Month. See s.n. 33.
37. Emperor En'yū had been on the throne ten years in Tengen 2 (979). *Honchō kōin shōunroku*, p. 433, shows the future Emperor Ichijō, the child with whom Senshi was pregnant, as his only offspring.

himself. "As long as I remain in the regency, I can make an Empress of Junshi no matter what happens."

Soon the third year of Tengen began [980]. Senshi's child was to arrive in the Third or Fourth Month. Lavish arrangements for the birth were made, both by the Palace Storehouse Bureau, which provided curtains and other requisites, all of white, and by Kaneie's wife,[38] who undertook additional preparations of her own. The event, it seemed, could not fail to be auspicious. Imperial messengers arrived at all hours of the day and night to inquire after the consort's health.

Toward the end of the Fifth Month, the long-awaited birth pangs appeared, and presently a fine baby boy was safely and easily delivered—not during the Fifth Month, but at the Hour of the Tiger [3:00–5:00 A.M.] on the First of the Sixth.[39] When a sword arrived from the Emperor, who had been notified with all possible haste, Kaneie's joy was beyond description. The reader may imagine the splendor of the celebrations during the first seven days.

Even in recent years, the gates of the Higashisanjō Mansion had been little frequented, but once the reigning sovereign's first male offspring had joined ex-Emperor Reizei's three sons in residence there, every nobleman in the capital hastened to pay his respects. After years of misery, Senshi's brothers were happy at last.

That year there was another fire at the Dairi, forcing the Emperor to take up residence in the Kan'in Palace, which had belonged to Kanemichi.[40] The current occupant, Major Counselor Asateru, moved elsewhere.

As I wrote earlier, the Regent Yoritada's daughter was living at Court as a Junior Consort, but she showed no sign of becoming pregnant. Yoritada must have found the situation a great disappointment.

Impatient to set eyes on his first son, Emperor En'yū commanded that the baby be brought to the Palace in secret, but Kaneie temporized, uncertain of what sinister designs others might be harboring in their hearts.[41]

38. Tokihime (d. 980), the daughter of a minor noble named Fujiwara Nakamasa (or possibly of Nakamasa's son, Yasuchika). She was Kaneie's principal consort and Senshi's mother. See s.n. 26; and *Sonpi bunmyaku*, 1: 54–56.

39. It was believed that a child born in the Fifth Month would harm his parents. See Nakamura 1962, pp. 13–14. The child was Prince Yasuhito (or Kanehito), the future Emperor Ichijō, who became Crown Prince in 984, reigned 986–1011, and died in the year of his abdication.

40. The Emperor actually stayed not at the Kan'in (n. 18), but at various places in the Palace compound and at Yoritada's Shijō Bōmon Mansion (south of Shijō and east of Nishinotōin).

41. The author suggests that Kaneie thought his enemies might harm the child to keep him from becoming Crown Prince.

The year had already produced a number of disturbing events, including a typhoon and an earthquake,[42] and it was not to the anxious Emperor's liking that the young Prince should remain in a private dwelling, but the temporary Palace was too cramped to accommodate additional residents, and he was obliged to content himself with sending messengers day and night to inquire after the baby's health.

The adorable little Prince's Fiftieth and Hundredth Day celebrations passed. Only qualms about Yoritada's displeasure kept the Emperor from visiting the Higashisanjō Mansion. Though Emperor En'yū was a man of great nobility, he was generally thought to be lacking in courage. Kaneie had probably concluded that this weakness made the Emperor undependable, for he still appeared very much on guard, even though his position might have been considered unassailable by then.

The fourth year of Tengen began [981]. The Emperor journeyed to Kamo and Hirano in the Second Month, apparently in fulfillment of a private vow of some kind. Quite possibly he prayed for the Prince. Now that he had become the father of a son, he was eager to abdicate.[43] It disturbed him that Senshi should linger at her father's house, but Kaneie thought, "I am not the Regent; why should I let her go?"[44]

Crown Prince Morosada's second sister, Princess Sonshi, had been presented to Emperor En'yū as a Junior Consort during Kanemichi's lifetime. The Emperor had found her attractive, but the Palace had burned to the ground almost immediately after her arrival, and people had begun to call her the Fire Princess. Before long she died.[45]

The Emperor, feeling that he could not ignore the Chancellor's wishes,[46]

42. There was a typhoon in 980 but no earthquake. The author may have been thinking of the great earthquake of 976.

43. Emperor En'yū worshiped at Hirano on the Twentieth of the Second Month. He visited Kamo in the Tenth Month of 980, but not, so far as is known, in the spring of 981. Hirano Shrine, situated in what is now Miyamoto-chō, Kamikyō-ku, Kyōto, was founded in 794, when its gods were transferred from Yamato Province to the new capital by Emperor Kanmu, who identified them with certain of his maternal relatives. Revered by the Heian Court as one of the Twenty-two Shrines, it enjoyed many special marks of Imperial favor. En'yū's visit in 981, which established a precedent for later Imperial progresses, may have been designed to secure divine assistance for his son, whom he hoped to make Crown Prince. There was a close connection between Hirano and the heir to the throne, who personally presented offerings at all of the shrine's festivals. *Koji ruien*, 7: 1396.

44. In the Tenth Month of 981 the Emperor returned to the rebuilt Dairi, where Senshi apparently joined him, since a reliable diary reports that she left the Palace almost immediately after Chōshi's death (see below). *Shōyūki*, 1: 10 (28 i Tengen 5).

45. Princess Sonshi was presented a month before the 980 fire. She cut her own hair in 982, thus renouncing lay life, and took formal Buddhist vows in 985, the year of her death.

46. For evidence of Yoritada's interest in the appointment, see *Shōyūki*, 1: 16–19 (23 and 29 ii, 3 and 5 iii Tengen 5).

showed himself disposed to grant Junshi the title of Empress, but Yoritada demurred. "What will people say if I set aside the mother of His Majesty's first son in order to give precedence to my own daughter?" he said. "It would be unwise to make an enemy of Kaneie."

"There is no reason for hesitation. Even if Senshi isn't appointed now, she will receive Imperial status some day. The world is uncertain; you had better make haste," the Emperor urged.

Greatly elated, Yoritada began secret preparations for the event. Unfortunately, it took him the rest of the year to finish, and meanwhile his plans became known to Kaneie, who retaliated by absenting himself from the Palace. Senshi's brothers also stayed home, and Senshi herself adopted a distant, formal attitude toward the Emperor. Listening to the rumors, Princess Shishi thought with indignation that Junshi's promotion was to blame for everything.

Soon a new year began [982]. A *kōshin* day chanced to fall during the First Month.[47] At the Higashisanjō Mansion where Chōshi was staying, and also in Senshi's apartments, the young ladies-in-waiting begged to be allowed to celebrate this first kōshin of the year, and on winning permission, they began great preparations. "It promises to be most entertaining. We'll spend the night visiting you in turns," said the consorts' three brothers.

On kōshin night, Michitaka, Michikane, and Michinaga did their best to amuse the ladies. The consorts busied themselves with versifying and similar elegant pastimes, and their attendants fought spirited battles at *go* and backgammon. "We should never have managed to stay awake all night if the gentlemen had not honored us with their presence," said the ladies as the first cocks crowed.

Toward dawn Chōshi dozed off, leaning on her armrest.

"You mustn't fall asleep now," cried one of her ladies. "The cock has

47. On the Twenty-seventh. The calendar date known as kōshin recurred every sixty days, when the Day of the Elder Brother of Metal (*kanoe* or *kō*), one of the "ten stems" (*jikkan*), coincided with the Day of the Monkey (*saru* or *shin*), one of the "twelve branches" (*jūnishi*). On the sexagenary cycle, see Webb and Ryan 1963, pp. 23–25. According to Taoist doctrine, every human body contains three malevolent worms that never leave except on kōshin night, when, after waiting for the host to fall asleep, they make a quick trip to Heaven bearing reports of his misdeeds, with the aim of shortening his life. In imitation of the Chinese, who tried to circumvent their ungrateful parasites by staying awake all night, the Heian nobility held kōshin vigils, whiling away the time with refreshments, games, stories, appropriate Buddhist prayers, and the composition of Chinese and Japanese poetry. (Most standard references favor the above explanation of the role of the three worms. For an alternative theory, see Morris 1967, 2: 88, n. 472.)

crowed; let her alone," said another. One of the gentlemen wanted her to listen to an impromptu verse. "Wake up!" he insisted. Seemingly deep in slumber, she made no response. He drew nearer, still calling out, and tried to pull her to her feet, troubled by something unnatural in her appearance. To his alarm, her flesh was cold. He snatched up a lamp, held it close, and saw that she was dead.

Stunned by shock and grief, the brothers managed to tell their story to Kaneie, who rushed to the scene in utter bewilderment. The sight that met his eyes overwhelmed him, and he sank to the floor, cradling his daughter's body in his arms. Agitated voices rang through the house, famous monks were summoned with frenzied haste, and messengers hurried off to arrange sutra-recitations at temples, but all was in vain. When Kaneie released Chōshi, she lay as though asleep, attired in four white damask robes and a red plum mantle,[48] with her beautiful long hair trailing beside her. We may imagine the feelings of the father who had loved her so dearly. The extreme youth of the Princes added to his distress.[49]

Ex-Emperor Reizei was astonished and dismayed by the news.

Kaneie attributed the tragedy to Motokata's ghost. Far from consoling him, the throngs who came with condolences merely added to his misery, nor was it of any help to remind himself that Chōshi's fate, hard as it was, must some day overtake us all. But it was necessary to be practical. The usual arrangements for the last rites progressed while the bereaved father shed helpless tears. It would be idle to say that we live in a world of wretched uncertainty.

The mourning period dragged on. Concerned for Senshi's safety, Kaneie transferred her and the infant Prince to another residence.[50] Granted that life is uncertain, Chōshi's death was beyond all experience. It was pathetic to think of her little sons, still too young to understand what had happened.

That year was the fifth of the Tengen era [982]. Yoritada's daughter Junshi was to be named Empress on the Eleventh of the Third Month, and the Regent's absorption in the preparations only deepened Kaneie's gloom. The ceremony took place according to plan, accompanied by scenes of in-

48. On "damask," see s.n. 34. A red plum mantle (*kōbai no mizo*) was a handsome heavy red outer robe, with a lining of plain purple silk (or, according to another explanation, of brown silk). The combination was considered appropriate for wear between the latter part of the Eleventh Month and the Second Month of the following year. EM, 1: 84, n. 10; Maeda 1960, p. 519.

49. The ages of Chōshi's sons (in sai): Okisada, seven; Tametaka, six; Atsumichi, two.

50. A reference either to Senshi's departure from the Dairi (n. 44) or to some subsequent move designed to thwart Motokata's spirit.

describable splendor. Yoritada's attitude was as one might expect, but the Emperor had surprised many people, and Junshi was nicknamed the Barren Empress by those who blamed Emperor En'yū for setting aside his first son's mother to honor a childless lady. Nevertheless it was a happy time for Junshi.

It was all very well for Kaneie to think, "If I live . . ." He was still dissatisfied and resentful. That Senshi's misfortune should have exposed him to gossip while he was still heartbroken over Chōshi's death—that, he felt, was an affliction such as few are called on to bear, and I need hardly say that the anger and bitterness with which he greeted the Emperor's decision made his old grievance against Kanemichi pale into insignificance. Death itself was almost preferable to the derision of society. His only consolation was to tell himself, "The story has not ended. We shall see what the future holds."

The gates to Kaneie's mansion seldom opened after Chōshi's death. The minister's sons also kept to themselves, refusing to emerge for even the most important events. Messengers from the Emperor called on Senshi daily, but not more than one in two or three took back an answer.

Princess Shishi of First Rank was also deeply distressed.

The beautiful little Prince had now entered his third year, and toward autumn the preparations for the Putting On of the Trousers began.[51] The Emperor commanded the Office of Palace Works to make whatever was needed for the ceremony. Arrangements were also set in train by Kaneie, who had found nothing to keep him busy after the final services for Chōshi, and so had been devoting most of his time to the affairs of his dead daughter's sons.

The widowed Kaneie had grown intimate with one of Chōshi's attendants, Tayū by name, who had so succeeded in capturing his fancy as to have become very much the mistress of the house.[52] There were numerous nurses on the premises to look after ex-Emperor Reizei's second, third, and fourth sons—Daini, Shō, Minbu, Emon, and others[53]—but the master's affections were completely engaged by Tayū, and he paid no attention to any of them.

---

51. *Hakamagi* or *chakko*. See s.n. 35.

52. Tokihime, Kaneie's principal wife, had died in 980. Nothing is known of Tayū.

53. Theories seek to identify Shō with a daughter of one of Senshi's nurses; Minbu with Tachibana Tōshi (daughter of a Minbushō official, Yoshifuru), a lady formerly in Tadahira's service; and Emon with a daughter of the poet Minamoto Kanezumi (fl. ca. 986–1013). EM, 1: 483, s.n. 99. Nothing is known of Daini.

In the hope of mollifying Senshi, the Emperor took pains to celebrate the young Prince's Putting On of the Trousers with all possible splendor. (He was really very much attached to Senshi, and would never have promoted Junshi if he had not been afraid of the Chancellor.) Kaneie had made up his mind to hold the ceremony during the winter at the Higashisanjō Mansion, but the Emperor said, "What an idea! Of course it must take place at the Palace." The Twelfth Month was settled upon, and everyone worked frantically to be ready in time. Senshi was also to go to the Palace for a stay of three days.

When the Prince journeyed to the Palace on the appointed day, after a last bustle of preparation, the splendor of the occasion may be imagined. As the Emperor beheld his son's startling beauty, he felt that he had sinned by slighting the mother of this handsome, promising child, who was destined one day to succeed to the Imperial throne. He arranged everything with great magnificence, and treated Senshi in his most conciliatory manner, but she remained cold and distant.

The Prince was indescribably beautiful in his trousers. "He is the very image of His Majesty when he was a little boy," said the Emperor's older ladies-in-waiting.

Carrying the Prince in his arms, the Emperor took him to Princess Shishi's apartments. The Princess was entranced. "You must not be unkind to Senshi unless you want him to suffer too," she warned. "I have had no intention of treating her harshly. What happened was unavoidable," he replied.

In addition to showering the Prince with elegant gifts, the Emperor took care to see that each senior noble, courtier, and lady-in-waiting received a handsome remembrance.

Senshi left the Palace with the Prince at dawn on the fourth day after her arrival. To Emperor En'yū's remonstrances, she replied only that she would return before long. Though the Emperor was disappointed, he must have felt that he had no one but himself to blame. Fond thoughts of the Prince filled his mind.

The first anniversary of Chōshi's death was observed in the same month.[54] Kaneie had merely been waiting for the Putting On of the Trousers to be finished. The minister arranged for memorial services shortly after the Twentieth, and all the old inconsolable grief flooded back as he supervised

54. If the author is correct, the service was early, since Chōshi had died in the First Month of that year (982). EM, 1: 88, n. 1.

the melancholy rituals. But Senshi's affair no longer distressed him, for he was satisfied that her promotion would come within a year or two at most.

Meanwhile the name of the era was changed to Eikan.[55] During the first year [983] everything went as usual from the First Month on, with the days slipping by uneventfully except when a public function was taking place. The Emperor, worried about the Prince's uncertain status, was more than ever obsessed by thoughts of abdication. He had also begun to suffer fearful torments from the visitations of malicious spirits. Ex-Emperor Reizei was in a pitiable state, with few intervals of sanity.

Soon the second year of Eikan [984] arrived. The Emperor reached a quiet decision. "This year without fail ... ," he thought. He was much disturbed by Kaneie's stubborn refusal to visit the Palace. To Senshi, who had commissioned numerous prayers on the Prince's behalf, he sent generous grants of ranks and offices.[56]

The seasonal observances passed swiftly. As the Seventh Month wrestling approached, the Emperor expressed a desire to have the young Prince watch the matches. Kaneie seemed reluctant to agree. Summoned to Court time after time, he found many pretexts for staying away—indispositions and other obstacles—and it was not until he received a peremptory command, with the matches just around the corner, that he finally put in an appearance. The Emperor addressed him with great cordiality.

"This is my sixteenth year on the throne," he said. "I had never anticipated so long a reign, but it must have been ordained, for here I have remained, willy-nilly. We shall all be busy with the wrestling this month, but next month I intend to step down. I want my son to be named heir apparent after the Crown Prince takes over, and I would like you to arrange for prayers at the temples so that all will go well. It has hurt me that you and certain others have shown displeasure with me, seemingly unaware of my affection for the boy. Even those who are blessed with large families love each of their children. How could I be indifferent to my only son?"

Kaneie assented respectfully and withdrew. Back home he held a whispered conversation with Senshi, ordered a light by which to inspect the calendar,[57] and sent messengers bustling off to arrange for prayers at temples. Although he made no announcement, the people in the mansion drew

---

55. Because of a drought and still another Dairi fire (Eleventh Month, 982). EM, 1: 88, n. 6.
56. The prayers were to secure the Prince a place in the Imperial succession; the offices and ranks, to serve as rewards to those responsible for arranging the services.
57. Presumably to determine an auspicious date for starting prayers.

their own joyous conclusions. His jubilant sons attended the wrestling matches, and he himself appeared at Court again in the best of spirits.

As the Eighth Month began, the great topic of conversation was Emperor En'yū's abdication on the Twenty-seventh. When the day came, His Majesty duly retired. He was succeeded by Crown Prince Morosada, and Senshi's son became the new heir apparent. It would be idle to call Kaneie's position enviable. His rise was of course not unexpected.

Ex-Emperor En'yū made the Horikawa Palace his residence.

The new Emperor, Kazan, was grown up enough to feel a lively interest in girls.[58] He soon showed by his behavior and speech that he was eager to receive daughters of the nobility as consorts, and Yoritada, who had been confirmed in his office of Regent, presented his second daughter, Shishi, in the Tenth Month.[59] This meant that others were shouldered aside in a rather cavalier manner, but the Regent could do as he pleased.

Yoritada had hurried Shishi into the Palace as soon as things had quieted down after the Accession Audience and the Imperial Purification for the Thanksgiving.[60] It is hard to say what Shishi looked like, since not even her own ladies were allowed a glimpse of her face until they had been with her for seven or eight years, but she is unlikely to have been ugly. Still, the Emperor did not seem particularly impressed. She *was* the Regent's daughter, though, and Yoritada probably felt confident of his ability to make her an Empress.

Meanwhile, the Emperor was sending daily letters to Prince Tamehira's daughter Enshi, of whose beauty he had heard glowing reports.[61] It would be a mistake, the Prince decided, to keep such a daughter shut up at home, and so he made his preparations and sent her off to the Palace. As the child of the late Emperor Murakami's favorite fourth son and Minamoto Takaakira's daughter, Princess Enshi could lay claim to a distinguished heritage in addition to her beauty. When she arrived amid ceremonies of the utmost magnificence, the Emperor was delighted with her, and the presentation proved a brilliant success.

58. He had acceded at the age of sixteen.

59. Yoritada, who was named Kanpaku on the day of Kazan's accession (27 viii 984), did not present Shishi until the Twelfth Month. For other inaccuracies in the following account of the new Emperor's consorts, see s.n. 36.

60. Shishi entered the Palace on the Fifteenth of the Twelfth Month, approximately two months after the Accession Audience (10 x 984), but well before the Purification, which took place in the Tenth Month of the following year, in accordance with the regular procedure for such events (s.n. 18). On the Accession Audience, see s.n. 37.

61. Enshi was about thirteen years old at the time. For a list of Prince Tamehira's children, see s.n. 38.

Two such consorts might have been expected to satisfy any sovereign, but presently Emperor Kazan was issuing impatient demands for Major Captain Asateru's daughter Shinshi. After some hesitation, Asateru decided to present her, persuaded that the Crown Prince's youth made that course the best means of realizing his paternal ambitions.[62] He did not worry that she might suffer from neglect. As Kanemichi's third and most popular son, he was still an influential figure at Court, and Shinshi's maternal grandparents had been Morosuke's daughter Tōshi (the Tōkaden Principal Handmaid) and Prince Shigeakira, Emperor Daigo's son. Shinshi herself was said to be exceptionally pretty. With so many advantages, Asateru thought, she could not fail to attract favorable notice, even though she would be entering the Palace late. He presented her in the Twelfth Month. Since he had inherited all the personal belongings of his devoted sister Empress Kōshi, to say nothing of Kanemichi's own treasures, the presentation was most elaborate.

Some time earlier, Asateru's affection for Shinshi's mother had cooled, and he had formed an alliance with the widow of Nobumitsu, the Biwa Major Counselor (the lady who was the daughter of the late Middle Counselor Atsutada). He was now completely estranged from his former spouse, even though she was rearing Shinshi and two of his sons.[63] Everything was done to make Shinshi's presentation flawless, but in such matters the parents ought to look after things together if they possibly can.

Although Nobumitsu's widow was a clever woman, it was hard to understand why Asateru had deserted a youthful wife for her sake. It was whispered that Asateru had acquired an extraordinarily mature stepchild in Naritoki's wife. Naritoki's popularity seems to have prevented open gossip, but there were those who pointed out that the widow was old enough to be Asateru's mother.[64]

Emperor Kazan made an almost embarrassing fuss over his new Junior Consort. The overshadowed former favorite, Princess Enshi, spent a gloomy and dissatisfied month while Shinshi constantly visited the Seiryōden and entertained the Emperor in her apartments. To judge from the sovereign's actions, one might have thought there was no other lady

62. The Crown Prince (the future Emperor Ichijō) was four years old in 984.

63. For information on Asateru's children, see *Sonpi bunmyaku,* 1: 52, which identifies Shigeakira's daughter as the mother of three of the sons, including Asatsune (973–1029), the only one to achieve kugyō status. It has been suggested that Asateru married the wealthy widow, described in the vulgate *Ōkagami* as old, swarthy, and pockmarked, in order to get the Biwa Mansion, which she had inherited from her father, Atsutada. EM, 1: 484, s.n. 103; Tsunoda 1963, p. 112; Satō 1929, p. 359.

64. See s.n. 39.

in the Palace. Those who watched could only conclude that the law of karma was at work.

Another year rolled around [985]. Beginning on the First of the First Month, a number of smart new ceremonies were adopted. The Chancellor, although somewhat puzzled and uneasy, accepted them with his usual willingness to follow the lead of others.

For some strange reason, Asateru's daughter Shinshi was spending fewer and fewer nights in the Imperial Bedchamber. At length His Majesty's invitations ceased altogether, and a month or two slipped by without so much as a note from him. In despair, Asateru asked himself what might have gone wrong. Try as he would, he could find no explanation for the disastrous turn of events; and meanwhile his daughter, the butt of mortifying ridicule, was being treated as though she were no longer a member of the Court. Shinshi managed to bring herself to stay awhile longer, but then she fled the Palace in embarrassment. The Emperor took no notice of her departure. It would be hard to find a more pathetic and tragic story in our times. Asateru closeted himself at home, declaring that it made his heart ache to visit the Palace.

The world is unlikely to forget such a thing. According to one theory, Shinshi's stepmother was at the bottom of it.[65] Or someone may have done something—perhaps a trick at the bridge used by the Emperor. At any rate, Shinshi ceased to visit the Seiryōden, the Emperor kept his distance from her apartments, and after her final incredible departure it was as though she had never come.

Naniokakimi[66] and others also stopped going to Court. It was a strange affair!

The Emperor had begun to send messages day and night to Naritoki's daughter Seishi and Tamemitsu's daughter Kishi. Pondering the sovereign's rude and dismaying abandonment of Shinshi, with whom he had been so infatuated, Naritoki scarcely knew how to respond. Even though Emperor Murakami had had ten or twenty consorts and concubines, he had arranged matters with admirable skill, treating all the ladies with kindness, and showing no preference to his favorites, but Emperor Kazan's behavior had been most erratic. No doubt it was this instability that led Naritoki to decide against presenting Seishi.

The Ichijō Major Counselor Tamemitsu, who was rearing a motherless

---

65. Possibly because she was the grandmother of Naritoki's daughter Seishi, who was then being groomed for marriage into the Imperial Family.

66. Tentatively identified as the childhood name of Noritomo, one of Asateru's sons. EM, 1: 484, s.n. 106.

daughter by himself,[67] had adopted an attitude of the utmost conservatism in all that concerned the girl, and he too was reluctant to accede to Emperor Kazan's request. But the Emperor continued to urge his suit through his uncle, Middle Counselor Yoshichika, whom he relied on to use his influence as the husband of Tamemitsu's oldest daughter, and at length Tamemitsu capitulated.

Meanwhile, Princess Enshi was still the Imperial favorite. The Emperor's treatment of Yoritada's daughter Shishi had been conventional from the start, so that Shishi was never subjected to embarrassing gossip. She spent four or five nights of every month in the Seiryōden.

Presently Kishi made a magnificent entry into the Palace. She was one of two children, a boy and a girl, born to a lady whose father was Atsutoshi, the eldest son of the Ononomiya Minister Saneyori, and whose brother was the noted calligrapher Sukemasa, the Minister of War. Kishi's father, Tamemitsu, was Morosuke's ninth son.

Since no grounds for distinctions existed, it would have been proper for all the Junior Consorts to be treated alike, but no sooner had Kishi settled into the Kokiden after her grand entrance than Emperor Kazan began to shower her with special attentions. Feeling, no doubt, a certain uneasiness, the overjoyed Major Counselor offered fervent prayers for her success, and many months passed with no alteration in the Imperial passion, which indeed was almost disgusting in its ardor. The scandalized rival consorts branded the affair unprecedented, predicted its swift end, and in numerous ways showed an unpleasant eagerness for Kishi's discomfiture.

Meanwhile, Kishi conceived. To the dismay of her attendants, she seemed scarcely able to swallow a morsel of fruit, and Emperor Kazan insisted on having all his own food offered to her before he would touch it, a demonstration of devotion that seemed excessive to Tamemitsu, watching nervously from the sidelines. In the third month she made the usual announcement and prepared to leave, but the Emperor found one excuse after another for detaining her, and the fifth month arrived before she could get away. The delay had troubled Tamemitsu, who was anxious to have his daughter in a place where she could receive every possible attention. Immediately after her arrival, he set all his people to work so that nothing should be left undone.

At first Kishi had blamed morning sickness for her inability to eat, but

67. Kishi's mother had been a daughter of Fujiwara Atsutoshi. On Tamemitsu and his children, see s.n. 40.

things had gone on in the same way for month after month, and she was now in an alarming state of emaciation. Her frantic father called for prayers of every description, but nothing stayed down, not even an orange. Her depression was pitiful to witness, and Tamemitsu cared for her with a heavy heart.

Emperor Kazan commissioned numerous Buddhist rituals of his own. He also commanded the Palace Storehouse Bureau to deliver everything necessary to Tamemitsu's house.[68] So many messages of inquiry were dispatched, often in the middle of the night, that the courtiers and Chamberlains considered themselves exceedingly ill-used, but anyone guilty of delay suffered the removal of his name from the courtiers' duty-board,[69] as well as the imposition of severe disciplinary measures—treatment not inappropriate, perhaps, for a Chamberlain of Sixth Rank, but scarcely to be borne without grumbling by the son of a great family. Furthermore, the Emperor refused to touch so much as an ordinary piece of fruit unless it was first sent over for Kishi to try, even though there was no point to the gesture, since she could eat nothing. His behavior was merely an additional worry to Tamemitsu, who could not help considering it abnormal.

Distraught with worry and love, the Emperor kept begging Tamemitsu to allow Kishi to come to the Palace, even if only for a few hours early some evening. At first Tamemitsu resisted, but in the end, realizing that Kishi was fretting about the Emperor's unhappiness, he agreed to send her for a day or two; and steps were taken to redecorate the Kokiden, where she was to stay. No good would come of it, predicted the spiteful ladies in the service of the other consorts.

The Emperor greeted Kishi with touching delight, lounged inside her curtains day and night, and refused to leave even to eat his meals. "What is anybody to think? He's acting like a madman," the Palace gossips whispered. Kishi was no longer the girl who had come to the Palace as a bride. After the baby's conception she had grown terribly thin, even while still in the Palace, and now her extreme emaciation made her almost unrecognizable. There was little to recall her old playfulness and charm as

68. Rewards for the monks, supplies needed for the rituals, etc.

69. *Nikkyū no fuda*, a board about five feet long mounted on the north wall of the Tenjō no Ma. It bore the names of all tenjōbito of Fourth, Fifth, and Sixth Rank, with space under each entry for the insertion of slips of paper, one per day, to show the total number of days on which the man had made himself available for duty during the course of a month. The expungement of a man's name from the roster meant that he could no longer enter the Courtiers' Hall.

she talked morosely of her approaching death. The poor unhappy Emperor sought to console her with tears and laughter by turns.

The escort and carriages came for Kishi after three days, but the Emperor refused to give her up. "Just one more night!" he kept saying. When seven or eight days had passed, Tamemitsu begged for her release, insisting that she could not receive proper protection away from home. In tears, the Emperor agreed. He came out to say goodbye, and stayed until the hand-drawn carriage[70] moved off. The honor moved Tamemitsu to tears of awe and gratification, which he did his best to suppress, fearful that they might bring bad luck.

To the great concern of the Emperor's ladies-in-waiting, the brief reunion had left him so agitated that his own health was imperiled.

Although Kishi had somehow managed to get along during the early months, she could no longer even raise her head after her return from the Palace. The end, it seemed, was merely a matter of time. Her weeping father redoubled his exertions, but it was all to no avail, and she died in her eighth month. I write nothing of Tamemitsu's feelings, which may be imagined. Emperor Kazan wailed with a frightening lack of restraint inside his curtains, deaf to the remonstrances of the nurses and others who tried to calm him. His grief was heart-rending.

At the Ichijō Mansion,[71] where it was necessary to consider practical matters, there were sorrowful preparations for the usual funeral ceremonies.

"When I brought her home, I hoped to see her an Empress riding in a litter.[72] How could I have dreamt of anything like this!" said Tamemitsu, flinging himself to the floor in tears.

The Emperor commanded his special favorites and intimates among the senior nobles and courtiers to accompany the body. He grieved alone throughout the night, tormented by the necessity of depending on others for an account of the last rituals.

---

70. *Teguruma*, a small-wheeled conveyance with a Chinese gabled roof and wide sides used as entrances and exits. The usual rule was that visitors to the Palace proceeded on foot from the outer Daidairi gates. A Prince, Imperial consort, Minister of State, high-ranking Buddhist monk, or other important personage was sometimes given special permission to use a teguruma, or, more rarely, an ox-drawn carriage (*gissha*) between a specific Daidairi entrance, usually Jōtōmon Gate, and another point closer to the Seiryōden, usually Sakuheimon Gate or Kenshunmon Gate for gentlemen, and a somewhat less distant place, such as the rear of the Kōrōden or the headquarters of the Military Guards, for ladies. *Koji ruien*, 32: 751; Ishimura 1958, 2: 418.

71. Tamemitsu's house. Kishi died in a house belonging to Fujiwara Tomomasa, a man of the provincial governor class. *Nihon kiryaku*, 2: 154 (18 vii Kanna 1).

72. An Empress, by special Imperial permission, could be carried in and out of the Palace in a litter.

Tamemitsu walked with faltering steps behind the carriage.

So Kishi was transformed into a wisp of cloud, and the days slipped by amid universal grief and shock. Going about the business of the sutras,[73] Tamemitsu wept without ceasing. During the entire mourning period, no consort visited the Seiryōden. (There was, it is true, an invitation to Princess Enshi, but she replied that she was unwell.[74])

In that atmosphere of melancholy, the second year of Kanna [986] began. From the First Month on, a sense of alarm and apprehension pervaded the capital. Strange portents multiplied, causing the Emperor to observe one period of ritual seclusion after another.[75] Through some inexplicable astrological conjunction, a great wave of religious fervor swept the upper classes, whose members talked of nothing but how this person or that had entered the life of religion.[76] Such tales, one may suppose, strengthened Emperor Kazan's sense of the tragic ephemerality of worldly things, and fired his disturbed mind with a passionate desire to free Kishi of defilement, "for I have heard," he mused, "that such women bear a heavy karma burden."[77] His acts of piety became extraordinarily frequent, and his agitated behavior worried the Chancellor and excited grave misgivings in Middle Counselor Yoshichika, the Emperor's uncle (who, however, kept his fears to himself).

The Emperor fell into the habit of listening to sermons delivered by the Holy Teacher Gonkyū, whom he summoned from Kazan for the purpose.[78] Pious reflections occupied his mind, and the phrase "wife, chil-

73. Extant records show that the *Lotus* and other sutras were copied during this period for presentation during memorial services at the Hosshōji. EM, 1: 484, s.n. 110. (The Hosshōji, founded by Tadahira in 925, was a great Tendai temple east of the Kamo River in the vicinity of Kujō Avenue, patronized by successive generations of Fujiwara leaders. It should not be confused with the Hōjūji, founded by Tamemitsu in 988 and usually associated with his name. See Chapter 4, n. 16.)

74. An invention. Enshi had not yet been presented at Court.

75. The portents included a rainbow, a snake on the veranda of one of the Daijōkan buildings, a ghost, the invasion of a room by doves, and a strange noise in the Giyōden. EM, 1: 485, s.n. 112.

76. Prominent figures who took Buddhist vows during the first few months of 986 included Princess Shishi of First Rank; the wife of an Imperial Prince; a Prince of Fourth Rank; one of Asateru's sons; and a Provisional Director of the Imperial Stables of the Left. EM, 1: 485, s.n. 113; Shōkai, 1: 218.

77. *Tsumi.* It was believed that a woman more than five months pregnant existed in a state of defilement (*kegare*, a kind of tsumi), and that she would have an adverse karma in the next life if she died in that state.

78. "Holy Teacher" translates Ajari (Skt. Ācārya), a title conferred on Tendai and Shingon monks by the state. (For Buddhist ranks and titles, see s.n. 41.) Gonkyū (b. 946), a monk patronized by Kaneie and Senshi, is thought by some commentators to have been encouraged by Kaneie to persuade the Emperor to abdicate. Shōkai, 1: 218; EM, 1: 485, s.n. 115. Kazan[ji] was another name for the Gangyōji, founded in 868 by the poet-prelate Henjō

dren, treasures, and regal estate"[79] sprang constantly to his lips. His favorite companion, Controller Koreshige,[80] and his uncle, the Middle Counselor, were greatly distressed. "This religious ardor is disturbing. It's all very well for ordinary folk to renounce the world, but an Emperor's case is different. The spirit that haunts ex-Emperor Reizei must be putting ideas into his head," they lamented. Meanwhile the Emperor's behavior had begun to betray an odd, uncharacteristic restlessness, a turn of events that prompted Yoshichika and Koreshige to spend their nights at the Palace.

On the Twenty-second of the Sixth Month in the second year of Kanna [986], there was a sudden clamor in the night. The whole crowd of people on duty—courtiers, senior nobles, and even common guards and servants —searched every inch of the Palace by torchlight, but Emperor Kazan was nowhere to be found. Arriving on the scene, the Chancellor and all the other senior nobles and courtiers all but ransacked the very courtyards. The uproar became general, and before dawn the barriers were ordered closed.[81] Yoshichika flung himself down in a frenzy of grief before the Sacred Mirror Chamber, the guardian deity of the Palace.[82] "What has become of my beloved master?" he sobbed.

Search parties, dispatched to monasteries and temples outside the city, unearthed no trace of the sovereign. The Imperial consorts were in tears.

When the short summer night had drawn to a dismal close, Yoshichika and Controller Koreshige set out to look for the Emperor at Kazan. There, to their horror, they discovered him, a slender young monk sitting stiffly

---

(816–90). A prominent Tendai institution during the mid-Heian period, it later lost its importance, although a small institution of the same name survives on the original site southeast of the present Kiyomizudera (Kitakazan-chō, Yamashina, Higashiyama-ku, Kyōto).

79. From the *Daihōdō daishūkyō* (Skt. Mahā-saṃnipāta-sūtra): "Wife, children, treasures, and regal estate do not accompany a man at the end of his life; the Buddhist precepts, charity, and upright conduct go with him in this world and the next." See EMZ, 1: 299.

80. Fujiwara Koreshige (or Korenari, 953–89), the offspring of a poor but gifted family, appears in contemporary sources as a poet, scholar, and bureaucrat of exceptional verve and talent. A protégé of Koretada, he became a Scholar (Gakushi) in the Household of Crown Prince Morosada. After the Prince's accession as Emperor Kazan, Koreshige joined with Yoshichika in the institution of a number of political reforms, exercising a de facto authority substantial enough to win him the nickname Regent of Fifth Rank.

81. The Three Barriers (Suzuka in Ise, Fuwa in Mino, and Ōsaka in Ōmi) were designed originally to protect the home provinces against eastern tribes. They retained only a symbolic importance in the tenth century, but messengers were always sent to close them on occasions of great national import, such as the death of an Emperor, Empress, or leading subject, or the accession of a new sovereign.

82. Following EMZ, 5: 464, we assume that "guardian deity of the Palace" (*sukujin, sugūjin*) is an epithet applied to the Sacred Mirror Repository (Kashikodokoro, or the Unmeiden). Some commentators take this more literally, as the name of a deity who lived next to the repository, protecting it and serving as an intermediary in prayers addressed to the mirror.

erect, his wide eyes glancing nervously about. They threw themselves down, heartbroken, and joined him in holy orders.

Nothing more shocking or heart-rending can be imagined. At every utterance of those familiar words, "wife, children, treasures, and regal estate," Emperor Kazan must have been contemplating just such a step. It was splendid of him to become a monk, but how had he learned the way to Kazan—and how had he managed to reach the place on foot?[83] To the shocked and dismayed Yoshichika and Koreshige, it was the most tragic of misfortunes.

The Crown Prince succeeded to the throne on the Twenty-third.[84] The new heir apparent was ex-Emperor Reizei's second son, Prince Okisada. The Emperor was seven years old, the Crown Prince eleven. Most fortunately for Kaneie, the Crown Prince, like the Emperor, was his grandson. (It was natural that that should have been so.)

Meanwhile, ex-Emperor Kazan had probably emerged from the burning house of the three worlds to tread the dewy earth of the four roads.[85] Very likely the soles of his feet would soon bear the sign of the thousand-spoked wheel, lotus flowers would blossom in his footsteps,[86] and a place would await him at the highest level of the first class in Amitābha's paradise.[87] But in this world the Palace lights had gone out for the men and women who had made him their support, and they wandered disconsolate in a realm of darkness.

83. According to Ōkagami, p. 53, Kazan was tricked into abdicating by Kaneie and his son Michikane. Michikane is said to have led the Emperor to the Gangyōji on the pretext that he too was going to become a monk, and to have ensured the success of his plot by picking up an escort of armed Minamoto warriors on the outskirts of the capital.

84. Ōkagami, p. 51, notes that Michikane took the precaution of delivering the Imperial Regalia to the Crown Prince even before Kazan left the Palace on the night of the Twenty-second.

85. In other words, he had renounced the world of illusion for a life of Buddhist piety. The metaphors are from Chapter 3 of the Lotus Sutra, which contains a parable likening the saving of mankind to the rescue of children from a burning house. The three worlds, aspects of the world of illusion and transmigration, are the realm of sensuous desire, the realm of form, and the realm of spirit; the four roads are the four noble truths (that life is suffering, that suffering comes from desire, that suffering can be ended, and that the practice of the Buddhist virtues will end suffering). See Sakamoto and Iwamoto 1964–68, 1: 166, 198; and Ch'en 1964, p. 379.

86. I.e. his virtue was probably comparable to that of a buddha. Lotus blossoms and thousand-spoked wheels, both appearing as wrinkles on the soles of the feet, are two attributes of a buddha—a ruler whose chariot wheels roll everywhere, and from whose feet lotus flowers fall like rain. For a picture, see EMZ, 1: 309.

87. According to one school of thought, there are three major categories of rebirth into Amitābha's paradise, each with three subdivisions. They are distinguished from one another by the kinds and locations of the lotus blossoms provided for reborn souls, by the speed with which the blossoms open, and by the length of time required for the person to attain perfect enlightenment.

Instead of remaining with the ex-Emperor, Middle Counselor Yoshi-chika isolated himself in a hermitage at Iimuro.[88] As for Koreshige, his conduct was more exemplary than that of the holiest saint.

Ex-Emperor Kazan had resolved to receive the Buddhist command-ments in the winter.[89]

Surprising events will be narrated in the following chapters.[90]

88. One of the Six Valleys at Yokawa on Mount Hiei.

89. Kazan is said to have gone through two such formal ceremonies, the first at the Tōdaiji in Nara, where the Hīnayāna commandments were administered, and the second at the Enryakuji on Mount Hiei, where he received the Mahāyāna commandments. *Shōkai*, 2: 29.

90. A stereotyped expression. On its use in other monogatari, see EMZ, 1: 309.

3

JOYOUS EVENTS

On the Twenty-third of the Sixth Month, as a natural consequence of the elevation of the new Emperor and Crown Prince, Kaneie was named Regent.[1] He received equality with the three Empresses, two Palace Attendant Escorts, and other Escorts from the Bodyguards and Military Guards of the Left and Right.[2] His brother, the Ichijō Major Counselor Tamemitsu, became Minister of the Right.

Ex-Emperor En'yū's Junior Consort Senshi was promoted to the rank of Grand Empress on the Fifth of the Seventh Month, and her three brothers, whose positions had previously been undistinguished, became senior nobles.[3] The oldest, Michitaka, a Middle Captain of Third Rank, was appointed Middle Counselor and Master of Senshi's Household; the second, Michikane, a Head Chamberlain, was made a Consultant; and the

1. The event in fact took place on the Twenty-fourth of the Sixth Month, 986. See EM, 1: 488, s.n. 132.

2. On equality with the three Empresses, see s.n. 31. The Palace Attendants (Udoneri) were minor functionaries in the Ministry of Central Affairs, chosen during the Nara period from among junior members of leading families, but later drawn from among men in the service of the great houses. According to the Yōrō Code, which fixed their number at ninety (a figure that fluctuated during the Heian period), their functions were to stand night duty at Court, perform miscellaneous tasks, and escort the Imperial litter. By mid-Heian it was usual for some of them to act as regental Escorts. Escorts (Zuijin) were armed guards assigned by the Court to accompany important members of the nobility when they traveled abroad. An ex-Emperor was entitled to fourteen, a Regent to ten, a Minister of State or Major Captain to eight, a Counselor or Consultant to six, etc. Three types were distinguished: (1) Udoneri Zuijin; (2) Konoe Zuijin (also called Honpu Zuijin), chosen from the Bodyguards; and (3) Kozuijin, drawn from the ranks of their personal retainers by lesser kugyō who, although entitled to the privilege, had received no Escorts from the Court. Eiga is probably in error in specifying that some of Kaneie's Escorts came from the Military Guards. According to Nihon kiryaku, 2: 159 (28 vi Kanna 2), the new Regent received the orthodox number of men from the orthodox sources, namely, two Udoneri Zuijin and four from each of the Bodyguards Headquarters.

3. Senshi, a Nyōgo, received the title because she was the new Emperor's mother. The incumbent Grand Empress, Reizei's consort Shōshi, became Senior Grand Empress on the same day. Nihon kiryaku, 2: 159 (5 vii Kanna 2).

third, Michinaga, a Lesser Captain of Fourth Rank, was promoted to Middle Captain of Third Rank.[4] Kaneie conferred the office of Master of the Crown Prince's Household on Asateru, the Kan'in Major Captain of the Left—a gesture that must have been a painful reminder to Asateru of his father's shabby behavior. It was embarrassing for the Major Captain to think that others might consider his appointment an illustration of the proverb.[5]

To transmit the Imperial Decree to Senshi, Kaneie selected a lady who called herself his daughter, a claim he recognized as quite possibly justified.[6]

Two ladies were named Assistant Handmaids and assigned to the service of the Crown Prince, where they were called Fujiwara Naishi no Suke and Tachibana Naishi no Suke. Everyone treated them with great respect. (Fujiwara Naishi no Suke, who had been known as "the daughter of Lord Morosuke," was full sister to a former Imperial consort. Tachibana Naishi no Suke seems to have been a daughter of the person called the Provisional Major Counselor.[7]) Since the Crown Prince was eleven that year, his Coming-of-Age ceremony was to take place in the Tenth Month.[8] Suishi, Kaneie's daughter by the Lady in the Wing Chamber, was to assume the office of Principal Handmaid and also to share the Prince's bed, and everyone was working day and night to get her things ready.[9] Thanks to this daughter, the Lady in the Wing Chamber, who

4. On their careers, see s.n. 42.

5. Unidentified. Possibly a saying based on the Chinese phrase *i te pao nu* ("Requite injuries with kindness"), which occurs in *Li-chi*, *Shih-chi*, and other works. EM, 1: 103, n. 12. Asateru's father, the late Regent Kanemichi, had demoted Kaneie from the office of Major Captain in 977.

6. The decree (*senji*) named Senshi Grand Empress. The lady is probably to be identified with the Senji listed among Kaneie's children in *Sonpi bunmyaku*, 1: 55.

7. Fujiwara Hanshi was the fourth daughter of Morosuke and the full sister of Emperor Reizei's Junior Consort Fushi. She formed a liaison with Michikane, gave birth to a daughter, Sonshi (984–1022), who later was named a Junior Consort, and became a nun in 1011. Tachibana Naishi no Suke, whose name appears to have been either Seishi or Tokushi, has not been definitely identified. "The Provisional Major Counselor" can only have been Yoshifuru (893–972), the sole Tachibana to hold that office during the period in question, but it is not certain whether Naishi no Suke was in fact his daughter or whether her father was Tachibana Nakatō, a provincial governor. She appears later in the text as the mother of children by Michitaka and his son Michiyori and as the wife of Fujiwara Arikuni (943–1011). These two women were prominent figures at Court, closely associated with Kaneie's family. Both were later enrolled among Emperor Ichijō's nurses and promoted to Third Rank. EM, 1: 488, s.n. 137; 1: 140, n. 4; 1: 515; s.n. 381; 1: 520, s.n. 422; *Murasaki Shikibu nikki*, p. 512, s.n. 53.

8. The actual date of the ceremony was the Sixteenth of the Seventh Month, 986. EM, 1: 462, n. 6; 1: 108, n. 5.

9. The Lady in the Wing Chamber (Tai no Onkata) was one of Kaneie's lesser consorts,

had had something of a reputation for loose behavior, had now become a personage of importance.[10] It only went to show, people said, what a child could do for one. (Suishi's sister, the younger daughter of the Lady in the Wing Chamber, had been named the Crown Prince's Mistress of the Wardrobe.[11] Michitaka was the younger girl's father.) The Lady in the Wing Chamber was of undistinguished birth, but it seems that her doting father, the Senior Assistant Governor-General, had spoiled her badly, allowing her to develop into a passionate, flirtatious woman.

I mentioned Michitaka just now. A certain rather overwhelmingly erudite man, the governor of several provinces, counted among his numerous children a favorite daughter, Kishi.[12] He had thought about marrying her off, but he was aware that men are a fickle lot, and it had seemed too risky a business. Resolving instead to let her go into service somewhere, he had succeeded in finding her a situation in the Imperial Palace during the reign of Emperor En'yū. For one of her sex, she handled Chinese characters with remarkable facility, and thus she had become a Handmaid in the Handmaids' Office, where she was known as Takashina Naishi. Although Michitaka was involved with a number of women, Kishi was the one he liked best. He made her his principal wife, and his devotion grew as she bore him three sons and three or four daughters. He had, or was said to have, several other children as a result of his incessant philanderings, but

probably to be identified with the Ōmi of *Kagerō nikki*. Her father, Fujiwara Kuniaki, served as Senior Assistant Governor-General of the Dazaifu. Suishi (974–1004) is said by *Ōkagami*, p. 170, to have been a great beauty and a favorite of her father. *Ōkagami* reports that she became a Principal Handmaid at the age of eleven (sai), but the correct date appears to be 987—i.e. the year following Crown Prince Okisada's genpuku. She entered the Crown Prince's palace as a consort early in 909 (xii Eiso 1), and remained at Court until her notorious affair with Minamoto Yorisada ended her public career (Chapter 4, below). EMZ, 1: 338; EM, 1: 104, n. 1.

10. "She is quite the sport, I hear," wrote Michitsuna's mother. *Kagerō nikki*, p. 199; translation from Seidensticker 1964, p. 87. She is known to have borne a daughter to Kaneie's son Michitaka.

11. This somewhat misleading expression probably means that the sister was given the title Mistress of the Emperor's Wardrobe and presented to the Crown Prince as a concubine. See EMZ, 1: 324.

12. The "overwhelmingly erudite man" was Takashina Naritada (926–98), who became Michitaka's father-in-law. A minor scholar-official from a family of poets, Naritada achieved kugyō status in 986 at the age of sixty, when Kaneie gave him Junior Third Rank, presumably in recognition of his relationship to Michitaka. Michitaka promoted him to Junior Second Rank, an exceptional honor, in 991. Later in 991, Naritada left the government, took Buddhist vows, and settled down with fanatical determination to the task of advancing the interests of his daughter's children and grandchildren. His oldest daughter, Kishi (d. 996?), was admired for her skill in the composition of Chinese and Japanese poetry and, with some reservations, for her learning, which was considered to be of an order not wholly appropriate for a woman. She is thought to have met Michitaka at Court sometime during the early 970's. See Kawakita 1968, pp. 159–69.

Kishi's offspring were his favorites. They were all precocious, probably because of their mother's intelligence.

Michitaka was a man of elegant appearance, delicate sensibilities, and faultless decorum.[13] His eldest son, Ōchiyogimi, who was the child of a mistress, had been taken from home to be brought up as Kaneie's son, and around this time bore the title of Middle Captain. The eldest son by Kishi was called Kochiyogimi.[14]

Kaneie's second son, Consultant Michikane, was an ugly, pasty-faced, hairy fellow, shrewd and domineering, with an ill-natured, censorious manner that people found intimidating. There was always something, it seemed, about which he felt compelled to lecture Michitaka. He had taken only a single wife, one of the numerous daughters of Imperial Household Minister Tōkazu, a son of Morosuke. Uninterested in romantic intrigues, he viewed the extramarital adventures of others with a cold, critical eye. Fujiwara Naishi no Suke in Senshi's palace had borne him a daughter whom he ignored.[15] He must have found it annoying that his wife, although she was the mother of numerous sons, had failed to give birth to a girl.[16]

Kaneie's fifth son, Michinaga, was a Middle Captain of Third Rank.[17] One wonders what he must have thought of his older brothers. He was entirely different from them in appearance and character—tactful, manly, pious, and considerate and protective in matters affecting his friends.[18] Indeed, his character was extraordinary and ideal in every respect! His devoted sister, Grand Empress Senshi, spoke of him as her son and favored him in innumerable ways.[19] Although barely twenty years old,[20] he avoided casual flirtations—not from any absurdly rigid scruples, but simply because he was unwilling to make an enemy or cause a woman pain. When his

13. Other sources confirm *Eiga's* appraisal and describe him further as lighthearted, amusing, and bibulous. For a discussion of his character, centering on the implications of his lack of political acumen, see Kawakita 1968, pp. 152–58.

14. For a list of Michitaka's children, see s.n. 43.

15. See n. 7. The daughter, Sonshi, became a Junior Consort in 1000, several years after Michikane's death, but was never an Imperial favorite. She later married Fujiwara Michitō (974–1039), the son of Naritoki.

16. On Michikane's children, see s.n. 44.

17. Actually a Lesser Captain of Fourth Rank. See s.n. 42. In referring to Michikane as Kaneie's second son and to Michinaga as his fifth, the author speaks from two different points of view. Michikane was Kaneie's third son and Tokihime's second; Michinaga, Kaneie's fifth and Tokihime's third.

18. Men who identified their fortunes with his, rather than attempting to rival him. See EM, 1: 106, n. 7.

19. Senshi was four years older than Michinaga. For an account of the methods she employed to advance her brother's interests, see *Ōkagami*, pp. 224–26.

20. Michinaga was twenty-one (sai) in 986.

affections were deeply engaged, he was careful to see that the affair was managed with discretion. People naturally began to hear about this unusual young man, and marriage proposals poured in from many quarters, but he rejected them all with the explanation that he wanted to think things over a bit. "I don't understand," thought Kaneie. "What does he mean, he wants to think things over?"

Kaneie had made himself responsible for rearing Chōshi's three sons. Now that Prince Okisada had become the heir apparent, the Regent was devoting more and more attention to Princes Tametaka and Atsumichi. Of the three, the Crown Prince and Prince Atsumichi seemed to him incomparable. The following year, he decided, would be a suitable time for the Coming-of-Age ceremony.[21]

With the advent of the Tenth Month, there was much excitement in anticipation of the Purification and Thanksgiving ceremonies. Since Emperor Ichijō was only seven years old, he was to be accompanied in the Imperial litter by his mother, whose ladies consequently had their hands full. The selection of an Acting Consort and all the other details of the ceremonies aroused lively interest.[22]

Presently it was time for the Purification.[23] At Kaneie's Higashisanjō Mansion, part of the north embankment had been demolished to make room for a viewing-stand from which the Princes and others could watch the procession, which was splendid beyond description.[24] Senshi and the Emperor shared a litter. Then the carriages approached—the twenty bearing Senshi's attendants, the ten allotted to the Emperor's ladies, and the one in which the Acting Consort rode—all so magnificent that they were quite, quite beyond words. I could not begin to do justice to the scene, but since everything followed the usual pattern the reader may imagine it. The Regent appeared toward the end of the procession, accompanied by impressively correct Escorts and a select retinue of well-bred, hand-

21. Since the Crown Prince's Coming-of-Age ceremony was scheduled for the current year, 986, the reference here is presumably to the ceremony for the five-year-old Prince Atsumichi. Prince Atsumichi's genpuku did not, however, take place until 993. EMZ, 1: 333.

22. Since it was considered desirable for an Imperial consort to participate in the Purification procession, the office of Acting Consort had been created to provide for such participation when an Emperor was too young for marriage. (Later, as the position became sanctified by custom, it was filled regardless of the Emperor's age and marital status, often by one of his Junior Consorts.) In 986, the Acting Consort for the six-year-old Emperor Ichijō was Kaneie's daughter Suishi. Shōkai, 2: 15; EM, 1: 489, s.n. 145; Wada 1953, p. 197.

23. The event took place on the Twenty-third of the Tenth Month. Nihon kiryaku, 2: 160 (23 x Kanna 2).

24. Some viewing-stands (sajiki) were temporary structures with wooden floors; others, like Michinaga's famous Ichijō sajiki, were semipermanent buildings boasting such amenities as cypress-bark roofs and railed verandas.

some outriders and other attendants.[25] As the party passed, Prince Atsumichi pushed open a blind at the Higashisanjō stand and leaned out. He
was dressed in an informal bombycine cloak, worn over a red robe and
several inner robes of various hues.[26]

"Hello, Grandpa!" he shouted to Kaneie.

"Behave yourself," the Regent scolded, but he smiled with affection as
he gazed at him. The onlookers must have been amused too.

Once the Purification was over, it was time to think about the Thanksgiving. The Crown Prince's Coming-of-Age, scheduled for the Tenth
Month, had been postponed until the Twelfth in order to allow everyone
to concentrate on the great ceremonies.

Soon the Eleventh Month began, bringing countless chores to be performed for the Thanksgiving, and the entire Court was caught up in agitated preparations for the curtain-raising and other ceremonies, such as
the Gosechi dancing, which was probably even more modish and brilliant
than usual that year.[27]

So time passed. The Crown Prince's Coming-of-Age ceremony was performed around the First of the Twelfth Month, and the Principal Handmaid Suishi at once came to wait upon him, taking up residence in the

25. On such occasions the Regent rode horseback or exercised the privilege, which he
shared with members of the Imperial Family, of using a "Chinese carriage" (*kara[bisashi]
no kuruma*), a large, elaborately decorated vehicle with a thatched, gabled roof. He was
accompanied by ten Escorts in special costumes, some mounted and others on foot, and by
unspecified numbers of additional attendants ranging in status from important courtiers to
low-ranking servants. See EMZ, 1: 336.

26. "Bombycine" (in the obsolete sense of "silk fabric") translates *orimono*, a term whose
exact meaning is no longer understood. The apparent morphology of the word suggests that its
original sense was simply textile, but in the mid-Heian period it was customarily used to
designate a particular category of silks that included, on the one hand, a rich fabric intermediate in cost between damask (s.n. 34) and brocade (s.n. 67), and, on the other, a relatively modest unpatterned cloth. Used without qualifiers, the word seems ordinarily to have
referred to the more sumptuous fabric, which the available evidence suggests was a changeable
damask—i.e. a damask with weft and warp in different colors—woven in a simple (non-
compound) warp-faced twill with patterning in weft twill or weft floats. The simpler orimono
may have been solid-colored unpatterned twills. Nishimura 1971–75, 2: 5–10; Akanekai
1975, pp. 131, 784; Hifuku Bunka Kyōkai 1969, 1: 110; EMZ, 5: 39; Reath 1927, p. 19.

27. Since this harvest festival was the first of the new reign (and thus, as the author points
out, a Thanksgiving rather than a First Fruits Service), there were five Gosechi dancers instead of the usual four (s.n. 18). The curtain-raising (*tobariage* or *kenchō*) was one of the
dramatic moments in the pageantry attendant upon a great state event in the Daigokuden or
Burakuin, such as an Accession Audience, a New Year Congratulations ceremony, or a Thanksgiving banquet. When the Emperor entered the hall and ascended the throne, he was shielded
from view by long-handled, Chinese style fans (*sashiba*), wielded by eighteen noblewomen
(*hatori nyoju*) in magnificent ceremonial costumes. After he was seated inside the throne
curtains, two Imperial Princesses or other high-ranking Court ladies revealed him to the gaze
of the assembled dignitaries by raising the south, or front, curtain. See *Koji ruien*, 1: 404.

Reikeiden.[28] The Prince was very young, but Suishi was already fifteen. Since she was Kaneie's daughter, she quickly received permission to ride in a hand-drawn carriage, and people treated her with as much respect and solicitude as though she were a Junior Consort. Her mother, the Lady in the Wing Chamber, was fortunate indeed.

Around that time Morosuke's eleventh son, Miyaogimi, was serving as Middle Counselor and Provisional Master of the Crown Prince's Household.[29]

Soon a new year began [987]. Since Grand Empress Senshi was staying at the Higashisanjō Mansion, the Emperor journeyed there on the Second of the First Month to pay his respects.[30] It was all very splendid, and there was much commotion as the Grand Empress's officials and Kaneie's Stewards expressed gratitude for their promotions in rank.

In the distribution of appointments on the last day of the month, Michitaka became a Major Counselor and Michikane a Middle Counselor.[31]

That year the era name was changed to Eien.

The Second Month passed amid the usual succession of observances in honor of the gods, with messengers being sent off to shrines and so forth.[32] The Emperor was to go to Iwashimizu in the Third Month, and there was much to do by way of preparation.[33] Michikane, who had been put in charge of the arrangements, appeared certain to win a promotion in rank.[34] Senshi rode with the Emperor in his litter as before, and it was an impressive and awe-inspiring event.

Minamoto Masanobu, the Tsuchimikado Minister of the Left, was the father of two daughters (children of his principal wife), whom he had reared with great care, hoping to see them become Empresses.[35] For some

28. The author's chronology is garbled. See nn. 8 and 9.

29. Miyaogimi was the childhood name of Fujiwara Kinsue (956–1029), a prominent figure of the day, whose mother was Princess Kōshi (a daughter of Emperor Daigo) and who had been reared in Princely style by Emperor Murakami and Empress Anshi. Both of the offices mentioned in the text were conferred on him in 986. He was later appointed Palace Minister (997), Minister of the Right (1017), and Chancellor (1021).

30. Probably a mistake. Senshi appears to have been living in the Dairi at the time. See EM, 1: 489, s.n. 148.

31. Both promotions, which were to provisional posts, took place in 986, not in 987.

32. See s.n. 45.

33. Other sources indicate that the Imperial visit took place in the Eleventh Month, rather than in the Third. The author may have misread source materials describing preparations for the Iwashimizu Special Festival, which was held on the Eighteenth of the Third Month in 987. EM, 1: 109, n. 18; 1: 489, s.n. 151. On Iwashimizu, see s.n. 46.

34. He was promoted to Junior Second Rank three days after the Imperial visit. *Kugyō bunin*, 1: 229.

35. Masanobu's principal wife was Fujiwara Bokushi, a daughter of the well-known poet

reason, Michinaga set his heart on marrying one of them.[36] He let Masanobu know how he felt, but the minister rejected his overtures.

"I never heard of anything so ridiculous," Masanobu said. "Does anybody think I'm going to let a young boy like him marry a daughter of
mine?"

Unlike most women, Masanobu's wife Bokushi was intelligent and perceptive. "What's wrong with taking Michinaga as a son-in-law?" she
asked. "I've seen him from time to time in processions and so forth, and
he impresses me as an unusual young fellow. Leave things to me. The
proposal isn't at all bad." Masanobu was still skeptical.

Masanobu had acquired a good many sons by other women—and daughters too, I dare say.[37] In addition to the two girls, Bokushi had given birth
to three boys, but two of them had already become monks, one while serving as a Controller and the other while serving as a Lesser Captain, and
there was great apprehension lest the family also be forsaken by the third,
who looked on life as a transient affair. Michinaga's proposal was thus most
welcome to Bokushi, and she plunged into preparations for the wedding.
Although Masanobu was not satisfied, it was useless to think of presenting
his daughter to either the present Emperor or the Crown Prince, both of
whom were far too young, and no other candidate of appropriate status
seemed quite suitable. (The Kan'in Major Captain, Asateru, for instance,
had an old wife—if indeed the woman was still alive—but Bokushi had
rejected him because of his distasteful connection with Nobumitsu's widow.[38]) The nuptials were celebrated as soon as the arrangements could
be completed.

Michinaga was treated with impressive consideration at the time of the
wedding. "Such attentions are ridiculous for anyone of his low rank. What
can they be thinking of?" Kaneie wondered. Michinaga visited his bride
with gratifying regularity.

Presently Michinaga became Master of the Left Capital Office.[39] Though

---

Fujiwara Asatada (910–67), who had been called the Tsuchimikado Middle Counselor.
Bokushi had probably inherited her father's house; hence Masanobu's sobriquet.

36. The text calls Michinaga the Middle Captain of Third Rank, a title he never held.
The prospective bride was the older sister, Rinshi, who was twenty-three at the time.

37. For a list of his children, see s.n. 47.

38. Although Asateru's first wife is described in Chapter 2 as youthful, the expression
used, chigo no yō ("like a child"), is possibly to be interpreted as a description of her personality. From Bokushi's point of view, the important consideration presumably would have
been not the wife's age, which was probably around thirty-six (Asateru's own age in 987),
but rather that he had turned his attentions elsewhere.

39. Both the wedding and the appointment to the Capital Office took place late in Eien 1
(987). It is not certain which came first. See EM, 1: 490, s.n. 155.

the post was by no means the kind of brilliant assignment sought after by young men, Kaneie had recommended him for it, pointing out that he himself had once held it.

The weddings of Kaneie's two other sons had seemed rather commonplace events, but the glittering splendor of Michinaga's had made a great impression, not least on the people in his service, who from that time on treated him with special respect.

It was reported that ex-Emperor Kazan was not yet back from his pilgrimage to Kumano,[40] undertaken after he had received the commandments at Mount Hiei in the winter of the previous year. Why was it, people wondered, that a former sovereign should have had to accustom himself to the rigors of such travels? He must have had a frightful karma. His uncle Yoshichika, the Middle Counselor Novice, had not gone along on the pilgrimage, but was leading an exemplary life at Iimuro. His, it seemed, was a renunciation of the world in the truest sense. In the Third Month, when the cherry tree in front of his cell was in full bloom, Yoshichika murmured some lines that long afterward came to the attention of others:

Mishi hito mo	The people I have known
Wasure nomi yuku	Are all forgetting me;
Yamazato ni	To my mountain home
Kokoro nagaku mo	Only ever-faithful
Kitaru haru kana.	Spring has come.

Controller Koreshige had also become a very holy man, as assiduous in his religious practices as a living buddha.

Kaneie's son Michitaka, the Major Counselor, was taking great pains with the education of his two daughters, Teishi and Genshi, in the hope of presenting them to the Emperor and the Crown Prince. Ōchiyogimi had married one of the numerous daughters of a man who was living at Yamanoi after having served as governor of many provinces.[41] Kaneie was of course devoted to Princes Tametaka and Atsumichi, but he also felt a deep affection for Ōchiyogimi, who was almost ignored by his own father.

40. I.e., to the three Kumano shrines in Kii Province: Hongū (Main Shrine), or Kumano-nimasu, in what is now Hongū-machi, Higashimuro-gun, Wakayama-ken; Shingū (New Shrine), or Kumano-hayatama, in Shingū-shi; and Nachi, or Kumano-nachi, in Nachi-ka-tsuura-machi. Though situated in different places, the three were organized as a single entity, unified by the "Kumano faith," a hybrid of Shintō and Buddhist beliefs, which had longevity and rebirth into paradise as its principal goals. Kumano was one of the great religious institutions of the Heian and Kamakura periods and was frequently visited by ex-Emperors and other notables, as well as by wandering ascetics and ordinary pilgrims.

41. Fujiwara Nagayori (d. 1010). The Yamanoi Mansion was situated north of Sanjō Bōmon and west of Kyōgoku. EM, 1: 490, s.n. 158.

Michitaka's one great desire, it seemed, was to secure rapid preferment for his other son, Kochiyogimi.

Meanwhile, at the Tsuchimikado Mansion the Lesser Captain forsook the world.[42] Masanobu was dismayed. "What a cruel blow!" he lamented. "Now that all our sons have gone the same way, no one is left to take care of their sisters." He even sought out the Lesser Captain to demand his return, which was going a bit far. His sons by other ladies were, by contrast, getting along very well in their careers.

After a time Michinaga's wife, Rinshi, began to feel out of sorts, and her periods stopped. Kaneie and Michinaga happily commissioned all the proper prayers, while Bokushi and Masanobu's mother looked after her in every possible way. The marriage was obviously a great success.

The situation of the Retired Emperor was admirable. But ex-Emperor Reizei led a pathetically empty life. As for this former sovereign, he wielded influence in many quarters.[43]

On the Third of the First Month in the second year of Eien [988], Emperor Ichijō visited ex-Emperor En'yū. It was a brilliant occasion, made still more impressive by the presence of Grand Empress Senshi. The ex-Emperor gazed at his adorable little son with inexpressible pleasure, and the Emperor took delight in performing for his father on his cherished flute. The ex-Emperor presented many gifts to the Emperor and Senshi.[44] There were also dazzling presents for the senior nobles and courtiers, as well as suitable remembrances for the Crown Prince's nurses, Fujiwara Naishi no Suke and Tachibana Naishi no Suke; for the middle- and low-ranking Court ladies; for Senshi's attendants; and even for the most humble guards and servants. The Emperor granted promotions in rank to officials in the ex-Emperor's service, senior nobles, and others.

42. Either Tokinobu (d. 1024) or Tokikata; see s.n. 47. EMZ, 1: 352.

43. An ambiguous passage. Interlinear notes in the text, which identify "the Retired Emperor" as Kazan and "this former sovereign" as En'yū, seem to require that the first sentence be interpreted as a rather strained reference to Kazan's life as a monk. Some commentators prefer to ignore the notes and treat the paragraph as an initial statement of the contrast between the lives of En'yū and Reizei. See EMZ, 1: 355.

44. The date of the occasion is probably a mistake for the first year of Shōryaku (990), when Ichijō, then ten years old, is recorded by reliable sources as having paid such a visit (*chōkin no gyōkō*). According to one description of the Shōryaku event, it was an elegant affair, with music on the lake for an audience that included the Imperial party in the fishing pavilion and twenty carriage-loads of Senshi's ladies on the eastern shore. Later the gentlemen performed, and ex-Emperor En'yū, delighted by the proficiency of his son, who was later to become one of the best flautists of the day, rewarded the Imperial flute teacher on the spot. The ex-Emperor's presents to the Emperor included a copybook, a belt, and a flute; the Emperor's to his father, a gold inkstone case and a warbler on a silver plum-branch. *Shōkai*, 2: 35; EMZ, 1: 355; Kaneko 1939, 1: 339.

Ex-Emperor En'yū's enviable situation always reminded people of ex-Emperor Reizei's melancholy lot. But empty as the mad former sovereign's life seemed, he was a veritable Kannon to the men and women in his service—a sacred being, manifesting himself on earth for the salvation of humanity. He would wear a robe or night-garment for a while and then take it off and give it away to one of the attendants waiting greedily to receive it—a practice that often left him disgracefully exposed to the winter cold. The occasional meetings with his sons, Princes Tametaka and Atsumichi, aroused him to pleased and affectionate interest, but Kaneie, intimidated by the formidable strength of the evil spirit, seldom permitted the boys to visit him. Such were the conditions under which he existed. He did, however, possess many rich estates and other treasures, all of which he dispensed with great generosity to the Crown Prince and his brothers.

Presently Rinshi experienced the symptoms and pains of approaching childbirth. The usual arrangements were made for sutra-readings and mystic rites, and urgent summonses went out to monks who were noted for their magical powers. Kaneie and Senshi besieged the house with nervous inquiries.

In spite of the relatives' apprehensions, the delivery proved uneventful, and Rinshi gave birth to a fine baby girl with little trouble.[45] Since the first daughter in that family always received great attention as a potential Empress, Kaneie sent repeated messages of congratulation. Michinaga's marriage had proved a triumphant success! I could not possibly describe the splendor of the ceremonies during the first seven days. Sumptuous celebratory banquets were sponsored by Rinshi's family on the Third Night, by Kaneie on the Fifth, and by Senshi on the Seventh.

After the birth of the baby, Michinaga's love for Rinshi was deeper than ever, and the two were inseparable. But in the meantime someone else had entered his life—a lady called Meishi, who was the carefully reared daughter of the late Emperor Murakami's brother, the Fifteenth Prince.[46] By birth, Meishi was the youngest daughter of Minamoto Takaakira, but the Prince had adopted her and made himself responsible for her upbringing, and she had later been received into Grand Empress Senshi's household, where people called her the Prince's Lady and treated her with the utmost respect. Every gentleman at Court hoped to meet her. Michitaka made a particular nuisance of himself (on the lookout, as usual, for a new love affair), but the disapproving Senshi put an end to his maneuvers. Perhaps

45. The future Empress Shōshi (988–1074). For a list of Michinaga's children, see s.n. 48.
46. On Meishi, see Chapter 1, n. 148.

karma had ordained that Michinaga should fare better, for he succeeded in getting to know the lady by making friends with one of her attendants. "After all, Michinaga isn't a frivolous sort," Senshi reflected. "Why shouldn't he have her?" She gave the pair her blessing and arranged the marriage.[47]

Michinaga's love for Meishi was quite genuine; and in any case he felt a keen sense of indebtedness to Senshi, so he made his new wife an affectionate and thoughtful husband. Even-tempered and placid by nature, Rinshi refused to brood over the affair, even though she found it embarrassing.

Kaneie turned sixty that year. Preparations were begun for a springtime longevity celebration, but difficulties with the arrangements made it necessary to postpone the event until the Tenth Month. Time passed swiftly, and presently the celebration took place in the Higashisanjō Mansion. A great many poems were inscribed on folding screens, but the excitement of the occasion left no time for copying them off. The young boys in the family performed with distinction as dancers. The Emperor honored the proceedings with his presence, as did the Crown Prince, and there were promotions for all of Kaneie's Stewards.[48] The two Stewards whom Kaneie valued most highly, Middle Controller of the Left Arikuni and Middle Controller of the Right Korenaka, were learned, highly respected men.[49] It was splendid indeed that they received advancements in rank.

That month also came to an end, and the Court began to look forward with impatience to the Gosechi ceremonies, which the Emperor and others would be able to view at leisure that year, undistracted by the solemnities of an Imperial Accession. The Shijō Empress Junshi, Masanobu's son Tokinaka (the Commander of the Military Guards of the Left), and certain provincial officials presented the dancers.[50] Senshi joined the young

47. Although the date of the marriage is uncertain, the author is probably correct in placing it after the marriage to Rinshi, who later emerges clearly as Michinaga's principal wife. (Note, for example, the preferential treatment accorded her children.) There is, however, a minority view to the contrary. EM, 1: 491, s.n. 164.

48. On longevity celebrations, see s.n. 49.

49. Fujiwara Arikuni, a well-known literatus, held responsible positions under Kaneie. He and his sons were later demoted by Michitaka, who resented Arikuni's support of Michikane in the power struggle after Kaneie's death, but he returned to favor under Michinaga, who made him Senior Assistant Governor-General of the Dazaifu (995) and Consultant (1001), and gave him Junior Second Rank. Taira Korenaka (944–1005), an official in the Controllers' Office for many years, became a Consultant in 992, a Provisional Middle Counselor in 996, and a Middle Counselor in 998. He ultimately attained Junior Second Rank. He died in Kyūshū after having been named Provisional Governor-General of the Dazaifu in 1001.

50. Junshi, the consort of Emperor En'yū, retained the title of Empress (Chūgū; later Kōgō)

Emperor on the night of the Imperial Rehearsal. There were all sorts of people behind the blinds in the Two-Bay Room, and any sensitive girl who did not happen to be especially pretty must have flushed scarlet and felt ready to faint with embarrassment. Empress Junshi's dancer was the most splendid of the group. What with the ladies-in-waiting commenting as they pleased on everything that caught their attention, it was a noisy occasion. At the next day's Imperial Viewing, it was easy to see that every girl attendant and servant had determined not to be outdone. They were all so attractive, each in her own way, that the spectators found it impossible to choose among them.

The Kamo Special Festival came toward the end of the month, after the Gosechi events.[51] The rehearsal was delightful, and on the festival day the ceremony of the Return in the Imperial presence was attended by Kaneie and all the other important senior nobles and courtiers.[52] One of the two dancers of Sixth Rank was Minamoto Kanezumi, a Chamberlain Lieutenant of the Left Gate Guards, who was known as Ue no Hōgan.[53] Kaneie was watching when Kanezumi took the winebowl in his role as dancer.[54] "First give us a poem in honor of the occasion," the Regent ordered, and Kanezumi promptly recited a line:

> Yoi no ma ni   During the night

"Excellent! Go on!" urged the company.

> Kimi o shi inori   We prayed for our lord,
> Okitsureba   And thus . . .

Kaneie was intrigued. "Hurry up! What comes next?" he said.

>   . . . we have faith
> Mada yobukaku mo   That his life will be as long
> Omōyuru kana.   As the hour has grown late.[55]

---

from 982 until 1000, when she became Grand Empress (Kōtaigō). *Shōyūki*, 1: 150 (19 xi Eien 2), which lists the sponsors of this event, fails to mention Tokinaka. On the Gosechi ceremonies, see s.n. 18.

51. The Kamo Special Festival was held on the last Day of the Cock in the Eleventh Month. There was also a "regular" Kamo Festival in the Fourth Month. See s.n. 50.

52. The focal point of the Kamo Return was a program of *kagura* ("sacred music"). See s.n. 51.

53. Hōgan, Lieutenant in the Imperial Police, was an additional office sometimes held by a Gate Guards Lieutenant. The term Ue meant that Kanezumi was entitled to frequent the Courtiers' Hall, a privilege accorded him because he was a Chamberlain. EMZ, 1: 370. Kanezumi was a well-known poet.

54. As part of the Return festivities, gentlemen of the Court presented the ceremonial winebowl to each of the dancers in turn. *Koji ruien*, 7: 1124.

55. There is a pun on *yobukaku*, which can mean either "late at night" or "rich in years."

Well satisfied, Kaneie took off one of his jackets[56] and gave it to him.

With the Gosechi ceremonies and Special Festival past, everyone felt that the year was all but over.

On the Nineteenth of the Twelfth Month, the Hell Screens and other things were taken out to be arranged for the Buddhist Names Services.[57] The frightening, pitiful pictures and the driving snow outside were reminiscent indeed of the poem about sending off the old year and welcoming the new;[58] and the voices of the courtiers struck the ear with a chilling effect as they chanted the holy names. There was a similar stir at the residences of other Imperial personages.

Next came the exorcism rites on New Year's Eve. The courtiers were amused by the young Emperor's delight when the rattle drums were presented.

So began the first year of the new Eiso era [989]. During the First Month, the Emperor visited his father at the En'yū Palace, where the former sovereign had been living since taking holy orders.[59] The customary forms were observed, with promotions for the ex-Emperor's staff.

Meanwhile Kaneie was occupied with remodeling Prince Moriakira's old Nijō Palace.[60] It had always been a beautiful house, and now, with the

56. *Akome no onzo*, an elegant lined garment, several of which might be worn under the cloak on formal occasions. See Rekisei Fukusō Bijutsu Kenkyūkai 1965, 1: 8–9.

57. The purpose of the Buddhist Names Services (*butsumyō[e]*), held annually during this period on the nights of the Nineteenth, Twentieth, and Twenty-first of the Twelfth Month, was to expunge sins accumulated during the year. The Jijūden picture of Kannon was transferred to the curtain-dais of the Seiryōden, and the Daytime Room was decorated with Buddhist images, pagodas, flowers, and censers. Seven screens were set up in the adjoining eavechambers, each covered with horrifying pictures of sinners undergoing torments in the hot, cold, and other hells described in Buddhist literature. The services, attended by members of the Court, consisted primarily of the recitation (by monks and others) of the names of 3,000 buddhas, a practice recommended in the *Sanzenbutsumyō Sutra* as a means of expiating sin.

58. An allusion to *Shūishū* 261, by Taira Kanemori (d. 990): Kazoureba / waga mi ni tsumoru / toshitsuki o / okurimukau to / nani isoguramu. ("Counting over the accumulating years, why should I be eager to send off the old and welcome the new?") To the Heian courtier, the word *tsumoru* ("accumulate," "pile up") was suggested both by the drifting snow and by the Hell Screens, with their reminder of man's burden of guilt. Kanemori's late-winter poem on the brevity of human life came to mind by a process of association, facilitated no doubt by the knowledge of the occurrence, in the same *Shūishū* context, of two poems linking sins and snow (258 and 260).

59. En'yū had taken Buddhist vows in 985, after having fallen ill of a disease that he attributed to Motokata's spirit. See EMZ, 1: 375. His residence was near the Ninnaji (Ukyō-ku, Kyōto). For a detailed account of Emperor Ichijō's visit, which took place in the Second Month, rather than in the First, see *Shōyūki*, 1: 161 (16 ii Eiso 1).

60. Nijōin, situated north of Nijō and east of Kyōgoku; not to be confused with the Nijō Palace of Empress Teishi (976[977]–1001), built later in the same general area. Kaneie needed an additional residence because the main part of his Higashisanjō Mansion had been turned over to his daughter, Grand Empress Senshi.

addition of every conceivable refinement, it gave promise of being quite perfect. The Regent's satisfaction mounted after each tour of inspection, and he urged the work ahead day and night, determined to have it finished in time for his New Year Banquet in the First Month of the following year.[61]

Of Morosuke's eleven sons and six daughters, Empress Anshi was the one whose descendants had monopolized the Imperial throne.[62] Tōshi and Fushi had remained childless. The line founded by Morosuke's eldest son, the Ichijō Regent Koretada, had proved undistinguished—Koretada's grandson, Emperor Kazan, was now a monk; the career of the son, Yoshichika, had ended in an astonishing manner; and only the youngest of the nine daughters had survived.[63] Asateru, the Horikawa Major Captain of the Left, had held onto his position of influence, but Akimitsu, the Hirohata Middle Counselor, was not highly regarded, and the others were still very low in rank.[64] Kaneie, although only the third son, was now Regent and head of the house, with a long, happy future in prospect. Minister of the Right Tamemitsu, the ninth son, was an exception among his brothers, since he was still in a position of prominence despite Kaneie's ascendency.[65] Of Kaneie's sons, Michinaga was the lowest ranking and the youngest, but his bearing commanded respect, and there was general agreement that he was the best of the lot.[66]

Time passed swiftly. During the oppressive heat of the Sixth Month, the Sanjō Chancellor Yoritada fell critically ill, and on the Twenty-sixth he died. He was Saneyori's second son. All the members of the Court were upset by the news, but their grief did nothing to change things. The reader may imagine the sorrow of Empress Junshi, ex-Emperor Kazan's Junior Consort Shishi, and Provisional Middle Counselor Kintō.[67]

61. *Daijin no taikyō*, a great formal banquet held annually by a Minister of State during the New Year season. It took place in the main room (*moya*) of his mansion, in contrast to the similar Appointment Banquet, an event held in the eavechambers to celebrate the master's appointment to ministerial office.

62. Morosuke had twelve sons and seven daughters, according to other sources. See s.n. 5.

63. As noted in Chapter 1, n. 167, not much is known about Koretada's daughters. *Sonpi bunmyaku*, 1: 381, lists only six, possibly because some of the others had died prematurely. See *Shōyūki*, 1: 100 (3 vi Kanna 1). The ninth married Prince Tametaka. EMZ, 1: 379.

64. Asateru and Akimitsu (944–1021) were sons of Morosuke's second son, Kanemichi. In 989 Asateru held Senior Second Rank and served as Major Counselor, Major Captain of the Left, Master of the Crown Prince's Household, and Inspector. Akimitsu held Junior Second Rank. A third son, Tokimitsu (948–1015), was a Consultant with Junior Third Rank.

65. Tamemitsu, then forty-seven, was Minister of the Right with Junior First Rank.

66. See s.n. 42 for the ranks and offices of Kaneie's sons by Tokihime, to whom the author is probably referring. Michitsuna (955–1020), a Middle Captain with Junior Third Rank, was below Michinaga on the official ladder.

67. Yoritada's children.

Yoritada received the posthumous name Rengikō, Upright and Excellent Lord. Though life is sad, there is little we can do about it. All too soon, the mourning period ended with a magnificent Buddhist service.

Because of the wrestling, the last of the Seventh Month usually slipped by unnoticed, but that year there seems to have been some talk of canceling the matches.[68]

At a special appointments ceremony, the Regent Kaneie became Chancellor; Major Counselor Michitaka, Palace Minister; Middle Counselor Michikane, a Major Counselor; and Michinaga, a Middle Counselor and Commander of the Right Gate Guards.[69]

Kochiyogimi became the son-in-law of the Minamoto Middle Counselor Shigemitsu, elder brother to the Reikeiden Consort (the mother of Emperor Murakami's seventh son, Prince Tomohira).[70] The attendant ceremonies far outshone the ones that had been arranged for his elder brother.

Saneyori's foster son, Sanesuke, was now a Consultant with a reputation as a fine gentleman.[71] Still a bachelor, he had received a number of overtures from noblemen with marriageable daughters, but for reasons of his own he had failed to respond. Everyone found his behavior curious.

Joint Coming-of-Age ceremonies were held for Princes Tametaka and Atsumichi.[72] Prince Tametaka came to be known as His Highness of the Board of Censors; Prince Atsumichi, as His Highness the Governor-General. Those offices were given them because three of Emperor Murakami's sons, Princes Tamehira, Tomohira, and Nagahira, held the ministries of Ceremonial, Central Affairs, and War. I should have mentioned earlier that the Ise Virgin was Princess Kyōshi, a younger sister of Emperor Kazan's Junior Consort Enshi, the daughter of Prince Tamehira.[73] Although there had been changes on the Imperial throne, Princess Senshi, Emperor Murakami's tenth daughter, continued to serve as Kamo Virgin.[74]

With the passing of time, the year drew to a close and the first year of Shōryaku [990] began. The Coming-of-Age ceremony for Emperor Ichijō took place on the Fifth of the First Month, and then, after a flurry of preparation, Kaneie held his New Year Banquet at the Nijō Palace. The re-

68. Presumably because of the Chancellor's death. The matches were in fact held. EMZ, 1: 382.

69. Kaneie became Chancellor in the Twelfth Month. The promotions of his three sons took place before Yoritada's death. EMZ, 1: 383.

70. See s.n. 52.   71. On Sanesuke, see Chapter 1, n. 57.

72. A mistake. The ceremony for Prince Tametaka was held in the Eleventh Month of 989, the one for Prince Atsumichi in 993.

73. On Enshi and Kyōshi, see s.nn. 36 and 38.

74. See s.n. 11.

modeled mansion was quite as beautiful and luxurious as the Regent had imagined it, and he presided in high good humor, assigning the place of honor to the Ichijō Minister of the Right, Tamemitsu.[75] The grounds were delightfully spacious. Michitaka's daughters watched the festivities from the elegant east wing, in which their father had taken up residence.[76] Some of the young gentlemen petitioned to be allowed to join them, but Michitaka would not allow it. The young Princes, Tametaka and Atsumichi, made a charming picture.

The great event of the Second Month was the presentation of Michitaka's eldest daughter, Teishi. Since Michitaka's wife Kishi was accustomed to the ways of the Imperial Palace, theirs was a fashionably social household, in which it was thought very wrong to keep the daughters in strict seclusion. Teishi, who was about sixteen at the time, became a Junior Consort on the night of her entrance into the Palace. Meanwhile Michitaka fretted because his next daughter was still only a child.

With no daughters of his own, Michikane must have found it hard to suppress jealous pangs. He had already built a grand mansion at Awata, furnished it with screens and partitions decorated with pictures of famous places and compositions by noted poets, ordered copyists to compile a collection of illustrated romances, and assembled a covey of ladies-in-waiting —all in anticipation of the birth of a daughter.[77] It was really rather amusing, people thought.

Fukutarigimi, the eldest of Michikane's sons, had fallen ill and died in the Eighth Month of the last year but one, and that too had been a bitter blow. The probable cause of the boy's death, according to some, was the extreme willfulness that had made everyone criticize him.[78]

Michitaka's third son, Takaie, a child of his principal wife, was then a Lesser Captain with Fourth Rank.[79] Takaie was something of a problem too, but not as much as Fukutarigimi. The fourth son, though still very

75. Tamemitsu had been guest of honor at a banquet held by Kaneie in the Twelfth Month of 989 to celebrate his appointment as Chancellor. The guest of honor at the New Year Banquet was the Minister of the Left, Minamoto Masanobu. EMZ, 1: 387.

76. Probably a mistake. Michitaka appears to have been living in the Higashisanjō Mansion. EMZ, 1: 388.

77. The mansion was on the far side of the Kamo River, probably in the general area of the present Shōgoin, Yoshida Shrine, and Shishigatani (Sakyō-ku, Kyōto).

78. Fukutarigimi (d. 989) had shocked the Court by throwing a temper tantrum at his grandfather's longevity celebration. See s.n. 49. The author implies that the hostile feelings of others caused the boy to sicken and die. EMZ, 1: 391. Ōkagami, pp. 199–200, describes him as "shockingly naughty and perverse," and attributes his premature demise to the curse of a snake he had tortured.

79. Takaie (979–1044) was eleven years old in 990. His rank was not Fourth but Junior Fifth Lower, and he did not become a Lesser Captain until 992. EM, 1: 493, s.n. 184.

young, had been made a Buddhist monk, the disciple of the Komatsu Bishop.[80] Except for Michiyori, nothing had been done yet about the careers of sons by other wives.

Kaneie had already been a widower for a number of years. He was more devoted than ever to his concubine, Naishi no Suke, whose status had become scarcely distinguishable from that of a wife. People of all kinds presented her with name certificates, and everyone congregated in her apartments whenever there was to be a distribution of Court offices.[81] She was the lady who had served Chōshi under the name Tayū.

At the beginning of Kaneie's regency, it had been pronounced inauspicious for him to remain single, and he had consequently married Princess Hōshi, Emperor Murakami's third daughter, whom he thought a charming and beautiful creature. (The Princess and the Emperor's third son, Prince Munehira, were the offspring of Arihira's daughter.) But she had failed to live up to expectations, and the marriage had soon ended, leaving her so ashamed that she had finally died. The incident was perhaps merely another sign of Naishi no Suke's good karma.

Kaneie had also started an affair with the granddaughter of Minister of Popular Affairs Motokata (a lady known as Chūjō no Miyasudokoro, who had been a minor Imperial concubine during Emperor En'yū's reign), but nothing had come of it.[82] The truth of the matter was that he had long ago concentrated his affections on Naishi no Suke. Although the Princes' nurses were quite as pretty, he never spoke to any of them, even in jest.

Meanwhile Kaneie's health had begun to fail. Recognizing the danger, his sons and Senshi tried every conceivable remedy. To the menacing spirits that had always plagued the Nijō Palace, the pathetic wraith of Princess Hōshi had now been added.[83] The brothers begged their father to go elsewhere. He refused to leave a house so perfectly suited to his taste, but presently the frightening course of the disease persuaded him to move

---

80. Michitaka's fourth son (exclusive of the offspring of casual liaisons) was the monk Ryūen (980?–1015). The Komatsu Bishop was Jitsuin (945–1000), an Enryakuji scholar-monk who spent his last years at a place called Komatsu Temple, believed to have been located in the area southwest of Omuro (Ukyō-ku, Kyōto). EMZ, 1: 392. (Ryūen himself was later known as the Komatsu Bishop. See Chapter 21, n. 8.)

81. A name certificate (*myōbu*) was a card listing the person's office, rank, name, and age. Its presentation was a symbolic act, pledging unlimited service in return for patronage.

82. Probably a daughter of Motokata's son Kanetada (935–1020), who was a Middle Captain during the reign of En'yū. Little is known of her. EMZ, 1: 394.

83. *Ōkagami*, p. 169, also ascribes Kaneie's illness and death to the malevolent influences at the Nijōin.

to the Higashisanjō Mansion, where the Princes, like everyone else, were frantic with anxiety.[84]

Kaneie petitioned to be relieved of the regency. The Emperor urged him to wait, but his condition grew desperate, and he resigned as Chancellor and Regent on the Fifth of the Fifth Month. There was not a dry sleeve anywhere, perhaps especially because the resignations came just at the time of the Sweet-Flag Festival.[85] It seemed appropriate to make him Kanpaku, but the crisis continued, and he entered holy orders on the Eighth of the Fifth Month. Although Michitaka was named Regent on the same day, it was impossible for him to derive any pleasure from the appointment while his father lay dying.

To Michitaka the end seemed imminent. In desperation, he converted the whole Nijō Palace into a Buddhist temple, telling himself that Kaneie could still live there if he recovered. At the Higashisanjō Mansion, all was misery and bewilderment as the malady continued to resist treatment.

Michitaka's situation was now splendid indeed. His wife Kishi had a large number of brothers—Akinobu, Michinobu, Sanenobu, and others— as well as a sister who had been selected to transmit the Imperial Decree (she was the wife of Tamemoto, the governor of Settsu), and a father who was still alive.[86] As head of the government, Michitaka could do just as he pleased. At the instigation of his wife's relatives, he hurriedly obtained Imperial sanction for Teishi's nomination as Empress, and the family began a great bustle of preparation at the very time when everyone was preoccupied with prayers for Kaneie's recovery. Thus Teishi became Empress on the First of the Sixth Month.[87] Most people felt that Michitaka had been wrong to go ahead with his daughter's elevation at such a time. Michinaga, who had been named Master of the Empress's Household, showed his anger by a brusque refusal to report for duty.

84. According to Ōkagami, p. 169, Kaneie died while still at the Nijōin, which had been converted into a temple, the Hokoin (or Hōkōin), shortly before his death.

85. The association is with ayame no ne ("sweet-flag roots"), a phrase that suggests weeping voices because of the homophone ne ("sound," "voice," "weeping voice"). On the Sweet-Flag Festival, see s.n. 53.

86. On Kishi's father, Takashina Naritada, see n. 12. The sister was called Senji because she had transmitted the Imperial Decree (senji) naming Teishi a Junior Consort. Senji's husband, Ōe Tamemoto, was a scholar-poet. In spite of their exalted connections, the brothers, of whom there appear to have been six, did not succeed in becoming kugyō. Sonpi bunmyaku, 4: 111.

87. The correct date is probably the Fifth of the Tenth Month, well after Kaneie's death. Teishi and the other Empress, Junshi (ex-Emperor En'yū's consort), were thenceforth called Chūgū and Kōgō, respectively. EMZ, 1: 401.

Meanwhile every effort to cure Kaneie failed, and his life ended on the Second of the Seventh Month. The entire Court was overcome with grief. True, he had turned sixty-two that year, but how bitter it seemed that he could not have been one of those who live to seventy or eighty! Since he had taken religious vows, he did not receive a posthumous title.

Naturally enough, Princes Tametaka and Atsumichi were inconsolable. Michiyori's plight was also sad. He was, to be sure, a Head Chamberlain, but he could not keep from worrying about the prospect of falling behind his younger brother, Korechika.[88]

The corridor and gallery apartments at the Higashisanjō Mansion were transformed into earthen-floored mourning chambers for the use of the Imperial personages and the dead man's sons.[89] The Crown Prince was deeply grieved.

The funeral and other ceremonies were performed with the utmost pomp and solemnity, and the later religious services were all quite perfect.

Arikuni had always been well disposed toward Michikane. Since he was also grateful for kindnesses shown him, he made it a practice to call fairly often at the Awata Mansion. It was a pity that his visits proved displeasing to Michitaka, whose father had always said, "Arikuni and Korenaka are my left and right eyes."[90]

During the mourning period, large numbers of specially commissioned Buddhist statues were installed in the central hall at the Hokoin Temple, as the Nijō Palace had been renamed; and the Forty-ninth Day services were held there toward the middle of the Eighth Month. The reader may imagine the nature of the occasion. The red plum by the east wing, which had been in dazzling full bloom for the grand New Year Banquet, was now nothing but a mass of undistinguished foliage. The Emperor, the Crown Prince, and everyone else made donations for the chanting of sutras.

Michitsuna, the oldest of Kaneie's sons, was then a Middle Captain of

88. In this section the author seems intent on presenting Michitaka in an unfavorable light; hence she makes Michiyori seem worse off than he was. Although it is true that Michitaka favored Korechika, one of his first official acts had been to elevate his older son, then nineteen, to the office of Consultant with Junior Third Rank. EMZ, 1: 403.

89. The floorboards were taken up, rush blinds were hung, and crude furnishings were installed. According to Ōkagami, p. 202, Michikane flouted convention by shunning the mourning chamber, used the hot weather as a pretext for keeping his blinds up, and read poetry with friends instead of praying. He justified his behavior on the grounds that Kaneie had unfairly denied him the regency, to which he considered himself entitled by virtue of his services at the time of Emperor Kazan's abdication.

90. See n. 49.

Third Rank. He must have been disappointed by his failure to become at least a Consultant before his father's death.[91]

Time passed swiftly, and soon the second year of Shōryaku [991] began. With Grand Empress Senshi and many others of the nobility still in mourning, the Emperor paid no New Year visit.

There had been no particular criticism of Michitaka's government, and the Regent himself was regarded as elegant and distinguished, but his aged, immensely learned father-in-law, Naritada (now called Takashina of Second Rank as the result of a recent promotion), was so very disagreeable by nature that everyone feared him. The brothers-in-law were installed in desirable provincial governorships, which had been distributed among them with a liberal hand. Many people resented the manner in which those gentlemen had used their positions for personal gain, and there was disgruntled talk of their humble origins.

Michitaka's wife Kishi was a devout Buddhist, always poring over some sutra or other. Her beneficences brought great pleasure to the monks at various mountains and temples.

Presently the state of ex-Emperor En'yū's health excited widespread concern. Already uneasy because there had been no Imperial visit that year, Emperor Ichijō resolved to hasten to his father's side at the earliest opportunity, and the journey took place as soon as an auspicious day could be selected.[92] The pain-wracked former sovereign gazed long and fondly at his son, who seemed very grown up now that he had performed the Coming-of-Age ceremony. Then he called for a list of his estates and other possessions and turned them all over to His Majesty. In spite of his youth, the Emperor was consumed with anxiety and grief. The ex-Emperor again looked at him for some time in silence, moved by the contrast with the usual Imperial visit. But it was dangerous to expose the boy to the malignant influences, and he hurried him off.

Several anxious days followed for the Emperor, and then, on the Twelfth of the Second Month in the second year of Shōryaku [991], the former sovereign's life came to an end. It was a time of indescribable grief and bewilderment for the monks, courtiers, secretaries, and others who had

91. Michitsuna, listed in reliable primary sources as Kaneie's second son, enjoyed a respectable later career: Consultant (991), Middle Counselor (996), and Major Counselor (997), with such prestigious additional posts as Master of the Empress's Household and Major Captain.

92. *Shōyūki* confirms that a visit was planned, but it does not seem to have been made. EMZ, 1: 412.

grown close to ex-Emperor En'yū through long years in his service. Kanchō, the Ninnaji Archbishop, was inconsolable.[93] (He was a son of the
Ninnaji Prince Atsumi and a brother of Minamoto Masanobu, the Tsuchimikado Minister.) Many shared the feelings of Gavāṃpati, who, stricken
with grief by Śākyamuni's death, turned to water and flowed away, saying,
"Now that the Great Teacher has entered nirvana, I shall follow him."[94]
"Heartbreakingly sad" is too pale a phrase for such an event. The Emperor reflected nostalgically on his last visit to his father.

93. The Ninnaji, the great Shingon temple at Omuro, stood near the residence where
En'yū spent his last years. Kanchō (916–98), a scholar-administrator remembered as the
founder of an esoteric study center and as the abbot of both the Ninnaji and the Tōji, had
administered Buddhist commandments to the ex-Emperor some years earlier.

94. Gavāṃpati (J. Kyōbonhadai) was a disciple of Śāriputra, the most brilliant of the
Buddha's disciples. EMZ, 1: 414.

4

UNFINISHED DREAMS

THE reader may imagine the majesty of ex-Emperor En'yū's funeral at Murasakino.[1] Deeply moved, Asateru, the Kan'in Major Captain of the Left, recalled the beauty of the same surroundings on a bygone Day of the Rat:[2]

Murasaki no	Purple-clouded plain
Kumo no kakete mo	Of Murasakino—
Omoiki ya	Could we have known then
Haru no kasumi ni	That we should see our lord
Nashite min to wa.	Mingle with the haze of spring?

Yukinari, the Assistant Commander of the Military Guards, was still very young, but after hearing Asateru's poem he sent a composition of his own to Koretada's grandson, Lesser Captain Narifusa:[3]

Okureji to	I hurried,
Tsune no miyuki wa	Not to be late,
Isogishi o	Whenever our lord traveled—
Keburi ni sowanu	But now this sad journey
Tabi no kanashisa.	Into smoke where I cannot go.

There were many others, always in the same melancholy, nostalgic vein. I doubt that anyone could remember them all.

---

1. According to other sources, the ex-Emperor was cremated near his residence, the En'yūin, south of Murasakino. EMZ, 1: 422.

2. A reference to En'yū's Day of the Rat excursion to Murasakino in 985, an occasion memorable, among other things, for the uninvited appearance and subsequent expulsion, by Asateru and Sanesuke, of the eccentric poet Sone no Yoshitada. EMZ, 1: 422; Ōkagami, p. 282. Asateru had resigned as Major Captain of the Left two years earlier; in 991 he was a Major Counselor. Kugyō bunin, 1: 232, 235.

3. See s.n. 54.

The funeral cortege returned to the capital.

Some deeply moving things happened during the mourning period. Noblemen who had been close to the ex-Emperor secluded themselves in temporary shelters at the funeral site.

It was during that time that Middle Captain Sanekata sent a friend a gorgeous spray of cherry blossoms, accompanied by a poem that everyone considered most apposite:

Sumizome no	This sad period
Koromo uki yo no	Of gray-dyed robes
Hanazakari	Comes in the season of
	flowering trees;
Ori wasurete mo	Forgetful of the time,
Oritekeru kana.	I have broken off a spray.

There were few events of brilliance during the period of national mourning.

Ex-Emperor Kazan continued to wander about on pious journeys. Once when he had fallen ill on the road to Kumano, he composed a poem, inspired by the salt-making fires of some seafolk:

Tabi no sora	Were the smoke from my pyre
Yowa no keburi to	To rise by night
Noborinaba	Into these travel skies,
Ama no moshiobi	Others might think it
Taku ka to ya min.	But a salt-maker's fire.

The ex-Emperor composed many similar poems during his travels, but no trustworthy person was there to preserve them, and they have all been forgotten. His wanderings once led him to a temple called the Enjōji, where the cherry blossoms were exceptionally fine.[4] As he strolled under the trees he murmured:

Ko no moto o	Making my home
Sumika to sureba	Beneath the trees,
Onozukara	Unwittingly
Hana miru hito ni	I am to become, it seems,
Narinubeki kana.	A blossom-viewer.

It was a pity that a former sovereign should have found himself in such dismal circumstances. His grandmother, Koretada's widow, was living at

---

4. The temple has not been identified. For theories, see EMZ, 1: 427.

the Eastern Palace with the former Regent's ninth daughter.[5] The old lady missed Kazan sorely, but his present status did not allow him to inhabit a layman's house in the capital.

Buddhist services for ex-Emperor En'yū were held at the En'yū Palace on the Twenty-eighth of the Third Month.[6] One may be sure that Emperor Ichijō was at pains to protect the interests of his father's favorite courtiers after the former Emperor's death.

Before the end of the year, there was a promotion to the Chancellorship for Tamemitsu, who had been Minister of the Right. Shigenobu, the Rokujō Major Counselor, replaced him. Shigenobu was a brother of the Tsuchimikado Minister of the Left, Masanobu.

A certain monk, remarkable for his skill as a chanter of sutras, often served at night in the apartments of the heir apparent, who was by then fifteen or sixteen years old. One evening, while entertaining the Prince with romantic stories, the monk happened to mention Naritoki's daughter Seishi. The Prince, much interested, summoned him nightly thereafter to recite the holy scriptures, and invariably managed to turn the subject of their casual conversations to Seishi. "I implore you," he said with every indication of sincerity, "to arrange the matter for me." The monk approached Naritoki, who reflected that Seishi could not stay single forever. He had done the right thing, he thought, in putting Emperor Kazan off. As far as the present Emperor was concerned, there was his youth to consider, as well as the fact that he had already named an Empress. But the Crown Prince was a different matter. To be sure, Kaneie's daughter Suishi had already entered the Crown Prince's Household, but that would make no difference. Naritoki began to prepare for the presentation of his daughter, who must have been about nineteen.

Naritoki's younger sister, Hōshi, had been a great favorite with Emperor Murakami, who had given her furniture and incidental requisites of every description, made expressly for her use. Since Naritoki had inherited all her rare and beautiful comb boxes, folding screens, and other objects,

---

5. Koretada's widow had reared Kazan. Although the ninth daughter was Kazan's aunt, her age may have been about the same as his. (Note that she later married Kazan's brother, Prince Tametaka, who was nine years the ex-Emperor's junior.) The Eastern Palace (Higashinoin; also called Higashiichijōin), situated south of Konoe and east of Higashinotōin, had belonged successively to an Imperial Prince, to Tadahira, and to Koretada. Since Kazan did in fact go there to live, as the author proceeds to reveal, it came to be known later as the Kazan'in. EMZ, 1: 429.

6. Other sources give the date as the Twenty-seventh of the intercalary Second Month. EM, 1: 130, n. 10.

he was free to concentrate on the wardrobes for Seishi and her ladies.

Seishi's mother was a daughter of the Biwa Major Counselor Nobu-mitsu, a circumstance that placed the family in an excellent relationship to the Crown Prince.[7]

Emperor Murakami had taught both Hōshi and Naritoki to play the thirteen-stringed zither, and Naritoki had in turn taught Seishi, who now played even better than her father, adopting a somewhat more modern touch that produced an exceedingly brilliant effect. One does not hear much about that sort of thing nowadays, so her accomplishment was all the more remarkable.

Naritoki's second daughter, Naka no Kimi, had been taught to play the lute. Observing that Naritoki and his wife were preoccupied with Seishi's affairs, Naka no Kimi's grandmother had taken the younger girl into her own home to rear, and the old lady, by now very infirm, was eager to find a suitable husband for her charge.[8] Naritoki's indifference must have been a source of great annoyance to her.

Soon all was in readiness, and early in the Twelfth Month Seishi joined the Crown Prince's Household, awakening old memories by taking up residence in the Sen'yōden.[9] Fortunately the Prince was delighted with her. "No one can slight my daughter now!" said Naritoki.

The Crown Prince showed no great interest in Suishi, but the atmosphere in her apartments was gay and sociable, and the Reikeiden corridor attracted courtiers who wanted a bit of relaxed conversation.[10] It was said that Seishi's reserve made people uncomfortable.

Seishi's elder brother Michitō was serving as Director of the Palace Storehouse Bureau.[11] People thought him a phlegmatic youth, very unlike his father.[12] Chōmeigimi, the brother who had been a Gentleman-in-waiting, had already taken religious vows. Naritoki often wished that Chōmeigimi, rather than Michitō, had been the one to remain active in secular affairs, for with Chōmeigimi, he felt, enormous success might have been achieved through the family's present connections.

Naritoki's nephew, Middle Captain Sanekata, was regarded as impres-

---

7. See s.n. 55.

8. The grandmother was Morotada's widow, the mother of Naritoki.

9. The former residence of her aunt, Hōshi.

10. The author is referring to the east corridor of the Reikeiden, where Suishi's ladies lived. EMZ, 1: 436.

11. There is no independent evidence to indicate that Michitō ever served as Director of the Palace Storehouse Bureau. He is known to have been an Assistant Commander in the Military Guards in 991.

12. Ōkagami, p. 97, describes Naritoki as cantankerous and self-important.

sively elegant and cultivated, and Seishi found his support a great asset. For the moment, at least, she could also count on the Crown Prince's absolute devotion, so that altogether she seemed very well off.

Michitaka's oldest brother, Michitsuna, was a Consultant. Michikane was Palace Minister, and Michinaga was a Major Counselor. Michitaka's oldest son, Michiyori, had become a Middle Counselor, as had Korechika, who had previously been a Middle Captain of Third Rank. Only the Regent's relatives, it seems, are ever promoted.

Since Michiyori's wife lived at Yamanoi, people called him the Yamanoi Middle Counselor.

Korechika's wife, the daughter of Major Counselor Shigemitsu, had given birth to a splendid baby boy, who was pampered outrageously by his grandmother and Michitaka. He was called Matsugimi.[13] Whenever he was taken to visit Michitaka, he and his nurse came back laden with gifts. The ladies-in-waiting must have been anxious for him to grow up.

The days and months slipped by, and presently the third year of Shōryaku [992] arrived. How wretchedly evanescent is man's life! People were already absorbed in preparations for the first anniversary of ex-Emperor En'yū's death, which was to be observed in the Second Month. The rites came and went, the gray mourning garb disappeared, and the Court shone again with the usual brilliant costumes.

The Regent, Michitaka, waited impatiently for some of his other daughters to grow up.

Michinaga's wives, Rinshi and Meishi, had both been pregnant since the preceding year. Beset as before by nervous qualms, Rinshi's father, the Minister of the Left, offered the customary prayers. Senshi saw to the rituals for Meishi.[14]

Michitaka had built an additional Buddhist hall, the Shakuzenji, inside the Hokoin precincts, and he was now engaged in elaborate preparations for the dedication.[15]

---

13. The grandmother was Shigemitsu's wife. Matsugimi was the childhood name of Michimasa (993?–1054).

14. We have supplied the name Senshi for the *miya* ("Imperial personage") of the text. *Shōkai*, 2: 99, and EMZ, 1: 442, appear to be in error in supplying Prince Moriakira (Meishi's foster father, who is listed in standard references as having died in 986).

15. The Hokoin was Kaneie's old Nijō Mansion. The Shakuzenji dedication, which took place in 994 rather than 992, was a major event of Michitaka's regency, described at length in one of the most elegant and witty sections of the *Pillow Book*. After elaborate advance preparations, the occasion began with a great formal procession through the city to the hall. Grand Empress Senshi, with fourteen carriage-loads of ladies, and Empress Teishi, with twenty—all magnificent in ceremonial robes—were the focus of attention. The daylong series of rituals included prayers, sacred dances, and the dedication of a complete set of the Buddhist

Death claimed Tamemitsu, the Ichijō Chancellor, on the Sixteenth of the Sixth Month. His posthumous title was Kōtokukō, Constant and Virtuous Lord. Since the death of his daughter, the Junior Consort Kishi, incessant religious observances had occupied his time—more so, indeed, than if he had been a monk. He had founded a magnificent temple called the Hōjūji, where, with admirable piety, he had celebrated the holy rites from morning to night.[16] His eldest son, Sanenobu, was Provisional Master of the Crown Prince's Household at the time, and another son, Tadanobu, held the title of Middle Captain.[17] During the Kamo Festival in the Fourth Month, Tadanobu had served as Imperial Messenger. Tamemitsu had equipped him with great splendor, but he himself had gone to view the procession in a shabby carriage, and had driven off after seeing him, unable to muster any enthusiasm for the remainder of the spectacle. People recalled the incident with deep sadness.

Tamemitsu had had three daughters who were full sisters.[18] The oldest, the Lady of the Central Hall, had been reared with the utmost devotion. Indeed, the existence of her two sisters had mattered little to the minister, who had seemed to care only for her and for Kishi. Since he had often remarked that beauty was everything in a daughter, the other two must have been plain.

During the mourning period, the Kamo Virgin sent Tadanobu a poem of condolence:

Iro kawaru	How deep lies the dew
Sode ni wa tsuyu no	On your sleeve
Ika naran	Of unaccustomed hue?
Omoiyaru ni mo	The very thought
Kie zo iraruru.	Overwhelms me with grief.

Those were sad days.

The Buddhist services for Tamemitsu were celebrated at the Hōjūji.

---

canon, its scrolls borne aloft on red lotus flowers by a procession of clerical and lay dignitaries. For details, see *Mak.*, pp. 284–300; Morris 1967, 1: 219–33; and EMZ, 1: 443.

16. The Hōjūji, probably founded in memory of Kishi (d. 985), stood southeast of the present Sanjūsangendō in Kyōto. It boasted a golden statue of Śākyamuni in its main hall, and was, says *Ōkagami*, p. 161, "an impressive achievement for someone who had never served as Regent."

17. Tadanobu (967–1035) later became a prominent figure at Court, admired for his literary ability and knowledge of ceremonial. Sanenobu (964–1001), depicted in *Ōkagami*, pp. 159–60, as dissipated and vain, is said to have died of pique when the younger Tadanobu was promoted over his head in 1001 to the office of Middle Counselor.

18. Shinden no Onkata (San no Kimi), Shi no Kimi, and Go no Kimi. The three, offspring of a daughter of Fujiwara Koretada, were half-sisters to the Imperial Consort Kishi, whose mother was a daughter of Fujiwara Atsutoshi.

Tamemitsu's house, the Ichijō Mansion, had been designed on an exceptionally grand scale. It proved difficult to maintain after the minister's death, and was soon in a sad state of disrepair. He had left the property, as well as all his other possessions, to the Lady of the Central Hall.

Meanwhile ex-Emperor Kazan had beeen paying an occasional visit to Koretada's ninth daughter at the Eastern Palace. One day he took it into his head to have his legs massaged by his old nurse's daughter, Nakatsukasa, whom he had seen on innumerable other occasions without paying her any attention.[19] Before long the two were on intimate terms, and the infatuated former sovereign was making himself at home in the palace instead of going back to his temple.[20] It was bad enough to have to witness his behavior oneself, thought Koretada's daughter. How much worse it would be when word of the affair got around, as it inevitably must!

Soon Kazan had quite settled down at the Eastern Palace, whence he issued political orders in a pathetic manner. Yoshichika, the Buddhist Novice at Iimuro, must have thought the ex-Emperor's behavior would come as no surprise to anyone familiar with his past eccentricities.

Senshi and the Regent greeted the news with great concern. "How can he get along without sustenance households?" they wondered.[21] "Perhaps it would be impossible to put provincial posts at his disposal, but it is only proper that he should have annual ranks and sustenance households. The way he is being treated shows a shocking lack of respect for a former sovereign." Appropriate grants were thus made. The ex-Emperor, who had found that life in the capital suited him very well, proceeded to build himself a house on the north side of the Eastern Palace. Then it apparently occurred to him that all this was rather an imposition on Koretada's daughter, and so he urged his brother Prince Tametaka, the President of the Board of Censors, to marry her. The Prince was willing, and the marriage took place.

For many years, Koretada's daughter had been a lady of exceptional piety. She had recited the *Lotus Sutra* some 2,000 or 3,000 times, and her

19. The ex-Emperor's nurse, the wife of a provincial governor named Taira Sukeyori, had presumably stayed on in his grandmother's household after his own departure. The daughter, Nakatsukasa, was also married to a provincial governor, Taira Suketada, by whom she had had a daughter. She seems to have served later as Mistress of the Wardrobe. EMZ, 1: 450.

20. Probably the Kazanji.

21. The Regent in question seems to have been Michinaga, rather than Michitaka. For a discussion of probable chronological errors in *Eiga's* description of ex-Emperor Kazan's activities, see EMZ, 1: 450–55. Although ex-Emperors and certain other members of the Imperial Family were entitled to sustenance households similar to those assigned to kugyō (2,000, in the case of an ex-Emperor), it appears that Kazan had forfeited his, as well as his claim to annual ranks and offices, by becoming a monk. EMZ, 1: 450.

chief concern after the marriage seemed to be to prevent the new state of affairs from interfering with her incessant devotions. Her husband, the Prince, was a tireless gallant, indiscriminate in his pursuit of women, and his nocturnal adventures caused much anxiety in those unsettled times.[22]

One day the Prince noticed a torn valance on a blind at the palace.[23] "Your blind looks as though it has had a run-in with the Imperial Police," he said.

"But it is a Censor who has come," ex-Emperor Kazan retorted wittily.

The ex-Emperor, who had always been rather flamboyant and hedonistic, now seemed to have cast off all inhibitions, as though heedless of the life to come. Nakatsukasa's daughter by Suketada, the governor of Wakasa, entered his service, and presently both mother and daughter were pregnant at the same time. The reader may imagine the dismay and horror with which Koretada's poor daughter viewed such a scandalous state of affairs.

Meanwhile, the overriding concern at Court was the illness of Grand Empress Senshi, which everyone recognized to be a matter of grave moment. The familiar evil spirits had made their presence known in the usual way, and there seemed little hope for her life. After paying her a visit, the Emperor returned dazed with grief. The malignant influences tormented her day and night, causing one fainting fit after another. At length she announced that her sole remaining desire was to become a nun. Her brothers were reluctant to agree but realized that her life was at stake. "After all," they said, "the important thing is for her to survive." So the deed was done. It was a terrible decision, but she must have felt driven to it by the will to live. And she did indeed recover, whether because of the step she had taken or because she had received every treatment available to the lay world—or perhaps because of her solemn vows to visit Ishiyama annually for the remainder of her life and to make pilgrimages to Hasedera and Sumiyoshi.[24] It would be a pale reflection of the truth to say that Emperor Ichijō was overjoyed.

22. Possibly a reference to the epidemics that swept the capital during the 990's. EMZ, 1: 456.

23. Probably at Kazan's residence.

24. Ishiyama, a famous old Shingon temple, was one of the Thirty-three Places sacred to Kannon, in what is now Ōtsu-shi, Shiga-ken. Its image of Kannon, to which miraculous powers were ascribed, was a cult object for people of all classes. Among its illustrious visitors were many Emperors from Uda on, and such literary figures as Murasaki Shikibu and Akazome Emon. Hasedera was another of the Thirty-three Places. Although the temple was relatively far from the capital (at Hatsuse in the present Shiki-gun, Nara-ken), its eleven-headed Kannon was deeply venerated by members of the Court circle. References in *Genji* and the *Pillow Book* suggest that it had a special appeal for noble ladies. See, for example, *Mak.*,

It was a great pity that Senshi had had to become a nun when she was scarcely more than thirty, but one must point out that she received the status of a Retired Emperor, with the title of Imperial Lady, and that annual offices and ranks were undoubtedly provided for her.[25] Untroubled by guards or by the necessity of dispatching messengers to the annual festivals, she led a tranquil, happy life. Men of pleasing appearance were chosen to serve as Secretaries in her household.

Before the year was out, the Imperial Lady journeyed to Hasedera with a retinue of senior nobles and other courtiers. The handsome young men were attired in hunting robes, and the older gentlemen wore informal costumes. It was a brilliant party—the Regent in his carriage, Senshi in a Chinese carriage, and carriage-loads of nuns preceding the conveyances of the ladies-in-waiting. The entourage included at least ten nuns, of whom some were recent arrivals and others ladies who had been with Senshi for years. One was a young girl, formerly called Miyuki, who had been named Ribata[26] after joining her mistress in holy orders. There were a number of new girls, who answered to such names as Homeki, Suiki, Hanako, and Shikimi.

At the temple, Senshi presented magnificent offerings to the sacred image, conferred largesse on the monks, and took her leave. She planned to visit Sumiyoshi in the Second or Third Month of that year.[27] Hers was an enviable life.

Michitaka was dissatisfied because his younger son, Korechika, was still only a Consultant and Middle Captain, whereas Michiyori was already a Middle Counselor. To Michiyori's chagrin, Michitaka proceeded to promote Korechika to the office of Major Counselor over his head.[28] Around that time, a serious illness compelled Asateru to resign as Major Captain of the Bodyguards, and Michikane attained a Major Captaincy, becoming

---

pp. 172–77; and Morris 1967, 1: 126–30. Sumiyoshi (Suminoe), on the shore of Naniwa Bay (now Ōsaka Bay), was the site of an important shrine whose deities were patrons of seafarers—and, from the Heian period on, of poets.

25. According to Nihon kiryaku, 2: 172 (10 ix Shōryaku 2), she retained her old annual offices, annual ranks, and sustenance households.

26. Skt. Revata, the name of an arhat mentioned in the Lotus Sutra.

27. "That year" translates kotoshi, presumably 992. Up to this point, the author has led the reader to believe that Senshi's renunciation of the world took place in 992. The Grand Empress in fact fell ill around the beginning of the Ninth Month in 991, became a nun on the Sixteenth of that month, and made the Hasedera pilgrimage in the Tenth Month. There is no independent record of a visit to Sumiyoshi in 992. EMZ, 1: 459–60.

28. As the author states earlier in the chapter, Korechika had become a Middle Counselor in 991; thus he was no longer a Consultant. His promotion to Major Counselor took place on the Twenty-eighth of the Eighth Month, 992. EMZ, 1: 463.

Major Captain of the Right. Naritoki assumed the title of Major Captain of the Left.[29] Third Rank was granted to all Assistant Chiefs who had been in service when Senshi was Grand Empress.[30]

The time had come for Michikane's daughter by Fujiwara Naishi no Suke of Third Rank to perform the Putting On of the Train.[31] The girl's mother made a great fuss about it, and Michikane supervised the necessary arrangements, though he took little interest in the affair.

Now that the Emperor had grown up a bit, Michitaka's title was changed to Kanpaku.[32] The Regent's middle daughter, Genshi, who had reached the age of fourteen or fifteen, was presented to the Crown Prince with great splendor and elegance. She took up residence in the Shigeisha, and Seishi withdrew to her father's house. Everything seemed to work to Genshi's advantage. The Prince, accustomed to Seishi's quiet tastes, responded to his new consort's gaiety and fashionable ways with almost embarrassing warmth. She made no special effort to appear modern, but he found her quite delightful, even to the exquisite color combinations peeping out beneath her hems and sleeves. Since she had received ladies' costumes and other presentation gifts from many quarters, all of her things were beyond criticism.

By comparison with her sisters, Michitaka's third daughter was extremely childish in appearance and manner. Wishing to do his best for her, her father arranged a match with Prince Atsumichi. The Prince, annoyed by the gossip about the arrangement, paid no attention to her after the wedding, but the Regent took particular care to look after his son-in-law's affairs, feeling that his behavior was only natural. The daughter came out of it very well, since she was received in the Southern Palace.[33]

---

29. Asateru had resigned as Major Captain of the Left in 989. Naritoki moved up from Major Captain of the Right on the First of the Sixth Month, 990, at which time his former post went to Michikane. EMZ, 1: 464.

30. "Assistant Chiefs" translates an unintelligible phrase, *sei* (Ueda *Daijiten* 5643) *no suke*, which appears to be the result of a textual corruption. There is some reason to believe that it should read Naishi no Suke (Assistant Handmaids). For a discussion of possible interpretations, see EMZ, 1: 464.

31. The daughter was Sonshi. For the Putting On of the Train (*mogi* or *chakumo*), see s.n. 56.

32. On 22 iv 993. The Emperor was thirteen.

33. Minaminoin, a residence associated with the names of Emperor Reizei's sons, Princes Okisada (Emperor Sanjō), Atsumichi, and Tametaka. It is thought by some commentators to have been part of Kaneie's Higashisanjō Mansion, and by others, including Matsumura, to have been part of the Reizeiin. (As indicated in Chapter 1, n. 151, the Reizeiin proper was destroyed by fire in 970 and not restored until 1008. It is conceivable, however, that some of its subsidiary buildings survived.) EMZ, 1: 469; Cranston 1969, p. 294, n. 369; *Nihon rekishi daijiten*, 19: 177.

In spite of her youth, Michitaka's fourth daughter became Mistress of the Wardrobe.

Takaie, Michitaka's youngest son by Kishi, had been made a Middle Captain of Third Rank.[34] He married the cherished daughter of Shigenobu, the Rokujō Minister of the Right;[35] and the minister, by then well along in years, was so pleased with the match that he always stayed up to look after things when Takaie arrived, even in the middle of the night. Unimpressed by Shigenobu's extraordinary kindness, Takaie neglected his wife for another woman, the daughter of Senior Secretary Kagemasa.[36] Michitaka scolded him for his shameful and disrespectful behavior, but there is little to be gained by reasoning with a man in love.

Tamemitsu's Ichijō Mansion had come into the hands of Senshi, who was refurbishing it in elegant style, apparently with the intention of getting it ready for the Emperor's use after his abdication.

Both of Michinaga's wives had given birth to sons. Rinshi's was named Tazugimi and Meishi's Iwagimi. Senshi's own nurses were looking after Iwagimi. Lady Tachibana of Third Rank had had a son and a daughter by Michitaka, as well a child by Michiyori.[37]

Seishi was several months pregnant. Her father, Naritoki, ordered prayers for her, happy and proud that her career in the Crown Prince's palace had gone so well. Since Genshi was with the Prince, Seishi felt that the pregnancy had come at an opportune time. Kaneie's daughter Suishi was living entirely at home, the subject of some very unpleasant rumors,[38] but

34. Takaie was named Middle Captain of the Left in 993 but did not attain Third Rank until the Eighth Month of 994.

35. Minamoto Shigenobu was the younger brother of Rinshi's father, Masanobu. As the author indicates, he held the title of Udaijin in 993. He became Minister of the Left in 994 and received posthumous Senior First Rank after his death in 995. Of his numerous sons, the only kugyō was Michikata (968–1044), a Middle Counselor from 1020 to 1043.

36. Fujiwara Kagemasa (d. 1023) was the brother of the Lady in the Wing Chamber, one of Kaneie's wives. As a Senior Secretary (Daijin), he was the top-ranking third-level official in the household of one of the Imperial personages (probably, it has been conjectured, Empress Teishi, Takaie's sister). EMZ, 1: 470.

37. Lady Tachibana was Tachibana Naishi no Suke. She was granted Junior Third Rank in 1010, after the events described here. The son by Michitaka was Yoshichika; the child by Michiyori was a daughter, mentioned in Chapter 13, where she is called Lady Dainagon. EMZ, 1: 472.

38. A reference to her liaison with Minamoto Yorisada (977–1020), the ablest of Prince Tamehira's sons, who was then a rising young tenjōbito. She is said to have borne Yorisada a son, Bishop Raiken, who presumably was present *in utero* during the famous scene that took place after Crown Prince Okisada asked Michinaga to investigate rumors of Suishi's pregnancy. Tsunoda 1963, pp. 80–87; EMZ, 1: 473. According to *Ōkagami*, p. 171, Michinaga pushed aside Suishi's curtains, ripped open her clothing, squeezed one of her breasts, and received a shower of milk in the face.

her behavior had not greatly affected the Crown Prince, who really cared only for Seishi, and who had indeed reached the point of looking on his relationship with Genshi as an irksome obligation.

Presently Korechika became Palace Minister. He was only about twenty years old.[39] Michinaga, who considered the promotion outrageous, began to keep to himself.

The Tsuchimikado Minister Masanobu died on the Twenty-ninth of the Seventh Month in the fourth year of Shōryaku [993]. Michinaga and the minister's sons assembled to take care of the melancholy last rites. The death was not unexpected, since Masanobu had been around seventy, but his wife, Bokushi, took it very hard. The successive Buddhist services were celebrated with the utmost solemnity. By that time Rinshi was pregnant again, and the old man had had his heart set on seeing the child safely into the world.

Two years after Kaneie's death, Michitaka stripped Arikuni of his offices and rank and confined him to his house. Michikane and Michinaga were appalled. People felt even sorrier for Arikuni when Korenaka was granted the post of Major Controller of the Left. While Arikuni was still in disgrace, his son lost his position as governor of Tanba.[40]

Soon the end of the old year ushered in the fifth year of Shōryaku [994]. For unknown reasons, it proved a troubled time. Great numbers of people sickened and died from the spring on, and their corpses littered the streets.[41] Unfortunately, the year was the one in which Seishi's child was expected. Rinshi's delivery was also imminent, and with matters in such a state the family was greatly concerned about her safety.

Rinshi's child, a daughter, was born without difficulty in the Third Month.[42] Despite the terrible conditions in the city, it was a happy event.

Around the Tenth of the Fifth Month, it became apparent that Seishi's confinement was at hand. A constant stream of messengers arrived from the Crown Prince, and Naritoki was tense with apprehension, but presently a fine little Prince entered the world.[43] Weeping for joy, Naritoki began to plan a series of magnificent celebrations. So passed the ceremonies during the first seven days—events so splendid that I must rely on the reader's

39. He received the office on the Twenty-eighth of the Eighth Month, 994, at twenty-one (sai), jumping over two Major Counselors (Asateru and Naritoki) and one Provisional Major Counselor (Michinaga).

40. See Chapter 3, n. 49, and EMZ, 1: 477–78.

41. Probably a smallpox epidemic. See s.n. 57.

42. The daughter was Kenshi (994–1027).

43. Prince Atsuakira (994–1051), the future Emperor Sanjō's first child. For a list of Emperor Sanjō's children, see s.n. 58.

powers of imagination to do them justice. The wet nurses assembled, and the Crown Prince waited impatiently for his first glimpse of his son.

"Of course it would be nice to let him see the baby as soon as possible, but the first meeting never used to take place until the child was five or seven years old," said Naritoki, who inclined to an old-fashioned, leisurely approach in the matter. The Prince insisted that he could not wait that long.

The pestilence ravaging the city was a source of deep concern to Senshi and Michitaka, especially since it was rumored that the next year promised to be even more terrible.

Emperor Murakami's ninth son, Prince Akihira, was living at Iwakura after having become a Buddhist Novice, as was his full brother, the late Emperor's third son, Prince Munehira.[44] (Prince Munehira had had two sons by a daughter of Masanobu. One of them, Lesser Captain Narinobu, had been adopted by Michinaga; the other, who had been given to the church while a boy, lived in the same place as his father.[45]) Prince Akihira had earlier married the daughter of Morosuke's son Machiosagimi, the Tōnomine Novice Lesser Captain, and the lady had given birth to a sweet baby girl. The Prince had found it hard to part with the child, but he was well aware that this is a transitory world, and so he had forced himself to accept the separation. Having heard stories about the little Princess's beauty, Michikane had taken her in, adopted her, and begun to rear her with great care. (The real reason for the adoption may have been the close relationship between Michikane's wife and the Prince's.[46]) By the time of which I speak, a great many eligible gentlemen had presented themselves as suitors, but Michikane had rejected them all. Then Provisional Middle Captain Kintō, the son of the late Sanjō Chancellor Yoritada, began to woo the lady.[47] Observing that even the most trifling note from Kintō

44. On Murakami's children, see s.n. 11. Iwakura was another name for the Daiunji, a temple founded in 971 by Fujiwara Atsutada in fulfillment of a vow by Emperor En'yū. Its reconstructed main hall survives at Ono-no-sato Iwakura, Sakyō-ku, Kyōto.

45. Narinobu (b. 979), who had assumed the Minamoto surname, was adopted by Michinaga and Rinshi (his aunt) after Prince Munehira's (951–1041) entry into holy orders. Known as the Shining Middle Captain (Teru Chūjō), he is remembered chiefly for his dramatic renunciation of the world in 1001, a step taken in concert with his friend Fujiwara Shigeie, the Radiant Lesser Captain (Hikaru Shōshō), because the two were depressed by the superior attainments of the "Four Counselors" of Emperor Ichijō's Court, Fujiwara Tadanobu, Fujiwara Kintō, Minamoto Toshikata, and Fujiwara Yukinari. The Prince's other son by Masanobu's daughter was the monk Eien (980?–1041?). EMZ, 1: 486; Dainihonshi, 4: 369; Honchō kōin shōunroku, p. 431; Hagitani 1971–73, 1: 189–90.

46. Machiosagimi was the childhood name of Morosuke's son Takamitsu. See s.n. 59.

47. Kintō had relinquished the post of Middle Captain in 992, the year of his appointment as a Consultant.

was written with incomparable grace and elegance, Michikane made up his mind to accept him. He furnished the east wing of his Nijō Mansion in splendid style, assigned ten accomplished and beautiful ladies-in-waiting, two girl attendants, and two maids to serve his foster daughter, and then, having done everything in his power to provide an agreeable setting, allowed Kintō to begin his visits.[48] Since the Prince's daughter was very lovely, the marriage proved a gratifying success.[49]

After a time Kintō redecorated the west wing of the Shijō Palace for his wife, explaining that he had found it inconvenient to visit her at Michikane's house.[50] Delighted by the lady's arrival, the late Emperor En'yū's consort, Empress Junshi, and ex-Emperor Kazan's former Junior Consort, Shishi, both arranged to meet her. Everything had gone just as Michikane could have wished, and he kept up a cordial correspondence with Kintō.

Michikane also adopted one of Tamemitsu's sons, Middle Captain Michinobu.[51] Michikane married him to his own wife's sister and in general assumed responsibility for his welfare.

As winter approached, Michitaka developed an insatiable thirst.[52] He grew alarmingly thin, and his visits to the Imperial Palace all but ceased. His distraught father-in-law Naritada, the Novice of Second Rank, not only offered prayers but also resorted to more extreme measures.[53] Kishi tried every imaginable remedy. Since the pestilence had abated somewhat with the advent of cold weather, people had just begun to relax when this fresh cause for anxiety arose.

In addition to his handsome son, Matsugimi, Palace Minister Korechika now had two pretty little daughters, whom he was rearing with all the care suitable for future Empresses.[54]

48. The mansion was north of Nijō and east of Machijiri across the street from Michitaka's house. It was also called the Machijiri Mansion. Tsunoda 1963, pp. 54, 72; Tsunoda 1969, p. 280.

49. The lady became Kintō's principal wife. Ōkagami, p. 93.

50. The Shijō Mansion was Yoritada's house south of Shijō, here called Palace because it was the residence of Empress Junshi.

51. Michinobu (972–94), a talented poet who died at the age of twenty-two, was Tamemitsu's third son. According to more reliable sources, he was adopted by Kaneie, not by Michikane. EMZ, 1: 489.

52. Michitaka's illness is thought to have been diabetes complicated by heavy drinking. Ōkagami, p. 175; EMZ, 1: 490.

53. It was widely believed that Naritada made a habit of supplementing the power of prayer with spells and curses. See EMZ, 1: 490.

54. Korechika's children by Shigemitsu's daughter were as follows. (1) Michimasa (993?–1054). Childhood name, Matsugimi. Highest rank, Jr. 3; highest official post, Middle Captain. Remembered as a poet and for his affair with the former Ise Virgin Princess Tōshi (1001 or 1002–1023), a daughter of Sanjō. (2) Ōhimegimi (b. ca. 993). Married Michinaga's son Yorimune. (3) Naka no Himegimi, also called Sochidono no Onkata (b. ca. 995). Entered

It was said of Korechika that he was almost too handsome and talented for a mere mortal courtier. Could it be, people wondered, that he was destined for an early death?

Michitaka's third son by Kishi (the one who had been given to the church) had been made a Bishop, and his younger brother, Takaie, had become a Middle Counselor. As for Michiyori, Michitaka remembered that Kaneie had had great plans for him, and so he made him a Major Counselor.

As the year drew to an end, the Regent continued to suffer from his craving for water.

Seishi had returned to the Crown Prince's palace with the little Prince. The baby's devoted father, unable to think of anything but his child, carried him about in his arms and attended to all his needs.

At the start of the new year, Empress Teishi reigned unrivaled in the Imperial Palace, but there was some doubt about the status of the Regent's other daughter, the consort of the Crown Prince.

In the First Month of this first year of Chōtoku [995], the pestilence returned with devastating virulence. It seemed that no one was to be spared. Senshi, already deeply disturbed by Michitaka's illness, began to fear that it might be impossible for the Regent to keep things running smoothly. The common folk had been dying in numbers so appalling as to make one think that all of them might soon be gone. Needless to say, a great many noblemen of Fourth and Fifth Rank had also perished, and it was rumored that the disease would strike next in the highest quarters.[55]

As though those terrible events were not enough, in the Third Month it began to appear that Michitaka's recovery was in doubt. One night the Regent went to the Imperial Palace. "I am suffering from a grave illness," he said. "May I ask that His Majesty issue an edict assigning temporary authority to the Palace Minister?" Feeling that it could do no harm to let Korechika look after things during his father's indisposition, the Emperor complied on the Eighth of the Third Month, and Korechika assumed control of affairs of state.

---

service of Empress Shōshi. *Sonpi bunmyaku*, 1: 308, lists, in addition, two obscure sons, Tadachika (999–1077) and Akinaga, by other women.

55. The chronicles report the deaths in 995 of two Regents (Michitaka and Michikane), the Minister of the Left (Shigenobu), three Major Counselors (Naritoki, Michiyori, and Asateru), two Middle Counselors, sixty officials of Fourth and Fifth Rank, and "innumerable" men of lower rank. Even though some of the victims died from causes unrelated to the epidemic, it was a terrible toll for one year, especially since most of the deaths were concentrated in two months, the Fourth and Fifth, when the incidence of the disease reached its peak. *Nihon kiryaku*, 2: 183 (1. vii Chōtoku 1); *Hyakurenshō*, p. 9 (8 v Chōtoku 1).

The Twentieth of the Third Month brought the death of the Kan'in Major Counselor Asateru, a victim of the pestilence. It was unspeakably dreadful. The other great lords were panic-stricken. "Today I grieve for another, not knowing the fate that awaits me tomorrow."[56]

In desperation, the dying Michitaka renounced the world on the Sixth of the Fourth Month. His wife promptly became a nun. Only the day before, Korechika had been granted Escorts and other perquisites;[57] but now everyone in the family mansion was dazed with grief and anxiety. On the Tenth, to the dismay and agitation of all, Michitaka's life came to an end.

Since Korechika's appointment had been only for the duration of Michitaka's illness, the Court buzzed with speculation after the Regent's death, and people almost forgot to mourn the father in their curiosity about the son's prospects. The young man's dictatorial methods had inspired widespread alarm and misgivings.

Michitaka's funeral had to wait until after the Kamo Festival. Even the timing of his death had been unfortunate.

In spite of Korechika's bereavement, he proceeded to issue orders dealing with every situation that seemed to him to invite improvement, including such matters as the lengths of robes and trousers. No doubt there were critics who blamed him for thinking of trifles at such a time. Would it not have been better to pretend to notice nothing amiss until the end of the mourning period?

Kishi's brothers, the provincial governors, were exceedingly apprehensive about the future. Their father, Naritada, dispensed with his own period of seclusion, recruited wonder-working monks for the recitation of prayers of various descriptions, and feverishly intoned petitions day and night.

On the Twenty-third of the Fourth Month, while everyone was still suffering from the shock of the Regent's death, the Koichijō Major Captain Naritoki breathed his last. Seishi's son, the infant First Prince, was left pathetically destitute of protection. Michinaga succeeded Naritoki as Major Captain of the Left, possibly because it was considered inadvisable to allow either of the two major captaincies to remain vacant for even a short time.

---

56. *Asu wa shirazu, ima wa kō nameri.* Probably an allusion to Tsurayuki's poem on the death of Ki no Tomonori (*Kokinshū* 838: Asu shiranu / waga mi to omoedo / kurenu ma no / kyō wa hito koso / kanashikarikere. ("Ignorant of the morrow—my last, perhaps—yet will I mourn another's fate while today endures, and I with it.")

57. At his own insistence. He was also pressing unsuccessfully to be named Kanpaku. *Shōyūki*, 1: 302–3 (10 iii–4 iv Chōtoku 1).

The funeral services for Michitaka were scheduled for the last part of the Fourth Month, following the Kamo Festival; and Naritoki's were to take place during the same period. Those were sad days.

Korechika, aware of the insecurity of his position, urged his grandfather to persevere in his efforts, and both Naritada and the monks under his direction performed rituals of kinds that are best left undescribed.[58] "Don't worry. Remember that Heaven, not man, determines the course of human events," Naritada said reassuringly. But the young minister's uncles talked to one another in nervous and pessimistic whispers, for they felt Michikane was greatly to be feared. Senshi favored Michikane's candidacy, and some hint of her attitude had evidently reached the general run of courtiers, who were adding to Korechika's worries by calling in droves at Michikane's house.

Meanwhile, Michikane had begun to suffer from disturbing dreams and giddy spells, as though some supernatural agent were trying to communicate with him. When he consulted the Yin-yang Masters, they advised a change of residence, but after he had begun to look for a suitable house, he was given to understand that the omens were auspicious after all. To his bewilderment, every divination seemed to yield a different result.

The news of the portents and precautions at Michikane's house caused Korechika to redouble his prayers. Alarmed by the situation, some people wondered openly if the Palace Minister's dogged efforts were not responsible for the strange events at his rival's residence; and finally their talk persuaded Michikane that it would be best to move. The time was late in the Fourth Month.

Michikane selected as his destination the home of Sukeyuki, a former governor of Izumo Province who had admired and trusted him in the years when everyone else had been currying favor with the Regent.[59] The residence, situated at Nakagawa close to the residence of the Minister of the Left, was an elegant establishment, with a lake, a stream, and a hill, built and originally occupied by Sukeyuki's father, Sukenobu, the Director of the Palace Storehouse Bureau, who had conceived of it as a refuge for Michikane when some other direction might prove unfavorable.[60] Suke-

---

58. Directed, presumably, against Korechika's rivals.

59. Fujiwara Sukeyuki (d. 995) was a poet and minor official. As the author goes on to indicate, he was a great-grandson of Tokihira: Tokihira—Atsutada—Sukenobu—Sukeyuki.

60. The Nakagawa, or Middle River (so called, according to one thory, in contradistinction to the Eastern River, or Kamo, and the Western River, or Katsura), followed a southerly course from its source north of the capital, passing east of what is now the Shōkokuji and continuing generally east of Higashikyōgoku Avenue to its confluence with the Kamo at Nijō. North of Ichijō, it appears to have been known as the Kyōgokugawa. In the vicinity of Ichijō

yuki was a grandson of Middle Counselor Atsutada, one of the sons of the minister Tokihira, which probably explained his low rank and general lack of success—or so some people thought.[61] In honor of Michikane's arrival, Sukeyuki made drawings on the screens and partitions in his own hand, contriving some exceedingly interesting effects. Michikane was happy there, and the house was besieged by visitors, but the new surroundings failed to cure him.

On the Second of the Fifth Month, a messenger brought an Imperial Edict naming Michikane Regent. Sukeyuki was overjoyed that the event had taken place while Michikane was living in his house, and his people also considered it a supreme honor. The crowd at the house was enormous —all the horses and carriages in the city, it seemed, had congregated there.

At Korechika's all was dejection. His coterie felt that they had been made ridiculous. "This has been a terrible miscalculation," they lamented. "How much better it would have been if Korechika had simply gone on as Palace Minister. A stopgap Regent! What a blunder! Is there a child anywhere who doesn't know that His Lordship has made a laughingstock of himself over this Regent business?" Their emotions were natural, for from their point of view it was a shocking turn of events.

Meanwhile, Michikane's ailment persisted. Thinking that he might be suffering from a disorder of the nervous system, his people treated him with magnolia-bark tea, but to no avail. Whether he stayed in bed or tried to remain active, he was in constant misery.

It was being said that Michikane's appointment had been entirely proper. How could a boy like Korechika be entrusted with the government? Michinaga also felt that things were finally being handled in a suitable manner. "If Korechika had not been in such a hurry to cut certain other things short, his own career might have been lengthened," said those who felt that he had neglected his father's memory in order to flaunt his authority by regulating the lengths of trousers and hunting robes.

By the Fourth or Fifth of the Fifth Month, Michikane was suffering from prostrating attacks of fever. Although he would have liked to commission sutra-readings and recitations, he was afraid that such measures

---

and Nijō, it gave its name to a villa area where members of the nobility sometimes went to escape the summer heat or to avoid a directional taboo. Readers of *The Tale of Genji* will recall the area as the site of the house owned by Kii no Kami where Genji met Utsusemi. Seidensticker 1976, p. 38; *Genji*, 1: 88; EMZ, 1: 504, 506; Kakimoto 1966, 2: 128; *Kagerō nikki*, p. 349, s.n. 97.

61. A reference to the supposed persecution of Tokihira and his descendants by the angry spirit of his defeated rival, Sugawara Michizane.

might be inauspicious at the outset of his regency, and so did his best to conceal his malady behind a façade of normality. In the Attendants' Office, crowded day and night with senior nobles and miscellaneous gentlemen of Fourth and Fifth Rank, and in the quarters assigned to the Escorts and Minor Attendants, where sounds of drunken revelry filled the air, nobody suspected his condition for a moment. Michinaga, calling daily to look after the necessary details, professed bewilderment at the persistence of what was without doubt a formidable affliction, but neither he nor anyone else dreamed that the Regent might die.

Since Michikane's condition had worsened at Sukeyuki's, he made up his mind to risk a return to the Nijō Mansion. He moved during the night of the Sixth. It was perhaps only natural that Korechika should have felt renewed optimism as he witnessed this and other indications of the Regent's difficulties. Secrecy was now out of the question at Nijō, where the household was astir with frantic activity.

With a new cause for alarm added to the pestilence that still raged, the senior nobles kept close to the Emperor, and all watches were fully manned by the Palace Guards and the Crown Prince's Guards.

At the Nijō Mansion, Michikane's wife, who was pregnant again, had dreamed that the new baby would be a girl. The diviners had concurred, and Michikane was looking forward to the birth with great eagerness, especially since his appointment as Regent had been, he thought, a portent auspicious enough to dispel any lingering doubts concerning the child's sex. Now, however, the sole concern of the household was the Regent's perilous state. Senshi sent one messenger after another, and Michinaga cared for his brother's needs with the utmost solicitude, making all his own possessions available as payment for the recitation of sutras—of which he ordered so many that he committed every horse in his stables and was obliged to fall back on carriage-oxen. Michikane's people, nervous and distraught, were barely able to walk without bumping into things.

Early in the morning on the Eighth of the Fifth Month, there were agitated reports that Shigenobu, the Rokujō Minister of the Left; Yasumitsu, the Momozono Middle Counselor;[62] and Seiin, a Buddhist Bishop,[63] had all died. Michikane's people reacted very sensibly. "What a commotion! It's unlucky to mention death when someone is ill. Say nothing to

---

62. Minamoto Yasumitsu, a grandson of Emperor Daigo.
63. Son of the literatus Ōe Tomotsuna (886–957). He was one of the monks who guarded the Emperor at night in the Seiryōden. *Nihon kiryaku*, 2: 182 (8 v Chōtoku 1); EMZ, 1: 515; *Dainihonshi*, 8: 52; *Sonpi bunmyaku*, 4: 91.

His Lordship," they admonished one another. But on that very day, during the Hour of the Sheep [1:00–3:00 P.M.], Michikane's life came to an end. The reader may imagine the scene at the mansion after that tragic event. It was like a nightmare, thought Michinaga. He left the house, his sleeve pressed to his face, as though in a dream. Because of the genuine affection that he and Michikane had felt for each other, he had cared for his sick brother with a touching disregard for his own safety. In Michitaka's case, one would scarcely have supposed a fraternal tie to exist, for after his death Michinaga had not so much as paid a call of condolence; but during Michikane's illness he had been a constant source of strength, and it was precisely the Major Captain's unavailing devotion, Michikane's people kept lamenting, that made the loss of their master so sad.

In spite of their display of grief, the men who had just entered the new Regent's service soon disappeared from the Nijō Mansion, leaving behind only those who had been with him for years. Exactly seven days had elapsed since his appointment. In the past, many gentlemen of his family had failed to attain the regency, but nobody had ever won it and then held it for so fleeting and dreamlike an interval.

When Korechika's astonishing presumptuousness had brought about his replacement as Regent, he had felt deep humiliation and resentment, but now he was happy again. "Whatever may happen later," he reflected, "this has been a swift change for the better." Naritada was still praying away, and his grandson probably felt even more certain of success than before, since he interpreted Michikane's death as a clear indication that he himself was destined to replace him. Such an attitude can scarcely have failed to provoke criticism.

Michikane had left no grown sons, but only two pathetic, shaggy-headed little boys.[64] His body was moved to the Awata Mansion that same night, preparatory to the celebration of the funeral on the Eleventh. It had been a sadly premature death. His favorite, Sukeyuki, who had rejoiced for him with such wholehearted pleasure, no longer wished to live.

After laboring with passionate devotion throughout the night of the funeral, Sukeyuki went away feeling ill. "I must have got too upset; I don't feel at all well," he said to his solicitous daughters.

Everyone was to stay at Awata during the mourning period.

Michikane and the others were not the only men of consequence who died. It seemed that not a soul was to be spared in those terrible times.

64. Kanetaka (985–1053) and Kanetsuna (988–1058), aged ten and seven in 995.

On duty one night at the Awata Mansion, Sukeyuki lay wide awake, obsessed by melancholy reflections. He murmured a verse:

Yume narade	Could I but meet
Mata mo aubeki	My lord again
Kimi naraba	Other than in dreams,
Nerarenu i o mo	I should not regret
Nagekazaramashi.	These wakeful hours.

He had been in poor health ever since the Eleventh. Early in the morning after that night at Awata, he went to his daughters' house. "I seem to be getting much worse. I really don't expect to pull through, so I've come to see you," he said. He told them about the poem, explaining that he had composed it on the preceding night as he lay sleepless at the mansion, and proceeded to copy it out for them on a sheet of white paper, which he extracted from underneath an inkstone. Then he went home and collapsed into bed. The members of his grieving household were frantic with anxiety. As he lay dying, he talked of nothing but his inability to attend the Buddhist services for Michikane. He died on the Twenty-ninth of the same month. Need I say that his family mourned? Sorrow knows no distinction of rank. One day his daughter composed this verse:

Yume mizu to	Alas! So little time has passed,
Nagekishi kimi o	And now I am the one
Hodo mo naku	Denied a dream wherein to see
Mata waga yume ni	The one who grieved
Minu zo kanashiki.	Not to see his lord in dreams.

The services for the dead noblemen took place one by one.

On the Eleventh of the Fifth Month, soon after Michikane's death, the Emperor entrusted the supervision of the nation and all its officials to Michinaga, who thus acquired the title of Regent and assumed a position of unrivaled authority.[65] For Senshi, who had always felt especially close to this brother, the appointment gratified a desire of many years' standing. Korechika shamelessly pinned his hopes on another sudden calamity like the one that had disposed of Michikane, and his grandfather prayed as hard as ever, certain that things could be made to take a turn for the better.

---

65. "Regent" translates Kanpaku, but the Emperor did not in fact give Michinaga that title. Rather, he was made Minister of the Right and invested with *nairan* ("private inspection") powers, which meant that he controlled all official documents. This made him, in effect, the Regent and led to his being informally called Kanpaku.

Meanwhile, the administration passed into Michinaga's hands. Observing Korechika's discouragement, his uncles and grandfather did their best to cheer him up. "Don't be so pessimistic. All you need to do now is stay alive. Surely you remember a Regent who lasted only seven or eight days! Anything is possible if you can survive. Stop behaving like a child. There's nothing to worry about as long as your old grandfather is here," they said. No doubt he found such talk comforting.

It was on the Nineteenth of the Sixth Month that Michinaga became Minister of the Right. Around the same time, there was a sad and shocking event: on the Eleventh of the month, Michiyori, the Yamanoi Major Counselor, died at the age of twenty-five after a short illness. The loss of such a popular and respected young noble was a source of great regret to Michinaga, who had intended to give Michiyori special preferment because he had been Kaneie's adopted son.

This latest event of a terrible year deepened Korechika's gloom.[66]

Senshi, who had in past years commissioned readings of the *Lotus Sutra*, now arranged a new series of recitations because of the frightful virulence of the epidemic.

The services for Michikane were held in the Awata Mansion around the Twentieth of the Sixth Month. His widow became a nun afterward.[67] Since she was expecting a child, people tried to talk her out of it, but she refused to be dissuaded. One can understand her feelings.

Empress Teishi had stayed on at home, prostrate with grief, but she could not remain there forever, and she finally returned to the Palace. The Emperor felt exceedingly sorry for her.

The Crown Prince's two consorts, Seishi and Genshi, were in the same pathetic situation.[68] The Prince grieved for them both. What would happen to Genshi, who had once been so self-confident, he wondered sadly. His devotion to his little son never wavered. He implored Seishi to bring the baby to his palace, but it seemed best to be cautious until the pestilence subsided, and she could not make up her mind to agree.

Tameyori, the governor of Settsu, composed a poem suggested by the sorrow and uncertainty of the times:[69]

66. Michiyori (971–95) was Korechika's half-brother.
67. Probably a mistake on the part of the author. Michikane's widow later married Akimitsu.
68. Seishi's father, Naritoki, and Genshi's father, Michitaka, had both died.
69. Fujiwara Tameyori (d. 998?) was a well-known poet. He was the uncle of Murasaki Shikibu.

Yo no naka ni	How large it has grown:
Aramashikaba to	The number of those
Omou hito	Who had wished
Naka wa ōku mo	Merely to remain alive
Narinikeru kana.	And who now are dead.

One of the Crown Prince's Lady Chamberlains, Koōgimi, heard it and wrote a reply:[70]

Aru wa naku	The living die;
Naki wa kazu sou	The dead multiply.
Yo no naka ni	How long
Aware itsu made	Shall we survive
Aran to suran.	In this transient world?

It became known that Sanesuke, the Ononomiya Middle Counselor, was visiting Prince Tamehira's daughter Enshi, who had been one of ex-Emperor Kazan's Junior Consorts. Michinobu, the Ichijō Middle Captain, sent Enshi a poem:

Ureshiki wa	How deeply, I wonder,
Ika bakari ka wa	May your happiness be felt?
Omouran	My misery seems to penetrate
Uki wa mi ni shimu	To the very marrow
Kokochi koso sure.	Of my bones.

Michinobu was apparently in love with the Princess himself.[71]

Oh yes, it was around that time that the title of Consultant was given to Arikuni, whom Michitaka had cashiered and confined to his home. It was a happy event for him. While people were still agreeing that the action had been entirely proper, Arikuni was named to fill a vacancy created by the recent resignation of the Senior Assistant Governor-General of the Dazaifu, an appointment that also seemed fitting.[72] He married the Emperor's nurse, Tachibana Naishi no Suke, and set off in great style for Kyūshū. "It is natural and gratifying that one of Kaneie's old favorites should rise in the world again after having been treated so shabbily by the

70. Koōgimi (d. ca. 1005?) is also known as Sanjōin Nyokurōdo Sakon. One of the Thirty-six Poetic Geniuses and a friend of Kintō and other literary figures, she was active as a poet over a twenty-five-year period from 979 on. About ninety of her poems are extant, including twenty in Imperial anthologies.

71. Since Michinobu had died in 994, the anecdote is out of order here.

72. Arikuni did not become a Consultant until 1001. The Dazaifu post fell vacant in the Tenth Month of 995, when the incumbent, Fujiwara Sukemasa, was dismissed at the insistence of the Usa Shrine priests, with whom he had quarreled.

late Regent," everyone said. Korenaka was then Major Controller of the Left.[73]

So began the winter [995]. Kanemichi's eldest son, the Hirohata Middle Counselor Akimitsu, had been married for a number of years to Emperor Murakami's fifth daughter, Seishi, whose mother had been the Hirohata Consort Keishi, and the couple had become the parents of two daughters and a son.[74] Akimitsu had always hoped to betroth one of the girls to an Emperor or a Crown Prince, but the rather delicate situation at the Imperial Palace had frustrated the first aspiration; and it had also seemed awkward to approach the Crown Prince, in whose household Michitaka's second daughter, Genshi, was already established. Now, however, he saw a chance to marry his oldest daughter, Genshi, to the Emperor, and he determined to act with all possible speed.[75]

Morosuke's eleventh son, Kinsue, was a Chamberlain Middle Counselor at the time.[76] He too had married a Princess, and she had borne him a daughter and two sons.[77] In the past, he had been deterred by fear of Michitaka—as, indeed, had all the other noblemen in the capital—but the new Regent's numerous daughters were still frolicsome little girls,[78] too young to worry about, and so Kinsue had begun to think of presenting the Emperor with his daughter, whose name was Gishi. (It was natural that he should have settled on the Emperor, since the Crown Prince had Genshi and Suishi as wives, to say nothing of Seishi, his first son's mother, whom the Prince loved with all his heart.)

Presently, Akimitsu's daughter entered the Palace and took up residence in the Shōkyōden. "The Emperor won't pay any attention to her. Akimitsu is much too old-fashioned," people said.[79] But they were mistaken. The Emperor treated her very well, and the presentation was a success.

In no mood to play second fiddle to Akimitsu, Kinsue proceeded to

73. And Consultant.

74. Akimitsu was a Major Counselor at the time. For a list of his children by Seishi, see s.n. 60.

75. Empress Teishi's position had become vulnerable because she no longer enjoyed influential family backing. She had also withdrawn from the Palace to go into mourning for Michitaka, thus providing Akimitsu with a favorable opportunity for Genshi's presentation.

76. Kinsue was in fact the twelfth (and youngest) son of Morosuke. He became a Major Counselor in the Sixth Month of 995.

77. On Kinsue's children, see s.n. 61.

78. "Numerous daughters" is probably an exaggeration. As far as is known, Michinaga's only daughters in 995 were Shōshi (aged seven) and Kenshi (aged one).

79. A girl from an old-fashioned family, the author implies, could not have been expected to succeed at Court.

present his own daughter, who moved into the Kokiden.[80] I need not say that he took care to make her entry more fashionable and elegant in every way than Genshi's, but the consensus appeared to be that the Emperor was unimpressed by the new arrival. He had, it seemed, taken a rather surprising fancy to Akimitsu's daughter instead.

The Palace had become gay and fashionable. Senshi commented merely, "If one of those ladies desires my affection, let her bear the Emperor a son."

The months and days sped by, with Genshi to all appearances the Imperial favorite. "Nothing like this has happened before," thought Empress Teishi in deep distress. "It's because my father isn't here anymore." But with the Emperor it was a case of "every encounter with another."[81] In his heart, he loved only the Empress.

Meanwhile, Senshi had taken possession of the Ichijō Mansion. The former occupants, Tamemitsu's daughters, had moved to a place in Taka-tsukasa, where Korechika was secretly visiting one of them.[82] The lady called Her Highness of the Central Hall, the third daughter, had been reared by her father with great care because of her remarkable beauty and disposition. "Beauty is everything in a woman," Tamemitsu had always said, and he had spared no pains in her upbringing. It was this Lady of the Central Hall whom Korechika was visiting.

Around the same time, ex-Emperor Kazan had begun to send love notes of great apparent sincerity to Tamemitsu's fourth daughter, Shi no Kimi. When the scandalized lady refused to respond, he resorted to personal visits, during which he demonstrated his devotion with great sophistication and gallantry. Such attentions, thought Korechika, could scarcely be directed toward Shi no Kimi; the ex-Emperor's true objective must be the Lady of the Central Hall.[83] "I find this affair upsetting," he said to his brother, Middle Counselor Takaie. "What shall I do?"

"Leave it to me," Takaie answered. "It's really quite simple."

One bright moonlit night, as the ex-Emperor was returning on horse-

---

80. Gishi's (974–1053) presentation took place in the Seventh Month of Chōtoku 2 (996); the presentation of Akimitsu's daughter, not until the Eleventh Month. EM, 1: 155, n. 28; 1: 499, s.n. 251.

81. Probably a tag from a poem or proverb to the effect that comparison with others merely heightens the attraction of one's old love. For other theories about the phrase, see EMZ, 1: 538.

82. The location of the house is uncertain. See EMZ, 1: 540. As the author indicates below, the third daughter occupied the principal apartments.

83. Presumably because Shi no Kimi was not pretty. See the author's surmise earlier in the chapter.

back from the Takatsukasa Mansion, Takaie and two or three suitable companions intercepted him, intending, if the reader will believe it, to "give him a scare"![84] They proceeded to fire off a number of arrows, one of which penetrated the ex-Emperor's sleeve. Although Kazan was an unusually brave man, there is a limit to anyone's courage, and he could scarcely have been expected to maintain his composure. Shaken and confused, he reached home on the verge of collapse.[85]

It would have been easy for ex-Emperor Kazan to complain to Emperor Ichijō or Michinaga, but the circumstances were not flattering, so he tried in embarrassment to hush the matter up, feeling that he could never live down the disgrace if it became known. Nevertheless the news reached both Michinaga and the Emperor; and indeed it soon became the chief topic of conversation everywhere. "A retired sovereign is an august personage," people said. "Though it must be admitted that nothing would have happened in the first place if ex-Emperor Kazan had been less frivolous, such a shocking act of lèse majesté cannot be ignored."

Korechika's guilt was compounded by the revelation that for years he had been sponsoring clandestine performances of the Daigen Service, a ritual that had been celebrated since antiquity exclusively by the Court, and never by any subject, no matter how exceptional the circumstances.[86] Furthermore, Senshi had become subject to puzzling spells of severe illness, in which malignant spirits sometimes figured—a turn of events that perturbed many people. There was no telling, they said, what the Palace Minister's lack of maturity might lead to next.[87]

So began the second year of Chōtoku [996].[88] During the Second and Third Months, families everywhere were busy with anniversary services for those who had died in the previous year, and a series of moving ceremonies took place, falling sometimes on identical or successive days. Some of the bereaved had started to wear ordinary clothing again, but others still appeared in garments of dark gray, and that too was most affecting. Then there was a great stir in anticipation of the next month's Kamo Festival. "Once the festival is over, the affair involving ex-Emperor Kazan will be settled," said some people. "Don't be foolish. They won't flush

84. The men with Takaie were probably some of the warriors whom Korechika appears to have been supporting. *Shōyūki*, 2: 3 (5 ii Chōtoku 2); EMZ, 1: 541.

85. The incident probably occurred in the First Month of 996 (Chōtoku 2). EMZ, 1: 542–43.

86. See s.n. 23, item 13.

87. It was being said that someone (presumably Korechika or his grandfather) had cursed Senshi. *Shōyūki*, 2: 5 (28 iii Chōtoku 2).

88. The author has already described a number of events that took place in 996.

Korechika out like a common robber," others argued. Still others were put off by all the gossip (of which the foregoing is only a sample), and showed in their behavior and speech that they felt sorry for Korechika. It was sad to think of what might happen to the young minister.

The lady known as Fujiwara Naishi no Suke had borne Michikane a daughter, Sonshi, to whom the father had paid little attention, despite his keen disappointment at his wife's failure to produce female offspring. Sonshi was grown up by now, and Naishi no Suke had determined to present her to the Emperor. Since Naishi herself was said to be Morosuke's daughter, the Fujiwara men had always treated her with great consideration, and no objection was raised to her decision. Michinaga took charge of all the arrangements.

Thus Sonshi entered the Palace, where she was known as the Kurabeya Consort.[89] Naishi no Suke, who had always been neglected by Michikane, had in recent years been receiving visits from Controller Korenaka, who now did everything possible to help with the presentation.

The ranks of the Imperial consorts were growing, but, as the Imperial Lady Senshi glumly observed, they had yet to produce a son. Senshi began to feel much better when Empress Teishi showed signs of being pregnant. Certain people were unimpressed and gave it as their opinion that the Empress was merely ill, but Senshi disagreed. "It's much too early to leap to conclusions," she said. "To judge from the Palace Minister's prayers and other activities, he, at least, seems to be convinced that a child is on the way. What a pity that he finds himself in such shocking difficulties just now." She could not help feeling sorry for him.

89. The significance of the appellation Kurabeya is unknown. For theories, see EMZ, 1: 548. Sonshi entered the Palace in 998, rather than in 996 as the author implies. She became a Nyōgo in 1000. After the death of Emperor Ichijō, she married Fujiwara Michitō, Naritoki's son.

5

THE
SEPARATION
OF THE BROTHERS

WHEN the Kamo Festival had drawn to a close, everyone seemed certain that the authorities would hand down the sentences so long discussed. For the unhappy Palace Minister and Middle Counselor, the suspense was very frightening and disagreeable, and they practiced strict ritual seclusion behind the locked gates of the Nijō Mansion. Empress Teishi, in wretched health as a result of her pregnancy, had been spending much of her time in bed. It was a cruel blow when, as was inevitable, rumors of her brothers' predicament reached her ears. If Korechika and Takaie were punished, she thought in despair, she would have nowhere to turn; far better for her to die first. But she could do nothing to affect the course of events.

"What is to become of us?" Korechika and Takaie said. "If we seek relief from our present troubles by throwing ourselves in the river or taking the tonsure, we shall still be suffering a hideous fate. Divine assistance is our only hope." They kept their prayer beads constantly by their sides, ate nothing, and lamented and worried night and day.

Extraordinary precautions went into effect at the Imperial Palace. On duty in the guards offices, where each commanded the services of innumerable warriors, were descendants of Mitsunaka and Sadamori—Former Michinoku Governor Korenobu, Lieutenant of the Left Gate Guards Koretoki, Former Bizen Provincial Official Yorimitsu, and Former Suō Provincial Official Yorichika.[1] The Crown Prince's Guards and the Palace

---

1. Minamoto Mitsunaka (912–97), one of the first chieftains of the Seiwa Genji line of warrior-aristocrats, amassed enormous wealth and influence by tying his fortunes to those

Guards mounted watches day and night, the barriers were secured,[2] and alarming rumors of impending police action began to circulate. Senior nobles and Imperial personages made preparations of their own. "For several years past, queer natural phenomena have been interpreted by diviners as portents of a crisis of arms. This must be the time," people said. Even insignificant townsfolk made ready to flee to the hills, oppressed by the tense, foreboding atmosphere.

Michitaka's brothers-in-law, Akinobu and Controller Michinobu, tried to rouse their nephews to action. "Things have reached a pretty pass," they said. "All this stir must mean the authorities are coming to arrest you. What do you propose to do about it?" But there was no hope of successful resistance.

Instead of swearing to share Korechika's lot, the senior retainers who had private rooms at his residence were carting away their belongings in frantic haste, with much attendant destruction and noise. It was a painful spectacle, but their master could scarcely order them to stop. And while Korechika was suffering the unspeakable embarrassment of knowing that those events were visible to outsiders, the entire Imperial Police Force surrounded the estate.[3] Villainous fellows streamed into the area, paralyzing traffic on streets and avenues for blocks around. The terror and panic inside the grounds were beyond words, but the main hall, where the family had assembled, was so pathetically silent that the building seemed deserted. The ruffians rampaged through the grounds, glaring menacingly into the rooms, while the group watching from behind the blinds and curtains grew faint with terror.

"There is no hope of escape now," said Korechika. "If only I could get away to visit Kohata, I'd be ready to go wherever they might send me, near or far." But the police and their lackeys were swarming everywhere; only a supernatural bird or beast could have eluded them.

"Even if I have to go in the middle of the night," Korechika said again, "I must bid a last farewell to my dead father's spirit." It was impossible

---

of the Fujiwara. (It was a party of his retainers who "guarded" Emperor Kazan on the night of the Emperor's abdication. See Chapter 2, n. 83.) Taira Sadamori (fl. mid-Heian) is remembered for his role in the suppression of Masakado's revolt, and as the architect of Taira military power in eastern Japan. Korenobu and Koretoki were Sadamori's son and grandson; Yorimitsu (948–1021) and Yorichika (b. 954), Mitsunaka's sons. All four held posts in one or another of the Guards Headquarters, the Imperial Police, or the Imperial Stables.

2. Ōsaka and other barriers commanding the routes into the capital.

3. Probably an exaggeration. There is no supporting evidence for the statement. The events described here took place on or shortly after the Twenty-fourth of the Fourth Month, 996. EM, 1: 501, s.n. 259; 1: 169, n. 27.

The Imperial Police at Korechika's residence.

to remain unmoved at the sight of the huge tears coursing down his cheeks like crystal beads; and Kishi, Empress Teishi, and the uncles all wept in bitter anguish. Meanwhile, the rabble poured into the courtyard, where the police struggled in vain to control them.

An official in formal attire shoved his way through the mob to a spot directly in front of the main hall. While those inside were still wondering at this new turn of events, he began to intone the words of an Imperial Edict. "For the crime of attempting to assassinate a former Emperor, for the crime of cursing the Emperor's mother, and for the crime of secretly performing the Daigen Service, a ritual never before celebrated by a commoner, the Palace Minister is appointed Governor-General of Kyūshū and banished from the capital. The Middle Counselor is appointed Provisional Governor of Izumo and banished from the capital." High and low inside the palace set up a frantic wailing.[4] Even the official who had pronounced the sentence failed to maintain his composure, and the police wiped away tears of pity. Listening behind locked gates, Korechika's neighbors wept in sympathy.

"You must leave now! The sun is setting!" the police shouted. Receiving no answer from inside, they reported back to the Emperor, who replied sternly that they must not allow matters to rest; they must insist.

Meanwhile, the day ended. Korechika had been praying for his father's spirit to lead him to the late Regent's grave that night. Toward midnight, as though in response to his entreaties, the noisy crowd fell asleep, and he stole out of the grounds, accompanied by his uncle Akinobu and two or three attendants. Perhaps he had silently made solemn vows that aided his escape.

The moon was shining when the party reached Kohata, but the area was densely wooded, and they were obliged to guess at the location of Michitaka's tomb. As they approached the spot, Korechika dismounted and pushed his way through the thick growth, numb with despair. Rays

4. The palace was the town residence of Empress Teishi, who had left the Imperial Palace on the Fourth of the Third Month, 996, to await the birth of a child. Called the Nijō Palace (or sometimes the Small Nijō Palace), it had been built for Teishi by Michitaka around 992 on the northern half of a site south of Nijō and west of Muromachi, next door to his own residence, the Higashisanjō Mansion. In 994, the Regent had added a residential complex on the southern half of the property for Korechika and other members of the family, but the new buildings had burned in 995, and in early 996 Korechika and Takaie were sharing the Nijō Palace with Teishi. Less than two months after the arrest of the brothers, a fire ended what proved to be Teishi's last sojourn there. The buildings were later used by the Empress's children. EMZ, 2: 22–24; Tsunoda 1969, pp. 227–83.

Korechika visits his father's grave at Kohata.

of moonlight filtered through the trees onto monuments and fences. He searched here and there. "It was just a year ago that he died," he thought. "The wood will still look new. But there were so many deaths in those days. Which one is it?"

He found the grave. Wracked with sobs, he poured out his story, and the startled creatures of the wild joined their cries to his. Even dumb animals, he thought with deep emotion, seemed to share his grief. "When you were alive, it was your pleasure to raise me above others," he said, "but now a cruel karma has banished me to a strange land far from the capital, and it is unlikely that I shall visit your grave again. Though I have committed no offense, the misdeeds of a previous existence have brought me to this extremity. If only I might hide tonight instead of going home! I can't bear the thought of disgracing you and dishonoring our name for generations to come. Help me! Takaie has also been sentenced to banishment, but the two of us are not even allowed to go in the same direction; we must follow separate ways. And quite aside from my own uhappy fate, there is the terrible effect on Her Majesty the Empress, who is several months pregnant, and who weeps incessantly, refusing even to sip a cup of hot water. It is most alarming—and most shocking when one considers her high station. No one is supposed to so much as pass in front of her guards' quarters without at least removing his hat, but now those unspeakable fellows have come crowding in almost to her chambers, tearing down blinds and reducing her to a shocking state of misery. Even if she manages to get through this safely, what will she do when it is time for the birth? I might have been able to help, but I shall be far away in some unknown place. I beg you to stay with her and protect her. And please visit the thoughts of His August Majesty and the dreams of the Imperial Lady, so they will believe in my innocence." Tears streamed down his cheeks. Since there was no danger of being overheard, Akinobu also wept aloud.

The party next set out in the opposite direction on the long journey to Kitano,[5] heading from the southeast to the northwest. The cocks were crowing as they arrived. With many tears, Korechika again recited his sad tale, ending with an admirably phrased vow that reflected his accomplishments as a scholar. He hurried off, unwilling to risk an encounter with the shrine officials, but it was already broad daylight. What ought he to

5. Kitano Shrine, situated in what is now Bakuro-chō, Kamikyō-ku, Kyōto. The shrine, founded around 947 in honor of Sugawara Michizane's spirit, was by the eleventh century a major religious institution. Korechika's intention was probably to appeal to the deified Michizane by pointing out that he too was a victim of false accusations.

do? An attempt to reenter the mansion might prove awkward; it would be better to await nightfall somewhere in the vicinity of the shrine. Though he could not help worrying as he imagined the pitiable state of those at home, he decided to spend the day near the racecourse of the Bodyguards of the Right.[6]

Back at the Nijō Palace, the police had been insisting that the banished men had already wasted a day and must set out at once, but presently they reported to the throne that only Takaie seemed to be inside; there was no sign of Korechika. "Disgraceful!" exclaimed the Emperor. "Isolate the Empress in a suitable manner and search the premises. Open the storerooms; look above the ceilings."[7]

"We must ask you to let us open the storerooms. Will the Empress kindly retire?" the police said. The people inside were obliged to hang makeshift curtains, and Teishi sat by while the police and their villainous accomplices ripped away the storeroom boards. It was a painful and degrading experience. "This, then, is what life is really like," thought the Empress, all but unconscious and quite beyond tears. Takaie sat dazed, dressed in a gray mourning cloak and trousers. The police officers hung back respectfully, but their lackeys rushed forward with a distressing air of triumph.

The police reported that they had looked everywhere for Korechika. "Perhaps he has taken Buddhist vows, but in any case he can't have left the capital. Make a thorough search," the Emperor commanded. The officers, who had faithfully obeyed orders in spite of their tears of sympathy, were heartily sick of their mission by now. What more, they asked, could be expected of them? But they searched on, while message after message arrived from the Emperor ordering them to guard the premises day and night. So that day also drew to a close.

The officers continued to bustle about, determined to stay awake all night, since they had been told that the Court, shocked and incredulous at the turn of events, had resolved to punish them all if Korechika escaped. Around the Hour of the Cock [5:00–7:00 P.M.], a plain wickerwork carriage with two or three attendants came hurrying toward the Empress's palace, its occupant unintimidated, it seemed, by the throng of police. Several officious lackeys in red robes rushed forward to challenge it. "What carriage comes to such a place?" they demanded.

6. The racecourse, site of the horse races in the Fifth Month, was southeast of the shrine in the same pine grove. EMZ, 2: 34–36.
7. There was room for concealment between the coffered ceilings and the roof.

"There's nothing to be alarmed about. His Lordship is returning from a journey to Kohata," someone answered. The lackeys moved away. The ox was unhitched at the gate, and the police, descending to the ground, arranged themselves in rows as the Palace Minister emerged.

Korechika appeared to be about twenty-two or twenty-three years of age. Meticulously groomed, plump, handsome, and fair-skinned, he seemed just such a man as Prince Genji, the Shining One, must have been. He wore three gray inner robes, thinly stuffed with cotton, and an unlined lower robe, a cloak, and trousers of the same color. People had always said that he was more accomplished and handsome than the usual run of senior nobles, and those who now beheld him found it impossible to restrain their tears. How tragic, they thought, that he should suffer so dreadful a fate! Most touchingly, he had refrained from riding through the gate, as though to say that he, at least, would show proper respect to the Empress.

With Korechika back, the police reported, "The Governor-General has just returned from a visit to Kohata."

"It is very late; you had better stand guard tonight and send him off in the morning at the Hour of the Hare [5:00–7:00 A.M.]," directed the Court. The police stayed up all night, while the Empress, Kishi, and Korechika sat together in unspeakable agitation, their hands joined.

The night drew to a close all too soon. The new day, everyone thought, must inevitably bring the end, but Korechika sat motionless, weeping aloud.

"Come on, it's time for you to be off!" shouted the officers. The Empress and Kishi seized Korechika's sleeves and held fast to them.

The police reported to the Court, and the Emperor sent back repeated instructions to reach through the curtains and pull the Empress's hands away. The officers, who were only human, felt in dismay that it had already been quite enough for their men to have stormed through the Empress's residence, breaking open storerooms. How could they possibly pull away her hands? "What will become of us if we are dismissed for dereliction of duty? Hurry, hurry," they begged.

Korechika had no choice but to leave. His people coaxed the frantically sobbing Matsugimi out of sight, and Korechika prepared to enter the carriage, taking with him a food pouch containing some tangerines and oranges and a single covered bowl. Takaie got into a matting carriage.[8]

Though Korechika would not have wished to commit the discourtesy of entering a carriage in the Empress's presence, Teishi and his mother fol-

8. *Mushirobari no kuruma*, a carriage covered with coarse straw matting. It was considered suitable for men of inferior rank.

lowed him outside. When the carriage was brought up, his mother climbed in after him, clinging to his waist.

"Korechika's mother is holding onto his sleeves; she intends to go with him," the police reported.

"We must not allow it. Get her away," came the answer. Of that, however, there seemed little likelihood. "I'll only go as far as Yamazaki.[9] I must go that far," she said. Since she was already inside, there was nothing to do but start the carriage on its way. It was the Twenty-fourth of the Fourth Month in the second year of Chōtoku [996].[10]

Korechika, who was to go to Tsukushi, headed southwest, while Takaie, destined for Izumo, turned northwest toward the Tanba Road. As the carriages moved away, the Empress cut off her hair with a pair of scissors and became a nun.[11]

"Korechika and Takaie have gone, and Her Majesty has taken religious vows," the police reported. How pitiful, thought Emperor Ichijō, that his pregnant consort should have suffered so greatly! Miserable at the thought of Teishi's unhappiness, he shed many furtive tears. Was not the ancient story of the "Song of Everlasting Sorrow"[12] very much the same sort of thing, he wondered sadly.

More people turned out to witness the departure of the brothers than one would find at the usual public spectacle, and they wept as they watched. It was too tragic a scene to be described by such threadbare words as pitiful and sad.

With the capital behind him, Takaie mounted a horse at the Tanba border and sent his carriage back. "Keep the ox in memory of me," he told the driver, who had been with him for years. Quite naturally, the man broke down in tears. So the carriage returned to the city, while its owner struck out along unknown mountain tracks.

At a place called Ōeyama,[13] Takaie wrote an affecting letter to the Em-

9. A town on the right bank of the Yodo River at the Settsu-Yamashiro provincial border (now Ōyamashiro-mura, Otokuni-gun, Kyōto-fu). During the Heian period, travelers heading west from the capital embarked there for the boat trip down the Yodo.

10. According to other sources, this was the date of the banishment decree, not of Korechika's departure. EMZ, 2: 48.

11. Other sources give the First of the Fifth Month as the date of Teishi's tonsure. *Ibid.*

12. Po Chü-i's poem describing the ill-starred love of Emperor Hsüan Tsung of China (685–762; r. 712–56) for his beautiful concubine Yang Kuei-fei (719–56). It ends with these famous lines, spoken by Yang Kuei-fei's wraith: "In the skies we shall be twin birds that fly together, / On earth we shall be trees with branches intertwined. / Heaven is enduring, earth long-living, but they will perish. / The everlasting sorrow will never come to an end." Translation from Payne 1947, p. 263.

13. A short stretch of mountain road on the Heian-Tanba route. It extended from Ōe

Takaie goes into exile. "With the capital behind him, Takaie mounted a horse at the Tanba border and sent his carriage back." The carriage ox has been unharnessed and the shafts rest on a stand.

press. "I have got this far without mishap. I am not good for much any more, but I feel certain that I shall return some day to be with you again, and my great concern is for your welfare in the meantime. I miss you dreadfully . . ."

He added a melancholy poem:

Uki koto o	Ōeyama is, I know,
Ōe no yama to	A mountain of trials—
Shiri nagara	Yet I had not thought
Itodo fukaku mo	To encounter
Iru waga mi kana.	Misery such as this.[14]

"Such are my present emotions," he wrote.

The grief-stricken and confused Empress seemed scarcely conscious of her surroundings. How sad, thought Emperor Ichijō and Senshi, that she should find herself in such a position—as though it were not enough to be pregnant!

On the same day, Korechika went as far as the Yamazaki barrier house,[15] escorted by four police officers of suitable rank, whose lackeys swarmed about the carriage in a distressing manner. The police officer who escorted Takaie was Commander of the Left Gate Guards Nobuyasu, a brother of the Nagatani Bishop.[16] It was all most astonishing and pathetic.

Korechika fell ill at the barrier house. The police escort reported to the Court that he would rest there until he felt better. His mother was with him, they said, still clinging to his cloak.

"Get him well and send him off as soon as you can, and see that his mother returns to the capital at once," the authorities replied. But the Emperor and Senshi, impressed by Takaie's great solicitude for Teishi and their mother, felt that such distant banishment was too cruel. With Michinaga's help, they persuaded ex-Emperor Kazan to agree to a less severe sentence, and it was announced that Korechika might stay in Harima and Takaie in Tajima. It would be idle to say merely that the news "delighted" Empress Teishi. She was pitifully happy.

Village in Otokuni District, Yamashiro, to Shino Village in Kuwada District, Tanba (now a part of Hyōgo Prefecture).

14. There is a pun on the name of the mountain ascended by the road (Ōeyama) and the *oboe* (orthographically identical with Ōe) of *uki koto o oboe*, "experience trials."

15. Site of an old barrier near the southern border of Yamashiro Province. According to *Shōyūki*, 2: 11 (5 v Chōtoku 2), Korechika stayed at Ishizukuri Temple in Nagaoka.

16. Fujiwara Nobuyasu, the son of a provincial governor, seems actually to have been Commander of the Right Gate Guards. He is unlikely to have been a brother of the Nagatani Bishop Kanzu (or Kanjū; esteemed by Michinaga and others for the efficacy of his prayers), who was a member of the Ki family. EMZ, 2: 57.

When it was learned at the barrier house that he was to stay in Harima, Korechika was overjoyed. He sent his mother home with tearful reassurances. "You must go back to the capital at once. I won't be far away at all, and that is a cause for great happiness. Furthermore, there is no reason why I should not be recalled, since I have done nothing wrong." He set out for Harima, and the two drew apart, traveling in opposite directions. Inexpressibly sad is too commonplace a phrase for such an occasion. When Kishi reached home and saw that her daughter had become a nun, she burst into convulsive sobs.

As Korechika journeyed toward his destination in Harima, he heard someone remark that the party had reached Akashi. He composed a poem:

Mono omou	To the darkness
Kokoro no yami shi	Of bewilderment
Kurakereba	And brooding memory,
Akashi no ura mo	Even Akashi Shore
Kai nakarikeri.	Brings no light.[17]

He himself must have noted, with a certain bitterness, the remarkable persistence of his ability to experience emotion. His mind lingered with resentment on the world's unkindness. Why was it necessary to send Takaie off somewhere else? Everything would have been all right if only both could have gone to the same place. Improvising, no doubt, on the ancient verse, "Though white waves rise, they cut no garment to bring together the two shores at Akashi and Suma," he wrote this:

Katagata ni	The two shores
Wakaruru mi ni mo	At Akashi and Suma—
Nitaru kana	Separated
Akashi mo Suma mo	Like the two of us,
Ono ga uraura.	One here and the other there.[18]

Moved to tears by his traveler's life, Takaie also composed a poem:

17. Akashi was a coastal area in southeastern Akashi District, Harima, now part of the Kōbe urban industrial belt. In premodern times, it was one of Japan's finest scenic areas, celebrated for its white sands and green pines, and for the view of Awaji Island across the sparkling blue waters of Akashi Strait. The poem contains a play on the literal meaning of the word ("bright," "light").

18. Suma was a coastal area in what is now Suma-ku, Kōbe. Like Akashi, it was admired by noble travelers and excursionists for its white beach, picturesque pine trees, and view of Awaji, and the two places were often bracketed in classical literature. Korechika's improvisation is based on a poem, attributed on doubtful authority to Kakinomoto Hitomaro (fl. ca. 680–700), that appears in the third Imperial anthology, Shūishū (477), for which see s.n. 62. The title of this chapter, uraura no wakare (literally, "The Separation of the Beaches"), derives from Korechika's poem.

Sa mo koso wa	It is quite true
Miyako no hoka ni	That one who travels from the capital
Tabine seme	Lodges in discomfort;
Utate tsuyukeki	Yet must it be so wet—
Kusamakura kana.	This pillow of grass?[19]

When Takaie arrived in Tajima, the governor of the province took it upon himself to do all sorts of things for him, going far beyond the Court's instructions.[20] Takaie was a considerate person, and others were always glad of an opportunity to serve him. Now that the exile had reached his destination, Nobuyasu was to return to the capital, but he found Takaie's melancholy situation so touching that he left behind his own son, Tomosuke (whom he had brought along on the journey), instructing him to act as the Middle Counselor's attendant.

At Harima, too, suitable accommodation was provided, and the police escort returned to the capital. It was not only those close to the banished men who rejoiced at the substitution of Tajima and Harima for the original distant destinations. But poor little Matsugimi was still inconsolable.

The Empress was tormented by a grief that never diminished, and her approaching confinement also haunted her thoughts as she grew great with child. A constant stream of messengers arrived from both Harima and Tajima. Kishi had been alarmingly ill ever since her return from Yamazaki, refusing food and even neglecting her habitual Buddhist devotions. Her brother, the Holy Teacher Seishō,[21] remonstrated with her, but she remained in a state of profound depression, unable, it seemed, to rally her spirits; and concern for her health added to the woes of Teishi and the others. Korechika's grandfather, Naritada, must have felt that something might still be accomplished through prayer, for he followed a strict dietary regimen and recited the holy names all day long.

All the letters sent to the exiles were melancholy in the extreme, but the saddest tidings were of their distraught mother. Now in critical condition, Kishi had taken to repeating a single monotonous refrain, even in her sleep. "Let me see His Lordship and then die. I want to die." (No doubt she in-

19. "Pillow of grass" translates *kusamakura*, a metaphor for sleeping on a journey. The grass is, of course, wet with tears.

20. The governor of Tajima in 996 was probably Taira Narimasa (brother of Korenaka), who figures in the *Pillow Book* as an official in Empress Teishi's Household. Since Narimasa seems to have remained in the capital during at least part of his tenure as governor, it is possible that the official in question was the provisional governor, Taira Yukiyoshi. EMZ, 2: 61; *Mak.*, p. 48.

21. A monk remembered chiefly for his poems in Imperial anthologies. He lived at Mount Hiei for a time.

tended the message to be transmitted to Korechika.) "Life is a transient affair. It would be terrible if she were to die with such thoughts in her mind," her brothers said. "I quite agree, but what can one do?"[22]

The Tenth of the Ninth Month passed. Teishi's confinement was approaching, and the illness of her mother, her sole support, caused her much anxiety. It seemed unlikely that Kishi would recover. Day or night, she never spoke except to murmur, "Ah, how I miss him." A succession of worried messages arrived from Harima and Tajima. Weeping, the sick woman composed a poem:

Yoru no tsuru	The crane at eventide
Miyako no uchi ni	Captive
Komerarete	In the city
Ko o koitsutsu mo	Weeps until dawn,
Nakiakasu kana.	Mourning its young.

When people inquired after her health, she would reply evasively, "Nothing is the matter with me."

Korechika could not decide what to do. He longed to see his mother and comfort her, but would not his sentence be increased if he let his concern take him back to the capital? Takaie had no intention of returning. Even if his mother were to die, he thought, he refused to be guilty of a second dishonorable act. What would people think?

Genshi was still receiving regular letters from the Crown Prince. The Emperor loved Empress Teishi dearly, but in deference to public opinion he sent his messages to her secretly through Ukon no Naishi.[23] Prince Atsumichi's wife, who seemed to be suffering from a mental disorder, now lived entirely at her family's residence. In spite of everything, Teishi still seemed to be in a more secure position than her sisters. If she were to bear a son, it would be splendid indeed, thought Senshi, already planning far into the future—for it was only proper, she felt, to show kindness to a lady so devoted to the Emperor. She was in truth deeply moved by Teishi's plight.

Already it was autumn. In the poignant sadness of the season, even the wind, sighing through the reeds, evoked thoughts of those faraway places in which just such melancholy rustlings would be increasing the misery of

22. The speaker is presumably either Korechika, Naritada, or one of Kishi's brothers.

23. A trusted lady-in-waiting, tentatively identified as the mother-in-law of Tachibana Norimitsu and/or the daughter of Fujiwara Suetsuna. She is described later in *Eiga* as assisting with the bathing ceremonies after the births of Teishi's two older children, Princess Shūshi (997–1050) and Prince Atsuyasu (999–1018). She also appears in the *Pillow Book*. EMZ, 2: 67; Kaneko 1939, 1: 56.

exile. Messengers arrived daily from Harima and Tajima. Kishi was so much worse that it was impossible to think of anything else. "If only I might see Korechika once more before I die," she repeated day and night. The Empress pitied her from the bottom of her heart. The uncles racked their brains for some way of getting Korechika and Takaie home—but that was a risky business. Kishi abandoned herself to tears of longing, and the people around her felt that it was impossible to predict what the future might hold.

The messages from the capital reduced Korechika to tearful vacillation. What was he to do? Discovery would mean the end of all hope. He would die without seeing the capital again. But he resolved at last to take the risk. "What more could happen to me?" he thought. "Could I be worse off? If the Court wants to punish me for visiting my dying mother—if the gods and buddhas want to blame me—then I shall simply accept it as fore-ordained." He set out for the capital, traveling day and night.

To return to the Empress's residence, he felt, would merely invite discovery. Taking elaborate precautions, he made his way under cover of darkness to Saiin, in the western sector of the capital.[24] His mother and the Empress stole away to join him, confident that there was no danger of being betrayed by the people there, who would surely remember the days before Michitaka's death when Kishi had visited them and done them many favors in spite of their inconvenient location.[25] The members of the family gazed at one another—the mother, Teishi and the other sisters, and Korechika himself—and the joy of the long-awaited reunion drew floods of tears from their eyes. They had bundled Kishi into a carriage and lifted her out again, mats and all. She had seemed scarcely conscious, but now she began to chatter away through her tears. "I won't mind dying after this," she said happily. It was extraordinary. Words like pitiful and sad are too commonplace for such occasions.

Korechika remained in concealment for a day or two, exercising the utmost discretion. But then the Court and the city began to buzz with rumors of his presence—inspired, perhaps, by a spirit of some kind—and a guard was stationed at Teishi's house. After investigating other likely places without success, the authorities rushed off an official messenger to

24. Saiin was an area in the general vicinity of Nishiōmiya and Shijō (Ukyō-ku, Kyōto), usually identified as the site of the Junnain, an early Heian town palace used by Emperor Junna (786–840; r. 823–33), which is said to have been known also as the Saiin (Western Palace). According to *Shōyūki*, 2: 24 (8 x Chōtoku 2), however, Sanesuke was told that Korechika was hiding in Teishi's residence. EMZ, 2: 70–71; *Uji shūi monogatari*, p. 446, s.n. 43.

25. Most members of the nobility lived in the eastern sector of the city.

survey the situation at Harima, where it was learned that the exile had indeed vanished. The search of suspicious places resumed, and presently word came that he was at Saiin.

The officials took an alarming view of the affair. "Ministers of State have been banished before, but none of them has ever slipped back into the capital. This is a grave matter; he must intend some harm to the government," they said.

It was concluded that Korechika would probably do the same thing again if he stayed so close to the capital. That was the root of the trouble. This time the place of exile must be Tsukushi itself, the Emperor decreed, and there must be a huge escort of police officers to take him there. The police surrounded the house and insisted that he come out at once, allowing him no chance to escape. No words of mine could describe the pathos of that second dreadful experience.

Korechika was to be accompanied in the carriage by his maternal aunt Senji, the wife of Tamemoto, the governor of Settsu.[26] His grief-stricken mother fell into a faint, but he himself assumed a fatalistic air. "There's nothing to get excited about. It was destined to happen," he said.

"Let me go too. I'm going too," Matsugimi shrieked as his father was about to leave. It was a pitiful scene. Someone improvised a stratagem to make the child stay behind, and the carriage was pulled out to begin its tragic journey. For Korechika, sunk in gloom, the whole unbelievable episode was like a dream.

The Empress was in despair. "At least it was comforting to hear that Harima, or whatever its name is, was quite close to the capital . . . It doesn't look as though Mother can survive much longer. How miserable I shall be with no one to take care of things when the baby comes," she thought.

It turned out that Korechika's presence had been revealed by Takayoshi, the Assistant Director of the Stables of the Right. The man, one of the many sons of Taira Chikanobu (a former governor of Echizen), was a singer who occasionally served in one of the choruses during performances of sacred music.[27] He received a promotion in rank for providing the information that relieved the Court of its anxiety. When he went to tell the good news to his father, Chikanobu no Ason responded with a shout of anger. "Whose house do you think this is, you heartless animal? No son of a man in my position acts as an informer; that's the business of rustic

26. Tamemoto was no longer the governor of Settsu at this time. EM, 1: 76, n. 7.
27. Chikanobu (945–1016) was a middle-ranking courtier who became a Consultant with Junior Second Rank in 1015. *Kugyō bunin*, 1: 248, 261–62.

louts and female street peddlers. Are you proud of yourself for wounding and grieving people with your disgraceful tale-bearing?" Takayoshi withdrew in confusion.

Some people said Korechika had merely got what he deserved, but those with a deeper understanding of human nature protested that it was wrong to blame him for returning. "With his dying mother begging even in her sleep for one last glimpse of him, he must have felt that he couldn't consider his own well-being. But what a pity! By now he must already have passed his original place of exile in Harima. Takaie was wise to stay away; he has his wits about him," they said.

For Korechika's mother, beset by anguished thoughts, the end was approaching. How little the word pitiful suffices to describe her condition! All her years of Buddhist piety seemed fated to come to nothing, thought her grieving brother, the Holy Teacher Seishō. Her father, having failed to profit from the lesson of his previous failures, was performing rituals day and night with frenzied determination.[28]

The Crown Prince sent Genshi many sympathetic letters asking how she was getting along. It was a great shame, he thought, that a lady who had once been so proud should suffer such mortification, and he longed to see her. Once Genshi sent him a poem, presumably in response to a letter:

Akigiri no	When I gazed out
Taemataema o	Through rifts
Miwataseba	In the autumn fog,
Tabi ni tadayou	It was sad to think
Hito zo kanashiki.	Of a wandering traveler.

With her distant brother in her thoughts, Empress Teishi recited these lines to herself:

Kumo no nami	He is far away
Keburi no nami o	Beyond cloud waves
Tachihedate	And smoke billows—
Aimimu koto no	Distant as the day
Haruka naru kana.	When we two shall meet.

As Korechika gradually drew closer to Tsukushi, the post-station functionaries in the various provinces received him with great kindness, weeping as they cared for his needs. When he reached his destination,[29] he found

28. In the hope of restoring Korechika to power.
29. He arrived in the Twelfth Month of Chōtoku 2, i.e. early in 997.

that provision for his reception had been made by the Senior Assistant Governor-General, Arikuni no Ason, [30] who had been told to expect him.

"I was very bitter after Korechika's late father took it into his head to strip me of office through no fault or negligence of my own, but my disgrace was nothing in comparison with the minister's. How terrible that he should come all the way to this unthinkable place! Regulations or not, I'll do what I can to make him comfortable." So Arikuni ran on as he saw to the preparations. The news of his activities caused Korechika such embarrassment that he longed to escape altogether from human society.

Arikuni sent a message by his son Yoshinari.[31] "I wish I could have called on you as soon as you got to this unthinkable place, especially since I have had little news of the capital, but as the administrator of the Nine Provinces,[32] I am not free to go about as I choose, and so I have not yet paid my respects. You have only to speak; I shall do whatever you ask. I feel certain that I have lived so long because fate wills me to continue in the service of my Lord's descendants." The innumerable boxes of gifts accompanying the letter added to Korechika's discomfiture, and he made no reply.

From that time on, Korechika ate monk's fare in ritual seclusion.

Meanwhile, not long after the Twentieth of the Tenth Month, Korechika's mother died in the capital. The family was prostrate with grief. It seemed a pity that the lady's father, the Lord of Second Rank, had lived so long. Much enfeebled by age, he could scarcely move about, and Akinobu, Michinobu, and Sanenobu were obliged to see to all the arrangements. Instead of having the usual cremation, they built a suitable resting place at Sakuramoto to receive the coffin.[33] It was all most affecting.

A messenger traveled day and night to bear the news to Tajima, where Takaie, choked with tears, ordered his garments to be dyed in somber hues. Someone also set out for Tsukushi, but it was not the sort of place that could be reached in a short time.

The later religious services were held in a suitable fashion.

Ten or fifteen days after the news had reached Tajima, the messenger arrived in Tsukushi. "So it has happened. How glad I am that we saw

30. On Arikuni, see Chapter 3, n. 49.
31. Not otherwise identified.
32. I.e. Kyūshū. The provinces were Bungo, Buzen, Chikugo, Chikuzen, Higo, Hizen, Hyūga, Ōsumi, and Satsuma.
33. "Resting place" translates ya, which here means tamaya, a structure in which a coffin was kept for a time before burial. Sakuramoto was an old name for an area in the present Shishigatani-chō, Sakyō-ku, Kyōto.

Korechika in exile in Tsukushi. Gifts arrive from the Senior Assistant Governor-General in a long chest carried on a pole and in a lidded box. Sails appear on the horizon.

one another," Korechika thought. He murmured a poem as he prepared
to change into mourning:

Sono ori ni	Ah! That then
Kitemashi mono o	I had donned
Fujigoromo	Mourning robes,
Yagate sore koso	For was it not
Wakare narikere.	Our last farewell?

In that wretched manner, Korechika's anxiety about his mother came
to an end. He had also been concerned about his sister's confinement, but
around the Twentieth of the Twelfth Month the Empress gave birth to
a Princess with little difficulty.[34] If she had been allowed to choose, Teishi
thought, she would have preferred a son, someone who could become a
source of confidence and joy. But she changed her mind after further reflection. "I am really very pleased. With so much hostility at Court . . ."
Although Teishi made no formal announcement to the Emperor, the event
naturally came to Senshi's attention, and so His Majesty learned of it.
How was Teishi managing, he wondered unhappily. Senshi too was moved
to sympathy by the thought of what the Empress must be enduring, and
she sent to inquire after her health.

Though the Empress had not made a great point of offering prayers,
some buddha or god must have helped her.

At the Emperor's direction, Ukon no Naishi presented herself for the
bathing ceremonies. Nervous and frightened as she was, she dared not
question an Imperial command. All the rites were observed in proper
style, there being certain prescribed forms in these matters—but what
splendid ceremonies would have celebrated such an event in the days of
Michitaka's glory! The thought of it made the Empress wretched.

Teishi and her ladies were a depressing sight in their dark mourning
robes, but the tiny princess was fair-skinned and dainty, and Ukon no
Naishi longed to show her to the Emperor.

It would have been unthinkable for any of the ceremonies during the
first seven days to be commonplace affairs.

When the news reached Tajima, Takaie accepted the child's sex with
fatalistic composure. "I am happy about it. Considering how we were
treated while Teishi was still childless, we're really better off. Many people
in ancient times suffered terribly from just such causes," he said. For

---

34. Princess Shūshi. For a list of the offspring of Emperor Ichijō and Teishi, see s.n. 63.

Teishi herself he felt deep sympathy. He wondered if anyone was taking proper care of her.

At Tsukushi, Korechika continued to mourn his mother. He had also been much concerned on the Empress's behalf, but someone had finally arrived to report that the confinement had taken place without incident.

After the Seventh Day, Ukon no Naishi prepared to return to the Imperial Palace. The Empress rewarded her with an extravagant assortment of gifts. "You have gone to so much trouble that I feel you are treating me as a stranger," said Ukon. "His Majesty only sent me because he thought you would feel free and relaxed in my company, but it seems he was wrong. I shall have no reply when he asks the meaning of this astonishing list of things." She repeated her thanks again and again.

When at length Ukon reached the Palace, the Emperor summoned her in an unobtrusive manner and questioned her closely about all that she had seen during her stay. Tears filled his eyes as she added one pitiful detail after another. "I am sure everything is quite as bad as she says," he thought.

When Ukon described the dainty little Princess, he responded with touching emotion, "I should like very much to see her. In ancient times, the first meeting between an Emperor and his child took place when the child was five or seven, and babies were not allowed to stay in the Palace at all, but such customs are, I believe, no longer observed. The Crown Prince walks around carrying Seishi's son, and Seishi herself is said to be pregnant again. How I envy him! Who knows when I shall see my daughter?"

"Her Majesty rewarded me with embarrassing liberality. She gave me a gorgeous set of robes, which I have laid aside for New Year's Day," Ukon said.

"Perhaps it is merely because I know few other women, but it seems to me that nobody is kinder or more thoughtful than Teishi," said the Emperor in an affectionate voice. Teishi's transformation into a nun had caused him great distress, and he suffered many secret pangs as he thought of the scandal that would erupt if she were to visit the Imperial Palace.

The next year [997] began, ushered in by the Congratulations on the First and a series of other impressive occasions. All was splendor in the brilliant springtime capital, but the exiles could not help thinking, "Is not the spring the spring of old . . ."[35] To them the season meant only that

35. An allusion to *Kokinshū* 747, in which Ariwara Narihira contrasts present misery with past felicity: Tsuki ya aranu / haru ya mukashi no / haru naranu / waga mi hitotsu wa /

the year of their banishment had receded into the past. Empress Teishi felt as though veils of mist hovered between her and the world of reality.

During Michitaka's lifetime, fire had destroyed half of the Nijō Mansion, which had originally included in its grounds both a northern and a southern compound; and the entire family had taken up residence in the remaining accommodations. Not long after Korechika's exile, the other half had also burned, and since Teishi's confinement had been imminent, Senshi had arranged for her to stay in a house belonging to Korenaka, the Taira Middle Counselor.[36]

"The little Princess must be adorable. Wouldn't you like to see her?" Senshi urged the Emperor. But the situation was delicate, and he probably found it difficult to reach a decision. He would naturally have wondered about Michinaga's reaction, and he must also have hesitated before inviting even the briefest of visits from an Empress who had pronounced religious vows. Senshi was touched by his evident desire to see the daughter of whom he spoke so often, but it was impossible for the child to come alone.

The daughter of Morosuke's son Tōnori was acting as one of the baby's wet nurses.[37] Among the other nurses were Ben and Shō no Myōbu.[38]

With the advent of summer, the baby seemed more captivating than ever. Almost every day brought pathetically anxious letters from the exiles.

Teishi's grandfather came to inspect the young Princess one night. The sight of him aroused the Empress's deepest feelings, and she burst into sobs, but the old man smiled happily as he beheld the dainty child.

"I count on you to look after me in your mother's stead," he said to Teishi, "and so I regret very much that I cannot visit you daily. People say you ought to go to the Palace, since the Emperor is so very anxious to see the baby. What do you intend to do? Nobody tells an old man anything."

---

moto no mi ni shite. ("Is not the moon the same? The spring the spring of old? Only this body of mine is the same body . . .") For discussions of the poem, see Brower and Miner 1961, p. 193; and McCullough 1968, pp. 52–53.

36. Teishi is known to have moved to the home of her uncle Akinobu (d. 1009?) after the fire on the Ninth of the Sixth Month, 996. There is no evidence of a subsequent move to Korenaka's house. EMZ, 2: 97.

37. Tōnori was known as Kitano no Saishō (the Kitano Consultant). His daughter, Lady Saishō, figures in the *Pillow Book* and the *Diary of Murasaki Shikibu* as one of the more important of Teishi's ladies.

38. Ben has been identified by Matsumura with a daughter of a provincial governor (Fujiwara Masatoki), who appears in Chapter 11 as the nurse of Princess Teishi (1013–94), the daughter of Emperor Sanjō and Fujiwara Kenshi, but the identification is uncertain. See Hagitani 1971–73, 1: 193. Kubota et al. 1962, p. 898, identify her with the poet of the same name, who, however, seems to have been active as late as 1076. Shō no Myōbu had been a lady-in-waiting in the household of Minamoto Masanobu. EMZ, 2: 97.

"I have wanted to do everything possible to make up to you for Mother's loss," she replied, "but I seem to have been so busy with little things, and now with the baby to take care of I don't know where the times goes. His Majesty assures me, with what seems to be great sincerity, that he won't be happy until he sees the Princess, and his mother has also asked me to bring the child to the Palace—I suppose because she feels obliged to respect his wishes. But with so many causes for hesitation, I can't make up my mind. It's the worry about Korechika and Takaie that upsets me most. The Emperor himself speaks of them with sympathy, I hear, and often says, 'In spite of everything, it would be unthinkable to let them stay in exile forever.'"

"I keep having dreams in which it seems that my grandsons are to be recalled, but unfortunately nothing has come of them yet," the old man replied. He continued in his most persuasive manner, "I really feel that you must decide to go to the Palace. After reciting prayers with great fervor, I went to bed and dreamed that you would give birth to a son; and my principal reason for coming today was to tell you that with such an omen you must go directly. I was afraid the news might get out if I wrote a letter." He spent the whole night in conversation, weeping and laughing, and took his leave at dawn.

Thus encouraged, Empress Teishi decided to visit the Palace. Akinobu and Michinobu bustled about, busying themselves with preparations of many kinds. The Empress's provincial households were uniformly slow in responding to requests for supplies, but someone in charge of a noble estate offered a contribution of silk, and with that the uncles were able to hurry things along. Everything seemed different now because the baby was to go along. Instead of a litter, which would have involved much old-fashioned ceremony, Teishi had decided to use a carriage. She was still very uncertain about the propriety of the journey, but the Emperor sent word that she was not to hesitate—she and the baby must come together. Since her grandfather had urged the same course, she made up her mind to go ahead. Nobody expected the gossips to remain silent.

In obedience to instructions from Michinaga that the Empress must have a proper escort, everyone went to Court on the night of the entry. Michinaga's attitude in the matter was most praiseworthy.

The moment Teishi arrived, Senshi took the young Princess in her arms. The child's dainty beauty brought a smile to her lips. As she gazed with deep emotion at the sweetly dimpled body and listened to the happy, incoherent prattle, she must have thought of the poet's lines about the response of tears to pathos.[39]

Teishi had been feeling terribly ill at ease, but when she met Senshi, there seemed no end of things to discuss. Meanwhile, the Emperor arrived to see the Princess. The laughing, babbling baby was irresistible. Why did this have to be his first glimpse of her, he wondered, the tears rising to his eyes. Though he said nothing of his feelings to others, he wished fervently that she had been a boy.

The Emperor went to call on Teishi. As was natural, she had had curtain-stands set up to preserve a proper distance between them, but he ordered the lights moved away and then began to converse with great informality, laughing and weeping. To the alarm of the ladies in attendance, "his heart went back to bygone days."[40] In the excitement of the moment, he seemed deaf to Teishi's agitated protests. He gossiped away about all sorts of things, and at dawn, when she was to leave, he said, "Do stay a bit longer—just four or five days, until the Princess learns to recognize me." By the first light of day, she proceeded to the Apartments of the Empress's Household, where she made the arrangements necessary for a brief period of residence.

Both the Emperor and the Empress were troubled by nervous doubts, but Emperor Ichijō was very much in love at the time, and he pretended to be unaware that people were critical of his behavior. Teishi's melancholy deepened as she reflected that she must now be the object of humiliating gossip. Remembering happier days, the Emperor's ladies pitied her with all their hearts.

After a few days, the Emperor moved Teishi to a building closer than the Household Apartments, which he pronounced too distant. Instead of summoning her to the Seiryōden, he went to her rooms, arriving in the dark and leaving before dawn. His passion seemed even more ardent than in the past, and one could not help wondering whether he cared at all for his newer consorts.

Teishi had planned only a brief visit, but the Emperor detained her with entreaties to stay "just a bit longer," until two months had elapsed.

---

39. *Kokinshū* 941 (anon.): Yo no naka no / uki mo tsuraki mo / tsuge naku ni / mazu shiru mono wa / namida narikeri. ("My tears, without being told, are yet the first to understand the sorrow and pain of this world.")

40. *Kokinshū* 734, by Ki no Tsurayuki: Inishie ni / nao tachikaeru / kokoro kana / koishiki koto ni / mono wasuresede. ("This heart of mine goes back to bygone days, too fond to forget past love.")

She had begun to feel out of sorts, and the cessation of her monthly periods made her fear that she might be pregnant. The Emperor, when he heard the news, felt certain that they had been lovers in an earlier life. It was all very natural, but even such trifles provoked the censure of others, and for Teishi it must have been a dreamlike existence.

When word of these events reached Tajima, Takaie busied himself with supplications to the buddhas and gods. Teishi's grandfather prayed harder than ever.

Meanwhile, by using her illness as an argument, Teishi had finally prevailed on the Emperor to let her go.[41] Gishi and Genshi had both taken up residence in the Palace, but neither had succeeded in usurping her place. Her problems preyed on the Emperor's mind, and he poured out his worries in a constant stream of letters. His messages arrived almost every other day, usually through the unobtrusive intermediacy of Ukon no Naishi. Teishi's overjoyed grandfather, convinced that his dream was coming true, prayed with frantic zeal.

Hearing about all this in Tsukushi, Korechika must have felt certain that he would be pardoned.

Takaie had long ago severed his connection with Shigenobu's daughter. He was now in love with a daughter of Kanesuke,[42] the governor of Iyo, and probably thought of little but seeing her again. Korechika pined for Matsugimi, far away in the capital. How well, at such times, the poem "The Living Pine Grove" seemed to reflect his own plight![43] Both were greatly to be pitied.

With the passing of time, the Empress grew great with child, and her melancholy deepened. It was too much, she said, to have her brothers so far away. The Emperor, who shared her misgivings, spoke frequently of the matter to his mother.[44]

41. The author probably makes this statement, which is unsupported by independent evidence, because (as is shown later) she mistakenly believed that Prince Atsuyasu was born in 998, rather than in 999.

42. A son of the Consultant Minamoto Koremasa.

43. *Shūishū* 1208, by Lady Shōnagon: Kyō made wa / Ikinomatsubara / ikitaredo / waga mi no usa ni / nagekite zo furu. ("Like the pines of the Living Pine Grove, I have lived on until today, yet misery makes my life a burden.") The author had gone to Kyūshū after an unhappy love affair with Fujiwara Naritoki. Her poem is a response to Naritoki's foster son, Sanekata, who had sent to inquire after her health when he visited the area as a messenger to Usa Hachiman Shrine. Ikinomatsubara (the Living Pine Grove) was a local scenic spot, now a part of Fukuoka City. It is introduced because its first two syllables are homophonous with the *iki* of *ikitaredo*, a form of the verb *iku*, ("live"). Similarly, usa ("misery") alludes to Usa Hachiman Shrine.

44. Possibly for dramatic effect, the author has taken liberties with the chronology. See the Introduction, pp. 34–35. Korechika and Takaie were pardoned in the Fourth Month of

In the winter Genshi showed signs of being pregnant. Her father, the minister, was giddy with joy, and the Emperor must have been pleased too. "If either of the two can manage to produce a son . . . ," thought Senshi.

When three months had elapsed, Genshi announced her condition and withdrew from the Palace. She made a brilliant departure in a hand-drawn carriage, accompanied by her ladies on foot. As the procession passed the Kokiden corridor, a crowd of Gishi's ladies looked on, pressed against a bulging blind. A pert child in Genshi's train glanced at the corridor, which was clearly visible in the torchlight, and called out, "At least your blind is pregnant!" "What impudence!" said the ladies. "We ought not to have watched." But in spite of their irritation with their rivals' superior airs, they could not help envying the circumstances of their departure.

After his daughter's return, Minister of the Right Akimitsu busied himself with prayers of every description. His consort was Michikane's widow. Poor Michikane! Not only his rank but also his wife had gone to Akimitsu. The minister was living at the Horikawa Mansion, to which he had made extensive alterations. Genshi's brother Shigeie was a Lesser Captain with an excellent reputation.

How swiftly the days and months sped by! Already it was the fourth year of Chōtoku [998], and little Princess Shūshi was three. One can imagine the frequency, and the loving devotion, with which Emperor Ichijō pictured her to himself, certain that she must be even sweeter than before.

Every precaution was being observed in preparation for the Empress's confinement in the Third Month, but there was no one to see to the prompt payment of her rents. The Palace Storehouse Bureau delivered articles necessary for the lying-in, and Senshi's thoughtfulness anticipated other requirements, so that the arrangements were somehow completed. Bishop Ryūen was most helpful.

After a period of anxiety, the first signs of labor appeared. Amid the bustle of excitement, Teishi felt miserably that she had no one to depend on. There was only the governor of Tajima,[45] who was, however, looking after her with great solicitude. When her grandfather heard that the delivery was at hand, he knelt in prayer with his head touching the floor— and perhaps it was in response to his frenzied pleas that a male child was born with no difficulty.[46]

---

997. Two months later, Teishi entered the Dairi, where she remained until the Eighth Month of 999, three months before the birth of Prince Atsuyasu. EMZ, 2: 114–16.

45. Taira Narimasa, brother of Korenaka. Teishi had moved to his house to await the birth. EMZ, 2: 120.

46. Prince Atsuyasu, born in Narimasa's house on the Seventh of the Eleventh Month, 999.

Overcome with joy at the birth of a Prince, the Empress's people sent word to Senshi. The Imperial Lady informed the Emperor, and a messenger appeared with a sword.

There was universal rejoicing and much gossip, not all of it in good taste. "Such is life," quipped someone. "'You aspire and your hopes are dashed; you try to get away and you can't'[47]—and a lucky thing for some people, too."

As before, Ukon no Naishi presented herself for the bathing rituals. In the ordinary course of events, one of the birth ceremonies would have been sponsored by the Court, but Emperor Ichijō temporized, reluctant to take the risk of offending Michinaga. Both the Emperor and Senshi were delighted when Michinaga, who may have guessed something of the Emperor's state of mind, took personal charge of the proceedings on the Seventh Night.[48] In addition to sending presents of silk and damask, Senshi provided for the Empress's other needs with great consideration.

On the Seventh Night, Fujiwara Naishi no Suke and some of the principal Palace Ladies and Lady Chamberlains came to help take care of the Prince. I am sure they all received suitable remembrances.

Teishi's grandfather was convinced that his dream had come true. "If you can manage to rear him safely, he will sit on the throne," he kept saying. "You must take very, very good care of him."

Messengers had been sent to Tajima and Tsukushi on the day after the birth. Takaie soon heard the news, which, needless to say, made him exceedingly happy. What a pity that there was no way of telling Korechika at once, he thought.

Now that Teishi's ladies had an Imperial Prince to care for, they congratulated themselves on not having left her service.

The bow-twangers for the bathing ceremonies and the learned Professors who read from Chinese texts were all chosen by Michinaga.

"Teishi has given us a fine child this time," said Michinaga. "Her line seems destined to survive. One scarcely expected the succession to leave Morosuke's descendants, but still it is gratifying to have such a birth in our father's family."

Korechika was deliriously happy when the news reached Tsukushi. "The Prince is the buddha by whose power we shall be recalled," he ex-

---

47. Possibly a proverb.
48. A contemporary diary, *Gonki*, 1: 86 (13 xi Chōhō 1), records the Seventh Night celebration but says nothing about Michinaga's sponsoring it.

ulted. Thereafter, his mind was completely occupied with thoughts of the future, and his dreams must have been rosy indeed.

Meanwhile, the Emperor was much concerned on the little Prince's behalf. The child, he felt, must not be left to shift for himself, and he longed to use the birth as an excuse for the recall of the exiles. After many consultations with Senshi, he approached Michinaga.

"As Your Majesty says, the Prince's birth would be an appropriate occasion for recalling them. I suggest that it be done," said Michinaga. The Emperor was overjoyed, but he replied in an offhand manner, "Very well, handle it as you think best." The recall edict was issued in the Fourth Month.[49]

That year, instead of the usual smallpox, a disease characterized by a heavy rash of bright red spots was claiming victims of all ages and classes. Some of the sufferers had died, and people were depressed and uneasy, both at Court and elsewhere. But the order for her brothers' pardon had raised Teishi's spirits to the skies. Her men set out at once, ahead of the official messengers, with orders to ride night and day. The gossips took a genial view of the affair. With such a splendid young Prince, it was only to be expected, they said.

The Kamo Festival and other events took place in the capital, and the end of the month arrived. Neither the Empress's messenger nor the Court's had reached Tsukushi, but Tajima was much nearer, and a great throng of important people went to greet Takaie. The occasion could not have been regarded as a source of prestige, but Takaie had never been happier. Setting out for the capital, he arrived on the Third or Fourth of the Fifth Month.

At first Takaie went to Kanesuke's house, but he found it impossible to frequent the premises openly because Michinaga's foster son Narinobu, the Minamoto Middle Captain, was often there, and Kanesuke consequently considered Takaie's presence a nuisance. Narinobu was said to be one of the two sons of Emperor Murakami's third son, Prince Munehira, the Minister of War (the one who had retired to Iwakura as a Buddhist Novice); the other son was a monk at Miidera.[50] Michinaga's wife had adopted Narinobu, and the young man had married one of Kanesuke's daughters. Takaie not only had started a clandestine affair with another

49. See n. 44. The real reason for the pardon was that Senshi had fallen ill.
50. Another name for the Onjōji (powerful ancient rival of the Enryakuji), situated in what is now Ōtsu-shi, Shiga-ken. The monk was Eien.

daughter, but had got himself banished into the bargain, so Kanesuke and his wife spoke of him in hostile tones, and he was obliged to skulk about when he was there.

Michinaga's wife had adopted Narinobu because he was her nephew; his mother was her half-sister.[51]

On the Fifth of the Fifth Month, Takaie composed a poem for his wife:

Omoiki ya	Could I have believed
Wakareshi hodo no	When we parted
Kono koro yo	In this very season,
Miyako no kyō ni	That today in the capital
Awan mono to wa.	We should meet again?

She replied:

Ukine nomi	At sweet-flag time
Tamoto ni kakeshi	Bitter tears
Ayamegusa	Fell on my sleeve,
Hikitagaetaru	But today when all is changed
Kyō zo ureshiki.	How happy I am!

Takaie could not restrain tears of joy when he visited the Empress. Gazing with deep emotion at the dainty little Princess and Prince, he felt as though a dream had become reality.[52]

It seemed that Korechika would never come. Akinobu and some others set out to meet him, and the sisters gathered—Genshi and Prince Atsumichi's wife. The fourth sister, who had been chosen as the infant Prince's foster mother, was busying herself on his behalf. Takaie went to see his wife only by night; the rest of his time he spent at Teishi's house.

Meanwhile, Naritada, a victim of the measles, was suffering from severe fainting fits, and his condition was said to be desperate. People found it most affecting. He begged to be allowed to see Korechika before he died, but of that there seemed little likelihood.

The epidemic raged on, sparing no one.

The Shōkyōden Consort Genshi had gone past the expected term of her pregnancy with a disturbing absence of birth symptoms. As a last resort, after prayers of all kinds had failed, she made a journey in the Sixth

51. See s.n. 64.

52. According to the *Eiga* chronology, the Prince was not born until almost a year after Takaie's return, which took place on the Twenty-second of the Fourth Month, 997. In fact, the birth took place more than two years after Takaie's return.

Month to Uzumasa, where esoteric rites and continuous recitations of the *Healing Buddha Sutra* were commissioned on her behalf.[53] She remained there after the first seven-day period of prayers and rituals, praying with redoubled fervor, and perhaps it was for that reason that symptoms appeared and she began to suffer. Her distracted father, Akimitsu, hastily informed Ukon no Naishi at the Imperial Palace, and the Emperor began to dispatch messages of inquiry. Senshi also sent word of her concern.

"It would be awkward if the child were to arrive at our temple," said the abbot and his monks. "On the other hand, it would be unwise for the lady to try to go home." Meanwhile, it became clear that the child was about to arrive. "Very well, she must remain. We can request forgiveness for the transgression later," they decided.[54]

Presently, an astounding spate of water gushed from Genshi's body. It was indeed very strange and unprecedented, her people admitted, but they assured one another that there must be some perfectly good reason for it. More and more fluid poured out, until at length her belly was flatter than a normal person's.[55] Nothing but water emerged, no trace of blood despite all the months of missed periods. The monks were dumbfounded, and Akimitsu was utterly undone—upset enough to remind one of the saying, "ill for seven days."[56] The minister clasped his knee in his hands and sat staring at the sky, feeling as though he had awakened from a dream.

Genshi's dismay and embarrassment were beyond comparison. Recalling the incident outside the Kokiden corridor, she felt that she could never show her face at the Palace again. Imperial messengers continued to arrive, but there was nothing to report. Though it was not unusual for a newborn child to die, this was something out of the ordinary, to say the least.

"It's embarrassing that such a thing should have happened, but at least she's safe, thanks to the buddhas," the temple monks said philosophically.

53. Uzumasa (now a place-name in Sakyō-ku, Kyōto) here refers to a Shingon temple, the Kōryūji (Uzumasadera). The *Healing Buddha Sutra* celebrates the miraculous powers of Yakushi, the Healing Buddha. There are two basic versions, one of which exists in four different translations, but in Japanese usage the title ordinarily refers to the one-chapter *Yakushi rurikō nyorai hongan kudokukyō*, translated ca. A.D. 650 by Hsüan-tsang. "Continuous recitations" can mean either habitual daily devotions or, as here, recitations for a specific purpose performed during a fixed period, usually of seven or twenty-one days.

54. The transgression was the defilement of a holy place by blood, a Shintō religious taboo that had been extended to Buddhism.

55. Although some elements in the story of Genshi's false pregnancy may be based on fact, this bizarre phenomenon, unreported in medical history, is not to be taken seriously. For comment, see EMZ, 2: 137–38.

56. Possibly a proverb.

The Emperor refrained from comment when he heard the news, but he felt very sorry for Genshi. "I wish Ukon had controlled her excitement and shown some discretion," he said to himself. "It would have been better if Genshi had never seemed to be pregnant." Senshi was also distressed.

The affair even became the subject of a popular ditty. The girl who had made the remark about the pregnant blind gave up her post in humiliation and stayed home. Nowhere was there so much malicious laughter as at the Kokiden. How supremely fortunate Genshi had appeared on the night of her withdrawal from the Palace, and how pitiable the sequel had been! We are constantly reminded of the ephemerality of worldly things.

The measles epidemic was raging in Tsukushi, too. In spite of Korechika's eagerness to leave for the capital, the Senior Assistant Governor-General urged him to wait until the disease had run its course, pointing out that it made travel hazardous and also that it would create problems for the servants who were to accompany him. With great reluctance, Korechika postponed his departure until the number of victims showed signs of falling off, but meanwhile his grandfather succumbed to the disease. Those were sad days.

Finally, Korechika set off for the capital in high spirits, his mind full of the little Prince who was the source of his good fortune. To Teishi and the others, impatiently awaiting his arrival, the long journey by land seemed to take forever.

Korechika reached the city in the Twelfth Month.[57] He went to the home of his father-in-law, the retired Major Counselor Shigemitsu, where his wife and the others greeted him with tears of joy. The place had deteriorated sadly since the old days. Too moved to speak, his wife gazed at him with wet eyes, and his own tears flowed in abundance as he stroked Matsugimi's hair. How the child had grown! Matsugimi rubbed his eyes and looked exceedingly happy, as was but natural.

Korechika recited a poem:

Asajifu to	Though the garden has become
Arenikeredomo	A tangled wilderness,
Furusato no	Tall indeed
Matsu wa kodakaku	Has the pine tree grown
Narinikeru kana.	At my old home.

57. Of 997, not of 998. EMZ, 2: 114.

And another:

Koshikata no	My life was spared
Ikinomatsubara	In the land of the Living Pine Grove,
Ikite kite	Whence now I return
Furuki miyako o	To behold with poignant emotion
Miru zo kanashiki.	The ancient capital.

His wife responded:

Sono kami no	How dreadful was my anguish
Ikinomatsubara	On that bygone day
Ikite kite	When you journeyed
Mi nagara aranu	Toward the Living Pine Grove,
Kokochi seshi kana.	Whence now you have lived to return.

"My first visit must be to the Empress," Korechika said. The haste with which he dashed off brought fresh tears to his wife's eyes.

Teishi also wept until her sleeve was drenched. "Let's talk about everything when we're more composed," she said.

Korechika was enchanted by the dainty charm of the children. He would have liked to hold the Prince in his arms, "but I feel it best to be very cautious," he said.[58] "How uncertain the world is! We must be thankful we have all survived." They wept bitterly as the talk returned again and again to their dead mother. Whether human beings weep for sorrow or for joy, the tears that rise to their eyes are the same. It was a pitiful sight.

Soon Korechika and Takaie chose an auspicious day on which to pray beside their mother's grave at Sakuramoto. They were both deeply moved, and tears streamed from their eyes as they imagined how happy she would have been if she had lived. It chanced that a heavy snow was falling. Takaie recited:

Tsuyu bakari	How sad to behold
Nioi todomete	The cherry trees
Chirinikeru	Whose blossoms have scattered,
Sakura ga moto o	Leaving only the hint
Miru zo kanashiki.	Of a lingering scent.

Korechika responded:

---

58. In mourning for his mother, he hesitated to touch the baby because he feared that the association with death might be unlucky. EM, 1: 195, n. 25.

Sakuramoto   Snow falls in soft flakes
Furu awayuki o   At Sakuramoto.
Hana to mite   Mistaking it for blossoms,
Oru ni mo sode zo   I break off a branch,
Nuremasarikeru.   And my sleeve grows wetter still.[59]

After addressing many sad speeches to their mother's spirit, they went home in tears, resolved that they would somehow manage to build a Buddhist hall on the spot.

59. Both poems contain the place-name Sakuramoto. In the second one, Korechika "confuses" the snowflakes with cherry blossoms, a symbol for his mother.

6

RADIANT FUJITSUBO

ICHINAGA's daughter Shōshi had reached the age of twelve.
Her Putting On of the Train took place that year [999], and then
Michinaga set about the preparations for her presentation.[1] Nothing was left undone. Her ladies-in-waiting were more elegant than the attendants who flocked to serve the Imperial consort in *The Tale of the First
Snow*,[2] and her folding screens and other furnishings were beyond comparison. The poems inscribed on the screens were composed by family
connections and others of exalted status. As the saying goes, "The more
important the poet, the more interesting the poem." Michinaga himself
contributed some lines, as did ex-Emperor Kazan and the Shijō Consultant Kintō. Kintō's poem accompanied a picture of wisteria vines in bloom:

Murasaki no	Sprays of wisteria
Kumo to zo miyuru	Seeming indeed
Fuji no hana	A purple cloud—
Ika naru yado no	What may be the dwelling
Shirushi naruramu.	This omen foretells?[3]

Ex-Emperor Kazan's composition accompanied a scene depicting a group
of young cranes in a garden:

Hinazuru o	So lovingly reared,
Yashinaitatete	The young crane—
Matsu ga e no	Hard it must be
Kage ni sumasemu	To send her to dwell
Koto oshi zo omou.	In the shade of the pine branch.[4]

1. Shōshi's mogi took place in the Second Month of 999, her presentation in the Eleventh.
2. *Hatsuyuki no monogatari*. It has not survived. See EMZ, 2: 153–55.
3. *Shūishū* 1069. Kintō uses "purple cloud" (*murasaki no kumo*) in both of its meanings: an auspicious cloud, and a metaphor for Empress.
4. "Crane" and "pine branch" are metaphors for Shōshi and Emperor Ichijō.

Those are but a small sample of the many poems composed. I shall not record the others.

Shōshi received Junior Third Rank on the Eleventh of the Twelfth Month in the first year of Chōhō [999]. She entered the Palace on the First of the Eleventh Month, some time after the Tenth,[5] accompanied by forty ladies-in-waiting, six young girls, and six servants. Her attendants had been selected with the utmost discrimination. It was not considered sufficient for a candidate to be personable and even-tempered: even if her father held Fourth or Fifth Rank, there was no hope for her if she was socially inept or lacking in the niceties of deportment, for only the most polished and elegant were accepted. Senshi and other personages sent suitable children to serve as girl attendants, and they were named accordingly—Inbito, the Person from the Imperial Lady; Uchihito, the Person from the Emperor; Miyahito, the Person from the Prince; Tonohito, the Person from His Lordship, and so forth. Although the reader will not need to be told that Shōshi was very lovely, I must mention her hair, which trailed on the floor for five or six inches. And her face and figure were more beautiful than I can say. In spite of her youth, she was so far from childish that it would be impossible to do justice to her grace and elegance. Her maturity astonished those who had entered her service with the notion that one so young was bound to make a poor showing as an Imperial consort.

The presentation took place after extraordinary attention to every detail of the preparations.

When one hears tales of earlier days, one can scarcely believe that ladies went about in public dressed in so few layers of clothing and with so little padding in their garments. One wonders how they managed to keep warm even at home, since ladies nowadays are always suffering from ailments caused by the weather, though they pile on so many layers that they are in danger of looking like frumps. But that was the fashion, and we must suppose that even a Junior Consort or Empress wore only a fraction of what we would consider an adequate costume.

Emperor Ichijō was by now an adult, and a discerning one at that. Shōshi's entrance was thus properly appreciated, even though she was a little uncomfortable at being subjected to the scrutiny of so discriminating an eye. Since the Emperor had been very young when Teishi was presented, a certain increase in maturity was only to have been anticipated, but he

5. "Some time after the Tenth" appears to be a textual corruption. "Twelfth Month" in the preceding sentence should read "Second Month."

had in fact acquired a depth of character and a distinction of bearing such as one scarcely expects from a sovereign in the present era of decadence. All the Ministers of State and senior nobles were delighted with him.

The late Regent Michitaka had been a man of exuberant tastes, interested in the most recent fashions, pleasure-loving, and gregarious, and the younger courtiers had always been irresistibly attracted to Teishi's corridors. Furthermore, although the Emperor had taken a number of other consorts—the ladies established in the Kokiden, the Shōkyōden, and the Kurabeya—none had succeeded in producing a child, whereas Teishi had given birth to two.

Shōshi took up residence in the Fujitsubo.[6] Shall I compare the splendor of her furnishings to the radiance of a precious jewel? A jewel glows dimly when it lacks the proper polish, but the apartments in the Fujitsubo sparkled and shone with dazzling beauty. No half-trained lady could have ventured to serve the mistress of such an establishment. Every object made of wood, even the merest curtain or screen frame, was covered with gold-lacquered designs and mother-of-pearl. To be sure, the bombycine jackets worn by all the ladies-in-waiting, and the trains with wave and shell patterns, conformed to styles prescribed since antiquity, but they somehow achieved a beauty so distinctive that one could only wonder how it had been managed. And anything that Shōshi herself wore, no matter for how short a time, was so exquisitely colored and perfumed that it seemed to deserve public recognition as a masterpiece. Shōshi visited the Imperial Bedchamber time after time.

On an auspicious day, Shōshi sent gifts to the Imperial nurses, maids, guards officers, and so forth; and presently even the humblest old kitchen servants were offering fervent prayers on her behalf. Even to nurses, she gave wardrobe boxes full of silk, damask, and bombycine robes, as well as other articles of various kinds. Ladies who had failed to win a place in her service felt keen humiliation and were pronounced failures by society, while those who happened to have been chosen were envied for their good fortune.

On the First, during the joyous excitement of the presentation, death claimed the Senior Grand Empress at Sanjō.[7] It may be imagined that

---

6. Actually in the northeast wing of the Ichijō Palace (Ichijōin), to which the Emperor had moved two days after the Dairi fire of the Fourteenth of the Sixth Month, 999. Shōshi first entered the real Fujitsubo on the Eleventh of the Tenth Month in the following year, when the Court returned to the rebuilt Dairi.

7. Princess Shōshi, consort of Emperor Reizei. She died on the First of the Twelfth Month (not on the First of the Eleventh, as the author implies), in a house at Sanjō owned by Tachi-

everyone at her palace was pitifully affected. How often we are reminded of life's uncertainty!

When the Emperor went to visit Shōshi at the Fujitsubo, the rooms were of course appointed with the utmost magnificence, and he was charmed by her appearance and manner as she made him welcome. How nice it would be, he must have thought, if his own daughter, Princess Shūshi, could be reared in exactly the same way. All his other consorts were quite grown up—almost excessively mature, in fact—but for Shōshi he could feel a fatherly affection. It was a delightful change after so many years, and he quickly developed a special fondness for her. The moment he crossed the Fujitsubo bridge, an ineffable fragrance penetrated deep into his robes. It was not the ordinary sort of concealed incense everyone burns nowadays, nor was it at all assertive, but it lingered in a manner that seemed to set it apart from the scents used by his other consorts. Even the most trifling articles in Shōshi's comb boxes[8] and writing case fascinated him by their elegance and novelty. His first act early in the morning was to visit her, and nothing that he saw failed to interest him, not even the shelves of the chests. One of her treasures was a book of poems illustrated by Hirotaka,[9] with verses in Yukinari's hand, which he examined with infinite pleasure. "It's much too amusing here; I am in danger of becoming a stupid fellow who knows nothing about affairs of state," he would say as he took his leave.

"You look so young that I feel like an old man beside you; it's really quite embarrassing," he would say when they were together in his private apartments during the daytime. He himself was barely twenty.

Though an Emperor is, to be sure, an Emperor, some of them are not quite what one might wish. One senses, perhaps, a certain lack of maturity. But Emperor Ichijō was almost unbelievably handsome and attractive. He drank wine in moderation, and his mastery of the flute never ceased to impress the people around him. As he was performing one day, he noticed that Shōshi was sitting with her eyes primly lowered.

"Why aren't you looking at me?" he demanded.

bana Michisada, the husband of the famous poet Izumi Shikibu (fl. ca. 1000). EM, 1: 202, n. 3.

8. *Mikushi no hako*, pairs of shallow, two-tiered boxes about a foot square. The upper trays held combs, scissors, tweezers, earpicks, comb cleaners, and hairdressing implements; the lower sections, some twenty small silver boxes containing mirrors, toilet articles, jewels, etc. EMZ, 2: 176.

9. Kose no Hirotaka was a great-grandson of Kanaoka, the founder of the Kose school of professional painters.

"When the flute is being played, one listens to the music; one doesn't watch the performer," she replied.

"That's the way you young people answer an old man of seventy. What a humiliating snub," he teased. The ladies-in-waiting marveled at the good fortune that allowed them to witness such happy scenes. Surely there had never been another couple to compare with those two!

All too soon, a new year began [1000]. Before the year was out, people said, some lady would receive Imperial status, and would not that lady be Shōshi? Teishi, busy with the Imperial children, showed no inclination to go to the Palace. The Emperor was uneasy and sad because he had still not seen his son.

Korechika had begun a thousand days of religious abstinence shortly after his return and was living a life austere enough to shame a monk. No doubt he viewed Prince Atsuyasu's existence as a beacon of hope. It was natural that he should have done so, and natural also that he should have prayed with frantic zeal on the Prince's behalf. Teishi herself seemed content—persuaded, perhaps, that the Prince would protect her position, despite her absence from the Palace.

Michinaga had told Senshi from the beginning that he relied on her to look after Shōshi's interests, and the Imperial Lady thus felt a heavy burden of responsibility for this particular niece,[10] but she was also well aware of Teishi's painful position.

Around that time, Shōshi was wearing Chinese damask mantles[11] with woven designs of double-flowering red plum blossoms, and the courtiers were also appearing in costumes of the utmost magnificence and modishness.

At the Tsuchimikado Mansion,[12] to which Shōshi was to return in the

10. She appears to have worked actively to secure the title of Empress for Shōshi. See EMZ, 2: 180.

11. "Chinese damask" (*karaaya*) is thought to have been the name given by the Japanese to a particular type of imported silk developed in China at the beginning of the Sung period (960–1279). It was a warp-faced twill with patterning in weft-faced twill, and with the diagonal lines of the ground and pattern running in opposite directions. The twill floats in both the ground and the pattern extended over five threads, producing a satiny effect. The cloth was woven in grège and beaten to make it soft and lustrous. "Chinese damasks" may have included imitations produced by Heian weavers. Nishimura 1971–75, 1: 7; Hifuku Bunka Kyōkai 1969, 1: 26–27.

12. Michinaga's great estate south of Tsuchimikado and west of Kyōgoku, which had come to him through Rinshi from his father-in-law, Minamoto Masanobu, and which was his principal place of residence during most of his adult life. Known also as the Kyōgoku Mansion and as the Jōtōmon'in (because of its proximity to Jōtōmon Gate), it was the birthplace of four Empresses (Shōshi, Kenshi, Ishi, and Teishi) and three Emperors (Go-Ichijō, Go-

following month, a great bustle of cleaning, repairing, and polishing was going on.

Shōshi left the Palace around the First of the Second Month.[13] People at Court noticed that the Emperor seemed lonesome and forlorn—but Shōshi's departure, they concluded, was doubtless a prelude to future events. The senior nobles and courtiers who formed her escort received presents of many kinds at the mansion before returning home.

With little to occupy him, Emperor Ichijō thought of using his leisure to see the young Prince, but he was exceedingly cautious in matters affecting Korechika and his family, and did not feel able to make his wishes known. Presently, Michinaga raised the subject. "This would be an excellent time for you to see the First Prince," he suggested. The Emperor was delighted. After consulting his mother, he proceeded to shower Teishi with messages of invitation.

Teishi hung back in embarrassment, until a kind letter from Senshi made her feel that perhaps she might go. Korechika did his best to encourage her. "What are you worrying about?" he said. "The Emperor will love you better than ever after he sees the Prince. Nobody is going to be unkind."

At the end of the Second Month, after a hectic period of preparation, Teishi was ready to enter the Palace.[14] Avoiding the ostentation of a litter, she and Princess Shūshi rode with the Prince in Michinaga's Chinese carriage, which had been sent to fetch the baby. Michinaga had also provided an escort of prominent gentlemen. Everyone agreed that he had displayed astonishing magnanimity.

Korechika marveled at his own lack of discernment. "I was unprepared for His Lordship's kindness," he admitted to his friends in private. "I expected him to do nothing for Teishi after his daughter's presentation, but he has shown gratifying generosity in making arrangements for the First Prince's journey. I would be incapable of such behavior."

Thus Teishi entered the Palace. Princess Shūshi had reached an appealing age, and the remarkable beauty of the young Prince must have drawn

Suzaku, and Go-Reizei). It burned on several occasions, the first in 1016, but continued to play an important role in the life of the Court after Michinaga's death, serving as a residence for Shōshi and, from 1037 to 1057, as a *sato dairi*. See EMZ, 2: 183–86.

13. As a preliminary to her elevation to Imperial rank. She moved not to the Tsuchimikado Mansion, but to a house in Nijō where Michinaga was then staying. EMZ, 2: 183.

14. Other sources give the date as either the Eleventh or the Twelfth of the Second Month. EMZ, 2: 188.

tears from his father's eyes. The Princess, who was four or five years old, chattered away in high spirits.

Since the night was auspicious, Senshi also saw the Prince. How closely he resembled the Emperor as a baby! She gazed at him with loving eyes, captivated by his dainty grace. The Emperor himself quite naturally felt that he could never be indifferent to the future of such a splendid child.

When Teishi had been in the Palace for a few days, Michinaga came to see the baby. He held him in his arms affectionately. What a pity, he thought, that the Emperor had not seen him until he was walking.[15] Parental love is something everyone understands.

The baby caught hold of Emperor Ichijō's flute in a delightfully appealing manner. Weeping and laughing in utter contentment, the Emperor repeated to Teishi day and night that there was nothing to mar his happiness except the uncertainty of human existence. But Teishi was not her usual self. She persisted in dwelling on dismal topics. "I felt that I ought not to come to the Palace this time, but I wanted to see you once more, and then too I was worried about the Prince's future, so I forced myself to do it," she told him with pathetic earnestness.

"Come, now! What makes you talk that way?" he asked.

"Somehow, I can't help feeling depressed," she answered. The same uncharacteristic pessimism shadowed every word she uttered.

"This is all very ill-omened," he protested.

"It doesn't matter what happens to me; it's just the child that I worry about," she said soberly.

The Third Month brought a decree elevating Shōshi to Imperial status. She was to be called Chūgū, and Teishi, who had previously held that title, was to be Kōgō.[16] The banquet was to take place soon afterward, on the Thirtieth of the Third Month, after which Shōshi was to reenter the Palace.[17] She was thirteen that year, a splendid young Empress indeed.

Meanwhile, Teishi determined each day to take her leave, and each day the Emperor insisted on keeping her. She had come in the Second Month. Her monthly period had arrived around the First, while she was still at

15. The Prince was actually only about three months old.

16. Other sources are unanimous in listing the date of the proclamation (*senmyō*) and the investiture proper as the Twenty-fifth of the Second Month, 1000, i.e. before the supposed date of the preliminary decree (senji). On the investiture ceremony, see s.n. 76.

17. The banquet celebrating Shōshi's appointment took place at the Tsuchimikado Mansion on the same date as the proclamation. She returned to the *sato dairi* on the Seventh of the Fourth Month. EMZ, 2: 194.

home, and there had been no indication of its return, even though the Twentieth of the Third Month had already passed. The circumstance was suspicious, and fears of being pregnant increased her sense of foreboding.

The Emperor addressed her with tender solicitude, worried by her strange behavior.

"I can't be happy about a pregnancy," she answered. "This is a dangerous year for me, and the astrologers have nothing but distressing predictions to offer. If I am really to bear a child, something dreadful may happen."

Teishi withdrew from the Palace on the Thirtieth of the Third Month.[18] She uttered many sad and moving speeches as she departed, and tears soaked through her mantle sleeve deep into the layers beneath. She could not rid her mind of the cessation of her periods, which seemed to her a particularly cruel twist of fate, and though she told herself that such brooding was unlucky, her depression persisted. Refusing food, she wept night and day. Korechika and Takaie recognized in alarm that the situation was serious. They dropped everything to arrange for prayers, but whenever they sent for a monk of any reputation or prominence, he put them off with excuses, unwilling to seem to be on intimate terms with the family. Since the intercessions of obscure clerics were unlikely to be fruitful, the brothers could do nothing but lament the impossibility of having the prayers they desired.

Meanwhile, there was a stir of preparation for the Kamo Festival and other events, but Korechika's family remained pitifully apart from it all. Bishop Ryūen and the Holy Teacher Seishō appeared regularly to recite the nocturnal prayers. Poor Teishi, busying herself with the needs of the Imperial children, wondered in tears how much longer she would be there to care for them.

Shōshi entered the Palace on the Thirtieth of the Fourth Month. The reader will perhaps be able to imagine the magnificence of the occasion. Her litter and other trappings were all new. She seemed born to the role of Empress as she sat in the Imperial litter, wearing a train and a formal coiffure.[19] All young girls are fresh and pretty, but Shōshi carried herself

18. The Twenty-seventh. She went to Narimasa's house. EMZ, 2: 198.

19. When serving meals and on certain other occasions, Heian Court ladies wore their hair in a special style called *migushiage* ("put-up hair"). Most of the hair was allowed to fall loose as usual, but some was drawn into a small roll above the forehead, tied with a white paper cord, and secured and decorated with hairpins. A similar term was used to describe the coiffure worn by great ladies and their attendants on state occasions such as the one described here, but it is not known whether the style was identical. EMZ, 2: 201.

with an impressive air of distinction. The Fujitsubo was now supplied with a dining bench, as well as a Korean dog and lion in front of the curtain-dais —appurtenances that made a splendid sight, even though they were only to have been expected in an Empress's apartments.[20] The younger ladies-in-waiting were fascinated.

The fire-huts at the Tsuchimikado Mansion had looked like something in a picture, but the ones in front of the Fujitsubo seemed a bit strange, possibly because people were unaccustomed to their presence.[21]

This time, to the chagrin of the less fortunate, the jackets worn by the ladies-in-waiting conformed strictly to status.[22] The bombycines of the privileged, which had attracted little attention when everyone was wearing the same kind of thing,[23] were now perceived to contain beautifully distinct patterns. On the other hand, ladies to whom bombycines were forbidden—even quite pretty young persons—found it impossible to make a decent showing, no matter how painstakingly their unfigured silk costumes[24] had been planned. It seemed all too natural that the female Palace servants should treat them with disdain.

"I used to think of you as a playmate I could relax with," said the Emperor, looking around him on one of his visits to Shōshi, "but I feel quite overawed now that you are so dignified. You've grown up amazingly since we first met. I'm sure you'll scold me for the slightest frivolity." The ladies in attendance, whispering among themselves, laughed heartily at his complaints.

Soon it was the Fifth of the Fifth Month, and the ladies appeared in

20. See s.n. 65.

21. Fire-huts (*hitakiya*) were used wherever an Emperor, Empress, Crown Prince, Ise Virgin, Retired Emperor, or Imperial Lady was in residence. They were small portable structures where members of the guards or other functionaries kept fires burning on moonless nights. Scattered references indicate that their basic purpose was to provide illumination, but little else is known about them. *Kojitsu sōsho*, 1: 552, 27: 93, 97; Ishimura 1964, p. 536.

22. "Jackets" translates *karaginu*, the outermost garment of a Heian lady's formal Court costume. Except with special authorization, only ladies-in-waiting of the upper class (*jōrō*) were entitled to wear the so-called forbidden colors (*kinjiki*), which in Michinaga's day seems to have been a term referring not only to colors, but also to fabrics and ornamentation—namely to red and green bombycine jackets and to stenciled trains (*jizuri no mo*). (It appears, however, that lower-ranking ladies-in-waiting sometimes received special permission to wear bombycine trains of other colors.) See Hagitani 1971–73, 1: 263–64.

23. The author is referring to the period before Shōshi's elevation, when a less formal atmosphere had prevailed.

24. "Unfigured silk" (*mumon*) may mean unfigured bombycine (*mumon no orimono*), i.e. a solid-colored, patternless twill. Commentators and reference works often equate it with plain silk (*hiraginu*), but the listing of mumon and hiraginu together in *Eiga* makes the interpretation difficult to accept, unless it is assumed that the distinction between the terms had to do with the presence or absence of printed figures, a view for which there appears to be no supporting evidence.

sweet-flag and China-tree jackets and mantles, elegantly appropriate to the season.[25] Three thicknesses of gossamer drapery,[26] dyed in shades of green, were hung on all the curtain-stands, and the eaves overhead were bursting with sweet flags above green-edged blinds. All the arrangements had been handled with exceptional taste and charm; even the presentations of the sweet-flag litters and medicinal balls were quite out of the ordinary.[27] The young ladies-in-waiting watched the proceedings with lively interest.

Meanwhile, the Emperor secretly longed to see Genshi, the Shōkyōden Consort. But he felt that he ought not to send a public figure to summon her, so for lack of anyone better he asked his old favorite, Ukon no Naishi, to deliver a letter in private. News of the affair somehow leaked out, and Ukon was afraid to show her face at the Palace, even though Michinaga said nothing. Michinaga passed it off as a joke. "How odd that Ukon doesn't come to the Palace. Maybe she doesn't like seeing me," he said. Others thought that he must consider Ukon's behavior exceedingly rude.

Obsessed by gloomy thoughts, Empress Teishi often tearfully begged her younger sister, the Mistress of the Wardrobe, to do her best as Prince Atsuyasu's guardian. Her sister also wept, pleading with her not to say such unlucky things. So the days and months passed. The Emperor, much concerned on Teishi's behalf, sent her many solicitous letters. The little Prince and Princess were the most delightful children imaginable.

Presently, it was time to think about the wrestling matches of the Seventh

25. "Sweet flag" (s[h]ōbu) and "China tree" (ōchi) were color combinations considered appropriate for summer wear. Opinions vary on the colors involved, but the consensus seems to be that sweet-flag robes were green (ao) with red (kōbai) linings, and China-tree robes pale purple (usumurasaki) with green linings. The modern term for the China tree (Melia azedarach var. japonica), a relative of the mahogany, is sendan. It produces pale purple flowers in summer.

26. See s.n. 66.

27. Two days before the Sweet-Flag Festival, it was customary for each of the six Guards Headquarters to present the Court with a sweet-flag "litter" (ayame no koshi or s[h]ōbu no koshi). The litters, which resembled small houses on stilts, contained sweet flags and aromatic yomogi (mugwort, similar to sagebrush) to be used for stuffing eaves and preparing medicinal balls. For a picture, see EMZ, 1: 204. Medicinal balls (kusudama), intended to prolong life and ward off disease, were presented to the Emperor by Court officials, to members of the Imperial Family and important subjects by the Emperor, and to one another by prominent members of society. Medicinal balls also figured in the Tango observances of the common people. Their exact nature appears to have varied over the years, but around 1000 they probably consisted of small balls of musk, aloeswood, and the like, contained in a brocade or net bag decorated with sweet flag, mugwort, long multicolored streamers, and, perhaps, nosegays of artificial flowers. In early Heian, they were worn on the Fifth of the Fifth Month as personal charms, a legacy from Chinese custom, but by Michinaga's day they seem ordinarily to have been attached to pillars in Palace buildings and private residences, where they remained until they were replaced by bags of rue berries (shuyu: Evodia rutaecarpa) on the Ninth of the Ninth Month.

Month. Needless to say, the heat was frightful. Since the Emperor had decreed that the Crown Prince was to attend that year, numerous special preparations were doubtless made. On the Seventh, Teishi sent a poem to Senshi:[28]

Kure o matsu	How goes it, I wonder,
Kumoi no hodo mo	In the heavens
Obotsukana	Awaiting nightfall?
Fumimimahoshiki	Would that I might tread
Kasasagi no hashi.	The Magpie Bridge![29]

The Imperial Lady replied:

Kasasagi no	Here "in the heavens,"
Hashi no taema wa	With no Magpie Bridge
Kumoi nite	To bring us together,
Yukiai no sora wa	I envy the skies
Nao zo urayamu.	Where they meet.

Wrestlers from the provinces arrived on about the Seventh Day, and thenceforth the Major Captains of the Left and Right[30] enjoyed few leisure moments. Since the Crown Prince was to be a spectator that year, everyone was determined that no detail should be neglected, and there was an amusing bustle of preparation.

Empress Teishi's melancholy deepened with each passing month.

28. The Seventh of the Seventh Month was the date of the Kikōden, or Tanabata Festival, a Court ceremony with mixed Chinese and Japanese origins, which celebrated the annual reunion, by means of a bridge of magpie wings spanning the Milky Way, of the Herdsman (the star Altair) and his wife, the Weaver Maid (Vega). Offerings of calligraphy, poetry, fruit, etc. were presented in the eastern courtyard of the Seiryōden, together with prayers for skill in the feminine accomplishments represented by the Weaver Maid, and for proficiency in the use of the brush. On the connection between the Tanabata Festival and the literary arts, see Ikeda 1967, p. 441.

29. *Kasasagi no hashi* (Magpie Bridge) is a metaphor for the stairway to the Imperial Palace; *kumoi* ("site of the clouds"; "the heavens"), for the Palace itself. There is a pun on *fumimimahoshi* ("would that I might tread") and *fumi mimahoshi* ("would that I might see [receive] a letter [from you]"). The surface meaning of the poem is, "Since I am worried about the possibility that something may happen to prevent the long-awaited meeting of the two stars tonight, I would like to be able to go to the Magpie Bridge and make certain that everything is all right." The concealed meaning is, "I am wondering how you are getting along at the Imperial Palace, where at present everyone is awaiting the Tanabata Festival. Since I cannot visit you, much as I would like to come to the Palace, will you not send me a note?"

30. Kinsue and Michitsuna.

7

TORIBENO

WITH the approach of the Eighth Month, Empress Teishi felt
more miserable and forlorn than ever, and she wept away
the days in a pitiful state of depression. Haunted by the sound
of the wind whistling over the reeds and by thoughts of dew under bush
clover, she gazed vacantly into space, her mind filled with nostalgic recollections.[1] She received heartening letters from the Imperial Lady Senshi,
as well as various articles dispatched from the Palace Storehouse Bureau
by order of Emperor Ichijō, to whom her pregnancy was a source of deep
concern. It was impossible to arrange the matter of ritual seclusion as she
wished. The proper sutra-readings were commissioned, although at two
altars only, but the monks were anxious not to appear remiss in more exalted quarters, and the only ones who came were unreliable substitutes
who kept falling asleep in the middle of their perfunctory chants.

"If the baby had arrived while I was still somebody who mattered, it
would have been a great event," the Empress thought. "Why did this have
to happen? Now I must count myself lucky merely to hear constant repeti-
tions of Amitābha's name." But the monks who answered the summons
to intone the sacred name were no more satisfactory than the others. They
rushed through the recitations as though eager to be off, and she finally
resolved to avoid the karma burden of anger by leaving everything to her
Household officials.

The visits of Korechika and Takaie were her sole consolation, but even
at such times she did nothing but weep. That in itself, she realized, was

1. Her melancholy deepened with the coming of autumn, regarded by the Heian Japanese as the saddest season of the year. There is an allusion to a poem by Fujiwara Yoshitaka:
Aki wa nao / yūmagure koso / tada narane / ogi no uwakaze / hagi no shitatsuyu. ("When
autumn comes, it is after all the evenings that move us—wind over reeds and dew under
bush clover.") *Fujiwara Yoshitaka shū*, p. 423.

an ominous portent, and she brooded incessantly about the futures of Princess Shūshi and Prince Atsuyasu. Bishop Ryūen turned up every night to stand duty. Without her brothers, she thought often, her plight would have been desperate indeed.

The Sen'yōden Consort Seishi had borne the Crown Prince a number of sons.[2] Her relations with him were intimate, and Michitaka's second daughter, the Shigeisha Consort, found it difficult to see much of him.

The Gosechi dancing and the Kamo Special Festival, coming one after the other, created a gay stir at the Imperial Palace. Young nobles who remembered earlier days came to talk to Teishi's attendants about the dancers, and Sei Shōnagon joined them as they gossiped, putting the inexperienced younger ladies in the shade with her wit and self-assurance.[3] The gentlemen found such company irresistible, and they were always to be found about the premises in groups of two or three.

Teishi's child was due that month. The Empress was suffering great discomfort, and the Reverend Seishō, who was in constant attendance at the house, presided over the offering of petitions, the acceptance of commandments,[4] and many other sad and moving scenes. Teishi had asked Korechika to provide the white furnishings, for although there was talk of supplies to come from the Imperial Palace, she felt that her Household should make its own preparations. Her ladies-in-waiting were also to have new robes, which involved much scurrying back and forth, but she herself had nothing to occupy and distract her, and her melancholy found expression in the themes of the casual scribblings with which she sought to while away the hours.

Korechika was still practicing abstinence, monkish as ever in his style of living and conduct. He now prayed solely for the Empress's safe delivery. Takaie put himself entirely at his sister's disposition, never leaving her residence even for a trip home. The remarkable charm of the young Prince and Princess was a source of great comfort to the brothers. Their own futures, they recognized, were uncertain in the extreme, but they hoped with all their hearts that at the least the Empress would somehow manage to survive.[5] Quite naturally, they looked after the two children with great solicitude.

2. See s.n. 58.
3. Sei Shōnagon was about thirty-five at the time. For her description of a Gosechi performance at which Teishi sponsored a dancer, see *Mak.*, pp. 139ff; Morris 1967, 1: 94ff.
4. *Jukai*, a ceremony in which a monk, nun, or layman swore to obey a set of Buddhist commandments.
5. To see her son on the throne.

The Twelfth Month began. Each day, the suffering Empress felt that the birth was at hand, and her fears increased when she realized that her brothers, aware of the great need for caution in that particular year, were facing the coming event with dismal foreboding. Impressive purification rituals and sutra-recitations went on without intermission; wonder-working monks bawled out their prayers; and the ravings of mediums, to whom an assortment of malevolent spirits had been transferred, added to the commotion. It was by then the night of the Fifteenth of the Twelfth Month in the second year of Chōhō [January 12, 1001]. Emperor Ichijō besieged the house with messengers begging for news.

Presently, the child was born.[6] Those in attendance were disappointed to learn that it was a girl—but after all, they reflected, the important thing was that the Empress had survived the ordeal. It was now a matter of the afterbirth. They prostrated themselves in prayer and sent payments for sutra-recitations to all the temples. Then it was discovered that the Empress was not drinking the hot water that had been brought, and at once there was great alarm and confusion. The afterbirth also seemed to be taking an inordinate amount of time.

"I don't like it," said Korechika. "Bring a light." He peered at the Empress's face, saw that it showed no sign of life, and touched her skin in alarm. The body was already cold.

In the uproar that followed, the monks milled around, still chanting doggedly, and everyone inside and outside the house prayed with frantic energy, but to no avail. Korechika held his sister in his arms and wailed.

Natural though his grief was, it was impossible to give way to it. He carried the child away and arranged the Empress's body in a reclining position. "Her low spirits worried me, but I never thought it would come to this. A long life brings nothing but sorrow," he said. Both he and Takaie repeated over and over through their tears, "If only we might go with her."

The removal of Princess Shūshi and Prince Atsuyasu to different apartments was another inauspicious and disheartening event. Everyone in the house had wept over the exile of the brothers until it had seemed that no tears could remain, but tears are one thing with which mankind is bountifully supplied.

The Emperor was informed. "How pitifully depressed she must have been. She seemed to have lost the will to live," he mused. His thoughts dwelt anxiously on the children, who were still very young.

Senshi was also shocked and grieved, but there was little she could do.

6. Princess Bishi (1001–8).

She had intended all along to take charge of the new baby, regardless of its sex, and she now sent one of her ladies, Chūjō no Myōbu, to act as its nurse.[7] Chūjō had planned to go home for a visit before assuming her duties, but Senshi gave her a present of some cloth for a dress and packed her off. "I was going to let you wait until after the New Year, but your first thought must be for the child," she told her.

When Chūjō reached the house where the Empress had been staying, Korechika received her with a tearful account of recent events. She carried little Princess Bishi off with her when she left. The baby's innocent expression moved her to tears, but she struggled to conceal them, fearing that they might invite misfortune. From then on Chūjō took care of everything, which was also most affecting.

The Emperor went nowhere, not even to visit Shōshi. He invited Shōshi to come to the Seiryōden, but she kept to her own apartments.

The Empress had scribbled things on a number of scraps of paper, which she had tied to her curtain streamers.[8] Korechika and the sisters took them down and read them. One said, "I feel that I shall die this time. Afterward, please do thus and so." Some of the notes were deeply affecting (they were intended, perhaps, for the Emperor). There was this poem:

Yomosugara	If he has not forgotten
Chigirishi koto o	The vows that were made
Wasurezuba	All through the night,
Koin namida no	I should like to see the color
Iro zo yukashiki.	Of the yearning tears he sheds.[9]

And this:

Shiru hito mo	It is time—
Naki wakareji ni	Bowed with grief,
Ima wa tote	I must set out in haste
Kokorobosoku mo	Toward that other world
Isogitatsu kana.	Where all are strangers.

And this:

Keburi to mo	Though my body
Kumo to mo naranu	Be not transformed
Minari to mo	Into smoke or clouds,
Kusaba no tsuyu o	Think of me as you gaze
Sore to nagameyo.	At dew on the grass.

7. Chūjō has not been identified. A woman of the same name appears in Chapter 8.
8. I.e. to the streamers on the backs of the curtain-stands inside the chōdai ("curtain-dais").
9. A reference to the contemporary belief that the deepest grief showed itself in tears of blood.

There were many such pitiful jottings. Concluding from the last poem that Teishi had not wished to be cremated, Korechika set about making the preparations for her burial. As a shelter for the body, he built a resting place surrounded by an earthen wall at a spot two hundred yards south of Toribeno Plain.[10] The rituals were to be exceptionally impressive, as was fitting for one of Teishi's exalted status.

It was heart-rending to watch the Imperial children, who understood nothing of what was going on.

Teishi had turned twenty-five that year.[11]

On the appointed night,[12] they put the Empress into a string-decorated carriage with fittings of gold. Korechika and other senior nobles formed an escort. A heavy snow was falling that evening, and the shelter where Teishi was to rest was completely buried. They dug it out, arranged the interior furnishings, unyoked the ox, and took the coffin inside. When it was time to go back, Teishi's brothers and her uncles Akinobu and Michi-nobu burst into tears. Observing that the building had already vanished beneath fresh snow, Korechika recited:

> Tare mo mina   Though no man's flesh
> Kienokorubeki   But melts one day,
> Mi naranedo   How grievous is the loss
> Yuki kakurenuru   Of this sister,
> Kimi zo kanashiki.   Vanished beneath the snow.

Takaie's poem:

> Shirayuki no   With no track
> Furitsumu nobe wa   On the plain
> Ato taete   Deep in fallen snow,
> Izuku o haka to   What will guide us
> Kimi o tazunemu.   To your grave?

Bishop Ryūen:

> Furusato ni   I wish only
> Yuki mo kaerade   Never to go home—
> Kimi tomo ni   Let me die
> Onaji nobe nite   Here on this plain
> Yagate kienan.   Beside my sister.

10. A strip of land between the Higashiyama hills and the Kamo River (southwestern Higashiyama-ku, Kyōto). It had been designated as a public cemetery and cremation site early in the Heian period.

11. Or possibly twenty-four (sai). The date of her birth is uncertain. EM, 1: 218, n. 5; *Dainihonshi*, 4: 104.

12. 27 xii Chōhō 2 (Jan. 24, 1001).

They were most pathetic. The events of that night were profoundly moving; I wish they had been captured in a painting for others to see.

"Tonight is the night," the Emperor thought. He mourned until dawn, his sleeves drenched with icy tears. Had it been the usual cremation, he might have hoped for a glimpse of smoke hanging over the plain, but now even that consolation would be denied him. A poem came to his mind:

Nobe made ni	My heart
Kokoro bakari wa	Has journeyed alone
Kayoedomo	To that plain,
Waga miyuki tomo	But you, perhaps, are unaware
Shirazu ya aruran.	Of its coming.

So he passed the night.

At daybreak, the members of the funeral party returned to Teishi's residence, where her people received them in a manner that was only to have been expected. During the journey, they had looked back constantly toward the shelter, their vision obscured by a curtain of falling snow, and all were in wretched spirits.

Sunk in grief, the mourners scarcely noticed the arrival of spring. As they grew conscious of the incessant clatter of horses and carriages outside, and listened with envy to the carefree shouts of attendants clearing the way for their masters, they found it hard to believe they all existed in the same world.[13]

Once the period of seclusion had ended, Senshi proceeded to the Sanjō Palace,[14] where she hoped to welcome the infant Princess Bishi in a day or two. The Emperor had thought to bring the other two children to the Imperial Palace after the final Buddhist services, but he could not help feeling sorry for Korechika and the others, who would then have had little opportunity to see them.

Choosing an auspicious day, Senshi sent for Princess Bishi. Korechika and Takaie would have liked to serve as escorts, but they were still in mourning, and so judged it best to be cautious.[15] Fujiwara Naishi no Suke went to fetch the baby, accompanied by a number of noble ladies and a

13. Since the Court was in mourning for Teishi, there were no official New Year festivities. The commotion might have been created by gentlemen paying seasonal calls on Senshi and Michinaga. EM, 1: 507, s.n. 316.

14. I.e. the Higashisanjō Mansion. She moved there from the Ichijō Palace on the Tenth of the Second Month. EM, 1: 507, s.n. 317.

15. Because the presence of people in mourning costumes might have been unlucky at this crucial juncture in the young Princess's life. EM, 1: 219, n. 30.

large contingent of Senshi's courtiers. That event, too, was infinitely distressing to the Empress's people.

Senshi was waiting when the party returned with the baby. The little Princess, though not much more than thirty days old,[16] was already sweet and plump, and Senshi's heart melted when she took her in her arms. It would be commonplace indeed to call the Princess's tragic and unexpected situation sad or shocking.

Korechika wept ceaselessly as he went about the business of arranging for religious services at the house. If Prince Atsuyasu and Princess Shūshi were to move to the Palace, he thought, he would lose his sole consolation.

It was rumored that one of Prince Tamehira's sons, the Minamoto Middle Captain Yorisada, was paying secret visits to Kaneie's daughter Suishi, the Reikeiden Principal Handmaid, who had all but ceased to appear at the Crown Prince's palace. The Crown Prince considered his relationship with Suishi ended, but he nevertheless felt a pang of sorrow when, presently, he learned that she had died.[17] Her mother, the Lady in the Wing Chamber, recited a poem as she gazed at a cherry tree in bloom:

Onaji goto	You are cruel,
Niou zo tsuraki	Cherry blossoms,
Sakurabana	To bloom in the same old way.
Kotoshi no haru wa	Will you not change your color
Iro kaware kashi.	For this year's spring?

Meanwhile, to the concern of all, Michinaga had come down with a serious illness at Sukekata's house, where he had been staying.[18] It goes without saying that the malignant spirit manifested terrifying strength. The patient was delirious, and every possible remedy was invoked. Empress Shōshi decided to withdraw from the Palace, thereby adding to the commotion, and Senshi was distraught with worry. But perhaps the innumerable vows were of some assistance, or possibly a god or buddha intervened, for the Yin-yang Masters announced that a change of residence would effect a cure. Divination indicated that the Tsuchimikado Mansion,

16. The baby's age would have been closer to fifty-five days. Other sources do not state that she was taken to Senshi's house.

17. Other sources state that Suishi died in 1004, not in 1001, as the author implies. EM, I: 220, n. 11.

18. Michinaga is known to have been ill in 998 and again in the summer of 1000, but not in 1001. Sukekata, a tenjōbito, was one of the sons of Rinshi's uncle Minamoto Shigenobu. EMZ, 2: 250, 252.

the house where the Principal Handmaid had lived,[19] was situated in an auspicious direction, and the move took place. The summer heat was almost unbearable, even for people in perfect health, and to Michinaga's attendants it seemed all too likely that he would succumb, but though the disease dragged on for an interminable period, he finally managed to throw it off. Everyone was astonished and delighted by such a splendid bit of luck.

Rinshi's younger sister, Naka no Kimi, the wife of Major Captain Michitsuna, had been pregnant since the preceding year. As the time for her confinement approached, the Yin-yang Masters advised her to move away from the Ichijō Mansion,[20] which they pronounced inauspicious. She went to a villa owned by a certain Holy Teacher at Nakagawa, a location said to be favorable, and there the baby was born. To everyone's delight, it was a boy,[21] but the afterbirth failed to appear, and Naka no Kimi died. Her aged mother was inconsolable. Michinaga was also greatly distressed. As a child of the same mother as his wife, and as her only younger sister, Naka no Kimi had been almost like a daughter to Rinshi, who was not on close terms with any of her numerous brothers. He and Rinshi had taken care of all the arrangements for Naka no Kimi's marriage to Michitsuna—and now, he thought sadly, it had come to this. For Michitsuna, the marriage had been a happy one, as well as a great social asset, and, quite naturally, his sense of bereavement was far more acute than if it had been an ordinary alliance. Holding the baby close, he would tell himself that at least this son was left to remind him of Naka no Kimi, but then his mind would turn to his wife's karma burden,[22] and he would fall prey to painful indecision. "How terrible my own karma must be. If only I might renounce the world and spend my days intoning the name of Amitābha Buddha. Still, there is the child to consider . . ."

The necessary things were done. As the period of ritual seclusion wore on, Michitsuna found a certain solace in caring for the pitiful child's needs.

19. Tentatively identified as a house formerly owned by Kaneie, east of Nishinotōin and north of Tsuchimikado. EMZ, 2: 251.

20. A former residence of her late father, Minamoto Masanobu, located south of Ichijō and east of Takakura.

21. Kanetsune (d. 1043). He may have been born the year before, in 1000. Two of Michitsuna's five sons, Dōmyō (d. 1020) and Saigi, became monks, and two others, Kanemune and Kanetsuna, died as tenjōbito. Only Kanetsune, because of his maternal connections, was able to become a kugyō (Consultant, Senior Third Rank). *Kugyō bunin*, 1: 294; *Sonpi bunmyaku*, 1: 337.

22. A woman who died in childbirth could expect the same fate as one who died during pregnancy. See Chapter 2, n. 77.

There were many eager aspirants for the office of wet nurse, but he soon turned everything over to Ben,[23] a lady of good birth whom his wife had admired and befriended, and who thus felt greatly in their debt. Naka no Kimi had promised Ben the post if the baby arrived safely, so it would have been difficult to select anyone else. Rinshi gave the choice her whole-hearted approval.

During the spring, preparations had begun for an official celebration to honor Senshi's fortieth year. The event had been planned for the spring, but Michinaga's illness had necessitated a postponement until the Seventh Month.[24] Senshi herself was occupied with arrangements for an Eight Ex-positions Service,[25] which she intended to make a great occasion. In the Seventh Month, everyone was concerned about the troubled times,[26] and the ceremonies were again postponed. Then fresh complications were created by Senshi's regular pilgrimage to Ishiyama, which always took place in the Ninth Month, and it seemed impossible to decide whether the anniversary festivities should precede or follow the journey.

Little Princess Bishi grew more appealing every day. Now at the crawl-ing stage, she frequently interrupted Senshi's Buddhist recitations. Senshi would stop and take care of her, scolding her for being a nuisance. Actual-ly, she was infatuated with the child. She took her to the Imperial Palace, and Emperor Ichijō was also captivated. He strolled about, holding the

---

23. Unidentified. EMZ, 2: 257.

24. The real reason for the postponement was the outbreak of an unidentified disease, which made it impossible to command the manpower needed for the preparations. As noted above, Michinaga is not known to have been ill in 1001. EMZ, 2: 259.

25. A celebration of the *Lotus Sutra*. Such services, called *hakkō[e]*, had been performed at Japanese temples since the end of the eighth century, in the mansions of the aristocracy since Tadahira's day, and at Court since the reign of Murakami. They flourished during the mid-Heian period under the sponsorship of Senshi, Michinaga, and Michinaga's sons and daughters, all of whom were devout believers in the magical powers of the *Lotus*. Typically, the services were held in fulfillment of a vow (often designed to help a deceased relative), the text of which (*ganmon*, "supplication"), composed in Chinese by a leading scholar, was ceremoniously presented as part of the ritual. As the name suggests, there were eight sessions, held twice daily over a four-day period, during which each of the eight books (*maki*) of the sutra was expounded and praised in turn. This process involved the participation of as many as sixty eminent monks from the great Nara and Heian temples: Questioners (Monja), who posed doctrinal problems; Lecturers (Kōji), who answered them; Judges (Shōgisha), who decided disputed points; Auditors (Chōju), who constituted the official audience; Clear-tone Singers (Bonnon), who intoned hymns in praise of the Buddha; and Tin-staff Chanters (Shakujō[shū]), who punctuated their chants at the end of each verse by shaking magical staffs to which metal rings were attached. See Chapter 22, n. 12. Music, bells, incense, sacred images, offerings of precious objects, vestments, and texts, and banquets for the attendant nobles added to the pomp and pageantry of these affairs, which were among the most im-pressive of Heian Buddhist events.

26. The epidemic.

Princess in his arms, and she grew accustomed to him at once, winning his heart by bursting into tears when he tried to leave.

"With such a child to care for, I shall never be able to sever my ties with the world," said the Imperial Lady.

Tears rose to the Emperor's eyes as he replied. "That's not such a bad thing, is it? She'll keep you from being bored." Senshi found his concern most affecting.

After returning from the Palace, Senshi made ready for her pilgrimage to Ishiyama in the Ninth Month,[27] while her bevies of ladies-in-waiting rushed about on errands of their own. The Imperial Lady was possessed by a strange melancholy as she supervised the preparation of image curtains,[28] clerical robes, and miscellaneous presents for the Ishiyama monks. To her attendants, watching with growing concern, her demeanor seemed exceedingly inauspicious.

Setting out from the capital, the party heard the plaintive cries of deer at Awataguchi and in the mountains near the barrier.[29] Overcome by a feeling of sadness, Senshi recited:

Amatatabi	Alas! Shall I never again
Yuki Ōsaka no	Behold my reflection
Sekimizu ni	In Ōsaka's barrier stream,
Ima wa kagiri no	To which I have come
Kage zo kanashiki.	These many times?

Lady Senji,[30] who was with her in the carriage, responded:

Toshi o hete	May the Barrier of Ōsaka,
Yuki Ōsaka no	So often passed,
Shirushi arite	Prove true to its name
Chitose no kage o	And detain our lady's image
Seki mo tomenan.	For a thousand years.

When Senshi arrived at her destination, the sight of the sacred hall brought on a new access of grief. "This is my last visit to the dear image I have revered for so many years," she thought in deep distress. Instead of

27. The pilgrimage began on the Twenty-seventh of the Tenth Month. EMZ, 2: 263.
28. *Michō no katabira*, which here means *tochō*, curtains hung on a chōdai or shrine containing a sacred image. *Shōkai*, 3: 193.
29. Both Awataguchi (an area extending eastward from the Sanjō Shirakawa Bridge to the base of the Higashiyama hills) and the Ōsaka Barrier were on the main route from the capital to Ōtsu.
30. Probably Senshi's half-sister, mentioned at the beginning of Chapter 3.

Senshi at Awataguchi on her way to Ishiyama. Curtains spill out on either side of the bamboo blinds at the front of the carriage; the shutters on the side windows are raised.

offering the usual prayers and services, she ordered a fire ritual,[31] in the hope of cleansing herself of defilement and ensuring an auspicious future karma. The temple monks were astonished and dismayed when they realized that all her petitions were concentrated on the last sad journey.[32] "We can't help wondering what is going through Her Ladyship's mind," they said nervously.

"Why do you find it odd?" asked Senshi. "This is my last pilgrimage, my final act of devotion to the deity I have chosen to worship until the end of my life." She presented damask curtains and silver bowls as offerings, gave vestments to the abbot and all the others, held a feast for the monks, added to the temple's lands, commissioned sutra-recitations of every description, and arranged for a myriad-light service.[33] When she was ready to leave, she burst into tears. Those who were with her were deeply saddened as they watched, and the monks prayed that she might continue to live for many years to come.

Senshi began the Eight Expositions shortly after her return.[34] In every detail, as may be imagined, the services far surpassed any of the similar rituals she had sponsored in other years. The Lecturers were an impressive sight as they spoke of the present world and the life to come.

It would be foolish to attempt descriptions of the ceremonies that now preoccupied the Imperial Lady. Their solemnity and grandeur were almost frightening. Michinaga understood the thoughts passing through her mind, and he saw to it that prayers were recited on her behalf at all the temples.

In the Tenth Month came Senshi's longevity celebration, held in the Imperial presence at the Tsuchimikado Mansion. It was an occasion of the utmost magnificence. Folding-screen verses were composed by some of the best poets, but I shall not record them all, since most followed the same general pattern. Controller Suketada wrote these lines next to a picture showing a lady and gentleman chatting beside a door on the night of the Fifteenth of the Eighth Month:

31. Goma (Skt. homa), an esoteric rite derived from the Hindu worship of Agni, the fire god. An altar was erected in front of an image of Fudō or a similar deity, magical formulas were recited, and offerings were thrown into a fire of sumac or some other wood. The fire, symbolic of wisdom, was believed to consume the petitioner's passions and illusions.

32. Into the next life.

33. Mandōe, an offering of 10,000 lights to a buddha or bodhisattva (here presumably to Kannon) as a prayer for the eradication of guilt and defilement.

34. The services were actually held by Michinaga as an adjunct to Senshi's longevity celebration, which occurred before the pilgrimage. The sequence of events was as follows: the hakkōe on the Fourteenth of the Ninth Month, 1001; the longevity celebration on the Ninth of the Tenth Month; and the Ishiyama pilgrimage on the Twenty-seventh of the Tenth Month.

Ama no hara	The dwelling is not, it seems,
Yado shi chikaku wa	Close to the sky,
Mienedomo	Yet the bright moon
Sumikayowaseru	Joins the caller there
Aki no yo no tsuki.	On an autumn night.[35]

To complement a picture of a kagura performance, Kanezumi wrote:

Kamiyama ni	Beneath the *sakaki* leaves
Toru sakakiba no	Plucked on the sacred mountain,
Motosue ni	They assemble in *moto* and *sue*
Murete inoru	To pray that our lady
Kimi ga yorozuyo.	May live forever.[36]

The dancers were young men from the family. As the festivities drew to a close, Michinaga's two little boys presented dances of their own— Meishi's son Iwagimi "Nassori," and Rinshi's son Tazugimi "Ryōō."[37]

The grounds of the mansion were spacious and elegant. The hills in the garden blazed with autumn foliage, and the leaves of the ivy vines on the islands shone with the brilliance of brocade,[38] trailing from the pines in

35. Suketada is probably to be identified with the poet and literatus of that name who was an adoptive son of Major Counselor Fujiwara Kanetada. The point of his poem is in the pun on *sumi*, a form of *sumu*, which can mean either "live" or "be clear," "be bright." The man is spending his nights at the house; the moon, as though to bless the match, comes to flood the scene with light. EMZ, 2: 269.

36. The authorship of the poem is uncertain. *Gonki*, 1: 228 (8 x Chōhō 3), ascribes it to Fujiwara Kanetaka, the second son of Michikane, with whom the poet Minamoto Kanezumi is often confused. See EMZ, 2: 270. In modern usage, the term sakaki ordinarily means the *Cleyera japonica*, a small tree related to the camellia, which is always to be found in the precincts of Shintō shrines. In earlier times, it seems to have been used for any one of an indeterminate number of evergreens associated with the worship of the indigenous gods, including fragrant varieties such as the star anise, or *shikimi* (*Illicium anisatum*). On moto and sue, see s.n. 51.

37. "Na[s]sori" and "[Ran]ryōō" belonged to the category of Court music (*gagaku*) known as *bugaku* ("dance music," essentially a Heian modification of instrumental dance music imported earlier from China and Korea). Bugaku compositions were divided into two categories: Left (*sahō*), mostly of Chinese origin, and Right (*uhō*), mostly of Korean origin, with the Left, as usual, considered superior. The dances were performed by two, four, or six persons, or, less often, by eight or by one, as here. "Ranryōō" featured an elaborately costumed dancer who held a golden baton and wore a fierce gold mask surmounted by a dragon. According to one tradition, the dance celebrated the bravery of a sixth-century Chinese king, Kao Ch'ang-kung, who hid his mild features behind an imposing mask and led 500 men to victory against a hostile army. As a Left piece, it was presumably considered suitable for Tazugimi, the son of Michinaga's principal wife. "Nasori," usually performed as a sequel to "Ranryōō," was a Right piece in which the dancer bounded energetically about the stage, wearing a blue mask and flourishing a six-inch stick. Although Tazugimi got the more desirable assignment, *Ōkagami*, pp. 272–73, reports that Iwagimi made so much better an impression that Senshi gave his teacher a promotion in rank. For a picture of the "Ranryōō" mask, see Kishibe 1969, photograph 22 (unpaginated).

38. "Brocade" translates *nishiki*, a term broadly used to designate any silk woven in patterned colors. See s.n. 67.

varying hues of crimson, dark red, green, and yellow. The same autumnal colors shimmered on the sparkling waters of the lake, and from the midst of the brocade the boats emerged, their music resounding with a chill beauty. Everything was quite, quite perfect; I can write no more, for words fail me.

Empress Shōshi occupied the west wing, the Imperial Lady the main hall, and Emperor Ichijō the south side of the eastern eavechamber. Rinshi was in the east wing, with the senior nobles in the galleries. The various officials of Fourth and Fifth Rank and the ordinary courtiers sat inside tents. Senshi's ladies were in the southwest gallery of the main hall, their gorgeous sleeves and skirts billowing out from behind the blinds.

The Emperor took his leave at the conclusion of the ceremonies. Not a soul was overlooked in the distribution of gifts and rewards to the senior nobles and courtiers. Since the time was the Tenth Month, the evening shadows gathered swiftly, and the affair soon drew to a close. Senshi returned to the Sanjō Palace on the following day. I know nothing about longevity celebrations in earlier times, but that one was splendid indeed! People could not help thinking it even better than the festivities in honor of Kaneie's sixtieth year, which had been observed while Senshi was still Grand Empress. The childish grace of Michinaga's young sons had drawn tears from every eye.

That month, Senshi went to stay at the Imperial Palace in preparation for the Eleventh Month, which promised to be exceptionally busy with the Gosechi dances and other religious events.[39] The delighted Emperor hastened to call on her. Little Princess Bishi was enchanting. Her father could not resist the temptation to play with her, and she responded to his attentions with bewitching coquetry. In the course of the conversation, Senshi said, "I have been feeling unaccountably depressed and nervous about the future. I wouldn't mind dying except that it gives me such pleasure to see you as you are now." She began to weep, and the Emperor was also moved to tears. "If anything were to happen to you, I couldn't go on living," he replied. "Though I knew ex-Emperor En'yū, I was only a young child, and so I survived the grief of his death. But to lose you would be unendurable." At that, Senshi dismissed the subject, handing him the child to play with. "I don't expect anything to happen at the moment," she said. "It's just that for some reason I have been less happy than usual."

39. The "other religious events" of the Eleventh Month were a series of ceremonies honoring the Sono and Kara gods and the deities of such important shrines as Hirano, Kamo, Kasuga, Matsunoo, Ōharano, Umenomiya, Yamashina, and Yoshida.

Senshi's longevity celebration at the Tsuchimikado Mansion. "As the festivities drew to a close, Michinaga's two little boys presented dances of their own. . . . The hills in the garden blazed with autumn foliage, and the leaves of the ivy vines on the islands shone with the brilliance of brocade, trailing from the pines in varying hues of crimson, dark red, green, and yellow. The same autumnal colors shimmered on

the sparkling waters of the lake, and from the midst of the brocade the boats emerged,
their music resounding with a chill beauty." Court musicians wearing "bird helmets"
ride in dragon-head and geki-head boats. Senshi is presumably seated behind the
blinds at the head of the stairs on the left.

In miserable spirits, the Emperor went off to visit Shōshi, whose beauty always made him forget his troubles as soon as he entered her apartments. He began to chat with tolerable calmness, but soon he remarked in a disconsolate voice, 'When I called on the Imperial Lady, her conversation was very gloomy. I'm worried about her." Although Shōshi preserved her modest and respectful demeanor, she must have been shocked and agitated by this news of the person to whose special care her father had long ago entrusted her. After talking about all manner of sad and amusing things, the Emperor took his leave. "Come early this evening," he said. "Tomorrow and the next day are ritual seclusion days; I won't be able to visit you." The sight of the two in such intimate conversation was enough to bring a smile of pleasure to any face.

On the last day of the month,[40] Senshi decided to withdraw from the Palace. More than usually reluctant to let her go, Emperor Ichijō lingered in her apartments until late at night. "You had better be off now," she finally said. "It's very late. I must go too." Most unwillingly, he went back, and she took her leave.

In the Eleventh Month, there was a flurry of activity in connection with the religious events, and in the Twelfth, everyone was busy with official and private preparations for the coming year. In the midst of it all, Senshi came down with a fever caused by boils. Michinaga was greatly alarmed. She herself supposed that she would soon recover, but the days dragged by, and she grew anxious and depressed. Recalling her talk of not feeling her usual self, the Emperor began to fear for her life. To the concern of his nurses, he lost his appetite and lapsed into a profound melancholy. Young as she was, Empress Shōshi also worried incessantly.

"You must let a doctor examine you; this is a dangerous business," Michinaga kept insisting, but Senshi refused. "If I'm sick enough to need a doctor, I probably won't survive, even if he does manage to save me for the time being," she told him.

Informed of the patient's symptoms, physicians diagnosed a parasitic infection. They prescribed a course of treatment that seemed to arrest the progress of the disease, and presently, to the relief of all, the boils began to drain. But the malignant spirits continued their persecution. Every conceivable religious ritual was performed; every possible avenue of hope was explored separately by the Court, Michinaga, and Senshi's own people. Each day, the Emperor hoped to be able to call on his mother, but time slipped by while an auspicious date was being sought.

40. The correct date is the Second of the Eleventh Month. EM, 1: 277, n. 24.

At length, the possessing spirits were transferred to four or five other people. The monks set up a clamor to drive them off, but then the onlookers learned to their dismay that Senshi had also been suffering from a curse uttered by one of the gods who lived in a corner of the Sanjō Palace.[41] As they say, "On a formidable mountain . . ."[42] There had already been ample cause for concern, but now it was evident that the Imperial Lady must move elsewhere. The choice fell on a house pronounced suitable by the diviners, the property of Middle Counselor Korenaka, the Governor-General of the Dazaifu.[43] The Emperor was to visit her on the day of her departure.

Fretful and demanding, Princess Bishi hung on Senshi and refused to leave her in peace, but the ailing Imperial Lady bore the baby's mauling patiently, unwilling to tell the nurses to carry her off. Moved by the depth of her love, the monks at her side wept as they prayed.

Senshi's protégés, accustomed for many years to living under the protection of the kindest and most considerate of patrons, were quite unable to think of anything except her illness. They all swore great vows to the gods and buddhas and waited on her in tears.

Meanwhile, the end of the month approached. Although the season was the busiest of the year, Senshi's perilous state cast a pall over the Court and the city.

It was under such conditions that Emperor Ichijō made his visit. Once the date had been set, Senshi waited with the utmost impatience for his arrival, which took place during the Hour of the Horse [11:00 A.M.–1:00 P.M.].[44] He hurried to her apartments, begrudging even the time spent in stepping down from the litter, and found little Princess Bishi running back and forth to Senshi's side, even though the Imperial Lady was clearly in pain. To have the child there at all, he thought, imposed far too great a strain. "Pick her up," he commanded the nurse Chūjō, but the protesting Princess insinuated herself into his mother's bosom. Senshi was scarcely recognizable. She gazed at the Emperor in silence as he shed tears of

41. I.e. of the Higashisanjōin. The gods, Hayabusakami and Sumifurikami, were enshrined in the northwest corner of the mansion's grounds as protectors of the premises. They had been granted Junior Fifth Upper Rank in 940 and Junior Fourth Lower in 987, and ultimately rose to Senior First in 1150. EMZ, 2: 284–86.

42. Conjectured to be an allusion to a proverb of the "It never rains but it pours" variety: "On a formidable [steep] mountain, there are also fierce beasts," or the like. EMZ, 2: 284.

43. Senshi appears to have moved not to Korenaka's house, but to a house owned by Fujiwara Yukinari. See EM, 1: 508, s.n. 331.

44. The date of the visit was the Sixteenth of the intercalary Twelfth Month, somewhat earlier than the text implies. Senshi moved on the Seventeenth.

helpless grief, reproaching himself for not having come sooner. Although she was weeping too, her eyes were dry. It was, he had heard, an unlucky omen,[45] and he broke down completely. I cannot describe how different it all was from his visits in other years, or how terribly inauspicious everything seemed. All the ladies-in-waiting were in tears. Michinaga went about with his cloak sleeves wringing wet, trying unsuccessfully to conceal his misery beneath a resolutely calm demeanor. In preparation for Senshi's move, which was to take place that same night, he was seeing to all the furnishings at the other house, and he bustled tearfully in and out of the room. The unhappy crowd of senior nobles, courtiers, and others in the Emperor's retinue talked of nothing but the Imperial Lady's chances of recovery. The Emperor was sobbing like a child.

Presently, the shadows began to gather. "You had better go soon," Michinaga told the Emperor in his most persuasive manner. "Otherwise it will be late at night before she reaches the other house."

"What sinful, callous behavior this position of mine forces on me! How can I leave her in such a state? The lowest fellow in the world would refuse to desert his mother at a time like this. An Emperor has a hard life. Let me at least go with her to the new place," Emperor Ichijō answered.

"I'm afraid it would be improper," said Michinaga. He again urged the Emperor not to tarry. Senshi said nothing, but she took her son's hand, as though distressed by his departure, and raised her weeping face to his. The throngs of attendants inside and outside the room burst into noisy lamentations. "Stop that! It's unlucky. There's no reason to carry on so," scolded the senior nobles, but they were also in tears.

"Where will Princess Bishi go?" the Emperor asked.

"Lord Michinaga said she was to join her brother and sister," replied the nurse Chūjō.

"That will no doubt be best," he said.

Darkness had fallen. The Imperial litter was announced repeatedly, and at length Emperor Ichijō took his leave, dazed with such grief as the reader may imagine. True, he was a ruler of men, but eminence carries with it no exemption from the anguish of filial grief. His misery was all too natural. As he prepared to enter the litter—lost, it seemed, in a world of his own— a stream of tears trickled from beneath the sleeve pressed to his face.

Michinaga had instructed all the nurses and ladies-in-waiting to stay with Senshi while he escorted the Emperor back to the Palace. The min-

45. An omen of death. EMZ, 2: 289.

ister rode absorbed in thought, worrying about what might be happening during his absence. At the end of the journey, the Emperor retired in silence to his bedchamber. It was impossible to think of anything but Senshi's condition; he sent off one messenger after another.

Back at the Higashisanjō Mansion, Michinaga ordered the nurses and a number of suitable attendants to take the young Princess to her sister's residence.

When it was time for Senshi to leave, the ox was unyoked from the carriage;[46] and Michinaga and Prince Tametaka carried her out and lifted her inside, still swathed in her bedclothing. Michinaga rode with her to the other house, where the ox was again unhitched, and they lifted her down. Princes Atsumichi and Tametaka, who had been nursing the patient day and night, also moved to the new location. The Princes were mere nephews, but they had always been second only to Emperor Ichijō in Senshi's affections, and now they waited on her in grateful remembrance of her many kindnesses, shedding floods of tears.

Everyone felt more hopeful after the move, but two or three days later the Imperial Lady breathed her last. It would be impossible to find a comparison for Michinaga's emotions. The Emperor, already numb with grief, reacted to the news by withdrawing into a private world of gloom, too miserable even to sip a cup of hot water. What can one say? Surely it was but natural.

The date of Senshi's death was the Twenty-second of the Twelfth Month in the third year of Chōhō [January 8, 1002]. The weather was frigid, with high snowdrifts everywhere, and so little remained of the year that the calendar rollers were visible.[47] Everything seemed to conspire to deepen the sadness of the mourners.

Three days later, the funeral procession made its way to Toribeno. A heavy snow was falling, but it may be imagined that neither Michinaga nor any other member of the Court was absent from the cortege. Needless to say, all the ceremonies were performed with great solemnity and dignity. With both Michinaga and the Emperor determined that everything possible should be done, it could not have been otherwise. Michinaga supervised the proceedings throughout the night, and at daybreak people began to leave. The snow was frightful. "How different this has been from

46. In order to bring the carriage closer to the building.

47. The Heian calendar, like a horizontal picture scroll (*emakimono*), consisted of pieces of paper pasted together into one long strip attached to a roller.

her past journeys," the mourners thought, the ice forming on their tear-drenched sleeves. Michinaga carried the remains to Kohata at dawn, and returned after sunrise to the mansion.[48]

Soon everyone at Court had made the transition to garments of black. The Emperor dragged through the days, still sunk in gloom, and there was mourning throughout the land.

All too soon, the year ended. Ordinarily, it would have been thought unlucky to weep on the First of the First Month, but such notions no longer had meaning. All the people who had enjoyed Senshi's favor were bewildered and distraught. It was decreed that the customary buddha-invocations and continuous sutra-recitations should be performed for the full forty-nine days. The Emperor copied a sutra in his own hand.

The Seventh of the First Month was the Day of the Rat, but the spring scenery at Funaoka went to waste. Kintō, the Commander of the Left Gate Guards, sent a poem to Senshi's Table Room:[49]

Ta ga tame no	For whom shall we pull up
Matsu o mo hikan	The pine trees
Uguisu no	On this day when the warbler
Hatsune kai naki	Trills in vain
Kyō ni mo aru kana.	Its first song?

No one who read it ventured to compose an answer.

Many touching things happened during the forty-nine days. Then it was time for the Buddhist services, which took place at the Kazan Jitokuji shortly after the Tenth of the Second Month.[50] The reader may imagine their nature. The offerings included the sutra copied by the Emperor, and Bishop Ingen officiated with great distinction as Lecturer.[51]

So ended the melancholy period of ritual seclusion.

The Kamo Festival that year was simplified in many ways. Cancelation was impossible, since the Festival was part of the regular Court calendar, but the authorities decided to dispense with the display of the Imperial Bodyguards, who are ordinarily the center of attention, and everything was done very quietly.

48. The journey to Kohata was made not by Michinaga, but by Michikane's son Kanetaka. EM, 1: 232, n. 15.

49. A room for ladies-in-waiting, modeled after the one in the Seiryōden.

50. The Jitokuji was a temple east of the Gangyōji, founded under Senshi's patronage around 985. Michinaga held numerous memorial services for his sister there. EMZ, 2: 299.

51. The sutra was actually offered several months later. Ingen (954–1028), a prominent Tendai monk who received many marks of favor from Michinaga, rose ultimately to the offices of Archbishop (1023) and Enryakuji abbot (1020). In early 1002, he was only a Master of Discipline, not a Bishop.

Around the Fifth or Sixth Month, the Crown Prince's consort Seishi fell victim to an illness. After a long period of confinement, during which she could not even see to the needs of Prince Atsuakira, she sank so low that the end seemed near, and her husband was in great distress. But then she suddenly recovered.

Meanwhile, Prince Tametaka, the President of the Board of Censors, had fallen into the dangerous habit of roaming about at night to visit women's houses. It made people uneasy, and there was a good deal of disapproving gossip. As it happened, a pestilence was raging that year with such virulence that no one's life was safe. The streets and avenues were clogged with stinking corpses, yet the Prince went blithely ahead night after night without paying the slightest attention. Perhaps that was why he finally fell ill and died.[52] His recent notorious infatuations with Shinchūnagon and Izumi Shikibu had been unpleasant for his wife, but she took his death very hard, and on the Forty-ninth Day she became a nun.[53] Always a devout Buddhist, she had read the *Lotus Sutra* 2,000 or 3,000 times and was well aware of the evanescence of worldly things. She now redoubled her pious exertions.

When ex-Emperor Reizei received word of the Prince's death, he said, "He can't have died. You'll find him somewhere if you keep looking." A parent's grief at the loss of a child is pitiful indeed. Crown Prince Okisada and Prince Atsumichi were both deeply affected.[54] Prince Tametaka had turned twenty-five that year.[55]

Ex-Emperor Kazan, who had been very close to the dead Prince, saw to all the arrangements.

It was of course an unhappy period, but nevertheless everyone was startled when a rumor spread that the Shigeisha Consort Genshi had died. This happened shortly after the Twentieth of the Eighth Month.[56] Many people were skeptical at first. "Really, what a story," they scoffed. "She can't have died as suddenly as all that. Nobody even said she was ill." But others replied, "It's true enough. Blood gushed from her nose and mouth,

---

52. On the Thirteenth of the Sixth Month, 1002. It appears, however, that his death was unconnected with the epidemic. EM, 1: 234, n. 8.

53. The Prince's wife was a daughter of Fujiwara Koretada. Shinchūnagon has not been identified. The poet Izumi Shikibu later became the mistress of Prince Tametaka's brother Atsumichi. She joined the coterie of literary ladies in Empress Shōshi's service after Prince Atsumichi's death in 1007. See Cranston 1969, pp. 3–24.

54. They were Prince Tametaka's brothers.

55. Or, according to other sources, twenty-six (sai).

56. On the Third of the Eighth Month, 1002, according to *Gonki*, 1: 226 (3 viii Chōhō 4). EM, 1: 234, n. 16.

and in an instant she was dead." It would be idle merely to call the event shocking or terrible. Life is uncertain, to be sure, but few go in such a bizarre and distressing manner. Society never tires of gossip, and people began to whisper some very unpleasant things about the relationship between the recovery of the Sen'yōden Consort Seishi, who had been so desperately ill, and the sudden death of Genshi. "Genshi died because Seishi did something dreadful to her," many said. Others argued that Seishi herself would not have thought of such a thing. "It must have been the nurse Shōnagon."[57]

Be that as it may, Genshi had been very young to suffer such a fate. Korechika and Takaie were inconsolable. The Crown Prince had never been in love with her, but he had thought that some day, when it was within his power, he would make her happy with a suitable position, and he mourned her with great sincerity and affection. "I think of her whenever I see certain color combinations or types of sleeves in a lady's costume," he said sadly.

"It was not easy for the Prince to be with her a great deal, but he liked her quite as well as he did Seishi," her brothers lamented again and again.

57. This passage has usually been interpreted to mean that Seishi or Shōnagon (tentatively identified as one of Seishi's old nurses) had either cursed Genshi or poisoned her. EM, 1: 509, s.n. 337; Kawakita 1968, pp. 181–83.

8

FIRST FLOWER

THAT winter, there was a Coming-of-Age ceremony at the Biwa Mansion for Michinaga's son Tazugimi, who had reached the age of twelve.[1] The cap of adulthood was conferred by Kinsue, the Kan'in Palace Minister. The mansion overflowed with guests, and the splendor of the host's presents may be imagined.[2]

So the year ended and a new one began [1003]. Yorimichi, who had become a Lesser Captain at the time of the appointments, was to act as the Imperial Messenger to Kasuga in the Second Month.[3] Since it was the first time that one of Michinaga's sons had been named Kasuga Messenger, the minister naturally took great pains with the preparations, devoting meticulous attention to every detail. Yorimichi was a plump, winning, little fellow, very dear to his father's heart. Those who joined him for the journey to Kasuga included every gentleman of Fourth, Fifth, or Sixth Rank with the slightest pretension to importance. After going to the Palace to watch the departure in the Imperial presence, Michinaga drove out in a carriage to view the procession on the road—a touching demonstration of parental affection.

On the day after the departure, there was a heavy snowfall. Michinaga composed a poem:

Wakana tsumu	The messenger I dispatch today
Kasuga no nobe ni	Is an anxious heart,

1. In fact, the event took place the following spring, on the Twentieth of the Second Month, 1003. In 1002, Yorimichi (992–1074) was still only eleven years old (sai). EM, 1: 239, n. 2.

2. Kinsue, for example, received a lady's costume, two horses, and a falcon. EM, 1: 509, s.n. 339.

3. Yorimichi went to Kasuga in the Second Month of 1004, a year after his promotion to the office of Lesser Captain, which took place on the Twenty-eighth of the Second Month, 1003. EM, 1: 239, n. 8.

Yuki fureba	For snow falls
Kokorozukai o	Where searchers gather tender herbs
Kyō sae zo yaru.	On the Plain of Kasuga.[4]

The Shijō Major Counselor[5] composed a reply:

Mi o tsumite	Concerned for the tender herbs
Obotsukanaki wa	In the endless snow
Yuki yamanu	On the Plain of Kasuga,
Kasuga nobe no	Well do I understand
Wakana narikeri.	Your fears.

Ex-Emperor Kazan, who had heard about the exchange, sent around a poem of his own composition:

Ware sura ni	Even my thoughts
Omoi koso yare	Stray in that direction . . .
Kasugano no	How, I wonder, fares the crane
Yukima o ikade	Toiling through drifting snows
Tazu no wakuran.	On the Plain of Kasuga?[6]

When at last the party returned on the following day, Michinaga celebrated the occasion with a banquet of extraordinary splendor. Considering the little envoy's youth, it was amusing to watch the solicitude with which he was waited on by the attendants, who seemed quite prepared to recognize him as a figure of authority.

The Imperial Palace now sheltered a whole family of children. Emperor Ichijō, who had asked Empress Shōshi to look upon Prince Atsuyasu as her own son, tried whenever possible to take the boy with him on his visits to the Empress's apartments. Teishi's two daughters, Princesses Shūshi and Bishi, were bewitching little creatures. The Emperor gazed at them with fond eyes, losing himself in sad memories of the past.

Mikushigedono, Michitaka's fourth daughter, had dropped everything to act as a mother to Prince Atsuyasu, whom Empress Teishi had commended to her care. Since Emperor Ichijō paid frequent visits to the Prince, he was bound to catch an occasional glimpse of her, and their chance encounters ripened into an intimacy that became the talk of the Palace. Shōshi was too young to mind, but there were whispers, it seems, that Mikushigedono herself found the affair unwelcome. Korechika and Ta-

---

4. The poem was sent to Kintō. It plays on *tsukai* ("messenger") and *kokorozukai* ("anxiety").

5. Kintō was still a Middle Counselor at the time.

6. The ex-Emperor uses the word even (line 1) because he is not a close relative of the crane (*tazu*, an allusion to Yorimichi's childhood name, Tazugimi).

kaie rejoiced in the karma that had led to such a splendid connection for their sister. (One may be sure that they ordered private prayers for her success.) The Emperor must have felt the pathos of the relationship, and Mikushigedono's own heart seems to have been "overcast as a peak shrouded in morning mist."[7]

After Prince Atsuyasu went to live in the Imperial Palace, Korechika and Takaie could no longer visit him as they pleased, but when they did manage an unobtrusive nocturnal call, they sometimes stayed for two or three days without anyone's being the wiser. The Prince and his sisters were delightful children, and their uncles forgot all their troubles while they were with them. If the Emperor happened to drop in on such occasions, they probably took the opportunity to exchange a few words with him in private.

Takaie made it a practice to call on Michinaga—who, far from disliking him, often sent someone to fetch him if he did not present himself. "He's not a bad fellow," Michinaga thought. "He was simply led astray by Korechika's cleverness."

Seishi's karma was no ordinary one, it seemed, for her union with Crown Prince Okisada had been blessed with many children. It was a matter of common knowledge that Michinaga intended to present the Prince with one of his daughters, the Principal Handmaid Kenshi, but the minister, unlike some of his predecessors, harbored no desire to bring about anyone's downfall, and he was delaying the presentation until a suitable occasion should arise.

Of the several daughters fathered by one of Rinshi's brothers (a gentleman known as the Imperial Auditor Controller), the second had once been married to Norimasa, the brother of Korechika's wife, but unexpected difficulties had ended the marriage, and the lady was now in service with Empress Shōshi. Michinaga had taken notice of her exceptional beauty and sensitivity, and he came to feel an attraction that deepened into love as their acquaintance progressed. Since the girl was her niece, Rinshi looked on the affair with a tolerant eye. Everyone agreed that Norimasa had been incredibly blind to neglect such a creature. She was called Lady Dainagon.[8]

As time went on, it began to appear that Mikushigedono was pregnant. She was feeling miserable, and her suffering moved Emperor Ichijō to deep sympathy and concern. After four or five months, the news got about.

---

7. An allusion to *Kokinshū* 935 (anon.): Kari no kuru / mine no asagiri / harezu nomi / omoitsukisenu / yo no naka no usa. ("In this cruel world there is no end to grief—my spirits, never brightening, are like the stubborn morning mist on the peaks where wild geese come.")

8. See s.n. 68.

There was no question of a formal announcement to the throne,[9] but she withdrew from the Palace to escape the gossips. She remained very much on the Emperor's mind, and he worried more than ever after he learned that her health was not mending. Innumerable prayers for a safe delivery were commissioned by Korechika, who thought it could be no worse for his sister to bear a child than to fail to conceive.

Lonesome and anxious without the Imperial children, Mikushigedono had begun to feel dreadfully ill after her departure from the Palace. Whether she kept to her bed or tried to move about, she was in constant pain. Korechika transferred her to his own house, where he did everything conceivable to help her, but she took a sudden turn for the worse, and within five or six days she died. She could not have been more than seventeen or eighteen.

To Korechika and Takaie, it was a bitter blow that an unborn child should so tragically have claimed the life of this beautiful, gentle girl, whose quiet refinement had equaled that of the late Empress Teishi herself. Because their dread of gossip was even stronger than their private grief, they sought to conceal their misery behind a mask of stoicism, but the first topic of conversation everywhere was the repeated disappointments suffered by their family. Not the least of their trials was the realization that Emperor Ichijō felt a deep, if unexpressed, sense of loss. It was quite certain, they felt, that he had been in love with Mikushigedono.

All too soon, the final rites were performed, and the period of ritual seclusion drew to a close. Korechika and Takaie both hurried to the Palace to take care of the children. Nobody could have helped feeling sorry for Prince Atsuyasu, who was inconsolable without Mikushigedono.

Presently, the second year of Kankō [1005] arrived. At the time of the appointments, Rinshi's son and Meishi's Iwagimi performed the Coming-of-Age ceremony and received the appropriate offices of Lesser Captain and Assistant Commander of the Military Guards.[10] The Kasuga Messenger, Lesser Captain Yorimichi, became a Middle Captain and was named Imperial Messenger for the Kamo Festival.[11] Michinaga had built

---

9. Because Mikushigedono was not an official consort.

10. "Rinshi's son" probably means the second of her two sons, Norimichi, who, however, performed the genpuku on the Fifth of the Twelfth Month, 1006. He was appointed Lesser Captain of the Right on the Second of the Twelfth Month, Kankō 4 (i.e. early in 1007). Iwagimi performed the genpuku on the Twenty-sixth of the Twelfth Month, Kankō 1 (1004), and was named Provisional Assistant Commander of the Military Guards of the Right in the Sixth Month of Kankō 2 (1005). EM, 1: 243, n. 29.

11. Both statements are inaccurate. Yorimichi is known to have been a Lesser Captain as

a long viewing-stand on Ichijō Avenue, elegantly equipped with a cypress-bark roof and handsome railings, from which in recent years he and Rinshi had viewed the Purification and Festival processions. That year, of course, he was deeply involved in the hectic business of getting the Messenger ready.

Everyone went to the viewing-stand on the festival day. Michinaga joined the party after watching the Messenger's departure, taking with him a number of courtiers and other gentlemen. Since all parents, even those in comparatively modest circumstances, consider it the highest of honors to have a son selected as Kamo Messenger and fit the young man out accordingly, it is small wonder that the preparations on that occasion were of the utmost magnificence. Words cannot describe the care with which the family had supervised every detail, even down to the costumes worn by the attendants, servants, and grooms who marched in the retinue.

Yorimichi's selection as Messenger had given the festival a special interest that year, attracting such exalted spectators as Prince Atsumichi and ex-Emperor Kazan, who both paraded back and forth in front of the viewing-stand in grand ceremonial carriages. Izumi Shikibu rode in the rear of Prince Atsumichi's conveyance. The ex-Emperor's gold-lacquered wickerwork carriage, marvelously constructed in all its details, seemed exactly right for the occasion. Its owner was attended by forty husky senior temple pages (all rather older than usual), twenty junior pages, and assorted footmen and lay servants. A group of variously costumed courtiers followed on foot behind the carriage, fluttering red fans as they passed and repassed the stand. Such an extravagant display would have been out of place in an ordinary year, thought Michinaga, but there was no denying that it enhanced the event for the Messenger. The senior nobles smiled broadly, delighted with the spectacle. "The ex-Emperor is still an elegant man, isn't he?" observed Michinaga. "He once said, I remember hearing, that he would come to add luster to the proceedings when Yorimichi served as Kamo Messenger, but I confess that I hadn't expected such a magnificent exhibition."

The procession moved along in perfect order, and the childish grace of the chubby little Messenger drew tears from his father's eyes as he passed. Every gentleman who knew what it was to love a child must have shared Michinaga's feelings. Young girls from the household staffs of Princes,

<hr>

late as the Third Month of 1006, and the Kamo Messenger in 1005 was Minamoto Masamichi (d. 1017), the son of Rinshi's brother Tokimichi. EM, 1: 243, nn. 30–32.

Ex-Emperor Kazan's carriage passing before Michinaga's Ichijō viewing-stand during the Kamo Festival procession. The headpieces of the attendants appear to be made of *aoi*.

great lords, and other noble families came along in bevies of ten, twenty, and thirty, each decked out after the current fashion in an incredible number of robes. "Where are you from?" Michinaga would ask, calling them over for a closer look. They would reply with the title of this Prince, that lord, or such-and-such a governor, and then he would admire the attractive ones and dismiss the others with a smile. It was an elegant and modish scene.

Around that time, Michinaga took pity on Korechika, who had been left with no official rank, and gave him sustenance grants and ministerial status.[12] Takaie had earlier been appointed Middle Counselor and Minister of War.[13] Everyone rejoiced at those happy events.

The Imperial Palace burned in the Eleventh Month, making it impossible to hold the Gosechi dancing. The Emperor, who took a very serious view of the repeated conflagrations, had made up his mind to abdicate if they continued.[14]

The third year of Kankō [1006] arrived. Intending to go into seclusion for a pilgrimage to the Sacred Peak,[15] Michinaga avoided social engagements from the First Month on, but he could not escape the usual round of ceremonies, and he began to wonder if it were not hopeless to attempt the expedition. It was by then the Fourth or Fifth Month.

During the first fifteen days of the Fifth Month, Michinaga's Thirty Expositions took place as usual.[16] In the last part of the month, there were to be horse races,[17] for which an elegant pavilion and track railings had been built at the Tsuchimikado Mansion. The original plan had been to invite the Emperor and Empress, but because of recent persistent rains, it seemed unlikely that the necessary preparations could be completed in time, and Michinaga had decided to settle for ex-Emperor Kazan, who

12. In 1005, Michinaga reinstated Korechika as a member of the deliberative assembly of nobles, seating him below the Ministers of State and above the Major Counselors. It was not until 1008 that Korechika received sustenance grants (*jikifu*) and equal status with the ministers (*jundaijin*).

13. He became a Provisional Middle Counselor in 1002.

14. There had been other fires in 999 and 1001.

15. Kinbusen, the site of the Zaōdō in the Yoshino Mountains (Nara Prefecture). Zaō Gongen, the divinity worshiped there, was considered to be effective in averting danger, prolonging life, and ensuring the prosperity of the petitioner's descendants. The preliminary period of purification for the pilgrimage lasted for twenty-one, fifty, or 100 days, during which the person lived away from home, abstained from wine, meat, and sex, avoided defilement, copied sutras, etc. The year 1007, rather than 1006, was probably chosen from the outset for Michinaga's pilgrimage, since it was in 1007 that he reached the age of forty-two (sai), considered a time of danger because the word for forty-two (*shini*) is homophonous with the word for death. EMZ, 2: 340, 366.

16. The Thirty Expositions of the *Lotus Sutra*. See the Introduction, p. 19.

17. Probably a mistake. The event seems to have taken place in 1004. EM, 1: 245, n. 38.

would, he thought, be better than no Imperial guest at all. "Will you do me the very great honor of coming to watch the races?" he asked, and the former sovereign, always ready to be amused, replied, "I believe it would help to relieve the rather severe depression from which I have been suffering lately. You may expect me on the appointed day."

Next came the business of preparing for the guest of honor. It would be lèse majesté not to give presents to the monks and nobles in the Imperial retinue, thought Michinaga—and what would be appropriate for Kazan himself?

When the day arrived, Michinaga paid his guest every possible courtesy, feeling that his presence added greatly to the occasion; and the ex-Emperor found the entertainment most amusing. I feel obliged to mention the embarrassment caused by the abominable racket the partisans of the winning team inflicted on the ears of the spectators after each contest.[18] But be that as it may, the event came to an end, and the ex-Emperor took his leave. A rare cream-colored horse, handsomely saddled, and a fine carriage-ox were among the many presents he received. Since night had fallen, Michinaga escorted him home, noting on the way what a sadly affecting impression this exalted personage made. He had indeed "cast off shackles that shackled yet."[19]

Thenceforth, Michinaga and ex-Emperor Kazan were on the best of terms. The ex-Emperor, who was an affectionate parent, sent over several letters asking to have his first and second sons—the ones by Nakatsukasa and her daughter—counted among the offspring of ex-Emperor Reizei.[20] That he should have made such a request was, Michinaga thought, touching proof of his extraordinary devotion to the boys. It was all very well to say that a man in holy orders had no business loving his children, but for his own part he saw no reason to oppose the scheme. "I quite understand, and I shall bring the matter to His Majesty's attention," he said.

Ex-Emperor Kazan was the eldest son of ex-Emperor Reizei, Crown Prince Okisada the second, the late Prince Tametaka the third, and Prince Atsumichi the fourth. Consequently, in the Imperial Edict that was issued on an auspicious day following Michinaga's representations to the throne, Nakatsukasa's son was designated the fifth son and her daughter's the

18. Embarrassing because such a lack of restraint was in questionable taste.

19. Presumably an allusion to a popular saying. The author means that Kazan, as a monk, ought not to have interested himself in worldly things like horse races.

20. The adoption, which led to the elevation of the boys to the status of Imperial Prince, took place in 1004, not in 1006. For a list of Kazan's known sons, all born after his retirement into holy orders, see s.n. 69.

sixth. Each boy was assigned the number of sustenance households usual for an Imperial Prince.[21] When Michinaga sent word to Kazan that the Emperor had ordered his provincial officials to set aside sustenance households for the Princes, the delighted ex-Emperor buried the messenger in an avalanche of presents. Michinaga saw the messenger after his return. "You're a lucky man," he laughed. "You've made a fine haul!"

The days and months slipped past, occupied by such events, and presently the end of the year approached. It was disappointing indeed, thought Michinaga, that a whole year had passed without his having been able to begin the purification for his pilgrimage to the Sacred Mountain. Next year without fail . . .

Around the Third Month [1006], ex-Emperor Kazan decided to hold some cockfights as a treat for his sons, the Fifth and Sixth Princes.[22] He doted on Nakatsukasa's boy, the Fifth Prince, but cared little about her daughter's child, the Sixth. Two teams of city boys were organized,[23] and they set about their duties with much commotion, fanning out into the countryside and quarreling over their finds. That sort of modern behavior, thought Michinaga when he heard about it, was not the right thing for Kazan to be associated with; he ought to have kept the affair quiet. The accommodations that were being prepared at the ex-Emperor's palace, and the plans that were being made, were astonishingly elaborate.

On the appointed day, musical performances and dances were presented at the music pavilions of the Left and Right that had been erected for the occasion. The host had sent invitations to Michinaga's sons, all of whom had accepted, and there were also other important young gentlemen in attendance. After the preliminary functions had ended, the cocks of the Left lost match after match to the victorious birds of the Right, until at length, to the secret amusement of the spectators, the ex-Emperor flew into a rage and began to grumble and complain. His behavior ruined the effect of his elaborate preparations, and the occasion ended in a manner nobody could have foreseen. It was an amusing episode.

As a result of the fire at the Imperial Palace, the Emperor had taken up residence in the Ichijō Palace. The Crown Prince had moved to the Biwa Mansion. By that time, Seishi had presented the Prince with two daughters and four sons.[24]

21. The grant for an unranked Imperial Prince (Shinnō) was 150 households.
22. It was a Chinese custom to hold cockfights on the Third of the Third Month.
23. Probably commoners who frequented Kazan's residence. The Team of the Left was to represent the Fifth Prince, the Team of the Right, the Sixth. EM, 1: 247, n. 36.
24. See s.n. 58.

Cockfighting at ex-Emperor Kazan's palace.

The Ise Virgin at the time was Prince Tamehira's daughter Kyōshi, who had held the position since she was a tiny girl.[25]

Those were times of rampant disease and death. Since the Emperor's character was irreproachable and Michinaga's conduct of the government was nowhere at fault, one must attribute the troubles to the degeneracy of the era.[26] Every year, some pestilence brought death and tragedy in its wake.

Winter arrived with its official events, the Gosechi dancing and the Kamo Special Festival, and then it was the fourth year of Kankō [1007]. How poignantly time's swift flight recalled the evanescence of worldly things!

Everyone was much occupied from New Year's Day on, and soon the First Month had slipped by. As the Second Month began, Michinaga prepared to purify himself for his journey to the Sacred Peak, but a number of people advised him not to set out too soon. "It would be better to begin the purification in the Fourth or Fifth Month," they suggested. "The mountains are at their best in the autumn." He accordingly postponed the purification, and then took great care to do nothing that might displease the gods. The house to which he moved belonged to a man called the Upward-looking Middle Counselor.[27] Things seemed very quiet with the Minister of the Left in seclusion. (Nevertheless, he still attended to official business.)

The pilgrimage took place in the Eighth Month. Since it was something Michinaga had very much wanted to do, and since no detail of the preparations had been neglected, the reader may imagine its splendor. A host of distinguished Buddhist prelates and all kinds of other people competed for places in the entourage, and the party also included the minister's sons and other relatives—so many, indeed, that he felt a certain uneasiness about the state of affairs during his absence. But all remained peaceful un-

25. The Princess, selected at the age of two in 986, held the office until 1011.

26. Yo no sue. The author combines orthodox Confucian political doctrine with an early expression of the idea, usually associated with late Heian thought, that the world had entered the "latter end of the dharma" (yo no sue; mappō), a 10,000-year period of decline presaging the final disappearance of the Buddhist religion. It was believed that mappō would begin 2,000 years after Śākyamuni's death—i.e. around 1050, according to one theory. EMZ, 4: 116. See also Chapter 15, n. 76.

27. Fujiwara Tadasuke (944–1013), said to have been so called because he was always looking up at the sky. Michinaga seems actually to have stayed at a house in the Muromachi area belonging to Minamoto Takamasa, who is probably to be identified with the man of that name who served as Assistant Master of Shōshi's Household. EM, 1: 249, n. 19.

til the return.[28] For years, the pilgrimage had been Michinaga's most cherished desire, and to everyone it seemed an official function.

With the arrival of the Twelfth Month, people began to bustle about
with a great air of excitement—all impatience, it seemed, for the advent
of balmy weather. There was something pathetic in their blithe disregard
of the uncertainties of human existence.

So began the fifth year of Kankō [1008]. The mists on the peaks were
transformed overnight, and the skies stretched calm and hazy to the horizon. The Kyōgoku Mansion was gay with the seasonal finery of the ladies
in attendance on Michinaga's second daughter, Kenshi (known to everyone by her official title of Principal Handmaid), and on her younger sister
Ishi. When Michinaga went to visit Kenshi, who was then fourteen or
fifteen years old, he found her seated in a chamber decorated with a charm-
ingly youthful touch. She wore a number of lined robes in different hues,
and her lustrous hair, of which every strand seemed polished, brushed the
hem of her red plum bombycine mantle, exceeding her height by seven
or eight inches. The aristocratic refinement of her features was softened
by a radiant charm that made her, Michinaga thought, almost too beautiful
for her parents' peace of mind.[29] There were seven or eight young ladies
in attendance, all looking happy and proud to be serving such a mistress.

Ishi was nine or ten, a beautiful child who resembled a tiny doll as she
trotted here and there. Over her inner robes she wore a semiformal coat
of yellowish green. Her skin was the color of gosling down—except that a
gosling's plumage is as white as snow, whereas in Ishi's complexion there
was the merest suggestion of pink. Everyone envied her nurse, Shōnagon,
who watched her charge with loving eyes.

The youngest daughter, Kishi, was about two or three. Michinaga started
to place the auspicious rice cakes on her head,[30] but her mother said, "She
isn't properly dressed yet. Wait a moment."

While the minister lingered at the mansion with his daughters, a succession of messengers arrived to remind him that he was overdue at the
Imperial Palace. It would be best, he decided, to leave without further
delay, and to take with him the many senior nobles and courtiers who had
gathered at the house to pay their respects. Just before setting out in his re-

28. Compare *Ōkagami*, p. 183, which reports a rumor that Korechika intended to "do
something awkward" while Michinaga was away.

29. Because the gods might take a notion to claim her.

30. A ceremony performed for small children of the nobility on the First of the First
Month or on some other auspicious day during the New Year season. Special rice cakes
(*itadakimochii*) from Ōmi, their number varying with the child's age, were placed on the
child's head, and words conducive to his or her future good fortune were pronounced.

splendent Court costume, he placed the rice cakes on his little daughter's head. The young nurse, Koshikibu, was an uncommonly pretty sight as she approached with the baby cradled in her arms.[31]

Michinaga's wife Rinshi, the mother of all those children, might still have passed for a girl of twenty.[32] Small and attractively plump, she was a charming figure, quite the equal of her daughter Shōshi as she leaned against an armrest, dressed in innumerable layers of white-lined robes, with the tapering ends of her rich, shining hair trailing to the hem of her mantle. Her attendants gazed at her with happy smiles. She reclined with an air of placid repose, fingering a small string of red sandalwood prayer beads, and unconsciously murmuring buddha-invocations; and her beauty moved Michinaga to praise. "Look at her!" he said to the nurse who was holding Kishi. "What do you think of the mother of these children? She is as young as her daughters! And her hair!" It was pleasant to see him gaze across at his wife, smiling with satisfaction. Meanwhile, Ishi was running in and out on errands of her own. "What a nuisance you are," said her father, checking her in midcourse.

Noting as he set out that the sun was already high, Michinaga made all possible haste to the Palace, with the party of callers from the mansion trailing along behind in their carriages. Empress Shōshi was in the Imperial Apartment,[33] amusing herself by writing out poems to improve her calligraphy. Then about twenty, she seemed even younger, probably because of her tiny figure. She was exceptionally slender—so frail-looking, indeed, that others worried about her—and at the risk of seeming to dwell on one topic, I must add that the length of her beautiful jet-black hair exceeded her height by at least two feet. She had magnificent white skin, and her cheeks were as red and plump as the ground-cherries little girls blow into.[34] She was wearing a set of gorgeous red robes and a white float-patterned mantle;[35] and to Michinaga she was a vision of loveliness as she

31. Koshikibu was the wife of a provincial governor, Fujiwara Yasumichi, whose mother had been Michinaga's nurse. EM, 1: 250, n. 23; Hagitani 1971–73, 1: 202–3.

32. Rinshi was forty-four.

33. Ue no Mitsubone, apparently a room in the Ichijō Palace named for the Fujitsubo Imperial Apartment in the Seiryōden.

34. Hōzuki (Physalis alkekengi). After squeezing out the insides of the fruit through a tiny hole, the child blew on the husk to make a noise.

35. Float-patterned (ukimon) seems to have described primarily damasks and bombycines with patterning in unbound weft floats. The patterns in such fabrics appeared raised, in contrast to the flatter, less conspicuous figures of bound-patterned (katamon) silks, in which the pattern was worked in a short-float weft-faced twill, with the diagonal lines of the ground and the pattern apparently running usually or always in the same direction. Sasaki 1951, pp. 107–11, also describes Nara-period examples of bound-patterned and float-patterned brocades,

leaned forward over her calligraphy, her hair cascading around her face. Her ladies awaited her pleasure in clusters of seven or eight. The ones who were permitted to wear special colors were a dazzling sight, and the others had contrived to put together smart costumes with various kinds of plain jackets and unfigured silk robes. Earlier Empresses had not included little girls among their attendants, but it had become fashionable in recent years for ladies to keep such children about them, and Shōshi was employing them for miscellaneous tasks. The girls—named, I believe, Yadorigi and Yasurai—were not particularly small, but their long hair, dainty figures, and ceremonial trailing robes,[36] worn without trousers, made them look like pretty, graceful children in an artist's painting.

After a short conversation with Shōshi, Michinaga proceeded to the Courtiers' Hall, where the usual ceremonies were performed with modish elegance.

The sight of Shōshi in the Imperial Apartment had made Michinaga think of his other daughters at the Kyōgoku Mansion.[37]

Shōshi's monthly periods had suddenly stopped. Her appetite had also vanished, but she had kept quiet throughout the Twelfth Month, not wishing to make a fuss about her condition. During the First Month, things went on in the same way, except, perhaps, that she seemed in constant need of sleep. "I understand that your period failed to arrive in the Twelfth Month," Emperor Ichijō said to her, "and that there has been no sign of it this month either, even though it's already the Twentieth. I know nothing about such things, but I suppose I had better speak to your parents." Shōshi was fearfully embarrassed, but to her great discomfort he brought up the matter during Michinaga's next visit, assuring her that there was no need for her to feel ill at ease. "Haven't you heard?" he asked Michinaga. "What do you mean?" Michinaga answered. "Don't you know the Empress isn't her usual self? Ordinarily she never sleeps; she's a regular night watchman. But nowadays it takes an extraordinary commotion

---

but it is not clear whether his use of the term reflects contemporary practice. The bound-patterned brocade is a 3/1 weft-faced twill with color patterning in an auxiliary weft that interlaces in the pattern areas in the same binding system as the ground. In the float-patterned brocade, an auxiliary weft floats unbound in the pattern areas. Nishimura 1971–75, 1: 6; Hifuku Bunka Kyōkai 1969, 1: 63, 140.

36. *Kazami*, the outermost robe worn on formal occasions by young girls in the service of Imperial consorts. The distinguishing feature of the kazami was its long separate panels, which trailed gracefully onto the floor. The sleeves were turned back at the wrists to show the garments underneath. Rekisei Fukusō Bijutsu Kenkyūkai 1965, 1: 56.

37. I.e. it had made him look forward to the day when the others would also be Imperial consorts.

to rouse her." "I had noticed that her face seemed thin, but what you say is news to me. She may indeed be pregnant," Michinaga said.

The minister proceeded to call in Tayū no Myōbu for a few private questions.[38] "Her last period came around the end of the Eleventh Month or the beginning of the Twelfth," said the nurse. "It is still only the Twentieth, so I had intended to wait awhile before bringing the matter up. She eats nothing and feels wretched. I did suggest telling you, but she replied, 'Don't say anything to him for a while. He would make the most absurd fuss. If I really begin to suffer, we can let him know.'" Tears sprang to Michinaga's eyes. He must have thought (with what elation one can imagine) that this was the miraculous result of his pilgrimage to the Sacred Peak.

The month ended amid the usual excitement over the distribution of offices. There could no longer be any doubt that Shōshi was pregnant. Rinshi had gone to the Palace as soon as she heard the news, and she was looking after her daughter with the greatest solicitude and anxiety.

In the Second Month, ex-Emperor Kazan began to feel ill. While everyone was expressing concern and inquiring after his health, he developed a fever caused by boils. It was clear that his state was critical, and the doctors held out little hope for his recovery. Among his many children by Nakatsukasa and her daughter, there were four Princesses, two by each mother.[39] "If I die, I shall take all the Princesses with me before the end of the forty-nine days," he kept repeating.[40] Nakatsukasa and her daughter shed floods of tears as they listened. (The ex-Emperor had given away the youngest of his daughters, Nakatsukasa's child, to Nakatsukasa's sister, Hyōbu no Myōbu, at the time of the baby's birth. "Rear this child as your own; I shall take no notice of her," he had said. Hyōbu no Myōbu had adopted her.)

Presently, the sick man lapsed into a coma, and on the Eighth of the Second Month he died at the age of forty-one, to the infinite grief and distress of the monks and others who had been his close attendants for years. "He was a fine man. We shall feel his loss," said Michinaga.

38. Probably the wife of Ōe Kagemasa. Originally a lady-in-waiting at Masanobu's house, she appears to have entered Rinshi's service after the latter's marriage, and later to have been attached to Shōshi's entourage. She was a poet of some note. In 1026, she joined Shōshi in taking Buddhist vows. EM, 1: 253, n. 31; *Murasaki Shikibu nikki*, p. 511, s.n. 29.

39. As indicated in s.n. 69, nothing is known of Kazan's daughters.

40. According to one theory, he was worried about the future of the girls, who had no influential relatives. Yosano 1962, p. 112.

On the night of the funeral, as she was preparing to put on the dread robe of mourning, Hyōbu no Myōbu composed a poem:

Kozo no haru	Last spring
Sakurairo ni to	I fashioned a costume
Isogishi o	In cherry blossom hues—
Kotoshi wa fuji no	This year I wear
Koromo o zo kiru.	A wisteria robe.[41]

Many other sad things happened.

During the period of ritual seclusion, death claimed each of the ex-Emperor's daughters except the youngest, the one whom Hyōbu no Myōbu had adopted. The strength of a high-born person's will is a fearsome thing, everyone agreed. "It must have been because he said, 'I shall take no notice of her,' that he spared Hyōbu no Myōbu's child," sobbed the ladies.

The Third Month arrived. It was time for the formal report on Empress Shōshi's pregnancy, but the announcement had had to be postponed because of the Light-Offering purification, which had begun on the First.[42] Need I describe the pride and joy that filled Michinaga's heart? After the selection of an auspicious day, prayers were commenced at temples everywhere. It would have been proper for Shōshi to retire to her own home, but she remained at the Palace in deference to the wishes of the Emperor, who had entreated her to wait until the Fourth Month.

Everyone had learned of her condition by then. Korechika's alarm may be imagined. If the child was a boy, people agreed, there could be no doubt about what would happen; and although it was impossible to predict the sex, with Michinaga's luck it was not likely to be a girl.

Around that time, Emperor Ichijō's second daughter, Princess Bishi, left the Palace, dangerously ill. Innumerable prayers, esoteric rites, and sutra-readings were commissioned, many of them by the Emperor himself, but the reports continued to paint a gloomy picture of the Princess's state, and her anxious father remained distracted with worry.

Empress Shōshi took her leave on the First of the Fourth Month.[43] It was a splendid occasion. Even the clustered pine trees at the Kyōgoku

41. "Wisteria robe" (fuji no koromo, originally a rough garment made of wisteria fibers) was a conventional term for mourning attire.
42. Gotō no kiyomawari, performed semiannually by the Emperor during the first three days of the Third and Ninth Months. The purification preceded the offering of lighted torches to the North Star, which was worshiped as a protective deity. No official business could be transacted during the purification period.
43. The Thirteenth of the Fourth Month is the correct date.

Mansion seemed greener than usual—symbols of a glorious future.[44] To supplement the countless prayers already being recited, Michinaga arranged for constant esoteric rites at three altars in the mansion, and for the continuous reading of sutras. Almost too anxious to sleep at night, he addressed a stream of prayers and vows to the Sacred Peak, begging for his daughter's safe delivery.

Meanwhile, Princess Bishi had sunk into a deep coma. But just when it seemed that she must perish, the Holy Teacher Monkyō[45] of Iwakura arrived, performed some rituals, and completely cured her terrible illness. In his delight, Emperor Ichijō made Monkyō a Master of Discipline—an act that probably caused many envious monks to think, "Such are the miracles wrought by a buddha's power!"

Since no Messenger was appointed for the Kamo Festival that year, Michinaga began his usual Thirty Expositions soon after the Twentieth of the Fourth Month.[46] The Fifth-Book Day fell on the Fifth of the Fifth Month—an intriguing coincidence of dates that must have prompted people to take special pains with the preparation of their offering-branches.[47] Since Empress Shōshi was among the spectators in the Buddha Hall, fresh green blinds were put up, even in the adjoining corridors, and the lower edges of the curtains made a cool rustle in the breeze from the Kamo River, their wave patterns standing out with sharp clarity.[48]

44. The pine tree was a symbol of longevity.

45. Monkyō (968?–1047?), a son of the calligrapher Fujiwara Sukemasa, was the Daiunji abbot.

46. Because the festival took place as usual in 1008, presumably with the Imperial Messenger playing his customary central role, commentators interpret this passage to mean that no messenger was sent by Empress Shōshi, who was in a state of ritual defilement because of her pregnancy. The author implies that Michinaga would have been unable to manage simultaneous preparations for two major events. EM, 1: 256, n. 8.

47. Both as the midpoint of the series and as the day on which offerings were presented, the Fifth-Book Day (*itsumaki no hi*) was the high point of an Eight Expositions or Thirty Expositions service. The lecture on the first chapter of the Fifth Book (the twelfth chapter of the sutra), the "Devadatta" chapter (Daiba[datta]bon), was regarded as particularly important because the text offered evidence that sinners and women were capable of attaining buddhahood. The chapter was also revered because it described how Śākyamuni, by gathering firewood and drawing water for the seer Asita, came into possession of the *Lotus Sutra*; and the Buddha's pious exertions were celebrated in an imposing "firewood procession" (*takigi no gyōdō*) of chanting monks and laymen, who made ritual offerings of wood and water. "Offering-branches" translates *hōmochi*, elaborate gifts attached to gold and silver sprays of flowers, branches, etc., which were also presented. Because the midpoint of Michinaga's services coincided with the date of the Sweet-Flag Festival, the worshipers devised various ways of alluding to the season—e.g. by attaching their offerings to artificial sweet-flag roots or leaves.

48. The purpose of the blinds and curtains was to provide privacy for Shōshi and her ladies.

In earlier years, Michinaga had devoted a great deal of thought to his Fifth-Book offerings, but now that the services had become part of his annual routine, he had decided to do things very simply. Others with a taste for elegance, their imaginations piqued by the possibilities of the situation, had produced some remarkable creations. (It was probably the difficulty of imposing restrictions that allowed them to do so.[49])

It was pleasant to watch the trim gentlemen of Sixth Rank and guards officers with their firewood and water buckets, and to see the nobles and monks marching in procession, each wonderfully elegant, handsome, and dignified in his own way. The chanting voices seemed a reminder of suffering, emptiness, and non-self, and the murmuring garden stream harmonized with their cadences, as though nature herself were also expounding the sacred doctrine.[50] The elucidation of the *Lotus* drew pious tears from every eye.

At the edges of the blinds, the bases of the pillars, and similar places, there were inadvertent displays of sleeves, and formal arrangements of skirts in sweet-flag, China-tree, pink, and wisteria combinations.[51] Even the sweet flags, massed at the eaves overhead, seemed more attractive and impressive than usual.

The much-discussed offering-branches proved exceptionally interesting. The younger people were fascinated by Takaie's creation, a silver sweet flag to which medicinal balls were attached. It was also entertaining to see the clever branches designed by the donors to accompany even such ordinary offerings as serving trays.[52]

The interior of the mansion, always elegant, was beyond comparison on such festive occasions.

Courtiers came in with Empress Shōshi's offerings, which were, I believe, serving trays. Perhaps with some notion of "wearing seasonal flowers,"[53] as the common folk say, the various Household officials and lesser ranks—Council functionaries and people of that sort—had devoted im-

---

49. I.e. it was difficult for Michinaga to prohibit extravagance in a pious cause.

50. An allusion to the *Muryōjukyō Sutra* (Skt. *Sukhāvatī-vyūha*), which compares the sound of water in the Pure Land to the voice of a buddha or monk expounding the dharma. EMZ, 2: 394.

51. "Formal arrangements of skirts" translates *kobareidetaru kinu no tsuma*, i.e. *idashiginu*, skirts deliberately revealed from behind the screens of rooms, of carriages, etc. On sweet-flag and China-tree combinations, see Chapter 6, n. 25. Robes intended to suggest the wild pink (*nadeshiko*) were dyed red (*kōbai*) or brown (*suō*) and lined with green (*ao*); wisteria robes were of pale purple (*usuiro* or *usumurasaki*) with green linings.

52. *Wakesara*. They are conjectured to have contained food offerings for the monks. See *Shōkai*, 4: 69.

53. Apparently a proverb. "Catching the spirit of the occasion"?

mense pains to their offerings, and they held their inferior contrivances proudly aloft in thin paper wrappings, very conscious of the ladies behind the blinds. Their behavior was amusing, since none of the ladies was paying any attention to people like them. The Emperor's envoy, Chamberlain Sadasuke,[54] received a formal reply from Michinaga after the ceremony, as well as a reward, which seems to have consisted of a bombycine robe in sweet-flag colors and a pair of deep red trousers.

That evening, the Empress was again present in the Buddha Hall, where she probably took advantage of the opportunity to chat with Kenshi. The light from the sacred lamps, mingling with the reflected glow of the basket-fires by the pond, shone with dazzling brilliance, and the pleasant fragrance of sweet flag filled the air. As the ladies-in-waiting returned to their rooms at dawn, they wound their way through corridors and galleries, along the veranda of the west wing, past the main hall, past Rinshi's chambers, where sutras were being recited, and past the apartments of the Empress, where continuous sacred recitations were also in progress. It was a chastening experience, even for those who, on private excursions to shrines and temples, had always tried, unsuccessfully, to impress people by surrounding themselves with bevies of young women, putting on an air of importance, ordering their servants to clear other travelers out of the way, and sauntering along with haughty expressions on their faces. To some of these last, indeed, the interminable journey through the great mansion appears to have brought a first intimation of their own insignificance.

When the Thirty Expositions drew to a close, Michinaga and the rest felt an agreeable sense of relaxation. Then Princess Bishi fell desperately ill. Everyone had been overjoyed when the monk Monkyō had snatched the Princess from the brink of death, enlisting, as people had thought, the miraculous powers of some buddha; but now the disease flared up again, took a swift turn for the worse, and claimed the little girl's life. She was nine years old. The Emperor was overcome with grief, his natural sorrow made more poignant by the memory of Senshi's great love for the Princess. And as for Korechika and Takaie—never, it seemed, had anyone suffered so many heart-rending tragedies. Princess Shūshi, who had reached the age of understanding by that time, was also piteously affected by her sister's death.[55] Why could it be, many people wondered, that

54. A minor Fujiwara, further identified in the text as an official in the Ministry of Ceremonial. He was probably chosen because he was related to Michinaga through Tokihime, Michinaga's mother, who was the aunt (or possibly the sister) of Sadasuke's father. EMZ, 2: 396.

55. Princess Shūshi, Teishi's other daughter, was eleven.

Korechika and Takaie seemed doomed to lose every relative they had?

Despite the numbing sense of bereavement felt by all, it was necessary to see the Princess properly buried, and that too was a source of grief. Even outsiders found it impossible to keep from weeping when Chūjō no Myōbu tearfully recalled how Senshi had chosen her to be the Princess's nurse.

Soon the Seventh Month arrived. The people at the Tsuchimikado Mansion felt great sympathy for Empress Shōshi, who had got almost too big to move about. The Emperor kept up a stream of solicitous inquiries.

It was being said that Genshi enjoyed a favored position among the Junior Consorts, but as a matter of fact the Emperor had almost no contact with any of those ladies. His only real pleasure came from his visits to Princess Shūshi, who was staying in the Palace. He often thought of his other little daughter, Princess Bishi.

With the coming of autumn, the beauty of the Tsuchimikado Mansion surpassed description.[56] The trees bordering the lake and the massed shrubs beside the stream blazed in a myriad shades of red and yellow, and the beauty of the atmosphere lent a special poignance to the voices that constantly chanted the sacred writings, their accents drifting on the cool breeze, and mingling all through the night with the perpetual murmur of the brook.

Everyone was busy with the Hokoin Eight Expositions until the First,[57] and then the Weaver Maid Festival came and went. One could not help reflecting that the people who occupied themselves with such events were like so many sheep bound for the slaughterhouse.[58]

Empress Shōshi's child was due in the Ninth Month. Michinaga had been praying that it would arrive in the Eighth, but he abandoned his supplications when others persuaded him that there was a fixed term in such matters, and that what he sought was wrong.

As the time drew near, every conceivable prayer was recited for the Empress's safety. Among the religious ceremonies, there was a Five Great Mystic Kings service, conducted throughout in a manner beyond criticism. Shōsan, the Kannon'in Archbishop, brought along an entourage of twenty assistants, each of whom took a turn at performing the sacred in-

---

56. This paragraph is virtually identical with the opening lines of Murasaki Shikibu's diary. See the Introduction, pp. 52ff.

57. Probably of the Seventh Month. This ritual, held annually by Michinaga at his father's former residence, usually ended around the Second of the Seventh Month. EM, 1: 512, s.n. 364.

58. I.e. they were seemingly unaware of the transience of life and the possible imminence of death. The simile, familiar from several sutras, appears *passim* in Heian literature. EM, 1: 512, s.n. 365.

vocations. Apartments in every corner of the grounds had been equipped as retiring rooms, even such places as the horse-racing pavilion and the library. Watching the monks stream back and forth between the out-lying buildings and the scene of the services, one could not help noticing that some of the older men were exceedingly ugly—and yet their faces commanded deep respect. It was a moving experience to follow one of those venerable figures in one's mind's eye as he proceeded back across the elegant Chinese bridges and through the trees to his quarters. The Holy Teacher Shin'yo, I believe, officiated in vestments of red[59] at the altar dedicated to Kuṇḍalī, and the Holy Teacher Shōzen bowed before Daiitoku.[60]

Immediately after the Five Great Mystic Kings service, the Ninnaji Archbishop Gakyō performed the *Peacock Sutra* ritual.[61] Thus rite fol-lowed rite in rapid succession, until a new day at last dawned.[62] It had been an ear-shattering, weird night, and those who were inclined to ner-vousness came away with giddy heads and racing hearts.

After the Twentieth of the Eighth Month, the senior nobles and other courtiers associated with the family spent most of their nights at the man-sion, dozing at the heads of stairways, on wing verandas, in galleries, and elsewhere about the premises. The younger gentlemen, who knew very little about music, competed at chanting sutras, sang modern songs, and debated the merits of one another's performances in a most amusing man-ner. On one occasion, Tadanobu, Tsunefusa, Yasuhira, and Narimasa per-formed together.[63] They pretended to be absorbed in the music, but their efforts to appear unconcerned were pathetically transparent.

59. Symbolic of fire, the destroyer of evil.

60. For a list of the chief officiants at the five altars, see s.n. 70.

61. Unlike the Five Great Mystic Kings service, which was performed by Tendai monks, the *Peacock Sutra* ritual (Kujaku [myōō]kyō no hō) was a Shingon specialty. The object of worship was Kujaku myōō (Skt. Mayūrasana), the Peacock King, so called because he was believed to ride a peacock. He was considered efficacious in bringing rain, ending floods, healing illness, and protecting women in childbirth. Gakyō (924–1012), a grandson of Emperor Uda, was a scholar-monk who held numerous high posts in the Shingon sect. Hagitani 1971–73, 1: 54–55, discusses evidence that the text should perhaps be emended to read Ninnaji Bishop (Ninnaji no sōzu), and that the monk in question was possibly not Gakyō (as indicated in an interlinear note in the text), but Rinshi's brother Saishin.

62. The author here describes events that did not occur until the Eleventh of the Ninth Month, the last night of Shōshi's labor. See EM, 1: 260, n. 14; and 1: 513, s.n. 366.

63. The text identifies the musicians by office, not by name. Fujiwara Tadanobu was Master of the Empress's Household. Minamoto Tsunefusa, a Consultant and Middle Captain of the Left, was one of Michinaga's Stewards; he later served as Master of Shōshi's Household. In 1008, Fujiwara Yasuhira (953–1017) was Commander of the Military Guards of the Left, Consultant, and Master of the Crown Prince's Household. He eventually became a Provisional Middle Counselor of Senior Second Rank. Minamoto Narimasa (d. 1041), one of Masanobu's

Shōshi had recently set her ladies to work making incense balls. The finished products were distributed, and servants brought censers for the Empress to test them.

So began the Ninth Month. The day of the Double Yang Banquet drew to a close, after festivities at which the chrysanthemums by the brushwood fences, symbolic of immortality, had seemed to presage a long and glorious future.[64] Empress Shōshi's pains had begun earlier that evening, and the mansion was in an uproar from midnight on. At the first flush of dawn on the Tenth, the Empress moved to a white curtain-dais.[65] The room's furnishings were all changed, an operation involving much activity on the part of Michinaga, Shōshi's brothers, and the officials of Fourth and Fifth Rank,[66] who hurriedly hung new draperies on the curtain frames and brought in mats.

The Tenth was a day of misery for Shōshi. The possessing spirits were driven into mediums, each attended by an exorcist bellowing prayers. Michinaga had already pressed into service all of the many monks who had been on duty at the mansion in recent months, and their ranks were now swelled by every cleric within call who enjoyed the slightest reputation as a miracle worker or ascetic. Deeply worried by the delay in the baby's arrival, the Emperor sent over a carriage-load of ladies with experience in such matters. Each of the possessed mediums was put inside an enclosure of folding screens, where the attendant miracle workers shrieked incantations in unison. The reader may imagine the noise and confusion.

Thus passed the night of the Tenth.

To Michinaga, the prolongation of Shōshi's labor was exceedingly strange and frightening. Gloomy thoughts, verging on the inauspicious,

---

grandsons, is identified here as the Mino Lesser Captain. Although he held numerous provincial posts, he died a tenjōbito. *Sonpi bunmyaku*, 3: 387, calls him an outstanding musician.

64. The Double Yang Banquet (*chōyō no en*), held on the Ninth of the Ninth Month, was so called because nine was a yang number. One of the Five Banquets (*gosechie* or *gosekku*) of the Court calendar, it imitated the chrysanthemum banquets of China, where legend attributed to chrysanthemum blossoms, and to their scent, the ability to ward off disease and prolong life. In the mid-Heian period, the observances consisted primarily of an official repast for courtiers and senior nobles at the Shishinden, with chrysanthemum displays, Chinese poems on relevant topics, music, and dancing. On the same day, at the Imperial Palace and elsewhere, the kusudama from the preceding Sweet-Flag Festival were replaced by bags of rue berries, again for prophylactic purposes. A related custom, observed by the aristocracy during most of the Heian period, involved swathing each chrysanthemum in floss silk before it was picked (to protect the blossom from dew, which might cause it to fade), and rubbing one's face on the Ninth with the damp, scent-impregnated cloth. Ishimura 1958, 1: 247–49.

65. It was customary for the delivery room to be furnished entirely in white.

66. Michinaga's Stewards.

occupied his mind, and it was only by surreptitiously wiping away his tears that he managed to preserve an air of composure. All the experienced older ladies were weeping. Someone suggested a change of location,[67] even if only within the mansion itself, and Shōshi moved to the northern eave-chamber. The older ladies stayed by her side. Everyone present was frantic with anxiety, and many were quite unable to control themselves. Bishop Ingen of the Hosshōji read aloud a supplication for the Empress's safe delivery,[68] weeping as he described everything Michinaga had done to propagate the teachings of the *Lotus*. The ceremony was extremely sad, but also impressive and reassuring. With every well-known Yin-yang Master in attendance, it seemed impossible that the gods could fail to respond to the calamity-averting rituals. There was a constant bustle of messengers departing with donations for the chanting of sutras. So the day passed, and the night as well.[69]

To the dismay of all, the Empress received Buddhist commandments.[70] Then Michinaga himself began to invoke the *Lotus Sutra*, and everyone felt much better. Never had there been such turmoil, but at last the child arrived safely. I shall leave it to the reader to imagine the scene as the throng of monks and others, high- and lowborn alike, prostrated themselves in prayer in the spacious hall during the wait for the afterbirth.

When all was over and the mother was allowed to lie down, Michinaga and the rest gave rein to their happiness. The baby was a boy,[71] an occasion for extraordinary rejoicing. Words like glorious are useless at such times.

Michinaga and Rinshi, their minds at ease, returned to their own apartments, where they distributed rewards to the Yin-yang Masters and the monks who had offered prayers. The older ladies stayed with the Empress, while the younger ones went off to rest in other rooms.

Elaborate preparations were made for the bathing ceremony. Rinshi had decided earlier not to be the one to cut the umbilical cord, feeling that it would involve her in sin,[72] but she was too happy to remember her qualms.

67. Probably to evade malignant spirits.
68. Ingen was Hosshōji abbot at the time.
69. I.e. the night of the Tenth. The sequence of events, garbled in the text, was as follows: on the Tenth of the Ninth Month, prayers by the Yin-yang Masters; on the Eleventh, Shōshi's move to the northern eavechamber, Ingen's prayer, and the birth of the child. EM, 1: 514, s.n. 377.
70. Although this meant only that she was requesting divine protection, the act was considered inauspicious as possibly presaging her departure from lay life.
71. Prince Atsuhira, the future Emperor Go-Ichijō (1008–36; r. 1016–36). Named Crown Prince in 1011.
72. Apparently a current belief. Its rationale is no longer understood.

The first suckling was to be performed by Consultant Arikuni's wife, Tachibana Naishi no Suke, who had been nurse to the Emperor; and the bath ceremony was to be conducted by ladies who had always been close to the Empress and were accustomed to her service.

I scarcely have the courage to venture an account of the proceedings. Needless to say, a sword arrived promptly from the Palace. (The Imperial envoy, Middle Captain Yorisada, must have received an exceptional reward, but the Ise Messenger happened to be still on his journey, and Yorisada could not enter the defiled mansion.[73]) There was also much excitement as people hurried in with bundles, bags, and Chinese chests, all of which apparently contained various parts of the white costumes to be worn by the ladies-in-waiting.

The bathing ceremony, which had been arranged for the Hour of the Cock [5:00–7:00 P.M.], was splendid beyond description. After the lamps had been lit, junior officials from the Empress's Household brought in the bath water, wearing special white garments over their robes of deep blue.[74] Everything was draped in white.[75] Nakanobu, the Empress's Chief Attendant, carried the water over to the blinds, where it was received, tempered with cool water, and poured into jugs by the two elegantly attired ladies in charge of the stands.[76] The jugs were sixteen in number. The costumes of the ladies-in-waiting, the bath aprons,[77] and the other garments were all of white. Sanuki no Saishō served as Bath Attendant, and Dainagon as Assistant.[78]

Michinaga carried the baby in. Kosaishō carried the Imperial sword, and Miya no Naishi walked in front with the tiger head.[79] Ten officials

73. Rather than being "still on his journey," the Ise Messenger set out on the day of the birth, bearing the usual annual offerings. Since the Palace observed ritual seclusion during the Messenger's absence, it was impossible for the Imperial envoy, Yorisada, to enter Shōshi's residence. A house was considered defiled for seven days after a birth.

74. The color prescribed for the Sixth Rank.

75. In *Murasaki Shikibu nikki*, p. 452, the author's source for this section, the white drapery is described as covering only the water stands, not "everything."

76. According to other sources, Nakanobu had a colleague on this occasion, variously identified as a Chief Attendant and as governor of Owari. Chief Attendant (Saburai no Osa) is known to have been the title of a post in the Attendants' Office of an important person's household, but little information is available concerning the duties involved. Nakanobu is probably to be identified with Mutobe Nakanobu, said by contemporary diaries to have been in service at the Tsuchimikado Mansion. EM, 1: 515–16, s.nn. 384, 385.

77. *Imaki*, worn by female attendants when they assisted at the baths of important persons.

78. At the *yudono no hajime* ("bath ceremony"), the Bath Attendant (Yudono) bathed the baby. The Assistant (Mukaeyu) poured water, received the child after the bath, etc. Sanuki no Saishō, also called Saishō no Kimi and Ben no Saishō [no Kimi], was Fujiwara Hōshi, daughter of Michitsuna and wife of Ōe Kiyomichi, the governor of Sanuki. She served as wet nurse to the new baby. On Dainagon, see s.n. 68.

79. Kosaishō is probably a mistake for Koshōshō (d. ca. 1013?), a close friend of Murasaki

of Fifth Rank and ten of Sixth served as bow-twangers. The learned Professor, Chamberlain Controller Hironari, stood beside the balustrade and read from the first chapter of the *Records of the Historian*.[80] The rites of bodily protection were performed by the Jōdoji Bishop.[81] It was amusing to witness the Bishop's bewilderment as showers of rice, thrown with great gusto by Lesser Captain Masamichi,[82] rained on his head.

The ladies in their white dresses were like figures in some marvelously elegant ink drawing. On inspecting the individual ensembles, each the product of long and anxious preparation, one observed that even the people authorized to wear forbidden colors tended to look much alike, since all were attired in bombycine trains and jackets of pure white. Among the others, the more mature wore unfigured white damask mantles and five inner robes—costumes that seemed ideally suited to their years. Their fans, similarly unostentatious, were decorated in a tasteful, pleasing manner with appropriate lines from old poems. The younger ladies, determined to make a good showing, had decorated their trains and jackets with embroidery and mother-of-pearl inlay, edged their sleeves with precious metals, and sewn on silver braid until the wearers sparkled like snow-covered mountains in the moonlight. I could not possibly do them justice.

The Third Night banquet was presented by the Master and other officials of the Empress's Household.[83] The Commander of the Left Gate Guards provided the banquet service for the Empress,[84] which consisted, as well as I could see, of aloeswood standing trays, silver plates, and things of that sort. The Minamoto Middle Counselor Toshikata and the Fujiwara Consultant Sanenari presented robes and swaddling clothes. The stiffened cloth in the corners of the clothes chests, the packing materials, the wrap-

---

Skikibu and a daughter of one of Rinshi's brothers, either Tokimichi or Sukeyoshi (951–98). Miya no Naishi is believed to be another name for Ben no Myōbu, a Tachibana lady formerly in the service of ex-Empress Senshi. EM, 1: 263, nn. 44, 46; *Murasaki Shikibu nikki*, pp. 510, 511, s.nn. 16, 26. On the tiger head, see s.n. 8.

80. Fujiwara Hironari (975–1028), a son of Arikuni, was one of the Crown Prince's two Scholars at the time. He became a Consultant in 1020. According to Michinaga's diary, he read from the *Classic of Filial Piety* (*Hsiao-ching*), not from the *Records of the Historian* (*Shih-chi*). *Murasaki Shikibu nikki*, pp. 453, n. 37, 512, s.nn. 55, 65.

81. "Bodily protection" translates *goshin*, thought by Matsumura (EM, 1: 263) to mean mudras and incantations designed to protect the baby during the bath, and by Hagitani (1971–73, 1: 254) to refer to the monk(s) who provided protection. The Jōdoji Bishop was Myōku. See s.n. 70.

82. Rinshi's nephew.

83. The Master was Fujiwara Tadanobu.

84. A mistake for Commander of the Right Gate Guards, a concurrent post held by Tadanobu. The Commander of the Left Gate Guards was Kintō. EM, 1: 517, s.n. 393; *Murasaki Shikibu nikki*, p. 454.

The bathing ceremony for Prince Atsuhira. "Michinaga carried the baby in. Kosaishō carried the Imperial sword, and Miya no Naishi walked in front with the
tiger head. Ten officials of the Fifth Rank and ten of Sixth served as bow-twangers.
The learned Professor, Chamberlain Controller Hironari, stood beside the balustrade
and read from the first chapter of the *Records of the Historian*. The rites of bodily

protection were performed by the Jōdoji Bishop. It was amusing to witness the Bishop's bewilderment as showers of rice, thrown with great gusto by Lesser Captain Masamichi, rained on his head." In the upper righthand panel, Shōshi sits with her ladies, screened on either side by curtain-stands.

pers, and the covered stands were all of the same white color, but each had been prepared with infinite care to reflect the donor's taste.[85]

The Fifth Night banquet was presented by Michinaga. It happened to be the Fifteenth of the month, and the thick autumn dew glittered in the unclouded light of a full moon. All the senior nobles and courtiers were in attendance, the more exalted seated on the west side of the east wing, with the seat of honor to the north, and the others on the north side of the southern eavechamber, with the seat of honor to the west. There were white damask screens to supplement the blinds in front of the main apartment. Beneath the bright moon, the Kangakuin students came parading along the border of the lake, where fires had been lit to illuminate the scene. The students presented the Empress with lists bearing their names, and were duly rewarded.

The scale of the festivities was astounding. Everywhere one looked, there were members of the lower orders—Escorts, people in the Empress's Household, men who had come with the senior nobles—gathering in convivial groups or dashing about on errands. The joy of the occasion could scarcely have held a personal meaning for them, but I suppose their high spirits came from the thought that they might bask in the new Prince's patronage some day. It was also interesting to watch the men attached to Michinaga's household, even insignificant fellows of Fifth Rank, as they sauntered to and fro in the bright light of the fires, the standing torches, and the moon, bowing proudly to the guests. The Empress's dinner was brought in by eight young ladies-in-waiting with their hair done up with white fillets, all so admirably suited to the office that no one could have had the least reservation about any of them. They bore in the silver trays one after another. The Empress was served that evening by Miya no Naishi, a stately, aristocratic lady. Since the young ladies carrying the trays were all very pretty, it was delightful to watch them.

There was an unpleasant argument about the paper betting stakes while Michinaga and the other senior nobles were playing backgammon.[86] Poems were composed, but I was too distracted by the noise to hear them properly,

---

85. Meishi's brother Toshikata was Provisional Master of the Empress's Household. He later served as Master of the Grand Empress's Household (appointed when Shōshi assumed the title of Grand Empress in 1012), and as Master of the Senior Grand Empress's Household (appointed in 1018), a post he retained until Shōshi became a nun. Sanenari was Provisional Assistant Master of the Empress's Household. Stiffened cloth (*oritate*) was used at the corners of chests and boxes for decorative purposes. "Packing materials" translates *irekatabira*, cloths in which garments were wrapped before being put into boxes for storage; "wrappers" translates *tsutsumi*, cloths in which clothing boxes were wrapped. *Murasaki Shikibu nikki*, p. 455, nn. 31, 32, p. 512, nn. 69, 70; *Kugyō bunin*, 1: 254ff; Sosawa and Morishige 1966, p. 88.

86. It was customary to play backgammon at birth celebrations. The argument concerned

and when I made inquiries, they proved to be so disorganized, and so complicated by allusions to particular circumstances, that it was hopeless to try to record them. The ladies were worried about having to recite poems if they were asked to drink.[87] Murasaki murmured some lines to herself in preparation:

Mezurashiki	May this moon
Hikari sashisou	Shining with wondrous light
Sakazuki wa	Make its rounds,
Mochinagara	Ever full,
Chiyo o megurame.	For a thousand generations.[88]

Since the Shijō Major Counselor Kintō was seated near the blinds, the ladies were even more worried about their voices and bearing than about the quality of their poems.[89]

So the banquet ended. Presents were distributed, all, presumably, in the usual style—a lady's costume and a set of swaddling clothes for each senior noble, and for courtiers of Fourth, Fifth, and Sixth Rank, respectively, a pair of trousers and a set of lined robes, a set of lined robes, and a pair of trousers and an inner robe. Both inside and outside the mansion, there was much festive activity late into the night, and then a new day dawned.

Since there was to be another celebration on the Seventeenth, Shōshi's ladies-in-waiting devoted the Sixteenth to putting together costumes different from the ones they had worn on the Fifteenth. Things were quiet that evening, and some of the ladies went boating on the lake in the garden, accompanied by the Consultant Middle Captain of the Left Tsunefusa and Michinaga's son, Lesser Captain Norimichi.[90] Many pleasant things happened.[91]

The Seventh Night ceremonies were sponsored by the Court. Chamberlain Lesser Captain Michimasa (the former Matsugimi)[92] came as an en-

---

the complicated etiquette involved in the placing of the bits of paper that were used as stakes in the betting. EM, 1: 265, n. 37; 1: 518, s.n. 402; Shōkai, 4: 109.

87. Custom required a poem of the person to whom wine was offered.

88. The reference is to Murasaki Shikibu. See the Introduction, p. 60. Word plays in her poem yield two other meanings: (1) May the splendid young Prince enjoy a long and glorious life; (2) Let the winebowl pass from hand to hand far into the night.

89. Kintō was a Middle Counselor in 1008. The ladies were nervous because his standards were known to be exacting.

90. Norimichi (996–1075) was a Middle Captain at the time.

91. Apparently a general comment on the busy season, rather than a specific reference to the boating, of which the author's source, Murasaki Shikibu nikki, p. 458, says little, except that the women, with their white dresses and black hair, made an attractive picture in the moonlight.

92. Korechika's oldest son, who was then fifteen.

voy, bringing a willow-wood box that contained a list of the Emperor's gifts. The list was shown to the Empress at once. Then the Kangakuin students marched in to offer their congratulations. They probably received rewards after presenting the lists of their names. Everything was even more impressive and elaborate than on the earlier nights. All of the Emperor's ladies-in-waiting were present for the occasion. Fujiwara Naishi no Suke and a number of Palace Ladies and Lady Chamberlains arrived in two carriages, whereupon the boating party went inside with some trepidation.[93] Michinaga received the visitors in an expansive mood, smiling broadly—as well he might, thought the onlookers. He presented each guest with a gift appropriate to her status.

On the following night,[94] the Empress looked especially lovely. Her face and body were noticeably thinner, and she seemed even more frail and delicate than usual as she reclined inside the curtain-dais. The ceremonies followed the same general course as on the previous occasions. Since the rewards for the senior nobles were offered from behind the Empress's blinds, they were transmitted by the two Head Chamberlains.[95] I believe the presents included garments belonging to the infant Prince, as well as the usual ladies' costumes. The rewards granted to the ordinary courtiers must have been such things as are customarily bestowed by the Court on formal occasions—oversized robes, quilts, rolls of silk, and the like. Tachibana Naishi no Suke, who had performed the rite of the first suckling, was given a silver-trimmed clothing box containing both a lady's costume and a bombycine semiformal jacket in wrappings of white cloth. She also received other gifts wrapped by the Empress.

Everyone changed back into ordinary costumes on the eighth day.

The ceremonies on the Ninth Night were sponsored by Yorimichi, the Provisional Master of the Crown Prince's Household. It was another memorable occasion, with the senior nobles seated near the Empress's blinds. Yorimichi's presents were displayed with modish elegance on a pair of tiered chests made of natural wood. There was a silver-trimmed clothing box decorated with a seascape in raised relief depicting P'eng-lai[96] and the like—a conventional subject, perhaps, but executed with superb skill and

93. From here to the end of the paragraph, the author inserts material recorded in *Murasaki Shikibu nikki*, p. 458, as taking place on the preceding evening. Murasaki says that Naishi no Suke and some other Court ladies arrived during the boating to pay a visit, and that Shōshi's attendants were nervous because they were only slightly acquainted with the callers.

94. I.e. the Seventh Night.

95. Meishi's nephew Yorisada and Rinshi's cousin Michikata. EM, 2: 453.

96. J. Hōrai. In Chinese legend, a fairy mountain in the eastern seas whose inhabitants are immortal. Often depicted rising from the back of a giant turtle.

taste. I mention the box only as an example; it would be beyond my powers to describe everything in detail.

The curtain-stands went back to normal that night, and all the ladies appeared in deep red robes. The unfamiliar color glowed with resplendent beauty through their transparent formal jackets.

So time passed. Empress Shōshi continued to guard her health with more than usual care, and it was the Tenth of the Tenth Month before she ventured out of her curtain-dais. Michinaga dropped in at all hours of the day and night, taking the Prince from the nurse's arms and holding him as though he were an indescribably precious object. One can easily understand his emotions. He even seemed to enjoy it when the baby wet on his robes.

Emperor Ichijō was to pay a call at the Tsuchimikado Mansion very soon. Much refurbishing and polishing had been taking place, and those who beheld the beauty of the house and grounds felt as though they were in the presence of some wondrous power capable of holding old age at bay—as though, indeed, the *Lotus Sutra* had manifested itself before their eyes. Since the purpose of the visit was to satisfy the Emperor's impatience to see his son, Michinaga experienced a greater sense of urgency than on similar occasions in the past. The event, he felt, must take place at the earliest possible moment, and he quite naturally lost many hours of sleep and neglected all other concerns in order to hurry things along.

The visit was planned for the latter part of the Tenth Month. Two boats, built for the occasion and drawn up for Michinaga to inspect, conveyed a vivid suggestion of living creatures with their dramatic, exotically beautiful dragon-head and *geki*-head prows.[97]

The Emperor was to arrive during the Hour of the Tiger [3:00–5:00 A.M.].[98] Long before dawn, the ladies at the mansion were fussing over their costumes. Since the senior nobles were to sit in the west wing, the Empress's ladies could afford to be somewhat casual, but Kenshi's attendants seem to have made much more elaborate preparations. A chair had been placed west of the Empress's curtain-dais in the richly redec-

97. The *geki*, a mythical white bird, was endowed by Chinese legend with the supernatural ability to withstand the force of the wind, and therefore was paired with the dragon, the master of the waves, to ensure safety on the water. At elegant entertainments, the two boats were usually occupied by musicians—the dragon-head (*ryōtō*) by performers of Chinese music and the geki-head (*gekisu*) by performers of Korean music. See the picture on pp. 242–43.

98. According to *Murasaki Shikibu nikki*, p. 462, he was expected during the Hour of the Dragon (7:00–9:00 A.M.). Although contemporary sources differ concerning the time, it is certain that he did not arrive until at least eleven o'clock in the morning. The date was the Sixteenth. Hagitani 1971–73, 1: 369, 377–78.

orated main hall. Ladies-in-waiting were seated behind blinds on the north and south sides of the chamber to the east.[99]

From beyond a slightly raised blind near the south pillar, there emerged two beautiful Imperial Handmaids with their hair dressed in formal coiffures, Ben no Naishi and Saemon no Naishi, who looked to the spectators like figures in a Chinese painting or celestial beings descended to earth.[100] They were charming, each in her own way, and their lustrous robes glowed with incomparable beauty. The Bodyguards performed their duties in regalia appropriate to the occasion.[101] It was Yorisada, the Chamberlain Middle Captain, who gave the Sacred Sword to the Handmaid.

Behind the blinds, the ladies authorized to wear forbidden colors were dressed in formal jackets of green or red, trains with stenciled patterns, and identical bombycine mantles in sapan colors.[102] Their glossy, fulled-silk outer robes, dyed in shades of red, suggested a scattering of autumn leaves, and their lined inner robes displayed the usual color combinations of green with yellow and the like. The other ladies were dressed according to their individual tastes in unfigured and plain silks. Their inner robes were similarly varied, and their trains were decorated with stenciled marine designs, on which the color of the water stood out with delightful freshness.

Among those present were four or five Imperial attendants who were also in the service of the Empress—two Handmaids, two Palace Ladies, and a serving lady. Wearing their hair done up in preparation for serving the Imperial repast, they went back and forth through the opening in the blinds from which the two Handmaids had previously emerged. The serving lady, Fujiwara Sanmi, was wearing a red jacket over yellow Chinese damask robes and a chrysanthemum mantle.[103] Chikuzen, Sakyō,

---

99. At this point, the Imperial litter arrives at the mansion. *Murasaki Shikibu nikki*, p. 463.

100. Their function was to resume custody of the Sacred Sword and Sacred Necklace, which always accompanied the Emperor. As was customary, the Sword and Necklace had been entrusted to the Bodyguards by the Handmaids' Office for safekeeping during the journey. Ben no Naishi is possibly to be identified with Fujiwara Gishi (widow of Rinshi's brother Sukeyoshi), who became a Naishi no Jō around 999 and took Buddhist vows with Shōshi in 1026. Saemon no Naishi was the sobriquet of Tachibana Ryūshi, who married the Middle Counselor Fujiwara Fuminori (909–96). *Shōkai*, 4: 122; Hagitani 1971–73, 1: 192–94; *Murasaki Shikibu nikki*, pp. 463–64; EMZ, 2: 464.

101. The costumes to be worn by the Bodyguards during an Imperial progress were prescribed in *Engishiki*. They included bows, arrows, and ceremonial swords. *Shōkai*, 4: 122.

102. *Suōiro*: brown with red linings.

103. Probably a mistake for Tachibana Naishi no Suke, who was also called Tachibana Sanmi, the Tachibana [Lady] of Third Rank. The usual chrysanthemum combination was white with a lining of brown (suō)—or, according to another theory, of green (ao)—but the

and the others all seemed to be dressed with great elegance too, but there was a pillar in the way that blocked my view.[104]

Michinaga entered the Imperial presence carrying the mewling infant, who sounded very young indeed. Sanuki no Saishō bore the sword.[105] The Prince was taken to Rinshi's seat west of the central door to the inner chamber.

The reader may imagine the pleasure with which Emperor Ichijō beheld the baby. Nevertheless, he could not help remembering how long he had been forced to wait for his first glimpse of Prince Atsuyasu. In such matters, he reflected, reliable assistance was everything; even an Emperor was helpless without someone on whom to depend. From there it was only a step to thoughts of the future, and secret grief for his oldest son flooded his heart.[106]

Night fell while the Emperor was still engaged in casual conversation with Empress Shōshi. Dancers presented "Ten Thousand Years," "Universal Peace," and "Festive Hall,"[107] and the stirring music of the flute, drums, and other instruments mingled delightfully with the sound of the wind sighing through the pines and the waves rippling on the lake. When Akimitsu, the Minister of the Right, heard the baby crying during "Ten Thousand Years," he remarked that the tiny voice harmonized to perfection with the strains of the music. Kintō and Tadanobu, the Commanders of the Left and Right Gate Guards, sang "Ten Thousand Years, a Thousand Autumns"[108] as a duet. "After today, I can't imagine why I was im-

diary indicates that yellow chrysanthemum (*kigiku*, yellow with a green lining) is meant here. EMZ, 2: 464.

104. "But there was a pillar in the way that blocked my view," is a direct quotation from the diary. Both Sakyō and Chikuzen were middle-ranking Palace Ladies (Myōbu). Sakyō has been tentatively identified as the wife of a provincial governor, Fujiwara Nagamasa. Almost nothing is known of Chikuzen, except that she became a nun with Shōshi in 1026. *Murasaki Shikibu nikki*, pp. 465, 513, s.nn. 95, 104.

105. The Imperial gift sent at the time of the baby's birth.

106. Because he recognized the impossibility of making Atsuyasu the next Crown Prince.

107. Three dances, all with Chinese antecedents, considered suitable for auspicious occasions. "Ten Thousand Years" ("Manzairaku") was set to music that, according to one tradition, had been inspired by a parrot belonging to Empress Wu (623–705) of the T'ang dynasty; "Universal Peace" ("Taiheiraku") dramatized the sword dance in which Hsiang Chuang of Ch'u attempted unsuccessfully to kill Liu Pang, the founder of the Han dynasty; and "Festive Hall" ("Katen") made use of a composition that was said to have been introduced at the Court of Emperor Ninmyō (810–50) by a returning Japanese ambassador to China. All the dancers were men in Michinaga's day, although "Ten Thousand Years" had at one time been performed by six women, and later by young boys. The martial "Universal Peace" was remarkable for the lavishness of the armor, helmets, and weapons worn by the four performers.

108. See s.n. 71.

pressed by earlier Imperial visits!" exclaimed Michinaga, moved to tears. To the other gentlemen, wiping their own eyes, his feelings seemed entirely natural.

Presently, Michinaga retired to a separate room. Joining him there, Emperor Ichijō summoned Akimitsu, whom he ordered to draw up a promotion list, a document raising the rank of every eligible person serving in the Empress's Household or acting as one of Michinaga's Stewards. Michikata took the draft to the Empress.

Because the new baby had been invested with the title of Imperial Prince, the senior Fujiwara nobles expressed their joy by forming a line and making obeisance in the Imperial presence.[109] (Members of other branches of the family did not participate.[110]) Then the promotions took place, and obeisances were performed by the recipients—Tadanobu, the Master of the Empress's Household (who had also been named Imperial Superintendent of the infant Prince's Household); Toshikata, the Provisional Master of the Empress's Household; Sanenari, the Provisional Assistant Master of the Empress's Household; and others.

The Emperor went in to spend some time with Shōshi, but all too soon the hour grew late and the carriage was announced. Michinaga emerged to see him off.

The next day an Imperial messenger arrived at the mansion before the early morning mists had dissipated. His promptness was evidence, one may suppose, of the Emperor's affection for the new Prince. The first cutting of the Prince's hair,[111] which had been postponed until after the Imperial visit, took place on that day, as did the appointment of the Stewards, Attendants, Superintendents, and other functionaries for his Household.

109. *Haimu* or *butō*. The performer of this Chinese-derived ceremonial act is said to have executed two standing bows; next turned the upper half of his body first to the left, with his arms outstretched in the same direction and his sleeves joined, then to the right, and then again to the left; and, finally, performed the same series of movements while kneeling on his right knee—a stylized indication that he was beside himself with joy and gratitude. The haimu was performed after the receipt of a reward, gift, promotion, appointment, etc.

110. I.e. the branches known as the Southern, Ceremonial, and Capital houses. The branch to which Michinaga belonged, the Northern house, was by far the most important.

111. *Ubuzori* or *teihatsu*, performed on a suitable day about a week after a child's birth. The exact nature of the ceremony in Michinaga's day is not known, but an account of the ubuzori of the future Emperor Antoku (1178–85; r. 1180–85) suggests that in the case of an Imperial Prince, a Minister of State placed on the baby's head such auspicious objects as pine twigs, symbolic of longevity; snake's beard, a hardy evergreen with medicinal properties; and sprigs of wild orange (*yama tachibana*) to ward off contagious disease. He then turned the head to the east and snipped off three locks, after which a nurse finished the haircut. Nakamura 1962, pp. 76–77.

The Empress's apartments, which had been abnormally bare of late, were restored to their usual shining beauty.

Rinshi was an admirable grandmother. The long-awaited birth of the Prince had filled her with satisfaction and joy, and she looked in on him at all hours of the day.

The Fiftieth Day ceremonies took place on the First of the Eleventh Month. The assembled ladies-in-waiting, attired in all the splendor that ingenuity could contrive, resembled the participants in some elegant matching game.[112] Near the Empress's seat east of the curtain-dais in the inner chamber, curtain-stands had been set up in an unbroken line between the north and south pillars. The Prince's repast had been arranged in the outer chamber to the south, and the Empress's to the west—probably the usual assortment of dishes, presented on aloeswood trays. For the Prince, there were six tiny pedestal trays, which were daintily appointed with attractive dishes, a beautiful chopstick stand depicting a beach scene,[113] and so forth.

The Empress's serving lady, Sanuki no Saishō, and her assistants were all wearing ornamental hairpins in their upswept coiffures. The Prince was to be served by Dainagon. A blind on the east was raised slightly, and the trays were brought in one after another by Ben no Naishi, Nakatsukasa no Myōbu, Tayū no Myōbu, and Chūjō, all ladies of impeccable appearance and demeanor.[114]

A daughter of Ōe Kiyomichi, the governor of Sanuki, had been in attendance at the mansion for the past several days. Her husband was Minamoto Tameyoshi, the Assistant Commander of the Left Gate Guards.[115] She was permitted to wear forbidden colors that night.

112. "The beautifully dressed ladies assembled in Her Majesty's presence looked very much like a pictorial representation of a matching game [monoawase]." *Murasaki Shikibu nikki*, p. 468. Heian monoawase assumed many forms: competitions involving artifacts (fans, pictures), competitions involving plants or flowers (wild pinks, chrysanthemums, sweet-flag roots), contests involving animal skills (cocks, songbirds, crickets), contests involving human skills (Chinese poetry, waka), etc. In every case, the appearance of the team members and their aides, and the manner in which they presented their entries, were as carefully considered as the entries themselves. See the "Picture Competition" chapter of *Genji* (2: 171–88; Seidensticker 1976, pp. 307–17). See also s.n. 16.

113. Perhaps of the type illustrated in *Ruijū zatsuyōshō*, p. 557, which shows two cranes crouching beak-to-beak on a curved, "beach-shaped" base. The chopsticks rested on the outstretched wings of the birds.

114. On Ben and Tayū, respectively, see nn. 100 and 38. Nakatsukasa, who later acted as nurse to Shōshi's second son (Go-Suzaku, r. 1036–45), is probably to be identified with Minamoto Ryūshi (a daughter of Minamoto Munetoki), apparently another wife of Fujiwara Yasumichi (n. 31). Chūjō (called Kochūjō by Murasaki Shikibu) is identified by some scholars with the woman of the same name who had been one of Princess Bishi's nurses. *Murasaki Shikibu nikki*, p. 511, s.n. 38; Hagitani 1971–73, 1: 194–97, 2: 209–10; EMZ, 2: 478.

115. She is probably the same woman as the nurse called Shō in the corresponding passage in *Murasaki Shikibu nikki* (p. 469). EMZ, 2: 478–79.

Rinshi emerged from the curtain-dais on her knees, with the baby in her arms. She was ceremoniously attired in a stenciled train and a red formal jacket, a moving expression of respect for the young Prince. Empress Shōshi was wearing a semiformal coat in sapan colors over five layers of robes in grape colors.[116]

Michinaga presented the rice cakes.

The senior nobles were seated on the veranda. They had been assigned places in the east wing as usual, but had moved closer, disposing themselves with a tipsy disregard for protocol—even Minister of the Right Akimitsu and Palace Minister Kinsue. From the direction of Michinaga's apartments, a number of magnificently attired courtiers filed in with boxes of delicacies,[117] which they arranged in a row parallel to the balustrade. When it proved difficult to make anything out by the light of the standing torches, Lesser Captain Masamichi and some other gentlemen were summoned to hold torches so that the boxes could be seen.[118] The ones destined for the Palace Table Room were all delivered that evening because a period of ritual seclusion was supposed to begin on the following day.[119]

Tadanobu, the Master of the Empress's Household, went up to the blinds to request permission for the senior nobles to enter the Empress's presence. Michinaga and the rest then took their seats, which extended from the position of honor (in the bay east of the central stairway) to the door at the corner on the east. Innumerable ladies-in-waiting were crowded inside. Approaching the row of bays in which Dainagon, Sanuki no Saishō, and Miya no Naishi were seated, the Minister of the Right pulled their curtains apart and began to flirt. He was too old for such frivolity, but one could not help being amused as he appropriated fans and cracked scandalous jokes. When Tadanobu brought him the winebowl, he sang "At the Foot

116. Grape colors (*ebizome*) are held by most scholars to have combined brown with a blue (*hanada*) lining.

117. Gifts for the guests from Michinaga. The boxes (*oribitsu*), made of thin, bent pieces of cypress, were similar in appearance to the modern *bentōbako* ("lunch box"), but of better quality. They are known to have numbered forty on this occasion. See the illustration in *Genji*, 1: 494.

118. Exterior illumination for nocturnal events was usually provided either (1) by standing torches (*tachiakashi*) made of resinous pine or bundles of reeds or bamboo—which, as their name implies, were planted in the ground—or (2) by servants holding similar devices (*taimatsu*). *Shishoku*, the torches held by Masamichi and his companions, were short taimatsu, about eighteen inches long, designed for interior use. Their tips were charred over a charcoal fire and rubbed with oil, and the grip section was paper-wrapped.

119. Whether at the Palace or at the Tsuchimikado Mansion is not clear. Since Michinaga's diary contains no entries for the next few days, the mansion seems the more likely. EMZ, 2: 482.

of Mount Miwa"[120] to delightful effect, though not at all in the usual manner.

Sanesuke, the Major Captain of the Right, went up to the east pillar of the next bay, where, instead of behaving like the others, he amused himself by counting the layers at the edges of the ladies' skirts and sleeves. He dreaded his turn at the bowl, but managed to pass it off with a conventional "Thousand Years, Ten Thousand Generations."[121] When Provisional Assistant Master Sanenari was ordered to take the bowl, he went around by the lowest seats rather than walk in front of his father, Kinsue, who was moved to drunken tears by his filial behavior. Even the ladies were impressed.

Anticipating a trying evening, Sanuki no Saishō and I[122] had agreed to steal away at the conclusion of the ceremonies. Just as we were about to leave, the eastern side of the room was invaded by a boisterous party of gentlemen—Michinaga's sons, Middle Captain Tsunefusa, and some others—and we were obliged to take refuge behind a curtain-stand. Michinaga caught sight of us and demanded a poem. The situation was so distressing and embarrassing that I could not refuse:

Ika ni ikaga	How to count them
Kazoeyarubeki	On this Fiftieth Day?
Yachitose no	So many
Amari hisashiki	The thousands of years
Kimi ga miyo o ba.	Of the young lord's life.

"Well done!" Michinaga exclaimed. After chanting the poem twice, he responded promptly:

Ashitazu no	Were ours the span
Yowai shi araba	Of the reed-dwelling crane,
Kimi ga yo no	Then might we count
Chitose no kazu mo	The thousands of years
Kazoetoriten.	In store for this lord.[123]

A man in his condition could not have produced such a ready reply unless the subject had been very much on his mind.

After the distribution of the customary rewards, Michinaga headed un-

120. See s.n. 72.

121. "Chitose yorozuyo." Probably a reference to a sacred music song (*kagurauta*), "Senzai no hō," in which the two choruses alternately chant phrases consisting almost exclusively of those two words. EMZ, 2: 484; Tsuchihashi and Konishi 1960, p. 331.

122. See the Introduction, pp. 58–61.　　123. The crane was said to live 1,000 years.

steadily inside. "It's no disgrace for me that the Empress is my daughter, and it does her no harm that I am her father," he said. "The Empress's mother is lucky too—she has such an excellent husband!" Rinshi left the room, embarrassed by his attempts at humor.

Empress Shōshi was to reenter the Palace on the Seventeenth, and once again her attendants were swept up in a whirl of preparation. On the appointed night, the ladies assembled at the mansion, including those who had been home on leave—more than forty in all, some with their hair dressed in formal coiffures. The hour grew late, and the departure took on a rather hectic complexion, with much argument about who was to ride in what carriage. Michinaga put an end to the discussion. "Established usage is to be followed. I shall allow no exceptions," he said. Lady Senji shared the Empress's litter.[124] Rinshi rode in a string-decorated carriage with the nurse Shō, who held the infant Prince in her arms. There were other conveyances following along behind, but it would be tedious to list them all.

The next morning, the Empress was at last free to examine the presents she had received from Michinaga the night before. They included a pair of comb boxes, the contents of which promised to be an inexhaustible source of wonder. There was also a pair of hand boxes, one of them filled with three poetic anthologies, *Early and Modern Times, Later Collection,* and *Gleanings,* each in five four-chapter volumes on white paper, with calligraphy by Yukinari and Enkan.[125] In the second box, there were copies of the private collections of early poets like Motosuke and Yoshinobu.[126]

124. She is to be distinguished from the Lady Senji in Senshi's service. Shōshi's Lady Senji was a daughter of Minamoto Koretaka (937–95), a grandson of Emperor Daigo who held the office of Middle Counselor with Senior Third Rank at the time of his death. Her given name appears to have been Chokushi. Hagitani 1971–73, 2: 19–20; *Sonpi bunmyaku,* 3: 461; *Kugyō bunin,* 1: 241; EMZ, 4: 42.

125. Hand boxes (*tebako*) were leather or lacquered tiered receptacles, about a foot long and eight inches wide, used as containers for everyday articles such as incense, cosmetics, toilet items, and calligraphy practice materials. The three anthologies, designated by the author in abbreviated form as *Kokin, Gosen,* and *Shūi,* were the first Imperial Japanese anthology (*chokusenshū*), *Kokinshū;* the second, *Gosenshū;* and either the third, *Shūishū* (ca. 1005) or Fujiwara Kintō's *Shūishō* (ca. 997), the smaller collection on which *Shūishū* was based. During the Heian period, Kintō's work was the more frequently copied. On Yukinari, see s.n. 28. He was a Consultant at the time. The other calligrapher, Enkan, a greatgrandson of Emperor Yōzei (868–949), was a monk who served as Hōryūji abbot. EM, 1: 273, n. 51, 1: 467.

126. In their day, both Kiyowara Motosuke (908–90) and Ōnakatomi Yoshinobu (921?–91) were highly regarded literati and poets. Both served on the *Gosenshū* compilation committee, both were on excellent terms with the Fujiwara leaders, and both were closely related

A few days later, on the Twentieth, the Gosechi dancers arrived at the Palace.[127] Empress Shōshi had given a costume to the girl presented by the Gentleman-in-waiting Consultant (a title that seems to have referred to Consultant Sanenari, the son of the Palace Minister). Another sponsor, Consultant Middle Captain Kanetaka, had asked the Empress for cord pendants, and she had sent along a set, accompanied by some incense balls, which were arranged in a pair of boxes decorated with artificial plum blossoms.[128]

From all accounts, the competition to turn out the best dancer had been unusually brisk that year. The girls came walking along with great aplomb, clearly visible in the light from a long row of torches that had been set close together near the temporary lattice screens masking the Empress's apartments on the east. Their behavior seemed ill-bred, but I suppose they were simply making the best of an awkward situation, since there was no other route for them to take.[129] Everyone commented on the brocade jackets worn by the ladies attending Naritō's dancer; they were a refreshing innovation, it was agreed, and showed excellent taste.[130] (Some objected that the ladies looked ungraceful—the result, they said, of wearing too many

---

to important woman writers. Motosuke was the father of Sei Shōnagon; Yoshinobu, the grandfather of Ise no Tayū (987?–1063?), who was one of the ornaments of Shōshi's literary salon.

127. The four sponsors, who figure in the following account, were (1) Fujiwara Nakakiyo, governor of Owari and nephew of Murasaki Shikibu's grandfather; (2) Takashina Naritō (d. 1010), governor of Tanba and Provisional Assistant Master of the Crown Prince's Household; (3) Fujiwara Kanetaka, Consultant, Middle Captain of the Right, and son of the Late Regent Michikane; and (4) Fujiwara Sanenari, Consultant, Provisional Assistant Master of Empress Shōshi's Household, and son of Palace Minister Kinsue. EMZ, 2: 497. The Twentieth was a Day of the Ox.

128. High-ranking friends, relatives, and patrons were usually expected to assist the sponsors in outfitting the dancers, in providing them with transportation, etc. "Cord pendants" translates [hikage no] kazura, a term used in the Heian period to refer to long white or green braided cords made of silk or paper-mulberry bark, four of which were suspended as ornaments from either side of a Gosechi dancer's head. The incense boxes were presumably decorated with the small sprays of artificial plum (kokoroba) that were also used as hat or hair ornaments by certain participants in the Thanksgiving and First Fruits services. Incense was an appropriate gift because caring for the incense burners was one of the tasks assigned to the dancers' girl attendants (warawa). Genji, 4: 531; EMZ, 2: 497; Morris 1967, 1: 94.

129. The dancers were arriving at the Ichijō Palace (the Imperial residence) for the Curtain-Dais Rehearsal, an event that probably took place in the east wing. They seem to have reached their destination by walking past apartments assigned to Shōshi and her ladies in the east section of the main building. The source of their difficulty was the presence of the Emperor and some other gentlemen, who had come to the east side of the building to watch the procession. EMZ, 2: 498; Murasaki Shikibu nikki, p. 478. A properly reared young woman was expected to do everything possible to avoid masculine eyes.

130. Murasaki remarks in her diary, p. 477, that they were attractive because they stood out in the darkness.

robes—but such criticism is old-fashioned.) Kanetaka's dancer and her entourage had also been fitted out with great care. Unfortunately, the countrified appearance of the two elaborately costumed scrub girls[131] provoked smiles among the spectators. Sanenari's group was perhaps the most modish. Seated behind the lowered blinds of the outermost chamber,[132] his ten ladies allowed only a glimpse of billowing skirts in the lamplight, and thus they managed to be far more impressive and elegant than others who made a point of displaying their finery in public.

The Empress presented huge silver boxes, filled with incense balls, to the dancer sponsored by the Master of the Crown Prince's Household, and Rinshi gave incense to the protégée of Masahira, the governor of Owari.[133]

After the Imperial Rehearsal that night, the Court looked forward eagerly to the Viewing of the Girl Attendants and maids.[134] When the time came and the procession began, everyone inside and outside the blinds watched with great excitement. The Emperor was present, and the infant Prince had also been brought in, so there were rice-throwers to add to the commotion.[135]

Naritō's little girls made an agreeable impression in trailing robes of olive gray, but Sanenari achieved a truly enviable color contrast by dressing the children in brown trailing robes and the maids in green Chinese jackets. Kanetaka's group wore trailing robes in sets of five; Nakakiyo's, grape colors in sets of three. The shades of the inner garments, which had been left to the discretion of the wearers, varied from pale to deep.

Since the room assigned to Sanenari's dancer was directly across from the Empress's quarters,[136] the edges of its blinds were visible above the temporary lattice screens, and the voices of the occupants were faintly

131. Latrine cleaners; two of the dancer's attendant servants.

132. Of the east wing. In order to view the dancing, the members of the Court had proceeded to the east wing and the adjacent corridors.

133. "Master of the Crown Prince's Household" should read "Provisional Assistant Master of the Crown Prince's Household," the title held by Naritō; "Masahira" should read "Nakakiyo." (Ōe Masahira, the literatus who was Akazome Emon's husband, had served earlier as governor of Owari.)

134. The Imperial Rehearsal (gozen no kokoromi) took place on the evening of the Day of the Tiger, not on the Day of the Hare, as the reader is led to believe by an unskillful cutting of the Diary. The Viewing of the Girl Attendants (warawa goran) took place a day later, on the Day of the Hare.

135. According to Murasaki's diary, p. 478, the Prince was present for the gozen no kokoromi the night before, rather than for this event. The purpose of the rice-throwing was to keep evil spirits away from the baby.

136. The Empress was probably staying in the eastern section of the main building; Sanenari's dancer, in the western part of the east wing.

audible. The Empress's people heard indirectly that Sakyō, one of the Kokiden Consort's ladies-in-waiting, was among the attendants looking after the dancer.[137] "How sad for her to be sitting in the background, watching the Court life she once knew so well! It would not be right to ignore her. We must send a message," they decided. "Which of the attendants was she in this evening's ceremony?" they asked. Tsunefusa and Narimasa both replied that she had been the one "over there." Someone added that she was still quite pretty, and so they rummaged through the Empress's fans until they found one decorated with a view of P'eng-lai.[138] They spread it on the lid of a box, gave it a border of coiled cord pendants, worked in an attractive array of mother-of-pearl combs and face powder, and sent it off by a person who was little known at Court, instructing her to leave it with the message that it was "for Lady Sakyō from Lady Chūnagon's room."[139] Just as they had hoped, the manner in which Sakyō's people said "Bring the gift inside" showed that their mistress thought it had come from the consort. The stratagem was a success. A poem was sent with an incense ball in a twisted letter:[140]

Okarishi	Among the courtly throng
Toyo no miyabito	At the Toyonoakari Banquet,
Sashiwakete	Your cord pendants
Shiruki hikage o	Stood out from the rest,
Aware to zo mishi.	Moving us deeply as we watched.

Sakyō was much embarrassed by the incident,[141] and Sanenari also felt that it would have been better for her if her presence had passed unnoticed. On the night when the Smaller Purification Tunics were worn,[142] Sane-

137. The Kokiden Consort was Sanenari's sister Gishi, who had become a Nyōgo in 996. The point here is that Sakyō, no longer in the consort's service, had suffered a humiliating loss of status.

138. In Murasaki's diary, pp. 480–82, it is clear that Shōshi's young ladies are using the picture of the legendary Chinese island of immortality to make fun of an aging former rival, but the attitude of the *Eiga* author is ambivalent, as is shown by her insertion of the sentence beginning "How sad . . . " and by her deletion of the malicious comments recorded by Murasaki. EMZ, 2: 506–7. See the Introduction, p. 55.

139. Chūnagon was probably one of Gishi's ladies. The idea was to make Sakyō think that she was receiving a present from the consort, her former mistress.

140. This sentence approximates the ambiguity of the original, which seems to be the result of a careless editing of the *Diary*. Murasaki, p. 481, says that the incense was among the gifts on the box lid. The formal communication known as a twisted letter (*tatebumi*) consisted of two parts: a strip of paper bearing a poem or other message, and a narrow outer envelope made of white paper, folded lengthwise, and twisted and bent at both ends.

141. Since Shōshi was the only consort present at the dances, it was apparent that the poem had come from her apartments, and that Sakyō's presence had been the subject of comment there.

142. The night of the Toyonoakari Banquet, the event at which the Gosechi dances were

nari's girl attendants and older ladies all appeared in green-and-white robes trimmed with red cords. Later, the Kamo Virgin heard about the conceit, found it amusing, and asked to see one of the costumes, which she pronounced very smart. She sent back the robe with a poem attached to the sleeve, scribbled on the edge of a sheet of green paper:[143]

Kamiyo yori	Rare indeed
Sureru koromo to	This manifold wearing
Iinagara	Of robes
Mata kasanete mo	Printed in green
Mezurashiki kana.	Since the age of the gods.

Soon it was time for the Kamo Special Festival. Michinaga's son Norimichi, the Provisional Middle Captain, was to serve as Imperial Messenger.[144] It chanced that the Court was to be in ritual seclusion on the festival date, and thus Michinaga, the other senior nobles, and the dancers all spent the preceding night in the Palace, whiling away the hours with gay and stylish pastimes.[145] Rinshi was present with Myōbu, Norimichi's nurse, who had no eyes for the amusing activities around her—or indeed for anything at all except the Messenger.[146]

It was on the same festival day that one of Sanenari's Escorts came up to one of Norimichi's, handed him the box lid that Shōshi's ladies had sent to Sakyō, and went off again. The lid held a silver mirror, an aloeswood comb, and a silver hair stick—all articles intended for the Messenger's use

---

formally presented. Young noblemen, selected by divination to offer food to the gods on the Day of the Hare, wore Smaller Purification Tunics (omi) both during the rituals on the Day of the Hare and during the banquet. The tunics, worn over the regular Court robes, were white unlined garments imprinted with green designs depicting plum blossoms, willows, birds, butterflies, etc., and trimmed with two red cords hanging down in front of the left shoulder. Cord pendants and kokoroba (n. 128 above) completed the costume. (The name omi referred to the relatively narrow cut of the garments, as compared with those worn by certain other participants in the Great Thanksgiving and First Fruits services, rather than to the extent of the preliminary purification required. The prescribed purification procedures were in fact extremely rigorous.)

143. The color of the paper was an allusion to the omi tunics. The Virgin was Emperor Murakami's daughter Senshi, then in her thirty-fourth year of service.

144. In 1008, the Kamo Special Festival took place on the Twenty-eighth of the Eleventh Month, five days after the Toyonoakari Banquet. Norimichi was twelve years old.

145. In order to participate in a Court ceremony held while the Emperor was observing ritual seclusion, kugyō and others were obliged to spend the preceding night at the Palace. EMZ, 2: 510. For the events preliminary to the Kamo Special Festival, see s.n. 50.

146. An inept abridgment of Murasaki Shikibu nikki. Rinshi and the nurse came to the Palace on the morning of the festival to watch the departure ceremonies. The nurse, identified in Murasaki's diary as Kura no Myōbu, was a subordinate wife of Ōnakatomi Sukechika (954–1038), the son of Yoshinobu. Murasaki Shikibu nikki, p. 483; p. 511, s.n. 23. Like Yoshinobu, whom he succeeded as Chief Priest of the Ise Grand Shrines, Sukechika was a prominent poet of the day.

in dressing his side hair. The inside bore a poem that was probably a reply to the earlier one, traced in reed-script characters of gold:[147]

Hikagegusa	Gazing at the brilliant throng
Kagayaku hodo ya	Of sun-bright pendants,
Magaiken	You were perhaps bemused,
Masumi no kagami	But my mind is unclouded
Kumoranu mono o.	As a limpid mirror.[148]

The Twelfth Month arrived, bringing with it the poignant realization that little of the calendar remained, and then the year drew to a close amid talk of the ephemerality of human existence—a span scarcely less brief, as many said, than the life of a flower or a butterfly.

Although little Prince Atsuhira was a fine baby, as beautiful as the full moon rising over the hills, his birth had been a painful shock for Korechika and his associates. To Korechika, it had meant nothing less than the end of all the secret hopes he had cherished so long. "I am fated, it seems," he thought miserably, "to be a perpetual butt of ridicule in this life. What a cruel blow! After that marvelous dream,[149] I was sure everything would turn out well in the end. 'For ordinary people,' as the saying goes, 'results are what count.' I have made it a habit to observe dietary purity, practice ritual seclusion, and pray earnestly to the gods and buddhas. And now this seems to be my reward." He consulted with his uncles Akinobu and Michinobu. "If I just go on hoping for something that will never happen, I shall simply subject myself to humiliation. I might as well be dead. What am I to do?" he asked.

"What you say is all too true," they answered gloomily, "but you can do nothing to change matters. We can only resolve not to give up hope as long as you are still alive." They wept as they spoke, and Korechika responded in a pathetic voice, "I know well enough that it makes no sense to go on thoughtlessly accumulating adverse karma in this way.[150] For a

147. The toilet articles were probably presented for use en route to the shrines. Hair sticks (kōgai) were long, narrow objects resembling flattened chopsticks, usually made of ivory or silver, that were used as hairdressing aids by both men and women. Their exact function is no longer understood. Reed script (ashide, ashidegaki) was an eccentric calligraphic style sometimes employed for the transcription of poetry. The characters, distorted to resemble natural objects, were incorporated into water-margin scenes depicting birds, reeds, rocks, etc.

148. "I am afraid you made a mistake the other night. The one who stood out was not I. But there is no mistake about this gift of a mirror; it is definitely intended for the Messenger." (Hikagegusa is another term for hikage no kazura.) Here ends the connection with Murasaki Shikibu nikki.

149. Unidentified. Probably an auspicious dream of his own, although the author may be alluding to Naritada's dream described in Chapter 5.

150. By concerning himself with worldly things.

man who understands the principle of cause and effect, it is foolish to cling to worldly ambitions. I have, of course, considered the possibility of becoming a monk and devoting my few remaining years to pious works that would help me in the next life. But a man who lacks a religious vocation is unlikely to succeed in casting off secular concerns by retiring to some forested mountain, intoning sutras, and living an ascetic's life. Buddha-invocations and chanting will do no good, I am sure, if I am still caught up in a host of worldly entanglements. That is why I have not been able to take the step."

Takaie and Bishop Ryūen agreed that the prospects were hopeless, but they refused to dwell on the matter, and actually seemed quite cheerful. They were less pitiful than Korechika, who seemed doomed to perpetual mental turmoil.

With the passing of the old year, the sixth year of Kankō [1009] began. There were the usual New Year events.

Prince Atsuhira was developing into a lovable little boy. One day, as Emperor Ichijō and Empress Shōshi were playing with him, the Emperor commented on the old custom that had kept small children out of the Palace, regardless of the Imperial desires. "To think that Princes and Princesses as delightful as this were not shown at Court until they were five or seven years old! Nowadays, one feels that nothing could be harder to bear. I never tire of this baby, no matter how often I see him, and I would be wretched indeed if he were not here—if I could be with him only in my thoughts. It was a very long time before I saw my oldest son, Prince Atsuyasu. When people talked to me about him, I used to be quite wild with impatience." His remarks showed admirable feeling.

Meanwhile, the First Month drew to a close. Except for a light trace around the Twentieth of the Twelfth Month, Empress Shōshi's periods had shown no sign of returning. It had something to do, she supposed innocently, with the birth of Prince Atsuhira. But then she began to suffer from the very ailments that had plagued her during the same season a year ago. Could it be that she was pregnant again? Some of her ladies were already whispering that this must be the case. Others objected that it was too early, to which still others retorted that it was common enough for one pregnancy to follow on the heels of another. After the long wait for the first child,[151] how splendid if he were to be joined immediately by a second!

Michinaga and Rinshi were delighted.

151. Ten years.

With the arrival of the Third Month, it became certain that the Empress was to bear a child. Michinaga's happiness was beyond description.

When the news leaked out, it was a source of great embarrassment to the other consorts who had been with the Emperor for years. Akimitsu and Kinsue, the ladies' fathers, must have felt ill-used indeed. After all, they probably reasoned, they belonged to the house of Fujiwara too; their misfortune could only be the result of a peculiarly inauspicious karma.

Although Shōshi had planned to leave the Palace toward the end of the Third Month, she stayed on for a time in deference to the Emperor's wishes.

Meanwhile, Michinaga's son Yorimichi had become Commander of the Left Gate Guards.

Since Michinaga was anxious to begin prayers at the mansion, Shōshi left the Palace around the middle of the Fourth Month. Concerned about her safety and lonesome for the baby, the Emperor lapsed into a state of depression.

At the Tsuchimikado Mansion, the young Prince was greeted joyfully by Kenshi, who had been awaiting his arrival with great eagerness. She carried him everywhere in her arms, leaving the nurses nothing to do beyond giving him the breast, a state of affairs they found much to their liking.

As before, every possible prayer was recited for the Empress. There was now a precedent for everything, and the same monks were charged with offering the same prayers, which they proceeded to do in exactly the same manner. Although the sex of the child was a matter of less importance than before, people must have felt that it would be immensely reassuring if Shōshi were to give birth to a second son, and it seems fairly certain that prayers for a boy were offered.

Shi no Kimi had moved into the Takatsukasa Mansion[152] after ex-Emperor Kazan's death. Michinaga felt that she would make a pleasant mistress, but she put him off, apparently unable to reach a decision, even though Rinshi also sent her various messages.

Meanwhile, a number of important gentlemen were showing themselves anxious to have Yorimichi as a son-in-law. Before anything was decided, there was an overture from Prince Tomohira on behalf of his daughter

---

152. The house where she had lived with her sister, the Lady of the Central Hall (Tamemitsu's third daughter), after turning over the Ichijō Mansion to Senshi. Kazan had probably taken her from there to his own residence.

Takahime.[153] The Prince, known as the Central Affairs Prince from Ro-kujō,[154] was the seventh son of a former sovereign, Emperor Murakami. His mother was Princess Sōshi, the Reikeiden Consort, and his principal wife was a daughter of the same Emperor's fourth son, Prince Tamehira, by a daughter of Minamoto Takaakira. The couple were the parents of three daughters and two sons.[155] Takahime had been reared with great care, and her lineage on both sides was beyond reproach.

Prince Tomohira was a man of extraordinary character. Impressively learned, he had gone so far as to acquire remarkable proficiency even in medicine and the yin-yang arts; he composed poetry of distinction in both Chinese and Japanese; and his superbly polished manners made others keenly aware of their own inadequacies. That he should condescend to think of Yorimichi was the greatest of honors, Michinaga declared, and he accepted the proposal with every mark of respect. "A man's career depends on his wife's family," he told Yorimichi. "The standing of that house is very high indeed; I think you cannot do better than to marry into it." Quiet preparations began, and the date of the wedding drew near.

As a matter of fact, Prince Tomohira had originally intended to present Takahime at Court as an Imperial bride, but for some reason—perhaps through the workings of karma—he had decided to give her to Yorimichi instead.

The nuptial ceremonies were conducted in the most up-to-date manner. There were twenty ladies-in-waiting, four girl attendants, and four maids; and all the arrangements were tasteful and elegant. Even the incense was not the sort of thing we use nowadays, but a marvelous concoction that made one wonder if it might not be the fragrant-robe scent so highly prized by our ancestors.[156] Takahime was fifteen or sixteen, with hair that seemed to Yorimichi very much like Kenshi's. He can have felt little doubt about her beauty.[157] Prince Tomohira appeared to be in excellent spirits.

153. Little is known of Takahime beyond what is stated in the text. She became Yorimichi's principal wife and ultimately held Junior First Rank.

154. The Prince's house, the Chigusa Mansion, stood east of Nishinotōin in the vicinity of Rokujō Bōmon. EMZ, 2: 530, 531.

155. Prince Tomohira's principal wife (and cousin) was called Nakahimegimi. On their children, see s.n. 73.

156. "Fragrant-robe scent" translates *kunoekō*, a famous old blend of Indian and Chinese incense herbs, cloves, aloeswood, musk, sandalwood, amber, and other ingredients, used for perfuming garments. The recipe had been lost before Michinaga's day. Ikeda 1967, pp. 279–80; EM, 1: 281, n. 27.

157. This presumably means that he could feel the texture and length of her hair in the dark, but could not see her face.

For the wedding banquet[158] a few days later, every member of Yorimichi's retinue was personally selected by Michinaga. The ceremonies in
the evening went off without a flaw. It would probably be wrong to attribute Yorimichi's ardor and the magnificence of his attire solely to the
bride's rank and lineage, but the match was undeniably a brilliant one.

Prince Tomohira considered the marriage a great success. To spare Yorimichi the necessity of constantly journeying to and from Rokujō, he decided to build the newlyweds a house in the upper city—for it was quite
possible, he feared, that the boy might otherwise encounter the demon
procession some night.[159]

With Takahime's future settled, the Prince felt he could now gratify
his old desire to enter holy orders. He was an imposing figure on every
occasion, and the Court had always sought his participation in the great
ceremonies and festivals, but he had never really been interested in such
things. It was all most regrettable.

With the time for Kenshi's presentation to the Crown Prince drawing
near, Michinaga was making the necessary preparations. Seishi received
the news in silence. She had long regarded the marriage as inevitable; the
only surprising thing was that it had not happened sooner. Her ladies expressed amazement at her lack of concern, but she made light of the matter and kept her unhappiness to herself. Her life henceforth must be devoted
to her children, she felt, and to such religious devotions as she could find
the leisure to undertake. To make a big fuss would simply put the Crown
Prince in a painful position; the sooner Kenshi came, the better. Of course,

158. *Tokoroarawashi.* In contrast to the private ceremonies on the first two nights of a
marriage, the tokoroarawashi publicly announced the man's acceptance by his wife's family
and the beginning of his residence in their house. It was preceded by a ceremony known as
the Third-night Rice Cakes (*mika no yo no mochii* or *mika no mochii*), so called because
it usually, although by no means invariably, took place on the third night of the marriage.
Rice cakes were served to the couple inside the bed curtains by the bride's mother or some other
senior family member, who thus symbolically discovered the groom and, by making him eat
food cooked over the family fire, incorporated him into the household. After eating at least
three of the cakes, the bridegroom put on a costume prepared by the family, and emerged for
his first formal meeting with his parents-in-law and other new relatives (who, in some
cases, saw him for the first time), an event that was accompanied by an elaborate banquet.
Meanwhile, his attendants were feasted and given presents in another part of the establishment. Nakamura 1962, pp. 162–68; Takamure 1966, 2:414–15; *Genji*, 5: 64; Seidensticker
1976, p. 903. See also Chapter 13, below.

159. The upper city was the area north of Nijō Avenue. The new house would have been
in the general area of Yorimichi's own residence at Tsuchimikado (on which see EMZ, 2:
547). The demon procession ([*hyakki*] *yagyō*), made up of various kinds of ghosts and
goblins, was believed to travel through the city on specified nights. For the famous story of
Morosuke's encounter with it, see *Ōkagami*, p. 127.

it was beyond her power to prevent the marriage, but nevertheless she behaved very well. An ordinary woman, even one of negligible status, would have been sure to annoy everyone with a flood of jealous complaints.

For Michinaga, preoccupied with the anxieties caused by Shōshi's condition, autumn arrived with astonishing speed. Since the child had been conceived in the Second Month, the birth was expected in the Eleventh, and there were so many thing to be done that he decided to let Kenshi's presentation wait until winter.

Around that time, there were numerous unpleasant reports of curses against the new Prince, invoked, it was said, by someone in Korechika's circle. Although the stories were probably false, they led to unfortunate results for Korechika, whose life became wretched indeed. Michinaga summoned Akinobu, the presumed author of the curses, and read him a lecture.[160] "You must not harbor such wicked designs. Prince Atsuhira is young, but the Four Heavenly Kings[161] are certain to protect anyone with his august karma. Curses can't even kill ordinary people like us, so how could they affect a child as blessed by fortune as the Prince? If you and your people have tried anything of the sort, you will be punished by Heaven. There will be no need for me to pass judgment on you," he told him. Akinobu retired with a respectful bow, too frightened and humiliated to speak in his own defense. Soon afterward, he fell ill, and within five or six days he breathed his last.

All of this made Korechika keep to himself more than ever. In the face of the incessant gossip about Akinobu's sudden death, he felt that life had become unendurable. He was feeling ill—a result, perhaps, of his depressed spirits and constant mental turmoil—but the indisposition, instead of destroying his appetite, seemed to make him gobble up great quantities of food. It was a strange departure from his customary behavior, and one that excited the gravest fears in his wife and Takaie.

During his semiretirement in recent years, Korechika had copied out each of the anthologies—*Early and Modern Times, Later Collection,* and

160. Other sources describe the discovery (late in the First Month of 1009, rather than in the autumn) of a written curse directed against Shōshi, Prince Atsuhira, and Michinaga, and the subsequent condemnation to death of a number of persons, most of them related to Korechika by blood or marriage. Korechika himself, although apparently not directly involved, was forbidden to appear at Court. Aside from this passage, there is no evidence that Akinobu was implicated. EMZ, 2: 536–38.

161. Jikokuten (Skt. Dhṛtarāṣṭra), Zōjōten (Virūḍhaka), Kōmokuten (Virūpākṣa), and Tamon (Vaiśravaṇa), warlike servants of Indra. They are believed by Buddhists to dwell, respectively, on the east, south, west, and north sides of Mount Sumeru, and to protect the faithful in the corresponding areas of the earth. Their menacing images frequently appear as a group in Japanese temples.

Gleanings. This feat was another indication of the immense erudition that set him apart from ordinary men.

Meanwhile, the esoteric rites, sutra-readings, prayers, and minor preparations for the Empress's delivery were all going forward in strict conformance to the precedents established earlier. Her pains began on the Twenty-fifth of the Eleventh Month, and the deafening shouts of the monks again resounded through the mansion. This time, there was no sign of any malignant spirit (a proof, one may suppose, of the efficacy of prayer), and the birth took place quickly and easily.[162] The one remaining worry, the afterbirth, was soon out of the way. And as though all that were not sufficient cause for rejoicing, the new arrival was a boy, a splendid infant in every way the equal of his brother. To Michinaga and the others, such astonishing good fortune was almost beyond belief.

The Emperor sent a sword as soon as he heard the news.

Everything was done in accordance with the precedents established after Prince Atsuhira's birth. The white robes worn by the ladies were winter costumes of gorgeous Chinese damask and bound- and float-patterned bombycine. Even the trousers were white—an admirable notion, since the total effect, by suggesting the dazzling plumage of a flock of cranes, hinted at a thousand years of life for the new Prince.[163] I shall not trouble you with an account of the bathing ceremonies, which followed the same pattern as before, with the same Professor. They were indescribably splendid, and the ceremonies on the Third, Fifth, and Seventh nights were even more magnificent than the earlier ones, because everyone was now accustomed to the rituals, and nothing was omitted.

Korechika had recently developed a persistent thirst. He was also consuming astonishing quantities of food, but, strangely, he had lost so much weight that he scarcely seemed the same person.[164] His health was miserable. How was it, he fretted, that someone who had always been exceedingly fat, even while observing religious dietary restrictions, could be reduced to skin and bones after returning to ordinary fare? Naturally enough, the uncertainty of Matsugimi's future was his great and overriding concern, the source of many painful reflections. It was small wonder that he lamented his changed circumstances.

Emperor Ichijō, lonesome for Prince Atsuhira and anxious to see the

---

162. Prince Atsunaga (1009–45), the future Emperor Go-Suzaku. He was named Crown Prince in 1022 and took the throne in 1036.

163. Trousers (*hakama*) were usually red. The crane was a symbol of longevity.

164. He is believed to have suffered from diabetes, the disease of which his father, Michitaka, had died.

new baby, insisted on the Empress's joining him as soon as possible. Since the Imperial Palace had burned, he was in temporary quarters. Crown Prince Okisada was staying at the Biwa Mansion.[165]

With the coming of the Twelfth Month, it was time for Kenshi's marriage to the Crown Prince.[166] The presentation, which had been so long in the planning, was carried out with spectacular magnificence. Indeed, it made one realize what an extravagant place the world had become. The wives and daughters of the senior gentlemen in Michinaga's service all assembled at the mansion to accompany the bride, whose retinue included forty ladies, six girl attendants, and four maids.

A long description of Kenshi's appearance would impress the reader as tiresomely familiar and repetitious, I fear, but it seems a pity to write nothing at all. She was sixteen, and her hair, even richer and more abundant than the elegant tresses of her sisters, shone with an almost theatrical beauty. The delighted Crown Prince treated her with the utmost consideration.

Life at the Crown Prince's palace must have been gayer and more fashionable after Kenshi's arrival. People had talked about "radiant Fujitsubo" when Empress Shōshi had first entered the Imperial Palace, but I could not possibly describe the splendor of even the most trifling of Kenshi's belongings. When one considers that ten years had elapsed since Shōshi's marriage, each bringing its own changes, it is not difficult to imagine the degree of luxury that had been attained.

Crown Prince Okisada treated Kenshi with a gracious consideration that she found rather embarrassing, coming as it did from one so much older.[167] Confronted with this slip of a girl after his many years of devotion to Seishi, the Prince had felt at first as though one of his own daughters had been installed at his side, but he was wholly enchanted as the days passed and he came to know her. He called her to his bedchamber by night, and during the daytime he visited her in her apartments, where he set out her belongings, inspected them one by one, and marveled at their beauty. Needless to say, he was particularly fascinated by the articles from the trays

165. A misleading passage. Imperial Palace here means not the Dairi but the Ichijōin, which burned in the Tenth Month of 1009. Various sources indicate that the Emperor moved to the Biwa Mansion on the Nineteenth of the Tenth Month, shortly after the fire. The Crown Prince, who had been living at the Biwa Mansion for some time, had gone elsewhere on the Fourteenth to make way for the Emperor. It was therefore Emperor Ichijō, not the Crown Prince, who was living at Biwa at the time of Prince Atsunaga's birth. EMZ, 2: 546–47.

166. The marriage seems rather to have taken place in the Second Month of the following year, Kankō 7 (1010). EMZ, 2: 547.

167. The Crown Prince, thirty-three in 1009, was eighteen years older than Kenshi.

and the tiny containers inside her comb boxes, which had been supplied by her mother and brothers in a spirit of keen rivalry. (Shōshi's wedding things, incidentally, seem to have been provided in the same way.)

Prince Okisada's other wife, Seishi, had inherited a pair of gold-lacquered comb boxes, made for an earlier Sen'yōden Consort by order of that lady's husband, Emperor Murakami.[168] The Prince had always liked nothing better than to examine their contents, but now they struck him as distinctly old-fashioned in comparison with Kenshi's. Emperor Murakami, who had better taste than any other sovereign, had personally supervised the creation of the articles in question, instructing the Office of Palace Works by word and by brush,[169] and sending back whatever failed to meet his standards. Yet to Prince Okisada, Kenshi's boxes appeared incomparable. His preference might, he knew, simply reflect the changed tastes of his time, but he remained convinced of their superiority, which seemed to him still another illustration of Michinaga's astonishing faculty for doing things well.

Seishi's folding screens were splendid works of art from the brushes of Tameuji and Tsunenori, with calligraphy by Michikaze himself on the colored-paper sections;[170] and they were as clean and bright as new, in spite of their age. Kenshi's were the work of Hirotaka, with calligraphy in what appeared to be Yukinari's hand. Confessing himself unable to choose between them, the Prince appealed to Michinaga and Yorimichi, who felt embarrassed and very much on their mettle in dealing with so mature, discriminating, and sophisticated a critic.

Magnificently attired in bombycine jackets and trains decorated with dramatic marine designs, Kenshi's bevies of ladies sat in groups, hiding their faces behind fans, whispering, and uttering mysterious laughs. They seemed a bit overwhelming to the Crown Prince, who was never quite at ease during his visits.

Seishi took care of the Prince's wardrobe, contriving elegant color effects and scents for even the least of his garments. There is a special air about any Emperor or Crown Prince, however young and childish, but

---

168. The author refers to Seishi's aunt Hōshi. The boxes had probably come to Seishi through her father, Naritoki, who was Hōshi's brother.

169. I.e. by drawing pictures.

170. *Shikishigata* (literally, "colored-paper shapes"). In the Heian period, the term *shikishi* (now a square "poem card") seems to have meant any piece of paper, regardless of color, shape, or size, that was designed primarily for use in recording poetry. Shikishigata were sometimes pasted or drawn on the surfaces of folding screens and sliding doors, where they served a similar purpose. The famous painters Tameuji (surname unknown) and Asukabe Tsunenori flourished around the middle of the tenth century. Tsunenori's name appears in the "Suma" chapter of *Genji* (2: 39; Seidensticker 1976, p. 237). On Michikaze, see Chapter 1, n. 163.

Prince Okisada's maturity, dignity, and refinement inspired a profound sense of awe in those who saw him. Kenshi put the other consorts in the shade with the exquisite sleeves and skirts that lent distinction to her most casual costume. Michinaga, it was clear, kept her amply supplied with beautiful robes.

"How do you feel about it all? Is your sleep troubled?" Seishi's attendants and others asked her. "The marriage ought to have taken place years ago," she answered. "I grieved for the Crown Prince because of the delay, and now that it has finally happened I am much relieved." She worked early and late on the Prince's elegant costumes, and saw to it that he received incense balls whenever she made new ones. It seems natural that he should have thought of her as a mother.[171]

Rinshi went back and forth on frequent visits to Shōshi and Kenshi, a state of affairs that was also just what one would have desired.

With the passing of winter, the seventh year of Kankō [1010] began. The usual ceremonies took place.

The advent of the new year brought a grave worsening of Korechika's condition, making it seem that the end might come at any time. Since every possible remedy had been tried during the past months, the despairing sufferer was at his wit's ends. He had been given ministerial grants two years earlier, and his situation would have been less pitiful if the local governors had been reliable and prompt in forwarding the revenues. When he had sunk very low, he summoned Lesser Captain Michimasa and the two girls, seated them in a row, and tearfully addressed his wife.

"I wonder how you will behave after I am gone. I have taken the greatest pains with the girls' education, because I have always felt I could somehow find a way to make them Imperial consorts if I lived—but what will they do now that I am to die? These days, it seems, even the daughters of Emperors and Chancellors are going into the service of Imperial personages as ladies-in-waiting, and no doubt many people will be after these two, but I shall be eternally disgraced if you allow them to get involved in any such arrangements. If one of them is talked into becoming the bride of some Prince or other gentleman, people will say the man has married her at my insistence, or because he knew I worried about her. You will never be able to give them the necessary support by yourself. If only I had asked the gods and buddhas to let them die before me! We can't even make nuns of them unless we want to be called mad—to say nothing of the very distinct possibility of their both winding up as com-

171. She was three years his senior.

panions to renegade monks. What a terrible pass we have reached! But be sure you will feel my anger if you make me a laughingstock after I am gone. Never dishonor my memory; never give others cause to laugh at me," he said.

Need I say that his bewildered daughters burst into tears? His wife sobbed brokenly, unable to reply.

"Although you have been dearest of all to me," Korechika resumed, speaking now to his son, the Lesser Captain, "I must leave you in your present inferior rank. What will you do when I am gone? Since you have character, I don't think this will end your career, but I can't help worrying about how you will make your way. Pay attention to what I say. Life may be hard, and you may begin to resent your low office and wish to be the equal of others, but I shall not allow you to remain alive for a fraction of an hour if you adopt the common practice of mouthing insincere flattery and humbly presenting your name certificate in pursuit of promotion. If you harbor any such notions, you had better forsake secular life and retire to some mountain forest." He wept as he spoke, and Michimasa's mind darkened with anguish. How inadequate it would be to describe the boy's feelings as sad! They were all too natural.

Takaie was overcome with emotion. "Why do you let your mind dwell on such things? Your sentiments are entirely proper, but nobody is going to do anything wrong," he said, with tears streaming from his eyes.

"For years, I have tried to be a father to you," Korechika replied, "and I need not tell you how sorry I am that everything has ended in failure for us both. From now on, you must be Michimasa's guide and mentor." He continued at great length in the same lachrymose vein.

While Korechika's immediate family and his niece and nephew, Princess Shūshi and Prince Atsuyasu, were thus absorbed in anxiety and grief, the Twentieth of the First Month came and went. It was time for the appointments ceremonies, and presently the sick man heard a great clatter of horses and carriages. The gentlemen of the Court, his people told him, were on their way to the Imperial Palace. His situation was most pathetic.

Korechika's elder daughter was still only seventeen or eighteen, a sweet, friendly girl, with flawless skin and fine, shining hair that trailed on the floor for four or five inches. She was a charming picture in her white robes, bound-patterned, red plum bombycine mantle, and red trousers. Her sister, about fifteen or sixteen and a bit larger in build, was dignified and calm, and no one could see her without marveling at her chaste beauty. Her abundant hair hung within three inches of the floor, promising well for the future. She wore several layers of colored robes, all rather soft—New Year's finery, it appeared, that had lost its stiffness.

Small and serene, the mother of these delightful creatures might have passed for a girl in her twenties. Her beauty was quite remarkable.

As for Michimasa—with his fine complexion and handsome features, he was as beautiful as a figure in a painting. He wore a light brown hunting dress with a green gossamer lining, a pair of deep purple bound-patterned trousers, and a glossy red cloak. His fair skin was flushed with weeping.

In days past, it had been said of Korechika that his great beauty and talents verged on the inappropriate for a courtier,[172] but the trials of recent years and the illness of the past months had wasted his once corpulent body. His complexion remained unchanged, but that in itself, the gossips said, was an ominous sign.[173] He was wearing a cap in bed as a courtesy to his daughters, and the four or five young ladies in attendance had made the gesture of putting on abbreviated trains of pale red.[174] It was a hushed, melancholy scene.

Korechika breathed his last on the Twenty-ninth of the First Month [of 1010], at the age of thirty-seven. To his daughters and Michimasa, who had refused to give up hope, his death came as a stunning blow, and they broke down in floods of frenzied tears, vowing not to survive him. If only their behavior might have done some good, it would not have been so inexpressibly pathetic. Their father's departure from the world had indeed been premature. One wonders if his illness and shortened life might not have been caused by the despair he felt when all his expectations, cherished with such confidence through years of adversity, were shattered by the successive births of Empress Shōshi's two male children—by the brilliant emergence, as it were, of the sun and moon.

I shall say nothing more about the grief and despair of Korechika's children. Takaie, Yorichika, Chikayori, and the other brothers were inconsolable, and one may be sure that Princess Shūshi and Prince Atsuyasu also felt a keen sense of loss. The reader will be able to imagine their feelings. Others too bemoaned the death of one who had, they said, already suffered more than his share of misfortunes.

For Takaie, secular life was now more painful than ever, and he spoke

172. The implication is that he should have been an Emperor.
173. It is not clear why this was ominous. According to one theory, it meant that his spirit would linger in the world after his death. Yosano 1962, p. 129.
174. "Abbreviated trains" (*shibira*) were worn by lesser ladies-in-waiting when they appeared before the master of the house. Korechika wore a cap because it was a breach of etiquette for a man to show his topknot. *Genji*, 5: 240, n. 6; EMZ, 2: 564.

to Bishop Ryūen of his growing desire to become a monk. In this miserable world, he felt, he no longer needed to consider anyone but himself. But when it came to the final decision, he was pitifully unable to take the step that would separate him from his beloved daughters, the children of Tōyori's daughter.[175]

Naritoki and his wife had both died before suitable arrangements could be made for Seishi's sister, Naka no Kimi (called the Younger Daughter at Koichijō). Determined to make a match equal to Seishi's, Naka no Kimi had taken it on herself to offer her hand to the Crown Prince's younger brother, Prince Atsumichi, and the Prince had installed her in the Southern Palace.[176] But the Prince's affection had cooled with the passing of time. He had conceived a violent passion for the wife of Michisada, the governor of Izumi; and Naka no Kimi had finally gone home to her grandmother at Koichijō, unable to endure his neglect.[177]

The Crown Prince and Seishi, well aware of the awkwardnesses that would have developed had they been responsible for the marriage, congratulated themselves on having had nothing to do with it. How differently fate had treated Seishi and Naka no Kimi! It was hard to believe the two were sisters.

It was because of the late Prince Tametaka's extravagant regard for his mistress, Izumi, that Prince Atsumichi had succeeded him as her lover. By that time, Atsumichi's first wife, Michitaka's third daughter, was leading a dubious life somewhere in Ichijō. People wondered what would become of Naka no Kimi.

Prince Tomohira died at about that same time.[178] Yorimichi looked after the final arrangements with gratifying and affecting devotion. I should

175. In Chapter 5, Minamoto Tōyori is called Kanesuke, the name by which he was known in later life. Takaie's long marriage to Tōyori's daughter produced a son, Tsunesuke (1006–81; ultimately a Provisional Major Counselor of Senior Second Rank), as well as the two daughters mentioned here. One daughter married Prince Atsunori (997–1054), a son of Emperor Sanjō; the other married Fujiwara Kanetsune, a son of Michitsuna. EMZ, 2: 568; Ōkagami, p. 192. See Sonpi bunmyaku, 1: 310, 313, for Takaie's numerous children from other alliances, of whom only one, Yoshiyori (1002–48), attained kugyō status.

176. Atsumichi had previously been married to Michitaka's third daughter. The Translation follows the account of Naka no Kimi's marriage in Ōkagami, p. 100. Eiga does not specify a subject for the sentence, and it is possible that a well-wisher or relative of the girl—a sibling, for instance—is to be understood as having proposed the match to Atsumichi.

177. The grandmother was Naritoki's mother, who had adopted Naka no Kimi. Tachibana Michisada seems to have separated from his flirtatious wife, Izumi Shikibu, around 1002 or 1003. Note that Atsumichi died in 1007, three years before most of the events described in this section. His affair with Shikibu probably began in 1003, after the death of her earlier lover, Prince Tametaka.

178. Prince Tomohira, Yorimichi's father-in-law, had died on the Twenty-ninth of the Seventh Month in the preceding year, 1009.

have mentioned earlier that Tamemitsu's daughter, Shi no Kimi (the one who had gone to live at the Takatsukasa Mansion after ex-Emperor Kazan's death), had moved to Tsuchimikado to become a companion for the daughters of the house—a step prompted by the many letters she had received from Rinshi. Michinaga took charge of her affairs, and presently his interest deepened into tender affection. He gave her a full staff of Stewards and other attendants, treated her with every mark of respect, and made her life at the mansion all that any woman could have desired. Her brothers, who had paid her little heed during the ex-Emperor's lifetime, soon became extremely cordial.

Empress Shōshi's older son, now in his third year, was irresistible as he ran busily here and there. In the Fourth Month, Michinaga let him watch the Kamo Festival procession from the Ichijō viewing-stand. He was a plump, fair-skinned little fellow with enchanting manners. As the Virgin passed, his grandfather raised the blinds and lifted him up. "What do you think of him?" Michinaga called out. The Virgin thrust a fan through the curtains of her litter—a sign, no doubt, that she had seen the boy. On the following day, she sent over a poem:

Hikari izuru	Now that I have seen
Aoi no kage o	The shining young *aoi*
Miteshikaba	Radiant as the emergent sun,
Toshi henikeru mo	I count my many years
Ureshikarikeri.	A blessing indeed.[179]

Michinaga's reply:

Morokazura	It was truly a mark of divine grace
Futaba nagara mo	That the *aoi*,
Kimi ni kaku	Though still a tender sprout,
Au hi ya kami no	Has thus encountered Your Ladyship
Shirushi naruran.	On the day of the double sprays.[180]

With two little grandsons running through the house, one behind the other, Michinaga seemed the most fortunate of mortals. It was small wonder that he treated Empress Shōshi with extraordinary respect.

179. The *Ōkagami* account of the episode (p. 124), which probably represents a conscious revision of this passage, says that both of Shōshi's sons were present. The poem is best understood as referring to both, since twin leaves were the distinguishing feature of the [futaba]aoi (on which, see s.n. 50).

180. "Double sprays" translates *morokazura*, which can mean either aoi or a Kamo Festival decoration made of katsura and aoi leaves, which was attached to blinds, worn on the head, etc. Here it is used in the second sense, serving as an ornamental adjunct to futaba.

Crown Prince Okisada's oldest son was Prince Atsuakira, known as His Highness the Minister of Ceremonial.[181] The Hirohata Middle Counselor Akimitsu, who had become Minister of the Right by that time,[182] took the Prince as a husband for his second daughter Enshi, the sister of Emperor Ichijō's Junior Consort Genshi. The bridegroom had anticipated some very old-fashioned marriage rituals, but everything proved to be quite attractively done. Unlike his popular younger brother Asateru, Akimitsu had never enjoyed a high reputation. Nevertheless, Asateru had died a Major Counselor, whereas Akimitsu, by dint of keeping himself alive, had managed to attain ministerial rank.[183] Prince Atsuakira had not expected a great deal of the marriage,[184] but to his surprise Enshi turned out to be remarkably pretty and good-natured. She was all anyone could have desired, and the two were soon very much in love. Although Akimitsu had always devoted most of his attention to his older daughter, the Junior Consort, he now came to feel that Enshi was by no means an ordinary girl —an opinion heartily endorsed by outsiders, who marveled at the lady's ability to monopolize the affections of so notorious a philanderer.

It was rumored that Yorimune, Michinaga's son by Meishi, was visiting Korechika's elder daughter, Ōhimegimi. There was nothing wrong about it, except that Korechika had been opposed to the idea of such a marriage. In the past, Yorimune had been much involved in romantic adventures. Indeed, he seemed unable to keep from flirting with every lady he met, and some of his affairs with waiting-women had even resulted in children. But aside from an occasional disagreeable lapse, he changed completely after he began to visit Ōhimegimi. He attended to all her needs with tender solicitude, moving her women to tears, and bound Ōhimegimi herself to him with a love that verged, she felt, on the immodest. Since Korechika's wife had always been partial to her other daughter, Naka no Kimi, she refused to put herself out for the young couple.

Meanwhile, Empress Shōshi sent letter after letter inviting Naka no Kimi to enter her Household. Disturbed by the notion of betraying her husband's last wishes, the mother was reluctant to let her daughter go, but she realized that some arrangement of the sort might ultimately be the

---

181. The Prince actually received this title after the accession of his father three years later, in 1013.

182. Akimitsu had been made Minister of the Right in 996.

183. Asateru had died at the age of forty-four in the epidemic of 995.

184. Presumably because, as noted in Chapter 4, Akimitsu's family had a reputation for being stuffy and old-fashioned.

best solution for Naka no Kimi's future, always provided that the girl was guaranteed acceptable treatment. It was pitiful to see her reduced to such circumstances. In this wretched world, all is as transient as the phantasms of a dreamer.

Everyone was shocked when Prince Atsumichi suddenly fell ill and died.[185] It was a tragically unexpected event.

Presently, Emperor Ichijō's eldest son, Prince Atsuyasu, performed the Coming-of-Age ceremony. The Emperor would have liked to make him Minister of Ceremonial, but since the office was occupied by Prince Atsuakira, and since the Crown Prince's second son, Prince Atsunori, held the title of Minister of Central Affairs, he gave Prince Atsuyasu the governor-generalship of the Dazaifu, a post that happened to be vacant at the time.[186] To the Emperor, this young son, so quick at his studies and sensitive in his judgments, was like a precious secret treasure; and his heart ached with frustration and pity whenever the two were together. Who could have dreamed that things would turn out as they had, he wondered sadly. He raised Atsuyasu to the First Degree of Princely Rank as a token of his love.[187] He had hoped to see everything done in proper order, but the boy's lack of outside support had made it all too clear that there was no hope of placing him in line for the throne. It was a bitter disappointment, and he never ceased to lament the Prince's unhappy fate. Divining his feelings, Empress Shōshi suffered with him. How splendid it would be, she thought, if she could somehow arrange for Atsuyasu to be placed in the line of succession while the Emperor still held the throne.

Emperor Ichijō had recently begun to talk of abdicating, "the sooner the better." The Empress was saddened, but others pointed out that she could look forward to a glorious future with two such fine sons.

185. He had in fact died in 1007.
186. As noted above, Atsuakira was not the Minister of Ceremonial in 1010, nor was his brother the Minister of Central Affairs.
187. The rank was conferred in the Sixth Month of 1011, on the day Emperor Ichijō informed the Crown Prince of his intention to abdicate. EMZ, 2: 586.

9

IWAKAGE

ALL Emperor Ichijō's talk was of abdication, but Michinaga withheld his consent. Meanwhile, the Emperor went into ritual seclusion because of a mysterious indisposition, a turn of events that left Empress Shōshi nervous and depressed. It was not long before the malady showed every sign of being serious. "I shall very likely get worse," the Emperor thought. "I must step down while my mind is still clear." A number of malignant spirits were harassing him. He was in the Ichijō Palace at the time, suffering cruelly from the summer heat, which was oppressive even to those in robust health; and his visitors and attendants were anxious and gloomy. It was by then the Seventh, Eighth, or Ninth of the Sixth Month [1011].

"I have made up my mind to abdicate now," he told Michinaga. "See to the arrangements." Michinaga acquiesced. "The usual thing is to grant the Crown Prince an audience first," he said. He set preparations in motion.

Both the Emperor and Shōshi hoped Prince Atsuyasu might be the next heir apparent.

When people learned of the Emperor's intention to receive Crown Prince Okisada in audience, they began to speculate about the Prince's successor. "With young Prince Atsuhira's brilliant connections, things look bad for us. He is sure to be nominated," said Prince Atsuyasu's party. But some of them still thought the oldest son would be chosen.

The Crown Prince went to the Ichijō Palace on the Eleventh. He made a magnificent showing. Everyone at the Palace was worried about the future, but the Prince's courtiers were in excellent spirits. It was all quite natural—but how pathetic it is that fortunes must alter so swiftly.

When the Prince arrived, the Emperor received him from behind his blinds with a few appropriate remarks. The clarity and firmness of his voice must have made the Prince wonder whether there was any truth to the alarming rumors that had been circulating. "After my abdication, I wish Prince Atsuhira to be named heir apparent," His Majesty began. "It would be right to appoint Prince Atsuyasu, but he lacks influential support. In matters of state, be guided by the men who have served me in positions of trust for many years. I have long wished to enter holy orders, and I intend to do so if I recover. But I don't expect to live much longer." It was most affecting, and the Prince brushed away tears as he took his leave.

Had Empress Shōshi been an ordinary woman, the news of Prince Atsuhira's selection would doubtless have delighted her, but she felt certain that the Emperor had wished his oldest son to succeed Prince Okisada, as would only have been proper. Prince Atsuyasu, too, she thought, must have hoped for the appointment in spite of everything. "With so much being made of the matter, I suppose His Majesty felt compelled to act against his conscience," she told herself. "The poor Prince is probably trying to console himself with the thought that he may have another chance some day. Prince Atsuhira is still young; it would have been all right to wait and see what the future might bring." To Michinaga she protested in tears, "I can't help regretting Prince Atsuhira's appointment. How terrible for Prince Atsuyasu to have his hopes frustrated after all these years!"

"I am happy to hear you express such generous sentiments," answered Michinaga, "and I share your feeling that it would have been proper to nominate Prince Atsuyasu. But since the Emperor has been quite specific, we can't very well say, 'No, no, you shouldn't have issued that command. Follow the order of birth.' Then too, you know, life is uncertain. If I can provide for Prince Atsuhira's future while I am still in charge of the government, I won't have any worries in the next world." What he said had its own logic, and the Empress was silenced.

Moved by the sick Emperor's pleas for her companionship, Empress Shōshi refused to leave his side for an instant. He was in great pain.

The abdication took place on the Thirteenth of the Sixth Month. After the Fourteenth, the ex-Emperor lapsed into a critical condition.

Prince Atsuhira was named Crown Prince. The appointment came as no surprise; everyone had expected it. Empress Shōshi found it distressing to watch Prince Atsuyasu, who had been nursing his father with great devotion throughout his illness. She knew what he must be feeling, and it seemed to her that her face must be red with embarrassment. Princess

Shūshi, already worried to distraction about the ex-Emperor, must have been miserable indeed after her brother's disappointment.

Since the Empress showed no interest in Prince Atsuhira's nomination, Michinaga bustled about by himself, making arrangements at the palaces of the new Emperor Sanjō, the Crown Prince, and the ex-Emperor. How indescribably fortunate he seemed!

Aware that his life was in grave danger, ex-Emperor Ichijō summoned Bishop Ingen, the Hosshōji abbot, to discuss his admission to holy orders. It would be inadequate to call such an event very sad. The Empress sobbed hysterically, and Prince Atsuyasu and Princess Shūshi were numb with grief. But the Crown Prince's nurses were in high spirits.

The ex-Emperor took the tonsure during the Hour of the Dragon [7:00–9:00 A.M.] on the Nineteenth of the Sixth Month. He seemed such a stranger afterward that Empress Shōshi was powerless to control her tears. The reader will understand her feelings.

Even after ex-Emperor Ichijō's renunciation of the world, it would have been possible for him to look forward to a splendid life as a respected and influential former sovereign. But everything depended on the restoration of his health, and of that, sadly enough, there seemed little prospect. Announcing that he wished to hear only buddha-invocations,[1] he ordered those around him to give up their religious rites. They insisted on continuing their fervent prayers for his recovery—some good, they thought, must surely result from his act of renunciation—but the progress of the disease was inexorable, and he succumbed around midday on the Twenty-second of the Sixth Month in the eighth year of Kankō.

Emperor Ichijō had become Crown Prince at the age of four, ascended the throne at seven, and reigned peacefully for twenty-five years, longer than any recent Emperor. Even Emperor Murakami, whose reign is always being cited as a glorious example, occupied the throne for only twenty-one years, and Emperor En'yū, who is praised as a good, indeed a saintly, ruler, for only fifteen. Everyone had been impressed by the fact that Emperor Ichijō had reigned so long—but now he was dead. I am unable to describe the emotions of all the courtiers, the Empress, Prince Atsuyasu, and Princess Shūshi, nor can I find words to write of Michinaga's distress.

Many sad things happened as the innumerable prayer altars were dismantled and the monks clattered off with their paraphernalia.

In the buoyant atmosphere of the new Emperor's Palace, people felt as

1. I.e. prayers for salvation.

though the morning sun had risen, but for the mourners at Ichijō the sky was heavy with clouds. (Perhaps their spirits revived a bit when they thought of the long, happy future awaiting the young Crown Prince. He was four that year, and the Third Prince was three. It was moving to see how easily their innocent minds were diverted.)

Ex-Emperor Ichijō and Empress Shōshi had once been inseparable, but now their paths diverged. Although the Empress stayed with the body awhile, she could not linger there forever, and at length she withdrew to her own quarters. The ex-Emperor's people changed the furnishings in the room and brought up lamps, and some of those who had been closest to him retired to a distance to begin their nightlong vigil. It was all very chilling and uncomfortable. For the first time in her life, Empress Shōshi knew the meaning of suffering. During the twelve or thirteen years since her presentation as a young girl, she had been with the Emperor early and late, always the unchallenged favorite, and inevitably his sudden death came as a dreadful shock. Her feelings were quite natural.

Since Princess Shūshi was at least fourteen or fifteen by then, she was aware of the significance of everything that happened, and her understanding was reflected in the sharpness of her grief. Prince Atsuyasu, though still very young, was a serene, confident lad, with a character that already commanded awed respect, and to one of his ready intelligence the loss of a father was hard indeed. The poor Prince had another sorrow that must have weighed heavily on his spirits.

The melancholy days dragged by, punctuated by the sound of voices intoning the sutras, and presently it was announced that the funeral would take place on the Eighth of the Seventh Month. To the anxious Empress, it seemed unwise to delay so long in a season of unbearable heat. If only the body had been immune to the hand of time, how gladly would she have kept it! But painful realities had to be faced.

On the Seventh of the Seventh Month, the eve of the funeral, Inspector Major Counselor Sanesuke sent a poem to the ex-Emperor's ladies:

Tanabata o	Could we but think
Suginishi kimi to	The Weaver Maid
Omoiseba	Our departed lord,
Kyō wa ureshiki	Joyful indeed
Aki ni zo aramashi.	This autumn day![2]

2. "If he were the Weaver Maid and we the Herdsman, we could look forward to meeting him tonight."

The nurse Ukyō replied:

Wabitsutsu mo	Despite our grief,
Aritsuru mono o	We have not lost him quite—
Tanabata no	But what of the pain
Tada omoiyare	In the Weaver Maid's heart
Asu ika ni sen.	When tomorrow dawns?

On the evening of the Eighth, they took the body to Iwakage.[3] Seldom had a procession been so imposing. It was, people thought, a spectacle worthy of the ex-Emperor's final journey. Could anyone suppose that Michinaga or any other senior noble or courtier failed to join the cortege? They reached the cremation ground, and soon the great and majestic sovereign was but an evanescent wisp of cloud. At such moments it is impossible to remain unmoved.

Long as the night was, it ended too soon. Around dawn, Prince Atsuyasu, Michinaga, and some others picked up the bones, and then all was over. It was a sad moment when Masamitsu, the Treasury Minister, set out with the remains.

The return journey was like a dream. By the time they reached the Ichijō Palace, the hour was already late. Yorimune recited a poem:

Izuko ni ka	Where might it have been
Kimi o ba okite	That we left our lord
Kaeriken	And started home?
Sokohaka to dani	How hard it is
Omōenu kana.	To clear one's mind ...

Kinnobu, the Director of the Palace Storehouse Bureau, recited:[4]

Kaerite mo	Now we are home—and yet
Onaji yamaji o	I long to tread again
Tazunetsutsu	That mountain track;
Nitaru keburi ya	To see if perchance there be
Tatsu to koso mime.	A like plume of smoke.

It was all inexpressibly sad.

For a few days, all the usual ceremonies and arrangements in the ex-Emperor's apartments had remained the same, even down to the most insignificant articles of furniture. One could almost have supposed that he

---

3. Still a wild foothill area, situated east of the present Kinkakuji and north of Kitano (Kagamiishi-chō, Kinugasa, Kita-ku, Kyōto). The spot was chosen by divination. EMZ, 3: 41.
4. A son of Tamemitsu.

was still alive. But now his old quarters were occupied by an image of Amitābha Buddha, brought in for the invocations, and monks seemed to be everywhere. It was most awe-inspiring and sad. The invocations at dusk, and again in the middle of the night, were especially moving.

Many things conspired to deepen the Empress's gloom. Once someone brought her a pink from the garden. The Crown Prince took it out of the jug beside her inkstone and tore off its petals, and a poem came to her mind:

Miru mama ni	The brimming dew o'erflows
Tsuyu zo koboruru	As I gaze.
Okurenishi	Sweet blossom,
Kokoro mo shiranu	You little know the grief
Nadeshiko no hana.	Of one who is left alone.[5]

On another occasion, observing that the ex-Emperor's apartments stood out with dramatic clarity in the bright moonlight, she wrote:

Kage dani mo	Who could have called it
Tomarazarikeru	A mansion of jade[6]—
Kumo no ue o	This cloud top
Tama no utena to	Where even his shadow
Tare ka iikemu.	Has ceased to dwell?

When the period of ritual seclusion ended, Buddhist services were held at the Ichijō Palace. It is unnecessary, I am sure, to dwell on their splendor, so I shall say no more. The Imperial personages were most pathetic.

Murasaki Shikibu composed a poem when the Empress moved to the Biwa Mansion after the mourning period:

Arishi yo wa	The days of old
Yume ni minashite	Are but a dream—
Namida sae	Desolate the house
Tomaranu yado zo	Where even tears
Kanashikarikeru.	Refuse to stop.[7]

Princess Shūshi moved to the Sanjō Palace, but Prince Atsuyasu stayed on at the Annex.[8] Empress Shōshi sent many kind messages to both.

5. Nadeshiko is used in both of its meanings, "pink" and "beloved child."

6. *Tama no utena*, a Chinese-style metaphor for a beautiful building or an Imperial residence. EMZ, 3: 45.

7. *Tomaru*, the verb of which *tomaranu* is an inflection, can mean both "cease" and "lodge."

8. Although the name Sanjōin usually refers to the post-abdication residence of Emperor Sanjō (see Chapter 12, n. 31), it might be taken here to mean the Sanjō house of Taira Narimasa, where Prince Atsuyasu had been born. It appears, however, that Princess Shūshi

In the Ninth Month, Controller Sukenari called on Princess Shūshi.[9] "During a recent visit to a mountain temple, I saw the place at Iwakage where the former Emperor was cremated," he said. "It moved me deeply, and I composed this poem":

Iwakage no	Indistinguishable,
Keburi o kiri ni	The smoke from Iwakage
Wakikanete	Blending with the mist—
Sono yūgure no	Again I felt
Kokochi seshi kana.	As on that night.[10]

The invocations and sutra-readings at the Ichijō Palace were to continue until the first anniversary of the ex-Emperor's death. Bishop Ryūen, the son of the late Regent Michitaka, who had been one of the celebrants during the forty-nine days, went back to his temple, leaving Jin'en,[11] the monk from Iimuro, to pray alone. Jin'en sent Ryūen a poem:

Kurikaeshi	To watch in a house
Kanashiki mono wa	Where the master
Kimi masanu	No longer dwells—
Yado no yadomoru	That indeed is grief
Mi ni koso arikere.	Beyond compare.

The Bishop's reply:

Kimi masanu	Sharper than your pain
Yado ni sumuran	In the masterless house—
Hito yori mo	The grief of another
Yoso no tamoto wa	Who must mourn from afar,
Kawaku yomo nashi.	His sleeve never dry.

The Crown Prince was living at the Imperial Palace by then. Empress Shōshi could not help worrying about him, and anxiety deepened her melancholy.

Seishi was still the only consort in residence at the Palace. Emperor Sanjō had written several times to ask Kenshi to come, but Michinaga seemed in no hurry to send her. Michinaga was acting as guardian for the

actually moved to Takaie's house at this time. In a large establishment, an Annex (bechinō) was probably a smaller version of the main hall (shinden). The one in question was situated on the grounds of the Ichijō Palace. EMZ, 3: 46–47.

9. Sukenari (988–1070), the son of Fujiwara Arikuni and Tachibana Naishi no Suke, was a scholar and minor bureaucrat who ultimately attained Third Rank, which he held from 1045 until he took Buddhist vows in 1052. Kugyō bunnin, 1: 297; EMZ, 3: 47.

10. The translation follows EMZ, 3: 47, which takes keburi to mean smoke from dwellings in the area.

11. A son of Fujiwara Yoshichika (Koretada's son).

Emperor—and, needless to say, for the Crown Prince as well.[12] Although there was nothing very new about his amazing good fortune, people never seemed to tire of discussing it.

Three of Emperor Sanjō's sons by Seishi had already performed the Coming-of-Age ceremony.[13] The fourth was still a child. The Emperor's oldest daughter was designated Ise Virgin.

Meanwhile, there was a great stir over the Accession Audience, the Imperial Purification, and the Thanksgiving. It was rumored that Kenshi was to be named Acting Consort,[14] but no official decision had been reached.

Around that time, a child was born to Korechika's oldest daughter, the one whom Meishi's son Yorimune had married. The baby was an exceptionally pretty little girl, and Michinaga took a great fancy to her, holding her in his arms and vowing to make her an Empress some day.[15] The ceremonies during the first seven days were performed in splendid style, with important personages as sponsors. One of the sponsors, I need hardly say, was Michinaga, who had made himself generally responsible for all the festivities. It was sad to recall Korechika's hopes for the daughter he had reared so carefully. "She is not at all badly off now," many people said, "but still, considering that Korechika intended to make her an Empress . . ." There was so great a fuss about every detail that I cannot possibly describe it all. The reader must call upon his imagination. After the baby's birth, Yorimune begrudged even the time required to put in an appearance at the Palace or his father's house.

Presently, Kenshi made another brilliant entry into the Palace.[16] The Emperor was a man whose tact, modern tastes, and sophistication lent distinction to his most casual act, and I need not say that he treated his young consort with the utmost consideration. Everyone seemed to be predicting a gala Purification.

12. Guardian (*ushiromi*) was a nonofficial position, which, the author implies, Michinaga held as the senior maternal relative. Since a new nairan decree had been issued to him on the Twenty-third of the Eighth Month, 1011, he was, in fact, the official surrogate of the Emperor, even though he had refused the title of Regent (Kanpaku). EMZ, 3: 51.

13. Princes Atsuakira, Atsunori, and Atsuhira, aged seventeen, fourteen, and eleven or twelve, respectively, in 1011. Prince Atsuakira's genpuku had taken place in 1006; the other two boys celebrated theirs on the Twenty-third of the Third Month, 1013, two years after the events described here.

14. For the Purification.

15. She married Emperor Sanjō's son Koichijōin (Prince Atsuakira), to whom she bore Prince Atsukata (1039–77) and the Consultant Minamoto Motohira. She was called In no Ue. For a list of Yorimune's children, see s.n. 74.

16. Probably around the Twenty-third of the Eighth Month, 1011, the date on which Emperor Sanjō conferred Nyōgo status on both Kenshi and Seishi.

Around that time, the Ise Virgin was living in the Palace in the Fields.[17] Her selection as Virgin was a great honor, but the sudden parting from her mother, Seishi, who had always been at her side, must have brought tears to her eyes. (No doubt she forced them back, realizing that they were inauspicious.)

Michinaga changed out of mourning early in order to see to the Purification and supervise other arrangements. The Crown Prince's Household officials had not yet been appointed, since their selection, it was thought, could not be undertaken with safety during a period of mourning. With the mourning now ending in any case, His Lordship made the choice of a Purification date the occasion for changing into ordinary attire.

Soon the Tenth Month began. Empress Shōshi was still in dismal spirits. Her tears rivaled the late autumn showers, and she took no interest in anything except the constant services for the ex-Emperor. The deep red leaves in the garden merely evoked sad memories. Watching little Prince Atsunaga, irresistible as he gamboled about, she longed more than ever to see the Crown Prince, who was reported to be growing up with amazing speed. Ordinarily cheerful and easygoing, she now went so far as to bewail her lack of a daughter. "If only one of my children had been a girl, how nicely I could have reared her," she said. This was perhaps a bit selfish, considering the brilliant future that had been provided for her older son. For poor Genshi and Gishi, who had no children at all, even a daughter would have been a great consolation.

There was much excitement about the Purification and other events, which were to be celebrated in an impressively modern fashion, but the Empress remained inconsolable. She felt drawn to Princess Shūshi, to whom she sent many messages. The Princess, scarcely less miserable, found it hard that she and Prince Atsuyasu could not live in the same house.

Everywhere there was careful attention to the services for the ex-Emperor. At the Ichijō Palace, where sutra-recitations and invocations never ceased, a forlorn handful of monks occupied the depressingly spacious apartments, and everyone who saw them was moved to nostalgic reminiscences about the days when the late sovereign was still alive. "Such indeed is the way of the world," people said.

During the ex-Emperor's residence at the Ichijō Palace, it had seemed

17. Princess Tōshi was named Virgin late in the Twelfth Month of the first year of Chōwa (January 1012) and entered the Palace in the Fields (Nonomiya) in 1013, two years after the events described here. EM, 1: 525, s.nn. 482, 483.

appropriate for Prince Atsuyasu to occupy the Annex, but now the Prince
felt, with some discomfort, that he might be considered an intruder. Just
as he was seriously debating possible alternatives, Michinaga offered to
give him the Southern Palace,[18] proposing that the Annex be turned over
to Prince Atsunaga. It did not seem a bad solution, and he decided to accept, on condition that he be allowed to stay until the anniversary of his
father's death.

Few of Emperor Ichijō's former ladies-in-waiting took service with the
new sovereign. Instead, they went off in various directions, some to the
Crown Prince, others to the Empress, and still others to Princess Shūshi or
Prince Atsuyasu. Probably they all felt that life at Court would thenceforth
lack the special tone their master had lent it, and that they had best seek
employment with some member of his family. Their grief as sharp as ever,
they never ceased to lament his loss.

Of course, the late Emperor's Junior Consorts, Sonshi, Gishi, and Genshi, were entitled to wear mourning. The somber garb was in a sense a
memento; there could be no distinctions of status. Genshi, in particular,
had loved her husband with all her heart, and it would have been strange
if she had shown no sign of grief after his death.

Since the ex-Emperor had died without disposing of his property, Michinaga undertook to apportion it. Genshi and Gishi both shared in the distribution at the Ichijō Palace. Michinaga was conscientious and fair, and
everyone expressed satisfaction, but it was a sad business, with numerous
poignant reminders of the dead man's many splendid qualities.

When ex-Emperor Ichijō had been about to cut off his hair, he had sent
Empress Shōshi a poem:

Tsuyu no mi no	How hard it is
Kari no yadori ni	To renounce the world,
Kimi o okite	Leaving you behind
Ie o idenuru	In this transient shelter
Koto zo kanashiki.	Of forms evanescent as dew.

She had been too distraught to compose a reply.

The wife of the Commander of the Left Gate Guards sent this to Gishi:[19]

---

18. Minaminoin. Evidence from a contemporary diary suggests that this was a residence
in the southern part of the grounds occupied by Korechika's Nijō Mansion (south of Nijō
Avenue and east of Machijiri). It should not be confused with the Minaminoin of the
Reizeiin. EMZ, 3: 61.

19. An interlinear note in the text identifies the Commander of the Left Gate Guards as

Kazu naranu	Rising and sleeping
Michishiba to nomi	In the rhythm of this transient life,
Nagekitsutsu	And lamenting ever
Hakanaku tsuyu no	To be of no more worth
Okifushi	Than a clump of roadside grass,
Akekure take no	With what impatience did I wait
Oiyukan	Morning and night
Kono yo no sue ni	For such happiness
Narite dani	As the day might bring
Ureshiki fushi ya	When my child,
Miyuru tote	Shooting up like a young bamboo,
Itsu shika to koso	Should grow to be a man.
Matsuyama no	But when in early spring
Takaki kozue ni	The eastern breeze
Sugomoreru	Began to blow,
Mada kozutawanu	Beguiling with scent of plum
Uguisu o	The warbler nestled snug
Mume no nioi ni	On Pine Mountain's lofty branch,
Sasowasete	Not ready yet to bear
Kochikaze hayaku	Tidings from tree to tree,
Fukinureba	Then with the melting
Tani no kōri mo	Of valley ice
Uchitokete	Came too a loosening
Kasumi no koromo	Sash of birth,
Tachiitsutsu	And with the rising cloaks of mist
Shizue made ni mo	That swirled among the lowest twigs,
Uchinabiki	Came a fashioning
Kishi no fujinami	Of swaddling clothes,
Asakaranu	And joy extending
Nioi ni kayou	To the humblest hearts.

Yorimichi, who held the title in 1011. The poem that follows, however, seems clearly to have been written by someone older and of lower social status than Yorimichi's wife Takahime. Possibly, as Matsumura suggests, the author was a lesser wife of Fujiwara Sanenobu, who had held the post some years before—a woman whom there is some justification for identifying as an older half-sister, by a mother of inferior status, of the Imperial consort Gishi. The poem itself is an unfortunate insertion, pedestrian and obscure, which seems to say that the widowed author, living in obscurity with her baby, is summoned to act as wet nurse for the Imperial consort's child (whose existence is otherwise undocumented). The child dies in infancy, whereupon the author leaves Gishi's service. In the last part of the poem, after commiserating with Gishi on the death of the Emperor ("the place where wild geese [i.e.—Nyōgo] flocked" is a metaphor for the Imperial Palace), she indicates that she has become a nun. The original, which is much less explicit than the English version, contains a number of puns, especially toward the end, which have not been translated. EMZ, 3: 66ff.

Murasaki no	Dwelling in the royal seat
Kumo no tanabiku	Where trail the purple clouds—
Asayū ni	Linked with no shallow bond
Ima mo midori no	To that purple
Matsu ni nomi	Of poolside wisteria bloom—
Kokoro o kakete	I concentrated every hope
Sugusu ma ni	On the pine tree, ever green.
Natsu kinubeshi to	In time I heard the voice
Kikoyu naru	Of summer's herald,
Yamahototogisu	The cuckoo from the hills,
Sayo fukaku	Calling as though to me alone
Kataraiwataru	In the dead of night.
Koe kikeba	I did not wonder what he meant,
Nani no kokoro o	Nor seek to question him,
Omou tomo	But pulled up sweet flags at the marsh—
Iiyaranu ma no	Long roots,
Ayamegusa	Symbols of long life—
Nagaki tameshi ni	And laid them on the eaves
Hikinashite	In happy hope
Yazuma ni kakaru	Of joys to come
Mono to nomi	Through our young lord.
Yomogi no yado o	Cleaning my humble home
Uchiharai	Amid its tangled weeds,
Tama no utena to	I thought of how some day
Omoitsutsu	I might dwell in a mansion of jade.
Utsusemi no yo no	For I had quite overlooked
Hakanasa mo	The transience of all things
Wasurehatete wa	In this inconstant world.
Chitose hemu	Then came our lord's Purification,
Kimi ga misogi o	And I prayed that the child
Inorite zo	Might endure a thousand years.
Kakinagashiyaru	Beside the shoals
Kawase ni mo	Where impurities were cast adrift,
Katae suzushiki	I started at the rustle
Kaze no oto ni	Of a cooling breeze,
Odorokarete mo	The waning year's
Iroiro no	Harbinger of change;
Hana no tamoto no	Yet heedless of its voice
Yukashisa o	Lost myself in dreams
Aki fukaku nomi	Of autumn's flowery sleeves
Tanomarete	Dyed in sumptuous hues.

Momiji no nishiki	When the Ninth Month came,
Kiri tatazu	Long Month of long nights,
Yo o nagatsuki to	And the mists never rose
Iiokeru	From the maple-leaf brocade,
Hisashiki koto o	I found an omen of longevity
Kiku no hana	In the ancient saw, "Long Month,
	long life."
Nioi o somuru	And when late autumn showers
Shigure ni mo	Painted with vivid brush
Ame no shita furu	The long-lived chrysanthemum,
Kai ya aru to	"What promise life now holds,"
	I thought.
Hakanaku sugusu	And thus the carefree
Tsukihi ni mo	Days and months slipped by,
Kokoromoto naku	Filled with eager dreams
Omou ma ni	Of future joys.
Kashira no shimo no	In the Month of Frosts
Okeru o mo	I paid no heed
Uchiharaitsutsu	To my whitening head,
Arihen to	Resolved to go on
Omoi munashiku	Just as before;
Nasaji to zo	Not to relinquish cherished hopes.
Koromo no suso ni	I sheltered him beneath my skirts
Hagukumite	And cared for him
Chiri mo sueji to	As for a precious gem,
Migakitsuru	Polished and dustless.
Tama no hikari no	But all unawares
Omowazu ni	Our shining light
Kienishi yori wa	Flickered and died.
Kakikurasu	Since then I have groped
Kokoro no yami ni	Through the blackness of despair,
Madowarete	Locked in a night
Akubeki kata mo	That knows no dawn.
Namida nomi	Nothing is left but tears
Tsukisenu mono to	Flowing without end,
Nagaretsutsu	Sweeping away all else.
Koishiki kage mo	The beloved image itself
Todomarazu	No longer remains;
Sode no shigarami	The weir of my sleeve
Sekikanete	Fails to arrest the flood.
Taki no koe dani	What care I that my wailing voice
Oshimarezu	Becomes a waterfall?

Madoiirite wa   Distracted by grief,
Tazunuredo   I have searched for him
Shide no yama naru   On mountain tracks,
Wakareji wa   But the living cannot tread the road
Ikite mirubeki   That branches off
Kata mo nashi   Toward the Mountains of Death.
Aware wasurenu   Alas! I can but hear
Nagori ni wa   The distant sound
Hikazu bakari o   Of your weeping voice,
Kazou tote   Like the cuckoo's plaintive cry,
Nakiwatarumeru   Child-calling bird,
Yobukodori   As you tell the days
Honoka ni kimi ga   In endless litany,
Nageku naru   Lost in grief
Koe bakari nite   For one you can never forget.
Yamashiro no   Now I dwell alone
Towa ni iwase no   By Suminoe's pines
Mori sugite   Beyond Iwase Wood,
Ware bakari no mi   Past Toba in Yamashiro.
Suminoe no   (How like a dream
Matsu yukikata mo   That once I prayed,
Nami kakuru   "May he never die!")
Kishi no manimani   My future is barren,
Wasuregusa   For others will, I fear, forget me
Oi ya shigeran to   As though I were forgetting-grass
Omou ni mo   Growing on Suminoe's wave-lapped
                                 shore.

Noki ni kakareru   No tie, it seems,
Sasagani no   Remains to bind us,
Minagara taenu   Not one as frail
Tayori dani   As spiders' webs
Musubazariken   Clinging to eaves.
Ito yowami   Weak indeed those bonds,
Kokorobososa zo   But the sorrow in my heart
Tsuki mo senu   Endures forever.
Munashiki sora o   When I grow weary
Omoiwabi   Of searching empty skies,
Kari no mureishi   I gaze toward the place
Ato mireba   Where wild geese flocked,
Hitori tokoyo ni   And behold you there
Okifushi mo   Doomed for all time to a widow's
                                 bed,

Makura no shita ni	A pool of tears
Ikeraji to	Ever beneath your pillow
Ukimi o nageku	As you lament your bitter fate,
Oshidori no	No longer wishing to live—
Tsugai hanarete	Like a mandarin duck,
Yo mo sugara	Parted from its mate,
Uwage no shimo o	That all through the night
Haraiwabi	Shakes frost from its plumage
Kōru tsurara ni	And sits exhausted,
Tojirarete	Locked in a sheet of ice,
Kishikata shirazu	Scarce knowing whence it came.
Naku koe wa	Startled, as in a dream,
Yume ka to nomi zo	I hear your wailing voice;
Odorokite	My spirit faints, borne down by grief.
Kiekaerinuru	Is it not vain
Tamashii wa	That a nun should waste her life
Yukue mo shirazu	In aimless search
Kogaretsutsu	Of a beloved form,
Tsuri ni toshi furu	Helpless as a fisherman
Amabito mo	When the boat he has rowed
Fune nagashitaru	For many a year to the fishing
Toshitsuki mo	Is carried off by some ocean stream?
Kai naki kata wa	For seek as I will—
Masaru tomo	Though I be zealous
Karu mo kakiyari	As fisherfolk
Motomuru mo	Gathering the kelp they reap—
Mirume nagisa ni	I shall never see his face again.
Utsu nami no	Would that I might pass from this world
Ato dani miezu	Like a wave striking a bare strand,
Kienan to	And vanish without a trace.
Omoi no hoka ni	But though I would not have it so,
Tsu no kuni no	I must live on
Shibashi bakari mo	For however brief a span
Nagaraeba	Here in the province of Tsu—
Naniwa no koto mo	In the land of Naniwa,
Ima wa tada	Where bountiful seaweed harvests
Amata kakitsumu	Drip their burden of brine—
Moshiogusa	And in my present state
Shio no tare o ka	Where may I turn for help
Tanomubeki	With my various affairs?
Keburi taesenu	If it should chance

Takimono no	That you think of me
Ko no katami naru	As a reminder of the child,
Omoi araba	Then humble though I be
Hitori nokosazu	I should like to ask
Uchihabuki	That you pity me and mine;
Koromo no suso ni	That you spread your wings
Hagukume to	And grant us shelter
Mi no hodo shirazu	Each and every one
Tanomumeru kana.	Beneath your skirts.

"The tears began to fall, and my brush could not set down the smallest part of what was in my heart," she concluded.

Gishi's reply:

"The mere sight of the words set down by your brush has drawn forth a flood of tears":[20]

Inishie o	I have been thinking
Omoiizureba	Of the distant past,
Yukigie no	Of the hardships we suffered,
Kakine no kusa wa	We two,
Futaba nite	Growing up like twin-leaved
Oiiden koto zo	Grasses in a hedge
Katakarishi	When the snow disappears.
Tsunogumu ashi no	All too soon
Hakanakute	The sprouting reed-leaves
Karewatataru	Withered away,
Mizugiwa ni	And the mandarin drake
Tsugawanu oshi wa	Dwelt forsaken
Sabishikute	By the water's edge.
Futari no hane no	The fledglings
Shita ni dani	(Already crowded while yet
Sebaku tsudoishi	Two pairs of wings
Tori no ko no	Offered shelter)
Kumo no naka ni zo	Made their uncertain way
Tadayoishi	Into the clouds.
Hiru wa onoono	By day they flew off,
Tobiwakare	Each on his own journey,

20. The poem attributed to Gishi, which is as undistinguished as the one she received, implies that the girls' father ("the mandarin drake") was left a widower when they were small. "Many are the birds who have joined the flock" presumably refers to Emperor Ichijō's children by his various consorts. "And sharper still your grief must be" says that a nurse, because she is constantly with her charge, feels his loss even more keenly than his mother does.

Yoru wa furusu ni	By night they came flocking
Kaeritsutsu	Back to the nest,
Tsubasa o koite	Hungry for a mother's wings.
Nakiwabishi	How sad it was
Amata no koe to	To hear that throng
Kiku bakari	Of grieving voices
Kanashiki koto wa	Lament the parent bird.
Hirosawa no	Ours were lives
Ikeru kai naki	Sorrow-filled
Mi naredomo	And scarce worth living,
Nami no tachii ni	Yet the two of us,
Tsuketsutsu mo	Going about our daily tasks,
Katami ni koso wa	Found strength and confidence
Tanomishika	One in the other.
Tare mo wa ga yo no	In those days you and I
Wakakereba	Were both still young,
Yukusue tōki	And we cherished hopes
Komatsubara	Deep-felt
Kodakaku naran	For that distant day
Eda mo araba	When our sons,
Sono kage ni koso	Sturdy as young pines,
Kakureme to	Would put forth lofty branches
Omou kokoro wa	Under whose friendly shade
Fukamidori	We might find shelter.
Ikushio to dani	Ah! How fervent was our faith,
Omōezu	Unswerving,
Omoisometeshi	And deep-dyed
Koromode no	As a deep-green robe,
Iro mo kawarade	One that has gone to the vat
Toshi fureba	Time and again.
Oiizuru take no	Years slipped by
Ono ga yoyo	And shoots of young bamboo
Ureshiki fushi o	Sprouted forth,
Miru goto ni	Bringing joy to each.
Ika naru yo ni ka	Was it not folly to believe
Karesen to	With every glad event
Omoikeru koso	That come what might
Hakanakere	Those shoots would never die;
Ashita no tsuyu o	That we two should never part?
Tama to mite	I polished the morning dew,
Migakishi hodo ni	Taking it for a gem,

Kienikeri	And it vanished before my eyes.
Yūbe no matsu no	Now I can but weep aloud,
Kaze no oto ni	Plucking my zither's strings,
Kanashiki koto o	Whose plaintive strains
Shirabetsutsu	Blend with the sound
Ne o nomi zo naku	Of the night wind
Muradori no	Moaning in the pines.
Muretaru naka ni	Many are the birds
Tada hitori	Who have joined the flock,
Ika naru kata ni	Yet only one has flown away
Tobiyukite	To unknown strands,
Shiru hito mo naku	To wander in bewilderment
Madouran	Where every face is strange.
Tomaru tagui wa	Many are those
Ōku shite	Who remain behind
Koishi kanashi to	To mourn him tenderly,
Omoedomo	But life for me is empty now,
Ima wa munashiki	Barren as that vast sky
Ōzora no	At which I gaze
Kumo bakari o zo	Morning and night,
Katami ni wa	Seeking a cloud,
Akekure ni miru	A reminder of him.
Tsukikage no	There is no way to cast off
Ko no shitayami ni	The terrible grief
Madoumeru	That crushes me—
Nageki no mori no	The sorrow
Shigesa o zo	Deep as shade
Harawan kata mo	Beneath a tree
Omōenu	Where moonbeams never fall.
Miru hito goto ni	It is but natural, I suppose,
Kotowari no	That every meeting with another
Namida no kawa o	Calls forth
Nagasu kana	A river of tears.
Mashite ya soko no	And sharper still
Watari ni wa	Your grief must be;
Ika bakari ka wa	Piteous indeed
Tatauran	Your brimming tears.
Fuchise mo shirazu	I picture to myself the dreadful gloom,
Nageku naru	The pain without surcease
Kokoro no hodo o	That torments your wounded heart,

Omoiyaru The sorrow that finds echo
Hito no ue sae Even among those others
Nagekaruru kana. Who but witness your despair.

She also sent this:

Kimi mo saba Let us rely on one another:
Mukashi no hito to Do you think of me
Omowanan As a link with the past,
Ware mo katami ni And you shall be to me
Tanomubeki kana. A keepsake from the dead.

IO

CORD PENDANTS

EMPEROR Ichijō's abdication, which took place on the Thirteenth of the Sixth Month in the eighth year of Kankō [1011], was followed on the Sixteenth of the Tenth Month by the new sovereign's Accession Audience. What earlier audiences may have been like I cannot say, since I did not see them, but Emperor Sanjō's was a magnificent event. The Emperor was a man in the prime of life, a splendid masculine figure. Although people were accustomed to regarding Michinaga as incomparable, everything has its limits, and he was obliged to follow on foot behind the Imperial litter. (It was a pity, in a way, because it must be admitted that Michinaga was a match for any Emperor. But of course the person escorted and borne aloft by the host of senior nobles and courtiers was the sacred Sovereign of Great Virtue.)

Soon there was a bustle of preparation for the Imperial Purification and Thanksgiving, two rituals of great importance to the Court and the nation. Unfortunately, just at that time ex-Emperor Reizei fell ill. Since his health had always been precarious, people tended to react calmly at first, but Michinaga paid him an alarmed visit. Although he appeared to be suffering, he began to bawl out the words of a song, while Michinaga looked on in puzzled concern. Such behavior was not unusual for him, but his mental confusion seemed to have assumed a new and disturbing dimension. It was particularly disconcerting that he showed himself perfectly well aware of the caller's identity. Bidding him a hasty farewell, Michinaga went to the Palace to report to Emperor Sanjō. "It looks very much as though the illness may prove fatal," he said. "What a terrible time for such a thing to happen! His death would be a national calamity."[1] The Emperor felt that he must call on his father. He wanted to go in the next day or

1. Because it would necessitate the postponement of the Purification and Thanksgiving.

two, he said—as soon as an auspicious date could be determined. "I understand your concern," Michinaga answered, "but you mustn't think of it. The malignant spirit is in complete control. It might be different if you could hope to find him lucid." As was but natural, the distraught Emperor burst into tears.

It was under such circumstances that the Purification arrangements proceeded. Seishi, to whom the role of Acting Consort had fallen, made haste to be ready.[2]

Ex-Emperor Reizei died on the Twenty-fourth of the Tenth Month. How inadequate are words like moving and sad! Emperor Sanjō was inconsolable.

For the ex-Emperor, who had lost all but one of his sons,[3] it was most fortunate that Emperor Sanjō was the survivor. What could the others have done for him? Emperor Sanjō had stagnated in the office of Crown Prince for many years, but the old man had managed to live until after his son's accession, and now, even though the Purification and Thanksgiving would have to be postponed, there would be a magnificent funeral, and the reigning sovereign would perform filial rites on his behalf. At the regular distributions of offices in past years, poverty-stricken provinces had invariably been allotted to Reizei. "I had intended to see that he was given the best after I ascended the throne," the Emperor mused sadly. "If only he hadn't died!"

The two great ceremonies were postponed until the following year. Meanwhile, there were the funeral arrangements, all of which became Michinaga's responsibility. The Emperor ordered his sons to attend the funeral services as his personal representatives—a moving and impressive gesture. The later Buddhist services were performed with great solemnity and splendor. Everyone had put on mourning, and the courtiers were a melancholy sight as they went about like crows in their outer robes of charcoal gray. Needless to say, it was all very drab, depressing, and gloomy. How unfortunate that such a thing happened just when all the preparations were being completed and the ceremonies themselves were about to begin!

Time passed swiftly. A change in the era name was decreed, and the new year became the first of Chōwa [1012]. The New Year season would have been festive in ordinary times, but Emperor Sanjō remained in se-

2. In Chapter 9, the author remarks that Michinaga's daughter Kenshi was expected to serve as Nyōgodai. As indicated here, however, the honor went to Seishi. EMZ, 3: 97.

3. Reizei's other sons were ex-Emperor Kazan (d. 1008) and Princes Tametaka (d. 1002) and Atsumichi (d. 1007).

clusion behind his curtains, making no appearance in the Courtiers' Hall.
It was a great pity. Since he was worried about possible unlucky conse-
quences, he also refrained from paying daytime visits to Kenshi, who was
staying in one of the Imperial Apartments.[4] But the arrival of the children
in their holiday finery created a pleasant diversion for the ladies-in-waiting,
who soon fell to chatting about earlier reigns. No recent sovereign had had
as many children as Emperor Sanjō, they said, but things had nevertheless
been lively under Emperor Murakami, whose large family had kept his
ladies on their toes day and night. And then there had been Emperor Uda's
reign, also very gay, not to mention Emperor Yōzei's children with their
elegant tastes. Once, someone said, one of Emperor Yōzei's sons had sent
the same poem to several ladies of his acquaintance:

Ku ya ku ya to	Which is worse—
Matsu yūgure to	The dusk,
Ima wa tote	When you wait and wonder,
Kaeru ashita to	Or the morning after,
Izure masareri.	When he says goodbye and leaves?

The Prince's favorite reply came from a lady called Hon'in no Jijū:[5]

Yūgure wa	I comfort myself
Tanomu kokoro ni	With hopeful thoughts
Nagusametsu	At nightfall,
Kaeru ashita wa	But I faint with grief
Kenubeki mono o.	When he takes his leave at dawn.

The ladies interspersed their anecdotes with amusingly frank observations about Emperor Sanjō's sons. One of them pronounced Prince Atsuakira, the Minister of Ceremonial, the best of the lot; another protested
that Prince Atsunori, the Minister of Central Affairs, was equally attractive; and a third gave it as her opinion that Prince Atsuhira, the Minister
of War, was irresistible.[6] Kenshi's attendants, a bit overwhelmed by so
much company, seemed more subdued than usual.

Meanwhile, everyone was predicting that a new Empress would be named
any day; the only question was whether the lady would be Kenshi or Seishi. In the midst of the speculation, the Emperor sent Seishi a poem:

4. Ue no Mitsubone. The Emperor was reluctant to visit her because he was in mourning.
5. Hon'in no Jijū (fl. ca. 940–60) was a Court lady who served two of Emperor Murakami's consorts, Anshi and Kishi; had affairs with three prominent Fujiwara gentlemen,
Koretada, Kanemichi, and Asatada; and established a reputation as a poet. Sixteen of her
poems appear in Imperial anthologies.
6. The boys were eighteen, fifteen, and about thirteen.

Harugasumi	Spring mists
Nobe ni tatsuran to	Are rising, I suppose,
Omoedomo	In the fields—
Obotsukanasa o	How long it has been
Hedatetsuru kana.	Since last we met![7]

He found her reply affecting:

Kasumumeru	The misty sky
Sora no keshiki wa	Speaks of spring,
Sore nagara	But for me the spring
Waga mi hitotsu no	Of your love
Arazu mo aru kana.	Has faded into the past.

To Empress Shōshi, it was unbearably sad that a new year had already begun, and she devoted herself with redoubled dedication to her religious exercises. On the Fifteenth of the First Month, all the gentlemen of the Court gathered at the Ichijō Palace for buddha-invocations. A brilliant full moon shone overhead as they departed at the conclusion of the services. Michinaga composed a poem:

Kimi masanu	In the masterless house,
Yado ni wa tsuki zo	The bright moon
Hitori sumu	Dwells alone—
Furuki miyabito	Of the old courtiers
Tachi mo tomarade.	Not one remains.[8]

Yukinari, the Middle Counselor and Gentleman-in-waiting, responded:

Kozo no kyō	When I gazed
Koyoi no tsuki o	At tonight's moon
Mishi ori ni	A year ago today,
Kakaramu mono to	I little thought
Omoikakeki ya.	Of such a thing as this.

There was great excitement as the time for the appointment lists approached. Observing that the Empress seemed to be recalling similar events during her husband's reign, Murasaki Shikibu composed a poem:

---

7. The Emperor, confined to the Palace and visualizing the spring scenery in the country-side, thinks with renewed affection of Seishi, who has been living in the city. Ambiguous phrasing permits a second level of meaning, which the author seems to have had in mind: "Although I should like you to rise, someone else stands in the way." Since the decision to make Kenshi Empress was announced on the Third Day of the First Month, it is possible that the poem was sent after the announcement. EMZ, 3: 107.
8. "Moon" is a metaphor for Shōshi.

Kumo no ue o	To one outside the clouds,
Kumo no yoso nite	Viewing from afar
Omoiyaru	The realm above the clouds,
Tsuki wa kawarazu	Only the moon, it seems,
Ame no shita nite.	Shines unchanged in the sky.

There were many such melancholy incidents. Dozing off toward dawn on a night when she had been particularly unhappy, the Empress saw a dim figure in her dreams whom she recognized as the late Emperor. She could not keep back her tears as she murmured:

Au koto o	Now that I cannot meet him,
Ima wa nakine no	When shall I see my lord again,
Yume narade	Unless in a dream
Itsu ka wa kimi o	Such as one dreams
Mata wa mirubeki.	When one cries oneself to sleep?

On several occasions, Emperor Sanjō remarked to Michinaga that he considered it proper to raise Kenshi to Imperial status. Michinaga always protested. "Seishi has been with Your Majesty for years," he would say, "and she also has a large family of children. It would be only right to promote her first. Kenshi's future will take care of itself; there is no need for haste." "Your attitude is not as I would have it," the Emperor finally told him in an aggrieved voice. "Do you object to the connection with me?" "If such is Your Majesty's pleasure, by all means issue the decree as soon as an auspicious date can be chosen," Michinaga answered. He left the Palace and set swiftly about the necessary preparations. Since there were no obstacles or other reasons for postponement, it was decided to make Kenshi an Empress, with the title Chūgū, on the Fourteenth of the Second Month.[9] Michinaga worked frantically to get things ready on time.

Though the ritual on the day of the investiture was merely the usual one, it seemed exceptionally dignified and impressive.[10] In the past, it had been almost impossible to distinguish the various ranks of Kenshi's attendants, who had all dressed as they pleased. Some of them had disapproved of such laxity, but many of those very ladies found their prescribed costumes a source of embarrassment on the day of their mistress's elevation. The timid and conservative were obliged by the regulations to put on bombycine jackets, whereas others who had prided themselves on their elegance were suddenly confronted by the devastating necessity of appearing in plain silk. The affair had its amusing side, but everything was different now that

9. See s.n. 75.　　　　　　　　　10. See s.n. 76.

Kenshi was an Empress. It was only natural that distinctions should be enforced, and thus that everyone should envy certain ladies who had formerly seemed undistinguished—like Ōsaishō no Kimi,[11] whom people had derisively nicknamed Granny, but who now waited on Kenshi in a stunning bombycine jacket in grape colors—and that no attention should be paid to others who had thought highly of themselves. All the ladies were secretly upset, but they concealed their distress as best they could, unable to complain to Kenshi. One could not help feeling sorry for them. Some very pretty daughters of gentlemen of Fifth Rank had been told to act as Lady Chamberlains, and they too were most pathetic as they stoically carried trays, ran errands, and performed similar duties, all of which seemed to them dreadfully humiliating.

Wearing a white costume and a formal coiffure, Kenshi took her place on the dining bench, with a fierce-looking lion and a Korean dog mounting guard beside her curtain-dais. The coiffure suited her admirably, lending an impressive air of dignity to her plump, girlish face, and everyone agreed that she made a perfect Empress. She was just nineteen. "It can't be more than three or four years since her presentation, and here she is already an Empress," people calculated. Grand Empress Shōshi had entered the Palace at twelve and received Imperial status at thirteen, but Kenshi was much more grown up. The fire-huts in the courtyard and the new guard station were staffed by low-ranking guards officers, who performed their duties with a great air of importance; and freshly appointed Chief Attendants and others bustled officiously about. The great banquet was to take place directly. Michinaga's oldest brother, Major Counselor Michitsuna,[12] had been selected to serve as Master of the Empress's Household, and almost all the other offices had been filled. It was rare indeed, people said, for two sisters to have the good fortune to become Empresses in succession.

Although the Emperor was anxious to promote Seishi, he could not bring himself to speak to Michinaga about it. Seishi herself did not mind, but various people who claimed connections with her ladies made a point of passing along the views of those outside the Court. "Her Ladyship must be miserable. It's a disgrace! I've never head of anything so unfair," the visitors said, putting on knowing airs. Some of the ladies showed Seishi letters from such people. "See what So-and-so has to say about it," they urged her.

"Why must they repeat those disagreeable things?" Seishi said seriously.

11. Unidentified.
12. Although second in order of birth, Michitsuna was the oldest of Kaneie's surviving sons.

"If people choose to gossip I don't want to know it. I have given up any idea of becoming an Empress, and now think only of what is to be my lot in the next world." Her protests merely provoked sage comments from the ladies. "Yes, but Her Ladyship is looking at things from a very special point of view—one that isolates her from human emotions and worldly concerns."

Since Michinaga was always amazingly sensitive to the feelings of others, he paid several visits to the Palace around that time. "With so many children, Seishi ought not to remain a Junior Consort. I hope you will promote her soon," he urged. "I quite agree," replied Emperor Sanjō ,"but judging from the stories my courtiers tell about earlier days, it appears that although in antiquity even a Palace Attendant's daughter sometimes became an Empress, no Counselor's daughter has been selected during more recent reigns, to say nothing of our own period."[13]

"The gentlemen are mistaken," answered Michinaga. "I am sure there is no such rule. Anyway, Your Majesty can simply issue a decree making Naritoki a posthumous Minister of State."

"Then I shall ask you to see to it," said the Emperor.

Michinaga transmitted the Imperial command to the Council of State. "Find an auspicious date on which to give Naritoki, the Koichijō Major Captain, the posthumous title of Chancellor. Be careful to avoid conflicts with important religious events, and read the proclamation of appointment at the Major Captain's grave," he said.[14] One of the Controllers received the order.

In the Fourth Month, after the main shrines had held their festivals, an auspicious date was chosen for an Imperial Messenger to visit Naritoki's grave. It was considered appropriate for Michitō,[15] the Master of the Palace Repairs Office, to participate in the ceremony, and thus he too made the necessary preparations and went to the grave. Naritoki was a lucky man, everyone said, to have had a fine daughter to bring him honors after his death. Naritoki's younger sister, Hōshi, the Sen'yōden Consort, had been

13. It was expected that the father of an Empress would be a Minister of State. However, Kōshi (842–910), the principal consort of Emperor Seiwa (850–80), was the daughter of a Middle Counselor, Fujiwara Nagara (802–56), who had been posthumously named Minister of the Left at the time of Kōshi's elevation to Imperial status—a precedent to which Michinaga makes oblique reference in his reply. Satō 1929, p. 32.

14. "Religious events" translates *kamigoto* ("[Shintō] god matters"). The festivals of Kamo, Inari, Yamashina, Hirano, Matsunoo, Umenomiya, Hirose, Tatsuta, Hiyoshi, and Yoshida Shrines all took place during the Fourth Month. According to *Kugyō bunin*, 1: 241, Naritoki's posthumous appointment was to the office of Minister of the Right.

15. Naritoki's son.

one of Emperor Murakami's special favorites, but she had never become more than a Junior Consort, and her one son had been feeble-minded— not at all what might have been expected of two such brilliant parents. It was splendid for the Koichijō Minister Morotada, people agreed, that his granddaughter should succeed where his daughter had failed.

Seishi assumed the Imperial title Kōgō on the Twenty-eighth of the Fourth Month. The Izumo Middle Counselor Takaie, a son of the late Chancellor, became Master of her Household—possibly because no one else was particularly eager to serve, or because he had heard that the office was going begging.[16] There was no competition for the other appointments, and nothing was done elaborately, but the usual forms were observed, and people exclaimed with tiresome frequency that Seishi was to be congratulated. One might call her, they said, the classic example of a lucky woman. "She is most fortunate—a model of feminine happiness," said Michinaga. "Though she has been alone all these years since the death of her parents, she has never committed an indiscretion or caused anyone the smallest concern. Isn't it wonderful that of all her children none should have been mentally retarded? People always shower Emperor Murakami with extravagant praise, but his eighth son, the child of Naritoki's sister, Hōshi, was an absolute dolt. Seishi has five or six sons and daughters, and there isn't a fool or idiot in the lot." With Michinaga himself talking in that vein, it may be imagined that others ran on at disagreeable length.

Empress Seishi had begun to think of remodeling the Koichijō house, and Emperor Sanjō was no doubt feeling happy because he had finally got his way. Everything seemed quite perfect. But Seishi could not keep from worrying about the future, and it is possible that the Emperor shared her apprehension. Once he sent her this poem:

Uchihaete	I am fated, it seems,
Obotsukanasa o	To go through life
Yo to tomo ni	A prey to unease—
Obomeku mi to mo	To fears I have already
Narinubeki kana.	Known for too long.

Her reply:

16. According to Sanesuke, who was then a Major Counselor, this was because Michinaga had let his opposition to the promotion be known. Sanesuke's diary and Michinaga's agree that Seishi's investiture (rikkō no gi) was attended by only four nobles of importance— Sanesuke himself, his brother Yasuhira, Seishi's brother Michitō, and Takaie. The other gentlemen of the Court were all in attendance on Kenshi, whose re-entry into the Dairi had been scheduled for the same date (27 iv 1012, rather than 28 iv). Shōyūki, 3: 11–16 (27 iv Chōwa 1); Midō kanpakuki, 2: 150 (same date).

Tsuyu bakari   If only there was someone
Aware o shiran   With but a shred
Hito mogana   Of human feeling—
Obotsukanasa o   Someone to say, "Come now,
Sate mo ika ni to.   You must not worry so."

One of the Emperor's chief concerns was the future of Princess Tōshi.

Even though the period of mourning for ex-Emperor Ichijō had ended, Grand Empress Shōshi remained sunk in gloom. She found it a cruel trial not to be able to watch the Crown Prince as he developed into a handsome little boy, and she never felt cheerful except when she was with the Third Prince, who trotted about the house in an irresistibly appealing manner.

Soon autumn gave way to winter. In Kenshi's apartments at the Imperial Palace, all was bright, new splendor after the Change of Dress,[17] a vivid reminder of the passing of time.

Everyone was caught up in a rush of preparation for the Thanksgiving Purification, which was to take place during the following month. Since Emperor Sanjō had stopped wearing mourning in the preceding month, and since the anniversary of the ex-Emperor's death had been duly observed, the Court was free to concentrate on the approaching ceremonies.[18] Michinaga's daughter Ishi,[19] the Principal Handmaid, was to be Acting Consort. Of her twenty carriages, three were to be supplied by Grand Empress Shōshi and three by Empress Kenshi, and both ladies were taking great pains to make an impressive showing. Everyone said that the carriages from the two Empresses would be the great sight of the Purification.

When the long-awaited day arrived, the Acting Consort's carriage and the others were so gorgeous that I could not possibly describe them. Some were thatched with cypress bark; others had been constructed to resemble Chinese ships, and the sleeves of the ladies and everything else followed the Chinese style. Gold and silver lacquer adorned the paneled entrances and exits.[20] As the procession moved along, the total effect of so much

17. *Koromogae*, a ceremony performed twice annually: (1) on the First of the Fourth Month, when tatami mats, lantern screens, and the like were replaced, and the heavy garments, room hangings, and curtains used during winter and spring were exchanged for new, lighter ones appropriate for warm weather; and (2) on the First of the Tenth Month, when corresponding preparations were made for the cold season.

18. The Purification took place on the Twenty-seventh of the intercalary Tenth Month; the Thanksgiving on the Twenty-second of the Eleventh Month. EM, 1: 328, n. 20.

19. Then thirteen.

20. Passengers entered from the rear and descended from the front.

magnificence, of so many mountain ranges, overflowing seas, and inlaid designs—the total effect, quite simply, dazzled the eyes of the spectators and paralyzed their powers of discrimination. Every lady in every carriage was attired in fifteen layers of clothing, and there were some whose Imperial mistresses had dressed them in garments of Chinese brocade.[21] But the reader must imagine for himself the unearthly beauty of that glittering parade. The horses and carriages of the great nobles and their sons—indeed, even their bows and quivers—were a rare and unprecedented sight. The past, I need scarcely say, has known no such spectacle, and there seems little prospect of anything like it in the future.

The short winter day drew to a close, and then there was the excitement of the Thanksgiving. The ceremonies on that occasion were solemn and dignified. The East's songs were composed by the Ise Chief Priest Suke-chika, a son of Ōnakatomi Yoshinobu, and the West's by Minamoto Kanezumi, the former governor of Kaga. Sukechika and Kanezumi were probably chosen because it was thought that they would produce outstanding poems, since Sukechika was Yoshinobu's son and Kanezumi was a close relative of Controller Kintada.[22]

Rice-Threshing Song of the East, "Sakata-no-kōri," by Sukechika:[23]

Yama no goto	Harvesting and heaping
Sakata no ine o	Mountain-high
Nukitsumite	The rice of Sakata,
Kimi ga chitose no	We thresh and offer it as first fruits,
Hatsuho ni zo tsuku.	That our lord may live forever.

Song for the Kagura,[24] by Sukechika:

21. Chinese brocades (*karanishiki*) were imported to Japan in large quantities during the mid-Heian period. Some notion of their structure may be obtained from the silk scraps found in the cavity of a wooden statue of Śākyamuni at the Seiryōji in Kyōto. The silks were apparently placed in the statue in China in 985 and brought to Japan *in situ* three years later. Two types of brocade from the statue have been described: a weft-faced compound tabby and a weft-faced compound twill. Nishimura 1971–75, 2: 7; Henderson and Hurvitz 1956, pp. 5–6, 34–38; Sasaki 1958, pp. 36–37.

22. Sukechika and Kanezumi were close friends. Kanezumi's grandfather, Minamoto Kintada (889–948), was a highly regarded poet during the reigns of Daigo and Suzaku.

23. Chanted by young girls as they threshed the offering-rice at the Thanksgiving site. Sakata-no-kōri in Ōmi was situated in what is now northeastern Shiga Prefecture. EMZ, 3: 140.

24. Performed on the Day of the Snake. Although the Yuki and Suki banquets were considered the principal events on the Day of the Dragon and the Snake, respectively, there were two feasts on each day, one at each of the two provincial banquet sites. The ceremonies on the two days were virtually identical, except that a kagura performance was offered on the Day of the Snake only, traditionally at the Seishodō. EMZ, 3: 140; Ishimura 1958, 1: 154.

Ōyashima	Since the beginning
Kuni shiroshimesu	Of the Imperial dominion,
Hajime yori	Countless are the gods
Yaoyorozuyo no	Who have guarded
Kami zo mamoreru.	The Land of the Eight Great Islands.

Entrance Music, "Takamikurayama":[25]

Yorozuyo wa	For a myriad ages
Takamikurayama	Shall we look up to him,
Ugoki naki	Eternally unchanging
Tokiwa kakiwa ni	And immovable
Aogubeki kana.	As Mount Takamikurayama.

Song for the Ha Passage, "Shikichi":[26]

Ōmiya no	Long shall it flourish—
Shikichi zo itodo	That site
Sakaenuru	Of the great shrine
Yae no kumigaki	Where stands the many-layered fence
Tsukurikasanete.	Fashioned of intertwined boughs.

Song for the Kyū Passage, "Kanayama":[27]

Kanayama ni	The fruitful rice plants
Kataku nezaseru	Of our native land
Tokiwagi no	Grow and multiply in profusion,
Kazu ni oimasu	Like the strong-rooted evergreens
Kuni no tomigusa.	On Mount Kanayama.

For the Departure Music, "Yasukawa":[28]

| Suberagi no | Now with the reign |
| Miyo o machidete | Of our Imperial lord |

25. The entrance music was presented while the musicians filed in to take their places. Takamikurayama, presumably an old Ōmi place-name, has not been identified.

26. Court music (gagaku) pieces usually consisted of three parts: (1) a "prelude" (jo), (2) a "breaking-away" (ha) movement, and (3) a "rapid" (kyū) finale. In present-day performances of the Chinese pieces in the repertoire (tōgaku), the prelude is in free rhythm but with melodic motion and drum (taiko) accents; the breaking-away movement is marked by a transition from a free to a fixed meter; and the rapid finale is the culmination of the preceding sections. Kishibe 1969, p. 24; Garfias 1975, p. 80. Shikichi, an unidentified Ōmi place-name, puns on shikichi, "building site." "Great shrine" refers to the Yuki Hall at the daijōsai site.

27. On kyū, see the note above. Kanayama has not been identified.

28. "Departure music" was played by the musicians as they withdrew after a performance. The Yasukawa, a river in Shiga Prefecture (Ōmi Province), empties into Lake Biwa.

Mizu sumeru	All is calm
Yasu no kawanami	As the rippling waters
Nodokokarurashi.	Of Yasukawa's limpid stream.

For the Entrance Music on the following day, "Nagaranoyama":[29]

Ametsuchi no	Long indeed
Tomo ni hisashiki	Shall his reign endure,
Na ni yorite	For his fame
Nagaranoyama no	Shall be eternal
Nagaki miyo kana.	As heaven and earth.

Song for the Ha Passage, "Yoshimizu":[30]

Yoshimizu no	Many are the good things,
Yoki koto ōku	Fair as Yoshimizu's stream,
Tsumeru kana	That we have piled in abundance,
Ōkurayama no	Making them tower
Hodo haruka nite.	Like Treasure-house Mountain.

Song for the Kyū Passage:

Yūshide no	Dangling braids
Hikage no kazura	Of paper-mulberry
Yorikakete	Cord pendants—
Toyonoakari no	Pleasant indeed,
Omoshiroki kana.	The Toyonoakari Banquet!

For the Departure Music, "Yasura-no-sato":[31]

Morobito no	The tranquility
Negau kokoro no	Of Yasura Village
Ōmi naru	In Ōmi—
Yasura-no-sato no	The heart's desire
Yasurakeku shite.	Of every man.

29. Nagarayama, a mountain west of the Onjōji in the present Ōtsu-shi, Shiga-ken, functions in the poem as a jo (introduction) for *nagaki*, "long." Like the Suki (West) music the author proceeds to list, the four Yuki (East) gagaku numbers just enumerated (i.e. the songs for the ha and kyū passages) were probably performed during the festivities that took place on the two days after the Day of the Hare, in which case "the following day" would have been the Day of the Snake, as *Shōkai*, 5: 105, identifies it. (EMZ, 3: 141, takes it to have been the Day of the Dragon.) As indicated in s.n. 18, the order of the principal events was as follows: offerings (Hare); Yuki Banquet (Dragon); Suki Banquet and kagura performance (Snake); Toyonoakari Banquet (Horse).

30. Yoshimizu survives as the name of an area in Moriyama-machi, Yasu-gun, Shiga-ken, on the left bank of the Yasugawa. Ōkurayama (Treasure-house Mountain) has not been identified.

31. A village in Kurita District, Ōmi.

Rice-Threshing Song of the West, "Ōkurayama,"[32] by Kanezumi:

Futaba yori	Though the years grow many,
Ōkurayama ni	Never shall it fail—
Hakobu ine	The rice transported
Toshi wa tsumu tomo	To Ōkurayama
Tsukuru yo mo araji.	Since time immemorial.

Song for the Kagura, "Nagamurayama":[33]

Kimi ga miyo	The folk will deck their heads
Nagamurayama no	With *sakaki* leaves
Sakakiba o	From Nagamura Mountain—
Yasoujibito no	Omen of our sovereign's
Kazashi ni wa sen.	Everlasting reign.

Song for the Ha Passage on the Day of the Dragon, "Tamamatsuyama":

Amatsusora	Under the clear skies
Ashita ni haruru	Of early morn,
Hajime ni wa	Even Tamamatsuyama,
Tamamatsuyama no	Mountain of Beauteous Pines,
Kage sae zo sou.	Seems close at hand.

Song for the Kyū Passage on the same day, "Inabusayama":

Toshi tsukuri	Since this is a reign
Tanoshikarubeki	In which men will prosper,
Miyo nareba	Growing their rice,
Inabusayama no	Our land has proved fruitful
Yutaka narikeru.	As Inabusayama, Hill of Plenteous Rice.

For the Entrance Music on the same day, "Sazareishiyama":

Kazu shiranu	For all the generations
Sazareishiyama	Until Sazareishiyama's countless pebbles
Kotoshi yori	Turn into boulders—
Iwao to naran	Even so long
Hodo wa ikuyo zo.	Shall his reign endure.

For the Departure Music on the same day, "Chitoseyama":[34]

Ugoki naki	Even immovable Mount Chitose
Chitosenoyama ni	Cries again and again

---

32. Presumably the name of a mountain in Tanba. Unidentified.

33. Unidentified (as are Tamamatsuyama, Inabusayama, Sazareishiyama, Tomitsukiyama, and Chijikawa below). The symbolism is auspicious because *naga* means long.

34. A mountain in Kuwada District, Tanba Province (now in Kyōto Prefecture).

Itodoshiku	In a mighty voice,
Yorozuyo souru	"May our Emperor live
Koe no suru kana.	A thousand years!"

For the Ha Passage on the Day of the Snake, "Tomitsukiyama":

Kimi ga yo wa	Auspicious as Tomitsukiyama,
Tomitsukiyama no	Mountain of Riches,
Tsugitsugi ni	Our Emperor's reign
Sakae zo masan	Shall prosper ever increasingly
Yorozuyo made ni.	For a myriad generations.

Song for the Kyū Passage on the same day, "Nagamurayama":

Yorozuyo o	For a myriad generations
Nagamurayama no	We shall endure, with lives
Nagaraete	Long as the name of Long Village Mountain,
Tsukizu hokoban	Never failing to transport
Mitsugimono kana.	The tribute rice.

For the Entrance Music on the same day, "Tominoogawa":[35]

Ame no shita	Never shall there be a barren autumn
Tominoogawa no	For the fields
Sue nareba	Bordering the lower reaches
Izure no aki ka	Of the fruitful Tominoo River
Uruwazarubeki.	In our fertile land.

For the Departure Music on the same day, "Chijikawa":

Nigori naku	The Toyonoakari Banquet—
Miewataru kana	For the first time
Chijikawa no	We gaze at the Chiji River
Hajimete sumeru	And behold limpid waters
Toyonoakari ni.	Free of impurity.[36]

Poems were composed and inscribed on folding screens for the occasion, but I shall omit them because they were not very different.

Thus ended the ceremonies that had claimed so much of the Court's attention since the preceding year. "How nice it would be," thought Emperor

35. Said to have been the name of a river in Ikaruka District, Tanba (now a part of Kyōto Prefecture).

36. Probably an allusion to the legend that the waters of the Yellow River flow clear once in every millennium, marking the appearance of a great sage. The poet uses the *chi* of Chijikawa, which can mean "a thousand," to suggest the Chinese legend and, in so doing, to praise the new Emperor. *Sumeru*, from *sumu*, "be clear," contains overtones of a homophone meaning "finish," appropriate because the Toyonoakari Banquet was the last major daijōsai event. EMZ, 3: 145.

Sanjō, savoring his new leisure, "if only Suishi and Genshi were still here." [37]

Empress Kenshi had begun to feel ill for no apparent reason. Michinaga worried at first, but having been told by her ladies that she had missed two periods, and having observed for himself her lack of appetite, he concluded that she might be pregnant. "It's very odd that her periods should have stopped last month," agreed her nurse, Naishi no Suke. [38] "I feel sure she must have conceived." And that was indeed the case. Michinaga and the Emperor were both delighted. "There's nothing to worry about," said Michinaga. "It makes no difference that she can't eat; she's supposed to be that way." He selected an auspicious date on which to begin prayers for a safe delivery.

The Twelfth Month brought busy days for everyone. At the Buddhist Names Services commissioned by the Emperor and other members of the Imperial family, solemn voices intoned the traditional *Buddhist Names Sutra*, recalling in moving fashion the poet's words, "May they vanish with the white snow." [39]

Soon came the end of the old year [1012], followed on the First by the Congratulations and other brilliant occasions. The officials selected to drink the leftover spiced wines in the Courtiers' Hall indulged in some improper and disagreeable behavior. [40] From the First on, all kinds of ceremonies had to be performed, and every day seemed taken up with a happy event.

Empress Kenshi was to withdraw from the Palace in the First Month. On the appointed day, she dressed her ladies in dazzling costumes; and that night there were ceremonies of a nature the reader will be able to picture for himself. Kenshi had acquired a reputation for traveling in style, but it is unlikely that any of her earlier journeys can have compared with this one. From her litter curtains down, all was brilliance and luxury. Since the Kyōgoku Mansion was situated in a proscribed direction, she proceeded to the Higashisanjōin. Emperor Sanjō, to whom she had grown very dear, felt unreasonably concerned about her.

37. Both had died before 1012.
38. Wife of Fujiwara Naritō, a tenjōbito who held a number of provincial governorships and other minor offices in the course of his career. EMZ, 3: 147.
39. See Chapter 3, nn. 57, 58. The allusion is to *Shūishū* 258, by Ki no Tsurayuki: Toshi no uchi ni / tsumoreru tsumi wa / kakikurashi / furu shirayuki to / tomo ni kienamu. ("May the grievous sins piled high through the year vanish with the white snow that darkens the sky as it falls.")
40. After the Emperor had partaken of the *toso* and other beverages during each of the *hagatame* ceremonies (see s.n. 23), the remainder, including the contents of the serving jugs, was consumed by designated "after-takers" (*shindori*), chosen for their ability to stay sober.

At the Higashisanjōin, Michinaga selected a propitious date on which to begin constant recitations of the *Great Wisdom, Kannon, Healing Buddha,* and *Life* sutras.[41] (Readings of the *Lotus* had begun as soon as the Empress's condition was made known.) As reciters he sought out monks who had lived for many years in mountain retreats, recluses who shunned human habitations. Continuous rites were also commissioned by the Court —altogether a most impressive array of prayers.

In those days, Akinobu, Michinaga's second son by Meishi, held the office of Director of the Imperial Stables of the Right. He was about eighteen or nineteen years old. What possessed him I don't know, but late one night the boy went to Gyōen, the Skin-robed Saint,[42] to ask to enter the Buddhist clergy. To become a monk, he told the Saint, had always been his dearest wish.

"Your father is devoted to you," Gyōen protested. "I know he would upbraid me."

"Such fears are unworthy of a holy man," Akinobu answered. "It shouldn't matter to someone like you if my father does object. You're wrong to feel that way. Even if you turn me down, I won't give up. Nothing can change my mind."

"You're right," Gyōen said. Shedding many tears, he made Akinobu a monk.

Akinobu borrowed one of the Saint's robes, gave him his own informal cloak, his trousers, and all his other elegant garments except one cotton-padded robe, and proceeded before dawn to the Mudōji on Mount Hiei,[43] accompanied by a monk the holy man had given him as an attendant.

---

41. (1) *Great Wisdom Sutra* (*Daihannya*[*haramitta*]*kyō*; Skt. *Mahā-prajñā-pāramitā-sūtra*), the fundamental philosophical work of the Mahāyāna school. Recited in the Nara and early Heian periods, in particular, as protection against many kinds of evils. (2) *Kannon Sutra* (*Kannongyō,* another name for the [*Kanzeon bosatsu*] *fumonbon,* the twenty-fifth chapter of the *Lotus Sutra*). Promises to save believers from "all trouble." (3) On the *Healing Buddha Sutra,* see Chapter 5, n. 53. (4) *Life Sutra* (*Jumyōkyō*), a text in which the Buddha explains how to avoid the miseries of old age, sickness, and death. Important in the eleventh century. See De Visser 1935, 2: 512.

42. Gyōen, an ascetic who is believed to have been a native of Kyūshū, had come to the capital around 1004 and founded the Gyōganji (popularly called Kawandō, Skin Hall), a temple that was highly regarded by people of all classes. "Saint" translates *hijiri,* a term used of hermit monks, wandering ascetics, and popular preachers. Such men often carried horn-tipped staffs, used berries for prayer beads, and dressed in deerskins, a practice Gyōen seems to have continued after settling in the city. For another famous account of Akinobu's renunciation of the world, which took place at the Kawandō in the First Month of 1012, not in 1013, see *Ōkagami,* pp. 209ff.

43. The Mudōji, on the south peak of the mountain, was part of the Enryakuji complex. It consisted primarily of a hall dedicated to Fudō. Akinobu lived there during much of his life as a monk, and died there in 1027.

Perhaps because of a word from the Teacher,[44] the boy's absence was discovered around daybreak. Michinaga sent search parties in every direction, and it was soon learned that he had taken vows at Gyōen's temple. In great distress, Michinaga sent a messenger to fetch Gyōen. The Saint was afraid to go, but after repeated summonses he had to present himself. Michinaga questioned him tearfully, and the Saint described his conversation with Akinobu. "I have caused you a great deal of trouble," he said. "Please forgive me." "Why should I blame you?" Michinaga answered. "A refusal wouldn't have stopped him. His mind was made up. I find it impressive, I must admit, for a young boy to turn his back on his family and decide on such a course without a word to anyone. His will is stronger than mine."[45] Michinaga hurried off toward Mount Hiei.[46]

Meishi was dazed with grief.

A number of people heard of Michinaga's departure and made haste to join him. The ascent seemed interminable, but at last he reached the temple. There was something inexpressibly appealing and awe-inspiring about his son's shaven head, so different from the anonymous bald pate of the typical monk; and he found it impossible to keep from weeping. His companions were also deeply moved.

"What made you decide to do it?" Michinaga asked through his tears. "Were you worried about anything? Did some act of mine seem harsh? Were you impatient for a promotion? Was there a girl you were in love with? As long as my influence lasted, I was ready to get you anything you wanted. I feel utterly miserable. How could you have done such a thing with no consideration for your mother or me?"

Overcome with emotion, Akinobu burst into tears. "I wanted nothing at all," he said. "It is just that always, even as a child, I have had my heart set on being a monk. I was ashamed to tell you, since that was not what you had in mind for me, and while I hesitated you raised me so high that I became involved in Court life against my will. But I am quite, quite sure that I will be most useful to everybody as I am now."

It might be best, Michinaga thought, for the boy to stay on at the Mudōji. While he was issuing the necessary instructions, messengers from the Im-

44. Probably a Mudōji monk, Bishop Kyōmei (965–1038), with whom Michinaga was on close terms. Akinobu became his disciple. EMZ, 3: 154.

45. Michinaga's diary entry for the day following Akinobu's departure records his own desire to become a monk. *Midō kanpakuki*, 2: 133 (17 i Chōwa 1).

46. Both the interview with Gyōen and the hasty journey to Mount Hiei appear to be inventions. It was Yorimichi who went to the Mudōji at once; Michinaga's visit took place three months later. EMZ, 3: 154.

perial ladies began to arrive, and soon the temple compound was astir.

Still in tears, Michinaga went back down the mountain to arrange for clothing and other requisites to be sent off at once. Meishi wept miserably as she prepared the robes.

Akinobu's brothers and his Imperial sisters also sent robes, but he kept only the ones from Meishi. The others he turned over to the Tendai monks. They were much too fine for him, he said; plain clothes would answer his present needs.

Michinaga and both Empresses sent furnishings for his cell.

It was an impressive and unusual entry into religious life.

Around that time, Emperor Sanjō asked Empress Seishi to come to stay at the Palace. She hesitated, wondering if it was the right thing to do, but Michinaga, who must have read the Imperial mind, took it on himself to bring the matter up. "Why doesn't Empress Seishi come back?" he asked. "It would be an excellent arrangement to have two Empresses in attendance on Your Majesty; Kenshi ought not to be the only one."

After many Imperial quotations of this remark, together with repeated injunctions against further vacillation, Seishi agreed to go.[47] She ordered a new litter and took great pains to make her procession opulent and beautiful. The entrance did not, to be sure, equal the spectacle on the night of Kenshi's departure, but identical ceremonies were observed. The Princess[48] rode in a string-decorated carriage. Lady Dainagon, the daughter of the Retired Major Counselor,[49] sat in the litter as the Empress's attendant. A number of ladies had recently entered Seishi's service, and the larger group made a pleasingly elegant showing.

The Empress took along three of her sons.[50] Prince Moroakira's hair touched the calves of his legs in back, and everyone who saw his pretty face wished for just such a little boy. Dressed in an informal costume, he bore the unmistakable stamp of royalty. No one could have mistaken him for a son of even the greatest noble.

After Empress Seishi's return, as may be imagined, she and Emperor Sanjō exchanged many interesting stories about things that had happened

47. She returned to the Palace on the Twentieth of the Third Month, 1013. Kenshi had left in the First Month.

48. Princess Shishi, the second of Emperor Sanjō's two daughters by Seishi. (The older daughter, Princess Tōshi, was serving as Ise Virgin.)

49. Minamoto Shigemitsu, so called because he had resigned his office in 992, six years before his death.

50. Atsuakira (994–1051), Atsuhira (999 or 1000–1050), and Moroakira (1004 or 1005–85). Atsunori, the second son (997–1054), remained in the city because of illness. EM, 1: 337, n. 32.

during their long separation. Gazing at the fire-huts in front of her apartments, the dining bench, and the other symbols of Imperial status, the Emperor said with evident emotion, "This is how I have always hoped to see
you. The realization of my ambitions for you means more to me than my
own good fortune." His one great regret was the absence of Princess Tōshi,
who had grown into a sweet young girl of twelve or thirteen.

Around that time, a number of gentlemen with daughters had begun to
show an interest in Michinaga's son Norimichi, the Commander of the
Left Gate Guards, but Michinaga and the boy's mother had come to no
decision about his marriage. Kintō, the Shijō Major Counselor, was the
father of two daughters, the younger of whom had been adopted at birth
and reared as a Princess by the Shijō Empress.[51] The older, Kintō's chief
joy, had been reared at home with meticulous care. Her mother was a
daughter of Emperor Murakami's ninth son by Takamitsu's daughter—
a Princess famous for her beauty, whom the Awata Lord Michikane had
adopted and eventually bestowed on Kintō. The Princess had become a
nun years ago, leaving her husband in effect a widower, but Kintō had
developed no new attachment. All his love was reserved for his daughter,
whom he now proposed to bestow on Norimichi. Since Norimichi greeted
his oblique overtures with every indication of pleasure, the affair was soon
settled, and Kintō set about the necessary preparations.

It would have been usual to marry so carefully educated a daughter to a
reigning sovereign or Crown Prince. At Emperor Sanjō's Court, however,
the outlook was hopeless. Empress Seishi had long ago borne the sovereign
several sons, and Empress Kenshi was someone with whom competition
was unthinkable. The Crown Prince was still only a mischievous little boy
of three or four. With both royal personages eliminated, who was left?
Kintō had observed that Michinaga's sons were regarded as the only young
men with really brilliant prospects, and so it was natural that he decided
on Norimichi. After a great many elaborate preparations, he received his
new son-in-law in the west wing of the Shijō Palace. No doubt he would
have liked to make use of the main hall, but Senior Grand Empress Junshi
was in residence there, and he probably did not feel like asking her to
move out. Junshi helped with the wedding arrangements.

Since the bride was only thirteen or fourteen, her abundant hair hung a
little short of the floor, but it was beautiful to the very ends, and Norimichi

51. Junshi, Kintō's sister. According to *Sonpi bunmyaku*, 2: 2, Kintō also had two sons,
the monk Ninnyū and Sadayori (995–1045), a poet and calligrapher who ultimately attained
the office of Provisional Middle Counselor with Senior Second Rank. *Eiga* attributes a third
son to him, the monk Ryōkai. The names of the daughters are unknown.

was captivated by her enchanting face. Thanks to Kintō's impeccable taste, the ceremonies were perfectly executed. The wedding banquet a few days later was also a splendid affair. The Senior Grand Empress, herself a woman of faultless taste, had taken a great interest in everything connected with the marriage—indeed, she and Kintō had made all the arrangements between them through constant consultations—and the results were extraordinary. No doubt Michinaga found numerous occasions to warn Norimichi to be on his best behavior. "The wedding ceremonies were most impressive. Kintō is a man who puts us all to shame, and it would be unfortunate if any thoughtlessness on your part were to injure his reputation," he said.

Junshi sent a number of her own robes, complete with appropriate accessories, to Norimichi's nurse, Kura no Myōbu.

Junshi was set on finding an equally good husband for her charge, Kintō's second daughter, before her own death.

At the Higashisanjōin, the days and months slipped by, bringing clear evidence that Empress Kenshi was pregnant. She was feeling wretched. The Emperor sent her messages twice a day, constantly bemoaned the time the child was taking to arrive, and commissioned an imposing array of prayers for a safe delivery.

II

THE

BUDDING FLOWER

Afte r ex-Emperor Ichijō's death, there were rumors of various kinds about his Junior Consorts and concubines. The Shōkyōden Consort Genshi was said to be carrying on a secret affair with the Minamoto Consultant Yorisada, a son of the late Minister of Ceremonial, Prince Tamehira. Her father, Akimitsu, heard the stories, investigated them, and saw with his own eyes that they were true. Wild with rage, he cropped off her beautiful hair and forced her to become a nun. There seemed no end to his persecutions. It was a shocking, incredible affair, and one that caused heated discussion, both in society and among the members of Akimitsu's household. Meanwhile, Yorisada continued his stealthy visits. "Get out!" Akimitsu said to Genshi. "I don't care where you go."

Genshi went to live with her nurse, who was the mistress of a monk named Bishop Jichisei.[1] Yorisada visited her faithfully, convinced that fate had ordained it all, and her hair soon grew to a presentable length.

Everyone agreed that Akimitsu had been shockingly unfair. Although Yorisada was, perhaps, just another young noble, his father had been Emperor Murakami's fourth son, and his mother was the daughter of Minamoto Takaakira. Furthermore, his character was wholly admirable. Was it not strange, people asked one another, that Akimitsu should have been so ill-natured? After all, the Kurabeya Consort Sonshi had been given in marriage by her mother, Fujiwara Naishi no Suke, to Empress Seishi's brother Michitō, the Master of the Palace Repairs Office.[2]

1. Jichisei (983–1027) was a Tendai scholar-monk, known also as a poet, who frequented the Imperial Palace. "Mistress" translates *kurumayadori*, which can mean either a villa maintained by a monk as a private retreat or, as here, a mistress kept in such a house. EMZ, 3: 183.
2. Sonshi was another of Emperor Ichijō's consorts. There was a further precedent in the

Empress Kenshi had taken up residence at Major Counselor Tadanobu's Ōimikado house after her withdrawal from the Palace early in her pregnancy.[3] Now, several months later, she decided to move to Tsuchimikado, just as everyone was expecting the baby to be born at Tadanobu's. Her host racked his brains for a suitable gift. She had moved to Ōimikado after a fire at the Higashisanjōin, where she had stayed first, and he was determined to find exactly the right farewell present to mark her departure. It would be best, he concluded, not to attempt anything elaborate. Expensive trifles were unlikely to intrigue a lady accustomed to every luxury. So he prepared a diary-like tale of life at Emperor Murakami's Court, made up of four large picture scrolls, with calligraphy by Sukemasa's daughter and Enkan,[4] and presented it to her in an elegant set of boxes, together with appropriate copybooks. She was delighted. To the ladies-in-waiting, he presented big partitioned cypress-wood boxes, filled with cosmetic powder and incense balls.

At the Tsuchimikado Mansion, all the prayers that had been used for Shōshi were recited again. With the weather so unbearably hot, Michinaga could not help worrying.

I should mention, perhaps, that a number of Tadanobu's Chief Stewards were honored by promotions in rank.

Kenshi's labor began on the evening of the Sixth of the Seventh Month in the second year of Chōwa [1013], while Michinaga was still fretting and offering prayers. Raising a deafening chorus of mystic incantations, the prayer-monks scattered rice furiously. A succession of Imperial messengers arrived, a cacophony of calamity-averting chants rang out, and during the Hour of the Dog [7:00-9:00 P.M.]—in answer, perhaps, to all their months of supplication—the child was safely delivered. There was a brief interval of noisy prayer, and then the afterbirth appeared. The monks were still quite fresh.

It was splendid that everything had gone so well, but when those in attendance avoided mentioning the child's sex, Michinaga realized that it must be a girl.[5] Although he was disappointed, he told himself that it was not so bad; this was not his first grandchild, and besides, Kenshi would

remarriage of one of Emperor Kazan's consorts to Fujiwara Sanesuke. It appears, however, that Yorisada had already taken another woman as his principal wife, and that Genshi was being treated as a concubine. See EMZ, 3: 184-85.

3. Tadanobu, a son of Tamemitsu, was Master of the Crown Prince's Household in 1013.

4. The calligrapher Sukemasa had died in 998. His daughter was the wife of Fujiwara Yasuhira. On Enkan, see Chapter 8, n. 125.

5. Princess Teishi, Kenshi's only child. Later known as Yōmeimon'in.

produce a son in time. He set about making the preparations for a bathing ceremony to be held that very night.[6]

No formal announcement was made to the Emperor. Naturally, however, he learned of the birth, and a messenger came from the Palace with a sword. It was not usual to send a sword to a newborn Princess, but there was no need to be constrained by the usages of the past in so flourishing an era, especially since the baby was Michinaga's grandchild; and thus a precedent was set. The messenger's reward was a magnificent robe, white as the plumage of the crane, which shines even in the dark.

One of the Crown Prince's nurses, Ōmi no Naishi,[7] was summoned for the rite of the first suckling. Numerous others were available, but Naishi was the daughter of one of Rinshi's own nurses, and she had also served Shōshi as a Handmaid.

The reader will be able to imagine the splendor of the bathing ceremonies performed during the next several days. Twenty men of Fifth and Sixth Rank were commanded to serve as bow-twangers. Those of Fifth Rank were Chamberlains. Since the baby was a girl, the Emperor was at pains to select handsome men.

No doubt everyone would have preferred a boy, but if people had spoken of the birth of Michinaga's first grandchild, the Crown Prince, as "the first blossom in the flowering of Michinaga's fortunes," then might not one say that the birth of this little Princess was a bud? For although the present might be a time of uncertainty and impatient waiting, the petals of a brilliant destiny would one day unfold.[8]

The white furnishings and all the other arrangements were just as they had been for Shōshi's confinements.

There were, it seemed, innumerable applicants for the office of nurse. Certain ladies in the Empress's entourage, the mothers of children fathered by men of some consequence, had apparently convinced themselves that their past services made them the only suitable candidates, but Kenshi had made up her mind to ignore their pleas and bring in new people from outside.

Despite the oppressive heat, each of the ladies took infinite pains to make

6. Princess Teishi was born around midnight on the Sixth, rather than early in the evening. The first bath actually took place only on the Eighth. EM, 1: 531, s.n. 507.

7. Tentatively identified by some scholars as Fujiwara Bishi, wife of Fujiwara Korenori (963–1033), who was one of Michinaga's Stewards. EMZ, 3: 195; Kugyō bunin, 1: 273.

8. Princess Teishi became the Kōgō of Emperor Go-Suzaku and the mother of Emperor Go-Sanjō (1034–73; r. 1068–72).

her white costume appear unusual and interesting, with most pleasing results.

Just as had happened after the births of Shōshi's sons, senior nobles of the first three ranks and ordinary courtiers of every rank down to Sixth presented themselves for the birth ceremonies, which were sponsored by Michinaga on the Third Night, by the Empress's Household on the Fifth, by the Court on the Seventh, and by Grand Empress Shōshi on the Ninth.

Since the Crown Prince was not yet weaned,[9] the new baby's attendants were soon deluged with messages demanding Ōmi no Naishi's return. There was no lack of volunteers to take her place. Kenshi was not entirely satisfied with any of them, but at length the honor fell to a daughter of the governor of Ise, a lady who was married to the late Regent Michitaka's son Chikayori, the Senior Assistant Minister of Central Affairs.[10] She put the Princess to the breast on the night of her arrival, freeing Naishi to go back to the Crown Prince. Lavish presents were bestowed on Naishi, and it was announced that her service would not be confined to the first suckling; she was to be counted among the Princess's regular nurses.

Since the infant Princess's hair was so long that it parted, they decided to let it hang naturally. How splendid it all was! Emperor Sanjō, charmed by glowing reports of her beauty, waited impatiently to see her.

Things happened to be fairly quiet elsewhere, and Michinaga took to appearing at odd hours of the night on errands connected with the baby. His visits upset the ladies, who were too oppressed by the intolerable heat to worry about appearances when they went to bed. The new nurse found the intrusions particularly embarrassing.

Realizing that the Emperor was anxious to see the baby, Michinaga had decided to arrange an Imperial visit to Tsuchimikado during the Ninth Month. (Empress Kenshi had been in poor health since the birth, and it seemed unlikely that she would be returning to the Palace very soon.) A great deal of preparatory polishing and repairing was going on at the mansion.

9. He was four years old.

10. The original reads: " . . . the honor fell to Toshitō's wife, who was a younger sister of the wife of the late Regent Michitaka's son Chikayori, the Senior Assistant Minister of Central Affairs. The nurse was a daughter of the governor of Ise." Evidence from *Midō kanpakuki* and elsewhere shows that the nurse, who was known both as Myōbu no Menoto and as Tayū no Menoto, was then Chikayori's wife, and that she probably had been married previously to Tachibana Toshitō, a provincial governor. "Governor of Ise" is a mistake for "Former Governor of Kaga," the title of the lady's father, Minamoto Kanezumi. "Toshitō's wife" is explained by commentators as the intrusion of an interlinear note, and "younger sister" as a corruption. EMZ, 3: 204-5.

The Emperor had hoped to hold the Fiftieth Day ceremonies at the Palace, but now they were to take place at the Tsuchimikado Mansion instead, because of Kenshi's inability to travel. Michinaga assumed responsibility for all the preparations. Supplies poured in from the Courtiers' Hall, from the Office of the Ladies-in-Waiting, and even from Grand Empress Shōshi's Household. It would have been impossible to count all the different varieties of boxed dainties and fruit baskets. The Emperor showed a gratifying interest in every detail of the proceedings, adding many admirable touches of his own. With the ceremonies scheduled for a date shortly after the Twentieth of the Eighth Month, the ladies worked early and late on their costumes, at the same time hurriedly preparing as best they could for the Imperial visit the following month.

All of Emperor Sanjō's principal ladies-in-waiting went to the Tsuchimikado Mansion for the baby's birth, and also for the Fiftieth Day celebration. The daughter of Tachibana Naishi no Suke (the Emperor's nurse), Minamoto Naishi no Suke, and other prominent gentlewomen, such as Sakari Shōshō, were registered on Kenshi's duty-board, and they seem to have been very faithful about visiting the mansion.[11]

Once the Ninth Month had begun, everyone sensed that the Imperial visit was imminent, and there was much rushing about. Aware that Kenshi's ladies would be magnificently attired, the attendants of her sister and mother, Ishi and Rinshi, were determined not to be outshone.[12] Great pains were also taken with the boat music. The visit itself I shall not describe in detail, since it followed the usual pattern. It was exactly like the one after the birth of Grand Empress Shōshi's son, the Crown Prince.

The mansion and grounds were a marvelous sight. To the delight of the spectators, the ivy on the island pines flamed with far greater brilliance than in ordinary years, as though caught up in the spirit of the occasion. The Emperor felt he had never beheld such dazzling splendor. And when the boats glided into sight as the dancing began, it seemed to him that such beauty must come from another world. The sound of the wind, sighing through the pines like the strains of a zither, blended harmoniously with

11. Tachibana Naishi no Suke's daughter has not been otherwise identified. According to one theory, she was the woman named next, Minamoto Naishi no Suke. Minamoto Naishi no Suke is mentioned *passim* in contemporary texts, which call her Lady Meishi and identify her as the wife of a provincial governor, Fujiwara Tokitaka. (Since there is no proof that these are one and the same woman, we have listed the two names separately in the Translation.) Sakari Shōshō, a daughter of the tenjōbito Fujiwara Sadataka (d. 981), was a *Goshūishū* poet. EMZ, 3: 207; *Sonpi bunmyaku*, 2: 59. The Empress's duty-board (*fuda*) was similar to the one in the Daibandokoro, on which see Appendix B, Seiryōden.

12. Ishi was then fourteen years old.

the music, and the ladies' dresses, billowing out at the edges of the blinds, were magnificent beyond description.

As soon as the Emperor went inside, he asked to see his daughter. Michinaga carried her in, and the Emperor took her in his arms to look at her. She was a plump, sweet infant, whose hair, he noted with some surprise, parted in the middle. When he spoke to her, she babbled enthusiastically, giving him a bright smile.

"Isn't she cunning? She seems to know me. I've never seen such an appealing baby. And what a head of hair! It will be down to her hips by next year," he said, already very much the adoring father.

He observed that Kenshi was wearing a set of Chinese damask robes in white chrysanthemum colors[13]—an auspicious reminder, he thought, of those other garments of white. "How did you manage in all that heat?" he asked. "It must have been terribly hard on your hair." But her hair lay coiled on her skirts in thick, luxuriant masses. "Really! What kind of hair is that for a mother?" he said. "Women who are old hands at child-bearing have pitiful, skimpy locks and sallow faces. You must be some sort of a freak. And the baby takes after you, I can see."

"Where is the nurse?" the Emperor asked presently. Michinaga himself took custody of the baby and carried her away. "The nurse is rather countrified in her ways," he said. "She's much too shy to show herself."

Stepping inside Kenshi's curtain-dais, the Emperor began to chat about the events of the past months, very much at his ease. "Just think," he mused, "this has been my first glimpse of that beautiful baby. She will have a splendid future. But life is hard for a man in my position. When I am worried about someone dear to me, it's sad not to be able to see the person at once." Then he said, "What do you say to having the baby brought here to lie between us? She's such a little doll. When Seishi's daughters were babies I thought them pretty, but they were ordinary by comparison. It's the long hair, I suppose, that makes this child so remarkably attractive. Come back to the Palace as soon as you can. You won't need any nurses there; I'll take care of her myself." Kenshi gave him a small, indulgent smile.

Soon twilight fell, and there began a nostalgic and moving musical performance, presented by the senior nobles. The faint sound of other instruments, drifting from an island in the lake, mingled with the lapping of the waves and the murmur of the wind in the pines.

Since the Emperor seemed in no hurry to emerge, Michinaga went to

13. White with brown linings.

fetch him. "It's getting late, and the music is quite nice. Perhaps Your Majesty should watch," he suggested. "I'm finding it enjoyable to listen from here. It's more interesting to hear a performance than to watch it. As for the dances, I've seen them all," the Emperor answered indifferently. Michinaga withdrew in something of a huff.

When darkness had settled over the scene, Michinaga came back again with his request, and the reluctant Emperor emerged from behind the curtains, repeating to Kenshi, "Don't forget, you must come very soon—within the next day or two if possible." Then His Majesty summoned the Major Captain of the Left[14] to write out a list of honors—sons of the house and Stewards were to have promotions, and the baby's nurse was to be granted Fifth Rank—and the Major Captain read off the names to the Empress, after which Michinaga performed the obeisance of gratitude. So the young Princess's nurse acquired Court Rank. Ōmi no Naishi also received a promotion. To the Emperor, senior nobles, and others, Michinaga gave the usual presents, all very handsome, as may be imagined.

The Tsuchimikado Mansion was amazingly favored by fortune. It is indeed cause for envy when a single private residence is honored by repeated Imperial visits, and when it sees its daughters depart for the Palace, one after another, to become Empresses. Even the humblest of the humble thought, with smiles of satisfaction, "This is what people mean when they talk about 'celebrated places'; this is what is called 'flowering fortunes.'" Human beings derive pleasure from the good fortune of others, just as they feel involuntary compassion in the face of suffering, and so all the common people greeted the successes of Michinaga's sons and daughters with admiration and joy.

After the Emperor's return, he thought of little but the baby. He sent off many messengers begging Empress Kenshi not to linger in the city. Kenshi, who had not fully recovered her strength, seemed content to stay at home, but he made such a nuisance of himself about it that she agreed to go to the Palace around the Tenth of the Eleventh Month. Since the Gosechi dances and the Kamo Special Festival were to follow almost at once, it may be imagined that her ladies had their hands full with the great quantities of robes required for their costumes. The younger ones seemed especially eager to make a gay and fashionable appearance after their long absence from Court.

Two more nurses for the baby had arrived. One was Ben no Menoto, a daughter of Masatoki, the governor of Awa, and the other was Nakatsu-

14. Fujiwara Kinsue.

kasa, a daughter of Takakata, a former official in Ise Province.[15] There also seemed to have been a considerable increase in the number of Kenshi's attendants during those months. One who came was Go no Onkata, the fifth daughter of the Hōjūji Minister of State Tamemitsu. Another was a lady who had been Mistress of the Crown Prince's Wardrobe while Emperor Sanjō was the heir apparent. (Her parents were the late Regent Michitaka and the Lady in the Wing Chamber; the Reikeiden Principal Handmaid Suishi had presumably been her sister.) A third was a daughter of Treasury Minister Masamitsu by Minamoto Takaakira's second daughter—a lady who also bore the title Mistress of the Wardrobe. And there were a great many other daughters of important men. Those were times in which the wives and daughters of all the great nobles entered Imperial service. If anyone stayed at home, the gossips interpreted it as a sure sign that she suffered from some dreadful defect. She might even be a cripple, they said. What a queer world it had become, with Chancellors' daughters leaving home to serve as ladies-in-waiting! The daughters of former sovereigns would be doing the same thing before long, people predicted.

There was little work for the nurses after Kenshi's arrival at the Palace. In a somewhat excessive display of parental love, Emperor Sanjō carried the tiny Princess about and dandled her in his arms all day long. Thenceforth, he had resolved, he would make himself responsible for even the most trifling of her furnishings.

Soon the year ended and the third year of Chōwa began [1014]. From the First of the First Month on, there was a fresh new feeling in the air. With the passing of the old year, the dwellers in the Realm Above the Clouds raised bright faces skyward, and the spring haze, appearing overnight, trailed banners of purple and lavender, as though sharing man's welcome to the new season. The sun shone mild and clear, a myriad birds chirped in swelling choruses, the buds on bare limbs suddenly burst into bloom, and new green clothed the hedge grasses. Searchers pushed through the reeds on the burnt fields at Ashitanohara, and at Kasuga too the Tobuhi watchman gathered the first tender sprouts of a "myriad generations"

15. Nakatsukasa, who appears to have been a woman named Fujiwara Kōshi (the wife of a minor courtier, Fujiwara Korekaze), was Kenshi's own nurse. Her name here is probably a scribal error for Chūjō, the otherwise unidentified person listed as the third of Princess Teishi's nurses in other sources, as well as in Chapter 19 below and in the version of this passage that appears in the Tomioka text. If so, it is possible that it was Chūjō, rather than Nakatsukasa, who was the daughter of Takakata, of whom, however, nothing is known. EMZ, 3: 224, 4: 419; Hagitani 1971–73, 1: 194–97.

spring. The breezes that melted the ice blew in gentle silence through the boughs, and the voices of warblers from the valleys lingered in the ear, singing, it seemed, of a long, happy reign. On the Day of the Rat, the pines at Funaoka impressed everyone with their eternal green, as though they were destined to live forever, transformed by the Imperial example. Even the bamboo leaves at the lip of the wine-crock seemed to presage a long and prosperous reign, and the rosebushes at the foot of the stairs to await summer with impatience.[16] It was all very pleasant and auspicious.

The Congratulations and other ceremonies went off in splendid style. The gorgeous, richly scented costumes of Kenshi's attendants occasioned no particular surprise, since her ladies invariably appeared to great advantage, even on occasions of much less importance. Certain of the gentlemen assigned to drink the leftover spiced wines seem to have disrupted the ceremonies in an unforgivable manner, a result of their having got disgustingly drunk and noisy.

In spite of the pressure of official functions, the Emperor found time to visit Kenshi's apartments.[17] Dressed in a splendid informal cloak and several dazzling inner robes, he seemed to the intimidated ladies a model of masculine beauty and breeding. Kenshi was half hidden behind green curtains. She wore eight or nine red plum robes under a float-patterned mantle of deep purple, and she too was an awesomely aristocratic and elegant sight as she languidly concealed her face behind a purple fan, decorated on one side with a huge painted mountain. The Emperor gazed in fresh astonishment at her long, abundant hair. The hair that inspired the saying "tangled locks on bombycine" must, after all, have been thin and scanty. Kenshi's beautiful tresses covered her whole skirt.

When the Emperor asked about Princess Teishi, the nurse Myōbu brought the baby in. Ben no Menoto bore the sword.[18] Observing that the Princess's hair had been trimmed at the ends, her father said in an affectionate voice, "Ah! Now she looks like a baby again." He carried her in his arms to show her the mirror cakes, all the while reciting the auspicious phrases in a long-winded manner that the onlookers found hilarious.[19] "He sounds like someone offering Hare Wand congratulations,"[20]

16. Many of the images in this passage are drawn from poems in *Kokinshū* and other collections. For the principal allusions, see s.n. 77; for additional details, see EMZ, 3: 227–29.

17. An invention. Kenshi was away from the Imperial Palace during the New Year festivities. EMZ, 3: 231.

18. The baby's guardian sword, presented by the Emperor after her birth.

19. See s.n. 78.					20. See s.n. 79.

one of the ladies whispered. He noticed the surreptitious titters and asked pleasantly, "What are you laughing at?"

The nurses had all done their best to make a splendid appearance, and the results were brilliant.

The Emperor chatted with Kenshi, laughing from time to time. How nice it would have been to paint the scene as the younger ladies sat in a group beside the curtains! Major Counselor Yorimichi put in an appearance, and he and the Emperor went off together after a little more talk.

Empress Seishi's son Moroakira, whose hair was exceptionally long, might have been mistaken for a girl in his informal costume.

At last the ceremonies ended, and everyone was able to relax. Inspired by some pine boughs covered with frozen snow, Emperor Sanjō sent Kenshi a poem:

Haru kuredo	Though spring is here,
Suginishi kata no	The ice
Kōri koso	Of a departed year
Matsu ni hisashiku	Has lingered long
Todokōrikere.	On the pines.

Her reply:

Chiyo fubeki	Though spring is here,
Matsu no kōri wa	The ice has been slow to perish
Haru kuredo	On pines
Uchitokegataki	Destined to endure
Mono ni zo arikeru.	For a thousand years.[21]

Toward the end of the First Month, there were the appointments, a source of joy to some and chagrin to others.

Kintō's daughter had been expecting a child since the preceding year. Her pregnancy was a matter of great concern for Kintō and the nun, and they ordered the recitation of innumerable prayers. They were not completely satisfied with their son-in-law, Norimichi, who continued to exhibit an adolescent penchant for casual romantic adventures, even though he seemed devoted to his wife.

Just as things were going along nicely at Court, the Imperial residence caught fire and burned to the ground. The Emperor and Kenshi went to Matsumoto.[22]

21. The Emperor's poem is presumably a complaint lamenting Kenshi's prolonged absence from the Dairi. Her answer implies that she was annoyed with him for some reason.
22. After the fire on the Ninth of the Second Month of Chōwa 3 (1014), the Emperor and

There had of course been fires during many reigns, but Emperor Sanjō, beset by other worries,[23] must have found the misfortune more than usually distressing. Orders for the construction of a new Palace were issued three days later. The responsibility for the rebuilding of the Shishinden fell to Empress Seishi's older brother, Michitō, who happened to be Master of the Palace Repairs Office at the time; and Senior Assistant Minister of Central Affairs Chikayori, the newly appointed Director of the Bureau of Carpentry, was to be in charge of the Seiryōden. (Chikayori was the husband of one of the baby Princess's nurses.[24]) It was decreed that each of the other buildings was to be erected by a provincial official, and Servants[25] from the Council of State accordingly set out in all directions. Work was to commence on the day of the Miare Festival in the Fourth Month.[26] Those who failed to complete their tasks by the Second Month of the following year were to suffer dismissal from their offices or provinces, whereas those who succeeded were to have their tours of duty extended or to receive promotions in rank. Faced with the Imperial ultimatum, the officials in the neighboring provinces and those responsible for the Shishinden and the Seiryōden all determined to get the frameworks of their buildings in place during the Fourth Month. It was astonishing, people thought, to see what could be done when the Court was involved.

On the day of the Iwashimizu Special Festival, just after the Twentieth of the Third Month, the new Princess was rather abruptly sent out of the Palace, probably because something was keeping her wet nurse away. Rinshi accompanied her, and she was also attended by her nurses and five or six high-ranking Court ladies. The next day, a poem arrived for

---

Kenshi went first to the tile-roofed Aitandokoro, a building in the Daijōkan compound that was used by the kugyō as a dining hall and, on occasion, as an office for the transaction of official business. For a description, see *Mak.*, pp. 214–15. On the Twentieth, they moved to the Matsumoto Zōshi (Matsumoto Apartment) in the same compound. Nothing is known of the Matsumoto Zōshi except that it occupied the site of a building once used as a residence by ex-Emperor En'yū. EMZ, 3: 239.

23. Perhaps an oblique reference to Michinaga's desire to replace Sanjō by the Crown Prince, Shōshi's young son.

24. See n. 10.

25. Servants (Shibu; also Tsukaibe) were minor Daijōkan functionaries. The Yōrō Code provided for 160 such positions, to be filled by the sons of men of Sixth, Seventh, or Eighth Rank. Wada 1953, p. 47.

26. A preliminary to the Aoi Festival, celebrated primarily at the Kamo Upper Sanctuary (Kamo Wakeikazuchi Jinja). The festival, held on the middle Day of the Monkey in the Fourth Month, welcomed Wakeikazuchi no Mikoto, the god of the Upper Sanctuary, who descended to the offerings provided, took up residence in a sakaki branch, and remained until the first thunderclap after the Aoi Festival. (The term *miare* has been variously explained as a name for the sakaki branch, as signifying the appearance of the god, etc.)

her from Kenshi in the Palace—suggested, I suppose, by the blustery wind that happened to be blowing:

Morotomo ni	If but the two of us
Nagamuru ori no	Watched together,
Hana naraba	I should not dislike
Chirasu kaze o mo	Even the wind
Uramizaramashi.	That scatters the flowers.

When Michinaga saw it, he composed a reply:

Kokoro shite	Take care
Shibashi na fuki so	Spring breeze—
Harukaze wa	Cease your blowing for a while,
Tomo ni mirubeki	And spare the flowers
Hana mo chirasade.	They must view together.

Rinshi's mother, the nun at the Ichijō Mansion, had often said to her daughter, "I feel I have lived ever so much longer just because I have seen Shōshi's youngsters. Now if only I might be allowed a glimpse of Kenshi's little Princess, I would wish for nothing more." Rinshi had been looking for a suitable occasion, and now she explained that circumstances had brought the baby to the Tsuchimikado Mansion. It was an ideal opportunity; she herself would take the Princess to see her great-grandmother. "How happy you have made me!" answered the nun. She sat hastily to work preparing for the visit.

Since it was not Rinshi's custom to mingle with the nurses, she took the baby separately in her own carriage. The nurses and the Princess's other ladies rode together, and there were three ordinary carriages filled with lesser attendants. They arrived to find the mansion beautifully decorated and the nun waiting in breathless anticipation. Rinshi carried the baby in.

"What a sweet infant!" exclaimed the nun as she gazed at the pretty, smiling face. "I'd love to hold her, but I am afraid she might cry." "No, of course she won't. Here, go to your great-grandmother," said Rinshi. The baby strained eagerly toward the old lady. "How happy I am!" said the nun, taking the baby in her arms and looking at her with affectionate eyes. "A long life is a great blessing. See how she lets me hold her! They say if a child won't let you hold him, it means nobody likes you. Somehow I must live to see all your daughters with Imperial children like this." Rinshi was deeply moved.

The nun treated the baby's nurses with great kindness.

On the following day, after a comfortable gossip, Rinshi set out for home. Among her mother's gifts to the Princess was a pair of incense-jar boxes, which the old lady had treasured in secret for years. The containers were filled with indescribably precious ancient incenses—the very names of which are no longer known—and with the choicest kinds of modern incense balls. Another gift, a box inlaid with silver and gold, contained such rarities as a copybook written by Michikaze. "I had put some things aside for the birth of just such a Princess," the nun said as she rummaged through her belongings. She gave each of the nurses a suitable costume and some silk, and provided handsome remembrances for the ordinary ladies-in-waiting. "I am not at all ready to say goodbye. I'll miss her terribly," she said.

After the baby had gone, the nun sat smiling to herself in fond recollection. Suddenly she felt a fresh surge of affection for her beloved Lesser Captain.[27] "It won't do any good to mope," she said. "I wonder if the Lesser Captain is anywhere around." The onlookers found her behavior rather absurd—or so it is said.

27. Probably her grandson Kanetsune (the son of Rinshi's sister and Michitsuna), who was thirteen or fourteen in 1014.

Supplementary Notes

SUPPLEMENTARY NOTES

Supplementary note 1

In 825 Fujiwara Fuyutsugu (775–826), one of the early architects of the Fujiwara hegemony, became the first Minister of the Left since 782. He married off his daughter Junshi (809–71) to the future Emperor Ninmyō (810–50; r. 833–50), son of his patron, ex-Emperor Saga (786–842; r. 809–23), and was given the posthumous title of Chancellor during the reign of his grandson, Montoku (827–58; r. 850–58).

The next Fujiwara leader was Fuyutsugu's second son, Yoshifusa (804–72), who was the first subject to serve as Regent and, with the exception of the monk Dōkyō (d. 772), the first subject to bear the title of Chancellor during his lifetime. His only child was a daughter, Meishi (829–900), whose mother was a daughter of Emperor Saga. Meishi married Emperor Montoku and produced a son who ascended the throne as Emperor Seiwa (850–80; r. 858–76).

Since Yoshifusa lacked male issue, he adopted his nephew Mototsune (836–91), the child of Fuyutsugu's oldest son, Nagara (802–56). Nagara seems to have been a man of limited ability, but—no doubt through Mototsune's influence—he received the posthumous titles of Sadaijin (877) and Daijō Daijin (879) during the reign of his grandson, Emperor Yōzei (868–949; r. 876–84), the offspring of Emperor Seiwa and Nagara's daughter Kōshi (842–910), who had also been adopted by Yoshifusa.

Mototsune became the key figure at Court after Yoshifusa's death in 872. He was named Regent in 876, on the accession of his minor nephew, Yōzei, and became Chancellor in 880. In 884 he deposed Yōzei, who was criminally insane, and replaced him with a son of Ninmyō, Emperor Kōkō (830–87; r. 884–87). Kōkō, a man of fifty-four, gave him written powers that made him the first Regent of a non-minor male Emperor. The powers were confirmed by Kōkō's successor, Uda, from whose reign the formal title Kanpaku dates.

Supplementary note 2

Mototsune's second son was probably not Nakahira, as *Eiga* states, but Nakahira's half-brother Kanehira (875–935), whose only claim to prominence seems to have been his skill as a performer on the lute (*biwa*). Kanehira never progressed beyond such modest offices as Imperial Household Minister and Provisional Head of the Grand Empress's Household. EM, 1: 474, s.n. 12.

Nakahira (875–945) eventually became Minister of the Left (in 937), but was far less influential than his younger brother, Tadahira.

Tadahira (880–949) succeeded Tokihira (871–909) as head of the house of Fujiwara (*uji no chōja*) after Tokihira's premature death at thirty-eight. As Figure 1 shows, it was he who became the ancestor of the main Fujiwara line. He is usually described as an easygoing, popular man with no administrative talents. In spite of his failure to cope with the rebellions of Masakado and Sumitomo, or with any of the other serious problems that troubled the government, he dominated the Court after Tokihira's death, becoming Minister of the Right in 914, Minister of the Left in 924, Sesshō in 930, Chancellor in 936, and Kanpaku in 941. He thus controlled the Court for thirty-five years, beginning with his assumption of authority as Minister of the Right at a time when the higher ministerial posts were vacant. He served as Regent for his two nephews, Suzaku (923–52; r. 930–46) and Murakami (926–67; r. 946–67), for nineteen years. He is often referred to by his posthumous name Teishinkō (Upright and Faithful Lord).

FIGURE I

Supplementary note 3

Ritual seclusion (*monoimi*), or abstinence, as it is sometimes called, was one of the conspicuous features of mid-Heian Court life. For most people, it was a device for avoiding the dangers that yin-yang theory discerned in such unusual phenomena as comets or the appearance of a deer in the garden, and in strange dreams, unlucky directions, and inauspicious dates; for those preparing to participate in Shintō religious observances, it was a means of cleansing oneself and avoiding defilement. Certain dates and directions were known in advance to be unlucky for people born at certain times, but in the case of questionable omens and dreams it was necessary to consult Yin-yang Masters for guidance. The ordinary Heian aristocrat could expect to spend from twenty to seventy days per year in ritual seclusion.

The strictness of the monoimi varied with the degree of danger to which the person was exposed. In extreme cases, the gates of the residence were shut, warning signs were posted to keep out callers, and no letters were accepted. Every building on the premises kept its blinds lowered, and the endangered person wore a "monoimi sign," observed dietary restrictions, cleansed his body, washed his hair, and behaved with the utmost discretion. When less rigorous precautions were prescribed by a Yin-yang Master, the gates might simply be left ajar, guests might be admitted, and the master might even emerge from the recesses of his chamber. Monoimi seems usually to have lasted for about two days, though the period was sometimes much longer.

When the Emperor was observing ritual seclusion, essential interviews were permitted, provided the courtier spent the preceding night at the Palace, spoke from outside the blinds, and kept his voice as low as possible. No one was allowed to enter the Palace on a monoimi day.

On the general subject of monoimi, see Okada et al. 1959–69, 3: 171ff.

The game of *go*, now well known in the West, is said to have entered Japan from China around the beginning of the eighth century. A popular upper-class pastime in the mid-Heian period, it is mentioned repeatedly in the *Pillow Book*, *The Tale of Genji,* and other contemporary writings.

"Backgammon" translates *sugoroku* (also *suguroku*), a game for two that differed only in details from its Western counterpart. Like *go*, sugoroku had entered Japan from China at an early date. It was banned in the seventh century because it had become a form of gambling, but the prohibition was ineffective. *Ōkagami*, in a famous passage (p. 184), describes a nightlong contest between Michinaga and Korechika, and comments on the value of the stakes involved whenever the two played. For details and illustrations, see *Nihon rekishi daijiten*, 11: 48–49.

Character parts (*hentsugi*) was another game of skill, the exact nature of which is no longer understood. Players were probably required to supply either the left-hand element (*hen*) or the body (*tsukuri*) of a partially concealed character in a Chinese poem or other context. (According to one theory, the object of the game was to make as many bona fide characters as possible by adding different *hen* to a designated tsukuri. Kitayama 1961, p. 708.)

Jackstones (*ishinadori*) was an exclusively female game. After scattering a number of small stones in front of her, a contestant threw a stone in the air and caught it, meanwhile picking up one or more of her other pieces in the same hand. The process was repeated until all of one player's stones were retrieved.

Supplementary note 4

Saneyori (900–970) succeeded Tadahira as head of the house of Fujwara in 949. As Minister of the Left, he was the senior official throughout Murakami's reign, although a number of factors—notably the early death of Jusshi (the daughter whom he married to Murakami), the success of Morosuke's daughter Anshi in the Imperial harem, and Morosuke's more genial personality—combined to diminish his influence. As a result of Morosuke's early death, it was Saneyori who became Regent and Chancellor on the accession of Morosuke's minor grandson, Reizei (950–1011; r. 967–69)—offices he retained until his death at the age of seventy under Reizei's successor, En'yū (959–91; r. 969–84). A correct and rather colorless man, he received the posthumous title Seishinkō

(Honorable and Prudent Lord). He was a good poet and the founder of a school of experts in the intricacies of Court ceremonies, old customs, and precedents. His residence at Ōimikado Karasumaru, the Ononomiya (Ono Palace, so called because it had belonged to an Imperial Prince who had later moved to Ono, at the foot of Mount Hiei), was one of the great showplaces of the Heian period. In Michinaga's day, the Ononomiya was the residence of Saneyori's grandson, Minister of the Right Sanesuke. For a description of its splendors, see Ōkagami, p. 90.

Morosuke (908–60) was Minister of the Right under Emperor Murakami. Although his death at the age of fifty-two cut short a career that would undoubtedly have encompassed the regency, his descendants became the dominant branch of the Fujiwara family. Like Saneyori, he had an encyclopedic knowledge of usages and precedents, which he recorded for posterity in a number of treatises. His Kujō Mansion was south of Kujō Bōmon and east of Machijiri.

Tadahira's third son (second, according to Sonpi bunmyaku, 1: 48) appears to have become a Buddhist monk while still a youth.

Morouji (913?–70), known as the Biwa Major Counselor, was a poet of some repute but does not appear to have been politically influential.

Morotada (920–69), a Major Counselor under Murakami, advanced to the status of Minister of the Right in the Twelfth Month of 967, shortly after the accession of Reizei. Two years later, operating in the near-power vacuum created by the death of Morosuke and the advanced age of Saneyori, he engineered a plot against the Minister of the Left, Minamoto Takaakira, which resulted in Takaakira's exile to Kyūshū and his own appointment as Minister of the Left. (Morotada's death seven months later was attributed by contemporaries to divine retribution.) The Koichijō Mansion, probably located south of Konoe and west of Higashinotōin, was another famous Fujiwara residence, owned successively by Fuyutsugu, Yoshifusa, Mototsune, Tadahira, Morotada—and, in Michinaga's day, by Morotada's son Naritoki, by Naritoki's daughter Empress Seishi, and by Seishi's son Prince Atsuakira. See Tsunoda 1963, p. 164.

Supplementary note 5

The correct numbers are twelve and seven. See Table 1 for a list of Morosuke's children.

Supplementary note 6

One of Morotada's sons, Sadatoki, lived only long enough to father a son of his own, Sanekata, who was reared by Morotada's other son, Naritoki. Naritoki (941–95), though less influential than the members of Morosuke's family, was a prominent figure until his death in the great epidemic of 995. Known as the Koichijō Major Captain, he held the concurrent title of Major Counselor, and when his daughter Seishi became Emperor Sanjō's Empress (1012) he received the posthumous title of Minister of the Right. In addition to Sanekata, he reared

TABLE I. Offspring of Fujiwara Morosuke

Name	Career	Remarks
Sons		
Koretada (924–72)*	Chancellor, Regent	
Kanemichi (925–77)*	Chancellor, Regent	
Kaneie (929–90)*	Chancellor, Regent	
Tōkazu	Treasury Minister	
Tadagimi*	Guards Commander	
Tōnori (d. 989)	Jr. 3 with no office (*hisangi*)	
Tōmoto	Master of Left Capital Office	
Takamitsu (b. ca. 940)	Lesser Captain	Became monk, 961
Tamemitsu (942–92)	Chancellor	
Kinsue (956–1029)	Chancellor	
Jinzen (943–90)		Tendai abbot
Jinkaku (955–1043)		Tōji abbot
Daughters		
Anshi (927–64)*	Empress of Emperor Murakami	
Tōshi (d. 975)*	Concubine of Emperor Murakami	Wife of Prince Shigeakira
San no Kimi*		Wife of Min. Takaakira
Hanshi (Tō [Fujiwara] Naishi no Suke)	Assistant Handmaid	Wife of Fuj. Michikane
Fushi	Junior Consort of Emperor Reizei	
Gashi		Wife of Min. Takaakira
Name unknown		Wife of Min. Shigenobu

SOURCE: *Sonpi bunmyaku*, 1: 51–59.
*Child of principal wife, a daughter of Fujiwara Tsunekuni.

his sister Hōshi's orphaned son, Prince Nagahira. Of his own children, Empress Seishi had the most successful career. Another daughter appears in contemporary writings as the estranged wife of Prince Atsumichi. His only son of importance was Michitō (974–1039), who rose eventually to the post of Provisional Middle Counselor.

Unable to compete on equal terms with her cousin Anshi, Morotada's daughter Hōshi (d. 967) nevertheless became one of Emperor Murakami's favorite Junior Consorts. Her verbatim recitation of *Kokinshū* for the Emperor is one of the celebrated anecdotes of the period. She was unfortunate in her son, Prince Nagahira, whose mental retardation is described in *Ōkagami*, pp. 97–99, as well as in the concluding episode of the present chapter.

Supplementary note 7

As indicated in subsequent notes, some of the women listed below were Concubines (Kōi), rather than Junior Consorts (Nyōgo). Anshi (927–64) was one of a series of Fujiwara Imperial consorts who used a combination of parental backing, charm, determination, and fecundity to help install Fujiwara grandsons as Emperors, and Fujiwara grandfathers and uncles as Regents. Married to Emperor Murakami while he was still Crown Prince, she dominated the Kōkyū until her death twenty-four years later, at the same time making her influence felt in most other spheres of Court life. She became a Junior Consort in 946, Empress in 958, Grand Empress in 967, and Senior Grand Empress in 969, the last two posthumously. She gave birth to three of Murakami's nine sons, including his two successors on the throne, and to four of his ten daughters. See s.n. 11.

Supplementary note 8

When an Emperor became the father of a son, it was customary for him to send a Lesser or Middle Captain with a guardian sword (*mamorigatana*) to be placed beside the baby's bed. See Nakamura 1962, p. 41.

There were two major categories of birth ceremonies:

1. Bath ceremonies (*oyudono* or *yudono no hajime*). These ceremonies were performed by families of all social classes shortly after the birth of a child. The following description applies specifically to Imperial offspring, but the procedure for children of noble houses was similar.

There were two bath ceremonies per day, the second a mere formality, on seven auspicious days selected by Yin-yang Masters soon after the birth. (Despite the name *yudono no hajime* ["the beginning of the bathing"], the first ceremony was not necessarily the child's first bath.) For reasons that are no longer understood, water from a favorably situated well or stream was put into sixteen jugs, after which a tub was filled and esoteric prayers were chanted over it by a Buddhist monk of high status. As further protection, a chunk of rhinoceros horn might be put into a white silk bag, sometimes with the addition of gold and other precious substances, and immersed in the hot water. The rhinoceros, as a notably strong animal, was believed to have potent protective capabilities. After the early part of the Heian period, wood of similar appearance was substituted for the horn, which was almost impossible to obtain.

When the bath was ready, two or three Professors (Hakase) took up positions in the courtyard, where they were joined by twenty archers, who formed a line with their backs to the hall. The baby was brought in, preceded by two or more ladies robed in white, of whom one carried the guardian sword and the others such things as rice (thrown to frighten away malignant spirits) and a tiger's head (possibly considered a protection because of putative medicinal qualities; see Hagitani 1971–73, 1: 251–52). As the bath progressed, each Professor in turn declaimed an auspicious passage from a Chinese classical text, repeating it three times, while the archers twanged their bows to ward off hostile influences. For details, see Nakamura 1962, pp. 46–56. See also Chapter 8 below. It appears that the Professors were not present when the child was a girl.

2. Birth celebrations (*ubuyashinai*). Heian families held formal celebratory banquets, with poetry and music, on the third, fifth, seventh, and ninth nights after a child's birth. Prior to each event, relatives and friends sent presents of white clothing for the mother and child, special foods, articles of furniture, etc. Each banquet had a different sponsor, although all took place at the mother's residence. When the mother was an Empress, the Third Night celebration seems usually to have been presented by her Household, and responsibility for one of the other events to have been assumed by the Emperor or ex-Emperor. The usual expectation, however, was that the baby's maternal relatives—grandfather, uncles, and perhaps Imperial aunts—would take the lead.

Features of the evenings included the congratulatory visits of the Kangakuin students (Chapter 1, n. 135), if the grandfather were the head of the Fujiwara house; the use of colored garments and furnishings on the Ninth Night, after the change from white (*ironaoshi*) that took place on the eighth day; and an ill-understood ceremony, the *megurigayu* or *susurigayu*, which was probably either a symbolic first feeding or an offering to ward off evil and ensure future prosperity. Nakamura 1962, pp. 60–72.

Supplementary note 9

Heian mourning customs were rooted in ancient Shintō beliefs concerning the polluting effects of a death in the family. The period of ritual seclusion, the wearing of special garments, and the final river-bank purification were all preserved from earlier eras, although the emphasis had shifted from the elimination of defilement to the expression of grief. As shown in Table 2, the closeness of the relationship determined the length of the period for which mourning dress (*fuku* or *buku*) was prescribed.

As paternal grandchildren, Anshi and Hōshi were obligated to wear mourning for five months. (It should be noted, however, that the prescriptions were not always rigidly observed.)

The person's relationship to the deceased also determined the length of his period of ritual seclusion (*imi*). There was a major distinction between mourning for a parent ("heavy mourning") and mourning for any other kinsman ("light mourning"). During light mourning, a bureaucrat took a leave of absence to enable him to remain in seclusion for a specific length of time, as indicated in Table 2.

A man who suffered the loss of a parent was supposed to resign his office and stay home for a year. Ways were found to circumvent the requirement, and it gradually became customary to reduce the period of seclusion to fifty days.

In early times, the bereaved wore garments made of untreated hemp or some other crude material. During the course of the Heian period, extremely complicated precedents and usages came to dictate the details of the attire considered suitable for individual members of the Court circle in specific mourning circumstances, but it can be said that the common material in mid-Heian was

TABLE 2. Periods of Mourning and Ritual Seclusion

Relationship	Period
Mourning Period	
Parent, husband*	One year
Paternal grandparent, foster parent	Five months
Paternal great-grandparent, maternal grandparent, paternal uncle or aunt, wife, sibling, husband's parent, son who was heir	Three months
Paternal great-great grandparent, maternal uncle or aunt, father's main wife, stepmother, stepfather in one's household, half-sibling by one's mother, child other than heir, grandson who was heir	One month
Other grandchild, paternal uncle's child, brother's child	Seven days
Period of Seclusion	
Parent	One year†
Husband, paternal grandparent, foster parent	Thirty days
Relative entitled to three-month mourning period	Twenty days
Relative entitled to one-month mourning period	Ten days
Relative entitled to seven-day mourning period	Three days

*Although not relatives, the Emperor and a servant's master also belonged to this category.
†Fifty days became conventional. See accompanying text.

plain silk, and that the commonest color was some shade of dark gray or black. See Ishimura 1958, 1: 169–74; Ishimura 1964, pp. 550–51; *Shōyūki*, 3: 160 (25 xii Manju 4); and EM, 1: 475, s.n. 24.

Supplementary note 10

The Heian Japanese had inherited from the Nara period the belief, first expounded by certain Indian Buddhists, that the individual entered a brief intermediate existence (*chūu*) before being reborn. On each seventh day until the forty-ninth, it was held, the soul had a chance at rebirth, and its fate could meanwhile be influenced by the acts of the living. *Tsuizen*, pious works to help the deceased, were consequently a major preoccupation of the bereaved family during the crucial period. Wealthy aristocrats usually arranged for elaborate Buddhist rituals on each of the seven days, culminating in a grand event on the forty-ninth, and for offerings (*kuyō*) of many kinds: clothing, medicines, vegetarian feasts and other gifts to monks; new temple buildings, statues, pagodas, and altar vessels; copies of sutras written out by important people, etc.

In *Eiga*, mention of Buddhist services immediately after a death usually refers to such "seven seven" activities. It was also common to hold services, with accompanying offerings, on the hundredth day after the death and on or about the first anniversary. Anniversary services, which were repeated annually in some cases, often centered around extended expositions of the *Lotus Sutra*.

Supplementary note 11
See Table 3.

TABLE 3. Offspring of Emperor Murakami

Name	Mother	Remarks
Sons		
Hirohira (950–71)	Fuj. Sukehime (d. of Motokata)	Governor-General of the Dazaifu
Norihira (950–1011)	Fuj. Anshi (d. of Morosuke)	Mentally ill; reigned 967–69 as Emperor Reizei
Munehira (951–1041)	Fuj. Masahime (d. of Arihira)	Minister of War; married sister of Michinaga's wife Rinshi; took Buddhist vows, 980
Tamehira (952–1010)	Anshi	Son-in-law of Min. Takaakira; Minister of Ceremonial
Morihira (959–91)	Anshi	Reigned 969–84 as Emperor En'yū
Masahira (960?–61)	Fuj. Hōshi (d. of Morotada)	Died young
Tomohira (964–1009)	Princess Sōshi (d. of Prince Yoakira)	Minister of Central Affairs; scholar, poet, calligrapher, musician; ancestor of Murakami Genji
Nagahira (965–88)	Hōshi	Minister of War; mentally retarded
Akihira (d. 1013)	Masahime	Took Buddhist vows, 984; called ninth son in *Eiga*, but said by some reference works to have been born in 954
Daughters		
Shōshi (948–51)	Anshi	Died young
Rishi (948–60)	Min. Keishi (d. of Moroaki)	Died young (*Eiga* omits name)
Hōshi (949–87)	Masahime	Married for a time to Fuj. Kaneie; later became nun
Kishi (949–86)	Princess Kishi (d. of Prince Shigeakira)	Ise Virgin, 975–84
Seishi (d. 998)	Keishi	Married Fuj. Akimitsu; mother of Genshi, Enshi, Shigeie
Rakushi (952–98)	Princess Sōshi	Ise Virgin, 955–67
Hoshi (953–92)	Anshi	Ise Virgin, 968–69

TABLE 3 (continued)

Name	Mother	Remarks
Shūshi (d. 970)	Sukehime	Died young (*Eiga* omits name)
Shishi (955–1015)	Anshi	Prominent at Emperor En'yū's court as Princess of First Rank; took Buddhist vows, 986
Senshi (964–1035)	Anshi	Kamo Virgin under five Emperors, 975–1031, then retired and became nun; presided over literary salon; poet

Supplementary note 12

Mizuhō amatadan nite . . . Zuhō (also *suhō, shuhō,* or *shiho*) were esoteric rituals celebrated by monks from leading Tendai and Shingon temples, in which the officiants made offerings of flowers, food, drink, incense, tapers, water, and the like; recited sutras, prayers, and incantations; performed magical hand gestures; made burnt offerings (*goma*; Skt. *homa*); and otherwise attempted to ensure prosperity, end a calamity, cure an illness, ensure the safe delivery of a child, or expel an evil spirit by achieving mystic unity with the buddhas or bodhisattvas enshrined on special altars erected for the services. Such rituals, and the elaborate preparations they entailed, played an important part in the lives of the Heian nobility. They varied in scale from small (one main altar combined with a fire altar, with one main officiant and ten or fewer assistants) through medium (two to four altars, each with an officiant and a maximum of sixteen assistants) to large (five or more altars, each with an officiant and from seventeen to twenty assistants); and the objects of worship, procedures, altar shapes, and offerings varied according to the ends sought.

In the present passage, *amatadan* ("many altars") almost certainly refers to a "large ritual" (*daihō*)—presumably of the type designed to subdue malignant spirits—and very likely to the five-altar ritual (*godanhō*), the commonest daihō. The objects of worship in the godanhō were Fudō, Kongō Yasha, Gōsanze, Kuṇḍalī, and Daiitoku—i.e. the Five Great Mystic Kings (*godaimyōō*), fierce forms assumed by the buddhas Vairocana (Dainichi), Amoghasiddi (Fukūjōju), Akṣobhya (Ashuku), Ratnasambhava (Hōshō), and Amitābha (Amida) in order to bring the dharma to beings who were otherwise unteachable. On the subject of malignant spirits and their exorcism in the Heian period, see McCullough 1973.

Supplementary note 13

A Heian youth's Coming-of-Age ceremony (*genpuku* or *genbuku*), which took place when he was from ten to fifteen years old, was one of the turning points in his life, a true rite of passage. Before it, he wore a child's hair style and costume and answered to a child's name; afterward, his coiffure, clothing, and name were those of an adult, he was eligible for marriage, and, if his family were sufficiently influential, he obtained Court Rank and began his climb up the official ladder.

The central act of the genpuku was the capping—the ceremonious placing of a man's cap (*kanmuri*, in the case of the nobility) on the boy's head by a dignitary known as a Kakan. A man of the highest possible status was selected for the Kakan's role. When the initiate was a Regent's son, the Emperor himself sometimes officiated. For a Prince, a Minister of State was the usual choice (in the case of the Crown Prince, his Mentor); for an Emperor, the Chancellor might fill the office.

The ceremony took place in the evening or late afternoon of an auspicious day. When the initiate was an Emperor or Crown Prince, the usual site was the Shishinden. For the son of a Counselor or Consultant being capped by a Minister of State or Regent, the function was held at the Kakan's residence.

In addition to the Kakan and the initiate, there were one or two other principal participants in the capping ceremony. The Nōkan, believed by most authorities to have served only when the Emperor was the initiate, loosened the childhood coiffure, cut the ends of the hair, bound the head with a fillet, and otherwise prepared the boy to receive the cap. (That office was usually performed by the Chief of the Palace Storehouse Bureau.) When there was no Nōkan, his functions were discharged by a Rihatsu, who also removed the fillet before the capping and adjusted the coiffure afterward. When the initiate was the Crown Prince, the Rihatsu was usually the Master or Provisional Master of his Household. In Prince Genji's case in *The Tale of Genji*, the Treasury Minister served.

After the ceremony the initiate retired to another room to change into a man's costume. Later there was feasting, and in the case of an heir apparent or other Prince the occasion was usually climaxed by the acquisition of a feminine bed partner (Soibushi), a girl of good family, often somewhat the boy's senior, who usually became his principal wife at a later date. Nakamura 1962, pp. 125–49; *Genji*, 1: 47–50; Seidensticker 1976, pp. 17–18.

Supplementary note 14

The best-known and most detailed contemporary account of an upper-class Heian funeral describes the funeral procession and cremation of Emperor Go-Ichijō in 1036. Since a similar, if less elaborate, pattern seems to have obtained for subjects, its main features are summarized below.

As was customary, Go-Ichijō's funeral procession set out for the cremation site at night. The vanguard consisted of twelve torchbearers and twenty monks in double columns, preceded by a yellow silk banner bearing a Buddhist mantra. Next came twenty men supporting four long silk screens (*hoshō*), two on the left and two on the right, which were intended to shield the coffin and principal mourners from vulgar eyes. The coffin, resting on a litter borne by twenty men, and further protected by a second, smaller set of screens (*kōshō*), was preceded by two men carrying a "light litter" (*hi no koshi*), on which a lamp burned. The coffin was followed by an "incense litter" (*kō no koshi*), containing a censer and vases of flowers. The bearers of both the light litter and the incense litter marched between the inner and outer screens, as did the Regent, Ministers of State, and other dignitaries, who followed next, wearing mourning garments and straw sandals, and holding peeled-wood staffs. Similarly accoutered, a great throng of lesser officials and minor functionaries streamed along outside the hoshō, some carrying torches.

At the cremation site, which was strewn with white sand and guarded by two torii, temporary structures had been erected for the use of the nobles and monks; and tentlike screens, firewood, water, and other necessities were in readiness. Designated nobles removed the coffin lid, inserted firewood, and lit fires. Buddha-invocations were chanted as the body burned. Personal belongings of the Emperor (toilet articles, an armrest, shoes, an inkstone box, etc.) were later consigned to the flames. Around eight o'clock the next morning, the fire was extinguished with rice wine, and the spot was sprinkled by the monks with dirt and sand. After the bones had been ceremoniously sealed in an urn, a Controller set out to take them to a temple, while the other mourners remained for the final rituals at the site, which included the erection of a stone stupa and the planting of trees. The dignitaries then went home, apparently by ox-carriage, stopping at the Kamo River for a brief purification. For details, see Ishimura 1958, 1: 167; Nakamura 1962, pp. 187ff; and *Sakeiki*, pp. 437ff (19 v Chōgen 9).

Supplementary note 15

Although it was not one of the Court's official annual observances (*nenjū gyōji*), the ancient Chinese custom of celebrating the appearance of the full moon on the Fifteenth of the Eighth Month with wine, music, and poetry was observed by Heian aristocrats from the mid-ninth century on. The festivities, which took place both at the Imperial Palace and at private residences, included such activities as boating and the composition of "moon poems" in Chinese and Japanese.

Emperor Murakami's entertainment, held on the Fifteenth of the intercalary Eighth Month, was primarily a poetry contest, with some thirty-five courtiers and ladies as participants. The sequence of events was (1) the garden contest described in Chapter 1, which was an extra frill to add interest to the occasion, (2) the poetry contest, with music and feasting, held in the same place (n. 111), and (3) the distribution of presents. See EM, 1: 480, s.n. 57; and Hagitani 1957–69, 2: 458–65.

Supplementary note 16

Although in later times suhama functioned only as accessories on festive occasions such as banquets and weddings, during the Heian period they were the favored receptacles for competing entries in the elegant contests to which the upper classes devoted much of their attention and wealth; and for important occasions their creation often required as much time and ingenuity as the selection of the contest entries. Thus there are records of a chrysanthemum competition in which the two suhama contained real sand and water and measured 8 by 6 feet and 8 by 7 feet, respectively; and of a poetry contest in which one suhama contained flowers, birds, and other decorations keyed to the assigned topics, each with an attached slip of paper containing a poem, while the other featured flowers made of gold, with silver leaves on which poems were inscribed. Hagitani 1957–69, 2: 404–5.

In the *Eiga* account in Chapter 1, there is nothing to indicate a direct connection between the entries in the garden contest and the suhama (or other containers) used later for the poetry contest. The entry of the Left differed from the usual suhama in that its decorations were painted, except for the silver foil fence and the live insects.

The Ōi River, at Saga Arashiyama in Kyōto, was the site of many elegant entertainments in the Heian period. Fires for illumination were hung in metal baskets from the sides of boats by the fishermen who worked the waters of the Ōi with cormorants.

Supplementary note 17

Table 4 compares the ages, ranks, and offices of the three appointees with those of Morosuke's three oldest sons, Koretada, Kanemichi, and Kaneie.

TABLE 4. Comparison of Appointees and Fujiwara Morosuke's Sons

Name	Age	Rank	Office as of the Ninth Month, 967
Tomohira	50	Sr. 4 L	Consultant
Morouji	53	Sr. 3	Middle Counselor
Morotada	46	Jr. 2	Major Counselor
Koretada	43	Jr. 3	Provisional Middle Counselor
Kanemichi	42	Jr. 4 U	Director of Palace Storehouse Bureau
Kaneie	38	Sr. 4 L	Middle Captain

Supplementary note 18

The ancient Shintō ceremonies known as *gokei* (Imperial Purification) and *daijōsai* (Great Thanksgiving Service) were always postponed when the Court was in mourning. Otherwise, they took place late in the first year of a new reign, or in the second year if the reign began after the Seventh Month. The gokei was the most spectacular of the preliminary events leading up to the daijōsai, which, like the less elaborate *niinamesai* (First Fruits Service) held in ordinary years, constituted a harvest thanksgiving ritual in the course of which the Emperor offered to the gods, and also personally consumed, food and drink made of the new grain—steamed rice, gruel, "white wine" (*shiroki*, a sweet wine), "black wine" (*kuroki*, wine mixed with ash), etc. By far the most important Shintō ceremony staged at the Heian Court, the daijōsai entailed complicated preparations that began months in advance, as indicated in the following abbreviated chronology.

Fourth Month. The daijōsai preliminary events usually began in the Fourth Month, with the selection by divination of two districts to supply the new rice. In the Heian period it became customary to choose an eastern district (*yuki*) from within Ōmi Province, and a western district (*suki*) from within either Tanba or Bitchū Province.

Eighth Month (first ten days). Messengers were sent to all provinces to conduct purification ceremonies. Offerings were presented at the Ise Grand Shrines and all other shrines in the Jingikan register.

Ninth Month. The new rice was harvested. Meanwhile officials were appointed, temporary structures were erected at the Kamo River, and other preparations were made for the Imperial Purification.

Tenth Month (last ten days): Imperial Purification (gokei). In Michinaga's day this event, which prepared the Emperor for his sacerdotal role, took place on the west bank of the Kamo River at the end of Nijō or Sanjō Avenue. The simple rites (a ceremonial hand-washing, followed by cleansing rituals performed by Jingikan officials) were preceded by a magnificent procession, which formed at the Imperial Palace to the rolling of drums. The Emperor rode in a phoenix litter, accompanied by all his gentlemen, some in Chinese carriages and others mounted on chargers with T'ang saddles and special trappings. Their Escorts wore costumes with lion and bear designs. Other fashionable vehicles carried the Junior Consorts and their ladies, gorgeously attired, and the Acting Consort (Nyōgodai), whose function was purely decorative but who nevertheless was the queen of the occasion.

Tenth and Eleventh Months. In a newly constructed sanctuary at Kitano, the food, wines, textiles, and other daijōsai offerings were made ready by kitchen workers, brewers, and weavers.

Eleventh Month

1. About a week before the daijōsai two main buildings and a number of smaller ones were constructed over a five-day period at the daijōsai site in front of the Daigokuden (later in front of the Shishinden or, on occasion, in the Daijōkan or Burakuin compound).

2. Last Day of the Ox (from this time on, there were daily events, falling, in order, on the days of the Ox, Tiger, Hare, Dragon, Snake, Horse, and Sheep): Gosechi Curtain-Dais Rehearsal (*chōdai no kokoromi*). This event, witnessed by the Emperor in the Jōneiden, was one of the preliminaries to the formal appearance of the Gosechi* dancers at the final daijōsai banquet. Although the five Gosechi dancers constituted only one of many groups who provided entertainment in the course of the daijōsai period, they figure far more prominently than any of the others in Heian literature, probably because each was a protégée of some member of the Court circle. Two of them, together with their ladies, girl attendants,† maids, and miscellaneous servants, were sponsored by men of the provincial governor class; three, by more exalted personages, such as Imperial consorts, kugyō, and tenjōbito. On or around the Day of the Ox, all five entered the Palace with their entourages and took up quarters

---

* An obscure term. It may mean "melodies of the five tones."

† *Warawa*, about ten years old.

in various sections of the Jōneiden, where a dance platform was provided and teachers were in residence to coach them. The Curtain-Dais Rehearsal on the night of the Day of the Ox (so called because the Emperor occupied the Jōneiden *chōdai**) was attended by the kugyō and tenjōbito, the last of whom danced and sang popular ballads outside the hall.

3. Day of the Tiger. Events on the Day of the Tiger included a spirit-pacifying ceremony; informal dancing, singing, and drinking in the Courtiers' Hall; and the Gosechi Imperial Rehearsal (*gozen no kokoromi*) in the Seiryōden eave-chamber. During the rehearsal, which took place at night, the girls performed on the veranda adjacent to the illuminated eastern garden, while the Emperor watched from behind bamboo blinds. Each dancer later left a comb wrapped in colored paper in front of the Emperor, who accepted one as a special token of approbation.

4. Day of the Hare. On this day, the daijōsai offerings were presented to the gods. The day began with offerings to 304 deities in the Jingikan. Meanwhile, around 10:00 A.M. a procession of several thousand people (according to *Engishiki* regulations) escorted the yuki and suki offerings from Kitano to the elaborately guarded daijōsai site for deposit in the new temporary buildings, where, with appropriate ceremony, the preparation of the rice and other sacred dishes began. Around 6:00 P.M., the premises were illuminated and preparations were made for the reception of the Emperor.

Earlier in the day, the Seiryōden was the scene of still another event centering on the Gosechi dancers, the Imperial Viewing of the Girl Attendants (*warawa goran*), a custom inaugurated during the reign of Emperor Murakami. Like the *gozen no kokoromi*, the ceremony took place in the eastern eave-chamber and veranda, furnished a pretext for drinking, dancing, and flirting on the part of the tenjōbito, and included the selection of a comb as a mark of Imperial favor.

The Emperor arrived at the daijōsai site around 8:00 P.M., purified himself, and proceeded to the Yuki Hall, one of the two main temporary buildings. Members of the Court, provincial officials and singers from the yuki province, and others participated in singing, dancing, and other preliminary observances. Then, at about 10:00 P.M., the yuki offerings of rice, fish, soups, dried foods, fruit, wines, etc. were presented to the gods and the sovereign. After the ritual consumption of his portion, the Emperor retired to the staging-room, thus completing the yuki half of the ceremonies.

The suki ceremonies, which were virtually identical, began at midnight and ended around six o'clock on the following morning (Day of the Dragon), thereby concluding the daijōsai proper.

5. Day of the Dragon. The principal event was the Yuki Banquet in the Burakuin (later in the Shishinden).

6. Day of the Snake. This day was devoted to ceremonies and festivities revolving around the Suki Banquet in the Burakuin. (See also Chapter 10, n. 24.)

* On chōdai, see s.n. 65.

7. Day of the Horse. This day saw a final great banquet in the Burakuin, the Toyonoakari no Sechie (Flushed Faces Banquet), centering around the presentation of "white" and "black" wine made from the new rice. In addition to performances of several other kinds, the Gosechi dances were at last formally presented.

8. Day of the Sheep and later. On the Day of the Sheep, there was a final round of presents for minor functionaries and others who had not shared in the largesse distributed at the banquets. On the last day of the Eleventh Month a purification ceremony took place at Suzaku Gate, and in the first third of the Twelfth Month the special purification status of the yuki and suki districts was terminated by local ceremonies.

The annual First Fruits Service (niinamesai), although basically similar to the daijōsai, was much less elaborate. The facilities of the Chūwain (later of the Jingikan or Kunaishō), rather than specially constructed buildings, were employed; the elimination of the Yuki and Suki Banquets advanced the Toyonoakari Banquet to the Day of the Dragon; there were only four Gosechi dancers instead of five, etc.

Supplementary note 19

The Ichijō Mansion, south of Ichijō and east of Ōmiya, was one of the great Heian houses. Koretada had inherited it from his father, Morosuke. After his death it passed into the hands of another of Morosuke's sons, Tamemitsu, who had married one of Koretada's daughters. Tamemitsu was probably the person who rebuilt it after it burned in 983. He is thought to have left it to his own third daughter, Shinden no Onkata, who seems to have occupied one of its lesser buildings, and to have sold the main house to Saeki Kintsura for presentation to Michinaga's sister Senshi. Senshi refurbished it with a view to making it a residence for her son, the Emperor, an aim shared by Michinaga, into whose hands the entire property eventually passed. Senshi's son lived there both before and after his abdication, and consequently is known as Emperor Ichijō. Tsunoda 1963, pp. 69–71; Kuroita 1971, pp. 1–21; *Shōkai*, 2: 176; EMZ, 1: 539–40. On the general subject of house ownership among the Heian nobility, see McCullough 1967, pp. 118ff.

Supplementary note 20

Ceremonies and festivities on the first Day of the Rat in the First Month (or sometimes on the second or third such day, or on a Rat Day in the Second Month) belonged to the large group of New Year observances that were aimed at ensuring good health during the coming months. In the Nara period they had taken the form of Court banquets, but in Heian times it was customary to go on outings to Kitano, Murasakino, or other nearby rural areas—partly, no doubt, in recognition of the Chinese view that to climb a hill and gaze in all directions on the Day of the Rat would "calm the yin and yang," but also in order to gather nutritious young greens (*wakana*), either for immediate consumption or for use at home or presentation to the Emperor (in the last case, a custom that became formalized as the presentation to the throne by the Palace Storehouse Bureau of a healthful soup made of various kinds of greens).

At these Day of the Rat outings (*ne no hi no asobi*), the participants strolled about picking parsley, shepherd's purse (*nazuna*), and other edible plants, and pulling up tiny pine trees, which, although also edible, were valued primarily as symbols of longevity—and, because of their green color, as harbingers of spring. The fruits of the guests' labors were consumed at an al fresco repast during which poems were recited.

With the possible exception of ex-Emperor En'yū's excursion to Murasakino in 985, Prince Tamehira's is the most famous of such outings, described in some detail not only in *Eiga* but also in *Ōkagami*, p. 121, which dwells on the magnificence of the procession through the streets of the capital, and on the crush of sight-seers' carriages. As *Eiga* indicates, hunting with falcons was part of the day's entertainment. The Prince sent the Emperor a pheasant around two in the afternoon, and after the return that night there was a gay party, with music and poetry, at which most of the adults got drunk. Ikeda 1967, pp. 532–35; EMZ, 1: 145.

Supplementary note 21

Ason was the second-ranking in a system of eight hereditary titles (*kabane*) established by the Court in 684. Highly prestigious because assigned to the Fujiwara, it was later granted to many new families of Imperial descent. Of the men named in the text, the first three were Minamoto and the last two were Fujiwara. See Table 5. The author has made a slight mistake in listing Yasumitsu's office.

TABLE 5. Leading Members of Prince Tamehira's Retinue

Name	Office in 964	Age in 964	Highest office
Min. Shigemitsu (923–98)	Middle Captain of the Left	41	Provisional Major Counselor
Min. Nobumitsu (927–76)	Head Chamberlain; Provisional Middle Captain of the Right	37	Provisional Major Counselor
Min. Yasumitsu (924–95)	Senior Assistant Minister of Popular Affairs	40	Middle Counselor
Fuj. Kanemichi (925–77)	Provisional Master of Empress's Household	39	Regent, Chancellor
Fuj. Kaneie (929–90)	Senior Assistant Minister of War	35	Regent, Chancellor

Supplementary note 22

The *tsuina*, an ancient Chinese ritual described in *Chou li*, is said to have been first observed at the Japanese Court in 706, a year of widespread pestilence. It figured prominently among the Heian *nenjū gyōji*, and vestiges of it survive in modern Japanese New Year's Eve observances. In the early Heian period its principal features were as follows.

The purpose was to drive pestilence demons from the Palace compound and ultimately from the capital, the latter task being undertaken by functionaries of the Capital Offices posted at the outer Daidairi gates. In preparation for the ceremony, which began during the Hour of the Dog (7:00–9:00 P.M.) on the last night of the year, the Emperor was presented with a stick and a set of rattle drums,* the Shishinden and Seiryōden gardens were brightly illuminated with torches, and members of the Court received peachwood bows and reed arrows.

While the Emperor watched from inside the Shishinden, a party of demon-chasers took up positions in the South Court. Their leader (*hōsōshi*) was chosen from among the minor Palace functionaries, primarily on the basis of his physical stature. He wore the costume prescribed in *Chou li*—a fierce, four-eyed golden mask and a black robe over red skirts—and carried a spear and shield. His colleagues, twenty in number, were young boys of the servant class, armed with rattle drums. They were followed into the courtyard by a group from the Bureau of Divination, whose leader read off a document warning disease demons to flee the country. Next the hōsōshi, supported by yells from the boys and assembled bureaucrats, uttered "demon-chasing shouts" and struck his spear three times against the shield, after which the demon-chasers and officials toured the Shishinden-Seiryōden area in pursuit of invisible demons, with the courtiers shooting their reed arrows. The party then proceeded to the main Daidairi gates, where their mission ended.

In the course of the Heian centuries, the Emperor stopped going to the Shishinden for the ceremony, the number of boy assistants dwindled to eight, and the demonic-looking hōsōshi himself became the target of the others' arrows, but the changes almost certainly occurred after the period in question here. *Koji ruien*, I: 1367–83.

Supplementary note 23

The official calendar was crowded to capacity during the first half of the First Month, not only because the New Year was a festive season, but also because the Court wished to take every possible precaution to ensure the personal well-being of the Emperor, the smooth functioning of the bureaucracy, and the peace and prosperity of the nation during the coming year. The origins and development of Heian New Year ceremonies are complex and frequently obscure, but

---

* Two small drums impaled on a pole. Balls attached to strings struck them when the pole was flourished.

the observances as a group (and often individually as well) can be said to have emphasized a combination of ancient Shintō beliefs connected with agricultural fertility; Chinese customs, both popular and official, embodying magical ways of promoting longevity; and other elements, both indigenous and imported, that bolstered the Imperial prestige or otherwise contributed to desired ends. As readers of *The Tale of Genji* know, those ceremonies that lent themselves to private use (e.g. the Obeisances to the Four Directions, the consumption of auspicious foods and drinks such as *mochigayu* and *toso*, and certain of the banquets) were also celebrated in the mansions of the great, a custom that added to the gaiety and hectic activity of the season.

For reference, some of the principal official New Year events are listed below. See also Wakamori 1957, Chapter 2; Ishimura 1958, 1: 176–210; and Ikeda 1967, pp. 502–37.

1. First Day, ca. 4:00 A.M.: Obeisances to the Four Directions (*shihōhai*). This important calamity-averting ceremony, first mentioned as a part of the Court calendar under date of 889, was performed by the Emperor in the eastern courtyard of the Seiryōden. In the Heian period, it consisted primarily of obeisances (a) to the tombs of the Imperial forebears, (b) to the particular star that was thought, in accordance with yin-yang doctrines, to govern the sovereign's destinies (his "affinite star," *zokushō*), and (c) to the "heavenly and earthly deities of the four directions."

2. First Day, ca. 8:00 A.M.: Congratulation of the Emperor (*chōga* or *chōhai*). Like the Imperial Accession Audience (*sokui*), which it closely resembled, the chōga was an elaborate T'ang-style ceremony in which the entire Court assembled with banners, incense, and drums at the Daigokuden to pay homage to the sovereign. Thought to date from 646, it was an annual event during the Nara period, but in early Heian it began to lose ground before a less pretentious ceremony with the same purpose, the *kojōhai*, which replaced it completely around 990.

3. First Day: Lesser Obeisance to the Emperor (*kojōhai*). In contrast to the chōga, which was a great public event, the kojōhai was a private ceremony in the eastern courtyard of the Seiryōden, in which only holders of the first six ranks participated.

4. First, Second, and Third Days: Presentation to the Emperor of Healthful Food and Drink (*hagatame*). On these three days, the Emperor was served with foods designed to promote longevity (radish, melon, salted trout, venison, boar meat, etc.), and with beverages believed to help prevent illness (toso, a Chinese drink; and other spiced wines and herbal concoctions). The attendant ceremonies, which took place in the Seiryōden, included many Chinese elements, such as the wearing of garments appropriate in color to the direction designated as auspicious for the Emperor during the coming year. See also Chapter 10, n. 40.

5. First Day: New Year Banquet (*gannichi no sechie*). The New Year Banquet concluded the major First Day observances. One of the most important

Court banquets of the year, it took place at the Burakuin, and later in the Shishinden. In addition to the usual feasting and music, it included such special features as the presentation of a new calendar to the Emperor by the Bureau of Divination and a report on the ice in storage. Thick ice at the beginning of the year was an auspicious omen.

6. Second, Third, or Fourth Day: Visit to the Imperial Parent(s) (*chōkin no gyōkō*). This ceremonial New Year visit by the Emperor to one or both of his parents dated from 834. An impressive occasion designed to serve as an example of filial piety, it consisted of a procession through the city to the parental abode; ceremonious bows by the Emperor to the ex-Emperor and/or Imperial mother; a banquet with music and dancing; the presentation of gifts by the host; and, finally, the bestowal of promotions in rank on members of the parental household, officials responsible for arranging the day's events, and others.

7. Second Day: The Two Imperial Banquets (*nigū no taikyō*). These banquets, which seem to have entered the Court calendar around 830, were provided by the Crown Prince and the Empress (or sometimes the Grand Empress) for courtiers who came to pay their New Year respects. On a smaller scale, therefore, they corresponded to the post-chōga sechie on the First. The guests were feted by the Imperial lady in the corridor west of Genkimon Gate (the gate directly north of the Jōganden), given presents, and sent off to the corridor east of the gate for the Prince's banquet.

On or about the same day, there were also highly ceremonious banquets (*taikyō*) in the homes of the Regent and/or one or more Ministers of State, as well as the Regent's Special Reception (*rinji [no] kyaku*), a banquet for New Year callers of Third or higher rank (as opposed to the taikyō for invited guests).

8. Second or Third Day: Party in the Courtiers' Hall (*tenjō no enzui*). At this affair, the Emperor looked on while the Head Chamberlains and lesser courtiers drank, sang, and danced informally in the Courtiers' Hall.

9. First Day of Spring: New Water (*wakamizu*). On the first day of spring, which usually fell near the beginning of the First Month, fresh water from a previously selected well was brought to the Seiryōden, where the Emperor drank of it, facing an auspicious direction and uttering a magical formula designed to reinforce its efficacy as a preventative of illness.

10. Fifth or Sixth Day: Promotions in Rank (*joi*). Appointments and promotions to the Fifth Rank and above were conferred at the Seiryōden. The ceremony was performed by senior Ministers of State and other officials, with the Emperor in attendance.

11. Seventh Day: Seventh Day Banquet (*nanuka no sechie*). Another important therapeutic ritual was the Seventh Day, or Green Horse (*aouma*), Banquet. Both because the horse was a yang animal and because green was the color of spring according to yin-yang cosmology, the Chinese sought to ward off illness during the year by viewing one or more "green" horses in early spring, preferably on the Seventh of the First Month, since both the day and the month were associated with the male principle. During the eighth cen-

tury the custom spread to Japan, where, in spite of some lapses, it persisted until modern times. The horses used seem to have been light grays, or possibly roans, colors that originally fell within the broad semantic compass of *ao* ("green"), and the word aouma was therefore usually written with Chinese characters meaning "white horse."

As formalized in the early Heian period, the event centered around a ceremonious parade, viewed by the Emperor and a throng of other spectators, in which twenty-one horses from the Imperial Stables were led through the Burakuin court yard (later, through the South Court of the Shishinden). Afterward the Emperor and members of the Court banqueted while dances were performed.

12. Seventh Day: Presentation of Young Greens (wakana). As indicated in s.n. 20, the presentation of young greens to the Emperor on the Seventh was an outgrowth of the custom of picking greens on the Day of the Rat. The shift in date, probably under the influence of the strongly auspicious nature ascribed to the Seventh, seems to have taken place by the beginning of the eleventh century, if not before.

13. Eighth to Fourteenth Days: Lectures on *Konkōmyōkyō* (*misaie*); Esoteric Rites at Shingon'in (*Shingon'in no mizuhō*); Rituals in Honor of the Mystic King Daigen (*Daigen no hō*). The second week of the First Month was devoted primarily to precautionary Buddhist observances, both exoteric and esoteric. The exoteric rites, performed as prayers for peaceful conditions and bountiful crops, consisted of an impressive series of daily lectures on the Golden Light Sutra (*Konkōmyōkyō*; Skt. *Suvarṇaprabhāsa-sūtra*), delivered at the Daigokuden with the Emperor and Court in attendance. The misaie was one of the major Buddhist events in the regular Court calendar, equal in importance to the Ninnōe.

Meanwhile, two sets of esoteric rituals were being performed elsewhere in the Palace compound to protect the state and the Imperial person. One series, the Shingon'in no mizuhō, was celebrated by Shingon monks in the Shingon'in, a hall near the Banquet Pine Grove in the open space northwest of the Chōdōin. The other, second only to the first as secret rituals of national import, invoked the special protection of a warrior divinity called the Mystic King Daigen, and took place in the Jōneiden or in the offices of the Popular Affairs Ministry. (Services in honor of Daigen were performed at other times as well—e.g. against foreign enemies—but always under official auspices. As *Eiga* notes later, in Chapter 4, the sponsorship of such services by a private person was a treasonable act.)

14. First Day of the Hare: Presentation to the Emperor of Hare Wands (*uzue*) and Hare Sticks (*uzuchi*). Uzue, bundles of wooden wands about five feet long, and uzuchi, attractively decorated strips of wood about three to five inches long, were presented to the Emperor on this day as a safeguard against evil spirits. For more details, see s.n. 79.

15. Eleventh to Thirteenth Days: Appointments to Provincial Posts (*agatameshi no jimoku*). Although it was possible to receive an official appointment

at any time during the year, the normal expectation was that the individual's name would appear on one of the semiannual lists, either in the spring, when the emphasis was on filling provincial vacancies, or in the autumn, when most of the central appointments took place. The spring appointments ceremony (also called *haru no jimoku*) consisted of three nights of high-level deliberations and decisions, held in the Seiryōden or in the Dairi apartments of the Regent. Voluminous lists of vacancies, performance records, recommendations, applications, and other materials had to be reviewed, and every step in the selection process was so hedged about by tradition that years of instruction and practice were considered a prerequisite to participation. Of all the Court's annual observances, the appointments ceremonies are said to have been the most difficult to master.

The Eleventh, Twelfth, and Thirteenth of the First Month (or, according to some sources, the Ninth, Tenth, and Eleventh) were the prescribed dates for the *agatameshi no jimoku*, but the rule was not rigidly observed. In the late tenth and early eleventh centuries, the event usually took place during the last third of the month.

16. Fifteenth Day: Seven-Ingredients Gruel (*nanakusagayu*). Another therapeutic measure, practiced by Emperor and commoners alike, was the consumption on the Fifteenth of nanakusagayu, a special gruel containing seven healthful ingredients: two kinds of rice, three kinds of millet, red beans, and sesame, according to *Engishiki*; white rice, red beans, soybeans, millet, chestnuts, persimmons, and cowpeas, according to a more adventurous recipe preserved by Morosuke's family. Nanakusagayu, or mochigayu (full-moon gruel), as it was sometimes called, was cooked over a fire made of hare sticks (see item 14 above), and remnants of the fuel, whittled into "gruel sticks," became the basis of a lighthearted pastime, frequently mentioned by Heian writers, in which childless women were struck on the buttocks by their friends to ensure male issue.

17. Sixteenth Day: Circle-Dancing Banquet (*tōka no sechie*). The last of the First Month's three great banquets (sechie) took place in the Shishinden halfway through the month, when the moon was full. The main entertainment was provided by a group of some forty youthful female dancers, mostly from the Naikyōbō, who performed circular figures under the moonlight in the South Court, stamping their feet in time to the music and chanting Chinese or Japanese verses appropriate to the season, such as good wishes for a long and prosperous reign. After the festivities at the Shishinden, the dancers visited the apartments of the Crown Prince and Empress, where they received additional refreshments and presents.

Readers of *The Tale of Genji* will recall memorable descriptions of similar performances by male dancers, who are depicted as having made the rounds of the principal private mansions after their official duties ended. Between 889 and 983, occasional performances of "male circle-dancing" (*otokodōka*) had in fact been presented at Court—usually on the Fourteenth, two days before the girls' dancing, and in the eastern courtyard of the Seiryōden, rather than at the Shishiden—but the custom had lapsed before Murasaki's day, and it is possible that *Genji's* reconstructions from secondhand evidence may not be completely reliable. The dancers' rounds, for example, may have been confined to the Palace precincts, as in the case of the female performers.

18. Seventeenth Day: Archery Ceremony (*jarai*). Held at the Burakuin or in front of Kenreimon Gate in the middle of the First Month, the Palace archery contest was another annual event imported from China, where it appears to have originated in remote antiquity as a magical means of driving away evil spirits at the start of a new year. The Emperor and Court viewed the efforts of two previously selected groups of archers—consisting, respectively, of gentlemen of the Court, ranging downward in status from Imperial Princes to holders of the Fifth Rank, and of officers of the Six Guards Headquarters—whose members competed on an individual basis within each group. On occasions when the Emperor failed to attend the ceremony, only the guardsmen performed. Prizes were bestowed for proficiency, and refreshments were served.

19. Eighteenth Day: Bowmen's Wager (*noriyumi*). The noriyumi archery contest on the morning of the Eighteenth, inaugurated in early Heian as an adjunct to the jarai, was actually the more elaborate of the two affairs. Two teams of marksmen from the Bodyguards and Military Guards, each led by a Major Captain, competed in the Imperial presence at the Yubadono (Butoku-den) for stakes of coins and textiles. The winners administered the cup of defeat to the losers, presented a dance, and went off to the home of their Captain for a banquet. (It should be noted that most of the references to noriyumi in Heian literary works are not to the regular annual event but to *tenjō no noriyumi*, contests of the same general type held from time to time between two teams of courtiers. See Ikeda 1967, p. 529.)

Supplementary note 24

The Horikawa Mansion and its famous gardens occupied a huge tract of land south of Nijō and east of Horikawa, in the vicinity of the present Kokusai Kankō Hotel in Kyōto. Said to have been built by Mototsune, the house had come to Kanemichi through one of his wives, Princess Nōshi, who was the mother of his favorite son, Asateru (951–95). Kanemichi had probably been living there since 950 or 951.

After the Dairi fire of 976, Emperor En'yū spent a year in residence at Horikawa with Kōshi, Kanemichi's daughter by an earlier wife (Princess Shōshi, also the mother of Kanemichi's oldest son, Akimitsu [944–1021]). Kōshi died there in 979. After another fire, in 982, En'yū returned to the house, which by then seems to have belonged to Akimitsu, for a sojourn of about three years, during which period he abdicated. Prince Atsuakira (994–1051), the husband of Akimitsu's daughter Enshi (d. 1019), also lived there from around 1010 until his marriage to Michinaga's daughter Kanshi in 1017. After the deaths of Akimitsu and Enshi, the mansion was sold by Enshi's sister Genshi to a rich provincial official, Fujiwara Tsunekuni, through the gift of whose heir, Minamoto Yukitō, ownership passed into the hands of Michinaga's descendants. See Tsunoda 1963, pp. 24–43, 77, 133, and *passim*; and Figure 2.

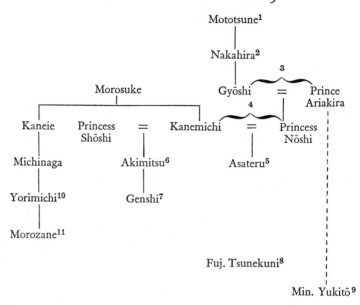

FIGURE 2. Successive Owners of the Horikawa Mansion

Supplementary note 25

Since the office of Kamo Virgin followed the pattern established for the Ise Virgin, it is convenient to consider the two together.

1. Ise Virgin (Saigū). Ise Virgins, said to have held office as early as the third or fourth century, were regularly appointed by the Court from the seventh century until the fourteenth. The beginning of a new reign meant the designation of a new Virgin, selected by divination from among unmarried Imperial or Princely offspring, to serve as High Priestess and Imperial surrogate at the Grand Shrines of Ise. Once chosen, the Virgin-designate was installed in an Initial Purification Cloister (Shosaiin) at the Palace, to remain until the Eighth Month of the following year. She then moved to the Palace in the Fields (No-nomiya), a second place of purification erected for her use at an auspicious site near the capital, which during the Heian period was always in the Sagano area west of the city.

Behind the brushwood fence and log torii of the Palace in the Fields, the Princess worshiped the Ise goddesses, avoided language suggestive of defilement or Buddhism, and otherwise prepared for her vocation. Finally, in the Ninth Month of the year after her arrival there, she performed a grand purification at the Kamo or Katsura River and went to the Imperial Palace, where, after a ceremony in the Daigokuden, the Emperor placed the comb of parting (*wakare no kushi*) in her hair and sent her off with an entourage of Court officials, who escorted her to the edge of the city. She then set out on the seven-day journey to Ise, performing a series of impressive purification rituals

at rivers along the way. Her progress was a great national event, involving purification rituals throughout the country, the construction of temporary accommodations for the procession at various places in Ōmi and Ise provinces, and
other extensive preparations.

The Virgin remained at Ise, worshiping regularly at both shrines and main-
taining strict ritual purity, until the death or abdication of the reigning sovereign,
or until she was given leave to retire on grounds of illness, the death of a parent,
or the like.

2. Kamo Virgin (Saiin). The principal function of Japan's thirty-five Kamo
Virgins, who held office successively from 810 to 1204, was to participate in
the great Aoi Festival of the Kamo Shrine, an ancient institution that had
assumed a prominent role in the social, religious, and political life of the ruling
class soon after the move to Heian. (The shrine's Upper Sanctuary survives at
what is now Kamikamo, Kita-ku, Kyōto; the Lower, at Shimokamo Miyakawa-
chō, Sakyō-ku. On the Aoi Festival, see s.n. 50.)

Appointed early in each new reign in the same manner as the Ise Virgin, the

TABLE 6. Known Offspring of Fujiwara Kaneie

Name	Career	Remarks
Sons		
Michitaka* (953–95)	Regent	
Michitsuna (955–1020)	Major Counselor, Sr. 2	Son of *Kagerō nikki* author
Michiyoshi	Junior Assistant Minister of Civil Affairs	
Michikane* (961–95)	Regent	
Michinaga* (966–1028)	Chancellor, Regent	
Daughters		
Chōshi* (d. 982)	Junior Consort of Emperor Reizei (968), posthumous Grand Empress (1011)	Mother of Emperor Sanjō, Princes Tametaka and Atsu- michi, Princess Kōshi
Senshi* (962–1002)	Junior Consort of Emperor En'yū (978), Grand Empress (986), first Imperial Lady (Nyōin) (991)	Mother of Emperor Ichijō; a major political figure after her son's accession
Senji		
Suishi (974–1004)		Marriage to future Emperor Sanjō ended after discovery of her liaison with Min. Yorisada

*Child of principal wife, Tokihime.

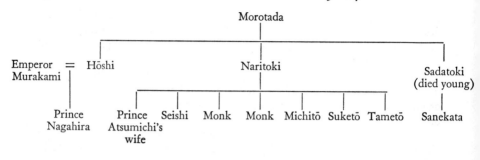

FIGURE 3

Saiin spent three years at a Shosaiin in the Palace, and then moved permanently to a Palace in the Fields at Murasakino near the Arisugawa River, north of the capital. There, like the Saigū at Ise, she avoided contact with defilement and Buddhism, kept branches of the sacred *sakaki* tree on the premises, and otherwise maintained a state of ritual purity. The terms of her tenure were essentially the same as those prescribed for the Saigū.

The Saiin's entries into the Shosaiin and the Palace in the Fields, her purification for the Aoi Festival, and her participation in the festival itself were all magnificent events in the mid-Heian period.

Supplementary note 26

Destined to be the last survivor among Morosuke's sons by his principal wife, Kaneie was able, before his death in 990, to assure brilliant careers for many of his own sons and daughters, who consequently play leading roles in the chapters that follow. His known children are listed in Table 6.

Supplementary note 27

Nobumitsu (927–76) was a grandson of Emperor Daigo; Atsutada (906–43), a son of Tokihira. Of Naritoki's children by Nobumitsu's daughter, the son, Chōmeigimi (b. 971?), whose adult name was Suketō, took Buddhist vows in 986. Their daughter, Seishi (972–1025), married the future Emperor Sanjō in 991, became a Nyōgo in 1011, and was named Kōgō in 1012. She bore six children, including Prince Atsuakira, who held the position of Crown Prince until pressure from Michinaga forced him to resign. Naritoki had seven children all together. See Figure 3.

Minamoto Nobumitsu's Biwa Mansion, probably located south of Konoe and east of Muromachi, was so called because of the loquat trees (*biwa*) in its grounds. After having been owned successively by Fuyutsugu, Nagara, Mototsune, Kanehira, Nakahira, and Atsutada, it had passed into Nobumitsu's hands through his wife, Atsutada's daughter. Around 1002, after the death of Nobumitsu and Asateru, her second husband, Atsutada's daughter sold the establishment to Michinaga, during whose tenure it was used from time to time as a residence by Emperors Ichijō and Sanjō, and by Sanjō's widow Kenshi. It burned in 1028. See Tsunoda 1963, pp. 68–69, 111–12.

Supplementary note 28

Yoshitaka's son was the celebrated calligrapher Yukinari, ancestor of the Sesonji family and author of the diary *Gonki*. He eventually became a Provisional Major Counselor. Minamoto Yasumitsu was a Consultant in 972. His house in the Momozono area (just northeast of the city) passed into the hands of Yukinari, who converted it into the Sesonji. See Figure 4, taken from *Honchō kōin shōunroku*, p. 426.

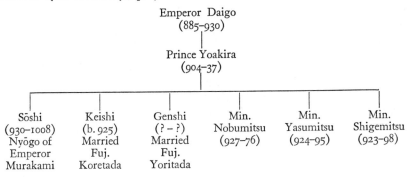

Emperor Daigo
(885–930)

Prince Yoakira
(904–37)

| Sōshi (930–1008) Nyōgo of Emperor Murakami | Keishi (b. 925) Married Fuj. Koretada | Genshi (? – ?) Married Fuj. Yoritada | Min. Nobumitsu (927–76) | Min. Yasumitsu (924–95) | Min. Shigemitsu (923–98) |

FIGURE 4

Supplementary note 29

According to *Sonpi bunmyaku*, Kanemichi had seven sons, most of whom appear to have been the products of casual liaisons. The only ones who advanced beyond the office of Middle Counselor were Akimitsu, the full brother of Empress Kōshi, and Asateru, the son of the Regent's principal wife. See Table 7.

TABLE 7. Sons of Fujiwara Kanemichi

Name	Career	Remarks
Akimitsu (944–1021)	Minister of the Left	Figurehead minister; competed unsuccessfully with Michinaga for power
Tokimitsu (948–1015)	Middle Counselor	
Asateru (951–95)	Major Counselor	Regarded by Kanemichi as his heir; died in epidemic of 995
Tōmitsu	Master of the Left Capital Office	
Chikamitsu		Took Buddhist vows
Masamitsu (957–1014)	Consultant	
Mochimitsu	Master of the Right Capital Office	

SOURCE: *Sonpi bunmyaku*, 1: 51–54. *Kugyō bunin*, 1: 214, lists Asateru as the fourth son.

Supplementary note 30

The Higashisanjō Mansion had originally been built by Fujiwara Yoshifusa next door to his father's Kan'in house, probably on a single block west of Machijiri and south of Nijō. After passing through the hands of Mototsune, his daughter Onshi, his son, Tadahira, and then Tadahira's daughter Kanshi and grandson Kanemichi, it had come to Kaneie, who is believed to have enlarged it by acquiring the adjoining block as a site for an additional structure, mentioned in contemporary writings as the Higashisanjōin Minaminoin (Southern Palace of the Higashisanjōin).

The mansion later belonged in succession to Kaneie's sons Michitaka and Michinaga, to Michinaga's son Yorimichi, and to Yorimichi's descendants for several generations. It played an important historical role, first during the hegemony of Kaneie and then under Michinaga, who furnished it magnificently and filled it with treasures to make it a suitable environment for his eldest daughter, Shōshi. Emperor Ichijō was born in the house in 980 and used it from time to time as a temporary residence after his accession. See Tsunoda 1963, pp. 65–66.

Supplementary note 31

"Equality with the three Empresses" (*junsangū* or *jusangū*) was an economic privilege conferred in the first instance on Fujiwara Yoshifusa, and later on all succeeding Chancellors throughout the pre-Meiji era, as well as on many members of the Imperial Family, Imperial consorts, maternal relatives of Emperors, and leading bureaucrats. Recipients enjoyed annual revenues (*nenkyū*)—i.e. annual offices (*nenkan*) and annual ranks (*nenshaku*)—equivalent to those awarded to the three categories of Empresses (Kōgō/Chūgū, Kōtaigō, and Taikōtaigō).

An Empress was entitled to three annual offices: one each at the third and fourth levels of the provincial administration, and a single low-ranking central post. This meant that appropriate vacancies were placed at her disposal at the time of the regular appointments ceremonies, with the understanding that she would select appointees and keep most or all of the perquisites prescribed for the offices. In addition, she was allowed to choose one candidate annually for promotion to Junior Fifth Lower Rank, and received the income from the eight *chō* of rice fields to which the holder of the rank was entitled. (On the specific perquisites granted to each rank, see Appendix A, p. 827.)

The nenkyū system was a Heian innovation designed to give the capital nobility a greater share of the wealth of the provinces, particularly the huge stores of rice collected by local officials as interest on seed-rice loans. The law provided that such rice was to be used to defray public expenses, but surpluses were shared among the principal local officials, for whom they became a source of income more important than rank fields, office fields, seasonal stipends, or the right to cultivate unused land. In the many provinces where the senior staff included only one official at the third level (*jō*) and one at the fourth (*sakan*), the two men appear to have shared about 50 percent of such annual surpluses.

Jusangū status thus conferred significant economic advantages, which were further strengthened by the customary simultaneous gift of from 500 to 3,000 sustenance households. As with other sources of revenue, however, the nenkyū system failed to survive the vicissitudes of the Heian period, and by the twelfth century, if not considerably earlier, "equality with the three Empresses" was nothing more than a status symbol.

Supplementary note 32

Of Yoritada's six children (*Sonpi bunmyaku*, 2: 2–4), the only ones to achieve a measure of prominence at court were Junshi, Shishi, and Kintō, all offspring of his principal wife, Princess Genshi, a daughter of Prince Yoakira. Junshi (957–1017) married Emperor En'yū in 978, became Empress in 982, advanced to the status of Grand Empress in 1000, and was named Senior Grand Empress in 1012, but her career as a consort was a failure because she bore no children. Shishi (d. 1035), a rather unsuccessful Junior Consort during the brief reign of Emperor Kazan, lived quietly in the family mansion at Shijō after Kazan's abdication. Kintō (966–1041), a leader in the cultural life of the Court during the first two decades of the eleventh century, was a scholar, musician, poet in Chinese and Japanese, literary critic, and arbiter of taste, but his official career languished after the death of his father in 989. In 1024, he resigned as Provisional Major Counselor after having stagnated in the position for fifteen years; and two years later he became a monk, relinquishing his remaining title of Inspector, which he had held since 1021.

Supplementary note 33

The wrestling matches (*sumai*) in the Seventh Month provided entertainment for one of the great periodic Court banquets (sechie).

As in other countries, wrestling has had a long history in Japan, where it appears to have developed in association with Shintō rituals, such as divination at the beginning of a new year to determine the probable nature of the harvest. Scattered references in *Nihon shoki* suggest that by the sixth century wrestlers from the provinces were being brought in to entertain the Court, but such events were sporadic and followed no set pattern. *Sechie sumai* is said to have begun in 737, when Emperor Shōmu ordered wrestlers to perform at the Tanabata Banquet, on the Seventh of the Seventh Month, as an adjunct to the main entertainment of the occasion, the composition of Chinese poetry. By 793 it was a regular annual event—a celebration of physical prowess considered equal in importance to the archery ceremony (*jarai*) on the Seventeenth of the First Month and the mounted archery (*umayumi*) on the Fifth of the Fifth Month. In the mid-Heian period, especially, it was one of the most lavish spectacles of the year. It remained a part of the Court calendar until 1174.

During its most flourishing period, the *sumai no sechie* was a three-day event in the latter part of the Seventh Month (the date having been changed to avoid the death anniversary of an early Heian Emperor). It was staged primarily by the two Major Captains of the Bodyguards, with the assistance of the War

Ministry and other departments of the government. Preparations began in the Second or Third Month with the dispatch of Konoefu envoys to the provinces to seek out experienced wrestlers and local strong men. Around the Seventh Month the recruits arrived in the capital, where they divided for training purposes into Left and Right camps, operated by the corresponding divisions of the Bodyguards.

In the mid-Heian period, the events centering around the principal banquet were as follows. (It should be noted that sites other than those indicated were sometimes used. For details, see the sources cited below.)

1. Twenty-fifth or Twenty-sixth Day: Practice bouts (*uchidori*). The sechie proper usually took place on the Twenty-eighth of a long month (thirty days) or the Twenty-seventh of a short one (twenty-nine days). Two days in advance, the Emperor went to the Jijūden to view the practice bouts in which members of each camp competed among themselves.

2. Twenty-seventh or Twenty-eighth Day: Banquets (*sumai no sechie*); wrestling matches (*meshiawase*). In the tenth and eleventh centuries, the usual site of the *sumai no sechie* was the Shishinden and its South Court. The festivities began early in the morning with the music of flutes, bells, and drums and the ceremonious entry of the Emperor, members of the Court, the opposing contingents, and a host of musicians, dancers, banner bearers, and lesser figures. The Heian tale *Utsubo monogatari* describes the brilliant appearance of the participants on one such occasion, dwelling in particular on the dazzling costumes of the Guards Captains, the products of many weeks of labor by the women in their families. During the course of the long day, the author continues, those present consumed three complete repasts, which were accompanied by music, dancing, and the composition of poetry. Meanwhile the wrestling proceeded, with the champions (*hote*) performing first rather than last as in the case of modern *sumō*. The contestants (*sumaibito*) wore hunting cloaks and tall caps, both of which they removed before coming to grips with their opponents, and were identified for the convenience of the spectators by artificial flowers in their hair, *aoi* (*Asarum caulescens* Maxim) for the Left and a gourd-shaped blossom (or gourd-flower?) for the Right. The Emperor personally decided close matches after hearing the opinions of the Captains and senior nobles. Since there was no ring, a throw was the usual method of achieving victory. After seventeen rounds or when darkness fell, the scores of the opposing sides were tallied, and the winners presented a dance performance.

3. Twenty-eighth or Twenty-ninth Day: Additional matches (*nukide*); Return Banquet (*kaeriaruji*). On the following day, the Court returned to the Shishinden to witness additional wrestling matches—exhibitions by the sechie stars, rematches to decide dubious cases, and contests between minor Guards officers. There was more feasting, both the Left and Right sponsored dances, and the noble guests received gifts from the Emperor. For each side, the final event of the *sumai no sechie* was the Return Banquet, to which the Major Captain invited his assistants and wrestlers. Ishimura 1958, 1: 243–45; *Koji ruien*, 44: 1017–1118; *Utsubo monogatari*, 2: 154ff.

Supplementary note 34

"Damask" translates *aya*, a term used of silks in which patterns were made by contrasting binding systems. (In our discussion of textiles, we follow when possible the usage recommended by the Centre International d'Etude des Textiles Anciens in its *Vocabulary of Technical Terms*, 1964.) The fabrics were usually monochrome, but there are literary references to two- and three-colored varieties, in which, presumably, warps and wefts of different colors produced a pattern that contrasted with the ground in color as well as in binding system (see Chapter 3, n. 26). Such polychrome damasks would have combined the essential characteristics of Japanese brocade (s.n. 67), which was woven in patterned colors, and of damask, which was woven in patterned binding systems; and the classification as one or the other may have depended on the observer—a common enough situation in the use of textile terminology. Damasks in the Heian period included tabbies with patterning in twill or floats (whether these were weft- or warp-faced, the sources do not say), but the usual variety seems to have been warp-faced twill with patterning in weft twill, with the diagonal lines of the ground and pattern sometimes running in opposite directions and sometimes in the same direction. There were also warp-faced twills with patterning in weft floats. Sasaki 1951, pp. 18–48, 97–98; Hifuku Bunka Kyōkai 1969, 1: 26–27; Nishimura 1971–75, 1: 5–8. For photographic illustrations of twelfth-century warp-faced twill damasks with the diagonal lines of the ground and pattern running in opposite directions, see Nishimura 1971–75, 1: Plates 43, 45–50. For an example with the diagonal lines running in the same direction, see Plate 44.

Supplementary note 35

The Putting On of the Trousers (*hakamagi* or *chakko*), a rite of passage for noble children of both sexes, marked the attainment of a certain stage in the child's development, usually celebrated at three (sai), but sometimes delayed until five, six, or seven. The ceremony, which appears to have dated from the early tenth century, was considered a milestone in a person's childhood, second in importance only to the *mogi* (see s.n. 56) or the genpuku. It centered around the formal donning of a skirtlike pair of trousers (*hakama*), presented by one of the family's senior members, who also tied the strings of the garment, thus performing a role comparable to that of the Kakan at a genpuku ceremony. For a Prince or Princess, the Emperor or ex-Emperor ordinarily tied the strings; for the child of a nobleman, the office was performed by his father, by a Minister of State, or by someone regarded as a successful father or grandfather.

Extant accounts of the hakamagi of Princess Teishi, the offspring of Emperor Sanjō and Michinaga's daughter Kenshi, illustrate the splendor of such events and the considerable advance preparation required. Around 4:00 P.M., an hour chosen by divination, the furnishings of the chamber were replaced by new curtains, screens, and lacquered or mother-of-pearl objects (a mirror-stand, a chest, a set of comb boxes, incense-jar boxes, a writing box, a brazier, etc.), all specially made by the Office of Palace Works in miniature sizes appropriate to the occasion. Around 8:00 P.M., the hour selected for the ceremony, the Emperor, senior nobles, and Princes entered and took their assigned places. The Princess then put on the hakama and the Emperor tied the strings.

Adjoining apartments were opened, new seats were occupied by the guests, and a formal banquet took place, with music performed by Court musicians, kugyō, and tenjōbito. The event ended with the usual presentation of gifts. See Nakamura 1962, p. 108; and *Utsubo monogatari*, 3: 574, s.n. 131.

Supplementary note 36

See Table 8.

TABLE 8. Consorts of Emperor Kazan

Name	Father	Date of presentation	Junior Consort	Remarks
Kishi (d. 985)	Fuj. Tamemitsu	28 x 984	7 xi 984	Died 18 vii 985 in 8th month of pregnancy; grief is said to have led to Kazan's abdication
Shinshi	Fuj. Asateru	5 xii 984	25 xii 984	Ignored after brief period of favor; left Palace
Shishi (d. 1035)	Fuj. Yoritada	15 xii 984	25 xii 984	Childless; lived with sister Junshi at Shijō after Kazan's abdication
Enshi (972–98)	Prince Tamehira	5 xii 985	Date uncertain	Neglected after brief period of favor; married Fuj. Sanesuke after Kazan's abdication

NOTE: Emperor Kazan reigned 27 viii 984–23 vi 986.

Supplementary note 37

The accessions of new Emperors in the Asuka and Nara periods appear to have been marked primarily by the transmission of the Imperial Regalia (the sword, mirror, and necklace), and by the more or less simultaneous issuance of an accession proclamation. From early Heian times on, the two main elements of such events became the focal points of two distinct ceremonies, the *senso*, or Accession ceremony proper, and the subsequent *sokui*, or Accession Audience. The senso included the physical transmission of the sword and necklace (the mirror remained permanently in the Kashikodokoro), the notification of the gods, and the symbolic seating of the Emperor on the Shishinden throne, all carried out under relatively private circumstances. The sokui, which took place at a later date, was by contrast a great state occasion, identical in most external details to the chōga. Like the chōga, it was held in the Daigokuden and its courtyard (later elsewhere in the Daidairi, or in the Shishinden of a *sato dairi*). Clad in formal Chinese costumes (*raifuku*, as opposed to *sokutai*, the usual Court dress), the civil and military officials filed into the courtyard, made splendid with special banners depicting the sun, the moon, the Green Dragon, the White Tiger, etc. The Daigokuden curtains were raised to reveal the sovereign on his throne, incense was ignited, and an Imperial Messenger stepped forward to read the accession proclamation. When the reading was completed, the assembled officials bowed twice and performed the elaborate dance of obeisance called *haimu* or *butō*. The military officers shouted "Banzai," waving their banners, and a Gentleman-in-waiting announced the conclusion of the ceremony. Kawabata 1966, p. 158. On raifuku, see Ikeda 1967, p. 176.

Supplementary note 38

See Table 9.

TABLE 9. Offspring of Prince Tamehira

Name	Career	Remarks
	Sons (all Minamoto)	
Norisada* (d. 1017)	Commander, Military Guards of the Right, Jr. 3	
Yorisada (977–1020)	Consultant, Sr. 3	Lover of Crown Prince's consort Suishi; soon after Suishi's death, married daughter of Tachibana Sukemasa; ca. age 35, began affair with Akimitsu's daughter Genshi
Tamesada		
Akisada	Gentleman-in-waiting, Senior Assistant Minister of Popular Affairs, Jr. 4 U	
Norisada*	Official in Board of Censors, Jr. 4 U	
Atsusada	Gentleman-in-waiting, Jr. 4 L	
	Daughters	
Enshi (972–98)		See s.n. 36 (Table 8)
Kyōshi (b. 984)		Ise Virgin, 986–1011

SOURCES: *Dainihonshi*, 4: 370; *Honchō kōin shōunroku*, p. 432; *Kugyō bunin*, 1: 269.
*The first characters of the names are Ueda *Daijiten* no. 3530 and no. 4261, respectively.

Supplementary note 39

As the author has already mentioned, Naritoki was married to Nobumitsu's daughter. Assuming that Naritoki (941–95) and his wife were of approximately the same age, she would have been some ten years senior to Asateru (951–95). Although Asateru and Naritoki owned houses of their own (the Kan'in and Koichijōin, respectively), they probably lived much of the time with their wives, who as mother and daughter occupied separate parts of the Biwa Mansion. See Figure 5.

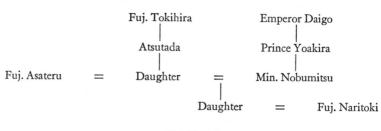

FIGURE 5

Supplementary note 40

As the author indicates, Morosuke's ninth son, Tamemitsu (942–92), was a Major Counselor in 985. He later became titular Minister of the Right (986) and Chancellor (991), but lacked the political power to ensure anything more than modestly successful official careers for his male offspring. Of seven sons listed in *Sonpi bunmyaku*, only three became kugyō—Sanenobu (964–1001), a Consultant; Tadanobu (967–1035), a Major Counselor; and Kinnobu (977–1026), a Provisional Middle Counselor. The Junior Consort Kishi (d. 985) was probably the second of his daughters. Other daughters who played minor roles in the history of the period were the third, Shinden no Onkata, Lady of the Central Hall (also called San no Kimi), with whom Fujiwara Korechika had a liaison; the fourth, Shi no Kimi, who was one of Emperor Kazan's mistresses after his abdication, and who later entered the service of Empress Kenshi and bore a child to Michinaga; and the fifth, Go no Kimi, who was also one of Kenshi's ladies-in-waiting. *Sonpi bunmyaku*, 1: 393ff; EMZ, 1: 446, 5: 464.

Supplementary note 41

After a monk had killed his grandfather with an axe in the sixth century, the Japanese Court had begun to appoint ecclesiastical officials to supervise and discipline the burgeoning monasteries and nunneries. By the Nara period, there were three principal categories of such officials, designated, in descending order of prestige, as Sōjō, Sōzu, and Risshi (Archbishop, Bishop, and Master of Discipline in the Translation), and known collectively as *sōgō*. Like members of the Daijōkan, *sōgō* appear to have differed from one another more in status than in their rather amorphous functions. As a group, they constituted an extremely powerful body, exercising broad authority from their Yakushiji head-quarters over all Buddhist establishments in the Kinai area.

In the eighth century, sōgō appointments were carefully weighed and sparing-ly bestowed. As late as 819, their numbers were restricted to one Sōjō, one Daisōzu (Major Bishop) one Shōsōzu (Lesser Bishop), and four Risshi. In the Heian period, however, the prestige of the offices attracted large numbers of candidates, and the resultant pressure, together with a resurgence of the hereditary principle, began to modify the size and composition of the body. When an Emperor's son took Buddhist vows, for example, he automatically became a Provisional Major Bishop; when a Regent's son entered the clergy, he became a Provisional Lesser Bishop. Soon after the middle of the eleventh century, the total number of sōgō approached sixty.

At the same time, sōgō authority diminished. Lesser officials attached to individual temples were granted permission to make internal appointments and handle miscellaneous business—functions previously performed by the sōgō—and certain temples early won complete exemption from sōgō jurisdiction. By the beginning of the Kamakura period, Sōjō, Sōzu, and Risshi were titles that retained a certain prestige but involved no substantive functions.

In the meantime, official titles of many descriptions were appearing within individual Buddhist institutions. The best known today are those of the men whose activities impinged most directly on the lives of the Court aristocrats, particularly (1) the abbots (variously known as Zasu, Chōri, Chōja, Bettō, etc.) at the major temples, (2) the Prayer-monks (Gojisō), who guarded the Imperial person at night in the Seiryōden, (3) the Leaders (Dōshi), who took charge of the great Buddhist rituals at Court, and (4) the Holy Teachers (Ajari), whose skill in the performance of esoteric rites made them familiar figures in the houses of the great.

The Heian period also produced a simple system of ecclesiastical ranks, three in number, that were intended to parallel the three sōgō offices. We translate their names, hōin (Dharma Sign), hōgen (Dharma Eye), and hokkyō (Dharma Bridge), as His Holiness, the Venerable, and the Reverend. In theory, the ranks were awarded to recognize distinguished scholarly and moral attainments. By the late Heian period, such criteria were habitually ignored, and before the formal abandonment of the system in 1873 the ranks had been conferred on innumerable warriors, physicians, sculptors, artisans, Confucian scholars, and other laymen.

Supplementary note 42

It will be noted that Michitaka was already a kugyō before his promotion. Michinaga, an Assistant Guards Commander of Fifth Rank, held an even less exalted position than the text states, and did not become a kugyō until 987. As Table 10 shows, however, the year 986 produced a succession of "joyous events" for each of Senshi's brothers.

Supplementary note 43

See Table 11 for a list of Michitaka's children.

TABLE 10. Principal Offices and Ranks Held by Sons of Fujiwara Kaneie and Tokihime

	Michitaka (953–95)		Michikane (961–95)		Michinaga (966–1028)	
Year	Rank	Office	Rank	Office	Rank	Office
984	Jr. 3	Middle Captain	Jr. 5 U to Sr. 5 L	Chamberlain, Lesser Controller	Jr. 5 L	Asst. Guards Cmdr.
985	Jr. 3	Middle Captain	Sr. 5 L	Chamb., Lesser Controller	Jr. 5 L	Asst. Guards Cmdr.
986	Jr. 3 to Sr. 2	Prov. Middle Counselor, Prov. Major Counselor	Sr. 5 L to Sr. 3	Head Chamberlain, Consultant, Prov. Middle Capt., Prov. Middle Counselor	Jr. 5 L to Jr. 4 L	Chamberlain, Lesser Counselor, Lesser Captain
987	Sr. 2	Prov. Major Counselor	Sr. 3 to Jr. 2	Prov. Middle Counselor	Jr. 4 L to Jr. 3	Master, Left Capital Office
988	Sr. 2	Prov. Major Counselor	Jr. 2	Prov. Middle Counselor	Jr. 3	Prov. Middle Counselor
989	Sr. 2	Palace Minister	Jr. 2 to Sr. 2	Prov. Major Counselor	Jr. 3	Prov. Middle Counselor
990	Sr. 2	Palace Minister, Regent	Sr. 2	Prov. Major Counselor	Sr. 3	Prov. Middle Counselor
991	Sr. 2	Palace Minister (resigned 7 vii), Regent	Sr. 2	Prov. Major Counselor, Palace Minister	Sr. 3	Prov. Major Counselor
992	Sr. 2	Regent	Sr. 2	Palace Minister	Sr. 3 to Jr. 2	Prov. Major Counselor
993	Sr. 2	Regent	Sr. 2	Palace Minister	Jr. 2	Prov. Major Counselor
994	Sr. 2	Regent	Sr. 2	Min. of Right	Jr. 2	Prov. Major Counselor
995	Sr. 2	Regent (died 10 iv)	Sr. 2	Regent (died 8 v)	Jr. 2	Min. of Right (nairan)*
996					Jr. 2 to Sr. 2	Min. of Left
997–1015					Sr. 2	Min. of Left
1016					Sr. 2	Min. of Left (resigned late 1016), Regent
1017					Sr. 2 to Jr. 1	Regent (resigned iii), Chancellor (resigned 1018)

SOURCE: *Kugyō bunin.*
*Private inspection powers. See Chapter 4, n. 65, above.

TABLE 11. Offspring of Fujiwara Michitaka

Name	Career	Remarks
Sons		
Michiyori (Ochiyogimi) (971–95)	Rose rapidly to Sr. 3 (xii 992) and Provisional Major Counselor (994)	Adopted by Fuj. Kaneie; called Yamanoi Dainagon
Yorichika (972–1010)	Middle Captain; Jr. 4 L	
Korechika (Kochiyogimi)* (973–1010)	Rose rapidly from Consultant (991) to Palace Minister (994); in exile, 996–97; later Sr. 2, but remained outside bureaucracy	Favorite son of Michitaka; lacked political ability; lost power struggle against Michinaga (see Kawakita 1968, pp. 168–75)
Takaie* (979–1044)	Provisional Middle Counselor (995); in exile; 996–97; re-entered government to serve as Middle Counselor (1002) and, with distinction, as Provisional Governor-General of the Dazaifu (1014); Sr. 2	Probably the ablest of Michitaka's sons (see Kawakita 1968, pp. 190–203)
Chikayori	Minor posts; Jr. 4 L	
Chikaie	Minor posts; Jr. 4 L	
Yoshichika	Lesser Captain; Jr. 4 L	Son of Tachibana Naishi no Suke
Ryūen* (980?–1015)	Named Bishop in 994 at ca. 15 (sai)	Called Komatsu Bishop
Daughters		
Teishi* (976 [977?]–1001)	Entered Palace of Emperor Ichijō (990); Junior Consort (ii 990), Chūgū (x 990); named Kōgō in 1000	Presided over literary salon and set tone of Palace life until death of father (Kawakita 1968, pp. 175–80); became nun, 996
Genshi* (981?–1002)	Consort of Crown Prince (future Emperor Sanjō; 995–1002)	Sudden death was attributed to machinations of her rival, Seishi, or of one of Seishi's attendants (Kawakita 1968, pp. 181–83)
San no Kimi*		First wife of Prince Atsumichi; mentally unbalanced; dropped out of sight after Prince terminated marriage
Mikushigedono* (ca. 983–1002)	Concubine of Emperor Ichijō	Died during pregnancy

*Child of principal wife, Kishi.

Supplementary note 44

Michikane's wife had probably given birth to only two sons by 986. As indicated in Table 12, the offspring of the marriage prospered moderately. In addition to those children and Naishi no Suke's daughter, Michikane appears to have had another son, Kanenobu (possibly by Tōkazu's daughter), of whom little is known. *Sonpi bunmyaku*, 1: 355. *Eiga* states, on dubious authority, that he was also the foster father of two children—a daughter of Prince Akihira and a son of Tamemitsu. See Chapter 4.

T A B L E 12. Offspring of Fujiwara Michikane and Tōkazu's Daughter

Name	Career	Remarks
	Sons	
Fukutarigimi (d. 989)		Identified as first son in *Ōkagami* (p. 199); died in childhood
Kanetaka (985–1053)	Consultant (1008), Middle Counselor (1023), Sr. 2	Adopted by Fuj. Kaneie
Kanetsuna (988–1058)	Middle Captain, Sr. 4 L	
	Daughter	
Nijō no Onkata (b. 995)	Lady-in-waiting to Michinaga's daughter Ishi	Born after death of father

SOURCES: EMZ, 1: 559; *Sonpi bunmyaku*, 1: 355.

Supplementary note 45

The Second Month, which came at the start of the new growing season, was a time of religious activity throughout the country. Shintō rituals of great antiquity were performed in the fields, shrines held festivals, and the Court devoted much time and energy to prayers for a successful agricultural year. The principal events on the Court calendar for the month were as follows.

1. Kasuga Festival (held twice annually on the first Day of the Monkey in the Second and Eleventh Months). The official importance attached to Kasuga Shrine, the ancient Fujiwara tutelary shrine at the foot of Mount Mikasa in Nara, corresponded to the prominence of the regental family in the political and social life of the nation. The shrine's festival, thought to date from around 850, was bracketed in Heian days with those of Kamo and Iwashimizu as the Three Festivals. In apparent imitation of the great Kamo Festival, it at first featured not only an Imperial Messenger, but also a Fujiwara Virgin (Saijo), whose riverbank purification and subsequent progress to Nara involved processions of great magnificence. The Virgin did not survive the ninth century, and in Michinaga's day the central role in the festival was played by the Imperial

Messenger, usually a Fujiwara Middle Captain, who journeyed to Nara with suitable offerings, accompanied by a splendid retinue of dancers and tenjōbito. Also in attendance at the festival were emissaries from other members of the Imperial Family; senior nobles; and Naishi. The main events were the presentation of offerings, including horses brought by the messengers; the recitation of an address to the gods (norito); sacred dances; and horse races.

2. Kinensai Festival (held annually on the Fourth Day of the Second Month). The basic element in the Kinensai, or *toshigoe no matsuri* (Harvest Prayer Festival), was a prayer (norito) for good crops, offered by the Jingikan at its Daidairi compound in the presence of the assembled Ministers of State and other bureaucrats. The prayer was addressed to the 3,132 gods and goddesses of the large and small shrines named in *Engishiki*—a list that can be regarded as having been compiled for the purposes of this event.

The Kinensai norito, which has traditionally been admired for its literary style, contains passages such as the following:*

> I humbly speak before you,
>   The Sovereign Deities of the Grain:
> The latter grain to be vouchsafed by you [to the Sovereign Grandchild],
>   The latter grain to be harvested
>   With foam dripping from the elbows,
>   To be pulled hither
>   With mud adhering to both thighs—
> If this grain be vouchsafed by you
>   In ears many hands long,
>   In luxuriant ears;
> Then the first fruits will be presented
>   In a thousand stalks, eight hundred stalks;
> Raising high the soaring necks
>   Of the countless wine vessels, filled to the brim;
> Both in liquor and in stalks I will fulfill your praises.
> From that which grows in the vast fields and plains—
>   The sweet herbs and the bitter herbs—
> To that which lives in the blue ocean—
>   The wide-finned and the narrow-finned fishes,
>   The sea-weeds of the deep and the sea-weeds of the shore—
> As well as garments
>   Of colored cloth, radiant cloth,
>   Plain cloth and coarse cloth—
> In these I will fulfill your praises.
> Before the Sovereign Deities of the Grain
>   I will provide a white horse, a white boar, a white cock,
>   And various types of offerings,
> And will present the noble offerings of the Sovereign Grandchild
>   And fulfill your praises. This I speak.

* Quoted with permission from Philippi 1959, pp. 17–18; the original appears in Kurano and Takeda 1958, p. 396.

The norito recitation was followed by the other major event of the Kinensai—the distribution of varying amounts of cloth, wine, farm tools, weapons, horses, and other goods to shrine representatives, gathered in the capital for the occasion, who were charged with the task of transmitting the offerings to their institutions.

Perhaps because the scale of the Kinensai was overambitious, it proved increasingly difficult to stage as the Heian period progressed. It was already failing in its objectives by the beginning of the tenth century, when, according to a contemporary observer, the shrine emissaries were appropriating the silk for their own use, drinking up the wine, and selling off the sacred horses to dealers outside the Palace gates. See Miyoshi 1922, p. 258. In an effort to prevent abuses, a large share of the responsibility for the Kinensai was delegated to provincial authorities, but the event continued to be bedeviled by corruption, inefficiency, and lack of economic resources.

3. Festivals of the Sono and Kara gods (held twice annually, on the first Day of the Ox after the Kasuga Festival in the Second Month, and on the last Day of the Ox in the Eleventh Month, immediately preceding the First Fruits Service). The Sono deity, usually identified with Ōmochinushi, and the Kara deities, usually identified with Ōnamuchi and Sukunabikona, appear to have been indigenous gods who were worshiped prior to the establishment of the Heian capital and whose shrines were situated in the area later selected for the Daidairi. The Court's original intention had been to move them, but they were left on their old sites when they indicated a desire to protect the Imperial Family—the Sono god to the north and the Kara gods to the south, in what became the western portion of the Imperial Household Ministry compound. Their festivals, said to date from around the middle of the ninth century, were elaborate affairs attended by Imperial Handmaids, kugyō, tenjōbito, and large numbers of lesser figures. The rituals, which were performed twice in identical fashion, first at one shrine and then at the other, consisted of the presentation of offerings by the Jingikan, a parade of horses, the performance of sacred dances, etc.

4. Ōharano Festival (held twice annually, on the first Day of the Hare in the Second Month and on the second Day of the Rat in the Eleventh). Ōharano Shrine, at the foot of Mount Oshio (Ukyō-ku, Kyōto), was a relatively young institution, established primarily for the convenience of Fujiwara ladies after the removal of the Court from Nara. Dedicated to the Fujiwara tutelary deities (the Kasuga gods), it was deeply revered by the family's members, and tradition required every Imperial consort of Fujiwara birth to visit it at least once. Its semiannual festival, inaugurated in 851, was celebrated with great magnificence. An Imperial Messenger was dispatched by the Court, bearing offerings comparable to those made at the Kasuga Festival; and other messengers represented the Crown Prince and the Empress. Private offerings were presented by the Regent, Ministers of State, and other Fujiwara dignitaries, many of whom attended the services in person. The reading of the norito, the parade of gift horses, the sacred dances, and the lesser events were similar to those at the

Kasuga Festival. (The Kasuga Virgin, when appointed, also did double duty as Ōharano Virgin.)

5. Kinenkokuhōhei Festival (held twice annually on auspicious days during the Second and Seventh Months). Like the Kinensai, the Kinenkokuhōhei (Offerings for a Bountiful Harvest) was a shotgun petition for good crops, addressed to the gods of numerous shrines; but whereas the Kinensai sought to enlist the aid of virtually every deity in the country, the Kinenkokuhōhei concentrated more modestly on the Grand Shrines of Ise and some twenty key institutions in the Home Provinces. The exact number of shrines involved was not fixed until 1068, after which it became customary to send offerings to the so-called Twenty-two Shrines: Ise, Iwashimizu, Kamo, Matsunoo, Hirano, Inari, Kasuga, Ōharano, Ōmiwa, Isonokami, Ōyamato, Hirose, Tatsuta, Sumiyoshi, Hie, Umenomiya, Yoshida, Hirota, Gion, Kitano, Mibu, and Kibune.

The main event of the Kinenkokuhōhei was a large gathering in the Court of Government (Chōdōin), when official messengers responsible for the presentation of offerings were ceremoniously dispatched to their respective destinations—an Imperial Prince to Ise and tenjōbito to most of the other shrines. The Emperor participated by viewing the offerings and by bowing in the direction of Ise after the departure of the Princely envoy.

Although the Kinenkokuhōhei appears to have been inaugurated around the beginning of the tenth century, it did not become a fixture on the Court calendar until the reign of Emperor Ichijō (r. 986–1011). It suffered frequent postponements, and, like the Kinensai, proved difficult to hold in the desired manner because the articles that were needed for offerings were not always available.

Supplementary note 46

The buildings of the great Iwashimizu Hachiman Shrine were situated on Mount Otoko near the capital, in what is now Yawata-machi, Tsuzuki-gun, Kyōto-fu. The shrine's three deities—Hachiman, identified with Emperor Ōjin (fifth century A.D.?); Ōjin's mother, Empress Jingū; and the goddess Himegami—were those worshiped at Usa Hachiman Shrine in Buzen, a shrine deeply revered by the Court because its oracle was credited with having saved the throne against a would-be usurper in the eighth century. Iwashimizu Shrine, founded by a Buddhist monk in 860 at the direction of Emperor Seiwa, shared the esteem enjoyed by the parent institution, and throughout the Heian period occupied a position of major importance in the life of the capital.

The Iwashimizu Release of Living Things Festival (*hōjōe*), celebrated on the Fifteenth of the Eighth Month, was a hybrid Buddhist-Shintō event inaugurated in the ninth century in imitation of a similar festival at Usa and extending over a two-day period in its fully developed form. On the first day, an imposing procession of senior nobles escorted the sacred god palanquin from the top of the mountain to the bottom, where offerings of food were presented, an Imperial prayer was read, sacred dances were performed, and the *Saishōō Sutra* (*Suvarṇaprabhāsa-sūtra*) was expounded. On the second, as recommended in the

Saishōō Sutra, birds were released from the mountaintop and fish were set free in a stream. The occasion ended with dances and wrestling matches.

Even more important in the lives of the Court circle was the Iwashimizu Special Festival (*rinjisai*), shown by contemporary accounts to have been a highlight of the year. Despite its name, which here can be taken to mean "additional" rather than "occasional" or "extraordinary," it became a regular annual event after the latter part of the tenth century, held on the second Day of the Horse in the Third Month. Its religious elements were those common to most great Shintō festivals: offerings, an Imperial Messenger, sacred music and dancing, and horse races. Of more immediate interest to most people at Court, however, were the events in the capital before the festival—especially the dance rehearsals.

The sacred music and dancing presented by the Court at the Iwashimizu Special Festival were of the type known as *azuma-asobi* or *azuma-mai* ("Eastern music," "Eastern dancing"), which flourished especially during the reigns of Emperors Kazan and Ichijō. An *azuma-asobi* program usually required the services of one or more singers, four or six dancers, and a small orchestra consisting of a Japanese zither (*wagon*, a six-stringed koto), a flute (*komabue*), an oboe (*hichiriki*), and a pair of clappers (*shakubyōshi*). The performers were usually members of the Bodyguards who came from musical families. A full program consisted of five sections: two introductory songs (*ichi no uta, ni no uta*); a first dance, "Suruga-mai," accompanied by songs with a strong folk flavor; a shorter second dance, "Motomeko," with more formal lyrics; and closing music (*kataoroshi*), during which the dancers retired.

A day or two before the festival, there was an elaborate formal banquet on the eastern side of the Seiryōden, attended by the Emperor and his entire Court. Immediately afterward, the gala trial performance (*shigaku*) took place. The women in particular seem to have looked forward eagerly to the spectacle, and to have watched in breathless admiration as the dancers described stately circles in the great eastern courtyard, keeping time to the music and waving their graceful sleeves. "One could gaze at them all day," writes Sei Shōnagon, "without having enough." *Mak.*, p. 197.

Later in the day, the Emperor inspected the horses to be raced by the guardsmen (*tōtsura no uma*).

On the day of the festival, there was an Imperial Purification ceremony in the Seiryōden, after which the Emperor worshiped the offerings displayed in the courtyard. The Emperor then retired for a change of costume and returned to witness the *niwa no za*, or departure ceremony. The officiating Head Chamberlain, having first assembled the kugyō and lesser figures, called in the Imperial Messenger and his party. Ceremonial cups were drunk, and the kugyō and others inserted artificial flowers in the caps of the performers—wisteria for the Messenger, who was usually a Middle or Lesser Captain, cherry blossoms for the dancers, and *yamabuki* (Japan globeflower: *Kerria japonica*) for the musicians. The Messenger's procession then set out for Iwashimizu, passing along streets lined with spectators of all classes.

In the early years of the Iwashimizu Special Festival, the Imperial Messenger

and his retinue, returning to the capital on the following day, proceeded directly to the Seiryōden courtyard for another banquet, a repeat performance of
"Motomeko," and the distribution of rewards. By Sei Shōnagon's day, as she
regretfully notes, this ceremony, the Return (*kaeridachi*), had been transferred
to the Butokuden, and the dancing had been eliminated. See Ikeda 1967, pp.
548–52; and, for vivid contemporary descriptions, *Mak.*, pp. 195–97, and *Ōkagami*, pp. 268–70. On *azuma-asobi*, see Tsuchihashi and Konishi 1960, pp. 274–
75, 422–25.

Supplementary note 47

See Table 13 for a list of Minamoto Masanobu's children.

Supplementary note 48

See Table 14 for a list of Fujiwara Michinaga's children.

TABLE 13. Offspring of Minamoto Masanobu

Name	Career	Remarks
Sons		
Tokinaka (943–1002)	Major Counselor, Jr. 2	Like his father, a famous flautist
Sukeyoshi (951–98)	Consultant, Sr. 4 L	Ancestor of Sasaki family (Ōmi Genji)
Michiyoshi (d. 998)	Third-level official in Ministry of Ceremonial, Sr. 6 U	
Tokimichi*	Provisional Lesser Controller, Sr. 5 L	Father of Masamichi, who was adopted by Masanobu; became monk
Tokinobu* (d. 1024)	Lesser Captain, Jr. 5 L	Became monk, 986?
Tokikata*	Assistant Guards Commander, Jr. 5 U	Appears to have become monk
Naritoki		
Saishin (954–1030)		Tōji abbot and other high clerical offices; a leading monk of the period
Daughters		
Rinshi (964–1053)		Principal consort of Fuj. Michinaga
Naka no Kimi (d. 1001)		Married Fuj. Michitsuna; mother of Kanetsune

SOURCES: *Sonpi bunmyaku*, 1: 337, 3: 386–87, 397; *Kugyō bunin*, 1: 244, 248; EMZ, 2: 256;
Kaneko 1939, 1: 339.
*Listed by *Sonpi bunmyaku*, 3: 386–87, 397, as child of principal wife, Bokushi.

TABLE 14. Offspring of Fujiwara Michinaga

Name	Career	Remarks
Sons		
Yorimichi* (Tazugimi) (992–1074)	Lesser Captain (1003), Sr. 3 (1006), Jr. 2 (1008), Provisional Middle Counselor (1009), Sr. 2 (1011), Provisional Major Counselor (1013), Palace Minister (1017), Jr. 1 (1021), Minister of the Left (1021–60), Chancellor (1061–62), Regent (1017–67)	Titular Regent at age 25; inherited power after Michinaga's death
Yorimune† (Iwagimi) (993–1065)	Middle Captain (1009), Jr. 3 (1011), Sr. 3 (1012), Jr. 2 (1013), Provisional Middle Counselor (1014), Sr. 2 (1018), Provisional Major Counselor (1021), Palace Minister (1047), Jr. 1 (1058), Minister of the Right (1060)	
Akinobu† (Kokegimi) (994?–1027)		Became monk
Yoshinobu† (995–1065)	Middle Captain (1013), Provisional Middle Counselor (1017), Sr. 2 (1019), Provisional Major Counselor (1021), posthumous Chancellor and Sr. 1	Instrumental in accession of Emperor Go-Sanjō; maternal grandfather, by adoption, of Emperor Go-Sanjō's son Shirakawa, who gave him posthumous title Chancellor
Norimichi* (996–1075)	Jr. 3 (1010), Sr. 3 (1011), Provisional Middle Counselor (1013), Sr. 2 (1015), Jr. 2, Provisional Major Counselor (xii 1019), Palace Minister (1021), Minister of the Right (1047–60), Jr. 1 (1058), Minister of the Left (1060–69), Chancellor (1070–71), Regent (1068–75), posthumous Sr. 1	
Nagaie† (Kowakagimi) (1005–64)	Provisional Major Counselor (1028–64), Sr. 2	Adopted by Rinshi

Chōshin (ca. 1014–72)	Archbishop	Tōji abbot; mother was Min. Shigemitsu's daughter

Daughters

Shōshi* (988–1074)	Fujitsubo Consort of Emperor Ichijō (1 xi 999), Junior Consort (7 xi 999), Chūgū (25 ii 1000), Grand Empress (ii 1012), Senior Grand Empress (1018)	A leading Court figure during peak of Michinaga's prosperity; mother of Emperors Go-Ichijō and Go-Suzaku; ladies-in-waiting included Murasaki Shikibu, Izumi Shikubu; became nun (19 i 1026); granted name Jōtō-mon'in on same day
Kenshi* (994–1027)	Principal Handmaid (xi 1004), consort of Crown Prince (Emperor Sanjō; 27 ii 1010), Junior Consort (23 viii 1011), Chūgū (14 ii 1012), Grand Empress (16 x 1018)	Bore only one child, Princess Teishi (Yōmeimon'in); thus not an influential figure
Kanshi† (before 999?–1025)	Consort of Koichijōin	
Ishi* (999–1036)	Principal Handmaid (viii 1012), consort of Emperor Go-Ichijō (iii 1018), Junior Consort (28 iv 1018), Chūgū (16 x 1018)	Nine years older than Emperor Go-Ichijō; mother of Princesses Shōshi (Chūgū of Emperor Go-Reizei) and Keishi (Chūgū of Emperor Go-Sanjō); died of smallpox
Kishi* (1007–25)	Principal Handmaid (xi 1018), Consort of Crown Prince (Go-Suzaku; ii 1021), posthumous Senior Grand Empress (1045)	Died at 18, shortly after giving birth to future Emperor Go-Reizei
Seishi†	Said to have been a Junior Consort of Emperor Sanjō	Wife of Min. Morofusa; may also have been called Ryūshi
Sonshi†		Wife of Min. Takaakira
Name unknown		

SOURCES: *Kugyō bunin*, passim; *Sonpi bunmyaku*, 1: 59–63; *Dainihonshi*, 5: 371–72.
*Child of Rinshi. †Child of Meishi.

Supplementary note 49

Longevity celebrations among the Heian nobility usually took the form of decennial observances held from a man's or woman's fortieth year on. They were sponsored by relatives, or occasionally by friends or patrons—even by the Emperor if the person being honored was sufficiently important—and always included a banquet, dances, and the recitation of poems. For especially exalted persons, there were also prayers at temples and largesse on a grand scale. See *Koji ruien*, 41: 344, 355.

The author's account of the celebration in honor of Kaneie contains some inaccuracies. Four separate events marked the occasion, all in the Third Month, rather than the Tenth: (1) on the Sixteenth Day, a celebration at the Hosshōji; (2) on the Twenty-fourth, sutra-recitations at sixty temples; (3) on the Twenty-fifth, a celebration at the Jōneiden under Imperial sponsorship; and (4) on the Twenty-eighth, an "after-banquet" (*goen*) at the Higashisanjōin. Two of Kaneie's grandsons are known to have danced at the Jōneiden celebration, which one of them, Fukutarigimi, almost ruined by throwing a temper tantrum. *Ōkagami*, p. 199. There is no record elsewhere of an Imperial visit to the Higashisanjōin in connection with the celebration. The author may have been confused about what happened where—or possibly, as EMZ, 1: 366, and *Shōkai*, 2: 44, suggest, she may have confused the longevity festivities with another occasion. For details, see EMZ, 1: 365–66.

Supplementary note 50

As at Iwashimizu and other important shrines, there were two major festivals at Kamo every year.

1. The Kamo Festival (held annually on the middle Day of the Cock in the Fourth Month). The "regular" festival (Kamo Festival, Aoi Festival, or simply the Festival) was one of the great religious and social events of the year, involving official and private preparations that began weeks in advance. The Emperor and the Virgin performed purification rituals, dancers and musicians rehearsed, guards officers were assigned to special ceremonial watches, offerings were prepared, and costumes, carriages, and horse trappings of the utmost magnificence were assembled in every aristocratic household, either for use in the official ceremonies or to impress fellow spectators.

The most important preliminary event was the Virgin's purification, which took place on the Day of the Horse at a spot on the Kamo River selected by divination. On the day of the purification, after the Emperor had personally inspected the outriders' horses and the Virgin's carriage-ox, there was a procession, watched by large crowds, that moved from the Imperial Palace to the Virgin's official residence at Murasakino and on to the river, where the ceremony took place.

On the Day of the Cock, the festival day itself, the focal point of interest was not the religious ritual performed at the Lower Sanctuary and duplicated at the Upper, but rather the great procession of military and civil officials, Court ladies, and attendants—some walking, others riding in ox-drawn carriages or on elaborately caparisoned horses, and all brilliantly costumed in formal robes, with flowers and leaves decorating their headgear, mounts, and carriages.

The principal figure in the procession as it left the Palace was the Imperial Messenger (usually a Middle Captain in the Bodyguards), who was charged with reading the Emperor's message to the gods. Other leading participants were the dancers, musicians, other guardsmen, and officials responsible for the offerings to be presented and for the horses to be paraded for the gods' enjoyment. In the latter part of the Heian period, there were also special emissaries from the Empresses and the Crown Prince, each with his own following.

The Virgin, borne in state on a litter from Murasakino, joined the procession with her retinue as it progressed slowly along the great Ichijō Avenue. Crowds of townsmen and peasants filled the streets, overflowing onto housetops and trees. Gorgeously attired ladies, courtiers, and exalted personages sat in lacquered carriages or luxurious viewing-stands, while their lackeys jostled against the commoners in an excited, unruly mass through which the Imperial Police, marching in the vanguard, cleared a passage. The houses along the way, the carriages and viewing-stands, and the spectators themselves were all gaily decked with garlands of real and artificial flowers, leaves of the katsura tree (*Cercidiphyllum japonicum*), and especially the aoi leaves that gave the festival its popular name, Aoi Festival. (Latter-day confusion between the *futaba-aoi* [*Asarum caulescens* Maxim], whose leaves were used as decorations for the Kamo Festival, and the *tachi-aoi* or hollyhock [*Althaea rosea*], has led to the common mistranslation Hollyhock Festival. Unlike the hollyhock, the *futaba-aoi* is a creeping, ivylike plant with attractive pairs of heart-shaped leaves growing directly from rooted horizontal stems. During the flowering season in May, a tiny reddish-purple bell-shaped blossom appears between each pair of leaves. See Kitamura 1966–67, 2: 321, and Plate 68, facing p. 315.)

At each of the two sanctuaries, the Virgin ceremoniously paid her respects, the Imperial Messenger intoned the rescript praising the gods and requesting their continued favor, offerings and *azuma-asobi* dances were presented, and horses were paraded and raced. The Virgin spent the night at the Upper Sanctuary, and on the following day there was another procession, the Return, less formal but equally colorful, which also attracted throngs of spectators. The Return culminated in a lavish Court banquet with rewards for the participants. Ishimura 1958, 1: 225–30.

2. The Kamo Special Festival (held annually, beginning in 899, on the last Day of the Cock in the Eleventh Month). As at Iwashimizu, the Kamo Special Festival (Kamo rinjisai) was a regular event in spite of its name. It followed the general pattern outlined for the Aoi Festival, but the Virgin played no role— an omission that caused the event to resemble the festival of any other great shrine honored by the dispatch of an Imperial Messenger, except that the proximity of Kamo to the capital was conducive to a more elaborate procession than usual. There was an especially close parallel with the Iwashimizu Special Festival in the Third Month: the *shigaku*, the inspection of horses, and the other preliminary events were virtually the same. The Kamo *azuma-asobi* rehearsal took place at night, however, so that, as Sei Shōnagon notes, the balmy spring air of

the Iwashimizu rehearsal was replaced by freezing cold and the sunshine by pine torches and bonfires. *Mak.*, pp. 77, 196. Another and more important difference was the retention of the Kamo Return (logistically a much simpler matter than the Iwashimizu Return). Reaching the city around midnight, the Imperial Messenger and his entourage went to the eastern courtyard of the Seiryōden for a full-scale Court banquet, at which they were given wine and otherwise honored. A musical performance followed, and the affair ended around dawn with the presentation of gifts of clothing or textiles to the Messenger, the dancers, and others. Ishimura 1958, 1: 253-55.

Supplementary note 51

The term *kagura* ("sacred music") can be used in a broad sense to mean any musical performance presented for the benefit of a Shintō deity (*azuma-asobi*, "Yamato-mai," "Kume-mai," etc.). Here, however, it is to be taken in its narrow sense as a specific kind of sacred music developed for Court use early in the Heian period. Because it was thought to be a remote descendant of the theatrical performance that had coaxed the Sun Goddess out of her cave, kagura was traditionally performed at night in an open area lit by fires called *niwabi* ("courtyard fires"), which functioned both as sources of illumination and as symbols of ritual purity. It retained certain exclamatory utterances and light features suggestive of its folk origins, but by the eleventh century it had become a carefully structured combination of poetry, music, and dance. Its most significant development took place under Emperor Ichijō, a sophisticated patron of the arts, who in 1002 instituted the biennial Naishidokoro performances, thereby stabilizing the form, encouraging high standards of performance, and reaffirming the essentially sacred nature of the music—a quality that had been in danger of eclipse because of the performance of kagura at banquets and on other social occasions. Most of what is now known of Heian kagura is based on accounts of Naishidokoro performances, which became annual events around 1075.

A Naishidokoro performance required the services of two choruses, called the *moto* and the *sue,* composed of around sixteen men all together; an instrumental group, usually made up of seven musicians (two Japanese zithers [*wagon*], three Japanese flutes [*yamatobue*], and two oboes [*hichiriki*]); and a Director (Ninjō). In most cases, the performers were subordinate Bodyguards officials with family specialties in appropriate branches of music. The Director, who gave the others their cues, made announcements, performed dances, and otherwise shaped the course of the performance, was usually an officer of Sixth Rank from the Ō family. Tanabe 1926, pp. 572-75.

After preliminary rituals by the Director, an introductory song, "Niwabi" ("Courtyard Fires"), was performed by the choruses. The next major portion of the program consisted of selections from a group of songs known collectively as *torimono* ("things taken"). So called from the auspicious objects successively flourished by the Director (a sakaki branch, a staff, a sword, etc.), the torimono were probably intended as invitations to the god to grace the occasion with his presence. Two songs accompanied the elevation of each object, the first sung by the First Chorus (*motokata*) and the next by the Second Chorus (*suekata*). The torimono section ended with a dance by the Director, after which there was an intermission, with wine and dramatic sketches.

There followed a second main block of songs (*saibari*), livelier in content, which were designed to entertain the god; a group of more serious compositions, the "divine departure" (*kamuagari*) music; and a second and final dance by the Director. The withdrawal of the Director signified the end of the performance. Tsuchihashi and Konishi 1960, pp. 257–362.

The usual Naishidokoro performance, which began in the early evening and lasted until the following morning, presumably included a generous selection of the approximately 100 songs available, even though each number was sung very slowly. Of the Kamo Return kagura, a relatively short affair, it can be said with certainty only that it was a performance "from 'Niwabi' to 'Asakura' and 'Sono koma' [two sending-off songs]." *Kuji kongen*, p. 79.

Commentators seem to agree that the kagura performance after the Kamo Special Festival was presented by the Imperial Messenger and his party. See also *Koji ruien* 7: 1124. We have found no evidence that a Director, chorus members, and extra musicians formed part of the procession to Kamo, or that kagura performances were presented at the two sanctuaries by the Court contingent, although it is conceivable either (1) that the entourage did include additional performers or (2) that someone doubled as Ninjō, that the full complement of kagura singers and dancers listed above was not always considered essential, and that the Imperial Messenger was thus able to present a kagura program (necessarily much abridged, since he reached the Upper Sanctuary around sundown and was usually back in the capital by midnight). For the Seiryōden performance, it appears that some *azuma-asobi* dancers may have functioned as singers, and that men who had not been to the sanctuaries were occasionally pressed into service as additional musicians. *Koji ruien*, 7: 1124. In any case, it would probably be a mistake to assume that the Return kagura was as complicated and formal as a Naishidokoro performance.

Supplementary note 52

See Figure 6.

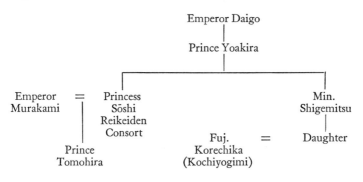

FIGURE 6

Supplementary note 53

The Sweet-Flag Festival (*tango no sechi*), celebrated on the Fifth of the Fifth Month at Court and elsewhere, represented an effort to ward off the diseases that tended to strike with the onset of hot weather. It embraced a variety of ceremonies and customs, most of them involving the aromatic leaves and roots of the sweet flag, or calamus (*Acorus calamus* var. *angustatus*), to which the Chinese and Japanese, like the medieval Europeans, ascribed medicinal properties. Sweet-flag leaves and/or roots were stuffed under the eaves of houses and Palace buildings, hung inside rooms, used in the preparation of "medicinal balls," worn as hair ornaments, and formally presented to the Emperor by Court physicians at a Sweet-Flag Banquet.

The sweet flag (the *Calamus aromaticus* of medieval European druggists) was known in the Heian period as *ayame* or *ayamegusa;* it is now called *shōbu.* Confusion with the modern ayame (*Iris nertschinskia*) and hanashōbu (*Iris ensata*, often called shōbu), both of which are irises, has led to the common English misnomer Iris Festival. The sweet flag's leaves and roots resemble those of an iris but have a distinctive fragrance; the tiny yellow-green flowers, massed together on blunt, tapering ears, are unlike those of any iris. See Kitamura et al. 1966–67, vol. 3, Plate 48, facing p. 175.

Supplementary note 54

On Yukinari, see s.n. 28. His cousin, Narifusa, who probably did not become a Lesser Captain until 998, had no official career of any consequence. See Figure 7.

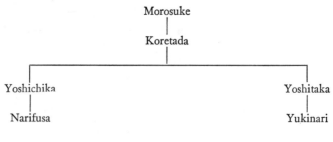

FIGURE 7

Supplementary note 55

Seishi's mother and Crown Prince Okisada were second cousins. See Figure 8.

Supplementary note 56

Like the genpuku for boys, the Putting On of the Train (mogi) for well-born girls was a rite of passage symbolizing the attainment of adulthood. It had originated around the beginning of the tenth century, when the adoption of the

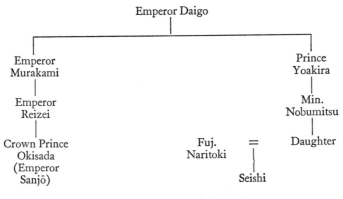

FIGURE 8

new free-falling feminine coiffure had destroyed the significance of the Putting Up of the Hair (*kamiage*), a ceremony that had traditionally taken place at the time of a girl's betrothal, in symbolic recognition of her sexual maturity. The mogi was less specifically linked to matrimony than the kamiage, but it too announced that a girl had reached marriageable age, and it was therefore performed around the onset of puberty. (The rule was not invariable. Michikane's daughter by Naishi no Suke was only eight years old, and Tamakazura in *The Tale of Genji* is represented as having been around twenty-two.)

The mogi usually took place at night in a room decorated for the occasion. It involved a bit of formalized hairdressing—a vestige of the kamiage—but its central feature was the ceremonious assumption of an article of adult wear, the *mo*, which was an elaborate train worn by noble ladies on formal occasions. The person who attached the train (Koshiyui) was an older relative or a prominent member of the Court circle, most frequently a woman. As with the genpuku, the symbolic act was quickly accomplished, but the advance preparations, the preliminary formalities, such as the reception and seating of guests, and the aftermath, notably the banqueting and the presentation of gifts, were extremely elaborate in leading families. See, for example, Chapter 19 of *Eiga*, which describes the mogi of Michinaga's granddaughter Princess Teishi. For a general survey of the subject, see Nakamura 1962, pp. 140–49; for illustrations of mo and of Nara and Heian hairstyles, see Rekisei Fukusō Bijutsu Kenkyūkai 1965, 1: 40–45, 48, 116.

Supplementary note 57

As shown in Table 15, there were repeated outbreaks of pestilence in the Heian capital during the period covered by the first thirty chapters of *Eiga*. The epidemic of 994–95, in particular, was long remembered for its catastrophic results. Prayers and offerings failed to moderate the virulence of the disease, which was probably smallpox; makeshift emergency facilities were overwhelmed by the numbers of the dead and dying; and the streets degenerated into a night-

mare of stinking corpses, preyed on by dogs and crows. More than half the inhabitants of the capital, including sixty-seven persons of Fifth or higher rank,
are said to have perished between the Fourth and Seventh Months of 994 alone.
Nihon kiryaku, 2: 178 (28 vii Shōryaku 5); EMZ, 1: 480–81.

TABLE 15. Major Epidemics in the City of Heian, 947–1025

Year	Disease
947 (Tenryaku 1)	Smallpox and dysentery
974 (Ten'en 2)	Smallpox
993 (Shōryaku 4)	
Fifth and Sixth Months	*Gaigyaku* (a contagious cough?)
Seventh and Eighth Months	Smallpox
994–95 (Shōryaku 5–Chōtoku 1)	Smallpox?
998 (Chōtoku 4)	Measles
1020 (Kannin 4)	Smallpox
1025 (Manju 2)	Measles

Supplementary note 58

See Table 16.

TABLE 16. Offspring of Emperor Sanjō

Name	Mother	Remarks
Natural Children–Sons		
Atsuakira (994–1051)	Fuj. Seishi	Named Crown Prince, 1016; resigned under pressure from Michinaga, 1017; assumed style of Retired Emperor with title Kochijōin; principal consorts: Fuj. Enshi (daughter of Akimitsu), Fuj. Kanshi (daughter of Michinaga)
Atsunori (997–1054)	Seishi	Minister of Ceremonial; Minister of Central Affairs
Atsuhira (999 or 1000–1050)	Seishi	Minister of Central Affairs; Minister of Ceremonial; Minister of War
Moroakira (1004 or 1005–85)	Seishi	Entered Ninnaji as monk Shōshin; highly regarded as ritualist
Natural Children–Daughters		
Tōshi (1001 or 1002–23)	Seishi	Ise Virgin, 1012–16; later liaison with Fuj. Michimasa
Shishi (1003 or 1006–48)	Seishi	Wife of Regent Norimichi

TABLE 16 (continued)

Name	Mother	Remarks
Teishi (1013–94)	Fuj. Kenshi	Jusangū (1015); consort of future Emperor Go-Suzaku (1027); Chūgū (ii 1037); Kōgō (iii 1037); Grand Empress (1052); Senior Grand Empress (1068); retired as Yōmeimon'in (1069); mother of Emperor Go-Sanjō and Princesses Ryōshi and Enshi; many poems in Imperial anthologies

Adopted Children–Sons

Name	Mother	Remarks
Atsusada (1014–61)	Fuj. Enshi	Minister of Central Affairs; Minister of Ceremonial
Atsumasa	Enshi	Became monk; lived at the Onjōji
Atsumoto (1023–32)	Fuj. Kanshi	Died in childhood
Atsukata (1039–77)	Daughter of Fuj. Yorimune	Minister of Ceremonial

Adopted Children–Daughters

Name	Mother	Remarks
Kenshi (b. 1018)	Kanshi	Married Fuj. Nobuie; called Reizei no Miya
Kashi	Daughter of Fuj. Yorimune	Ise Virgin, 1046–51
Eishi	Enshi	

SOURCES: *Honchō kōin shōunroku*, pp. 430–31; *Dainihonshi*, 4: 380–81, 513–14.

NOTE: The adopted children, most of whom were born after Sanjō's death, were offspring of Prince Atsuakira (Koichijōin). They were given the status of offspring of the Emperor so that they could bear the titles Imperial Prince (Shinnō) and Imperial Princess (Naishinnō).

Supplementary note 59

The wives of Michikane and Prince Akihira were first cousins. See Figure 9. The adoption is not mentioned in other sources.

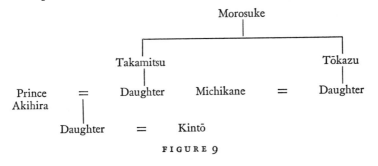

FIGURE 9

Supplementary note 60

See Table 17 for a list of Akimitsu's children by Seishi.

TABLE 17. Offspring of Fujiwara Akimitsu and Princess Seishi

Name	Career	Remarks
	Son	
Shigeie	Jr. 4 L, Lesser Captain	Became monk, 1001
	Daughters	
Genshi	Shōkyōden Junior Consort of Emperor Ichijō (996)	Married Min. Yorisada after deaths of Ichijō and Suishi
Enshi (d. 1019)	First wife of Crown Prince Atsuakira (Koichijōin)	

SOURCES: *Sonpi bunmyaku*, 1: 51; Tsunoda 1963, p. 170 and *passim*.

Supplementary note 61

Kinsue's wife was Princess Ryoshi, a daughter of Prince Ariakira.

Sonpi bunmyaku, 1: 120, lists a daughter, Gishi, and two sons, Sanenari and the monk Nyogen, as her children. The mothers of Kinsue's other two sons, Chikakata and the monk Shinkaku, are not listed. See Table 18.

TABLE 18. Offspring of Fujiwara Kinsue

Name	Career	Remarks
	Sons	
Sanenari (975–1044)	Middle Counselor, Sr. 2	
Chikakata	Senior Assistant Minister of War, Jr. 4 U	
Nyogen (977–1021)	Bishop	Enryakuji monk
Shinkaku (990–1084)	Archbishop	Abbot of Tōdaiji, etc.; called Kanjuji Archbishop
	Daughter	
Gishi (974–1053)	Kokiden Junior Consort of Emperor Ichijō (996)	Became nun, 1026

Supplementary note 62
   Shūishū 477:

Shiranami wa	Though white waves {rise, {cut,
Tatedo koromo ni	They do not combine [the cut
Kasanarazu	pieces] into a garment;
Akashi mo Suma mo	Akashi and Suma are {reverse sides [of a garment]. {[separate] beaches.
Ono ga uraura.	

   The poem draws on two meanings of *tatedo*, a form of the verb *tatsu*: "rise," "rear up," and "cut [out]" (as of fabric for a garment). There is also a pun on *ura*, which can mean either "back," "reverse side," or "beach."

Supplementary note 63
   See Table 19 for a list of Emperor Ichijō's children by Teishi.

TABLE 19. Offspring of Emperor Ichijō and Fujiwara Teishi

Name	Career	Remarks
	Son	
Atsuyasu (999–1018)	Governor-General of the Dazaifu; Minister of Cere- monial (1016)	Unable to become Crown Prince be- cause of Michinaga's opposition; his only child, Genshi (1016–39), was adopted by Fuj. Yorimichi and became Emperor Go-Suza- ku's Empress
	Daughters	
Shūshi (997–1050)	Princess of First Rank (1007), status of "equality with the three Empresses"	Lacked influential support; isolated after Emperor Ichijō's death; took Buddhist vows while still a young woman
Bishi (1001–8)		Died in childhood

Supplementary note 64
   See Figure 10.

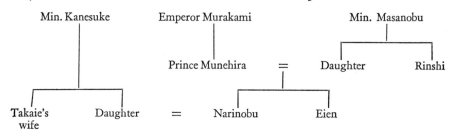

FIGURE 10

Supplementary note 65

The dining bench (*daishōji*) was a combined individual seat and table used by a member of the Imperial Family. It consisted of two rosewood tables inlaid with mother-of-pearl, each about three or four feet long, two feet wide, and a foot high, which were placed together, covered with mats edged in black-and-white damask, and equipped with a round cushion and an arm rest. The food was served on small individual tables. For an illustration, see *Genji*, 1: 488.

The curtain-dais (here *michō*; also called [*mi*]*chōdai*, or, in the case of an Empress, *hamayuka*) faced south in the principal apartment of an upper-class residence and served the master or mistress as both private sitting room and bedchamber. Its base, a black-lacquered platform about a foot high and nine feet square, was surmounted by a ceiling (*akarishōji*, resembling the modern shōji) supported on three pillars, approximately six and one-half feet high, in each of the four corners. Curtains trailed the floor at the corners, and there were also pillar-to-pillar curtains on the four sides. The curtains on the south, east, and west sides were rolled up to the height of the two-foot *kichō* that stood inside. Both the stationary curtains and the kichō were decorated with long silk streamers. The floor was covered with two large tatami mats, surmounted by additional matting (*tsuchishiki*), by cushions, and at night by bedclothing. For illustrations, see Ikeda 1967, p. 162.

Like the daishōji, the Korean dog and lion (*koma inu shishi*) were appurtenances of royalty. These sizable beasts sat facing one another on opposite sides of the chōdai entrance, the dog white with a horn and a closed mouth, the lion yellow with an open mouth. Their ostensible functions were to keep the curtains from blowing in the wind and to ward off evil spirits, but they were essentially status symbols.

Supplementary note 66

"Gossamer" (*usumono*) was a general term for sheer silks, especially silk gauzes. The chief silk gauze in use among the Heian nobility appears to have been *ra*, a Sino-Japanese term for which usumono was sometimes used as a Japanese equivalent. Ra was based on an alternating-gauze binding system (we follow the terminology of Emery 1966, pp. 180–92), in which alternate ends

were shifted to the left (or right) over two ends shifting in the opposite direction, bound in their transposed positions by picks, and then recrossed to their
original positions. In unpatterned ra, the binding system was plain alternating-
gauze throughout. In patterned ra, a figure was formed by the contrast between
a plain alternating-gauze binding and a complex variation thereof in which the
ends were worked in groups of four instead of two, producing interstices in the
fabric extending over three picks. See Sasaki 1951, p. 35, for a chart of the system. The Shōsōin fabrics include a simpler kind of gauze called *sha*, which was
apparently also used in the Heian period. Sha was woven in a plain-gauze binding system in which alternate ends (the doup ends) were regularly crossed to
the left or right over adjacent ends (the fixed ends), and then recrossed to their
original positions after being bound by picks. This binding system produced
gauze crosses linked by ends vertically, instead of diagonally, as in an alternating-gauze weave. In a variation of the system, ends were worked together in
threes instead of in pairs, but the crosses remained vertical. There were unpatterned and patterned varieties of sha, the patterned variety having either a
tabby ground and a plain-gauze figure, or vice versa. Sasaki 1951, pp. 33–39;
Hifuku Bunka Kyōkai 1969, 1: 63, 424–25; 2: 485–87; Akanekai 1975, p. 428.

Supplementary note 67

The rich store of seventh- and eighth-century fabrics preserved at the Hōryūji
and in the Shōsōin includes a wide variety of brocades: slit (*k'o-ssu*) and interlocked tapestries; warp-faced compound tabbies and twills; weft-faced compound twills; tabbies and twills with weft-float patterning; warp-faced twills
with patterns in weft twill; double-cloth tabbies with patterns in chiné warps
or in wefts of polychrome yarn composed of different colored threads loosely
twisted together; etc. But it is unlikely that all those weaves and techniques
were known to the Heian nobility. Textile historians assume, for instance, that
the warp-faced compound tabbies and twills and the interlocked tapestries were
no longer in use at the beginning of the Heian period.

Descriptions of the few surviving pieces of Heian brocade (almost all from
the end of the period) indicate only two types. One is a weft-faced compound
twill, in which the weft is divided into two, three, or four series of different
colors. A main warp interlaces with one weft series in weft twill, the series
changing as the color of the pattern requires. The remaining weft series are
separated to the rear with the aid of a pseudo pattern-shed warp (called a wick
warp by Japanese experts), the paired ends of which appear on neither the face
nor the reverse of the fabric. The pattern-shed ends also serve to lengthen the
floats of the picks on the face, thus intensifying the effect of the weft colors in
the pattern. The other type of brocade that can definitely be placed in the Heian
period is a warp- or weft-faced twill with patterning in weft twill. An auxiliary
pattern weft interlaces with the warp in the pattern areas and either floats unbound on the reverse or is secured there in twill binding.

There is evidence to suggest that a third type of brocade was also in use,
although no examples of it survive. It was a double-cloth tabby, in which two

sets of warps of the same color interlaced in double-tabby weave with two sets of wefts in different colors. See also Chapter 20, n. 13. Sasaki 1951, pp. 46–147; Sasaki 1958, pp. 29–39; Nishimura 1971–75, 2: 3–10; Simmons 1962; Burnham 1967. For photographic illustrations of Heian brocade, see Nishimura 1971–75, vol. 2. Plates 21, 30–32, 34, 38, 75, and 99 are weft-faced compound twills; Plate 33 is a warp-faced twill with patterning in weft-faced twill. For an example of Nara-period double-cloth brocade, see Plate 71.

Supplementary note 68

Lady Dainagon was probably a daughter of Masanobu's son Sukeyoshi. Her name was Renshi. Minamoto Norimasa, a provincial governor, was one of Shigemitsu's sons. EMZ, 2: 333. See Figure 11.

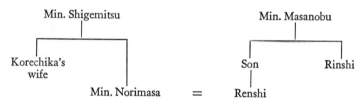

FIGURE 11

Supplementary note 69

For a list of Kazan's known sons, see Table 20. (Nothing is known of his daughters.)

TABLE 20. Sons of Retired Emperor Kazan

Name	Mother	Remarks
Akinari (998?–1035)	Nakatsukasa's daughter	Minister of Central Affairs; probably ranked as Reizei's 6th son
Kiyohito (ca. 998–1030)	Nakatsukasa	Kazan's favorite; President of the Board of Censors; probably ranked as Reizei's 5th son
Kakugen (1000?–1065)		Tōdaiji abbot; Daigoji abbot
Jinkan (1002?–51)		Took Buddhist vows as a child; Tōdaiji abbot; Ishiyama abbot

Supplementary note 70

As shown in Table 21, the chief officiants at the five altars were all prominent Tendai monks.

TABLE 21. Chief Officiants at the Five Altars

Altar	Officiant	Remarks
Fudō	Shōsan (939–1011)	Onjōji abbot, 991; Kannon'in Archbishop, 1002. The Kannon'in was part of the Daiunji, a subsidiary of the Onjōji
Gōsanze	Kyōen (949?–1019)	Maternal uncle of Fuj. Sanesuke; Hōjūji abbot; prayed for Emperor Ichijō during illness of 1011; Archbishop, 1011; Tendai abbot, 1014–19
Kuṇḍalī	Shin'yo (941?–1029?)	Grandson of Fuj. Akitada; credited with improvement of ex-Emperor Sanjō's eyes, 1015; Bishop; Onjōji abbot, 1025; Archbishop, 1028
Daiitoku	Saigi (983–1047)	Son of Fuj. Michitsuna; Bishop; called Shōzen in *Eiga*
Kongō Yasha	Myōku (946–1020)	Son of Prince Ariakira; named Bishop in 1013 after efficacious prayers for ex-Emperor Sanjō; lived at Jōdoji, on site of present Ginkakuji; Tendai abbot, 1019–20

Supplementary note 71

"Ten Thousand Years, a Thousand Autumns" is a *rōei*, a type of vocal music especially popular during Emperor Ichijō's reign. Rōei lyrics, sung to the accompaniment of Chinese musical instruments, consist of short excerpts from Chinese poems (usually a fourteen-word couplet) or, less often, of *waka* (thirty-one-syllable Japanese poems). This example, which is very old, makes use of a couplet from a poem by the early T'ang literatus Hsieh Yeh. Unlike most later rōei, it retains Japanese approximations of the original Chinese pronunciations instead of translating the words into Japanese:

> Kashin reigetsu kan bukyoku   In this auspicious season,
>   our joy knows no limit;
> Banzei senshū raku biyō.   For ten thousand years and one
>   thousand autumns, our happiness
>   will not end.

See *Wakan rōeishū*, p. 250; and Tanabe 1963, p. 110.

Supplementary note 72

Mount Miwa, traditionally considered sacred, stands within the confines of the present Kashiwara-shi, Nara-ken. The author apparently intends a reference to an ancient anonymous poem (*Kokinshū* 982):

Waga io wa	My cottage stands
Miwa no yamamoto	At the foot of Mount Miwa.
Koishikuba	If you miss me, pray come to call.
Toburaikimase	Mine is the gate
Sugi tateru kado.	Where the cryptomeria grows.

According to *Murasaki Shikibu nikki*, p. 470, Akimitsu's song was "Mino-yama" ("The Hills of Mino"), a *saibara* often sung on festive occasions:

Minoyama ni	Ah, the splendid oaks,
Shiji ni oitaru	Thick-growing
Tamagashiwa	On the hills of Mino!
Toyonoakari ni	Ah the pleasure of meeting,
Au ga tanoshisa ya	The pleasure of meeting,
Au ga tanoshisa ya.	With wine-flushed faces!

The saibara, like the *imayō* ("modern song") and rōei, was a major Heian vocal genre. The lyrics, of which over sixty are extant, were for the most part Nara-period folk songs, set to Chinese music early in the Heian period. "Mino-yama" was one of the few that approximated the tanka form. Most of the others were less polished, although there was a tendency to favor five- and seven-syllable lines. The "Umegae," "Takegawa," "Agemaki," and "Azumaya" chapters of *Genji* are all named after saibara, attesting to the popularity of the genre during its heyday in the late tenth and early eleventh centuries. Tsuchibashi and Konishi 1960, p. 410.

Supplementary note 73

One of Prince Tomohira's two sons, Yorishige, was adopted by a minor official, Fujiwara Koresuke, and never became a kugyō. (He is said by Matsumura to have been the child of a different mother.) The other, Minamoto Morofusa (1008–77), whom Yorimichi adopted, rose to the office of Minister of the Right (1069) with Junior First Rank. In addition to the daughters by Nakahimegimi, the Prince had a daughter who married Yorimichi's brother Norimichi. EMZ, 2: 528; *Sonpi bunmyaku*, 2: 43, 3: 485; *Honchō kōin shōunroku*, p. 433. See Figure 12.

Supplementary note 74

See Table 22 for a list of Yorimune's children.

Supplementary note 75

As indicated in Chapter 10, n. 7, the decree (*senji*) announcing the decision was issued on the Third Day of the First Month. The official proclamation (*senmyō*) on the Fourteenth of the Second Month made the changes shown in Table 23.

TABLE 22. Offspring of Fujiwara Yorimune

Name	Career	Remarks
	Sons	
Kaneyori* (1014–63)	Middle Counselor, Sr. 2	
Toshiie* (1019–82)	Minister of the Right, Sr. 2	
Yoshinaga*	Palace Minister, Sr. 2, posthumous Chancellor	Adopted by Michinaga's son Yoshinobu
Motosada	Minister of Punishments, Sr. 4 L	
Yoshisue (d. 1077)	Middle Counselor, Sr. 2	
Raikan	Provisional Major Bishop	Called Tokudaiji Bishop; Tōji abbot
	Daughters	
Enshi* (1016–95)	Reikeiden Consort of Emperor Go-Suzaku (ca. 1042)	Reared by Princess Shūshi; bore a daughter, Princess Seishi, shortly after death of Emperor Go-Suzaku
In no Ue*	Consort of Koichijōin	Mother of Prince Atsukata and Min. Motohira
Shōshi	Consort of Emperor Go-Sanjō (1066)	Lived in Shōkyōden; took Buddhist vows after death of husband
Name unknown		Wife of Minister of the Right Morofusa; mother of Major Counselor Morotada

SOURCE: *Sonpi bunmyaku*, 1: 245–51.
*Child of Korechika's daughter Ōhimegimi.

TABLE 23. Changes in Imperial Consorts' Titles, 1012

Name	Old title	New title
Junshi	Grand Empress	Senior Grand Empress
Shōshi	Empress (Chūgū)	Grand Empress
Kenshi	Junior Consort	Empress (Chūgū)

SOURCE: EMZ, 3: 111.

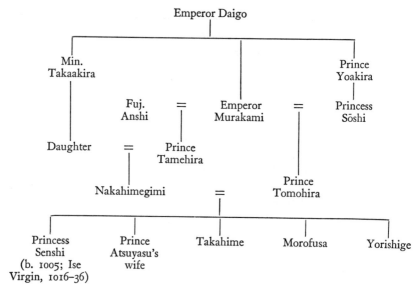

FIGURE 12

Supplementary note 76

The formal investiture of an Empress (*rikkō no gi* or *rikkō no sechie*) began with a council of nobles at which the proclamation (senmyō) was drawn up. The senmyō was then read aloud at the Shishinden, usually in the Imperial presence, and Household appointments were made according to a list drawn up by the minister in charge of the ceremony. Meanwhile, an Imperial messenger (a Middle Counselor, designated at the council meeting by the minister in charge) proceeded to the lady's residence to announce the promulgation of the senmyō. Chamberlains and other functionaries were also dispatched from the Court to deliver the symbols of Imperial status—a chair, dining tables, guardian animal figures for the chōdai, special footgear, etc. See s.n. 65.

Wearing a white Chinese jacket, a white gauze train, Imperial footgear, and a formal coiffure, the new Empress later received the congratulations of the senior nobles, guards officers, and other courtiers, who were then entertained on the premises at an elaborate banquet, while she herself dined in state. *Gōke shidai*, pp. 451–53; EMZ, 3: 116. For a brief description of Kenshi's investiture, which took place at the Higashisanjō Mansion, see *Midō kanpakuki*, 2: 128 (14 ii Chōwa 1).

Supplementary note 77

1. "A myriad birds chirped . . ."—*Kokinshū* 28 (anon.):

Momochidori	Spring,
Saezuru haru wa	With its myriad chirping birds,

Monogoto ni	Brings renewal
Aratamaredomo	To every living thing,
Ware zo furiyuku.	Yet I grow older still.

2. "Searchers pushed through the reeds on the burnt fields at Ashitanohara
. . .," a reference to the custom of going out into the fields in early spring to
pick young greens, which were valued both for their taste and for their health-
giving properties. There are allusions to two poems.

Kokinshū 252 (anon.):

Kiri tachite	Mists hover
Kari zo naku naru	And wild geese call.
Kataoka no	The leaves will have turned
Ashitanohara wa	At Ashitanohara
Momiji shinuramu.	In Kataoka.

Kataoka is now part of Ōji-machi, Kitakatsuragi-gun, Nara-ken. Ashitanohara
has not been identified.

Gosenshū 3 (Taira Kanemori; d. 990):

Kyō yori wa	Whom shall I invite
Ogi no yakehara	To set out with me today
Kakiwakete	In search of young shoots
Wakana tsumi ni to	Amid the reeds
Tare o sasowamu.	On the burnt fields?

3. "And at Kasuga too the Tobuhi watchman gathered the first tender sprouts
of a 'myriad generations' spring." Tobuhi[no], Beacon-fire Field, was part of
Kasuga Plain at Nara. A watchman had been stationed there during the Nara
period, charged with the duty of lighting a beacon to warn the Court of an
emergency. There are allusions to two poems.

Kokinshū 18 (anon.):

Kasugano no	Watchman at Tobuhi Field
Tobuhi no nomori	On the Plain of Kasuga,
Idete miyo	Go out and look, that we may know
Ima ikuka arite	How many days must pass
Wakana tsumitemu.	Before we pick the tender shoots.

Kokinshū 357 (Naishi no Kami [Fujiwara Banshi]; fl. ca. 900):

Kasugano ni	As I pluck the tender shoots
Wakana tsumitsutsu	On the Plain of Kasuga,
Yorozuyo	The god [of Kasuga] will know how I rejoice
Iwau kokoro wa	That your life will span
Kami zo shiruramu.	A myriad generations.

Kokinshū 357 was written on a folding screen to congratulate the author's brother on reaching the age of forty (sai). A gift of young greens symbolized a wish for the recipient's good health and long life.

4. "The breezes that melted the ice . . ."—*Kokinshū* 2 (Ki no Tsurayaki; 884–946):

Sode hijite	On this first day of spring,
Musubishi mizu no	Are breezes melting
Kōreru o	The icebound waters
Haru tatsu kyō no	That once I scooped up,
Kaze ya tokuramu.	Drenching my sleeve?

5. "The voices of warblers from the valleys . . ."—*Kokinshū* 14 (Ōe Chisato; fl. ca. 900):

Uguisu no	If there were no songs
Tani yori izuru	Of warblers
Koe naku wa	Emerging from the valleys,
Haru kuru koto o	Who would know
Tare ka shiramashi.	That spring had come?

6. "They were destined to live forever, transformed by the Imperial example." —*Shūishū* 24 (Ōnakatomi Yoshinobu; 921–91):

Chitose made	After today the very pines,
Kagireru matsu mo	Trees that live a thousand years,
Kyō yori wa	Will endure for ten thousand generations,
Kimi ni hikarete	Following the example
Yorozuyo ya hemu.	Set by our lord.

The poem was composed for an Imperial Prince's Day of the Rat outing.

7. "Even the bamboo leaves . . .," a rōei drawn from a poem by Po Chü-i (772–846)—*Wakan rōeishū*, p. 84:

Motai no hotori no chikuyō wa haru o hete juku su
Hashi no moto no shōbi wa natsu ni itte hiraku.

With the passing of spring, the bamboo leaves at
the lip of the wine-crock mature;
With the start of summer, the roses at the foot
of the staircase bloom.

Bamboo leaves were added to rice wine as clarifying agents during the brewing process. In Po Chü-i's poem, as often, they function as a metaphor for the wine itself, which, brewed in winter, ripened in the course of the following spring. For other allusions in Japanese literature to this famous couplet, see *Wakan rōeishū*, p. 262, s.n. 147. The auspicious significance ascribed to the leaves by the *Eiga* author rests on a word play involving two meanings of *yo* ("reign" and "the space between two joints on a bamboo stalk") in the phrase *sue no yo haruka ni*.

Supplementary note 78

"Mirror cakes" translates *mochii kagami*, the old name for the round, flat *kagami mochi* displayed in modern Japan during the New Year season. From the Muromachi period on, mirror cakes were among the hagatame dishes served on the first three days of the First Month. During the Heian period, they appear to have had no direct connection with the hagatame ceremony, but rather to have functioned partly as religious offerings and partly as seasonal decorations, arranged then, as now, with garnishes of citrus fruits, greenery, etc. By the eleventh century, it had become customary for members of the upper classes to face the *mochii kagami* on New Year's Day and chant auspicious poems that were, in effect, prayers for the head of the family and other household members. The poem most often recited on such occasions is believed to have been a *Kokinshū* tanka punning on the name of Mirror Mountain in Ōmi (Gamō-gun, Shiga-ken).

Kokinshū 1086 (Ōtomo Kuronushi; d. ca. 900?):

Ōmi no ya	Because in Ōmi
Kagami no yama o	A Mirror Mountain has been raised,
Tatetareba	We can see in advance
Kanete zo miyuru	That our lord will live
Kimi ga chitose wa.	For a thousand years.

See Yamanaka 1972, p. 107; *Genji*, 2: 377; and Seidensticker 1976, p. 409.

Supplementary note 79

Hare wands (uzue) were slender five-foot rods, covered with paper at the top, which were tied together in bundles of two, three, or four, and presented to the Emperor in the Shishinden by members of the Guards on the first Day of the Hare in a new year. The wood came from trees associated with the yang principle in yin-yang cosmology (camellia, peach, plum, etc.), and the choice of the Day of the Hare represented an attempt, based on Chinese precedent, to utilize the evil-dispelling powers of a yang animal associated with spring and the east. The custom flourished particularly in the mid-Heian period, when the wands were presented on tree-dotted landscape trays—often with the tips held in the mouth of the animal corresponding to the Emperor's lucky direction (hare for the east, horse for the south, etc.). After the Shishinden ceremony, the wands were taken to the Daytime Chamber of the Seiryōden, where they served not only a protective but also a decorative purpose. Uzue were also presented to members of the Imperial Family by the Court, and to one another by the nobility in general.

Nothing specific is known about the form assumed by the "congratulations" (*hogai*), which appear to have consisted of good wishes or auspicious phrases pronounced by a person presenting wands.

Uzue should not be confused with the similar *uzuchi* ("hare sticks"), which were also given to the Emperor and others, either officially or privately, on the first Day of the Hare; and which also served as magical protectors and spring-time decorations in the Daytime Chamber and the houses of the nobility. An uzuchi was a short, thin, round or square peachwood stick, about three to five inches long, with a perforation at the paper-wrapped top, from which colored streamers and other decorations were suspended. Yamanaka 1972, pp. 144–49; Ishimura 1958, 1: 201–3; EMZ, 3: 234.